Software Quality and Productivity

Software Quality and Productivity

Theory, practice, education and training

Edited by

Matthew Lee

Department of Information Systems
City Polytechnic of Hong Kong
Kowloon Tong
Hong Kong

Ben-Zion Barta

Ministry of Education, Culture and Sports
Jerusalem
Israel

and

Peter Juliff

School of Management Information Systems
Deakin University
Victoria
Australia

SPRINGER-SCIENCE+BUSINESS MEDIA, B.V.

First edition 1995

Originally published by Chapman & Hall in 1995
MyCopy version of the original edition 1995

DOI 10.1007/978-0-387-34848-3

A catalogue record for this book is available from the British Library

∞ Printed on permanent acid-free text paper, manufactured in accordance with ANSI/NISO Z39.48-1992 and ANSI/NISO Z39.48-1984 (Permanence of Paper).
www.springer.com/mycopy

CONTENTS

Preface x
International Program Committee, Organizing Committee and Sponsors ix

PART ONE Keynote papers

1 Towards the 21st Century's software quality, state-of-the-art and international standard in JTC1/SC7
M. Azuma 3

2 Software quality and productivity improvement
R.G. Dromey 10

PART TWO Requirements, Design and Development Methodologies

3 Progress towards RACE: a 'soft-centred' requirements definition method
D.W. Bustard 29

4 MOOSE: A method designed for ease of maintenance
R.I. Ferguson, N.F. Parrington and P. Dunne 37

5 BPR for developing information systems – a case study
E. Coakes and J. Coakes 45

6 Towards a methodology for 24 hour software production using globally separated development teams
I. Gorton and S. Motwani 50

7 MetaMet – a soft systemic way toward the quality of information systems
P. Kokol and B. Stiglic 56

8 Changing programming paradigm – an empirical investigation
J. Miller, G. Darroch, M. Wood, A. Brooks and M. Roper 62

9 Application-oriented methods for systems development – a review
D. Millington and I.M. Tulloch 66

10 A proposal for composing software design process
S. Mochizuki and T. Katayama 72

11 Team-based software development using an electronic meeting system: the quality pay-off
S. Sawyer and P.J. Guinan 78

12 Designing with non-functional requirements
C.J. Theaker and J. Whitworth 84

13 Modelling the requirements of process controlled systems
T.K. Sateesh and P.A.V. Hall 88

14 Compiling heterarchical programs by means of Petri nets
B. Evans 92

PART THREE Object Oriented Analysis, Design and Development

15 Type checking classes in Object-Z to promote quality of specifications
J. Chen and B. Durnota 99

16 An axiom-based test case selection strategy for object-oriented programs
T.H. Tse, F.T. Chan and H.Y. Chen 107

17 AMI: a case tool based on artificial intelligence techniques for an interactive modelling for analysis
L. Lasoudris, M. Maurice-Demourioux and R. Voyer 115

18 Object-oriented framework for requirement specification
S. Liao, J. Ma and L. Lasoudris 123

19 A structured object-oriented view on systems modeling
G. Wu and G. Dedene 127

20 Construction of a WYSIWYG LaTeX typesetting system using object-oriented design
J.H.M. Lee, J.C.K. Leung and C.C.K. Wong 135

21 A re-engineering approach for object-oriented database design
J. Fong and I. Kwan 139

PART FOUR Software Process and Capability

22 Software process model specification
M. Baldi and M.L. Jaccheri 149

23 Soft systems methodology – a process view
G. Tate 156

24 BOOTSTRAP – improving the capability of software industry with database support
J. Jarvinen 162

PART FIVE Project Management

25 On the optimal timing of software development cycle
H.A. Wan 173

26 Information systems project manager's critical success factors: in-house verses outsourced development
H. Rehesaar and A. Rose 177

27 Measuring the value and performance of your IT department
T. Lynch 183

PART SIX Quality, Reliability, Standards

28 ISO standards in software engineering
J. Billington 189

29 An investigation of desired quality attributes for different types of software
T. Musson and E. Dodman 193

30 A unifying model for software quality engineering
I. Tervonen 200

31 Quality achievement: current practices and the way ahead
J. B.Thompson 206

32 Software reliability models for practical applications
M. Xie 211

33 Assessing the quality of requirements engineering products
R.E.M. Champion 215

34 Re-certification of software reliability without re-testing
C. Wohlin 219

35 SAFE: a programming language for software quality
B.K. Oliver and R.G. Dromey 227

36 Impact of organisational maturity on software quality
M. Tan and C.Y. Yap 231

37 Using strongest postconditions to improve software quality
S. Pan and R.G. Dromey 235

PART SEVEN Specifications, Metrics, Assessment

38 Experience in software inspection techniques
D.A. Brunskill and A. Samuel 243

39 Measuring process improvement: integrating software process assessment with quality cost evaluation
M.P. Neilson and T.P. Rout 250

40 Mutation versus all-uses: an empirical evaluation of cost, strength and effectiveness
W.E. Wong, A.P. Mathur and J.C. Maldonado 258

41 Software quality: the user's point of view
M. Xenos and D. Christodoulakis 266

42 Complexity measures for system development models
E.H. Ferneley, D.A. Howcroft and C.G. Davies 273

43 Composite complexity measures (CCM)
P.S. Grover and N.S. Gill 279

44 Automated testing tool for NATURAL®
S.-L. Hung, L.-f. Kwok and K.C.-k. Law 284

45 Analysis of data collected from software development case studies
R. Hunter 290

46 A framework for software development technical reviews
L.P.W. Kim, C. Sauer and R. Jeffery 294

47 A model-based approach for software test process improvement
L. Lian, F. Fujita, S. Kusumoto, K.-i. Matsumoto, K.Kikuno and K. Torii 300

48 Size estimation for C programs with different applications
C.J. Lokan 308

49 Cyclomatic complexity as a measure of the structure of knowledge-based/expert systems
T.T. Moores 314

50 S/C: a software size/complexity measure
Y.R. Pant, J.M. Verner and B. Henderson-Sellers 320

51 A critical re-examination of cyclomatic complexity measures
B. Henderson-Sellers and D. Tegarden 328

52 Reliability through cooperative work in software testing
T. Tuikka 336

PART EIGHT Reusability

53 Code reusability mechanisms
X. Castellani and H. Jiang 345

54 Rule-based reasoning approach for reusable design component retrieval
S.-T. Lai and C.-C. Yang 353

55 A multi-layer metrics combination model for reusable software components
S.-T. Lai and C.-C. Yang 361

PART NINE Integrated Environments, Case Tools

56 Environment for three dimensional graphics user interface development
Y.K. Chan, S. Kwong, C.H. Lee and K.L. Chan 369

57 PEACE: process evolution and adaptation CASE environment – its framework and requirements
T. Yoshida, A. Murata and M. Azuma 378

58 Software development environments to support model consistency
V.E. Veraart and S.L. Wright 382

PART TEN Education and Training

59 Process oriented instruction for software engineers (POISE): perspectives and experiences
S. Thummalapalli and R.K. Todi 389

60 OO methods in teaching: current experience and future possibilities
G. Lovegrove, P. McLaughlin, J. Chabik and P. Standen 395

Index of contributors 401

Keyword index 402

PREFACE

The International Federation for Information Processing (IFIP) is a body which aims to co-ordinate the various facets of computing/information processing across the world. IFIP has an infrastructure of Technical Committees (TCs), each of which has a number of Working Groups (WGs). TC-3 is concerned with computers in education. Within this, W.G. 3.4 is a Working Group whose brief is education and training for IT professionals and advanced end-users while the brief of W.G. 5.4 is the quality and certification of industrial software.

The specific aims of WG3.4 include :

- the promotion of effective education and training of IT professionals and advanced end-users;
- the maintenance of up-to-date IT professional education curricula;
- the dissemination of knowledge on current best practice in IT education;
- the exploration of technological advances in the delivery of training and education; and
- the consideration of internationally recognised qualifications for professional certification and registration.

The Working Conference entitled "First IFIP/SQI International Conference on Software Quality and Productivity (ICSQP'94)" was produced with the co-operation of IFIP, the Software Quality Research Institute of Australia, the Hong Kong Computer Society and the City Polytechnic of Hong Kong.

The aim of the conference was to provide a forum for discussion among researchers and practitioners interested in the efficient production of quality software systems. The two major themes running through the conference were quality and productivity.

A total of 2 invited papers and 58 papers accepted from those submitted to the conference form the scientific and professional contents for the 3 days of lectures and discussions. To safeguard the quality of the conference, all the accepted papers have been subject to a peer group evaluation process. These papers shall provide the basis for three days of continued interest among the participants and ensure lively debates within the formal sessions of the conference and, not less important, during the free meetings in between the formal sessions.

As would be expected from any contemporary conference focusing on software productivity, many papers addressed the issues involved in object-oriented design and development. The shift to object-orientation as a major, if not predominant, paradigm for software development promises to deliver the increases in productivity which have been the goal of developers for the past two decades.

Issues relating to education and training bear out the necessity for education providers to have flexible curricula which can change to reflect advances in current theory and practice. The sharing of experiences from such a wide variety of sources is one of the major attractions of these conferences.

The production of quality software systems depends on reliable methods of producing software specifications and their subsequent evaluation against those requirements. Many of the papers addressed issues related to software metrics and the approaches able to be applied to software testing.

There was much discussion of design and development methodologies and their role in the issues of both quality and productivity and of the perennial problem of software reusability. The movement towards object-orientation as a design paradigm has had reusability as one of its major cornerstones. The papers in these proceedings should provide a source of current thinking and practice in this area.

We trust that readers of these proceedings will obtain much of the benefit enjoyed by those who participated in the conference.

We wish to express our thanks for the authors of the paper and to those who laboured long and hard to bring the conference itself to fruition and to enable these proceedings to be compiled.

The editors.

INTERNATIONAL PROGRAM COMMITTEE

Dr Ben Zion BARTA (Chair)	Israel
Professor Sandro BOLOGNA (Co-Chair)	Italy
Professor R. Geoff DROMEY (Co-Chair)	Australia
Professor Peter JULIFF (Co-Chair)	Australia
Dr Matthew K. O. LEE (Co-Chair)	Hong Kong
Prof Phillip Sallis	New Zealand
Prof M Azuma	Japan
Prof M Maiocchi	Italy
Prof J Billington	Australia
Prof Dave Bustard	United Kingdom
Mr Mike Deutsch	United States
Prof N Fenton	United Kingdom
Prof C Ghezzi	Italy
Prof Dick Hamlet	United States
Prof Robin Hunter	United Kingdom
Prof Graham Tate	Hong Kong
Prof Su Yunlin	People's Republic of China
Mr Terry Rout	Australia
Dr Min Xie	Singapore
Dr Chuk Yau	Australia
Dr June Verner	Hong Kong
Dr T H Tse	Hong Kong
Dr Ernest Lam	Hong Kong
Dr B Kitchenham	Hong Kong
Dr John Edwards	United Kingdom
Dr Trevor Moores	Hong Kong

ORGANIZING COMMITTEE

Dr Matthew K. O. LEE (Chair)	Hong Kong
Dr S. L. HUNG (Co-Chair)	Hong Kong
Mr T. P. Rout (Co-Chair)	Australia

SPONSORS

International Federation of Information Processing (IFIP):
W.G.3.4 (Education and Training of IT Professionals and End Users)
W.G.5.4 (Industrial Software Quality and Certification)
Software Quality Research Institute (SQI), Australia
Hong Kong Computer Society
City Polytechnic of Hong Kong
Department of Information Systems
Department of Computer Science

The City Polytechnic of Hong Kong supported the Conference as part of its 10th Anniversary Academic Conference Programme.

PART ONE

Keynote Papers

1

Towards the 21st Century's Software, State of the art and International Standard in JTC1/SC7

Motoei Azuma
Department of Industrial Engineering and Management, Waseda University
3-4-1, Okubo, Shinjuku-ku, Tokyo 169, Japan

1. INTRODUCTION

Efforts towards better software quality have been made for over three decades. In sixties to early seventies (1960 - 1971), most of the efforts were focused on testing and debugging. Then software engineering emerged. The following latter seventies and early eighties (1972 - 1982) are considered to be the age of software engineering, especially structured techniques such as structured analysis, design, coding and testing. After then (1983 - 1994) CASE tools have been the key topics driven by such technologies as Object Oriented, Artificial Intelligence and Graphical User Interface. Unix based workstations and personal computers have made great progress during this period. Another remarkable advance have made in the field of software management including software metrics, TQM (Total Quality Management) in software and process improvement.

Nevertheless, much efforts have yet to be made. This paper focuses on recent technologies in the area of software management and related international standard in ISO/IEC JTC1/SC7.

2. APPROACH AND MODEL

There are three approaches for improving software quality and productivity. They are information science approach, industrial engineering approach and human factors approach. Software management is an industrial engineering approach which applies industrial engineering technologies into software production. The main goal of software management is to develop or maintain a better quality software product at a lower cost by a target date. However, it is not enough. Managerial effort to improve the organization, where staff are working in better environment and trying to achieve better results, is considered to be more important.

The goals of software management are metrication, standardization, and automation (Figure 1). Metrication means to make an attribute of management object to be measurable. In every area of industry, if they want to manage any object, such attributre of the objects as productivity, human performance, cost and quality must be measurable.

Standardization is the important driving force for better management. Both product standards and process standards have contributed to the progress in various industries. Product standards helped consumer to select a product from wider variety of products, and helped to aquire a parts for maintenece. Process standards made it possible that the process be automated and that inexperienced workers make a good job.

Automation means to automate effort required for management, such as data collection and analysis. By automation a manager can concentrate on decision making for exceptional matter and risk management.

The author developed a cause effect model (Figure 2) which shows relation between environmental factors, process and results of the process, and made joint questionnaire survey on software management in EC (EU) and Japan based on it. There are both external and internal environmental factors which are directly influential on the process or have indirect influence

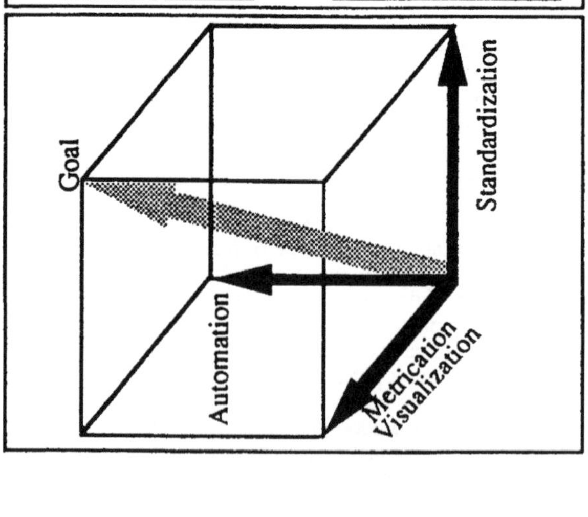

Fig.1 Management Approach

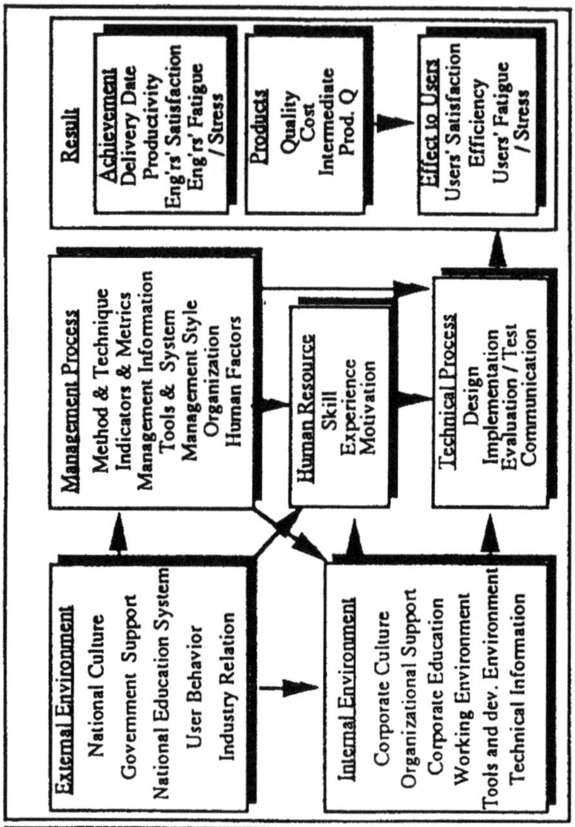

Fig.2 Software Management Cause-Effect Model

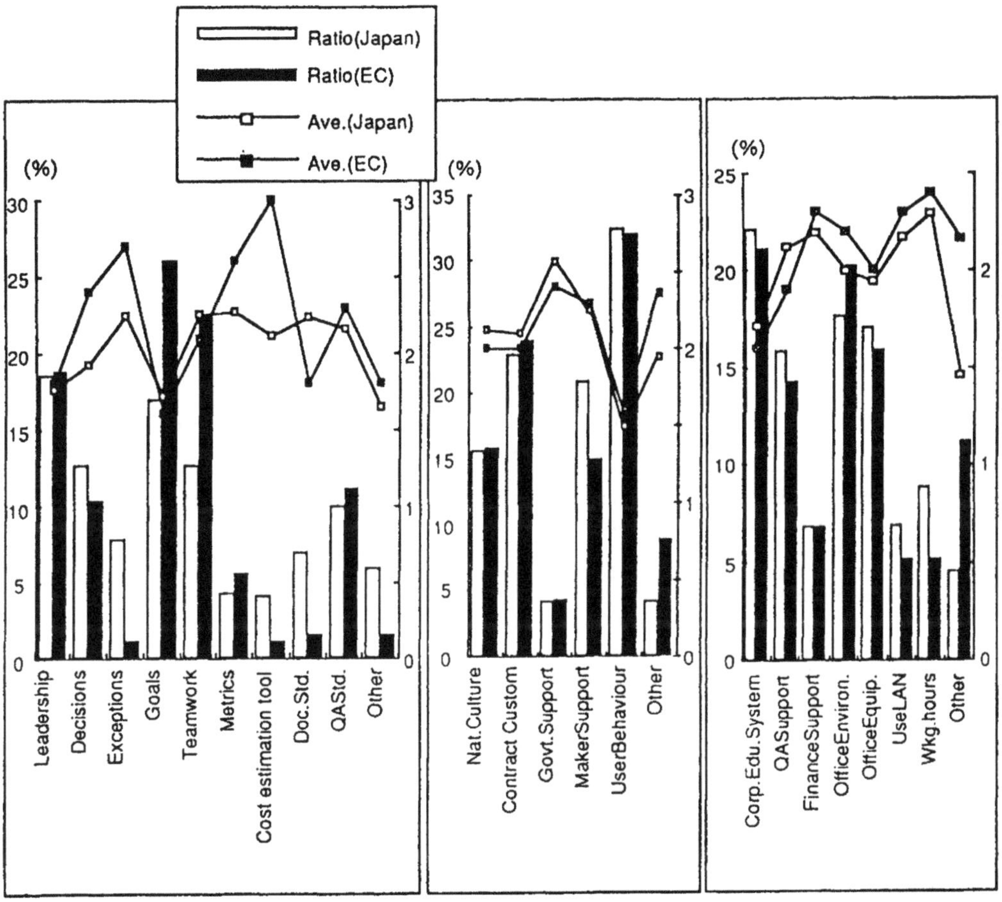

Fig.3a Influential Management Factors

Fig. 3b Influential External Factors

Fig.3c Influential Supporting Functions

through management or human factors. Some interesting results, such as influential factors were clarified (Figure 3) [1].

3. ENVIRONMENT AND SUPPORT

3.1 Organizational Support

Because of very rapid growth in information technologies, a software engineer has too many things to study and the volume of new information in the area beyond human capability to handling. Therefore the support by professional staffs is vitally important. A successful organization receives organizational support from such staffs as software engineering laboratories, fiance department and quality assurance department. Some companies have software engineering laboratories for developing and transfering technologies. Quality assurance and Software engineering are selected as important organizational supporting functions by EC/J survey. Corporate education function is also recognized as important. Most of Japanese large company have good corporate education system. External consultants may be helpful especially for those companies which are not large enough to have independent supporting organizations. Guides for these supporting functions should be established soon.

3.2 Tools Environment Support

Workstations and personal computers have made grate progress in cost performance. UNIX and MS-DOS have been also successful. GUI (Graphical User Interface) is now very popular, and Macintosh. MS-Windows and X-Window are widely used. In earlier days, UNIX based programming support environments were centralized, but they became personalized. And recently these personalized environments are connected to each other with local and wide area network and form distributed systems. This distributed environment is more difficult and time consuming to manage. Yet many organizations do not have any professional staff for system management support.

Many kinds of tools to support software works were developed. Among them, CASE (Computer Supported Software Engineering) tools are getting well-known. But, unfortunately, because of wrong pricing policy (too expensive), they are not widely used. Because of diversity of computer hardware, network and software, recent tools and their environment are not so easy to integrate and maintain. That is why tools integration and management support is also selected as important supporting function.

Standards such as CDIF (CASE Data Interchange Format) by CDIF Technical Committee in USA and PCTE (Portable Common Tool Environment) by ECMA(European Computer Manufacturers Association) TC33 in Europe are expected to solve this problem. SC7/WG11 has many projects in this field. SC7 decided to accept CDIF documents as onputs to the WG11 works. SC7/WG4 has projects on CASE tool selection and implementation.

4. PROCESS ASSESSMENT AND IMPROVEMENT

One of the essential concept of traditional Japanese TQM is to improve quality by process. This means that a person in charge of a process is also responsible for quality. He/she must think the person in charge of the next process as a customer. So he/she must try to improve the process. Major Japanese computer mainframers have made efforts to apply this concept into software. SWQC in NEC, which tried to improve a process by means of QC group activity, is well known as a successful case.

Process assessment has become suddenly fashionable since SEI published its method [2]. There are two possible reasons of it. Various attempts to analyze Genjo (current status) of software process and make Kaizen (improvement) have been made in many companies where TQM was applied in software. These companies needed more formal checklists, criteria for Genjo Analysis and guidelines for Kaizen. Other companies needed more generic guidelines for process improvement. SEI method met these requirement. However, it is still at the entrance of the technology development for process improvement. The technology to make the human process evollutional, and the environment which adapt to the process are possible goals for it. IEEE transaction on Software Engineering had a "Special section on the evolution of software process" in December 1993, and IEEE Software edited "Measurement Based Process Improvement" issue in July 1994. Many conferences and workshops on software process, such as ICSP (International Conference on Software Process), ISPW (International Software Process Workshop) and European Workshop on Process Modeling have been held.

In JTC1/SC7, WG7, WG8 and WG10 are working on developing standards in the software process field. DIS 12207 Software Life Cycle Process was developed by WG7 and circulated to the P-member bodies for the final ballot closing on August 28. WG8 has projects on configuration management and quality assurance. WG10 is working on developing a series of standards on process assessment.

5. PRODUCT QUALITY EVALUATION AND METRICS

Many works have been done in this field individually or sometimes relatedly. They include quality model, Metrics and methodologies and their supporting tools. The followings are some examples of them.

5.1 Quality Model

The concept and technique of quality deployment is well known as one of the important techniques in Japanese TQM. When we evaluate quality of anything, for several characteristics. For example, quality of a car is evaluated taking such characteristics as, e.g., reliability, performance, safety, comfort and drivability, into consideration. Relative weight (Importance) of each characteristics varies depending on nature of the target and user's purpose. Quality characteristics (or factors) can be deployed. This structure is called quality model.

Boehm [3], McCall [4], developed quality model in 1976 and 1977 respectively. Several models followed in Japan. Based on these experiences, INSTAC (Information Technology Research and Standardization Center) of JSA (Japanese Standards Association) made a five-year-research on quality evaluation standardization. The model developed by INSTAC was used as a input for ISO/IEC 9126. ISO/IEC 9126 (Information technology - Evaluation of software product - Quality Characteristics) defines six quality characteristics and subcharacteristics [5]. ISO/IEC 9126 has been widely used even before it was published as international standard.

5.2 Metrics and Indicators

There are only a few well known metrics that are used. Examples are Complexty metrics, Cyclomatic number, module metrics, such as, Fan-in and Fan-out, Cohesion and Coupling [6], [7], [8]. However, only a limited number of companies are using these metrics.

In order to utilize these metrics, it is important that there are some guides to utilize these metrics for specific purpose and guides to develop a metric when necessary. And engineers must be well educated. ESPRIT (European Strategic Program for Research in Information Technology) supported a project METKIT (Metrics Education and Training KIT) which developed a tool kit for metrics education [9].

INSTAC developed a series of indicators and metrics which were contributed as an initial input to support JTC1/SC7 project 7-13 (ISO/IEC 9126 Series).

Function Point is another topics for standardization in the area of software metrics. Though FP is not a metrics to measure quality but a metric to measure a size of software, it is important not only for scale and cost estimation of a project but also for quality management, because many quality indicators are normalized by a scale of a software. SC7/WG12 is a very new working group to standardize the Function Point supported by International Function Point User Group.

5.3 Quality Requirement

In order to develop or acquire better quality software, requirement should be stated clearly for every quality characteristic. It is desirable that requirement is shown with quantitative evaluation criteria using metrics. However, most of requirement technologies are focusing only on functional requirement, and sometimes on efficiency requirement. Usability is an another area of topics but not in software engineering community but in ergonomics community. There are several good check lists developed by Shneiderman and ESPRIT which are useful for both usability requirement and review [10], [11].

Six quality characteristics and subcharacteristics defined in ISO/IEC 9126 can be applicable for this purpose. ISO/IEC 12119 (Information technology - Quality Requirement and Testing) describes quality requirement and testing directives based on ISO/IEC 9126, which are also applicable if the target software is a consumer software. However more effort is necessary to develop and validate indicators and metrics to state quality requirement and criteria qualitatively.

5.4 Evaluation Methodology

In USA, Murine [12] developed SQM (Software Quality Metrics) based on McCall model. He placed a Metric level under the criteria of McCall Model and developed metrics, though most of the metrics are subjective and ad hoc. A metric is a rule and method to measure an attribute of software. Basili et al. are organized the TAME project [13] and are developing a system for quality management. Their approach is called GQM, that is, Goal, Question and Metric. Nance and Arthor of Virginia Polytechnic developed a methodology sponsored by US Navy [14].

In Japan Azuma (the author) et al developed SQMAT [15], and IBM Japan developed SQULAS in 1982. based on Japanese traditional quality deployment approach. Since then, major Japanese computer companies have developed its own quality system, which caused new problem to the software users. Miyoshi et al. [16] tried to evaluate software development environment quality.

In Europe, ESPRIT project took major role in developing information technologies. ESPRIT had another project on software metrics called SCOPE. SCOPE was used as a initial input to the Evaluators' Guide written bellow.

JTC1/SC7/WG6 (Convenor: M. Azuma) is developing the following series of guides for evaluation of software product to support ISO/IEC 9126.

Part 1	General Guide (Co-editor: M. Azuma, N. Bevan, S. Nishiyama)
Part 2	Managers' Guide (Editor: T. Ipoly)
Part 3	Developers' Guide (Editor: H. Schafer, J. Boegh)
Part 4	Buyers' Guide (Editor: J. Harauz)
Part 5	Evaluators' Guide (Editor: P. Robert)
Part 6	Evaluation Module Guide (Editor: J. Boegh)

6. HUMAN FACTORS

Human capability is more diverse in mental area than physical are. An Olympic marathon runner can run two times faster than a city runner in speed. However, expert programmer can be 30 times efficient than novice programmer in productivity. Therefore more effort should be focused on this area including motivation, team, human relation, education and training, and working environment.

Software psychology is one of the most important research area in human factors where B.Shneiderman made initial contribution [17]. Dr. Fujigaki made interesting research in the Techno-stress field [18] and published a book (in Japanese) on it. Concerning the team structure, once the chief programmer team, egoless team and matrix team and so on were area of interests. But it seems that most of researcher in the area lost their interest in this field.

Working environment was another topics. The author proposed the initial idea of Satellite Office. The experimental office was built in a suburb of Tokyo [19]. It aimed to offer software engineers such environment that one or a small group of software engineers can work in a satellite office which is located in urban residential area, outside of the main office, co-operatively with engineers in the main office or in another satellite office as if they were working by sitting side by side in the same office.

A CSCW (Computer Supported Co-operative Work) and a groupware are geting growing interest and concern of many researchers, manageres and users [20], [21]. But it seems that definitions of these terms have still not concensus. CSCW is a generic name of the concept or work style which represents that a group of people work co-operatively by means of computer support. Groupware is a name for the technology or software to support CSCW. CSCW/ Groupware is one promising technology area for supporting software development and maintenance process, becuse still software process is man power intensive work and it should be co-operative. CASE tools must have CSCW feature in near future. However, it will take longer before a new work item for international standard in this area will be proposed.

7. CONCLUSION

Conputer science and engineering approaches, industrial engineering and management approaches and human factors approaches are not exclusive but complementary or co-operative to each other. Advaces were made in these area, such as CASE tools, software metrics, quality assurance and CSCW for the past ten years. Some of them were co-operative. It is important that new technologies are harmonized and that researchers in this field will always keep it in their mind. Efforts for standardization will be increased and the process will be accelrated.

However, because of reasons as follows, more effort must be done for the quality and productivity improvement of software.

(1) Emerging new technologies in information systems, such as multi media and vertual reality, require new software engineering. New concepts may be necessary for this problem. There is egg and chicken relation between information technologies and software engineering.

(2) No matter how deliverately requirement is analyzed, it will change. Evolutional software process paradigm and its supporting environment and adaptive software look like promising solutions.

(3) Human brain process is difficult to understand. Developing a CASE tool with groupware functionality and adaptive to the user looks like promising alternative solutions.

REFERENCES

1 Software Management Practice and Metrics EC and Japan, Proc. AQuIS 93

2 W.S.Humphrey, Managing the Software Process, Addison-Wesley, 1989

3 B.W.Boehm et al., Quantitative Evaluation of Software Quality, Proc. 2nd ICSE(International Conference on Software Engineering), pp592 - 605

4 McCall et al., Rome Air Develop Center Report, TR-77-369, 1977

5 ISO/IEC 9126: Information technology - Evaluation of software - Quality characteristics and guides for their use.

6 R.Dumke, Softwareentwicklung nach Masz, Vieweg, 1992

7 N.E.Fenton, Software Metrics A rigorous approach, Chapman and Hill, 1991

8 K.H.Moller, and D. J. Paulish, Software Metrics, Chapman and Hill, 1993

9 M.Bush and M.Russel, Software Engineering Measurement: A Modular Course, Proc. COMPSAC 91, pp571 - 576

10 Schneiderman, Designing the user interface, second Edition, Addison-Wesley, 1992

11 S.Ravden and G.Johnson, Evaluating Usability of Human-Computer Interfaces, Ellis Horwood,1989

12 G.E.Murine et al., Measuring Software Product Quality, Quality Progress, Vol.17, No.5, pp16-20, 1984

13 V.R.Basili and H.D.Rombach, The TAME Project : Towards Improvement-Oriented Software Environments, IEEE Trans. on Software Engineering, Vol.14 No.6, pp758-773, 1988

14 Arthur, J.D. and Nance, R.E., Developing an automated procedure for evaluating software development methodologies and associated products- A final report, Technical report SRC-87-007, Systems Research Center and Virginia Tech, 1987

15 T.Sunazuka and M.Azuma, Software Quality Measurement and Assessment Technology, Proc. 8th ICSE, pp142 - 148, 1985

16 Miyoshi, Azuma,An Empirical Study of Evaluating Software Development Environment Quality, IEEE Tr. SE Vol. No.

17 B.Shneiderman, Software Psychology, Winthrop, 1980

18 Y.Fujigaki, Interactive Approach to Reduce the Stress of Working Group in Information Technology, Proc. 11th Congress of International Ergonomics Association, pp1265-1267, 1991

19 K.Fujino et al., The Near Future Office Environment in the C&C Era - C&C Satellite office -, NEC RESEARCH & DEVELOPMENT, No.81, pp1-7, 1986

20 D.Diaper and C.Sanger Eds., CSCW in Practice: An Introduction and Case Studies, Springer-Verlag, 1993

21 I.Greif Ed., Computer-Supported Cooperative Work: A Book of Readings

2

Software Quality and Productivity Improvement

R.G. Dromey
Software Quality Institute,
Griffith University, Nathan, QLD., 4111, AUSTRALIA

Abstract

For there to be order-of-magnitude improvements in the quality of software and the productivity of software development and evolution there needs to be a much more strategic approach to software engineering. Such an approach needs to place a balanced emphasis on both software products and software development processes. A set of factors that are likely to make the most significant contributions to quality and productivity improvement are identified and discussed.

Keyword Codes: D.2.0 D.2.4, D.3.0, K.1.0, F.3.1
Keywords: Software Engineering, Reengineering, Reuse, Software Metrics

1. INTRODUCTION

For a long time in software engineering the dominant focus has been upon all that is associated with *software development*. What has become clear over recent years is that if we want to produce quality software, cost-effectively then it will be necessary to focus on improving both the *products* of software development and the *processes* used to develop software. Both *software* and the *processes* used to develop software may be subjected to three things:

- **development**
- **evaluation** (evaluation = assessment, measurement, inspection, audit)
- **improvement**

As the following diagram illustrates, up until recently the focus in software engineering has been in the top left-hand corner rather than in the other five segments. The challenge that we face is to raise the maturity of our knowledge, tools and practices associated with these other five segments. As progress is made in these areas it will make increasingly important contributions to the quality of software and the productivity of software development.

SOFTWARE	PROCESS
Software Development	Process Development
Software Evaluation	Process Evaluation
Software Improvement	Process Improvement

(shaded) Traditional focus of Software Engineering

(unshaded) Quality and Productivity-Oriented Software Engineering

2. PROBLEM DOMAIN

In broadening the focus of software engineering to concentrate on quality and productivity improvement [1] a number of key problems need to be addressed:

- We need to develop a much more mature understanding of what constitutes quality software. Progress on this problem through the construction of better *quality models* is a prerequisite for (a) building quality into software, (b) evaluating the quality of software and (c) improving the quality of existing software.

- Much currently produced software and large tracts of legacy code is of poor quality and must undergo rework restructuring and/or reengineering. More powerful *reegineering* methods and tools are needed. A major problem looming is the need to protect and exploit existing software investments in the face of massive changes in computer architecture expected over the next ten years.

- Software is difficult and costly to maintain and yet there is a high demand to modify and/or enhance it because organisations must keep adapting to changing environments. We must build on the contribution that object-oriented techniques have made to making software more *resilient to change*. Object-oriented techniques only partly solve the problem.

- The high cost of developing software c.f. other technology means that we must find ways to make *reuse* of existing software effective in order to improve productivity and quality. Environments must be developed that make all forms *reuse* easy to practice for computing professionals. Again object-oriented techniques only partly solve the problem.

- There are ever-increasing needs to develop highly complex systems for poorly understood problems. A priority is to find less vulnerable ways of responding to such problems through more effective means of identifying the real requirements for such systems. Developing a system is a learning process, rather an activity with clear preset goals.

- It is not well-established how to create, and maintain, effective and repeatable software development processes that produce quality software, economically. In responding to this we will need to come to terms with the role technology needs to play in modelling, managing and guiding processes executed by software engineers
- Estimation of cost and schedule for large software projects remains very difficult. We need to develop methods of estimation and risk assessment that model tangible reality rather than reflect seat-of-the-pants understanding.

3. FRAMEWORK FOR IMPROVEMENT

A rigorous framework for engineering quality software that responds to the problems we have identified must be sought [2]. To achieve this goal it will be necessary to strike a balance between the *empirical* and the *formal* and between a *software process* [3] and a *software product* [4] orientation. No single approach alone, is powerful enough to comprehensively address the problem of engineering quality software. An integrated set of methodologies are needed to specify, design, implement, measure, assess, manage, re-engineer and reuse industrial and commercial software and the processes used to develop such software. At the highest level there are three key issues that must be addressed if we are to make substantial gains in software engineering.

Product Quality

To improve software product quality an intensive effort, building on current empirical and scientific/mathematical methods' research, is needed. Useful models and standards for various aspects of software product quality must be defined. These must be supported by tools to assist building quality into software, measuring, assessing and assuring the quality of software and improving poor software by applying powerful restructuring and re-engineering methods. In our quest to improve product quality we should not underestimate the importance of the role that programming languages play. Languages must play a greater role in all aspects of software development rather than simply supporting the implementation.

Process Effectiveness

The effectiveness of the processes used to develop software has a very significant impact on both the quality of software produced and the productivity of the development, maintenance and evolution of software. Defined, repeatable and assured processes are needed to cost-effectively produce quality software - that is, *a quality process is needed to produce quality products*. To improve the productivity of software development and software utilisation several approaches must be pursued. One approach involves focussing on key aspects of *process improvement*. Another approach involves reducing the need to develop new software by effective *reuse* of existing software in the development of new systems. A third approach involves integrating specification, design and implementation into a much more seemless environment. Productivity is also heavily dependent on the effective and strategic deployment of human resources throughout projects.

Technology Transfer

Technology transfer must also play a vital role in improving the quality of software and the productivity of software development. It is generally recognised in software engineering that there is a large gap between state-of-practice and state-of-the-art. This is reflected in such identified problems as low usage of superior software inspection methods that have been available since the 1970's and low uptake of technology to support software testing. Already there are best-practices being used by a select few to achieve remarkable gains in quality and productivity. *The greatest challenge we face is to transfer proven technology to the vast majority who practice software engineering.*

In the discussion which follows we will endeavour to respond to some of the problems that have been identified. Our focus will mainly be on product issues that have the potential to influence both quality and productivity as these are areas that have been somewhat neglected in the software quality debate thus far.

4. PRODUCT QUALITY IMPROVEMENT

There are a very diverse range of things that influence the quality of software. It is therefore very easy to expend effort exploring avenues that are likely to have little payoff. What we must do is identify which factors are likely to make the *most significant* contributions to improving software quality and focus our efforts accordingly. Here we suggest that there six key drivers that have the greatest potential to deliver the highest payoff in improving software product quality

- **product quality model**
- **automated inspection**
- **language**
- **reegineering**
- **measurement**
- **reuse**

We will seek to explain why these factors are the most important and identify how they can contribute to software product quality and productivity improvement. We will also discuss what can be done to exploit these product quality drivers.

Much of the effort to date directed at improving software product quality has focused on the process, establishment of quality management systems and gaining accreditation for those systems. What has guided this focus has been the view that a quality process is needed to produce quality software. Such efforts however are unlikely to lead to substantive improvements in software product quality unless they are guided by comprehensive models of software product quality for each of the key deliverables of development: *the requirements specification, the design, and the implementation.* As the Roman philosopher Senaca wisely put it: *when you know not what harbour you are sailing for any wind is the right one.* What has happened thus far is that many organizations have adopted Quality Management without having a clear idea about what quality software is. As a result *there are plenty of organizations that have costly certified Quality Management Systems but the bottom line is that their software has not shown any marked improvement.*

A very high priority for improving software product quality is therefore to construct suitable models that systematically and comprehensively capture what we mean by quality software. Without such models we have no focus at which to direct our efforts to produce quality software through improvement and refinement of the processes that are used. *You cannot build quality in to software if you don't know what quality is no matter how good your intentions!* Having a model for software product quality can also have a strong influence on each of the other key *quality drivers*.

Up until now there has been very little interest in specifically designing programming languages to facilitate building quality software. Existing languages leave essentially all of the responsibility for building quality into software to the programmers. They do little to provide an environment that supports and encourages the building of quality software. In fact, many languages actively encourage practices which are well known to seriously detract from the quality of software. Good models for software product quality can influence language designers to design better languages that support building quality into software. For example, programs that have structures that result in the execution of statements that use uninitialized variables should not be able to even compile! Embodying sound quality principles within programming languages and their compilers is by far the most efficacious way to realize product quality objectives. We will now make a claim which to many will seem controversial as a way for the future. However existing beliefs and folklore must be challenged if order-of magnitude progress is to be made. *We suggest that programming languages which embody quality principles have the potential to make the single most far-reaching impact on software product quality for the least investment.* Good language tools are an indispensible prerequisite for producing quality software.

It is well recognized in the quality community [5] that in order to improve products and processes it is necessary to make meaningful *measurements*. In many situations it is clear what must be measured. With software however it is far from clear what needs to be measured. This situation has not stopped many organizations from feverishly trying to measure a whole range of things about software in the vain hope that once they have got the measurements they will somehow know how to use such measurements to substantially improve the quality of their software. Unfortunately most of these efforts have had very little useful impact. The reason for this is that they are not linked in any systematic way to a model of software product quality. *The most desirable situation for the application of measurement for improvement is to be able to define an ideal for some property and then make measurements of a product to see if the ideal is realized.* If the ideal is not realized then their is a basis and guidance for improvement. Existing measurement theory for software has not sought such an approach to measurement.

Although the goal should always be to build quality into software it is also necessary to ensure that it has actually been built-in, given human fallibility in the execution of complex tasks. For a long time it has therefore been recognized that *inspections* have an important role to play in producing quality software. Despite this, they are rarely applied effectively and when they are employed properly they are costly to implement given their labour-intensive nature. The whole process of inspection has been hampered by the lack of suitable models of software product quality. Once stable models for software product quality are available it then becomes possible to automate significant aspects of the inspection process and thereby improve the efficiency and effectiveness of inspections.

In most engineering disciplines *reuse* is widely practised. Unfortunately in software engineering this has not been the norm. Given the current labour-intensive nature of software development, the fact that reuse is not significantly exploited makes software development a very costly activity. Object-oriented design and implementation is being hailed by many as the solution to our reuse problems. We have no argument with the idea that O-O can make an important contribution to reuse. However O-O is far from a complete solution to our reuse needs. Key challenges that we face in the reuse area are: how to meaningfully identify and retrieve reusable functionality, how to exploit reuse at much higher levels than O-O allows and how to reclaim reusable software from the vast tracts of legacy code in existence.

In our quest for software product quality improvement we cannot afford to ignore existing software. In any one year the amount of new software created is *small* compared with the amount of existing software that has been built up over many years at huge cost. The major problem we face in regard to existing software is that much of it is of poor quality which makes it troublesome to maintain and change. What is more in today's competitive environment there is always ongoing pressure for organizations to change. And, invariably, this flows through to generating a need for organizations to change their existing software. There is therefore substantial demand to develop powerful means to reengineer poor quality software into restructured software that is much less costly to change. We should also look to apply powerful *reegineering* tools to newly developed software, as it is developed, to ensure that it does not end up as software that will be costly to maintain in the future.

In what follows we will make a number of suggestions for tackling the key factors that have the greatest potential for contributing to an order-of-magnitude improvement in software product quality and software development and maintenance productivity.

QUALITY STRATEGY
Tangible → Intangible

4.1 Model for Software Product Quality

Considerable effort has gone into setting up accredited Quality Management Systems and a plethora of process standards. These efforts must be balanced by an equally substantial focus on software product quality if significant improvements in quality and productivity are to be realized. To date there have been very few attempts to tackle the problem of software product quality systematically and comprehensively. Efforts in this whole area have largely stalled because of:

- the perceived scale of the problem
- the diversity of quality defects in software
- the difficulty of factoring high level quality attributes down to the implementation level

These barriers can be overcome by adopting the strategy of always proceeding from the tangible and measurable to high level less tangible quality attributes. Both empirical and formal means are needed in this undertaking.

4.1.1 Empirical Model

There is plenty of empirical advice scattered throughout the literature about what constitutes good software. However none of this advice amounts to a systematic model for software product quality. We suggest an appropriate starting point for developing such a model is to make the observation that programs are constructed using *structural forms* (e.g., variables, expressions, assignments, loops, etc). A basic characteristic of *forms* is that they possess *properties*. The form-property model [6] can facilitate (i) building quality into software, (ii) detecting quality defects in software (iii) and the systematic classification of quality defects. A focus on quality defects is also able to make a positive, if indirect, contribution to building quality into software by telling us *what not to do*. In considering software the two principal categories of structural forms are those that describe *processes* (that is, the executable statements and statement components of the language) and those that describe *data* (the variables, records etc). To illustrate the process of applying the form-property model we will use several simple examples.

Examples:
Consider the fundamental structural forms: *variables* and *expressions*. To be free of quality defects they should possess a number of defined properties. Here we will simply list the *quality-carrying* properties of variables and expressions:

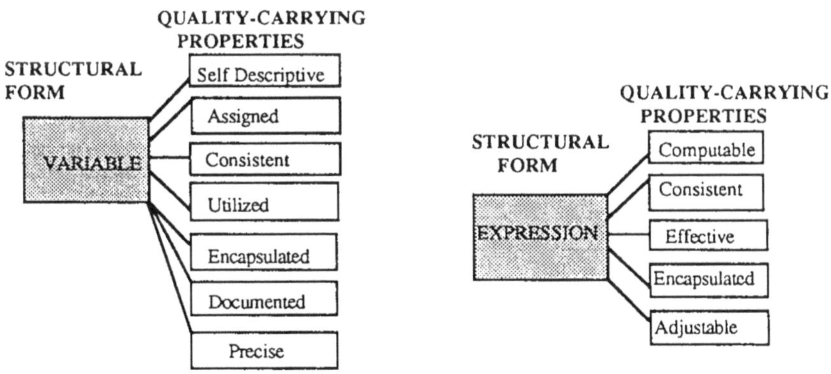

To *build-quality-into* variables and expressions when we implement programs we should therefore ensure that all of the above properties are satisfied. *In a similar way we can associate a set of quality-carrying properties with each of the other structural forms used in programs for a particular programming language.* The result of this exercise is something tangible that programmers and others can use to produce quality software.

In the case of expressions, for example, violation of any of these properties represents a *quality defect* that destroys the expression's integrity. There are also other problems that can arise with expressions. For example, an expression may contain an *unassigned* variable. However, because of the precedence rule used in the classification discipline that is employed this defect will be classified as a *variable integrity* defect rather than as an expression integrity defect even though it impacts the computation of the expression.

This model for software product quality enables us to construct a powerful quality defect classification discipline. The discipline fits our normal intuition regarding defects. It focusses on the *source of the problem* rather than on the consequences of the defect. In the previous example there is no defect directly with the expression. Rather the problem resides elsewhere - the variable should have been assigned before being used in the expression. *A crucial requirement in developing such a framework for categorizing quality defects is that the process is repeatable.* That is, two people confronted with the same defect should arrive at the same classification for that defect. The present proposal attempts to achieve repeatability through the use of bottom-up structural precedence. (e.g. in the example above since variable may be contained within an expression, the variable classification for the defect assumes precedence).

Examples

Defects that violate the quality-carrying properties of expressions are given below:

uncomputable -	divide by zero
inconsistent -	contains side-effects
ineffective - contains	computational redundancy
unencapsulated	uses variable from outside its scope
unadjustable -	contains numbers

All of the above types of defects detract from the quality of expressions. Therefore to build quality into expressions when we implement programs we should avoid these types of defects.

An important additional feature of the empirical model of software product quality that we have described is that it makes direct links between *product characteristics* and high-level *quality attributes*

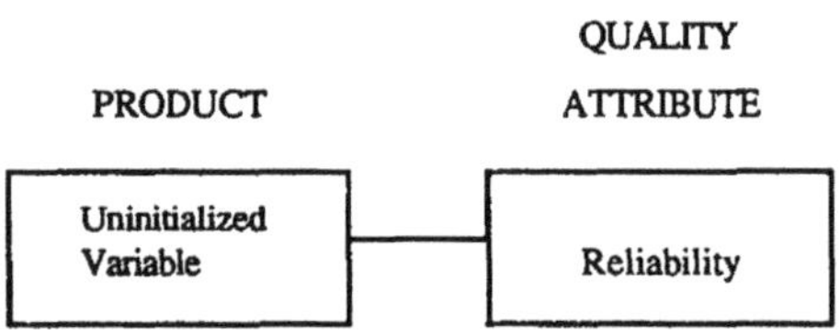

Property of Variable:	Assigned
Quality Attribute:	Reliability
Variable Defect:	Unassigned

In developing this model the intent is to identify and associate a set of properties with each structural form that may be used in a program. The accompanying constructive theorem may then be used to make an assertion about the quality of a given piece of software.

Constructive Theorem

If each of the properties associated with a particular structural form is satisfied when that structural form is used in a program, it will contribute no quality defect to the software.

In other words a program is quality-defect-free when none of the quality-carrying properties of any of its structural forms are violated. On the other hand, there is the complementary assertion that if any of the properties associated with a structural form are violated in a program then each violation will contribute a quality defect to the software.

This model for software product quality is put forward as a framework that may be criticized, refined and if necessary corrected. No claim is made in the expanded treatment of this model [6] that we have listed a complete set of quality-carrying properties for each structural form. For example, at an earlier informal presentation of this model someone in the audience pointed out that an important quality-carrying property of numeric variables is that they have the appropriate *precision*. This is a perfectly reasonable observation and precision has therefore been added to the quality-carrying property-list for variables. What is important is that such an addition to the model does not destroy it but instead constitutes a refinement. For something as complex and difficult to define as software quality it is important to have a model that is easy to refine both in terms of identifying additional quality-carrying properties and in attaching such properties to particular structural forms. Over time such a model has the potential to evolve into a powerful definition. Another advantage of the form-property framework is that it is easy to adapt to any kind of programming language. *It is a systematic, generic yet simple model for software product quality that guides us down the path from the tangible towards quality.*

The fully developed model for software product quality [6] is quite extensive. Here we have only attempted to summarize some of the features of the model. The model is important in that it allows us to achieve our two primary goals. It gives us *direct advice* on building quality into software and at the same time it may be used to assist in the systematic, repeatable classification of quality defects in software. *These are critical steps towards scientific understanding and engineering applicability.*

4.1.2. Formal Model for Software Product Quality

While the empirical model we have described is very useful in practice there are still many deficiencies in software that it cannot easily capture. We suggest that this approach needs to be complemented with a formal model for software product quality. Such a model can assist us in three important ways:

- it admits constructive verification and detection of a wider class of defects
- it provides a basis for improving and re-engineering software
- it points to a powerful measurement discipline for software quality

The feature of formal methods is that they allow us to focus on the *semantics* of programs. A powerful theoretical tool that can be used to help capture the semantics of program structures is the strongest postcondition [7,8]. In developing a framework for assessing, improving and measuring software quality we may exploit the application of strongest postconditions. Their important advantage is that they allow the derivation of specifications from program components. Such specifications formally and accurately characterize program semantics. A conceptual definition of a strongest postcondition is given below.

Strongest Postcondition
Given any Hoare triple {P} S {Q}, the strongest postcondition Q is the final state such that for any variable set, if the initial value set satisfies P, then the final values must satisfy Q. The strongest condition at the execution point after execution of S under the precondition P is denoted by sp(P,S).

Since the strongest postcondition describes the strongest condition at each execution point, we can use it to identify a number of significant quality defects. For example, an unreachable branch is one where the precondition, i.e. the strongest postcondition of the previous statements, implies the negation of the corresponding branch guard.

Unreachable Branch
Given any multi-branch statement $\textit{if } C_1 \rightarrow S_1 \;[]\; C_2 \rightarrow S_2 \;[]\; \ldots \;[]\; C_n \rightarrow S_n \textit{ fi}$, *under precondition P, where* $n \geq 2$, *a branch* $C_i \rightarrow S_i$ *is called unreachable if* $P \Rightarrow \neg C_i$.

This definition formally captures an ideal for branch statements. It tells us that all branches of an if-statement should be reachable. It also defines the logical (semantic) property that is exhibited by a branch when it violates the ideal by being unreachable.

Example

Under the precondition $x=a \wedge y=x$, only the second branch in *if* $x+y>2a \rightarrow z:=x+y \; [] \; x+y \leq 2a \rightarrow z:=(x+y)/2$ *fi* is reachable

The results of strongest postcondition calculations may also be exploited to identify *redundant assignment* statements.

Redundant Assignment

An assignment S is redundant under a given precondition P if sp(P , S) ≡ P .

This definition once again expresses the *ideal* for inclusion of an assignment statement in a sequence of statements. An assignment statement should only be included in a sequence if the strongest postcondition that holds *after* execution of the statement is not equivalent to the precondition that holds *before* the assignment executes. In other words every state-changing statement must change the state of a computation - otherwise it is redundant.

Example

Given $x:=1$; $y:=x+3$, *if* $x+y>2a \rightarrow y:=4 \; [] \; x+y \leq 2a \rightarrow z:=(x+y)/2$ *fi* under the precondition **true**, strongest postcondition calculations enable the redundant assignment $y:=4$ to be found.

Elsewhere [9] a comprehensive treatment is provided which shows how methods based on the use of strong postcondition calculations may be used to construct a powerful formal model for defining, measuring and improving software product quality.

4.2 Automated Inspection - product evaluation

The empirical model of software product quality that we have sketched above is well-suited to directly linking defects associated with product characteristics to the quality attributes of the ISO-9126 Software Product Evaluation Standard [11]. For example, we have already seen how a defect in which a variable is *unassigned* in an expression directly impacts the *reliability* quality attribute.

A tool called PASS-C (Program Analysis and Style System[12]) which is based on the above empirical form-property model has been developed as a rule-based static analysis system. This system, which contains a large number of rules, is able to analyze the text of C programs and report the presence of a wide range of quality defects. The system is like a compiler in that it pinpoints the line number where each defect occurs and it indicates the nature of the defect. The system classifies the various defects both as product structural form integrity violations and as quality attribute violations such as maintainability, efficiency or reliability problems etc. It also provides a set of summary statistics about the quality of the program being analyzed and its rating against an industry average product quality profile. A typical high-level product quality summary is as follows:

PASS-C Sample Output Abridged

Total Loc processed : 13129
Total quality defects : 1210
Quality defects / KLoc : 92.16
•
•
•

Quality Attributes	Defects	Product Attributes	Defects
Functionality	65	Correctness	423
Reliability	402	Structural	348
Efficiency	151	Modularity	199
Maintainability	1206	Descriptive	240
Portability	148		

Reliability Profile

Times Fired	Rule	Rule Description
4	Rule 6	Hidden Loops
82	Rule 7	Uninitialized Variables
2	Rule 11	Loops that Make No Progress
12	Rule 15	Redundant Conditional Assignment
2	Rule 18	Premature Initialization
48	Rule 25	Duplicate Output
18	Rule 28	Unassigned Address Parameter
62	Rule 29	Function Side Effects
•		
•		
•		

Maintainability Profile

Time Fired	Rule	Rule Description
56	Rule 1	Redundant Declarations
133	Rule 2	Global Variables
20	Rule 3	Poor Naming Conventions
•		
•		
•		

Systems like PASS-C have the potential to make an important and productive interim contribution to assuring the quality of software as it is developed. They allow a significant model of software product quality to be implemented in a very efficient way. Such tools should be on every programmer's workbench aiding him/her to efficiently monitor the quality of software as it is developed and thereby providing the means to build in quality during development. Of course, in the future as quality support is integrated into programming languages the need for such "quality compilers" should largely disappear.

4.3 Language Contribution

We must not underestimate the importance of language in producing quality software cost-effectively [10]. An often quoted example is the difficulty of performing arithmetic computations using the Roman number system. In contrast our present system makes such computations straightforward and mechanical. What we are suggesting is that most existing programming languages do not facilitate building quality software. By implication we also suggest that with better languages the enormous task of building quality software will become significantly easier. This is a strong claim but one which we believe is defensible.

In making a case for this position we will start by presenting a view held by many linguists (and others): *the language that we use to express solutions to problems strongly influences and limits our thinking*. If this is the case, and if it also applies to programming languages then it has significant implications for the shape/architecture of such languages. We claim that the dominant programming languages that are currently in use are most suited for implementing intensive processing activities/computations - that is, algorithms and functions. Unfortunately most of the real world that we want to model consists systems and subsystems of various forms that interact with one another in a variety of different ways. Within such systems/subsystems there is often plenty of computation and large numbers of objects of varying complexity. However computations across systems rarely dominates.

Intensive computations tend to be confined within functions/programs. On the other hand only the *results* of intensive computations tend to be exchanged between programs or subsystems. Existing languages, because of their computational focus, have neglected to provide adequate support for effectively modelling large systems made up of loosely-coupled computationally-intensive programs and subsystems. This forces us to violate the fundamental principle of correspondence which demands that *the structure of the solution should mimick the structure of the problem.* This state of affairs has two important consequences:

- it distorts our thinking about problems that need to be solved using software, and
- it distorts the architecture of software systems which in turn detracts from their quality and their architectural transparency with respect to the problems that they solve.

If we are able to overcome these design flaws in existing languages then we will need languages that support not only programming but also design and reuse at a much higher level (i.e. at the system/subsystem level). Another consequence of such a change in language architecture would be that it would obviate the need for separate CASE tools. *What we must do is come to the realization that programming languages should support design as well as implementation of computations because design is intimately connected with modelling the interaction between subsystems and programs.* Integrating design and implementation is worthy step forward that has the potential to make a very substantial impact on the quality of software and the productivity of software development.

People no longer want to build just programs. There is an increasing need to assemble powerful systems and subsystems - however most programming languages do not support this. Instead they are structurally too flat. This causes us to distort our thinking when trying to solve large problems . Our languages should make it easy to design not only algorithms and programs but also rich systems structures made up of many interacting programs and subsystems. Object-oriented programming languages go only part of the way by modelling objects. In order to control complexity and achieve natural interaction between subsystems and extensive reuse we need to limit the interaction between objects. The object-oriented approach only deals with low level reuse. Much greater progress will occur when we start to reuse whole systems and subsystems rather than just objects.

The language SAFE which seeks to respond to the quality-support deficiencies with existing languages is discussed elsewhere [13].

4.4 Reengineering

In our quest for product quality improvement we must not ignore the very large body of software already in existence. In any one year the amount of new software written is very small compared with the huge amount of software already in existence which keeps most large organizations operational. The problem with this large resource of legacy code is that much of it is of questionable quality and difficult to maintain. However so much money has already been invested in this software that it cannot be easily thrown out and replaced by new and better software. In many instances organizations are stuck with having to maintain and modify large tracts of poor quality software. The problem with this is that it is a very costly and labour-intensive activity.

Strongest postcondition calculations provide a powerful framework for formally re-engineering software to produce improved program structures that satisfy the original specification [14]. In this section we will show how formal methods may be used to remove redundant statements and simplify the bodies of loops.

4.4.1 Removing Redundant Statements.

Strongest postcondition calculations coupled with simplifying logical equivalence transformations provide a powerful means for removing redundancy from complex structures.

Example:
Consider the following highly redundant Abstract Program **AP** suggested by Manna [15].

```
If p(y) → x:=y; do ¬p(x) → x:=f(x) od
[] ¬p(y) →
    x:=a;
    If p(x) → do ¬p(x) → x:=f(x) od
    [] ¬p(x) →
        x:=f(x);
        If p(x) →
            x:=a; do ¬p(x) → x:=f(x) od
        fi
    fi
fi
```

The strongest postcondition calculation for this Abstract Program under the initial precondition **true** yields[]:

sp(**true**, **AP**)
≡ sp(**true**∧p(y), x:=y; *do* ... *od*) ∨ sp(**true**∧¬p(y), x:=a; *If* ... *fi*))
:
≡ (p(y)∧x=y) ∨ (¬p(y)∧p(a)∧x=a) ∨ (¬p(y)∧¬p(a)∧x=f(a))

The calculated strongest postcondition characterizes the behaviour of the above program and the formally transformed *equivalent* program below from which all logical redundancy has been removed:

```
If p(y) → x:=y
[] ¬p(y) → If p(a) → x:=a []¬p(a) → x:=f(a) fi
fi
```

4.4.2 Restructuring Complex Loops

Loops are frequently poorly structured. We may use a similar approach to that described in the previous section to identify the reachable branch set for loop structures. The formal process for re-engineering branched loop structures is called *loop rationalization*. It is described in detail elsewhere[14]. Here we will only briefly summarize the process. We start with a branched loop body and assume that **Inv** is the invariant of the loop (when the loop invariant **Inv** is not available the weakest invariant **true** is used). We then proceed to calculate the strongest postcondition for each branch, i.e.

do G →

$$
\begin{array}{ll}
\textit{if}\ C_1 \rightarrow S_1 & \{sp(G \wedge \mathbf{Inv} \wedge C_1, S_1) \\
[]\ C_2 \rightarrow S_2 & \{sp(G \wedge \mathbf{Inv} \wedge C_2, S_2) \\
[]\ \ldots & \\
[]\ C_n \rightarrow S_n & \{sp(G \wedge \mathbf{Inv} \wedge C_n, S_n) \\
\textit{fi} &
\end{array}
$$

od,

where

$$\forall i \forall j((i,j \in [1,n] \wedge j \neq i) \Rightarrow (C_i \Rightarrow \neg C_j))$$

and

$$C_1 \vee C_2 \vee \ldots \vee C_n \equiv \mathbf{true} \text{ for } i,j \in [1,n].$$

These n postconditions $sp(G \wedge \mathbf{Inv} \wedge C_i, S_i)$ determine the successor set of each branch, that is, $\beta_i = \{1,2,\ldots,n\} - \alpha_i$, where $\forall j(j \in a_i \Rightarrow (sp(G \wedge \mathbf{Inv} \wedge C_i, S_i) \Rightarrow \neg (G \wedge C_j)))$. We may assign each branch $C_i \rightarrow S_i$ to a separate node of a directed graph, then connect all nodes that β_i indicates, to form the *branch successor graph* [14].

<u>Example:</u>

Given the following poorly formed loop structure taken from a commercial program :

```
while ((Option = getopt(arge, argv, Voptions)) !=ERROR) {
        if ((char) Option == Optionq) {
                QuitFlag = TRUE;
                if (LevelFlag) {
                        Error = TRUE;
                        break;
                }
                if (SubsytemFlag) {
                        Error = TRUE;
                        break;
                }
                else {
                        if ((char) Option == Optionl) {
                        LevelFlag = TRUE;
                        if (QuitFlag) {
                                Error = TRUE;
                                break;
                        }
                        LevelStr = optarg;
                        }
        }
        else {
                if ((char) Option == Options) {
                        SubsytemFlag = TRUE;
                        Subsystem = optarg;
                        if (QuitFlag) {
                                Error = TRUE;
                                break;
                        }
                }
                else {
                        if ((char) Option == "?") {
                                Error = TRUE;
                                break;
                        }
                }
        }
}
```

Stage I: Guard Resolution

As part of the loop reegineering process we must first resolve the guards associated with each branch. This amounts to calculating all their strongest preconditions - that is we find the condition that applies directly before execution of the assignments in the branch. The result of this process is shown below:

```
while ((Option = getopt(arge, argv, Vailoptions)) != ERROR) {
    if (...== Optionq)∧LevelFlag { QuitFlag = TRUE; Error = TRUE; break; }
    [] (...== Optionq)∧¬LevelFlag∧SubsytemFlag { QuitFlag = TRUE; Error = TRUE; break; }
    [] (...== Optionq)∧¬LevelFlag∧¬SubsytemFlag){ QuitFlag = TRUE; } - - third branch
    [] (...== Optionl)∧QuitFlag { LevelFlag = TRUE; Error = TRUE; break; }
    [] (...== Optionl)∧¬QuitFlag { LevelFlag = TRUE; LevelStr = optarg; }
    [] (...== Options)∧QuitFlag {SubsytemFlag = TRUE; Subsytem = optarg; Error = TRUE; break; }
    [] (...== Options)∧¬QuitFlag { SubsytemFlag = TRUE; Subsytem = optarg; }
    [] (...== "?") { Error = TRUE; break; }
    fi
}
```

Branches that no do cause termination are shown in **bold**

Stage II: Calculation of Strongest Postconditions for Each Branch

The strongest postconditions that apply after each branch is executed must then be calculated. The calculation for the third branch is shown below.

Precondition for Execution of Third Branch

((Option = getopt(...))== Optionq) ∧ ¬LevelFlag ∧ ¬SubsytemFlag

Third Branch

{ QuitFlag = TRUE; }

Strongest Postcondition After Execution of Third Branch

((Option = getopt(...))== Optionq) ∧ ¬LevelFlag ∧ ¬SubsytemFlag ∧ QuitFlag

Successors Accessible After Execution of Third Branch

Comparing the strongest postcondition result with each of the branch guards it is clear that the branches 1, 2, 5, and 7 will not be accessible directly after the third branch has executed. The successors of the third branch are therefore:

{3, 4, 6, 8}

In a similar way we can perform strongest postcondition calculations to determine the successor sets for each of the other branches. We may then use this information to build the branch successor graph for the loop structure. The branch successor graph for our example above is shown in the leftmost part of the figure below:

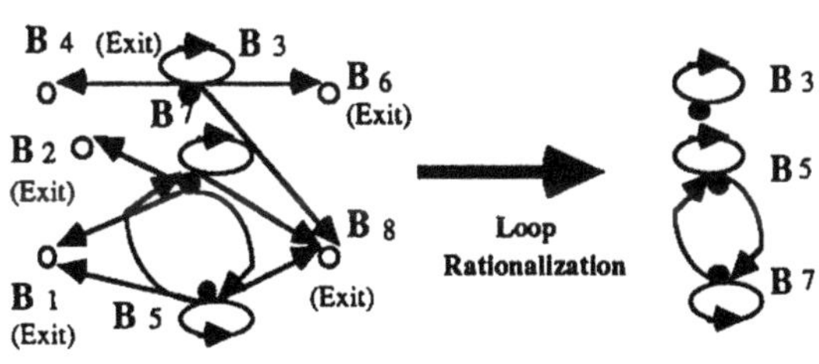

Stage III: Loop Rationalization

Once the BSG has been constructed we have the information we need to transform the loop into a normalized form. Loop rationalization involves removing all the terminating branches from the loop body (i.e. those shown in stage I that are not in bold). These terminating branches correspond to leaf nodes in the BSG. The result is shown below.

```
do ((Option = getopt(...)) == Optionq)∧¬LevelFlag∧¬SubsytemFlag → QuitFlag = TRUE
[] ((Option = getopt(...)) == Optionl) ∧¬QuitFlag → LevelFlag = TRUE; LevelStr = optarg
[] ((Option = getopt(...)) == Options) ∧¬QuitFlag → SubsytemFlag = TRUE; Subsytem = optarg
od;
if (Option == Optionq)∧LevelFlag → QuitFlag = TRUE; Error = TRUE
[] (Option == Optionq)∧¬LevelFlag∧SubsytemFlag → QuitFlag = TRUE; Error = TRUE
[] (Option == Optionl)∧QuitFlag → LevelFlag = TRUE; Error = TRUE
[] (Option == Options)∧QuitFlag → SubsytemFlag = TRUE; Subsytem = optarg; Error = TRUE
[] (Option == "?") → Error = TRUE
fi
```

We will explain later details of the accompanying metric calculations involved for this example. If a loop structure has a branch-successor graph (BSG) that is made up of only strongly connected components then it contains no latent inefficiencies and redundancies. On the other hand, if a BSG is not strongly connected it can be improved by processes of *loop rationalization* and *loop normalization.* Loop rationalization is a re-engineering technique based on strongest postconditions calculations that leads to the removal of all terminating branches from the loop body. In our example above these transformations have led to the construction of a loop with a considerably simpler body. Its BSG (see rightmost graph above), consists only of strongly connected components.

4.5 Measurement

There is a large body of knowledge [16] relating to patterns of composition, structuring, modularization and methods of consistency, proof and verification which provide important, but not metric indications of quality. The one thing that links most, if not all these indicators of quality, is *semantics*. If semantics can be used as the basis for software measurement then it has the potential to provide more direct and meaningful measures of software quality. Strongest postconditions allow us to tap the semantics of program structures. Their important advantage is that they may be used to derive specifications directly from program components. Such specifications formally and accurately characterize program semantics.

To support the semantics approach to measurement it is necessary to have an accompanying quantitative discipline. There are two primary choices: *absolute* versus *relative* measurement. To date most software metrics have focussed on absolute measurement. In the present proposal we will seek to exploit the principle of always measuring things with respect to an *ideal.* A primary motivation for measurement is to seek improvement. Measurement with respect to an ideal has the important property of being *constructive* in relation to quality improvement and re-engineering [17]. The key challenge is to find ways to meaningfully characterize the ideal. The exploitation of semantics for software measurement is directly compatible with, and supportive of, the application of this relative measurement principle. Based on the principles of formal semantics and relative measurement we can define a number of important measures of software quality.

In applying the proposed measurement methodology *strongest postcondition calculations* are used to evaluate software and return a number of values, called ρ-numbers. These numbers, which are ratios, each provide indications of quality relative to an ideal for the particular property that is being measured. If a chosen software component exhibits the ideal with respect to the property that is being measured then the corresponding ratio will have the value 1.

In what follows we will illustrate the flavour of the approach by considering a *reachability* ratio. We claim the reachability ratio provides a much more informative and useful metric than the McCabe Number because it can be used to guide the improvement of the software.

The ρ_d-number is used to measure the reachability of a branched software component. It defines the ratio of the number of reachable executable branches for a component relative to all possible branches that the syntax (not the semantics) indicates should be reachable for that component. The reachability of a multi-branch statement is defined as:

$$\rho_d = \text{(number of reachable branches)/(total number of branches)}$$

$$= (n - n_u)/n$$

where the number of unreachable branches n_u under a precondition are ascertained by applying the necessary implicative requirements for execution. Obviously, $1/n \leq \rho_d \leq 1$. Reachability calculations for a loop structure are given below.

Example:

We can calculate the internal reachability for the poorly structured loop in section 4.4. In this case the BSG has 8 nodes and ideally each node should be accessible from every other node. Counting up the edges and self-rings in the BSG we find that there are only 13 connections instead of $8 * 8 = 64$ and so the internal reachability for the loop structure is only:

$$\rho_d = 13 / 64.$$

This indicates that there is a lot of unnecessary structure in the loop. The validity of this measure is supported by the fact that, as we have shown in the previous section, five branches are able to be removed from the loop body in the re-engineered implementation.

Other formal measures that can be formulated along these lines relate to redundancy, reusability, cohesion and logical consistency in the use of variables. These measures are discussed in detail elsewhere [17].

4.6 Reuse

Earlier in our discussion of language contributions to quality and productivity improvement we considered how they should be designed to support the reuse of large and complex systems and subsystems. Here we wish to consider a more fundamental reuse problem which .is inhibiting existing reuse efforts. *Clearly until reuse technology can be made easy to use, versatile and powerful large numbers of software professionals are not going to show a serious interest in reuse*. Object class libraries go part of the way to addressing this problem. However the fundamental problem that we still face in reuse is how to characterize the functionality of software components so they are easy to store and retrieve from large libraries. People have proposed keyword and facet-based systems [18]. However such systems by no means constitute a general, widely applicable solution to the problem because of the tenuous links between keywords and functionality.

The use of formal specifications offers some hope in that formal specifications in some instances at least are able to accurately capture functionality. There is however the problem that there are many different ways of formally characterizing the same functionality. Fortunately there is one possible way to overcome this obstacle - we can exploit the idea of constructing a *canonical notation* from formally expressed specifications. What a canonical notation does is allow us to map differently expressed but formally equivalent specifications to a single unique canonical form. We would suggest that this approach offers some prospect for in the longer term building powerful reuse systems. Early results using such an approach are discussed elsewhere [2]. At the very least, such an approach has the potential to support the construction of safety critical software.

Conclusion

Order-of-magnitude improvements in software quality and productivity will require a concerted and systematic effort on a number of fronts. There is a need to combine the contributions of both empirical and formal approaches. A process orientation is certainly important but it will need to be guided by comprehensive and systematic models of software product quality. Better languages offer the greatest scope for building quality into software directly. Formal methods also offer considerable opportunities for re-engineering, reuse and meaningful measurement that can point directly to quality improvement and the development of powerful tools that will help us to produce quality software. In our efforts to produce quality software cost-effectively there is plenty of scope to be industrious - the challenge is to be effective.

REFERENCES

1. V.R.Basili, J.D.Musa, *The Future Engineering of Software: A Management Perspective*, Computer, 90-96, September 1991

2. Dromey, R.G., *A Framework for Engineering Quality Software* Australian Software Engineering Conference, Sydney, September (1993)

3. Paulk, M.C. et al. *Capability Maturity Model for Software*, Technical Report CMU/SEI-91-TR-24, Software Engineering Institute, Pittsburgh, Pennsylvania, 1991.

4. *Technology for Evaluation and Certification of Software Product Quality*, SCOPE, ESPRIT Project 2151

5. Deming, W.E., *Out of the Crisis*,

6 Dromey, R.G., *A Model for Software Product Quality*, IEEE Trans. on Soft. Eng. (accepted for publication)

7. Back, R.J.R.: *A Calculus of Refinements for program Derivations*, Acta Informatica 25, 593- 625, 1988

8. Dijkstra, E.W., Scholten, C.S.: *Predicate Calculus and Program Semantics*, Springer-Verlag 1989.

9. Pan, S., Dromey, R.G., *Software Quality Improvement Using Formal Methods* , Research Report, Software Quality Institute, (1994)

10. Dromey, R.G., McGettrick, A.D.: *On Specifying Software Quality*, Software Quality J., 1-31, 1992.

11. *ISO-9126 Software Product Evaluation - Quality Characteristics and Guidelines for Their Use* (1991)

12. *PASS-C: Program Analysis and Style System for C*, Software Quality Institute, Technical Report, (1993)

13. Oliver, B., Dromey, R.G., *SAFE: A Programming Language for Software Quality* , First Asia-Pacific Conference on Software Quality and Productivity, (1994)

14. Pan, S., Dromey, R.G., *Loop Rationalization* , Computer Journal, (submitted for publication) (1994)

15. Manna, Z: *Properties of Programs and the First-Order Predicate Calculation*, Comm. ACM., 16(2), 1969.

16. Kennedy, K.: *A Survey of Data Flow Analysis Techniques in Program Flow Analysis: Theory and Applications*, Prentice-Hall Englewood Cliffs, N.J., 1981.

17. Pan, S., Dromey, R.G., *A Formal Basis for Measuring Software Product Quality*, Research Report, Software Quality Institute, (1993)

18. Freeman, P.E. (Ed), *Tutorial: Software Reusability*, IEEE Computer Society (1987).

PART TWO

Requirements, Design and Development Methodologies

3

Progress Towards RACE: a 'Soft-Centred' Requirements Definition Method

D.W. Bustard

Department of Computing Science, University of Ulster, Cromore Road, Coleraine, BT52 1SA, Northern Ireland

Abstract

This paper summarises some recent work by the Requirements Definition Group at the University of Ulster and other collaborators on developing a better requirements definition method for computing systems. The method, RACE (Requirements Acquisition and Controlled Evolution), is gradually being shaped through a series of intermediate research studies. In essence, the approach has been to establish requirements for RACE, identify individual techniques that meet those requirements, experiment with the combined use of the techniques and finally build the method. In practice, RACE has been influenced significantly by Checkland and Wilson's Soft Systems Methodology (SSM) and this forms the core of the method. The paper discusses eight main requirements for RACE and describes four of the intermediate studies. Plans for future work are also outlined

Keyword Codes: D.2.1; D.2.2
Keywords: Requirements/Specification; Tools and Techniques

1. INTRODUCTION

Despite an increasing clarification of what 'good practice' means in software engineering [1, 2], and a general willingness by industry to follow that practice, the goal of routinely completing computing projects to specification, on time, and within budget, remains well out of reach [3]. The obvious implication is that some aspects of the software engineering process need to be improved and the best place to start is probably right back at the beginning of the process, in the requirements definition phase, where the greatest potential benefit can be obtained [4, 5]. The purpose of this paper is to describe the rationale for, and basic characteristics of the requirements definition method, RACE, Requirements Acquisition and Controlled Evolution, currently under development at the University of Ulster in collaboration with co-workers in other establishments. The method is being designed from scratch, on the assumption that a thorough revision of current thinking is needed to produce significant benefits. The RACE method is, however, building on known concepts and techniques that are considered valuable, such as the Soft Systems Methodology [6, 7], object-oriented development [8], and risk management [9].

The development of RACE has, as might be expected, involved a specification of its requirements. The specification has been produced as a list of the essential attributes of any acceptable method. For example, these include "it must support evolutionary system development" and "it must support the use of formal description techniques". None of the requirements identified is particularly novel. Consequently for each requirement there is a considerable amount of material in the literature describing how to deal with this aspect of analysis, and highlighting specific techniques that are applicable. There is, however, no existing requirements definition method that comes close to covering all of the requirements specified. The approach to developing RACE has, therefore, involved selecting from appropriate existing support techniques and examining how they might be used in combination.

The work is currently in this experimental phase and the second section of the paper summarises four particular areas of study. This is preceded by a discussion of the eight main requirements of RACE that have been identified.

2. RACE REQUIREMENTS

When considering the desirable attributes of a requirements definition method, or indeed any method, it is perhaps tempting to start by putting down broad general characteristics such 'easy to learn', 'easy to apply', and so on. These are obviously important but unfortunately are at such a high level that they provide little help in clarifying the method. The initial approach taken with RACE has been to set out attributes that are much more specific to requirements definition although still general enough to give substantial flexibility in the design of the method. The broader quality attributes will be considered later when the method is being assembled.

So far, eight main attributes of RACE have been isolated. These are:

1. It must deal with the broad problem situation and not be specific to computing

Computing systems do not exist in isolation and are rarely a goal in themselves. They are developed to support some wider system and are introduced because of a need to make changes to that system. This wider system is the *problem situation* and any useful requirements definition technique must address requirements for the wider system before considering specific computing needs. Indeed, the analysis technique must be sufficiently neutral to allow the conclusion, in some circumstances, that the system change need not include computing facilities.

2. It must support both goal driven and problem-driven approaches to analysis

There are two broad approaches to solving any problem: *goal-driven* and *problem-driven* and it is unsatisfactory for a requirements definition method to support one to the exclusion of the other. In essence, the goal-driven approach means identifying some desirable position and then deciding how best to reach that position; the problem-driven approach means investigating the current position and then deciding how to best to improve it. Both approaches have their uses. For example, if no documented goals exist or if a major change to a system is envisaged, then the goal-driven approach is desirable. Alternatively, if a system is largely satisfactory and only needs minor enhancement then the problem-driven approach is preferred.

3. It must allow for multiple perspectives

Most systems defy precise definition. In general, a system exists for multiple purposes and individuals construct personal viewpoints of the system using various combinations of these purposes. For example, a restaurant may exist to supply sustenance, to provide entertainment, to facilitate business discussions, and so on. The actual nature of the restaurant will depend on the precise emphasis placed on each of these purposes by the proprietor. Allowance must be made for supporting such multiple perspectives in managing requirements. More precisely, this means enabling multiple system perspectives to be identified and explored, and having some way of combining the perspectives in one system in a balanced way. It must be appreciated, however, that there is therefore no notion of identifying the 'right' system, only of composing a system that is effective given the preferences of the client and others in the problem situation. In many circumstances opinions will differ so some means of resolving conflict is also required.

4. It must support collaborative requirements definition

There are several different ways to view the role of an analyst in the requirements definition process. At one extreme the analyst can be seen as a passive gatherer of requirements, responsible for documenting the needs of those in the problem situation, the *problem-owners*, and identifying any conflicts. At the other extreme, the analyst has the role of 'expert problem-solver', responsible for clarifying the problem and developing possible solutions. Neither of these extremes is satisfactory. Certainly the analyst must be a good listener but it is equally important that the analyst contributes to the solution of the problem to take advantage of his or her own expertise. Similarly, although the analyst can help to solve the problem, ownership of the final solution must lie with the problem-owners, making it essential that they be directly involved in problem solving. The conclusion, therefore, is that the process of defining requirements is best treated as a collaborative problem-solving activity with the analyst and problem-owners having similar status. The requirements definition method must therefore support such a collaborative approach.

5. *It must address risk issues*
Requirements definition, like any creative process, is a cycle in which proposals are made, evaluated, and then revised and refined as necessary. Developing an initial proposal for change is largely a positive activity concerned with identifying what a system is required to do. Evaluation is much more negative, tending to focus on ways in which the proposed system or change process may fail. These opportunities for failure are *risks*. The requirements definition method must provide a mechanism for identifying such risks and for managing them appropriately. In some cases the identified risks can be avoided; in others it is necessary to develop contingency plans to deal with the associated failures should they occur.

6. *It must support evolutionary system development*
All useful systems evolve, meaning that they go through a sequence of development changes. This evolution can be forced by need or be part of a planned programme of change. The latter approach allows for the possibility of making the initial change through a sequence of intermediate steps [10, 11]. This has the benefit of simplifying each change step and thereby reducing the risk of failure. Gilb [10] states that each phase should make a change that is of measurable benefit to those in the problem situation. The intention is that once a particular phase is complete the benefit of the change is assessed and the planned programme revised accordingly. The requirements definition method must support such evolutionary development in an appropriate way.

7. *It must address the needs of subsequent system development*
Any requirements definition method must be well integrated with the larger software development process to which it belongs. It is clearly impractical to link up to all, or even a substantial majority of existing development methods but there is a need to demonstrate such integration. The link must consider how the specified requirements will be used in subsequent development. For example, this would include the use of the requirements specification in software design and acceptance testing. The change control mechanism for requirements must also be considered, covering both initial development and system maintenance.

8. *It must support the use of formal description techniques*
The use of formal description techniques in specifying requirements offers several potential benefits including (i) the development of a deeper understanding of both the problem situation and the changes proposed to alleviate that situation; (ii) the avoidance of misunderstandings in subsequent system development based on the requirements; and (iii) having a precise statement of needs against which to evaluate the final system. Traditionally, formal techniques have been more associated with proving the correctness of a final implementation and of supporting a refinement approach to program development in which an initial formal specification is successively transformed into a coded implementation. While this is possible, in principle, the effort involved means that it can only be attempted for critical parts of large systems, or where safety concerns are paramount, or where formal proof is mandated. This paper takes the view that formal descriptions are of benefit in general software development but that their use should be optional. Like the previous requirement, there is then a need to demonstrate how this can be achieved in at least one case.

The next section considers four intermediate studies that are contributing to the definition of RACE by examining the use of techniques that go part of the way towards meeting the stated requirements.

3. INTERMEDIATE STUDIES

The discussion so far has been slightly misleading in implying that the requirements for RACE were developed before identifying relevant support techniques. In practice, the two evolved together through an investigation of existing analysis methods in search of worthwhile ideas. In all of this work, the most significant 'discovery' was Checkland and Wilson's Soft Systems Methodology (SSM) [6, 7], which now forms the core of the RACE method. This section describes four RACE studies, all of which involve SSM. The first examines the value of SSM as the development base for RACE. SSM meets several of the stated requirements but its most attractive characteristic is that it is a 'lean' technique, meaning that all of its individual elements having a clear purpose. The requirements that SSM does not meet can be handled by introducing other techniques. The second study, for example, considers how risk management and SSM can be combined. The third study examines the integration of SSM with traditional computing analysis techniques. This covers both structured analysis [12] and object-oriented development. Finally the fourth study looks at the use of formal description techniques as a means of strengthening the SSM process and assisting with the link to computing analysis techniques.

3.1 The Use of Soft Systems Methodology for Requirements Definition

Soft Systems Methodology (SSM) has emerged as the core of the RACE method. It meets two of the listed requirements in full and one in part:

1. It must deal with the broad problem situation and not be specific to computing

SSM is a general problem-solving technique. It is not specific to any problem area although recently it has been promoted extensively as an aid to the development of information systems [7]. Its areas of application have included public utilities, health, agriculture, industry, law, defence and scientific systems [13, 14]. SSM is a very well established technique. It was first conceived in the early 1970s and then refined by use in real problem situations, mostly in industry. It is now relatively stable. Overall then, SSM is a good match for the requirement for a technique that deals with the broad problem situation; it is particularly attractive because it has proven its value over many years.

2. It must support both goal-driven and problem-driven approaches to analysis

SSM is a strongly goal-driven technique. It focuses on the basic purposes of a system and on the behaviour necessary to achieve those purposes. Its particular strength is in dealing with 'messy' situations where there is uncertainty about the nature of the problem and/or disagreement about the options for its solution. In principle, all problems can be approached in this way and this provides a good counter to the common tendency to underestimate the extent of problems initially. However, although such a general approach can always be used effectively for any new problem situation, thereafter, it should only be used again when a major review is required. Thus, while SSM can provide a goal-driven technique for RACE, a problem-driven technique must also be found and integrated appropriately.

3. It must allow for multiple perspectives

SSM's support for multiple system perspectives is one of its major strengths. The first stage of SSM is to identify as many reasons as possible why a system exists and to express these reasons succinctly as system *root definitions*. Each root definition is expanded into a *conceptual model*, defining the activities necessary for the system to meet its purpose and also indicating relationships among the activities. The conceptual models are combined into a single *consensus model*, which when evaluated and refined subsequently becomes the *required system model* [15]. This latter model reveals the desirable system changes when it is compared with the problem situation. The SSM approach to multiple perspectives is particularly appealing because it concentrates on a small manageable number of identified system purposes, as distinct from considering the viewpoints of individuals in the problem situation, which are likely to differ for everyone involved.

In summary, SSM successfully addresses two and a half of the requirements for RACE. Of equal importance, is the fact that SSM has no features that are irrelevant to, or conflict with, the remaining requirements. Thus, SSM seems an ideal starting point for the development of RACE, particularly so because it also covers the very earliest phases of problem investigation and is well tried in practice.

3.2. Enhancing SSM With Risk Management Techniques

Risk is the possibility of loss or injury and risk management is the process of determining risks and responding to them. Risk management can be divided into two main activities [9]: *risk assessment* and *risk control*. Risk assessment involves (i) identifying the risks concerned; (ii) analysing the threat of those risks in terms of their probability of occurrence and the magnitude of the resulting loss; and (iii) prioritising the risks accordingly. Risk control covers (i) risk management planning, to develop plans for addressing each major risk; (ii) risk resolution, to implement the plan that will either eliminate the threats or keeping them at an acceptable level; and (iii) risk monitoring, to assess the effectiveness of risk resolution and take corrective action as necessary.

Risk is not addressed explicitly by SSM. Certainly SSM includes recommended practices that reduce risk, such as implementing system changes incrementally or having a monitoring and control mechanism within a system, but there is no direct, systematic treatment of risk. The expected benefits of considering risk explicitly are that (i) the process of system change should be smoother; and (ii) the resulting systems should be more robust. Risk management is particularly relevant to SSM because of its goal driven approach to analysis, which tends to identify substantial system changes, carrying relatively high risk.

Risk investigation, being a process of critical evaluation, is best considered after a creative phase of analysis yielding phase products ready for assessment and refinement. On that basis there are four stages of SSM where risk could be addressed:

1. When the problem situation has been described: this would consider risks in the current situation to identify opportunities for improvement and give a base for subsequent evaluation of change proposals.
2. When root definitions of relevant systems have been produced: root definitions contain a list of system constraints. Thus, identifying risks at the root definition stage can help to determine additional system constraints for inclusion in each root definition.
3. When conceptual models have been derived from the root definitions: risk can be considered (i) after each conceptual model has been constructed, to ensure that it has been adequately formed; and (ii) when the consensus model has been developed (by combining the individual conceptual models), to ensure that the resulting model deals adequately with the separate risks and to examine risks resulting from interaction and conflict among the models.
4. When feasible, desirable system changes have been determined: all proposals at this lower level of detail can be examined for risk and refined accordingly.

In practice, examining risk after the first problem analysis phase is not recommended because it requires the analyst to explore the problem situation in more detail than is desirable. The analyst must not be overly exposed to the problem situation, initially, to avoid the practical difficulty of being lured into modelling what exists rather than what should exist. Risks associated with the current system can instead be considered at stage three when conceptual models are being evaluated with respect to the problem situation.

Further details on the proposed risk management additions to SSM, and an example of its use, can be found in [16]. Overall the approach is appealing because it strengthens SSM without interfering with its basic operation.

3.3. Integrating SSM With Computing-Oriented Analysis Techniques

The possibility of using SSM with a computing-oriented analysis technique was proposed as long ago as 1985 [17] and has since been followed up by many related investigations [18, 19]. One significant development has been the recent establishment of a link between SSM and the government standard analysis and design method, SSADM [20]. This work was commissioned by the CCTA in the UK [21]. The link has been facilitated by the fact that there is a strong resemblance between the conceptual models of SSM and dataflow models of SSADM (similar to those found in any Structured Analysis technique): both are concerned with describing system behaviour and both are structured in a similar way. This connection has also been explored as part of the RACE study [15] and a technique for linking conceptual models and dataflow diagrams has been proposed. In summary, the proposal is:

1. Perform a complete SSM analysis, developing full hierarchical conceptual models and validating them to produce required system models.
2. Construct an *interaction table* for each model, identifying the interaction of each activity with other *processes*. A process is either an activity or a *repository* of information. A repository may be an individual, a document, a computer disc, or any other form of information consumer or producer.
3. Construct dataflow diagrams from the interaction tables and conceptual models. The interaction tables provide the technical content for the dataflow diagrams and the conceptual models give layout guidance. This is desirable to help the analyst understand the relationship between models.

This process of converting conceptual models to dataflow models is relatively straightforward and can largely be automated. The link between SSM and object-oriented analysis (OOA) is also being considered [22]. This is much more problematic, however, because SSM produces behaviour oriented conceptual models whereas OOA starts with static data oriented object models. Nevertheless, the ever growing popularity of OOA means that some satisfactory link must be found.

For any link it is always possible to take a *loosely coupled* approach, meaning that the knowledge gained in applying the first technique is use in the application of the second without any specified rules or guidelines. A check is then performed to ensure that the models produced in each case are consistent. Such an approach is unsatisfactory in several ways, including: (i) it is hard to teach; (ii) it is hard to apply consistently; and (iii) change control is difficult. A *tightly coupled* approach, like that suggested for dataflow modelling, is clearly preferable because it allows for some automation of consistency checking and can even assist with the initial development of the computing-oriented models.

The link for OOA is currently being investigated. In effect, this means defining a method of transforming SSM models into object models. A starting point has been to investigate existing OOA techniques to see to what extent they are compatible with SSM concepts [14]. This work has identified four techniques that provide a reasonable fit, namely those due to Jacobsen [23], Reenskaug [24], Booch [25] and Gibson [26]. Further research is being undertaken using a selection of these techniques.

3.4. SSM and formal descriptions

As indicated earlier, SSM conceptual models are imprecise: the meaning of each activity has to be deduced from the term used for its name, and the links between activities are really just indications of relationships, without any accompanying definitions. Precision can be added in the computing-oriented analysis phase but there is benefit in introducing it at the end of the SSM phase. Specifically, it can help to avoid misunderstandings about what exactly is being proposed as a result of the SSM analysis and so help identify problems earlier in the process. Precision in the SSM analysis can also strengthen the link with the subsequent computing-oriented analysis.

Work is currently being done on the particular case of supporting the specification of conceptual models using LOTOS, a process algebra-based formal description technique [27], in conjunction with developing a link to Structured Analysis. This combination is being considered because the underlying notations used by each technique are all based on describing behaviour and so are largely compatible. This will allow attention to be concentrated on the main issue of how best to manage the combined use of such a collection of techniques. Once this relatively homogeneous case has been examined the research will be extended to consider the use of less compatible formal descriptive notations and computing-oriented analysis techniques.

The research started by looking at the broad issue of the role of formal descriptions in the software development process [28]. In this field, much work has been done on the development of formal notations, rather less on the development of formal techniques and very little on the production of formal software development methods. The expression 'formal methods' perhaps needs some clarification. It is often used as a blanket term to cover the related activities of constructing, analysing, transforming, and verifying formal descriptions. The word 'formal' is used here in the sense that all of the activities have a sound mathematical basis. It does not mean, however, that there are step-by-step procedures identifying the precise way to perform the activities, either singly or in combination [29]. In that sense the word 'method' is misleading and 'technique' would give a rather clearer picture of what is intended.

Defining a relationship between SSM conceptual models and LOTOS processes gives a formal semantics to this currently informal notation. It also provides a means of saying more about the relationship between activities. Through LOTOS, the conceptual model activities can be treated a set of communicating processes and the order and effect of communication specified. The meaning of the resulting description can be portrayed as an *action tree* showing all possible behaviours as event sequences [30]. Also these permitted behaviours can be projected on to the conceptual models to provide a simulation that may facilitate communication with the client.

Another advantage of this work is that it gives a good starting point for computing-oriented analysis. The formal description provides a precise specification on which the subsequent development can be based and/or assessed. Also, since dataflow diagrams can be derived from SSM conceptual models in a largely automated way, the formal description provides a means of portraying system behaviour through an simulation of the dataflow representation. Again this may facilitate communication with the client.

4. CONCLUSION

This paper has summarised the current position of some research directed towards the identification of RACE, a better requirements definition method for computing systems. The main desirable attributes of RACE have been identified and explained, followed by a brief outline of four studies concerned with investigating techniques that are likely to form part of the method. SSM has emerged as the core of the method and the studies have all built around it. The influence of SSM has even permeated the language used in this paper (e.g. 'problem situation' and 'problem-owner'). This research is, however, at a relatively early stage. The implications of several of the requirements have still to be explored in detail and there are many remaining inter-connections between techniques to examine. Nevertheless, the results so far have confirmed the initial belief in SSM [32] and its combination with other techniques seems to be giving additional value without having any detrimental effect.

Acknowledgements

This research is being undertaken as part of the RUNES project (Requirements Understanding, Negotiation, Expression and Scrutiny), funded by the University of Ulster. RUNES, is broadly concerned with investigating techniques for improving the requirements definition process, and the development of tools to support that process.

I am very grateful to the many people who have contributed to and influenced this work in various ways, including Raymond Oakes, Des Vincent, Mark Norris, Dave Horncastle, Brian Carey, John Wright, Anthony Alston, Adam Winstanley, Sally McClean, Philip Morrow, Pat Lundy, Des Greer, Trevor Dobbin and Eoin Heslin.

REFERENCES

1. Humphrey W: *Managing the Software Process*, Addison Wesley, 1989
2. DTI: TickIT, *Guide to Software Quality Management System Construction and Certification*, Issue 2.0, Febuary 1992

3. Norris M, Rigby P, and Payne M: *The Healthy Software Project*, Wiley, 1993
4. Boehm BW: *Software Engineering Economics*, Prentice Hall, 1981
5. Davis AM: *Software Requirements, Object, Functions and States*, Prentice Hall, 1993
6. Checkland PB and Scholes J: *Soft Systems Methodology in Action*, Wiley, 1990
7. Wilson B: *Systems: Concepts, Methodologies and Applications*, 2nd Edition, Wiley, 1990
8. Wilkie G: *Object Oriented Software Engineering: The Professional Developer's Guide*, Addison-Wesley, 1993
9. Boehm BW: *Software Risk Management*, IEEE Computer Society Press, 1989
10. Gilb T: *Principles of Software Engineering Management*, Addison-Wesley, 1988
11. Cobb RH and Mills HD: *Engineering Software Under Statistical Quality Control*, IEEE Software, **7** (6), November 1990, pp 44-54
12. Yourdon, E.: *Modern Structured Analysis*, Prentice Hall, 1989
13. Mingers J and Taylor S: *The Use of Soft Systems Methodology in Practice*, Journal of the Operational Research Society, **43**(4), 1992, pp. 321-332
14. Dobbin TJ and Bustard DW: *Combining Soft Systems Methodology and Object-Oriented Analysis: The Search for a Good Fit*, Proceedings of the 2nd Information Systems Methodologies Conference, Edinburgh, August 1994
15. Bustard DW, Oakes R and Heslin E, *Support for the Integrated Use of Conceptual and Dataflow Models in Requirements Specification*, Colloquium on Requirements for Software Intensive Systems, DRA Malvern, May 1993, pp. 37-44
16. Bustard DW and Greer D: *Enhancing Soft Systems Methodology with Risk Management Techniques*, Proceedings of 2nd International Conference on Software Quality Management, Edinburgh, July 1994
17. Stowell F: *Experience with Soft Systems Methodology and Data Analysis*, Information Technology Training, May 1985, pp. 48-50
18. Mingers, J.: *Comparing Conceptual Models and Data Flow Diagrams*, Computer Journal, **31**(4), pp. 376-378, 1988
19. Stowell F (Ed.): *Soft Systems Methodology and Information Systems*, Systemist, **14** (3), August 1992
20. *SSADM Version 4 Reference Manual* , NCC/Blackwell, Oxford, 1990
21. CCTA: *Using Soft Systems Methodology for SSADM Feasibility Study*, 1994
22. Alston AJ, Wright PJ and Bustard DW: *COBRA: A Methodology for CIS Object-Oriented Business and Requirements Analysis*, Proceedings of the 1st Information Systems Methodologies Conference, Edinburgh, September 1993, pp. 99-112
23. Jacobsen I, Christerson M, Jonsson P and Overgaard F, *Object-Oriented Software Engineering - A Use Case Driven Approach*, Addison-Wesley, 1993
24. Reenskaug T, Andersen EP, Berre AJ, Hurlen A, Landmark A, Lehne OA, Nordhagen E, Ness-Ulseth E, Oftedal G, Skaar AL and Stenslet P, *OORAA: Seamless Support for the Creation and Maintenance of Object-Oriented Systems*, Journal of Object-Oriented Programming, October 1992, pp. 27-41
25. Booch G, *Object-Oriented Analysis and Design with Applications*, Benjamin-Cummings, 1994
26. Gibson E, *Objects - Born and Bred*, Byte, October 1990, pp. 245-254
27. ISO - Information Processing Systems - Open Systems Interconnection - LOTOS - A Formal Description Technique Based on the Temporal Ordering of Observational Behaviour, ISO 8807, 1989.
28. Lundy P and Bustard DW: *Making Formal Methods Work: What's being Done and What Can be Done*, Proceedings of 2nd International Conference on Software Quality Management, Edinburgh, July 1994
29. Woodcock J and Loomes M, *Software Engineering Mathematics*, Pitman, London, 1988
30. Winstanley A and Bustard DW: *EXPOSE: An Animation Tool for Process-Oriented Specifications*, Software Engineering Journal, **6** (6), November 1991, pp. 463-475
31. Bustard DW and Winstanley AC: *Making Changes to Formal Specifications: Requirements and an Example*, IEEE Transactions on Software Engineering, Vol. 20, No. 8, August 1994
32. *SSM in Computing*, Workshop Notes, University of Ulster, April 1994

4

MOOSE: A method designed for ease of maintenance

R. I. Ferguson, N. F. Parrington and P. Dunne

University of Sunderland, School of Computing and Information Systems, Priestman Building, Green Terrace, Sunderland, Tyne/Wear, SR1 3SD, UK ,Tel. +44 091 5152508, Fax. +44 091 5152781, Email - i.ferguson@sunderland.ac.uk

Abstract

The problem of change as manifested in perfective and adaptive maintenance is presented along with some of the qualities that software must possess in order to minimise the effects of change. These qualities can be provided by the Object Oriented paradigm. This paper describes the current work on a Method for Object Oriented Software Engineering (MOOSE) that has ease of maintenance and re-use as primary design objectives. A prototype CASE tool to support the method has also been developed: details and proposals for its re-engineered capabilities are given. No attempt is made to completely define the method, instead a general description of its features, particularly those pertinent to maintainability, is presented.

keyword codes : D.1.5; D.2.2; D.2.7

keywords : object-oriented programming; tools and techniques; distribution and maintenance

1. THE PROBLEM

Lehman's first law states that any system's requirements will change over time and that for the software to remain useful, it too must change. [1]. The Software Engineer is thus faced with the prospect, that no matter how well the stages of elicitation, specification, analysis and design are performed, a significant amount of the system produced will need re-engineering over its lifetime.

Software Maintenance activities are frequently categorized (following Swanson [2]) as "Perfective" - consequent on change of requirement, "adaptive",- due to change in operating environment - "corrective" - bug fixing or "preventative" [3].

The key factors influencing maintainability are complexity and modularity [4]. Complexity is a measure of how difficult a piece of code it to understand. If a piece of software has been refined into a set of smaller sub-problems then it is said to be modularised. If the individual modules have low external coupling and high internal cohesiveness, then the system will be easier to maintain as the effect of changing any one piece of code will be limited to the module in which the change occurs. Another factor affecting the maintainability of a system is the ease with which a programmer can maintain a mental model of what the system does, and how it is built.

2. A SOLUTION

One paradigm that claims to improve these factors is the Object Orientation (OO).Rooted firmly in modularity, its modelling approach is closer to human ways of reasoning than procedural methods [5], and it isolates the effects of change through its use of information hiding[6]. Object orientation gives a system the flexibility required by Lehman's 1st law. Requirements do not have to be artificially frozen at design time (as assumed by the traditional software development lifecycle).They may evolve with time and the system development process needs to take this into account.

3. METHOD - MOOSE

A method is currently being developed at the University of Sunderland to take advantage of the object oriented paradigm. It remains flexible enough that engineers can work in their own manner, yet provides sufficient constraints to facilitate the production of high quality code. It uses prototyping to allow ease and accuracy of requirement elicitation, while the use of formal specification ensures that there exists an unambiguous definition of each module's purpose. It rigorously employs the ideas of modularity but still allows an experimental programming approach to be taken where required. The method is known as MOOSE - Method for Object Oriented Software Engineering

3.1 - Fundamental concepts

MOOSE is closely linked with its supporting CASE tool, JACI (Just Another CASE Implementation). The notations used by MOOSE have been designed with tool assistance in mind and would prove awkward to handle without the aid of the tool. Moreover, inconsistencies in the underlying database can be introduced by working on a system with a tool that is not part of JACI. This must not be permitted, as it is from this database that the executable code is generated.

3.2 - Underlying Concepts

MOOSE is modular. Every piece of software built via the method is treated as a module, whether it is a complete air traffic control system or a three line routine. The basic unit of modularity is the OO "class" Each module can be treated separately from any other module in the system. When necessary, a module can consist of, or use, smaller sub-modules which can likewise be refined, ultimately into problems of a manageable size. This process of refining can therefore be described as recursive and it produces a hierarchy of modules. In fact, several different hierarchies are produced depending on the relationships between modules.

One concept crucial to MOOSE and the supporting tool is that of the module framework. This isn't a code template; rather it is a database schema with fields for storing all the information that is required to completely describe one module.:

Table 1: MOOSE module framework 'fields'

natural language description of the module
the formal specification of the module
analysis diagrams
design diagrams
sub-modules
some representation of the procedural logic of the modules
function members
the code itself
house-keeping and project management information.

All stages (activities) of MOOSE result in some deliverables. It is these deliverables that are stored in the fields defined by the module framework. Thus if a framework for a system level object is complete., then a complete specification for a whole system will exist. In fact, this top-level framework has a physical counterpart in the tool's database.

3.3 - Components

The MOOSE method is built on "approaches", "activities" and "techniques".

3.3.1 - Approaches

The approaches available to a software engineer are "top-down", "prototyping" and "experimental-programming" which represent the three main ways in which software can be constructed [7].

One of the reasons that three different approaches can be taken, is that deliverables arise from "the wrong activity". For instance, if an experimental-programming approach is being taken to build a module, when the module is complete, a design must exist for it, which can be "backfilled" into the module framework design diagram field. In many cases it should be possible to automate large parts of this process..

3.3.1.1 - Top-Down

The top-down approach is the classical method of software production. It involves starting with a rough description of a problem and gradually refining that description into smaller sub-problems which are then repeatedly refined until each problem is codeable. Associated with this approach is the idea of sequentially performing analysis, design and coding with each stage not commencing until the previous one has been completed. MOOSE permits this approach but allows backtracking and iteration of activities.

3.3.1.2 - Prototyping

MOOSE encourages the use of three types of prototyping[8];throwaway, evolutionary and incremental. Prototyping is used primarily to identify user interaction with the system and to map interface items (menus, buttons, etc.) onto classes that can implement that means of interaction. Tool support for this is available via the Tcl/Tk prototyping langauages.[9]

3.3.1.3 - Experimental programming

Experimental programming has been referred to as programming without a specification. [10]. It is particularly useful for designing new algorithms, but likely to cause maintenance problems if the code developed is not subsequently documented. MOOSE allows this approach with the caveat that it is best done in conjunction with the JACI CASE tool, which gives significant help with retro-documenting.

3.3.1.4 - Mixing approaches

Within software development, different approaches are appropriate depending upon the level of the desired system that is being worked on. A "top- down" approach is more appropriate for high-level (top of system) work - for things that might be termed "application objects". Experimental-programming is better for code closer to machine level - "utility objects."

Perhaps the most powerful approach is to combine approaches. This combines the structure of top-down with the exploratory power of experimental programming. This would permit (for instance) the use of a top down approach to develop a basic understanding of the system, the use of prototyping to ensure correct user interaction and the use of experimental programming to get the latest sort-routine working at optimum speed.

3.3.2 - Activities

The three activities of the method are "analysis", "design" and "coding". These are not the usual distinct phases of traditional software development but form a continuum, although each activity still has associated deliverables. This continuum arises for 2 reasons, i) the OO paradigm uses the same modelling concepts throughout development, ii) MOOSE uses a unifying notation which is applicable throughout the lifecycle.

3.3.2.1 - Analysis

Analysis in MOOSE is achieved by identifying the entities that make up a system and the relationships between them. The relationships are then categorised and refined. The data necessary to represent those entities are then added followed by the operations that can be performed on them. Each identified entity is then refined recursively. Analysis uses a natural language description of the problem (PEP) as its starting point. The entities identified from this description are then shown on a form of modified Entity-Relationship diagram [11] known as the analysis diagram.

The relationships between the objects that have been identified are then examined. Relationships fall into four significant categories based on those used by Booch [12]: "has_a", "is_a_kind_of", "contains" and "uses". A hierarchy of classes is associated with each category. The cardinality of each relationship (1:1, 1:M, M:M) is identified.

3.3.2.2 - Design

In the design activity, each module identified on the analysis diagram is converted to an individual design diagram. Modelling of things "systemic" [13] to this level then commences. This includes: addition of data members to classes, addition of function members, derivation of a formal specification,algorithm design, addition of parameter passing information

3.3.2.3 - Coding

If the "top-down" approach of MOOSE has been used exclusively, a complete set of design diagrams will exist following completion of the design activity. The diagramming notation has been so designed as to reduce coding to a mechanical process. Although it is not yet implemented we expect that to a large extent, code generation can be automated. Conversely, if an exclusively experimental-programming approach has been taken, coding may well be the first activity undertaken.By using the editors built into JACI, the code is entered directly into the system database. From there, it can be reverse engineered into diagrammatic form, in real time thus providing design documentation 'on-the-fly'.

3.3.3 - Notation - analysis diagrams

Analysis diagrams are closely related to Entity-Relationship diagrams. Their main features are as follows:-

3.3.3.1 - Modules

The presence of a module simply indicates the existence of an entity in the real-world system being modelled. These are designed to look like the "class" of the design notation. Each module must have a unique name; using JACI, they can be expanded to their corresponding "class" diagram at the click of a button.

3.3.3.2 - Relationships

Relationships indicate a link of some sort between two entities. Each relationship must have a name. Conventional "crows feet" indicate the cardinality of the relationship.

Fig. 1 - Modules and relationships

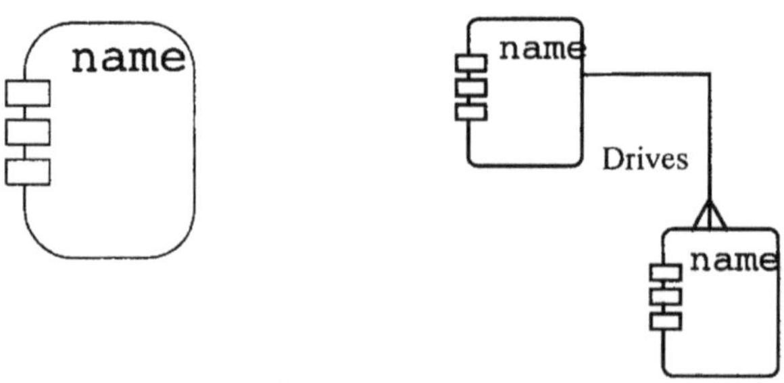

3.3.3.3 - Categories

Relationships fall into 4 categories, each of which is implemented in a different way. An "is_a_kind_of" relationship indicates inheritance of some kind is required. A "contains" relationship is implemented using a container class. "Has_a" relationships indicate participation in a whole/part hierarchy. The "uses" type of relationship implies the use of pointers to maintain links between instances of two classes. From the identification of these relationships part of the design can be inferred automatically The identification of "is_a_kind_of" and "has_a" relationships leads to the construction of hierarchies of entities. It can be useful to identify the existence of such structures on separate analysis diagrams.

3.3.4 - Notation - design diagrams

A single design can be made up of a series of design diagrams. For every entity identified on an analysis diagram, a corresponding diagram should exist.Design diagrams contain a lot of "link" information (which we have dubbed "hypercase links"), between diagrams, subsections of diagrams and other parts of the MOOSE database. Modules (classes) are shown thus:-

Fig. 2 - Classes / datamembers / function members

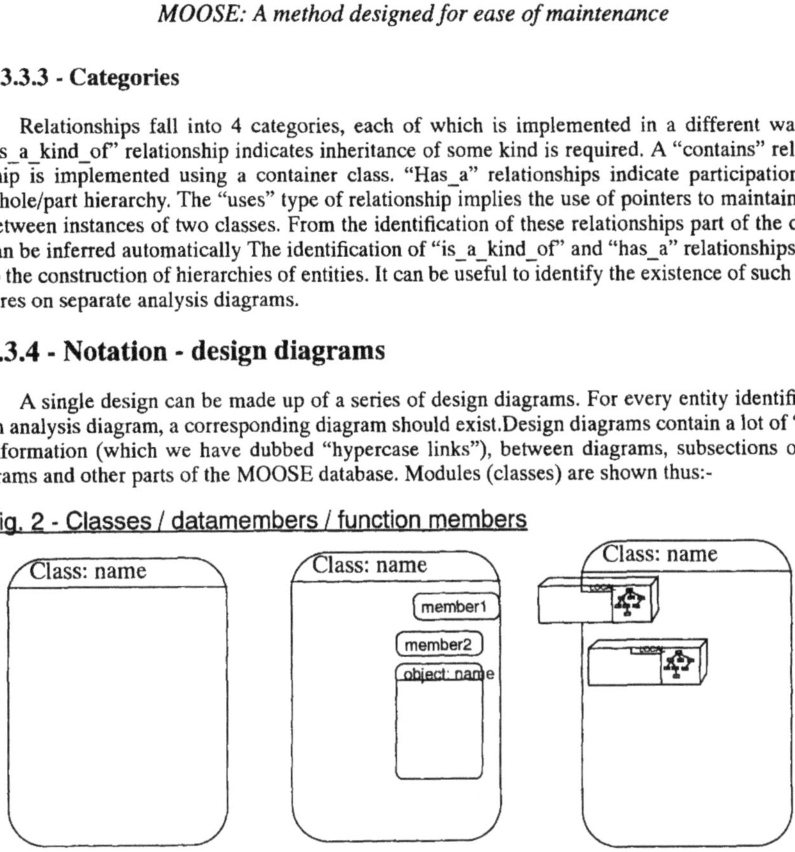

3.3.4.1 - Data members

Data members can be added to a class by placing them on the right hand side of the owning classes' bounding box. The member may be of either object or non-object type. The visibility of a member is indicated by its position: inside the class - private, touching the edge of the class public. The C++ "protected" visibility is dealt with below (Section 3.3.4.7 - "Inheritance")

3.3.4.2 - Function members

Function members are added on the left hand side. Implementation functions appear entirely within the bounding rectangle of the owning class. "Policy" methods are shown partially protruding from the bounding box.

3.3.4.3 - Function icon

The function member "icon" has several parts: i) name of the function (or method), ii) a local variable area/ "landing area" for formal parameters.(See "function calls" below), iii)a code icon. In JACI, access to the code representations are accessed via "clicking" on this icon. The impossibility of having the code represented directly in this space is a consequence of designing the notation with tool support in mind.

3.3.4.4 - Parameters

Three types of formal parameter are supported, based on the Ada standard parameter declaration; .in, out, in/out

Fig. 3 - Functions / Parameters

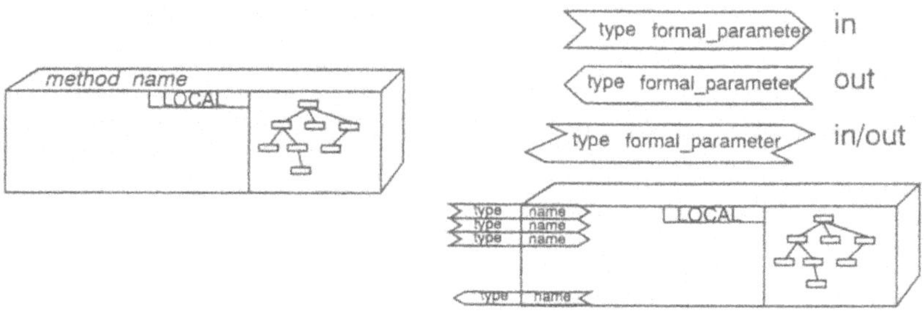

3.3.4.5 - Procedural logic

Procedural logic can be represented in three ways in MOOSE; pseudocode; JSP and directly in the target language code. (Although MOOSE itself is language independent.)The code icon is shown here as 'exploding' to a JSP diagram editor. A prototype diagram-text translator has been implemented allowing the simultaneous display/editing of code and JSP.

Fig. 4 - Procedural logic / Function Calls

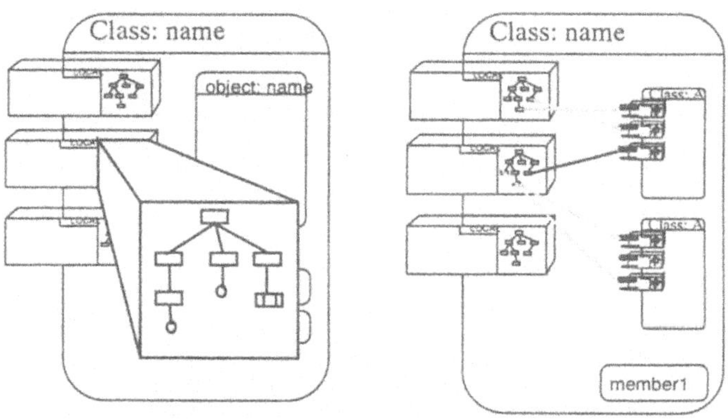

3.3.4.6 - Function calls (message passing)

Function calls ("message passing" is the OO term) take place between methods. They originate with the methods of the class being designed and are targeted on methods of member data. In MOOSE, they are simply shown as un-annotated lines. If every possible function call were shown simultaneously on a design diagram the result would be an extremely cluttered diagram. To avoid this, the number of links shown at any one time are limited by visibility controls.

3.3.4.7 - Inheritance

On a class' defining design diagram, any members which are defined as "protected" (accessible only to the methods of descendant inheriting classes) are shown in a different colour to "private" or "protected" members. In any descendant class, only the public members inherited will be displayed. Inheritance is shown in the following fashion. The idea being that descendants appear to be "built upon" their ancestors.

Fig. 5 - Inheritance

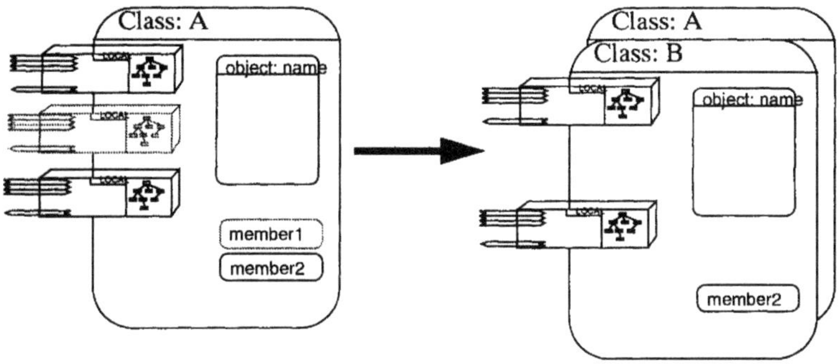

3.3.4.8 - Genericity

No special graphic notation is required to define a generic (template) class. Any variables (usually parameters of the classes method) that are of unknown type at design time are represented on the diagram prefixed with a designatory identifier surrounded by "<" and ">" characters in much the same manner as they are treated in C++. e.g. <T> my_variable.

3.3.4.9 - Container classes

Some representation of the containment of data in structures like arrays, queues etc. was desirable to match the programmers metal model of the implementation. The following notation allow messages to be sent to the container class and the data contained within it. The container class can be defined using the elements of notation already described; however when a container appears in a diagram as a member object, the following "square box" convention is required. This way both the methods of the container class and the contained class are "exposed" for potential use the owning classes methods.

Fig. 6 - Containers

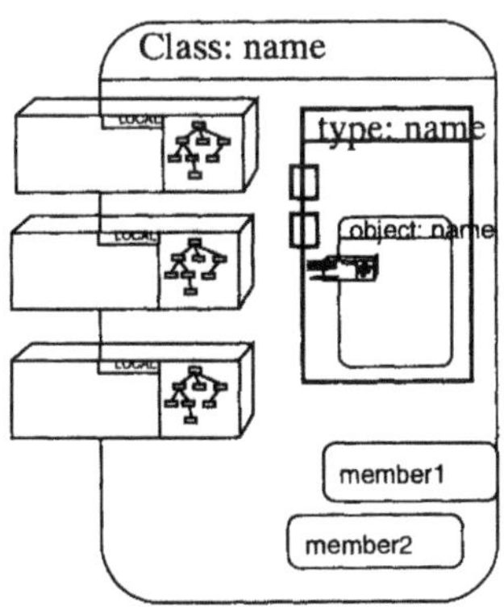

3.3.4.10 - Tool Support

MOOSE will be supported by an integrated CASE toolset based on a 2 tier PCTE database. Named JACI, the toolset currently exists in prototype form only.When complete, it will include editors to cope with all the notations of MOOSE. A network of "hypercase" links allow navigation between the different representations of entities. The links reach to every possible representation of any given entity in the database and between related entities. The common database should also allow the integration of facilities such asthe AI based NLP tools, the expert "method navigator", automatic translation between representations where possible. and the browser/librarian allows perusal of existing modules facilitating reuse.As a consequence, an engineer should rapidly be able to access all of the sources of information from which a given module was produced.

4. CONCLUSION

There are four main reasons why MOOSE produces code that is highly maintainable: i) the generated code is well modularised ii) the modelling method is intuitive and matches human thought process, iii) genericity/inheritance and the library encourage re-use iv) documentation availability. Provided the whole database is committed to the re-use library each module will always have its specification and design documentation available.

5. FUTURE WORK

Since the analysis and design diagrams form such a complete specification of a module's properties and behaviour, it has been proposed, but not investigated, that the diagrams could actually be executed, forming the basis of a truly "visual" language. Such a language, based on a readily understandable notation, could have major consequences for maintainability.

References

1 Lehman, M.M. and Belady L. "Program Evolution. Processes of Software Change." London, Academic Press

2 Swanson, E.B. "The Dimensions of Maintenance", Proc. 2nd Intl. Conf. Software engineering, IEEE, Oct 1976, pp. 492-497

3 Pressman, R.S. (1992) Software Engineering: A Practitioners Approach 3rd Ed, p. 664, McGraw-Hill, NY, USA

4 Curtis, B. and Sheppard, S.B. (1979) Identification and validation of quantitative measures of the psychological complexity of software. Software Management Research Report, General Electric

5 Wiener, R.S. and Pinson, J.P., (1988), "An Introduction to Object-Oriented Programming and C++", Addison-Wesley, p. iii

6 Meyer, B., (1988) "Object-oriented Software Construction", Prentice-Hall, pp7-25, "Aspects of Software Quality"

7 Pressman, R.S. (1992) Software Engineering: A Practitioners Approach 3rd Ed, p. 22-37, McGraw-Hill, NY, USA

8 Ince, D.,(1993) "Prototyping" in "Software Engineers Reference Book" ed. McDermid, J., Butterworth-Heineman

9 Ousterhout, J., "Tcl and the Tk Toolkit",(1994), Addison-Wesley

10 McDermid J. and Rook, P.,(1991) "Software Development Process Models" in "The Software Engineers Reference Book", ed. McDermid, J., Butterworth-Heineman

11 Chen. P., "The Entity-relationship Model -towards a unifying view of data", ACM Transactions on Data Base Systems, Vol.1, 1, March 1976, pp 9-36

12 Booch. G. "Object Oriented Analysis and Design" 2nd Ed, Benjamin-Cummings, ch.5 pp176-180

13 Checkland. P.,(1981), "Systems Thinking, Systems Practice", Wiley

5

BPR for Developing Information Systems - a case study

Elayne Coakes and Jim Coakes

School of Business Systems, Faculty of Business, University of Luton, Luton, Beds, LU1 3JU
School of Business, Thames Valley University, Slough, Berks, SL1 1YG

Abstract

The use of BPR techniques in CIS development is useful in the strategy, analysis and requirements definition phases, but only if it is part of a business wide quality improvement initiative. Its major strengths lie in techniques for balanced empowerment of stakeholders and levelling of power from an hierarchical base point. In addition, using BPR techniques in CIS development may impact positively on the quality of the CIS.

This paper reports a detailed case study in the use of BPR techniques in CIS development. The system was developed during 1992 and implemented at the end of 1993. In 1994, as this paper is being written, the system is being used successfully and stakeholders are looking for further enhancements to extend its area of operation. It is clear from this that expectation success has been achieved and that in terms of software quality the system fulfils many of McCall's criteria.

Keyword Codes: D.2.1,H.4.1
Keywords: Software Engineering, Requirements, Information Systems Applications, Office Automation.

1. INTRODUCTION

The Company under review is an international engineering, construction and project management contractor, which is currently shifting from individual attainment to group quality. To achieve this they had recently introduced a comprehensive policy of continuous improvement through BPR.

2. COMPUTER INFORMATION SYSTEM (CIS) DEVELOPMENT

In Hirschheim and Klein [1989][1] four paradigms of Information Systems development are discussed:

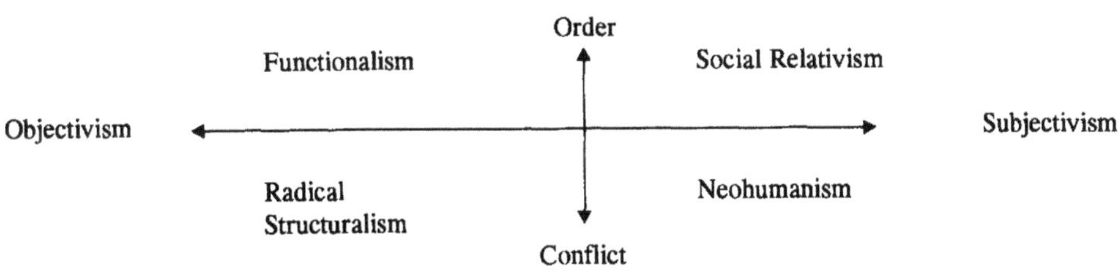

They identify the story of the Analyst as Systems Expert (the orthodox approach to systems development) as lying within the functionalism paradigm. The assumption to be made is that specification should be as objective as possible. The resolution of issues is not within the domain of the systems developer, he is primarily the expert. Business Process Re-engineering, we would argue, falls into the story of the Analyst as Facilitator within the Social Relativist paradigm. The system developer should work from within the users' perspectives and help them find their preferred views, his role being to find out what system makes sense. Thus any system that meets with the approval of the affected parties is legitimate. The facilitator helps stimulate reflection and co-operation, using appropriate tools and methods, and favours strong participation.

The assumption behind this story corresponds to Lyytinen and Hirschheim's view [1987][2] that expectation failure (where the CIS does not fulfil stakeholder's expectations) is related to the values and perceptions of information system stakeholders.

2.1 Developing Better Systems

Two major areas are identified as producing systems that are more successful, 'conflict resolution' and (improving) 'requirements definition'. A recent Price Waterhouse[3] survey found that of all respondents 45% mentioned poor requirements definition, 34.5% little user involvement and 29.5% political issues, as reasons for CIS failures.

2.1.1 Conflict Resolution

Mumford [1983][4] says:

'all change involves some conflicts of interest. To be resolved, these conflicts need to be recognised, brought out into the open, negotiated and a solution arrived at which largely meets the interest of all parties in the situation... successful change strategies require institutional mechanisms which enable all these interests to be represented, and participation provides these.'

Activities are ultimately controlled by those who perform them. People who do not have a say in the decisions on how these activities are to be changed, may not abide by those decisions. Jones and Kydd [1988][5] would go on to say that equivocality (ambiguity or the absence of clarity) resolution is critical to realising improved productivity. The use of group meetings, integrators and face to face contact help to resolve equivocality.

2.1.2 Requirements Definition

The Company traditionally used Information Engineering (IE) as the preferred development methodology. IE falls into the functionalism paradigm. Under IE the specification is designed to be as objective as possible and it lays great emphasis on data analysis as data is more stable than processes. Diagrams are used for communication and users are encouraged to participate in system design. The difficulty is that users may not understand completely the terminology and technical language used. Fitzgerald [1990][6] argues that the traditional approach to software documentation produces documents that are poorly understood by users. Kit Grindley [1991][7] quotes a manager as saying : 'How would you describe a journey into the unknown, a place where your compass doesn't work, the sun and the stars are replaced by elusive rainbows... The language is strange, the customs new, the pathways intricate and mysterious and you depend on local guides and native bearers.'

Mumford [1985][8] says that any definition of system requirements should concentrate first on business problems and needs. She advocates the use of a design group consisting of users and their representatives as well as technical specialists to debate system process and design.

2.2 BPR in CIS Development

A corporate culture embodies the shared values, meanings and understanding about what is important for the organisation . Job structure follows naturally from culture and so Kydd and Jones

(1989)[9] assert one of the reasons so many IS development methodologies fail is the difficulty in changing job structure without first changing culture. Yet most IS implementations change job functions and structure axiomatically. BPR expressly sets out to change culture and mind-set.

2.2.1 A Measure of Success - Improved Software Quality.

How do we assess software quality? Pressman [1992][10] defines software quality as:

'conformance to explicitly stated functional and performance requirements, explicitly documented development standards, and implicit characteristics that are expected of all professionally developed software..... Software requirements are the foundation from which quality is measured. Lack of conformance to requirements is lack of quality.'

McCall et al [1977][11] identify ten quality factors: maintainability; flexibility; testability; portability; re-usability; interoperability; correctness; reliability; efficiency; integrity and usability. But many of these quality measures and metrics are inappropriate in looking at BPR at work. BPR and continuous improvement techniques measure quality by process improvement and therefore CIS development designed using these techniques need to use this type of measurement also. We will show in the case study that process improvement and the use of BPR techniques help resolve conflicts, improve requirements definition and produce quality software.

3. CASE STUDY

The Company needs to account carefully for national and international telephone charges. Substantial charges are incurred working on projects across the Eastern Hemisphere and Europe, and a charge from any phone needed to be allocated to a staff member, a department or a client project.

3.1 Initial Situation - How Did The Process Become So Complex?

A CIS for *recharging telephone costs* had been developed by outside consultants in 1984, and transferred to a new platform in 1990. The CIS became more complex as particular features and requirements has been built in. The system used batch processes to handle 2 weeks' phone calls at a time to produce journal vouchers and other input for the financial billing systems. These processes also identified incorrect data well after it had entered the system. When the old CIS had problems, and outputs had to be produced under time pressure, sometimes an extra data correcting batch process would be added in to make the faulty output usable by a financial system. Sometimes this extra process became a regular feature of future runs of the system.

3.2 Systems Analysis And Development - How Did BPR Techniques Help?

The Company had recently introduced BPR, training senior management in the approaches and outcomes at residential courses run by external consultants. However, at this point the supervisors and other staff had only received a brief introduction to BPR. Initial staff reaction to BPR was 'Oh no not another cure all management technique, it will be like all the others, they come in every few years then fade away'. This highlights a degree of cognitive dissonance between staff and management.

The MIS manager responsible for running the inefficient legacy system mentioned above, was keen on the benefits of BPR, so he set up a project to examine the processes associated with the telephone charging system. Senior IT and quality management were kept fully informed of the proposed project and its progress.

The MIS Manager set up a team to examine the processes, bringing in the following stakeholders:

- ñ Staff 'on the ground': Phone operator(s), IT staff responsible for laborious 2 weekly batch work and accounts clerks who received data for further processing.
- ñ Management: IT Department, Accounting and Office Services.

Meetings were set up to review the project. As BPR was very new to the Company at the time, a trained facilitator was added to the team to help maintain a 'BPR direction' and assist with implementing the new techniques. There was initial nervousness about this new way of solving problems. This was particularly evident where equal rank was maintained in the meeting room, in an otherwise very hierarchical organisation. At the early meetings it took several hours to agree the basic direction, aims and mission, but this served to maintain 'goal congruence' later among team members. Team members were not given time allowances for attending, but it was assumed that a successful outcome would reward team members with a saving of future efforts. When work pressure was heavy it was therefore hard to keep busy people in the team.

After agreement of aims, the team moved on to assessment of processes, starting off by using *Brainstorming* to develop ideas of the steps involved in the process. The team identified the departments and groups involved in each process. There was then enough information to draw up *Deployment flow charts* (DFCs) of the processes. DFCs show process flows, highlighting stakeholder responsibility at each stage. These graphic and comprehensive charts provided a powerful level of insight and understanding of the whole process to an extent which surprised all members. To clarify the (rather complex) DFCs, 'Affinity diagrams'[i] were used, grouping together related processes. In order to make decisions, *light voting*, where participants put a number of points against the various options, was used. This deflated divisive and rigid positions on decision options. When a conflict arose in a meeting, the aim was to resolve it by discussion and sharing of information. Clearly for this information sharing to work fully, it was important that all participants attended meetings regularly.

3.3 Software Quality - Does BPR Improve It?

The work performed on this project earned an award from the Company for Continuous Improvement. In particular, the Company was impressed by the team's self starting approach and initiative in improving processes, in line with the principles of BPR. The main users stated that the system fulfilled their key objective of providing correct data, on time, to the finance department. In particular, it now takes two to three days to process a two week period's phone calls, instead of seven to ten days, with one period's work sometimes causing chaos by running into the next period's work. Switchboard staff estimate that they now put half as many hours into processing the data, declining from 25 to 15 hours per week, although the process is still far from fully automated, only relieving them of two work processes. The system's screens and menus were also felt to be very usable.

The system is now reliable, and has not required IT Department intervention at all during the last two working periods (May 1994). The previous level of IT staff involvement was around 25 person hours per week. Users do, however, have a very long list of required enhancements, but there are no IT resources to satisfy these needs. Should staff become available, the system would be relatively easy to amend. Such a large enhancement list (rather than a bug fix list) can be seen as indicating a desire to expand the system's area of involvement. Note that documentation is significantly incomplete and yet the system is operating successfully.

3.4 BPR vs Other Methodologies

The Company's usual methodology for system development is Information Engineering. BPR was used to supplement the strategy and analysis stages of the methodology. Essentially, BPR re-emphasised the importance of involving all stakeholders in the development throughout the essential early stages. BPR diagrams such as DFCs are directly comparable with Data Flow Diagrams as used

---

[i] Based on the KJ Method developed by Jiro Kawakita in the 1960's and as taught to the company by Technology Exchange Center (TEC) Inc., Santa Ana, California, 92701

by most system development methodologies. But with BPR, the way the analysis is performed is of more importance than the actual data and the processes.

4. LESSONS LEARNED

Lessons learnt during the process included:

ñ No process is sacred or fixed

ñ All relevant stakeholders must be brought into the development process and involved fully at the requirement definition phase.

ñ Discussions are most effective when staff rank is ignored.

ñ BPR techniques help empower individuals and break down departmental barriers.

ñ Commitment of the whole development team, of both IT and non IT staff to shared goals, will contribute significantly to the success of the system.

5. CONCLUSION

The use of BPR techniques in CIS development is useful in the strategy, analysis and requirements definition phases, but only if it is part of a business wide quality improvement initiative. Its major strengths lie in techniques for balanced empowerment of stakeholders and levelling of power from an hierarchical base point.

The case study system was developed during 1992 and implemented at the end of 1993. In 1994, as this paper is being written, the system is being used successfully and stakeholders are looking for further enhancements to extend its area of operation. It is clear from this that expectation success has been achieved and that in terms of software quality the system fulfils many of McCall's criteria.

REFERENCES

1. Hirschheim, R. and Klein, H.K.: 'Four Paradigms of Information Systems Development', *Communications of the ACM,* 32 10, October 1989, pp199-1216.
2. Lyytinen, K. and Hirschheim, R.: 'Information Systems Failures - a survey and classification of the empirical literature', *Oxford Surveys in Information Technology*, 4, 1987, pp257-309.
3. Price Waterhouse Survey of Computer Failures, 1989.
4. Mumford, E.: 'Designing Human Systems', Manchester Business School., 1983.
5. Jones, L.H. and Kydd,C.T.: 'An Information Processing Framework for Understanding Success and Failure of MIS Development Methodologies', *Information and Management*, 15, 1988, pp263-71.
6. Fitzgerald, G.: 'Achieving Flexible Information Systems: the case for improved analysis', *Journal of Information Technology,* 5 , 1990, pp5-11.
7. Grindley, K.: 'Managing IT at Board Level: the hidden agenda exposed', Pitman, 1991, pp149.
8. Mumford, E.: 'Defining Systems Requirements to Meet Business Needs: a case study example', *The Computer Journal*, 28 2 , 1985, pp97-104.
9. Kydd, C.T. and Jones, L.H.: 'Corporate Productivity and Shared Information Technology', *Information Management* 17, 1989, p277-282.
10. Pressman, R.: 'Software Engineering: A practitioner's approach', McGraw-Hill. 1992, pp150.
11. Mccall, J., Richards, P., Walters, G.:'Factors in Software Quality', NTIS AD-A049-014, 015, 055. November 1977.

6

Towards A Methodology for 24 Hour Software Production Using Globally Separated Development Teams

Ian Gorton[a] and Sanjeev Motwani[b]

[a] Ian Gorton, School of Computer Science and Engineering, University of New South Wales, PO Box 1, Kensington, Sydney 2033, Australia

[b] Sanjeev Motwani, Asia Pacific Systems Engineering Centre, BT Australasia, 1 Market St, Sydney NSW 2000, Australia, E-mail: {sanjeev, ian}@apsec.bt.com.au

Abstract

The potential advantages of utilising software development teams which reside in different time zones are discussed. The experiences of an experimental study which attempted to share a software project between teams in Australia and India are then related. The results of this study show that, co-operative software development on a global scale is feasible, productivity gains are achievable and potentially enhanced product quality is an important by-product.[+]

Keyword Codes: K.6.1; K.6.3; D.2
Keywords: Project and People Management ; Software Management; Software Engineering

1. INTRODUCTION

As the global market for software continues its rapid growth, many multinational companies involved in software production are establishing development groups around the world. Ostensibly these groups usually aim to support the local customer base for their company's products, and on occasions may participate in strategic product development efforts. More often than not however, the development of a specific product is localised to a single site. This is in main due to the perception that developing complex software systems is an inherently difficult task, and introducing unnecessary communications barriers between the personnel involved will only make the task more difficult[1].

In this paper we argue that geographically separated development teams should be viewed as an opportunity to improve and re-focus an organisation's software development practices. With modern communications networks, support tools and suitable software engineering and management practices, significant time differences between teams can be exploited to reduce product development times.

We take the approach that a software development project may be divided amongst geographically separated teams possessing partially overlapping or disjoint working hours. These teams will have a fast and reliable data communications network, and may also communicate by telephone and facsimile. In order to make the time differences work to their advantage, the development teams must collaborate on a shared task. For example, one team will work upon the task during their normal working hours. At some stage before the end of their day part or all of the task will be handed over to a collaborating team to continue with during their normal working hours. Near or at the end of the collaborating team's working

[+] Ian Gorton would like to thank BT Australasia for their support in the BT Research Fellowship scheme. Ian Gorton and Sanjeev Motwani would like to thank Mark Norris, David Beale, Martin Deacon, Udaykumar Revankar, Sunil Chavan, Michael Rohanek and Ponampalam Balakumar for their participation in this project.

day, they will hand the task back for continuation by the original team. In this manner, a team would be able to build upon the progress made by the co-operating team 'overnight' - a phenomena we call the *overnight gain effect.*

It is envisaged that the effective use of development teams across time-zones could have a number of beneficial effects for an organisation involved in software development Overlap of development activity, giving potentially 24 hour continuous development effort could significantly reduce time-to-market for software products. It could also lead to better utilisation of available skilled employees, minimising duplication of expert skills in different locations around the world. Product quality may further be enhanced due to the introduction of global perspectives during the development effort, and costs may be reduced by exploit low operating overheads and skilled staff in developing nations[2]

However, to exploit such a working environment, it will be necessary to implement procedures and methods to organise, monitor, control and synchronise distributed team efforts. For example, individual teams must be able to ascertain precisely which parts of a project have been completed, which are still in progress, and which are still to be tackled. Co-ordination of team activities will inevitably incur some overhead, and management of such a decentralised effort will be inherently more complex.

The motivation for this work arises from the establishment of a new BT software development centre in Sydney, Australia. For the Sydney group to actively and effectively participate in BT's global development processes, there is a need to extend and re-design existing development methodologies to take into account the problems and opportunities associated with distributed teams. Consequently, in order to understand the fundamental work factors which affect developers working in a globally distributed environment, we are conducting a series of progressively more complex experimental studies on live software projects. These will culminate in a large development trial using several teams in a number of locations. This paper describes the second study, which used two one-person teams located in Sydney and Bombay to develop a database package.

2. MODELS OF DISTRIBUTED WORKING IN SOFTWARE DEVELOPMENT

We propose three major models for organising distributed teams to take advantage of time differences: co-operative (peer-to-peer), delegation (supervisor/worker) and consultative (expert consultation). Each model has its own strengths and weaknesses, and can be used as a guide to match team organisations to project requirements and specific tasks.

When teams are organised to operate co-operatively, teams will exist on an equal basis and share closely related activities. For example, two teams may work on functionally dependent modules in a system. When the first team completes coding a module, it may pass the module and test specifications to the second team for testing. The second team will run the tests, and fix any errors which it can detect in a reasonable amount of time, only passing back problems to the first team in severe cases. In return, as the second team completes modules, it passes the code and test specifications to the first team for testing and repair where possible. Co-operating teams could also utilise each other for quality assurance activities. To effectively co-operate in such activities, teams should be comfortable when working together, be of similar status and possess a similar skill set. Effort in identifying tasks which are of suitable duration and complexity would also be required, and communication and management overheads would be unavoidable.

The delegation model of co-operation across time zones would seem most applicable to development, testing and support phases of software development. For example, a dedicated test team could accept completed modules and test specifications from a supervising development team. The test team would run tests and report back on their success and failure. The development team would then fix errors and pass the fixed code back for regression testing. A similar team structure could be operated during the maintenance and support cycle of a system. Supervisor/worker teams are not uncommon in large software developments [3]. Their advantage is a clear separation of responsibility between teams, easing control and management overheads. When operating in disjoint time zones, the scope for exploiting the overnight gain effect is significant, and reduced product development cycles could be expected. Further, the worker team does not require the experience or expertise of the supervisory team. This should lower the level of technical discussion between teams, giving concise and structured interactions, and reducing the likelihood of technical disputes.

Consultative teams would seem to offer broad scope for exploitation of the overnight gain effect in software development. Expert teams with skills ranging from reviewing development proposals to enhancing existing systems could be deployed. In certain circumstances, these teams would be used as organisation-wide resources, in others they may be dedicated to a particular project. Tasks of short duration could be dealt with rapidly and feedback be returned to the client on their next working day.

3. AN EXPERIMENT IN SOFTWARE DEVELOPMENT ACROSS TIME ZONES

During September 1993 an initial experimental study was held within BT's Asia Pacific Systems Engineering Centre (APSEC) in Sydney. This study simulated two geographically separated single person teams by placing an imaginary barrier between two developers in the same office. This initial study was mainly used to test out how task assignments and synchronisation could be organised, and how each team's progress could be monitored and controlled.

With the experience of the first study, a more ambitious second experiment was planned. Two single person teams were established to operate using the delegation model to develop a PC-based database package. The program development team was based in Sydney, with the program test team based in Bombay, India. In addition a local project leader was assigned to each team to monitor overall progress and deal with organisational issues. The time difference between Sydney and Bombay is five and a half hours, thus allowing a three hour overlap of core working hours. This was deemed important as it would allow unforeseen problems to be immediately discussed and corrected over a telephone. The study was planned to operate for approximately one week during December 1993 with the aim of developing and testing the major input and query screens in the database project.

The Sydney team was given sole responsibility for designing and developing the software, and producing test specifications. A design specification for the project was completed prior to the study commencing: this acted as the base reference document for both teams. As parts of the system were implemented, they were passed over to the test team in Bombay, which ran the appropriate tests and reported back on their success or failure. Due to the time difference between the two teams, from the development team's perspective, testing would have occurred 'overnight', allowing the overall project to progress at a faster rate (Sydney is five and a half hours *ahead* of Bombay).

No direct data link existed between the Sydney and Bombay sites. A BT private network with reasonably fast delivery for small files was however available for email messages. File transfers between sites were thus achieved using a modem connection. While this was certainly slow compared with other forms of communication, the amount of data to be transferred daily was relatively small (maximum of 300KB) and consequently did not consume too much time.

For this mode of working to be successful, a number of project control and communications mechanisms were established to help overcome the distributed nature of the project teams.

3.1 Task Assignment

A Task Assignment (TA) form was designed to enable the development team to assign tasks to the test team. A TA was to be submitted by the development team each day, and it was to specify which modules should be tested and which test specifications should be used. In addition, any previously reported faults that had been fixed and should be re-tested were to be specified. As well as fields for general reference (e.g. source, destination, expected duration) the TA contained an area for allocating contingency work. Due to the nature of distributed work across time zones, unexpected problems (e.g. corrupt files, ambiguity in test specifications) could delay a project for longer than when such problems can be discussed face to face. In such circumstances, the contingency work allocation would be used to guide the test team to work on areas that could be profitably exploited in the near future.

3.2 Test Specifications and Fault Reports

Test specifications were drawn up by the development team. For each user screen in the system, a detailed list of tests were specified. A set of standard test cases was also created to ensure overall consistency between screens in the system. Whenever a test case in a test specification produced an error, the test team was to create a Fault Report (FR). A FR must contain sufficient information to allow the error to be reproduced by the development team. Each FR submitted by the test team was to be listed in the daily status report to ensure that FR's did not for some reason 'go missing', and to provide a check-list for the development team.

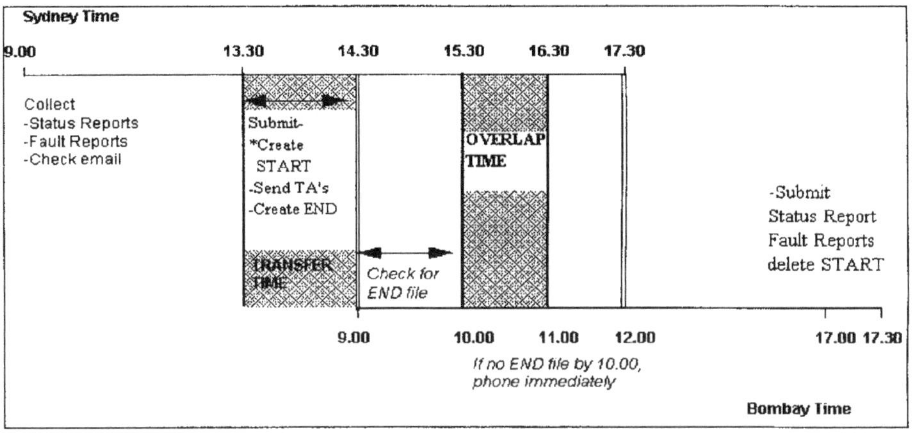

Figure 1 **Daily Schedule for Development and Test Teams**

3.3 Status Reporting

A status report (SR) was to be submitted by the test team using email at the end of each day. The SR should indicate exactly what has been accomplished and what problems have occurred. This information should include the exact status of each task that has been assigned, and identify tests that have been completed and test cases which will require action by the development team.

3.4 File Transfers

Two distinct types of file transfers are required in a distributed team project. First, the current files associated with the project development such as program code, executables, test data and test specifications must be maintained in a common area. When using the delegation model, only the development team is allowed to alter these files. Consequently the development team must ensure that the latest versions of all development-related files are made available to the test team. In general these files are too numerous and large to be conveniently or reliably transferred by electronic mail. Second, project control files such as TA's, SR's and FR's must be exchanged daily. TA's are transferred from the development team to the test team, and SR's and FR's are transferred from the test team to the development team. In general these files are small in size (one or two pages of text) and can be transferred conveniently via electronic mail.

It is important to note that the successful transfer of both categories of files is not alone a sufficient condition for progress. Not only must the files be transferred successfully, they must also be available at the start of the working day of the team which is to utilise the files. Consequently, a daily schedule of activity was drawn up to clearly specify the deadlines by which certain activities were to take place. This daily schedule is shown in Figure 1. Two important time periods are highlighted in the schedule, namely *transfer time* and *overlap time*. *Transfer time* is the period allocated for the development team to make the latest versions of the project files available to the test team. To ensure partial transferred files were not accessed during transfer time, a simple file locking mechanism (using the START and END files in Figure 1) was implemented. *Overlap time* was the period designated for direct telephone conversations between the two teams.

4. EXPERIMENTAL OBSERVATIONS

The study ran from the 15th to 22nd December. For the majority of this time, program development and testing successfully overlapped. Each day newly developed screens were passed to the test team during transfer time. The development and test team then proceeded independently until the end of the development team's work day. The test team continued testing until their work day ended, and transferred back status and fault reports for the development team to collect when they returned in the morning. In this manner, enhanced productivity in terms of actual progress on the project during the trial period was achieved due to the overnight gain effect. Many lessons were learned in the process of designing, performing and monitoring the experimental study. Some of these are summarised below.

High Quality Planning is Essential: We consider the planning stage to be crucial to a project's success. The scope for severe problems to arise when using distributed teams is considerable. It must therefore be absolutely clear what the roles and responsibilities of each team are, and how they are to communicate and interact[1]. Soliciting input from the development teams during the planning stage, and obtaining feedback on plans ensures that team members are well informed and leads to project guidelines which everyone is content to follow.

Ensure that communications networks are adequate: A reliable and fast communications network is essential for projects which use globally separated teams, as failures in the network have the potential to cause havoc. Projects should ideally utilise existing networks which have been in use for a reasonable period of time and for which the performance characteristics and failure rate are well known. Well before a project commences, estimates of the communications load should be made. This should involve estimates of the maximum file size that will need to be transferred, the amount of files transferred on a daily basis, and overall traffic expected on the network. In addition, a back-up network should be established to ensure that the project can continue co-operatively in the event of a network failure

Monitor File Transfers: It should never be assumed that file transfers are successful. Measures must be instigated to monitor all file transfers and ensure that some form of crash recovery mechanism is automatically invoked.

Review All Project Documentation: When direct contact amongst team members is not possible, minor inconsistencies, mistakes or ambiguities in project documentation can potentially cause a delay of a day or more due to time differences. To help remove these problems, quality assurance methods such as peer review should be utilised extensively on all materials which will be passed to other sites.

Allocate Multiple Tasks: Despite all attempts to eradicate errors and provide reliable communications, problems inevitably occur. It is therefore essential that the problem does not stop a team from performing any productive work until the issue can be cleared up - this could mean a whole day of lost productivity. To guard against such delays, multiple, independent tasks should be allocated and be current at any particular time. This allows a team to continue working on other parts of the project until obstacles on a task are removed. In our trial, contingency tasks in TA's played this role effectively.

Minimise Distractions to Key Team Members: If a strong daily dependence exists for work allocations between two teams, distractions which delay one team temporarily can adversely affect the related team. This kind of problem can be minimised by ensuring that sufficient tasks are outstanding so that temporary productivity lapses have little overall impact (see previous point).

Problem Resolution: A project needs problem resolution procedures for technical or managerial issues which arise as the project progresses. This can be especially problematic in projects with distributed teams, as the potential for direct communications is limited. An important issue for one team may not seem so crucial from another team's perspective. Other problems may call for some synchronised action at each site. If one team neglects to perform this action, all other teams are delayed. In our study we defined a shared issues table to track and maintain the status of all unresolved problems. Each team leader was assigned the responsibility of maintaining this table, and ensuring that appropriate actions were taken. However, despite taking these measures, not all problems were dealt with in an effective and timely manner. For example, some requests in email or fax messages were missed or ignored, and occasionally incorrect actions were carried out due to a lack of background information. It was felt that the distributed responsibility for problem resolution (amongst team leaders) was not effective. One possible solution would be to assign a single person to be responsible for global problem resolution. In this manner, a project-wide perspective on problems could be maintained.

Be Prepared for Cultural Differences: Considerable differences in cultural backgrounds and attitudes towards work are seen amongst western societies. These differences are even greater when teams from diverse, non-western nations participate in a project. Some examples of the cultural differences encountered in our trial were varying degree of command over written and spoken English, differing work ethic, and the expected level of formality in communications.

Choose Key Team Members Carefully: Working in a distributed environment places additional pressure and demands on key team members. We observed that communications failures between sites cause genuine emotional distress, and the inherent reliance on other teams for progress causes pressure to mount to considerable levels. For these reasons, experienced and highly motivated staff should be used to fill important positions. Moreover, good communications and negotiation skills are essential.

5. FURTHER WORK AND CONCLUSIONS

The potential advantages of deploying globally separated software development teams have been presented, and three models for their organisation have been discussed. In performing an experiment in distributed working across time zones, some important issues and potential problems were observed, and guidelines for running such a project were tested. At this stage, after two small-scale studies in distributed working, considerable insight into the inherent problems of this approach has been developed. Several solutions have been proposed and validated during both studies. Next we intend to further test these solutions in a more extensive study involving more personnel and a larger time difference between teams. While the project has so far focused on exploiting a delegation development model, we aim to experiment with the co-operative model. Although the problems of teams working co-operatively are probably the most significant, we feel this may have the greatest potential for exploiting concurrent activities using globally separated teams[4].

The project will also consider how CSCW tools could help distributed teams interact and share information. We envisage that work flow and scheduling system in the manner of that proposed in [5] could help considerably with activity co-ordination. Such a system would provide a unified view of the project development files, and control access and file transfers between sites.

REFERENCES

1. Truett,L.F. et al, Co-ordination of Software Development Activities Among Sites that are Geographically Separated, in COMPSAC-17, (Nov 1-5, Phoenix), IEEE, 1993, pp 70-75
2. Press, L., Software Export From Developing Nations, IEEE Computer, 26, 12, (1993), pp 62-67
3. Norris, M and Rigby, P., Software Engineering Explained, John Wiley and Sons, UK, 1992
4. Prasad, B., Morenc, R.S. and Rangan,R.M., Information Management for Concurrent Engineering: Research Issues, Concurrent Engineering: Research and Applications, 1, 1, March 1993, pp 3-20
5. Gronbaek, K., Kyng, M., and Mogensen, P., CSCW Challenges: Co-operative Design in Engineering Projects, Communications of the ACM, 36, 4, (June 1993), pp 67-77

7

MetaMet - A Soft Systemic Way Toward the Quality of Information Systems

Peter Kokol and Bruno Stiglic

The Faculty of Technical Sciences
62000 Maribor
Slovenia

Abstract

The quality of information systems (IS) is strongly related with the quality of the IS design process and both are fundamental issues in successful IS construction and use process. In the paper we present a MetaMet a quality oriented IS design approach which should result in quality information systems.

Keyword Codes: H.1.0; D.2.0; D.2.1
Keywords: Information Systems, General; Software Engineering, General; Requirements/ Specifications

1.INTRODUCTION

The quality of information systems (IS) is strongly related with the quality of the IS design process and both are fundamental issues in successful IS construction and use process (successful in terms of all affected and involved parties and individuals). There are various definitions of software quality and various ways how to achieve it. The most usual approach [9] is on achieving more effective control of the IS design process, emphasising the need for improved project management and the introduction and subsequent enforcement of standards. In such manner the most effort has been devoted for the search of new metrics to monitor errors, reliability, usability, maintainability etc. In that way the quality is defined as [10]:

The totality of features and characteristics of a product or service that bear on its ability to satisfy stated or implied needs.

However, there are also some other more soft oriented views to IS quality. Their proponents emphasise that considering technical aspects of design process by itself is insufficient. The design process is multidimensional and must be treated as a learning, communication and negotiation process. In such manner the quality is defined as [9]:

Quality is perceived in terms of those external product attributes which are relevant for the particular types of users; or

Quality is judgement by customers of users of a product or service; it is the extent to which the customer or users believe the product or service surpasses their needs and expectations.

As seen from above two definitions the "soft" IS quality should not be considered as intrinsic to an IS, but it exists in the relationship between customer/user and product, where customer/users includes all involved and affected parties and product can include goods and services (see Fig. 1). Thereafter the quality is socially constructed phenomenon that is customer/user and situation dependent and changes over time in response to changes in environment, values, beliefs etc. Concerning above definitions and statements we can conclude that quality IS design is (or at list it should be) a very human intensive process. Such processes can not be tackled with "hard engineering approaches" but in more "softer way " using principles advocated by Checkland or Flood [4, 5]. According to their work we predetermined two main issues that must be considered in the manner to design successful information systems:

- we must obey to principles of participance, continuity, holism and endless learning. That means that we must take into account the whole "system" (not only involved but also affected participants of the IS design process and related environments, process, product etc.) and must consider the uncertainty of the situation (the value system of participants will change during the process, unexpected events will occur, situation can be changed etc.),
- we must be able to answer two *"basic questions"*.

  Question 1. *which* from many possible computerised information systems (IS) to design? and

  Question 2. *how* to design the selected one?

  Above two questions seems very reasonable and natural for any IS design situation, but are very rarely explicitly answered.

We argue that the design of an IS in the systemic and participative manner is closely related to the epistemology of *soft system design* (Checkland 1981, 1990; Flood 1991) and should be as shown in Figure 2. The *"conventional " IS system design* is closely related to hard-system thinking [4, 5]. It is in general concerned only with Level 0 design and one process. In contrary the systemic and participative design should be performed by three processes on two design levels. Taking into account all these facts we can state that the IS design methodology able to result in successful and quality systems should confront to characteristics shown in Table 1. As a result to above of above discussion and as a possible response to the software crisis we constructed a new IS design methodology called MetaMet (MetaMethodology). Their characteristics of MetaMet are very similar to characteristics required in Table 1. Thereafter it is our belief that MetaMet represent a possible way toward the improvement of IS quality.

Table 1. The required basic characteristics of MIS design methodologies

Current MIS Design Methodologies	New/Changed MIS Design Methodologies
sequential	iterative
unparticipative	participative
one - dimensional	multi - dimensional
mono - lingual	multi - lingual
one - aspect	multi - aspect
one - levelled	multi - levelled
systematic	systemic
technological system	human activity system
waterfall model	extended operational model
situation insensitive	situation sensitive
partial	holistic
control abstraction	knowledge abstraction

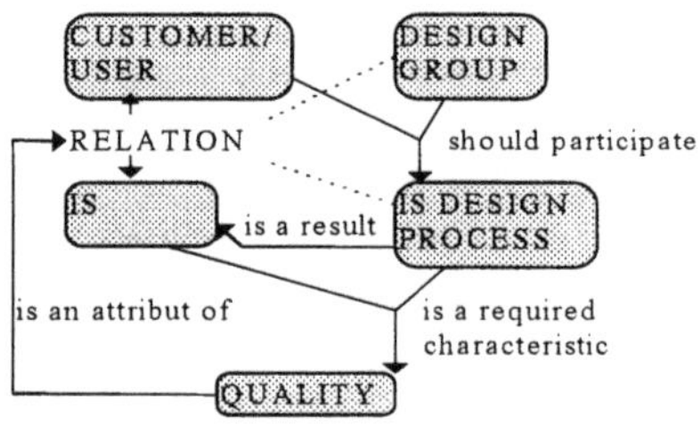

Figure 1. The Notion of Quality

2. RELATED RESEARCH

Many new software design paradigms have been proposed as a response to the software crisis. These range from solely technological to most elaborate paradigms, based on theory. Operational, prototyping and transformational paradigms [1] are most prominent among them. They try too incite user participation in order to deliver executable code early in the design process, and automate the production of software. Other approaches are more general and are usually based on AI or similar concepts. Their aim is to support a part of actions performed during the IS design process and are independent of the methodology used. A recent and very promising IS design approach called "Evolution of Software Processes" is based on the emerging view that software processes - like software - also needs to be evolved lest they become obsolete. The aim of the evolution is to fulfil the needs of the people who perform the process and the developmental and organisational goals to be achieved.

Despite many advantages of new software design paradigms and approaches it is argued [2, 8] that it is unreasonable to rely on only one paradigm, because the tools and techniques for one set of circumstances need not be appropriate for others. Various solutions based on metadesign and modelling of software design paradigms like domain analysis, metamodeling, system factory etc. were proposed recently in the manner to enable more flexible design in different design situations.

However, the majority of above approaches differs from the MetaMet in at least one of following features:

- they are concerned only with modelling, evolution etc. of the software processes and not with their design
- they are concerned only with some aspects, dimension and phases of the metadesign
- they do not provide a well defined metadesign methodology, theory or framework
- they are often to technological and neglect political, cultural and other dimensions of system design
- their metadesign life cycle follows the waterfall model
- they are concerned only with large systems.

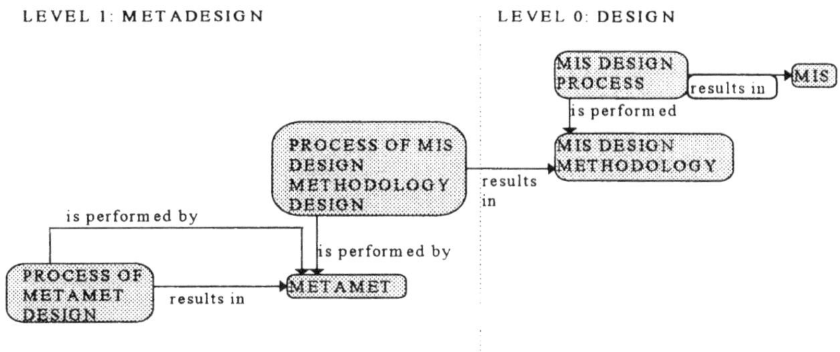

Figure 2. Two Levelled MIS Design

3. TWO LEVELLED DESIGN - WHY

All things are in state of flux

- Heraclitus of Ephesus

In those rare situation in which the question 2 is explicitly answered, it is normally transformed into the form *Which methodology to use to design this IS?* and it is our belief that this is simply not enough. Generally speaking in addition to the famous saying of Heraclitus presented above they are four claims supporting our view.

- First the IS design occurs in two contexts: the context within which the designer operates and the context produced by the *designing design* itself.
- Second the IS design can be defined as a *process* [Osterveil 1987, Kokol 1993] performed in a *specific design situation*, according to a *specific life cycle design paradigm* and using a *specific methodology*.

Analysing design processes, design situations, paradigms and relations between them [6, 7] (Kokol 1992b) we assert that:

1. there are no definitely good or bad design methodologies, they are good or bad only if associated with a specific design situation

2. there are design situations (or at least they will be in the future) for which no known design paradigm is appropriate.

- Third there is a variety of different IS design paradigms and it is very unbelievable that the IS design group has an expertise in selecting and applying the best of them.
- Fourth, it seems clear that software quality will be brought into the centre of the design process and thereafter we need software quality oriented processes and a way to design, measure and manage them (*"the product can not be better than its design process"*).

In that manner the simple selection of "the best" IS design methodology is at least very difficult if not impossible. Thereafter we assert that to enable successful IS design in all design situations we must first *design* (this design can in many situations be reduced to selection, but nevertheless this selection is carried out in a systemic fashion) an appropriate design paradigm. This activity was called the *metadesign* or *Level 1 design.*

4.TWO LEVELLED DESIGN - HOW

During the seventies the symptoms of the software crisis became visible also in our country and in the beginning of eighties it became critical. As a consequence we tried to overcome the crisis with the use of unconventional methodologies and latter on with the construction and application of new design paradigms. At that time we also introduced the idea of metadesign and more recent the approach now known as metaparadigm [7]. In last years we strive to improve the metaparadigm in the systemic manner and the results off our effort IS MetaMet presented in following sections.

Meta met is defined as

a process in which a problem situation containing a manual IS is transformed into an improved situation - employing a computerised IS - appreciating the epistemology of MetaMet, the characteristics of the problem situation, recent developments in IS research and science in general (standards, norms, technology, etc.) and the principle of uncertainty performed in an endless learning loop.

According to above definition the MetaMet should support following activities:

- formal description (metamodeling) of design paradigms, design process and design situations;
- formal evaluation and comparison of design paradigms;
- metadesign of design paradigms, where metadesign is treated in a very broad sense as invention of new design paradigms, adoption of known design paradigms, composition of known design paradigms, selection between design paradigms etc.;
- design of the IS using the metadesigned paradigm
- be able to learn and accumulate the knowledge from current MetaMet's applications and be able to reuse this knowledge in further applications;
- appreciate current state "of the art" in IS designs, system theory, science in general etc.

One of the most important Metamet's characteristics is that the design process should be performed during an infinitive learning loop. As a consequence the design and metadesign should advance in parallel. First an intuitive methodology is constructed reflecting the initial users and design group vision. The methodology is then used in IS design concurrently with the construction of the primary design methodology In the case of conflicts, new requirements, changing environment and other factors of *uncertainty* the primary methodology is improved according to new conditions. During the MetaMet's use the SSM [4] is employed as a metadesign methodology.

5.EVALUATION OF THE METAMET USE

It is natural to ask question such as: *Does the metaparadigm work?, Is it good? Is it more usable then approach X?, etc.* But, as for any system approach, such questions can not be answered. There is in principle no way in which it could be proved or disproved that using the MetaMet is "*the best*" way to design information systems. In addition the traditional scientific evaluation method (empirical assessment of a given hypothesis) is not appropriate for the information system research [8]. But in the manner to implement the endless learning loop mentioned in previous sections we must be able to, at least, approximately rate the successfulness of using metaparadigm. This can be de done in two ways:

- we can employ the measurement approach proposed by Conrath [3]. Conrath suggests, in spite that no single measure can be adequate for an IS evaluation, that an IS should be assessed using four constructs: user satisfaction, system effectiveness, value and utilisation. In our case we implemented the Conrath's approach with a blind questionnaire that is answered by all known involved and affected persons. A symbolic median value is then calculated and it represent an overall view of the IS successfulness.
- we can evaluate the resulting IS design paradigm with the semi-formal approach introduced by Kokol [6]. This approach enables one to compare various design paradigms according to different dimensions. Using questionnaires answered by all relevant people we obtain a median value similar to above which represent the overall quality of the design methodology being designed and used.

After assessment of results of the MetaMet use in various design situations we can conclude that the MetaMet is a very promising method for the design of successful and quality information systems.

REFERENCES

1. Agresti W W: *New Paradigms for Software Development*, IEEE CS Press, New York, 1986.
2. Avison DE, Wood-Harper AT: Multiview-An Exploration in information systems development. *Australian Computer Journal, 18*(1986)174-179.
3. Checkland P and Scholes J: *Soft Systems Methodology in Action.* John Wiley & Sons, Chichester 1990.
4. Conrath D W, Sharma R S: Evaluation Measures for Computer-based Information Systems, *Computers in industry 21*(1993)267-272.
5. Flood R L, Jackson M C: *Creative problem Solving: Total System Intervention*, Wiley, 1991.
6. Kokol P, Stglic B, Zumer V: Software Design Tools Evaluation in Context of a Metaparadigm, *Proceedings of AQSDT'92*, Nahouraii E (ed.), New Orleans, IEEE CS Press, pp. 34-41, 1992a.
7. Kokol P: Metaparadigm: A Soft Systemic MIS Design Approach. *Journal of Medical Systems 17*(1993b)47 - 57.
8. Kokol P: Software System Design with the Metaparadigm, *Cybernetics and Systems 1994*, Trapl R. ed., World Scientific, Singapore 1994, pp. 385 - 390.
9. Vidgen R. T., A. T. Wood Harper: Establishing and managing a Relevant Notion of Quality. *Proceedings of SQM 93*, Elsevier 1993, pp. 117-132.
10. ISO: *ISO 8402: Quality Vocabulary*, ISO 1986.

8

Changing Programming Paradigm - An Empirical Investigation

James Miller, Gerald Darroch, Murray Wood, Andrew Brooks and Marc Roper

Dept. Computer Science, University of Strathclyde,
Livingstone Tower, Richmond Street, Glasgow G1 1XH, Scotland

Abstract

This paper outlines an investigation into the ability of experienced programmers to effectively change programming paradigm. In particular it investigates programmers changing from imperative to object-oriented programming. This is achieved by comparing code samples from the new and experienced object-oriented programmers. Each sample is presented to a tool which makes a number of automatic measurements. The comparison has revealed large style differences between the two sets of programmers. The two groups having very different ideas on what constitutes an object, resulting in significant variations in the concepts of the responsibility or extent of a class, and inheritance and associated operations. These differences will typically result in major variations in the quality and reusability of the software produced.

Key Codes: D1.5; D2.8
Keywords: Object-Oriented Programming; Metrics

1. INTRODUCTION

Object-oriented techniques are viewed by many as the most exciting development within the field of software construction. Companies and organisations are rushing to retrain their technical personnel in this new medium and in the process change experienced imperative programmers into novice object-oriented programmers. But what are the consequences? Can experienced proficient imperative programmers be considered ready to construct new systems after a short re-orientation or does the change in paradigm require time to mature with the retrained personnel? Programmers are expected to master additional concepts (such as inheritance, function overloading and polymorphism) and successfully integrate them into their existing 'toolkit' of techniques for system construction. Will the retrained personnel produce 'better' systems or will it lead to a reduction in quality? This study attempts to help answer these questions.

2. OVERVIEW OF THE EXPERIMENT

The main objective behind this project is an attempt to characterise the principal differences (in terms of coding style) between novice and experienced object-oriented programmers. It should be noted that the novice object-oriented programmers are themselves experienced programmers in other paradigms). In order to achieve this goal the project team carried out an empirical evaluation on code produced by both novice and experienced subjects. Evaluation took the form of submitting code samples from both groups to an attributes tool(OOATS) (produced for this project). The tool calculates various measures[1, 2, 3, 4] for each sample of work and produces a 'characterisation' of the code in terms of various object-oriented properties. The properties can be grouped into three overlapping categories: responsibility or extent, complexity and inheritance properties of an object. These properties were subsequently summed for each group, and the two summations were statistically compared for significant differences.

The selection of a set of measures to characterise an object-oriented program is (currently) a subjective process. Little is understood about what contributes to good or bad object-oriented code to fully characterise the process. Hence we have chosen a list of measures as a starting point. It is hoped as the study is extended the number and type of measurements will increase. No claim is made that this set of measurements provide any particular insight, simply an interesting basis for exploration.

3. EXPERIMENTAL DESIGN AND ANALYSIS

3.1 Subjects and their Experience

The study has collected sample code from both camps: novice and experienced. Novice object-oriented programmers were people who had at least three and as many eight years traditional programming expertise, but had only recently transferred paradigm. All programmers in the novice group were experienced C programmers. The code selected was their first attempt at producing a significant (> 1000 lines) object-oriented system. In addition it was verified that the programmers' objective was to produce 'good quality' object-oriented code and not just a working solution. Programmers in the experienced object-oriented group all had three years or more object-oriented experience. All programmers in the experienced group were experienced C++ programmers. The study was carried out in C++. It was hoped to minimise any ability and familiarisation factors by the choice of languages and participants' backgrounds.

3.2 Measurements

All measurements were automatically produced via an object-oriented metrics tool produced for this study. The tool measured the following characteristics for each program:

Average number of methods per class
Average number of instance variables per class
Average size of method per class
Average class 'complexity'
Average method 'complexity'
Average instances of function overloading per class
Average instances of operator overloading per class
Average number of 'children' classes
Maximum depth of inheritance per program

The method 'complexity' is calculated using McCabe's Cyclomatic number (as suggested by Graham[3]) and the class complexity is the sum of the class' method complexities as suggested by Chidamber and Kemerer[1]. All other measurements are self-explanatory.

3.3. Analysis

The results from a t-test on each measurement will be described in this section. The t-test was selected because of its effective performance with small samples[5]. From the collected programs, 31 samples from each camp were identified for analysis, via random sampling. The Null hypothesis is "that the means of the two samples are equal" (i.e. We have found no difference between the novice and experienced programmers) and hence the alternative hypothesis is "that the means are different" (i.e. we have found a difference). The t value for each measurement is:

Table 1. t-test values for each measurement

Measurement	*t Value*
Average number of methods per class	5.069*
Average number of instance variables per class	8.307*
Average size of method per class	0.312
Average class 'complexity'	5.250*
Average method 'complexity'	0.485
Average instances of function overloading per class	3.715*
Average instances of operator overloading per class	5.355*
Average number of 'children' per class	5.700*
Maximum depth of inheritance per program	5.970*

* means the null hypothesis has been rejected and the alternative accepted. All results are stated at the standard 5% significance level.

4. DISCUSSION AND CONCLUSIONS

Although great care must be taken to draw general conclusions from experiments with small sample sizes, we believe the results show that significant differences (in style) exist between novice and experienced object-oriented programmers. In seven out of the nine attributes measured our experiment has found a statistical difference. The 2 attributes where no difference was detected (Average size of method per class, Average method 'complexity') are attributes with directly comparative attributes within imperative programming (Average function size, Average function 'complexity'). Hence one might surmise that total programming experience rather than specific experience within an individual paradigm is the most important factor and hence due to the two camps having similar experience no difference would be expected.

These results are contrary to the study by Wilde and Huitt[6], they reported finding (in professional commercial work) median method sizes of "1 executable statement for C++ programs and 3 noncommented lines for Smalltalk programs". Although not explicitly measured by the tool, the average size of methods in our study is approximately 10 uncommented statements (in both novice and experienced). This is closer to typical figures for imperative systems. (Estimates for imperative systems vary greatly depending on experience of programmers, language used, etc. Typically, they are even larger, e.g. in a study by Basili and Perricone[7], they quote an average of approximately 100 lines of commented Fortran).

The significant differences in the other measurements seem to indicate that the novice and experienced subjects have very different ideas on what constitutes an object. The novice programmers are producing a series of relatively independent objects with functionality exactly meeting the specification. Whereas the experienced programmers are producing larger objects (with additional functionality) fully integrated into their class hierarchies. For example, the novice programmers produced objects with 6 methods on average (range 1 to 23) whereas the experienced programmers produced objects with 25 methods on average (range 1 to 131); the novice programmers produced objects with, on average, less than one instance of function overloading (range 0 to 5) whereas the experienced programmers produced objects with, on average, three instances of function overloading (range 0 to 16). See Table 2 for a full description of averages and ranges.

We could surmise that the experienced programmers are overspecifying their system in an attempt to provide reusable components (additional methods, operator and function overloading - resulting in increased class 'complexity'). This in turn allows them to easily build an extensive hierarchy (with their reusable components) and in turn accounts for their increased use of inheritance (number of children, maximum depth of inheritance).

Table 2 . Averages and ranges for each measurement

Measurement	*Novice*		*Experienced*	
	Ave.	Range	Ave.	Range
Average number of methods per class	6	23	25	131
Average number of instance variables per class	4	16	2	11
Average size of method per class	10	37	9	35
Average class 'complexity'	13	77	38	245
Average method 'complexity'	1.5	5	1.5	14
Average instances of function overloading per class	<1	5	3	16
Average instances of operator overloading per class	<1	1	4	17
Average number of 'children' per class	0.1	3	0.5	8
Maximum depth of inheritance per program	0.2	2	1	4

In conclusion, this study casts doubt that organisations using novice programmers will in the short term reap the perceived benefits of object-oriented construction and suggests that the paradigm change is not a straightforward process. It further suggests the programmers will require a period of time to adapt their style and thinking patterns to accommodate the new paradigm. We would again warn against generalising the results of this study due to its limited sample size. Currently we are investigating extending the study both in terms of sample size and measurements collected, such as connascence[8] and the Law of Demeter[9].

REFERENCES

1. CHIDAMBER, S.R. AND KEMERER, C.F. Towards a metrics suite for Object-Oriented design. In *OOPSLA*, 1991, pp 197-211.
2. COPPICK, J. AND CHEATHAM, J. *Software Metrics for Obejct-Oriented Systems.* ACM press, 1992.
3. GRAHAM, I. *Object-Oriented Methods.* Addison-Wesley, 1993.
4. LORENZ, M. *Object-Oriented software development: a practical guide,* Prentice-Hall, 1993.
5. BULMER, M.B. *Principles of statistics.* Dover, 1979.
6. WILDE, N. AND HUITT, R. Maintenance support for object-oriented programs. *IEEE Transactions on Software Engineering,* 1992, Vol.18, (12), pp 1038-1044.
7. BASILI, V.R. AND PERRICONE, B.T. Software errors and complexity. In M. Shepperd, editor, *Software Engineering Metrics Volume 1: Measures and Validations,*.1993, pp 168-183, McGraw-Hill.
8. PAGE-JONES, M. Comparing techniques by means of encapsulation and connascence. *Communications of the ACM,* 1992, vol.35, pp 147-152.
9. LIEBERHERR, K.L. AND HOLLAND, I.M. Assuring good style for object-oriented programs. *IEEE Software,* 1989, vol 6, pp 38-48.

Application-Oriented Methods for Systems Development - A Review

D. Millington and I. M. Tulloch

Department of Computer Science, University of Strathclyde, 26 Richmond Street, Glasgow G1 1XH, United Kingdom.

Abstract

The need for *application-oriented methods* has not yet been established, but a method which supports the incorporation of domain knowledge into the development life-cycle is known to be attractive. This paper discusses the development of computer applications using methods and tools which in some way reflect the nature of the underlying applications. It identifies the objectives of such an approach, and discusses work carried out in the health-care domain, including the HEAL language which is currently under study at Strathclyde University. In addition, the basis of a pre-fabrication method (PFM) is outlined.

Keyword Codes: D.2.1; D.2.2
Keywords: Software Engineering, Requirements/Specifications; Tools and Techniques

1. INTRODUCTION

An earlier paper by Millington, Gray and Tulloch [1] discussed the role of application-oriented *tools* for software development in the creation of new systems. Software engineering tools are built to support the application of particular *methods*. This paper reviews the area of application-oriented methods - a topic merely touched on in the earlier paper. The basic question to be considered is "How far may any method for systems analysis and design be application-oriented and what advantages would result ?". The answer to this question is explored by considering work in the health-care applications domain in particular.

2. OBJECTIVES OF APPLICATION-ORIENTED METHODS

The prime objective of methods and tools oriented towards a particular domain of applications is increased user participation in systems development. This is achieved through expressing application requirements and designs in terminology similar to the normal language of the application area, and by providing tools which convert such requirements and designs into operational computer systems. The consequences are:

• improved software quality, particularly in respect of 'fitness-for-use'.

• improved software productivity, through automating more of the translation and transfer processes required to move from a user-model of a required system to an implemented model.

Methods and tools should therefore recognise commonly-occurring entities, as well as commonly-occurring tasks and their sequencing. For example, in the health-care domain, they should 'know' what a patient record is (at least in a default version) and what "make an appointment" means.

3. APPLICATION-ORIENTED METHODS FOR HEALTH-CARE SYSTEMS

3.1 Background

The contents of this section reflect the authors' involvement with the development of health-care (particularly hospital) applications over many years. Three distinct areas of activity relating to this domain are now discussed :-

(i) **HEAL** (HEalth Applications Language), which is currently under study at Strathclyde University in Glasgow.

(ii) The **CBS** (Common Basic Specification), which was developed centrally for the National Health Service within England and Wales.

(iii) Projects under the European Community's AIM (Advanced Informatics in Medicine) Research and Technology Development Programme.

The first two relate to specific work which sought to provide an applications-oriented context for *methods* used in systems analysis and design. On the other hand, the AIM projects had a stronger emphasis towards the provision of *tools and environments* for developing health-care applications.

3.2 HEAL (HEalth Applications Language)

Work on HEAL developed from a past hospital systems analysis study [2], which originally set out to express the data processing functionality occurring in each of a hospital's departments or areas of activity (over 70 in all). That it was necessary to record similar requirements in different areas prompted the analysts involved to formulate a formal syntax for specifying the processing procedures required.

Each procedure commenced with a verb (from a set of 21) and had its own defined specification structure. One example was SCHEDULE, defined as

> "arrange a timetable of activities or an activity within a timetable, STORE the details in the appropriate file(s), and initiate any consequent actions necessary". **(1)**

where STORE was another procedure pitched at a more basic level. The formal syntax of SCHEDULE was defined as

> Schedule event for individual / location (into file). **(2)**

where (i) the parentheses indicates an optional clause within the procedure, (ii) the stroke ('/') indicates permissible alternative nouns which may be used and (iii) the underlined words are replaced by specific examples in practice. For example, an actual invocation of SCHEDULE recorded in the original study was

> Schedule outpatient clinic for patient. **(3)**

The "consequent actions necessary" in definition (1) above were expected to be different for different actual events. In the case of the event represented by (3), these might include initiating a booking for patient transport and the scheduling of pre-clinic X-ray and ECG examinations for some categories of patient.

This specification language was developed primarily as a *method of systems analysis*. It was also envisaged to be used in both design and implementation; however, for several reasons, this did not occur. Tulloch [3] used this work as a basis for considering the design of **HEAL**, an implementation language for health-care applications.

Current studies are concerned with how HEAL could be implemented. Possible delivery systems include fourth-generation languages and object-oriented systems; indeed the latter appear, at least initially, to offer an attractive implementation route.

3.3 Common Basic Specification

Within the National Health Service for England and Wales, the extent to which hospitals and health authorities worked with similar *data* was recognised early in the development of computer use. Its recognition was formalised first in the reports of the Steering Group on Health Services Information (the Korner Committee) and in the consequent "Korner Data Model" [4]. From these was developed a wider "NHS Data Model" [5], which sought to support data modelling work involved in developing health-care applications.

The NHS Information Management Centre later supplemented this model by incorporating *processing* information. This led to the formulation of the Common Basic Specification (CBS), a model which claims to provide precise definitions of all NHS activities and the data they require, making "available in one source all the basic material required by anyone specifying information requirements in the NHS" [6].

The nature and use of the CBS are outlined by Dallimore [7]. It sets out to provide a generic model of health-care systems requirements, which can be tailored to the needs of a specific hospital (or hospital department). The CBS itself does not include implemented components for specific software/hardware environments, but it clearly offers the prospect of modular construction of applications through reuse of components.

The initial version of the CBS model was developed using SSADM (Structured Systems Analysis and Design Method) - the established mandatory method for developing software applications for the UK government.

In practice the CBS appears to have received a mixed reception from its intended users i.e. health authorities and external systems suppliers. This may be due to

- a perceived inherent complexity of the model, and/or
- a reluctance to apply the necessary effort and resources (e.g. training) to use the model

Nonetheless, the CBS appears to be the most extensive (and the most promising) attempt so far to incorporate domain knowledge and the principle of reusability into both the analysis and design phases of health-care application development.

3.4 European Initiatives

Hospitals and other health-care facilities throughout Europe share similar functions and organisational structures. Consequently, the need for and the perceived benefits of domain-oriented methods and their supporting tools are of interest within this wider context. The Committee of the European Communities (CEC), through its Research and Technological Development programme entitled "Advanced Informatics in Medicine" (AIM), recognised and supported this area of research.

In the preliminary phase of AIM (1989 - 1990), two projects - HEALTHBENCH and HELIOS - concentrated on methods and tools for health-care application development *in general*, rather than on the development of specific applications.

HEALTHBENCH set out to identify an appropriate architecture for an integrated software engineering environment to support the development of health-care applications. It surveyed the use of general-purpose software tools in the development of such applications [8], to gauge *inter alia* their perceived limitations. The project subsequently determined a general architecture for a health-care software engineering environment [9]. This perspective was developed further by Millington, Gray and Tulloch [1].

HELIOS set out to specify a "Software Engineering Environment" and a "Ward Information System" which would include an "Image Management Subsystem". It appeared to employ elements of an application-oriented method in its work [10]. Its successor in the current phase of AIM (1992 - 1994) is HELIOS II, whose quoted objectives are "to develop a fully integrated medical software engineering environment supporting analysis, design and implementation of medical applications and to use this platform for building significant parts of a multimedia medical workstation" [11]. One component of the environment being developed is an object-oriented database management system, which will "provide the developers with a core set of medical classes needed to construct basic medical applications" (ibid). In this case, a *general* method is employed (i.e. the object-oriented method), and the application-orientated perspective is achieved by providing a pre-defined set of reusable classes.

4. APPLICATION-ORIENTED METHODS AND TOOLS IN OTHER DOMAINS

Millington, Gray and Tulloch [1] reviewed the use of application-oriented tools in general, noting in particular the work of the ATMOSPHERE project [12] under the CEC's ESPRIT programme of research and development. The ATMOSPHERE project has designed system engineering environments for five different application domains (i.e. embedded aerospace systems, distributed information processing, digital computer networks, communications, and process control). Each environment is intended to support the methods appropriate for its application domain - but this does not necessarily imply methods which are used only for that application domain and not for other domains.

A particular advantage of *object-oriented* methods is seen to be their potential to create reusable components of applications systems. Such components inevitably relate to a particular application domain, and the topic of *domain analysis* is identified as a major theme in the context of reusability. Arango [13] provides a valuable comparison of published domain analysis methods, and maps these onto a "Common Process". He also identifies *evaluation* (or alternatively *validation*) of domain analysis as a topic barely touched on so far. That requires consideration of the subsequent use of the results of domain analysis. In respect of this paper's theme, even if it may be argued logically that domain analysis as a method should not itself be domain dependent, the use of its results may be - but this aspect has still to be explored.

5. THE FUTURE OF APPLICATION-ORIENTED METHODS AND TOOLS

Earlier sections have shown that domain-orientation has influenced the work of systems development at several points in the system life-cycle. However, a fundamental question remains - "Is there a need for application-oriented methods for analysis and design, or is the need solely for software engineering tools which incorporate domain knowledge within general methods?".

If the need is for application-oriented methods, it is necessary to identify the particular capabilities required of the method beyond those of general methods. Indeed structured methods of analysis and design have for real-time and control applications different expressive capabilities from those required for the bulk of business and administrative applications. However, it may be argued that "real-time" and "control" do not identify *application domains*; rather they are *types of processing* which may occur across a range of application domains.

Irrespective of the answer to the first part of the above question, the answer to the second part appears to be a definite "Yes" - there *is* a need for tools enabling domain knowledge to be used within general methods. The present popularity of object-oriented methods is largely built upon their promise of enhanced "re-usability" of system components within a range of applications. Such components may very definitely include application domain knowledge. However although re-usability has been exploited in the implementation phase in object oriented programming, its use in other phases of the life-cycle appears to have received only limited attention so far.

If re-usability of system components is to be taken seriously there is a need to develop a "pre-fabrication method" (PFM) which supports the use and management of system components within and across the analysis, design, implementation and maintenance phases of systems development. Such a method requires not only that a development life-cycle should be meaningful for an individual component, but also that there should be well-established techniques for the integration of components into the overall system. Such integration techniques need to be available at each phase of the development cycle, and might be expected to entail more than just the provision of a library or catalogue facility. They also need to cover the documentation for the final system (e.g. user documentation), as well as that which is part of the development process. Figure 1 gives a simple diagrammatic representation of the basic requirements for integration.

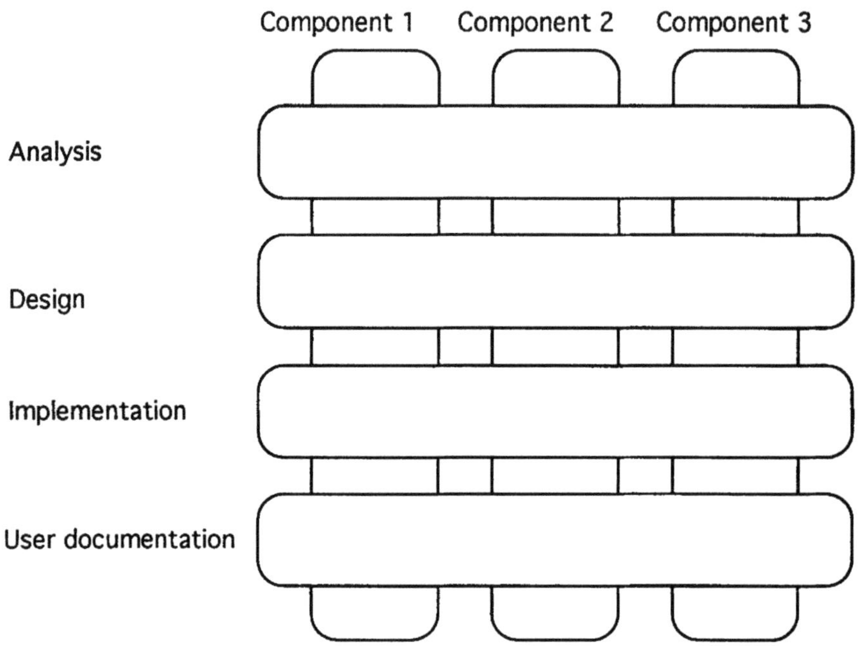

Figure 1 Integration needs

The set of techniques comprising PFM should additionally cover the requirements for ensuring quality through appropriate verification and validation checks in each phase. Again techniques have to be concerned not only with individual components, but also with their integration mechanisms.

This provides an agenda for further defining a PFM and appropriate tools for its operation. Significant inputs for this task will be experience to date with

- applications software libraries
- generic analysis and design specifications such as the CBS previously discussed.

The PFM is likely to be used by the end-user application developer; therefore it, rather than methods of domain analysis, is the prime contender to be application-oriented.

6. CONCLUSIONS

It is established that the incorporation of generic application domain knowledge into software development can improve quality and productivity, through its support of re-usability. How this knowledge is made available for incorporation into a specific application needs further study. The approaches of HEAL and the CBS are two distinctive attempts to achieve this within the health-care domain, but a more extensive pre-fabrication method (PFM) is required - one which is applicable to *all* phases of application development.

Since application development will be undertaken increasingly by end-users, it is likely that a PFM will itself be application-oriented, reflecting particular characteristics of the user community as well as the underlying application domain.

REFERENCES

1. Millington, D., Gray, E. and Tulloch, I.M.: 'Application-oriented tools for software development' in: Stowell, F., West, D. and Howell, J. (eds), System Science: 'Addressing Global Issues', (Plenum Press, 1993), pp. 361-366.
2. Nuffield Medical Data Processing Unit, Notes to accompany a session entitled 'Methods of Systems Analysis in the Liverpool Project', given to the National Health Computer Services Group, April 7th, 1970.
3. Tulloch, I.M., 'Application Specific Languages (Including Introduction to HEAL)', M. Phil. dissertation, University of Strathclyde, Glasgow, 1992.
4. Steering Group on Health Services Information: Reports on the collection and use of information about activity in hospitals and the community in the National Health Service, H.M.S.O., London, 1984.
5. 'The National Health Service Data Model', Vol.1. Management Summary, NHS Corporate Data Administration, Birmingham, United Kingdom, 1986.
6. 'Introduction to the Common Basic Specification', NHS Information Management Centre, Birmingham, United Kingdom, 1990.
7. Dallimore, T.: 'Common Future', *British Journal of Healthcare Computing*, 1991, Vol.8, (3), pp. 26-28.
8. Millington, D., Tulloch, I.M. and Gray, E.M., 'Current Use of Software Tools in the Development of Medical and Health Services Computer Applications - a Survey', *Journal of Information Technology*, 1991, Vol.6, pp. 86 - 93.
9. Hooymans, M., 'HEALTHBENCH - Health Information Decision Support Workbench -General Architecture of Healthbench', in: Timmers, T. & Blum, B.I. (eds), *Proc. IMIA Working Conference on Software Engineering in Medical Informatics*, Elsevier, Amsterdam, The Netherlands, 8 - 10th October 1990.
10. C.E.C., Exploitation of results from the AIM exploratory action, C.E.C., DGX111/F/A11516, Brussels, 1990.
11. AIM 1993 - Annual Technical Report on RTD: Health Care, CEC, DGX111, Brussels, 1993.
12. Obbink, H., 'Systems Engineering Environments of Atomsphere', *Proc. European Symposium on Software Development Environments and CASE Technology*, Springer-Verlag, Berlin, 1991, pp. 1 - 17.
13. Arango, G., 'Domain Analysis Methods' in: Schafer, W., Prieto-Diaz, R., & Matsumoto, M.(eds), Software Reusability, Ellis Horwood, London, 1994.

10

A Proposal for Composing Software Design Process

Sumio Mochizuki[a] and Takuya Katayama[b]

[a]Shukutoku Junior College, 1150-1, Fujikubo, Miyoshi-cho, Iruma-gun, Saitama-ken, 354, Japan (Previous affiliation: Mitsubishi Space Software Co.)

[b]Department of Computer Science, Faculty of Engineering, Tokyo Institute of Technology 2-12-1, Ookayama, Meguro-ku, Tokyo, 152, Japan

Abstract

We described a real industrial process in terms of HFSP(Hierarchical and Functional Software Process).[1] After analyzing design process of our experienced engineers, we discovered two describing methods, that is, object-centered process and phase-centered process which can respectively show the design process from their different points of view. It can be considered that they extracted generic object-centered process from their rich design experiences, and applied it to real design works, converting it into the phase-centered process suitable to design the objective system. In this paper we described the two process description methods and the way how to convert object-centered process into phase-centered process on the basis of object transition. We clarified the method how to compose the phases for a concrete system design and how to execute object-centered process in a phase.

Keyword Codes : D.2.10 ; K.3.2 ; H.0
Keywords : Software Engineering, Design ; Computer and Information Science Education ; Information Systems, General

1. INTRODUCTION

We wanted to describe formally our real design process. In the research, after analyzing design process of our experienced engineers, we discovered two describing methods: Object-centered process and phase-centered process. [2] [3] Comparing them, we discovered that transition of objects is the important key. We clarified the method how an experienced engineer design a concrete system, applying these models.

2. PRODUCTION AND TRANSITION OF OBJECTS

Various objects are produced in the middle of the design works. Some objects produced are modified by the next process. These are the temporary products, which we call intermediate objects. The final results, which we call final objects, are retained until the design works are finished, and they are included as the parts of the fundamental design document. After observing real design processes, we discovered there are the following two types of transition.

a. Type Ⅰ transition · · Input objects are converted to the output objects of different kind.
b. Type Ⅱ transition · · An input object and its output object are of the same kind.

In designing a large-scaled system, some of the objects are produced repeatedly. Converting their rough contents into detailed contents, the designer can get consistent final objects. Fig.1 shows the transition of object groups in accordance with execution of the first level process for designing the Data Acquisition System for checkout of artificial spacecraft (DAS shortly), as a real example of Type Ⅱ transition. In this figure the process is executed from left side to right side, and the transition of the object group is shown by three rough state. Arrow shows Type Ⅱ transition of each object between the processes.

3. TWO MODELS FOR DESCRIBING DESIGN PROCESS

In the past research, we analyzed, described and evaluated a real fundamental design process for a practical system (DAS), using HFSP. [2] [3] We discovered the following two models.

Phase-Centered Process (○ ; Intermediate object ● ;Final object ◒ ; Intermediate object between ○ and ●)

Note : Req. =Requirements

Object Group	Object \ First level process	1 Analysis of User's Req.	2 Design of System Specification	3 Software Design	4 Check and Review
——	a Requirements Specification b Hardware Specification c Computer Specification d OS Specification				
A Investigation of User's Req.	1.a System Operation Req.	●	●	●	●
	1.b System Function Req.	●	●	●	●
	e Performance Req.	●	●	●	●
B Investigation of System Operation	f System Operation Sequence	○	●	●	●
	g Mode Transition Diagram	○	●	●	●
	h Output on CRT		●	●	●
	i Man-Machine Interface Specifications	○	●	●	●
C Investigation of System Function	j Function Block Diagram		●	●	●
	k Interface Specifications between Functions	○	●	●	●
	l Function Tables	○	●	●	●
	m Data Processing Method	○	●	●	●
D Feasibility Study of System Specification	n Results of Feasibility Study of System Specification		●	●	●
E Investigation of Data and Processing	o External Interface Specifications	○	◒	●	●
	p Task Structure		○	●	●
	q Data Flow Diagram		○	●	●
	r Interface between Tasks			●	●
	s Task Specifications			●	●
F Decision of Control and Timing	t Control Flow Diagram			●	●
	u Control Specifications			●	●
	v Timing Chart	○	◒	●	●
	w Task Priority			●	●
G Feasibility Study of Software Design	x Results of Feasibility Study of Software Design	○	○	●	●
H Total Check	y Fundamental Design Documents		○	◒	●

Figure 1 Transition diagram of the objects by executing first level phase-centered process for designing the practical system DAS.

3.1 Object-centered process

In the fundamental design of a practical system, many objects of the same kind which are produced through type II transition. Object-centered process renames and treats objects of the same kind as a single object. After this renaming, the remaining objects are of the different kind, and these objects could be processed through type I transition. For the DAS process, collecting and classifying these objects into the groups in accordance with their contents, we get the eight object groups in Fig.1. The first level object-centered process, which produces these object groups, are shown in Fig.2. These object-centered processes are executed from upper to lower in accordance to the relations between objects. There are only type I transitions in this object-centered process. This object-centered process can express concisely and comprehensibly static relations between the objects and can describe various design procedures of the similar systems in an application area as a common process, therefore this might be called a generic model.

3.2 Phase-centered process

The object-centered process places importance on generality and static relations between objects. On the other hand the phase-centered process intends to describe the real design processes which could be enacted. In designing a very simple system, the contents of the objects are also simple, and we can enact its object-centered process as it is. However, in the case of designing a large-scaled system, we have to produce many objects having deep and complicated logical structure. As the objects in object-centered process are generated through object refinement repeating process, the object-centered process cannot be enacted directly unless it is unfolded into an executable process as shown in Fig.2, where such refinement is explicitly described. From the standpoint of project management, design works should necessarily be divided into phases which are the first level phase-centered processes. Here we assume the following characteristics for the phases. (1) Objects which have close relation with each other are defined in one phase. (2) The purpose of design works in each phase is to define the final objects which are allotted to the phase in the project plan. (3) Repeating and preliminary execution of processes are necessary in a phase for designing a large-scaled system. (4) Final objects are defined sequentially in accordance with the execution of phases. There is no redoing of phases in principle. (5) Phase has an interface with project management, including review of schedule, cost, and quality.

4. DETERMINING PHASES

In this and next sections we propose a method of composing enactable phase-centered process from an object-centered process.

4.1 Determining fundamental phases

Observing the object groups, we can find that there are two types of object groups. One consists of the object groups which have close relations between them and should be defined in one phase to avoid redoing in design works. The other consists of the object groups which can be defined in each different phase. As the results, we get the phases which define object gorups mentioned before. We call them fundamental phases. Fig.1 shows an example in which some object groups are defined in one phase. In the figure the final objects that are included in *Investigation of System Operation* group, *Investigation of System Function* group and *Feasibility Study of System Specification* group are defined in *Design of System Specification* process. These objects in *Investigation of System Operation* group and *Investigation of System Function* group have close relations each other, as parts of the system specifications. Changes of objects in one object group may affect the objects in the other object group, and large redoing may be needed. Therefore the final objects in those two object groups are needed to be defined in one phase. Similarly the objects in *Investigation of Data and Processing* group and *Decision of Control and Timing* group define software design totally, and have close relations each other. Therefore their final objects are to be defined in one phase. On the other hand the other object groups such as *Investigation of User's Requirements* and *Total Check* are defined in each different phase. After the investigation we get phases and call those phases fundamental phases, which are shown in Table 1.

4.2 Defining phases

When a designer designs a concrete system, he composes appropriate phases on the basis of fundamental phases. At first he describes object-centered process correspondent to each funda-

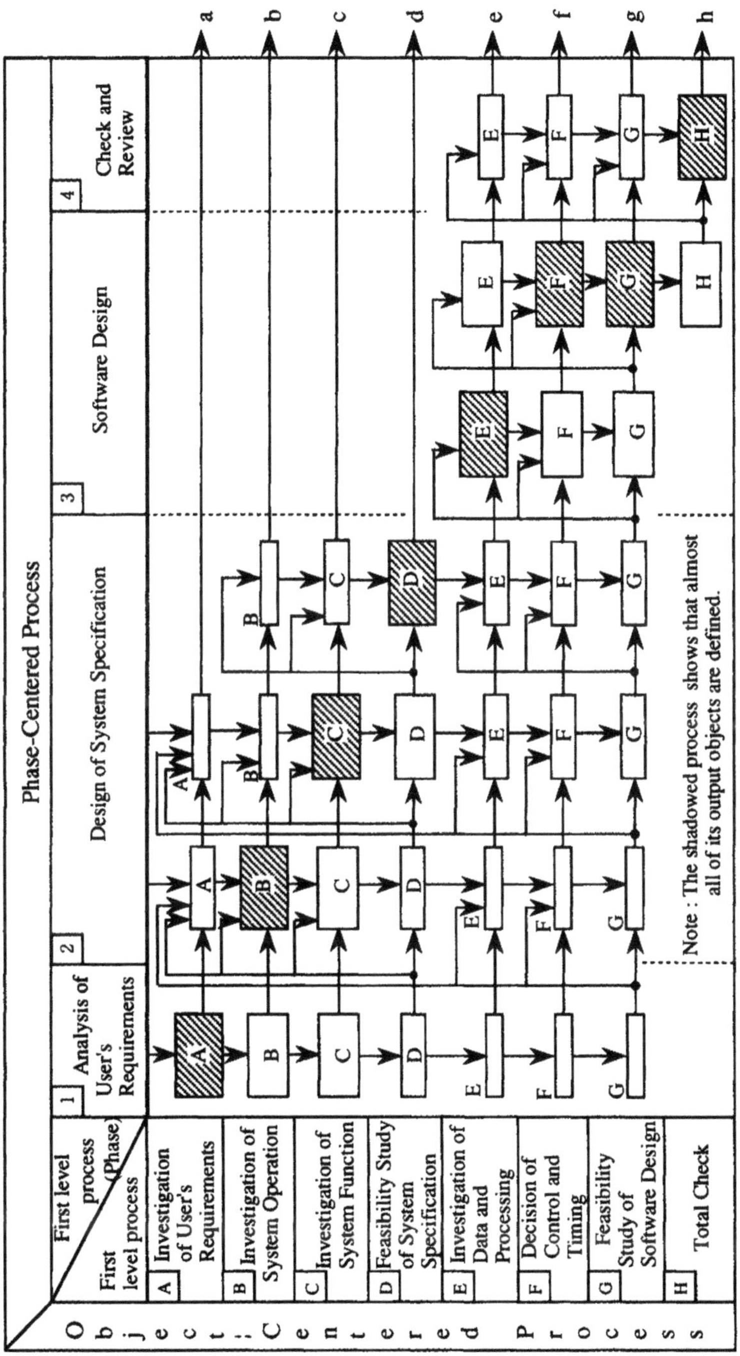

Figure 2 Phase-centered process for designing the practical system DAS.

mental phase as shown in Fig.3. That is, each fundamental phase is given object-centered process which produces the object groups allotted to the fundamental phase in Table 1. Furthermore, the fundamental phases are evaluated by their degree of difficulty in applying them to the objective system. Though it might be hard to measure quantitatively the degree of difficulty, their appropriateness could be evaluated, as follows.

(1) Weight of fundamental phases

We denote the weight w(a) which expresses degree of difficulty of process "a" in object-centered process. This w(a) cannot be defined precisely, but the experienced designer can define it experientially from scale and complexity of the system. A fundamental phase includes processes, and its weight is given by summing up the weights of the included processes.

Table 1 Fundamental phases and phases for different-scaled systems.

Object group	Fundamental Phase	Phase for designing a system: Large-scaled system.	DAS.	Small-scaled system.
Investigation of User's Requirements	Analysis of User's Requirements	Analysis of User's Requirements (1)(2) · · ·	Analysis of User's Requirement	Analysis of Requirements
Investigation of System Operation	Design of System Specification	Design of System Specification (1)(2) · · ·	Design of System Specification	
Investigation of System Function				
Feasibility Study of System Specification				
Investigation of Data and Processing	Software Design	Software Design(1) (2) · · ·	Software Design	Software Design
Decision of Control and Timing				
Feasibility Study of Software Design				
Total Check	Check and Review	Check and Review	Check and Review	———

(2) Composition of phases

There are upper limit value Wmax and lower limit value Wmin for the weight of an executable phase. When the weight of the fundamental phase W(q) exceeds those values, the fundamental phase is regarded to be inappropriate for real design works. The appropriate phase for real design works are composed on the basis of fundamental phase as follows;

a. $Wmin < W(q) < Wmax$ · · The design works included in the fundamental phase q are appropriate, and it can be used as the phase for real design.

b. $Wmax < W(q)$ · · Weight of the fundamental phase q is too difficult. However, as fundamental phases cannot be divided to smaller ones, the fundamental phase q is repeated, that is, phase q(1), phase q(2), etc. and intermediate objects are obtained gradually.

c. $W(q) < Wmin$ · · Phase is the objective of project management. The design works included in the fundamental phase q are so small that project management for it is redundant. Therefore some neighboring phases should be combined into one phase which is shown in Table 1 so that its size is appropriate to management works.

5. COMPOSING PHASE-CENTERED PROCESS

In the previous sections, we could decide the phases, the objects defined in each phase, and the processes which define the final objects in the phases. The processes were executed repeatedly, and executed preliminarily in a phase as follows.

5.1 Repetition of processes in the phase

In case of designing a simple system, the objects allotted to each phase can be defined only by executing the processes included in each phase without repetition. In case of designing a practical system, the objects, which are to be defined in a phase, cannot be defined completely by executing only once the processes in the phase. In this case the processes are repeated and executed successively in the phase, until output objects of the phase are defined finally.

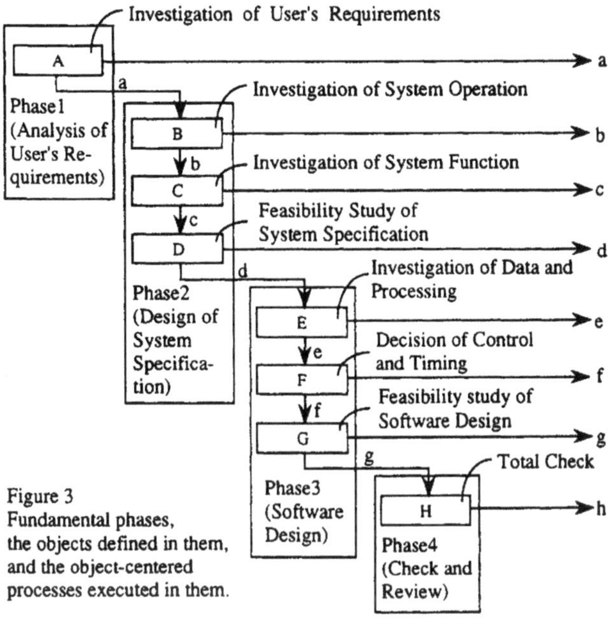

Figure 3
Fundamental phases, the objects defined in them, and the object-centered processes executed in them.

5.2 Preliminary execution of the processes in a phase

In order to define the final objects in a phase, some processes in the later phase are preliminarily executed for checking and reviewing if the obtained objects are reasonable. We call this checking processes "Preliminary execution of the processes".

Fig.2 shows the real design process of practical system DAS as an example of the phase-centered process. The phases are shown in the upper column, which are executed from left to right. The processes in a phase are executed from top to bottom in a column, and the next right column are executed. In this phase-centered process, there are repeats of three times in *Design of System Specification* phase, and repeats of two times in *Software Design*.

6. CONCLUSION

In this paper we described two process description methods: object-centered process and phase-centered process. Furthermore, we described the method how to convert object-centered process into phase-centered process on the basis of object transition. After analyzing the objects produced in the DAS design, we clarified the method how to compose the phases for a concrete system design and how to execute object-centered process in the phases.

REFERENCES

1. Katayama T., "A Hierarchical and Functional Software Process Description and its Enaction", Proceeding of the 11th International Conference on SoftwareEngineering, 1989, pp.343-352.
2. Mochizuki S., Yamauchi A., Katayama T., "Describing and Evaluating Fundamental Design Process of Checkout System for Artificial Spacecraft by Process Model HFSP", Transactions of Information Processing Society of Japan, Vol. 33, No. 5, May, 1992, pp. 691-706.
3. Mochizuki S., Yamauchi A., Katayama T., "Two Models for Describing Software Design Process: Object-Centered Model and Phase-Centered Model", Proceedings, the 5th International Conference on software Engineering and Knowledge Engineering, June, 1993, pp. 291-295.

11

Team-Based Software Development Using an Electronic Meeting System: The Quality Pay-Off

S. Sawyer[a] and P.J. Guinan[b]

[a] School Of Information Studies, 4-206 CST, Syracuse University, Syracuse NY 13244 USA
[b] School of Management, Boston University 704 Commonwealth Ave., Boston MA 02215 USA

Abstract

To determine the effects of a home grown Electronic Meeting System (EMS) on product quality. We surveyed 40 software development teams and their project sponsors. Teams were part of a single software development laboratory which itself is part of a large international organization. A model of intra-group conflict management which incorporates using an EMS to reduce work uncertainty is a significant predictor of product quality. Further, teams with higher levels of experience relied less on the EMS. This leads us to believe that using the EMS acts as a conflict management surrogate for less experienced teams.

Keyword codes: D.2.2, H.5.3, K.6.3
Keywords: tools and techniques, group and organization interfaces, software management.

1. INTRODUCTION

This paper reports on product quality improvements realized by software development teams at a large software development laboratory. The changes in quality are one by-product of team-based software development using an electronic meeting support (EMS) system. This EMS was developed in-house, specifically to support software development. These EMS are suites of software tools available in specially designed meeting rooms, often with facilitation [1,2,3]. Research reported on here focuses on two questions:

(1) What characteristics of software development teams affect product quality?
(2) How does using an electronic meeting system affect product quality?

The EMS represents one intersection of two major developments in the organization of technologically sophisticated work [4]. First, organizations increasingly rely on groups, or teams, as the locus of work [5,6]. Second, organizations increasingly rely on technology to support work [7,8,9].

The research site is a software development laboratory: one site of a large international company. This site develops complex sub-system software. Both the scale and complexity of the development effort required to produce this type of software dictate using software development teams. Software developers at the site are accustomed to working in teams; and, they expect that appropriate software will be available to support their efforts.

In recent years developing software at this site has been rapidly growing more difficult. The size and complexity of the software products are expanding. Products are being ported to multiple platforms and core modules of the older products are being refined and re-written to improve system performance. These challenges are magnified by the organization's turbulence. The lab has had three site managers and two division managers in three years, and experienced difficulty in competing for new product areas.

2. THE ELECTRONIC MEETING SYSTEM

The EMS used at this site grew from the work experiences of the teams themselves. It began with a laptop computer, LCD projector, and a projector screen in a conference room. The concept has matured to where more than 20 meeting rooms at the site, representing 60% of available meeting space, have been configured as EMS. These EMS have a dedicated work station projecting onto a large screen. The screen is normally located at one end of the room and is the dominant feature. Rooms also have electronic whiteboards, facsimile machines, telephone lines, video equipment, and ergonomic layouts.

The EMS's computer is tied into the organization's local and wide area networks. These networks provide access to all software and work products accessible at any developers individual station. The workstation is identical to developer's systems. The facsimile, telephone, and whiteboards allow for additional communication and idea capture -- both in the room and to other sites and other EMS. Video allows for meetings to be taped and reviewed. This preserves the history behind decisions, provides training tapes, and helps to document projects.

3. THEORETICAL BASIS

The research stems from two existing lines of research. Research on group process suggests a causal relationship where group and individual characteristics affect the processes of working together, which in turn affects team performance [10,11]. The EMS-use research focuses on how EMS use affects both the process and the outcomes of team-based work [12,13,3]. Major components of the model are:

Team-Member Experience: From the observations and exploratory interview it was clear the developers and managers felt team member experience was a critical input. Previous group process research also posits the importance of team-member experience as a determinant of performance [14,15,16,10].

Group History: Exploratory interviews also indicated that teams had extensive group history. In addition, literature on ISD discusses group history as an importance predictor of performance [17,18,19].

Group Focus and Infrastructure: Hackman [14,15,16] defined a set of elements to characterize group processes. These can be described as elements of group focus or group infrastructure. Group focus encompasses team member's commitment to working together, the degree to which the work is an exciting challenge, the clarity of the group's goals, and the strength of the group's norms. Group infrastructure includes the material and technical resources available to the group and the team leaders managerial style.

Group Process: Process-oriented studies of software development have focused on relating the process of reducing intra-group conflict to improving performance [20,21,22,19]. Since groups of people bring differing levels of experience to a problem, as well as a broad range of views, conflicts between team members is endemic to tasks such as design [23,24,25,26]. In addition, EMS-use research often employs intra-group conflict management as the theoretical basis for their work [27,28].

Technology: Our view of technology builds on previous work by Fry and Slocum [29,30,31]. Technology is seen as a way to either reduce the uncertainty of the worki facing the group or to support the interdependence between team members.

Figure 1: Research Model

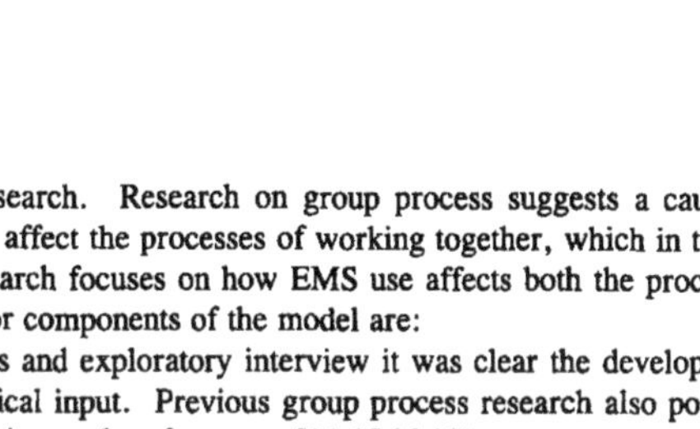

Product Quality: The performance variable is an aggregate measure of the quality of the final product [33]. We used stakeholder assessments of performance. Stakeholders are individuals who are not on the team but are directly affected by the product. Thus, their view of quality may be the most crucial evaluation of performance [33] when product quality is a critical performance measure [34].

Figure 1 presents the research model. The model posits that the group's conflict management process is affected by the experience of the individual team member, the length of time the group has been together, the degree to which the group is focused on their work, and the amount of project infrastructure provided to the team. The process is also affected by the use of the EMS as functionally characterized by its' ability to reduce work uncertainly (making tasks easier to perform) and its' ability to support team interdependence.

These are seen as a set of moderators and mediators to the software product's quality as measured by stakeholders.

Two hypotheses are developed from the model presented in Figure 2. The first hypothesis posits that the intra-group conflict management process of team-based software development is a moderation model, accounting for differences in software product quality [35]. Moderation means that the relationship between two variables is dependent on the level of a third variable. In this model, the group input elements' effect on product quality, are moderated by the conflict management process.

H1: The intra-group conflict management moderates the group and team-member inputs. This accounts for differences in software product quality.

The second hypothesis posits that using the EMS mediates the process of developing software. The interaction of intra-group conflict management and EMS using is a more powerful predictor of the process effects on software product quality. This is a mediation model [35] as the interaction between process and technology use becomes a significant predictor of product quality.

H2: EMS use mediates the intra-group conflict management. This accounts for additional differences in software product quality.

4. RESEARCH METHOD

This is a field-based study employing, cross-sectional surveys of development teams coupled with longitudinal data collection involving interviews with team members and observation of team meetings [36,37,38]. Over 16 months, 60 interviews and surveys of 40 teams were collected. During this time, more than 30 work days have been spent al the site observing meetings and collecting the data. A key-informants method was used to gather survey data [39,40,33]. Key informants are members of the team who provide a broad sample of the entire team. Researchers contacted each team directly about participating, describing the feedback they would receive if they participated.

4.1 Sample

Forty teams participated. The sample represents approximately 50% of the project teams at this site, and includes teams from all departments. At the individual level, 128 respondents from the 40 teams represent about 20% of all developers. For each team surveyed, key stakeholders were contacted to provide an external evaluation of software product quality. All respondents were assured of their anonymity: results are aggregated to team levels. Teams average 2 years as a unit. Team members average 9.8 years of professional experience and 7.9 years with this company.

Stakeholders were identified by the teams and these stakeholders were approached independent of the teams. Stakeholders were drawn from both customer and managerial positions to reduce organizational bias. For each team, from one to three stakeholders completed a survey. These stakeholders had an average of 13.7 years of professional software development, had managed software development for 8.3 years, and had been with this company an average of 10.2 years.

4.2 Instrumentation

To conduct the research two survey instruments ware employed: one for team members and one for stakeholders. This reduces method bias by separating independent and dependent variables [36,41]. Indicators for group history and team-member experience were developed from the exploratory interviews and observation. All other variables were measured using previously developed scales [16,6,26,27,42]. The dependent measure is a scale of quality in terms of the product's flexibility and maintainability [33].

5. ANALYSIS

This research focuses on two questions. First which characteristics of team-based software development best predict software product quality? Second, how does using an EMS affect software product quality? Since a mediation model is posited, path-analytic methods of analysis are used [35,43,44,46]. Further, EMS use is seen as an interaction effect [47,35].

Path models decompose the total effect of one variable on another into direct, indirect, and spurious elements. They imply a causal ordering, and all paths must be calculated. Total effects are the zero-order correlations. Direct and indirect effects are calculated using the standardized coefficients of multiple regression and the linear path relationships between the model variables [44,45].

To test H1, a path model of the team-member and group inputs, group process, and outcome variables was estimated. The model is not significant ($F=2.05$, $p=.097$, adjusted $R^2=.121$). Thus, Hl is rejected. The moderated conflict management model of software development team process provides no significant predictors of software product quality.

To test H2, a path model of the team-member and group inputs, the interaction of the group process and EMS, and outcome variable was estimated. Testing for the interaction effects of the conflict management process and both technology variables indicated that only one interaction team was significant. Further, since the significance of the coefficient of the interaction team cannot be evaluated when first-order teams are included, the path model for H2 differs from H1's path model in that the process team reflects the interaction of EMS use to reduce work uncertainty and intra-group conflict management [47,35].

Table 1: Path Calculations of Interaction Model

Path Effects:	Total	Direct	Indirect	Spurious
TME-CM/EM	-.1794	-.5735	-.0235	-.4176
GH-CM/EM	.2516	.3889	-.1373	.0000
GF-CM/EM	.5068	.5985	.3212	-.4129
GI-CM/EM	.4793	.0692	.4087	-.0014
TME-QUAL	.1899	.2832	.1638	-.2571
GH-QUAL	.0989	-.1125	.0334	.1780
GF-QUAL	.4493	.2830	-.1061	.2724
GI-QUAL	.2910	-.1915	.4549	.0276
CM/EM-QUAL	.4194	.4579	.0000	-.0083

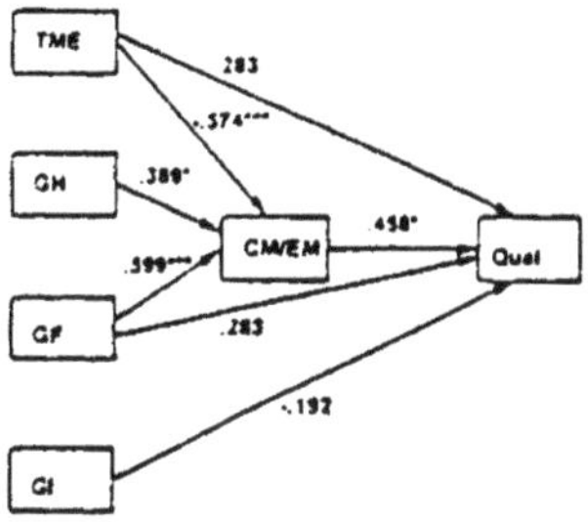

*p : .05 = *.p : .01 = **.p : .001 = ***. paths less than .011 not shown*

Figure 2: Final Path Model

Table 1 presents the path calculations and Figure 2 summarizes the most important paths. The model is significant ($F=2.98$, $p=.025$, adjusted $R^2=.207$). H2 is accepted: using an EMS moderates software development team intra-group conflict management and affects stakeholder views of software product quality. That is, there is a synergy between using the EMS to reduce work uncertainty and the management of intra-group conflict. The interaction team is a significant predictor of the variance in software product quality. Further, team-member experience, group history, and group focus are significant contributors to both software product quality and the interaction of EMS use to reduce work uncertainty and manage intra-group conflict.

6. DISCUSSION

This research has been motivated by two issues. First, the need to better understand the effects of intra-group conflict management has on software product quality. Second, to better understand the effect using an EMS has on software product quality. The data show that as team-member experience increases, the synergistic effect of EMS use to assist in intra-group conflict management decreases. This may mean that more experienced teams have developed successful conflict management processes. Thus, for these teams, using the EMS may not be as valuable for assisting in managing conflict or reducing work uncertainty. Interviews with developers and managers indicate that the way the EMS is used varies by the team's aggregate experience. Less experienced teams used the EMS to help them explore and define issues and to establish work processes. More highly experienced teams used the EMS to report on project status and deliverables.

The data further show that group history and focus are significant predictors of the EMS/conflict interaction. The model in Figure 2 also indicates there is a significant affect to produce quality through managing intra-group conflict and using an EMS to assist in this process. This supports the contention that process-focused models of software development provide both insight into how teams go about software development and what affect these processes have on outcomes.

This result is particularly interesting in that the EMS providesa vehicle for team members to more easily manage conflict. The large screen and ergonomic design make it easy to work in the room so that everyone can focus on the same work product [48]. More importantly, by facing the work product, and not each other, the product becomes less attached to any one person: it is shared by the team. Thus, it may be easier to criticize a dis-embodied product on the common screen than to face a colleague and disagree. It is also easier to accept criticisms since it is directed toward the work and not toward the developer. While managing conflict often means confronting criticism and trying to synthesize disparate views, using this EMS eases the difficulties in face-to-face confrontations by focusing attention on the common work-product, and not on the individual team members.

7. IMPLICATIONS

The opportunity to study actual software development teams, using EMS to perform their work, in their natural setting, makes this work valuable for both researchers and practitioners. For both parties, the EMS studied is interesting in that it grew from the experiences and needs of the teams. Its' simplicity is a key issue for continued study.

The site's software developers believe that quality has improved. While a causal relationship can not be made, data provided by the site indicates that, since teams began using the EMS, there has been a 50% reduction in defect rates of shipped products. Furthermore, these EMS are in high demand, with the 21 rooms booked 89% of the year, and often booked to 120% of capacity during peak periods. The EMS are part of these ISD team's normal work.

The results should be interpreted with the following limitations in mind. This is a single site, these developers are very experienced, well educated (89% have a college degree and 33% have an advanced degree), and familiar with team-based work (on average team members have worked on 10 ISD projects). Further, the EMS is atypical to what is reported in the literature (See McLeod, 1992) in terms of structure and functions. This site's use of their EMS reflect both the experience of the teams and the unique development of this system to meet their needs.

References

1. DeSanctis, G. and Gallupe, R., "A Foundation for the Study of Group Decision Support Systems." Man. Sci., May 1987, Vol. 33, No. 5, pp. 589-609.
2. Grey, P., Vogel, D. and Beaulair, R., "Assessing GDSS Empirical Research," European J. Op. Res., 1990.
3. McLeod, P., "An Assessment of the Experimental Literature on Electronic Support of Group Work: Results of a Meta-Analysis," *Human-Computer Interaction*, 1992, Vol. 7, No. 4, pp. 257-280.
4. Ellis, C., Gibbs, S., and Rein, G., "Groupware: The Research and Development Issues," MCC Technical Report Number STP-414-88, December 1988.
5. Goodman, P., "Impact of Task and Technology on Group Performance," in **Designing Effective Work Groups**, P. Goodman (ed), San Francisco: Jossey-Bass, 1986.
6. Chung, W. and Guinan, P., "Effects of Participative Management on the Performance of Software Development Teams," Proc. of the 1994 SIG CPR Conference, The ACM, April, 1994.
7. Susskind, C., "**Understanding Technology**, Baltimore: The Johns Hopkins University Press", 1973.
8. Zuboff, S., "**In the Age of the Smart Machine**", New York: Basic Books, 1988.
9. Postman, N., **Technopoly**, Alfred New York: A. Knoptf. 1992.
10. McGrath, J. and Altman, I., **Small Group Research**. New York: Holt, Rinehart and Winston, 1966.
11. McGrath, J., "Studying Groups at Work: Ten Critical Needs for Theory and Practice," in **Designing, Effective Work Groups**, P. Goodman (ed), San Francisco: Jossey-Bass, 1986.
12. Pinsonneault, A. and Kraemer, K., "The Impact of Technological Support on Groups: An Assessment of the Empirical Research," Decision Support Systems, June 1989.
13. Dennis, A., Nunamaker, J., and Vogel, D., "A Comparison of Laboratory and Field Research in the Study of Electronic Meeting Systems." J. of MIS, Winter 1990-1, Vol. 7, No. 3, pp. 107-135.

14. Hackman, J., "The Design of Work Teams," in **The Handbook of Organizational Behavior**, Boston: Addison-Wesley, 1987.
15. Hackman, J., "A Set of Methods for the Research on Work Teams," Research Program on Group Effectiveness, Yale School of Organization and Management, Technical Report # 1. December 1982.
16. Hackman, J. and Oldham, J., **Work Redesign**. Boston: Addison-Wesley, 1980.
17. Boehm, B., "Improving Software Productivity," Computer, September 1987, pp. 43-57.
18. Rash, R. and Tosi, H., "Factors Affecting Software Developers' Performance: An Integrated Approach," MIS Q., 1992, Vol. 18, No. 23, pp. 395-409.
19. Walz, D., Elam. J, and Curtis, B., "The Dual Role of Conflict in Group Software Requirements and Design Activities," Draft manuscript, February 1992.
20. Robey, D. and Farrow, D., "User Involvement in Information System Development: A Conflict Model and Empirical Test," Man. Sci., January 1982, Vol. 28, No. 1, pp. 73-85.
21. Robey, D., Farrow, D. and Franz, C., "Group Processes and Conflict in Systems Development," Management Science, October, 1989, Vol. 35, No. 10, pp. 1172-1191.
22. Curtis, B., Krasner, H. and Iscoe, N., "A Field Study of the Software Design Process for Large System," Comm. of the ACM, November 1988. Vol. 31, No. 11, pp. 1268-1287.
23. Thomas, K., "Conflict and Conflict Management," in **Handbook of Industrial and Organizational Psychology**, M. Dunnette (ed), Chicago: Rand McNally, 1976. pp. 889-936.
24. Thomas, K. and Pondy, L., "Toward an Intent Model of Conflict Management Among Principal Parties," *Human Relations*, December 1977, No. 30, Vol. 12, pp. 1089-1102.
25. Pondy, L., "Organization Conflict: Concepts and Models," *Admin. Sci. Q.*, Vol. 12, pp. 296-320.
26. Green, S. and Taber, T., "The Effects of Three Social Decision Schemes on Decision Group Process," *Org. Pref, and Human Behavior*, 1980, Vol. 25, pp.97-106.
27. Poole, M., Holmes, M. and DeSanctis, G., "Conflict Management in a Computer-Supported Meeting Environment," *Man. Sci.*, August 1991, Vol. 37, No. 8, pp. 926-953.
28. Sambamurthy, V. and Poole, M., "The Effects of Variations in Capabilities of GDSS Designs on Management of Cognitive Conflict in Groups," *Info. Sys. Res.*, September 1992, Vol. 3, No. 3. pp. 224-251.
29. Slocum, J. and Sims. H, Jr., "A Typology for Integrating Technology, Organization, and Job Design," *Human Relations*, 1980, Vol. 33, No. 3, pp. 193-212.
30. Fry, L., "Technology-Structure Research: Three Critical Issues," Acad. of Man. J., 1982, Vol. 25, No. 3.
31. Frey, L. and Slocum, J., Jr., "Technology, Structure, and Workgroup Effectiveness: a Test of a Contingency Model," *Acad. of Man. J.*, 1984, Vol. 22, No. 2, pp. 221-246.
32. Sproull, L. and Goodman, P., "Technology and Organizations Integration and Opportunities," in **Technology and Organizations**, P. Goodman and L. Sproull (eds), San Francisco: Jossey Bass, 1989.
33. Henderson, J. and Lee, S., "Managing I/S Design Teams: A Control Theories Perspective," *Man. Sci.*, June 1992. Vol. 38, No. 6, pp. 757-777.
34. Gold, C., "Total Quality Management in Information Services," Ernst and Young Center for Business Innovation, Research Note, September, 1992.
35. Venkatraman, N., "The Concept of Fit in Strategy Research: Toward Verbal and Statistical Correspondence." *Acad. of Man. R.*, 1989, Vol. 14, No. 3, pp. 423-444.
36. Dillman, D., "**Mail and Telephone Surveys**," John Wiley & Sons, New York, 1978.
37. Selltiz, C., Jahoa, M., Deutsch, M. and Cook, S., **Research Methods in Social Relations**, New York: Holt Rinehart, 1959.
38. Aday, L., "**Designing and Conducting Health Surveys**," San Francisco: Jossey-Bass, 1989.
39. Seidler, J., "On Using Informants: A Technique for Collecting Quantitative Data and Controlling Measurement Error in Organization Analysis, Amer. Soc. R., December 1974, Vol. 39, No. 12, pp. 816-831.
40. Lee, S., Goldstein, D. and P. Guinan "Informant Bias in I/S Design Team Research," Boston University Working Paper Number 89-25, November 1989.
41. Dawis, R., "Scale Construction," *J. of Counseling Psych.*, 1987, Vol. 34, No. 4, pp. 481-489.
42. Kraut, R. and Streeter, L., "Coordination in Software Development," Carnegie-Mellon Univ., Draft, 1993.
44. Spaeth, J., "Path Analysis," in **Introductory Multivariate Analysis**, D. Amick and H. Walberg (eds), Berkely: McCutehan, 1975.
45. Duncan, O., "Path Analysis: Sociological Examples, *Amer. of Soc.*, 1966, Vol. 72, pp. 1-16.
46. Blalock, H., **Theory Construction**, Englewood Cliffs, NJ: Prentice Hall, 1969.
47. Allison, P., "Testing for Interaction in Multiple Regression," *Amer. J. of Soc.*, 1977, Vol. 83, No. 1, pp. 145-153.
48. Spillers, R., Sawyer, S., Guinan, P. and Farber, J., "Experiences with Team-Based Software Development," *Proc. of the 1994 SIM Conference*, SIM Press, 1994.

12

Designing with Non-Functional Requirements

Colin J Theaker and Jenny Whitworth

School of Computing, Staffordshire University,
Beaconside, Stafford ST18 0AD, England

Abstract

A major class of software and systems engineering projects are critically dependent upon the attributes of the final system as much upon its functionality. These attributes reflect the quality of the design and implementation of the product, yet in most circumstances, they are treated in a very loose and haphazard fashion during the system development. From very poor requirements specifications, the successful implementation of a system all too often depends upon the intuitive skills of experienced designers. There are many documented examples of systems which have failed as a result.

This paper examines a framework for systems design and implementation that addresses both the problems of correct functionality and also the specification and tracking of non-functional requirements, through to an auditable solution. The objective is to provide an environment in which design engineers (and project managers) can consider design trade-offs and make informed judgements accordingly. The research is ongoing and so the paper outlines some of the longer term aspirations of the project.

Keyword Codes: D.2.1; D.2.8; D.2.6; D.2.10
Key words: Non-functional requirements, system attributes, process modelling, object orientation, CASE and workbench tools, real-time systems.

1. INTRODUCTION

The class of computer-based systems which include reactive, real-time and embedded systems presents us with some of our greatest challenges when it comes to designing and implementing the software. The constraints that are imposed on the final product development may significantly impact upon whether the product itself is a success or failure, with factors such as cost, performance and time-to-market playing a significant role. The nature of reactive systems is also that they are involved in control applications, where issues of safety and reliability may play a dominant role. The 'quality' aspects of system development are therefore often more important than simply providing the expected functionality.

This paper discusses an approach for systems engineering which addresses the wider issues of software development and the quality attributes which are associated with the system. In broad terms we shall refer to these as the **non-functional attributes** of a system, to distinguish them from the logical behaviour (or functionality) that is embodied in the algorithmic implementation of the software. The range of these is very open-ended, but might include performance, reliability, cost, size, etc.

Once a system has been implemented, it is generally feasible to measure the attributes of the system and thereby validate that the requirements have been met. Some may be relatively easy to quantify, for example size and cost may be measured directly. Other attributes may take on a stochastic distribution, whilst others may only be estimates of future behaviour, such as the prediction of future software reliability based on past performance. The situation we would like to achieve is one in which a designer can recognise that these non-functional requirements are present, and that during the design process, they are refined in a manner similar to the function attributes. The refinement process naturally relies upon engineering expertise for both the functional and non-functional partitioning. In many cases the different types of attribute are heavily interrelated. A significant part of the design process, which currently relies largely on intuition or 'gut feeling', is to apply design trade-offs in a quantifiable way so that desired attributes are optimised and that the design is 'safe' [1] with adequate tolerances.

2. CURRENT PRACTICES

Although recognised as an important factor in the design and management of systems [2], in most cases the non-functional characteristics are neither (well) specified as a requirement nor measured, and the achievement of a satisfactory solution to this nebulous problem too often rests in the skill and expertise of experienced practitioners. Even when a well-engineered solution is manifest, with no control or measure of the attributes during system development, the final quality may be unrecognised and subsequently lost for future developments. This is clearly poor engineering practice and equally poor economics.

Within specific design methods, temporal aspects are probably the one area in which non-functional attributes have been most widely addressed. In considering temporal behaviour, some methods have incorporated stochastic techniques. For example, Stochastic Petri nets [5] support the modelling of a system using Petri nets and at the same time use random variables to specify the time behaviour of the system. These nets are obtained by associating an exponentially distributed random variable with each transition of the net. The variable defines the delay from the enabling to the firing of the transition. An alternative approach that has been adopted is to attach an interval of time $[t_{min}, t_{max}]$ to each transition. This interval represents the minimum and maximum time that may elapse between the enabling and the firing of a transition. PRM-Nets [4] have been used to develop performance models of parallel programs at the implementation stage. These nets support the modelling of both the software and hardware structures as well as the mapping of software process to physical processors. Other models have adopted a deterministic approach. In CSP [3], the process a-->P models a system which first engages in the event a and then behaves as P. In timed CSP [1], the process $a\text{-}^{t}\text{->}P$ will behave as P precisely t time units after the event a has occurred. These various methods highlight the different approaches to incorporating time within the various development methods.

Apart from these, where any mechanisms are used, they tend to be of a very ad-hoc nature and are ancillary to the main development process rather than being an integral part of it. They mainly take the form of simulation systems, such as [7], which can be used very effectively in determining overall system architectures and configurations, particularly for hardware/software systems in which the hardware structure may be one of the biggest issues. However unless they become part of the main development process, the use of such techniques will only be viable on those systems (and parts of systems) for which the parallel effort in developing a simulation model will be worthwhile.

3. MOOSE

The work described in this paper is part of a much larger collaborative project concerned with the tools and techniques to support systems engineering, entitled MOOSE, or **Model-based Object Oriented System Engineering** [6]. The focus of the work is on the tools and techniques for the development of

---

[1] 'Safe' in this context applies as much to the development process and the likelihood of achieving a successful product as to any issues of safety criticality.

executable models of systems, through which their functionality can be explored along with the design issues which result by considering the non-functional requirements.

The models we are concerned with here are generated at the very early stages of the life-cycle. The models are executable and this distinguishes the work from other forms of design notation, such as DFDs and ERMs. By using these models from the start, the look and feel of a potential product can be demonstrated, the functionality refined, and an evaluation of its technical feasibility explored.

An object oriented approach has been adopted in which a system is represented as a network of collaborating objects. A system may be refined hierarchically to allow the elaboration of systems of objects into further subsystems. Initially the objects are considered to be *uncommitted* as no assumption is made as to how they will be implemented. The system allows systematic consideration of the design options available for each object, and through the interactions between objects, allows for a dynamic view of the system behaviour. In considering performance requirements (processors, stores etc.) to support an implementation, we could use the system as a vehicle for hardware/software co-design to obtain optimum design trade-offs. In this respect, consideration of the non-functional requirements becomes even more important.

Support for the modelling process is based upon a standard CASE tool, namely Select Yourdon. Diagrams are captured and edited using the standard system, but to overcome limitations in the graphical notation, specific naming conventions have been adopted for the textual annotations to allow the distinctive nature of each object to be identified. The captured database can be interrogated by other software packages to provide additional functionality over and above the standard tool. This mechanism also allows us to enhance the model with a variety of different textual notations to support different aspects of the design process. For example, a language has been defined which allows the model to be 'exercised' to examine the dynamic behaviour of a system. Its functionality can be reviewed and in particular, the interactions between objects closely scrutinised. Similarly the different non-functional requirements of each object can be represented and refined.

The consideration of non-functional requirements starts with the initial specification of the product. Although current practice in generating such specifications is very poor, good guidance on how this may be addressed may be found, for example, in [2]. We have chosen to restrict our activity principally to performance (and other temporal aspects) and reliability. These have interesting differences, not least in the state of the art for their specification and analysis, but they also exhibit many similarities.

In reality, most non-functional attributes would exhibit a stochastic distribution in their behaviour. Such distributions are difficult to apportion during the design refinement and add complexity to the analysis process. Current engineering practice (if done at all) might be to consider single values such as typical or worst cases. The notations we are currently considering therefore lie between these extremes, representing ranges of values and probabilities of falling outside the ranges. Notations of this form are capable of providing very powerful analysis information. For example, with temporal behaviour we could obviously identify logical inconsistencies such as race conditions or incorrect sequencing of events. We could also quantify the performance behaviour, such as typical (mean), best case and worst case responses and also the likelihood of the behaviour falling outside acceptable criteria. This would allow us to identify appropriate levels of hardware performance (in a cost effective way) or to design appropriate recovery mechanisms into the system.

Starting at an initial context diagram with its overall requirements specification, the design refinement progresses. At each refinement, the requirements, both functional and non-functional, are further apportioned to the constituent objects. This is naturally where the skill of the designer is used to derive an appropriate partitioning. The interaction between the objects is important, for example, objects interacting sequentially or in parallel would obviously produce different timing behaviour. With 'rules' in place, it is possible to validate at each stage of the refinement if the partitioning is acceptable in meeting the higher level requirements and to assess the tolerances which ensue.

A verification against the requirements will take place once an actual implementation has been derived (or once we are sufficiently sure of its implementation). In the case of functionality, this may be a simple check list to identify whether the function is present or not. With non-functional requirements, we need to measure the values of the actual attributes of the system. It is worth noting that the overall system may still meet its requirements even though individual sub-systems fall outside the tolerances apportioned to them. However, an awareness of the 'hot spots' is still useful for the management of subsequent developments.

4. FUTURE DEVELOPMENTS

This project is still in a comparatively early stage, particularly for the inclusion of non-functional requirements in the design process. Some tool support has been developed, a number of models have been captured of actual and potential systems, and routes to synthesis are being explored. Issues relating to non-functional requirements are still a subject for debate, particularly with respect to the notational aspects.

The refinement of requirements is one of the more challenging areas, particularly if one considers the support that could be given to the designer at that stage. Whilst certain techniques, such as complexity analysis or function point analysis could help in certain areas, we must still recognise that some of the attributes are unmeasurable even when the system has been implemented, and we are forced to predict future behaviour based on the past. Building up an historical perspective through the collection of metrics is obviously a desirable form of support.

There are issues relating to the refinement which will be addressed as part of this project. For example, as an executable model of the system exists, there is naturally data available relating to the dynamic behaviour. It is proposed to make use of this in connection with the performance analyses. The identification of how objects interact and how the inverse can be utilised in the design process is the subject of further work.

ACKNOWLEDGEMENTS

The work described in this paper has been partially funded by the SERC (project number GR/J09840). The authors would like to acknowledge the help provided by the collaborators on this project, including Professor D Morris at UMIST, Professor R Phillips at the University of Hull, and their respective colleagues. We would also like to thank the companies who have provided support in terms of tools and applications to model, in particular to Select Software Tools Ltd and to ICL.

REFERENCES

1. Davies J., Jackson D.M., Reed G.M., "Timed CSP -Theory and Practice", LNCS Vol. 600, pp640-675.
2. Gilb T., "Principles of Software Engineering Management", Addison-Wesley.
3. Hoare C.A.R., "Communicating Processes", Prentice Hall.
4. Hull M.E.C., O'Donoghue P.G., "Timed Petri net Approach to Performance Modelling with the MOON Method", *Software Engineering Journal*, Vol 9, No 3, pp 95-106.
5. Marsan A., Balbo G., Conte G., "Performnce Models of Multi Processor Systems", MIT Press.
6. Morris D., Evans D.G., Schofield S., "Model-based Object Oriented System Engineering (MOOSE) - A Design Method and Notation", To be published.
7. SES Workbench, Software Engineering Software Inc., Austin Texax.

13

Modelling the Requirements of Process Controlled Systems

T.K. Sateesh and P.A.V. Hall

Computing Department, Faculty of Mathematics and Computing
The Open University, Milton Keynes MK7 6AA, United Kingdom

Abstract

Computer controlled systems with strict timing requirements are ubiquitous. Temporal requirements are often the timing restrictions imposed by the application environment. Real-time properties concerns quantitative timing constraints. We introduce the concepts of Timed Requirements Language (TRL) a language invented primarily for the exposition of temporal properties of process controlled systems. TRL is designed to project operational behaviour through time. TRL is based on event model and realises the behaviour of system with strict timing constraints. TRL treats functionality and timing in the same framework.

Keyword Code: D.2.0; D.2.1; D.2.2
Keywords: Software Engineering, General; Requirements; Tools and Techniques

1. INTRODUCTION

Requirements of a system evolve as a set of simple needs. These needs are comprehended with many essential properties of that class of system. The technique employed for the evolution of requirements are pertinent only to a particular class of system as the properties differ from one class to another. In defining requirements the goal is to maximise the functionality of system while minimising the failure. Requirements are derived from a wide range of concepts. The focus here is to capture real time requirements of systems. A major application of computers has been in the control of physical processes like industrial plant control, nuclear reactors, flight control systems and patient monitoring systems. These systems are characterised by hard response time and dynamic environment. Process controlled systems normally interact with external world entities. A system can be described from external user's point of view. External description establishes associations among activities which occur within different subsystems of a system. Sequence of interaction among components provides a description of the system operation and furnishes the operational behaviour of the system. Requirements specification based on real world models are transparent and easy to understand. System interactions are related to the communication among components and environment. In order to avoid any misunderstanding requirements must be expressed in a formal representation. A formalism specifies a class of objects under discussion in an unambiguous and general manner [9]. For easy analysis requirements are required to be stated in a language understandable by computers.

Process controlled systems have to satisfy stringent timing characteristics. Timing constraints arise while maintaining the stability of plant. These timing constraints depend on the physical characteristics of plant. System needs are required to be represented in a language that incorporates timing feature. As Leveson [6] observes 'most real-time specification languages have only simple primitives for timing, such as a time-out, that do not adequately capture the complexities of time and therefore are inadequate for fully specifying and modelling requirements'. A requirements language must facilitate the description of temporal properties that are meaningful for these systems. Substantial work has been carried out by a number of researchers in the requirements specification of real-time systems like [1] [8]. The works on temporal requirements [3] [8] [5] has influenced us. Our language philosophy builds on these works and simplifies system evolution to handle possibly unforeseen requirements. In this article we introduce the concepts of timed requirements language (TRL) to specify real time aspects of the systems. TRL is designed to specify systems where temporal aspects are of considerable interest. TRL promotes a descriptive method. TRL emphasises understanding what takes place and when it takes place in the system, which are system behaviours.

2. MODEL OF SYSTEM

System modelling starts with informal requirements and a set of assumptions on the system and environment. A model is a simplified representation of something to be developed. In general model is an abstraction of the system. Model gives description of the function of the real system. Model incorporates the essential feature of the system. A model of a computational paradigm is a set of direct or indirect observations that can be made of a computational process [4]. A system is composed of interacting components. Behaviour arises out of time ordered interactions between subsystems. These interactions provide a qualitative description of how the system works. A system description constructs a model of a system. This model identifies the approximate structure of system by recognising the important incidents that occur. The word structure refers to a partial description of system showing it as a collection of parts and showing relations between the parts. Balzer [2] argues that system requirements must be a cognitive model. It must describe a system as perceived by its user community. The object it manipulates must correspond to the real objects of that domain.

A simple model of a real time system can be described by the time ordered interactions between subsystems. System is connected by physical devices which operate in their own time scales. Computer is said to operate in real-time if actions carried out by the computer relate to the time scales of the external tasks. Typically the requirement of a computer is to complete a set of operations within a prespecified time. Majority of tasks fall into this category. Events occur in real time without any reference to the operations inside computer. The sequence of actions is determined by the events occurring in the environment. Controller has to synchronise its operations with that of environment. Environment is an active part of the system. It is the responsibility of the controller to overcome any unsatisfactory behaviour of environment. While system modelling, environment has to be modelled first. This becomes essential to capture the lag time and response time requirements.

2.1. An Approach to Modelling

Functional requirements originates from a sense of causation. A letter can not be read unless it is received, and a customer gets what he orders. The requirement is a chain that mirrors this causal relationship among several events occurring in a system. Real-time systems interact with physical devices which are monitored and controlled. A complex system is a combination of interacting components. In all these systems one device energises the other. The behaviour of a system is the causal relationship among real world events. Requirements evolve from this simple set of behaviour. Requirement of a system involves the order of occurrence of events and also constraints on the time of occurrence. We make use of event based model to capture the behaviour of system. The behaviour of a software system may be characterised by the sequence of events which occur. Distinct events carry distinct labels. Each event is assumed to occur instantaneously. Event occurrence marks a point in time, which is significant for the analysis of dynamic behaviour of the system. Thus event serves as a temporal marker. Continuous events which consume a definite time interval and is vital for reasoning are represented by two atomic events like start of the event and end of that event. By atomicity we mean that the events are indivisible.

In event model, one is interested in the ongoing process involving real world entities (i.e., how an event is caused, how an event affects other events, and which event is dependent on other events). Description of behaviour produces a chronological relationships between corresponding transactions. With real-time systems we are interested in the precise sequencing of operations and the detailed timing and control characteristics of external devices. Behaviour is a sequence of exchange of information between the co-operating units. Behavioural descriptions has to be operational to aid the easy analysis of system behaviour. Data flow diagram shows only the flow of data and is not interested in the sequence of activities occurring. Event sequence represents a finer detail of activities involved in processing the action. Behavioural specification describes constraints on observable behaviour. A constraint imposes a restriction on the behaviour of a system. A commonsense description of the system's behaviour envisions the relationship between the components of system and their potential behaviour. Functional description of system is described in terms of the exact role of its components. The component model is responsibility driven rather than data driven. We can model the functions as agents cooperating with each other to achieve the goal. Agent characterises the resources and the task assigned to it. Agents can be either concrete or abstract. A concrete agent may have a representation in system like a button, a printer and so on. An abstract agent may have no direct representation in system, instead it models a behaviour which is a set of operations that it can be requested to carry out. Abstract agent models a certain responsibility of system. Responsibility of a system as conceived by a user emphasises the utility point of view.

3. MODELLING LANGUAGE

Functional behaviour is a collection of operations which selectively manipulates the agents to provide an intended function. TRL describes behaviour using only the interactions with which the system and its environment communicate. Behaviour of a system is defined by behaviour expression. Behaviour expression is a sequence of interaction of events.

behaviour : behaviour expression --> setof (sequenceof (TimedEvent))

In other words behaviour expression consists of a set of events that can take part.

A behaviour definition is of the form

(behaviour ($e_1, e_2,$ .. e_n))

where behaviour is the language construct that binds events (e_1 , e_2 , . . e_n). System activity is asserted by defining bodies of processes. Processes are used to describe the dynamics of the system. Process consists of a sequence of behaviour expressions, where each expression is justified by expression previous in the sequence. With TRL computations are described in terms of processes. We treat all communication mechanisms by manipulation of events. TRL treats the system as a set of processes. Process reflects a synoptic view of system consisting of a sequence of events that the real system may engage.

A **process P** is a set of behaviour expressions of the form

(behaviour ($e_1, e_2,$ .. e_n)) . . . .

(behaviour ($e_1, e_2,$ .. e_n))

In TRL every event is a timed event. A timed event associates a time parameter with event. It is expressed as (button_pressed, t1) where t1 is timing parameter associated with event 'button pressed'.

3.1. Language Constructs

Requirements can be elicited by stepping through the scenario in which events motivate the system to behave in a particular pattern. A triggering mechanism provides the basis for describing these scenarios. Events are defined as what happens to the environment. This provides a qualitative reasoning about observed or postulated behaviour. Such a reasoning is quite useful for generating explanations on what can happen and how the things that happen can interact. System description is derived from the behavioural description of components and their interconnections. Behavioural description of each component reveals its objective.

Causal ordering manifests relation between <triggering event> and <action sequence>. Action sequence describes the complete pattern of behaviour. Action sequence may consist of one or more events. In other words each event may *energise* finetly one or more events. *Energise* is a strict partial ordering on events with utmost one immediate predecessor event. Action sequence may be represented by a single event or as a composition of events. It is possible to specify several action events which all meet the same selection criteria. Action sequence is to be performed one at a time and in the order they are written. A system can react to several types of events. For example an automated library assistant (ALA) can react differently depending on the type of order received. ALA depending on the order received generates a collection of events or a single event.

```
IF (command = reserve, t1) THEN (proceed to reserve a book, t2)
    ELSIF (command = overdue_notice, t3) THEN (proceed to issue notice, t4)
    ELSIF (command = check_status, t5) THEN (proceed to check the status, t6)
    ELSIF (command = help, t7) THEN (provide help, t8) FI
```

A boolean condition may also be associated with the triggering event. Triggering operation takes place only if the condition is satisfied. An absence of a condition is evaluated as condition = true. Following Martin-Löf's constructive type theory [7] we define types as predicates that state the properties of system or its components. For example a book can only be reserved if it is available in library. This is expressed as

```
IF (command = reserve, t1) ASWELL (book is available) THEN
        (proceed to reserve a book, t2) FI
```

Defunct behaviour is also built into TRL. Behaviour function on defunct behaviour (NIL) is an empty set. Other constructs like 'do' and 'with' are used to capture the other scenarios of system activity.

3.2. Representation of timing constraints

Timing constraints are an essential part of real-time requirements. Dasarathy[3] provides a classification of timing constraints. A slightly different approach to temporal requirements is employed in [5]. Timing constraints of both types can easily be expressed with TRL. More complicated timing constraints can be expressed involving event associated timers. The timing constraint is expressed as a relation between the timing parameters, like

IF (command = reserve , t1) THEN (proceed to reserve a book , t2)
WHERE (t2 <= t1+5) ^ (t2 > t1 +1) FI

WHERE specifies a condition on the time period between events. Temporal requirements are the qualitative and quantitative statements about the required temporal order of activities. Timing constraints are explicit specifications of the behaviour of system components. Timing constraints in TRL are specified by timing relation(s) between events. Any timing constraint user defined or system derived can easily be expressed. Timing constraints like the latest allowable start time, the earliest allowable start time and the interval during which a task is allowed to start are easily specified. Timing constraint can involve the constraint over many events. An operation like measuring the level of water in a tank or measuring the temperature of furnace is to be accomplished periodically. Periodic behaviour represents such repeated actions. Repeated behaviour is associated with a predicate. As long as this predicate evaluates true, specified action is observed. Periodicity of repetition is specified. Periodic behaviour is represented with 'while' construct. TRL treats functionality and timing in the same framework. Naturally it is possible to build several behaviours for the same system. These can be developed independently to simplify the task of requirements evolution. Here we are not describing the language in detail. It is not essential to this paper, as here we are only considering the concepts of language.

4. CONCLUSION

TRL has been designed to specify systems where temporal properties are of interest. The essential feature of the language is being descriptive and this is appropriate for modelling real time aspects of activity. Description requires the identification of events contained in system. As this method is parametrized with respect to events in a system, it allows to treat different systems in a uniform way. In essence, TRL provides a notation for the description of system models.
The importance of obtaining conceptual model requirements has been underlined by various researchers. TRL has been used with some real-time systems. PREET (Process-oriented REquirements Elucidating Tool) checks the validity and consistency of requirements expressed in TRL. Also PREET provides description of the temporal and functional behaviour through timed transition diagrams. It helps to experiment with the description of systems, as the descriptions can easily be modified and then analysed for their suitability.

REFERENCES

1. Alford M.W, 'A Requirements Engineering Methodology for Real-time Processing Requirements', IEEE Transactions On Software Engineering, January 1977, pp. 60 - 69
2. Balzer R.M. and Goldman N.M, 'Principles of Good Software Specification and their Implication for Specification Languages', in Proceedings of the Specifications of Reliable Software Conference, April 1979, pp. 58 - 67
3. Dasarathy B, 'Timing Constraints of Real-time Systems: Constructs for Expressing Them, Methods for Validating Them', IEEE Transactions On Software Engineering, SE- 11 (1) Jan 1985, pp. 80 - 86
4. Hoare C.A.R, 'Let's Make Models', in LNCS - 458, Ed J.C.M. Baeten and J.W. Klop, Theories of Concurrency: Unification and Extension, Springer Verlag, 90 pp. 33
5. Jahanian F and Mok A.K, 'Safety Analysis of Timing Properties in Real-Time Systems', IEEE Transactions on Software Engineering, Se-12(9), Sept. 1986, pp. 890 - 904
6. Leveson N.G, 'The Challenge of Building Process-control Software', IEEE Software, November 1990, pp. 55 - 62
7. Nordström B and Smith J, 'Propositions And Specifications of Programs in Martin-Löf's Type Theory', BIT 24(1984) pp. 288 - 301
8. Zave P, 'An Operational Approach to Requirements Specification for Embedded Systems', IEEE Transactions on Software Engineering, vol. SE-8, May 1982, pp. 250 - 269
9. Zeigler B.P, 'Multifaceted Modelling and Discrete Event Simulation', Academic Press, Orlando 1984

14

Compiling Heterarchical Programs by Means of Petri Nets

John B. Evans

Department of Computer Science, University of Hong Kong, Pokfulam Road, Hong Kong

Abstract

We present a method for compiling a program which does not have a conventional tree-like hierarchy of control. Such a structure can arise quite naturally in applications which are strongly user-interactive or contain significant elements of transaction processing, dynamic modelling or process control. Having a heterarchical structure, the application program is capable of being executed simultaneously at an unlimited number of points. Thus a program involving parallel distributed processing, interleaving between processors or multithreading might take advantage of this approach. The encompassing execution strategy is based on the idea of tokens moving through a variant of a Petri net under the control of a firing protocol. We describe an approach to modelling control structures with Petri net semantics and means taken to provide complete reactivation control at run time.

Keyword Codes: D.1.5, D.3.3
Keywords: Object-oriented programming, Language constructs and Features

1. DISCRETE-EVENT SYSTEMS AND PETRI NETS

A discrete-event system is a dynamic system which changes at certain points in time by the instantaneous movement of entities from one state to another. Such a system can be described in terms of entity interactions, any number of which may be simultaneously taking place in parallel. Although the interactions may persist, their initiations and dissolutions are taken to be instantaneous. The system is a discrete-event system; that is, that all change in the system is seen as instantaneous. In many cases this is an assumption which is easy to make: either it is approximately true, or a finite duration can be resolved into a pair of bounding instants. The state of the system as a whole can be thought of the totality of all the states currently taken up by all the component entities. A discrete-event system is thereby a valuable abstract means to specify a wide variety of existing or hypothetical systems.

Discrete-event systems, with their concern for parallel happenings are obvious candidates for some kind of *Petri net* [1] description. In brief, a Petri net is a directed bipartite graph with a net of nodes consisting of a set of *places* (represented by circles) and a set of *transitions* (represented by bars). Being directed, the arcs are of two types: those connecting places to transitions, and those connecting transitions to places. One way of capturing a discrete event system is to associate the *places* with *states* in which the interactions occur and *transitions* with *state-changes.* Entities can be modelled by *tokens* of the net (represented by small discs) which can occupy places which denote the particular interactions being undergone. An association of places with tokens is called a *marking* of the net.

The dynamics of a Petri net are given by an application of the Petri *firing rule* which applies to any transition. If we consider all the places which are associated with a given transition, that is the places which are connected by an arc *from* the place *to* the transition (i.e. the *input places* of the transition), then if each member of the transition's set of input places contain at least one token, the transition can be said to be *enabled* for firing. On *firing* one token is removed from each input place and one token is entered into each *output place*, with complementary meaning. Note that for any transition, its input and output places are not necessarily disjoint. With such an association, the idea of discrete events translates into instantaneous firing.

We propose a variant of the Petri net, the Devnet [2], for which we seek to make the following correspondences to discrete-event systems:

• *place* becomes the state in which the entity may reside for some non-negative duration of time. In applied systems research, the concept of state is closely associated with that of *activity*— the idea being that an entity in a state is actually *doing* something productive. We may maintain this association as long as we are prepared to accept that durations in which entities wait idly for resources, or for some condition to arise, are also counted as 'activities'.

• *transition* becomes a generic event which defines and controls the change from one state to another. Such events can delimit activity durations and initiate entity interactions.

• *token* becomes the individual entity, typed as a member of an entity class. The class definition may include attributes which themselves are typed. Equivalently, we may consider tokens as *objects* representing instances of their respective class. The tokens are coloured according to their class. The instantaneous marking of a Devnet corresponds to the overall configuration of the discrete-event system given by the totality of entities-in-state.

• *arcs* denote the connections between state and event, or between the activities and the events which start and terminate them. More particularly, arcs which are input to a transition indicate an enabling relationship, while arcs which are output from a transition indicate the possible routes of tokens dispersed by the transition's firing. Since arcs refer to the passage of tokens, they are coloured according to the class of entity they transport.

• *firing* then becomes an event occurrence, an activation of an enabled transition where the controls and consequences defined in the event are made manifest on behalf of a specific entity, or collection of entities. Firing involves moving tokens from places input to the transition to places in its output set. In the Devnet we allow some kinds of event to be triggered after a time-delay from their enablemenent.

One particular simulation language, ***Simian*** [3], has an intimate relationship with the Devnet. The compiler constructs a data-structure representation of the Devnet as the temporal aspects the Simian program are being compiled, in order to guide the activation and reactivation of the program at run time. Compilation pragmatics are thus reduced to a protocol of pursuing tokens across transitions, with due regard to token matching, expressed priorities and conflict resolution. By incorporating the Devnet into the object program in this way gives a more coherent and intelligent interpretation of the system described, which in turn enables the design of the Simian language to be *declarative* at an extremely high level.

Given any unmarked Devnet, we can tell which transitions may be in mutual conflict. For any marked Devnet we can tell which transitions are not enabled, and thus the set of transitions whose enablement status should be further investigated. The precise workings of how a Devnet may drive a program is described later. In addition to the typical *Petri interaction*, the Devnet allows *message interaction* in which the state of a remote place may affect (either enable or inhibit) a transition's ability to fire, a *delay interaction* in which an enablement commences a count-down to a later firing for a particular entity in the input place.

The three-way association of entity-event-time (or, in net terms, token-transition-time) is taken as fundamental, forming the *engagement* data-structure, which is the means by which all entity interactions are implemented in Simian. Also present in the data structure is the idea of entities coming together in *collaboration*, as specified in the Petri interaction, for the duration of particular activities. This aspect of object handling has received scant attention from language designers adhering to the OOP paradigm. On transition firing, input tokens can be fused together for collaboration or separated for dispersal. The unfolding of the system dynamic is then seen as a series of making and breaking of engagements as time advances, as prompted by the Devnet structure.

2. THE DEVNET: CONTROL STRUCTURES

There is a large number of ways in which an entity may be guided along a route. We consider here three general classes of route: choice, iteration and parallel, corresponding to roughly similar features from the control structures of algorithmic programming languages. For the first two classes, a new feature is added to the Devnet, that of a transition which may have *disjunctive* sides. This feature allows the modelling of non-deterministic enablement and dispersal. The separation into upside and downside enables the consideration of the enablement and dispersal properties of the transition separately. Each side can then be broken into a number of segments which represent disjunctive alternatives to the functioning of the respective side. Each segment is considered separately as regards enablement or dispersal.

In the case of the *choice* structure, we have a subnet which is preceded by a transition with a disjunctive downside. This indicates that when the transition fires, a choice is made and one of the two output routes, and thus one of the subnets, is chosen. When either of the subnets is completed, this has the effect of firing of the closing transition which has a disjunctive upside, indicating that only one upside need be enabled for the transition to fire. In this way the Devnet supports the Simian program structure:

`IF - THEN - ELSE - FI`

where a choice is taken based on an evaluation of the Boolean expression immediately after the `IF`. With an obvious extension a more general structure is supported:

`CASE - IN ... OUT - ESAC`

In a similar way, making use of a transition with disjunctive upsides and downside, the iterative structure

`FOR .. FROM .. STEP .. TO .. WHILE .. DO - OD`

can be supported. When handling iteration, one must always bear in mind the possibility that the initial evaluation will lead to not entering the loop body at all, and, for temporal programs, this requires that all loop control logic be associated with a single transition. An infinite loop does not require any control, but is just a linear sequence turned on itself.

3. FIRING PROTOCOL OF THE PRIMATE ALGORITHM

Having an internal representation of the Devnet as a pathfinder for the Simian executive program enables entities to be advanced in a *circumspect* way, taking into account a system-wide perspective. The executive algorithm of Simian, Primate, by making use of the topological properties of the Devnet, will take note of all the conflicts and reactivations which might otherwise be forgotten or swept under the carpet. Moreover, any number of entities can be advanced simultaneously without giving any particular advantage or hindrance to any one of

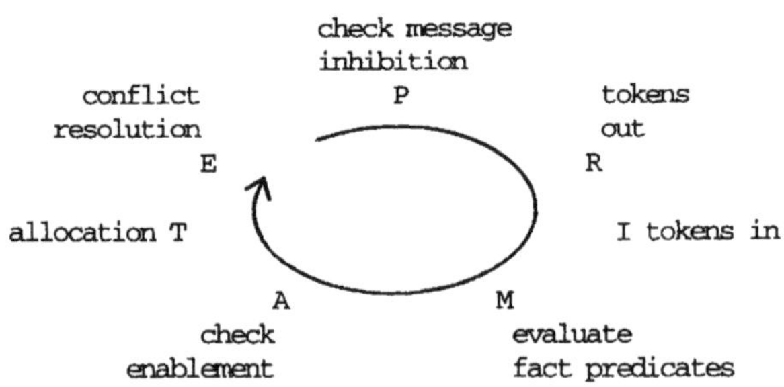

Fig. 1: The Primate algorithm: an outline.
Normal entry is at P, but M, A and E starts are possible. The cycle can be exited after P, M, A, T or E.

them, while maintaining respect of the conditions of priority and conflict resolution, etc. which the simulationist has stipulated.

The first stage (see Fig. 1) is concerned with ascertaining the next event and the particular engagement containing the entity, or set of entities, to be advanced. For ease of description, we will assume here that there is only one engagement, although the algorithm can handle an arbitrary number of coincident engagements. Then the engagement's immediate future is pursued, resulting in a new configuration of the model, giving a new Devnet marking. Finally the consequences of the new marking are analysed to detect whether additional token movement is possible. If so the cycle is continued from the second stage and the cycle is repeated until there is no more token movement possible.

4. CONCLUSIONS AND FURTHER WORK

Although this discussion has been couched mainly in terms of the Simian compiler, a methodology using some variant of Petri nets should be of value in the compiler for any language accepting general heterarchical [4] programs. In pursuing this approach we have departed from three conventional assumptions, *viz*, that the "natural" structure of program control is tree-like and hierarchical; that objects do not form associations, divide and re-divide (especially across class boundaries); and that diagrammatic representations of programs are for necessarily *preliminary* excursions into programming.

We have tried to show that the Devnet diagram, as a qualitative expression of system properties, has some definite benefit as a portrayal of the outline of a system's dynamic. In the form of a data-structure serving as an activator for a heterarchical program it can serve:

- for detecting conflict possibilities;
- as an internal model of event interdependencies;
- to automatically reactivate entities;
- as a basis for driving a back-end animation.

Promising future work on the Devnet might extend its application into the area of the monitoring of control systems involving human controllers, automatic transport, inventory control and in the area of AI planning, both of which are areas with significant dynamic and decision components. By subsuming so much abstract structure into the compiler, we arrive at a higher-level platform upon which to base the design of languages, in the medium of which specific dynamic structures can be definitively *expressed.* The declarative nature of such utterances no longer bears much relation to what was conjured up by the label "programming". Instead a bridge is built between the modes of *specification* and detailed execution. Ultimately the effect of such a close system modelling will amount to a prelude to automation and improvement of the system under study [5].

REFERENCES

1. Reisig, W. *Petri Nets: An Introduction*, Springer-Verlag, Berlin, 1985.

2. Evans J.B. 'The Devnet: a Petri Net for Discrete Event Simulation', (Rozenberg, G., Ed.) *Advances in Petri Nets* 1993, *Lecture Notes in Computer Science,* **674**, (Eds: G. Goos, J. Hartmanis), Springer-Verlag, Berlin, 1993, 91-125.

3. Evans, J.B. *Structures of Discrete Event Simulation: An Introduction to the Engagement Strategy*, Ellis Horwood, Chichester, UK, pp. 279, 1988; ISBN: 0-7458-0103-X.

4. Boden, Margaret *Artificial Intelligence and Natural Man*, Second Edition, MIT Press, London, 1987.

5. Evans, J.B. 'System Synthesis: An Object Petri-Net Methodology', Proceedings of the *European Simulation MultiConference 1994*, Barcelona, June 1-3 1994, 202-206, and University of Hong Kong Department of Computer Science Technical Report TR-93-09, pp. 13.

PART THREE

Object Oriented Analysis, Design and Development

15

Type Checking Classes in Object-Z to Promote Quality of Specifications

J. Chen and B. Durnota

Department of Software Development, Monash University, PO Box 197,
Caulfield East 3145, Australia

Abstract

Formal specification of software requirements has been recognised as an essential ingredient to improve the quality of delivered code. When integrated with the structuring mechanisms of object-orientation, formal specifications can provide a powerful tool for the software developer. However, the formal specification of particularly large systems needs to be supported by tools which assist the specifier or reader of the specification either to understand and/or to reason about a specification. The simplest form of reasoning is that of type checking. This paper develops a simple but useful set of rules for type checking the object-oriented formal specification language Object-Z. Although type checkers exist for Z, at present none exists for Object-Z. The lack of a type checker for Object-Z is a hinderence to a wider and more consistent use of this specification language as an integral component in developing high-quality software products.

Keyword Codes: D.2.1; D.2.2; D.1.5
Keywords: Requirements/Specifications; Tools and Techniques; Object-oriented Programming

1. INTRODUCTION

The construction of software conforming to a client's requirements has been a major challenge of software engineering. Formal specification, as an important part of formal methods, has been an active area in recent years, firstly within the academic and research community and now attracting serious attention from industry. One of the most successful formal specification languages is Z, developed by the Programming Research Group at Oxford and is being used by many industry companies [1].

Object-Z is an object-oriented extension of Z developed in order to overcome some of the limitations of Z [2,5], especially with regards to the specification of large systems. Although Object-Z is largely based on Z, there are important differences such as the notion of *class*, *class type* and *class inheritance*.

However, the formal specification of particularly large systems needs to be supported by tools which assist the specifier or reader of the specification either to understand and/or to reason about a specification. Reasoning can range from the easier, more syntactic level of type checking, through to a wider semantic analysis (such as consistency checking), and ultimately to theorem proving.

The work described in this paper concerns the type checking issue of Object-Z specifications. Although type checkers exist for Z, at present none exists for Object-Z. This has hindered a wider and more consistent use of Object-Z.

Type checking Z specifications has been previously investigated and several type checkers have been developed [6]. From several recent industry surveys and reports of using Z, type checkers are regarded as an important tool in the construction of formal specifications [4, 9]. Especially for specifications of large size or complex or involved team work, type checking is a simple and effective way to improve the quality of specifications.

In this paper, we focus on type checking the components of Object-Z related to defining or referring to class types. We will briefly discuss other aspects of type checking Object-Z, which can be based on the work done to Z. A detail report on type checking Object-Z is under preparation[3].

Formal specifications provide a means to precisely describe the requirements of software. Therefore using formal specification could help in achieving better quality of software. However such a benefit cannot be taken as granted without suitable tool support as various stages of specification construction. One of the important quality criteria is that the specification itself be consistent. We regard the consistency as having different degrees. These degrees of consistency range from type consistency, selected aspect consistency and total consistency. Realistically, most software developments would require the type and selected aspect consistency. In some cases, especially in safety-critical software development, the total consistency may be required. We believe our work described in this paper is an important step towards a tool set for supporting quality assurance of formal specification.

The rest of this paper is organised as follows. In Section 2 we give a brief description of class types in Object-Z and other background knowledge needed in this paper. Section 3 discusses typing rules for class type checking in Object-Z. Finally we discuss further work in Section 4.

2. CLASS TYPES IN OBJECT-Z

Z is a model-based specification language based on typed set theory and with structuring constructs called schemas [8]. Object-Z is an object-oriented extension to Z developed to allow the structuring of large specifications [2, 5, 7].

A Z specification consists of a number of *state schemas, initial state schemas* and *operation schemas.* The values of variables defined in a state schema define a state of the system we are modelling. An operation schema relates input to output variables, as well as changes to state variables before invocation of the operation schema to that after invocation. The *predicate* part of a schema imposes constraints amongst values of variables (*invariants, preconditions, postconditions*).

Object-Z bundles all the operations pertaining to a given state schema into a *class.* Classes are templates for *object* instances of that class. Classes may be defined via (potentially multiple) *inheritance,* and variables may reference objects -- this is called *instantiation.* A class definition parameterized with generic types has the following form:

ClassName [generic parameters]
visibility list
inherited classes
type definitions
constant definitions
state schema
initial state schema
operation schemas
history invariant

An example of an Object-Z class definition is the following one of a bounded stack of items of type *T:*

Stack[T]

$max : \mathbb{N}$

$max \leq 100$

$items : \text{seq } T$

$\# items \leq max$

INIT
$items = \langle \rangle$

Push
$\Delta(items)$
$item? : T$

$\# items < max$
$items' = \langle item? \rangle \frown items$

Pop
$\Delta(items)$
$item! : T$

$items \neq \langle \rangle$
$items = \langle item! \rangle \frown items'$

The constant *max* is the bound on the stack. The state variable *items* models the stack as a sequence of items of type *T*. Initially, the stack has no items. The *Push* operation prepends an input *item?* to *items* -- only if there is room left in *items*. The Δ-list gives the state variables that are changed by the operation -- *items* in this case. The *Pop* operation outputs the head *item!* from *items*, and then equates the new value of *items* to the tail -- provided *items* is not empty.

2.1 Instantiation

Any object may have any other object as its constituent. This is done by a variable referencing either an individual object or an aggregate. Consider our generic stack in which the generic type *T* has been replaced by **N** and some of the variables are renamed, thus giving a stack of natural numbers:

$$NatStack == Stack[\mathbb{N}][nats/items, nat?/item?, nat!/item!]$$

Class *StackPair* contains two individually named references s_1 and s_2 to stacks of natural numbers:

StackPair

$$s_1, s_2 : NatStack$$
$$s_1 \neq s_2$$

$$\#s_1.nats \leq \#s_2.nats$$

INIT

$$s_1.\mathit{INIT} \wedge s_2.\mathit{INIT}$$

$$Push_1 \mathrel{\widehat=} s_1.Push$$
$$Push_2 \mathrel{\widehat=} s_2.Push$$
$$[other\ operations]$$

Push₁

$$s_1, s_2 : NatStack$$
$$s_1.max : \mathbb{N}$$
$$s_1.nats, s_1.nat' : \operatorname{seq} \mathbb{N}$$
$$nat? : \mathbb{N}$$

$$s_1 \neq s_2$$
$$\#s_1.nats \leq s_2.nats$$
$$\#s_1.nats' \leq s_2.nats'$$
$$\#s_1.max \leq 100$$
$$\#s_1.nats \leq s_2.max$$
$$\#s_1.nats < s_2.max$$
$$s_1.nats' = \langle nat? \rangle \frown s_1.nats$$

Since it is intended the references s_1 and s_2 do not change, they are declared as constants. We have also required that the size of the first stack does not exceed the size of the second stack. The dot notation '.' is used to reference features of an object, such as it's state variables. The expanded definition of operation $Push_1$ is given alongside.

One sometimes wants to reference an object of a particular class or any of its derivative subclasses. This is achieved using the ↓ prefix. Thus:

stack: ↓ *Stack*[N]

declares *stack* as a reference to a stack of natural numbers, or to any subclass of stack, where the actual natural number type N has been substituted for the generic type parameter.

IndexedStack[T]

$$Stack[T]$$

$$index : \mathbb{N}_1$$
$$items \neq \langle\rangle \Rightarrow index \in \operatorname{dom} items$$

SetIndex

$$\Delta(index)$$
$$n? : \mathbb{N}_1$$

$$n? \in \operatorname{dom} items$$
$$index' = n?$$

Push

$$\Delta(index)$$

$$items \neq \langle\rangle \Rightarrow index' = index + 1$$

Pop

$$\Delta(index)$$

$$index = 1 \wedge items' \neq \langle\rangle \Rightarrow$$
$$index' = 1$$
$$index \neq 1 \Rightarrow index' = index - 1$$

2.2. Inheritance

Inheritance allows classes to be incrementally specified by reusing previous class definitions. Type and constant definitions and schemas of the inherited classes and those declared explicitly in the derived classes are merged. Schemas with the same name are conjoined. renaming can be used to avoid unintended name clashes during merging in the inherited class. As an example, an indexed stack can be defined by inheriting from the generic stack.

3. TYPING RULES FOR CLASS TYPES AND OBJECT REFERENCES

In this section, we discuss class type checking issues with respect to each of the uses of class types in Object-Z as described above. We first consider typing rules for the signature parts of classes in the case of inheritance and instantiation respectively. Then we discuss typing rules to expressions of Object-Z with class or class feature references.

3.1. Typing Rules for Class Signatures

3.1.1. Inheritance

When we define a new class in Object-Z, the new class may inherit features from existing classes. Semantically, the features of the new class is the collection formed by merging the features of inherited classes and newly defined features of the current class.

Class type conflicts may occur from this merge. For example, if there is an operation *op* defined in one of the inherited classes and a new operation with the same name *op* is defined in the current class, this should be regarded as a conflict of calls (type) components. A typing rule corresponding to this is as follows:

Let *op* be an operation defined in an inherited class C_1 of a class C. We say that *op* in C is *type correct* if there is no other operation with the same name defined in C, except by explicit redefinition. (Redefinition must conform to the typing rule below.)

We may indeed intend to use the same name of operation but with a new definition in the current class. A redefinition facility can be used in such situations. From a typing point of view, the redefinition of the operation *op* should conform to the following rules:

Let *op* be an operation defined in a class C. Suppose that *op* is redefined in an inherited class C_1 of C. We say that the redefinition of *op* in C_1 is *type correct* if the signature of the new *op* in C_1 is the same as that of C.

In case an operation is explicitly removed in the definition of a new class, no specific typing rules are required with respect to inheritance of classes in defining a new class. However, there are rules on the use of such classes with respect to instantiation of classes.

Object-Z allows multiple inheritance in the definition of a new class. Semantically, the newly defined class is the collection formed by merging the inherited classes together with newly defined features of the current class. It is possible that the merge of more than one inherited class may cause type conflicts. The following typing rules are corresponding to such situations:

Let C_1 and C_2 are two inherited classes of class C. We say the merge of C_1 and C_2 is *type correct* if the following conditions are satisfied:
1. Any common attributes (constants and variables) of C_1 and C_2 should be of the same type.
2. Any common operation of C_1 and C_2 should have the same signatures.

typing rule.

3.1.2. Instantiation

A class is considered to be *type correct* if, at least, its declarations and operations are type correct. Then, the first typing rule is simple but important:

Let *r: ClassName* be a constant or variable declaration in a class, where *r* is a constant or variable name. We say that the declaration is *type correct* if:
1. Class *ClassName* is type correct.

Class *ClassName* is an existing class.

The reason for requiring this rule is simple. If *ClassName* is not defined yet, then all references of the features of the *ClassName* in the current class or any class inheriting the current class are not defined (often called *message not understood* in object-oriented programming languages).

The second typing rule concerns reference of inheritance hierarchies:

Let *r*: ↓ *ClassName* be a constant or variable declaration in a class *C*. We say that the constant or variable declaration is *type correct* if the following conditions are satisfied.
1. Class *ClassName* and every class inherited from *ClassName* are *type correct*.
2. There is no operation defined in *ClassName* which is removed from any of the classes inherited from *ClassName*.

The first condition is not difficult to understand as a feature reference to *ClassName* or any of its inherited classed could be undefined if they are not type correct.

Recall that the notation ↓ is introduced for reference to any class in a class inheritance hierarchy in Section 2. The intuition of the second condition is that, if any of the operation defined in the root class of a class inheritance hierarchy is removed from a class inherited from the root class, a feature reference to that operation in an object reference to that class may cause reference undefined. In order to avoid such situations, the second condition must be imposed.

3.2. Typing rules for expressions with class references

There are two main types of expressions in Object-Z as in classical first-order logic: the terms and the predicates. *Terms* correspond to function applications, and *predicates* are predicates associated with state schemas, initialisations, operations schemas and definitions in a class. Two tasks are involved in type checking expressions, and they involve the notion of well-typedness:

A term is *well-typed* if:
1. It is a constant or variable of a declared type (this declared type is called the *type* of the term), or
2. It is of the form $f(t_1,\ldots,t_n)$, where all the t_j are well-typed, and of type T_j and the declared type of f is $T_1 \times \ldots \times T_n \rightarrow T$. Then T is called the *type* of the term.

A predicate is *well-typed* if:
1. It is of the form $R(t_1,\ldots,t_n)$, where all the terms t_j are well-typed, and of type T_j and the declared type of the relation symbol R is $T_1 \times \ldots \times T_n \rightarrow T$, or

2. It is of the form $\neg P$ for a well-typed predicate P, or
3. It is of the form $P \wedge Q$ for well-typed predicates P and Q, or

Similarly for other logical connectives and quantifiers.

Then, an expression is *type-correct* if it is well-typed.

For example, suppose that $+$ is a two-place operation symbol requiring both arguments to be of type *integer*. Then $x + y$ is well-typed if and only if both x and y are of type *integer*, and the type of the expression is *integer*. Suppose that $=$ is a two-place predicate symbol for equality. The predicate $E_1 = E_2$ is well-typed if and only if E_1 and E_2 are two well-typed expressions and are of the same type.

Type checking expressions and predicates of Object-Z can be largely based on the type checking method used for Z expressions and predicates, except the well-typedness of expressions with class feature references.

Let us now consider the typing rules for expressions of Object-Z with class feature references. Other aspects of type checking of Object-Z expressions and predicates are the same to that of Z expressions and predicates[6]. There are two typing rules for expressions with class feature references:

Let $r.op$ be an expression occurring in a class definition, where r is a constant or variable of the class, and op is an operation. We say that $r.op$ is *well-typed* if the following conditions are satisfied:

1. r is declared as an object instance of class C or of any of its subclasses -- as $r: C$ or $r: \downarrow C$,
2. $r: C$ or $r: \downarrow C$ is a *type correct* declaration, and
3. op is an operation defined in C.

Let $r.att$ be an expression occurring in a class definition, where r is a constant or variable of the class, and att is an attribute (a constant or state variable). We say that $r.att$ is *well-typed* and of type T if the following conditions are satisfied:

1. r is declared as an object instance of class C or of any of its subclasses -- as $r: C$ or $r: \downarrow C$,
2. C or $r: \downarrow C$ is a *type correct* declaration, and
3. att is an attribute of C and of declared type T.

4. FUTURE WORK

We have described type checking classes and object references of Object-Z specifications in this paper. We regard type consistency is an important aspect in improving the quality of specifications. This work is part of our effect towards quality formal specifications of software in general, and Object-Z specification in particular.

Future work based on this paper includes: (1) combining Z type checking with class type checking reported in this paper to achieve a unified type checking system for Object-Z, and (2) integrating type checking with other tools for analysing and reasoning Object-Z specification to provide a CASE tool for quality specification construction.

References

1. Barden, R., Stepney, S. and Cooper, D., "The Use of Z", in *Proc. of 6th Z User Workshop*, Nicholls, J.E. (ed.), Springer-Verlag, 1991, pages 99-124.
2. Carrington, D., Duke, D., Duke, R., King, P., Rose, G. and Smith, G., "Object-Z: An Object-oriented Extension to Z", in *Formal Description Techniques, II (FORTE'89)*, Vuong, S. (ed.), North-Holland, 1990, pages 281-296.
3. Chen, J. and Durnota, B., "Type Checking Object-Z Specifications", in preparation.
4. Craigen, D., Gerhart, S. and Ralston, T., *An International Survey of Industrial Applications of Formal Methods*, two volumes, U.S. Department of Commerce, MD 20899, 1993.
5. Duke, R., King, P., Rose, G. and Smith, G., "The Object-Z Specification Language - Version 1", Technical Report No. 91-1, Software Verification Research Centre, The University of Queensland, May 1991.
6. Reed, J.N. and Sinclair, J.E., "An Algorithm for Type-Checking Z", Technical Monograph RG-81, Oxford University, 1990.
7. Rose, G., "Object-Z", in *Object Orientation in Z*, Stepney, S., Barden, R. and Cooper, D. (eds.), Springer-Verlag, Chapter 6, 1992.
8. Spivey, J.M., *The Z Notation: A Reference Manual*, International Series in Computer Science, Prentice-Hall, 1989.
9. Weber-Wulff, D., "Selling Formal Methods to Industry", in *Proc. of FME'93: Industrial-Strength Formal Methods*, Woodcock, J.C.P. and Larsen, P.G. (eds.), LNCS 670, Springer-Verlag, 1993, pages 671-678.

16

An Axiom-Based Test Case Selection Strategy for Object-Oriented Programs*

T.H. Tse [a], F.T. Chan [b], H.Y. Chen [c]

[a] Department of Computer Science, the University of Hong Kong, Pokfulam Road, Hong Kong.
Email: tse@csd.hku.hk. Tel: (+852) 859 2183. Fax: (+852) 559 8447.

[b] School of Professional and Continuing Education, the University of Hong Kong, Pokfulam Road, Hong Kong.

[c] Department of Computer Science, the University of Hong Kong, Pokfulam Road, Hong Kong. (On leave from Jinan University, Guangzhou, China.)

Abstract

Because of the growing importance of object-oriented programming, a number of testing approaches have been proposed. Frankl et al. propose the application of the functional approach, using algebraic specifications for the generation of test cases and the validation of methods. Given a specification, Frankl et al. propose that equivalent terms should give observably equivalent objects, and offer general heuristics on the selection of equivalent terms for testing. Their guidelines, however, are only supported by limited empirical results, do not have a theoretical basis, and provide no guarantee of effectiveness.

In this paper, we define the concept of a fundamental pair as a pair of equivalent terms which are formed by replacing all the variables on both sides of an axiom by normal forms. We prove that an implementation is consistent with respect to all equivalent terms if and only if it is consistent with respect to all fundamental pairs. In other words, the testing coverage of fundamental pairs is identical to that of all equivalent terms, and hence we need only concentrate on the testing of fundamental pairs. Our strategy is mathematically based, simple, and much more efficient. Furthermore, it underscores the usefulness of axiom-based specifications.

Keyword Codes: D.2.1; D.2.5; D.1.5
Keywords: algebraic specifications, functional testing, object-oriented

1. INTRODUCTION

Object-oriented programming is considered as an increasingly popular software development method for the 1990s. Since testing is one of the most quality critical and time-consuming phases of the software development process, it is important to investigate into the testing of object-oriented programs. As indicated in [1], the important change from the testing of conventional programs to the testing of object-oriented programs is that the latter programs are not necessarily executed in a predefined order. The sequence of invocation of methods in a class is not specified explicitly.

---

* This research is supported in part by a Research and Conference Grant of the University of Hong Kong.

Operations are allowed to be called in any order once an object has been created. Methods across different classes can be combined in various ways. Furthermore, many new testing problems related to inheritance, polymorphism, overloading, encapsulation, aggregation, and state-dependent behavior have arisen [2]. It is generally accepted, therefore, that object-oriented program testing is quite different from the conventional counterpart.

A number of papers on the testing of object-oriented programs have been published [3–14]. Most of the papers discuss the nature of the problem and potential solutions, using approaches such as functional testing, structural testing [5,9], and state-based testing [13,14]. In particular, Frankl et al. [4,7,8] propose the application of the functional approach [15,16] (or black-box testing) to object-oriented programming. They propose the use of algebraic specifications both as a means of selecting test cases for objects and for validating the results of testing. Different test cases are generated from algebraic "terms" satisfying the axioms in the specification. A set of automatic tools have been developed integrating test case generation with the execution and verification of test results. Unfortunately, there is a fundamental problem in the theory behind the equivalence of terms, and the proposed heuristics for the selection of terms is only formulated from limited empirical results.

In this paper, we propose an improved theoretical foundation for Frankl's functional approach, and a more efficient strategy for selecting equivalent terms as test cases. Our strategy reduces the domain of test case selection from a polynomial function of the set of axioms to a linear function. On the other hand, we formally prove that the testing coverage is as good as that proposed by Frankl et al.

2. A SUMMARY OF FRANKL'S FUNCTIONAL TESTING APPROACH

In their functional testing approach, Frankl et al. use algebraic specifications [17–19] of abstract data types (ADTs) to specify classes in target programs. A series of operations on an ADT is known as a term (or called a "word" in Frankl et al.). Let u_1 and u_2 be two terms of an ADT. Let s_1 and s_2 be the respective sequences of operations in a given implementation. According to Frankl et al., one term is equivalent to another if and only if one can be transformed into the other using axioms as rewriting rules. The test suite (s_1, s_2) reveals an error of the implementation if u_1 is equivalent to u_2 but the operation sequences s_1 and s_2 produce observationally different objects.

Based on the above idea, Frankl et al. constructed a set of testing tools called ASTOOT. First of all, it accepts an algebraic specification and an implementation of the given class. It then accepts a term u_1, and generates an equivalent term u_2. Test drivers are created automatically by a driver generator to check and execute the operation sequences s_1 and s_2 corresponding to u_1 and u_2, respectively. Finally, the results of the executions of s_1 and s_2 are compared. If they do not give the same observational result, an error is found.

In Frankl's approach, test cases are generated by a compiler and a simplifier. The compiler translates the two sides of each axiom of an algebraic specification into a pair of ADT trees as a transformation rule. A conditional axiom in the specification will give rise to a branch in the ADT tree. The simplifier inputs an original term u_1 provided by the user, translates it into an ADT tree, and applies the transformation rules in the form of the pairs of ADT trees to obtain an equivalent term u_2.

Two important problems are raised: How do we select an original term to be input to the simplifier, and how do we select paths through the resulting ADT trees, in order to increase the likelihood of exposing errors? To explore these problems, Frankl et al. performed two case studies, testing erroneous implementations of priority queues and sorted lists. After running several thousand test cases, they recommended the following tentative guidelines on the generation of test cases:

(i) Select long original terms, with various ratios of different operations.

(ii) For the case of conditional axioms, choose a variety of parameters so that all possible paths in the ADT tree would be traversed.

3. EVALUATION OF FRANKL'S APPROACH

There are a number of merits in Frankl's functional approach and the associated tools:

(a) An integrated set of automatic tools are provided for test case generation, test driver generation, test execution, and test checking.

(b) After running a program with a test case, we must examine the result of execution against the specification of the program. This so called oracle problem is a major concern in program testing. The use of algebraic specifications is an elegant solution.

(c) Frankl's approach takes a suite of methods as a test case, instead of taking an individual method. This concept is especially useful in object-oriented programming, where the sequence of events does not depend on a predefined calling method but on a suite of messages passing among objects.

There are, however, some problems in Frankl's approach:

(i) The definition of the equivalence of terms has a fundamental problem. Consider, for example, the two terms *"([5] | [1] | [4] | [2]) . sorting"* and *"([4] | [5] | [2] | [1]) . sorting"* in a specification for bubble sort (see Example 1 in the next section). They are regarded by most people as equivalent, and they also produce equivalent results when implemented correctly. However, they cannot be transformed into one another by left-to-right rewriting rules. Furthermore, transformation using axioms as rewriting rules is uni-directional. Thus a term u_1 being equivalent to u_2 would imply that u_2 is not equivalent to u_1. Frankl's papers are based on this fallacious definition.

(ii) The guidelines on the selection of equivalent test cases are supported only by two empirical studies, do not have any theoretical basis, and hence provide no guarantee of effectiveness.

4. AN AXIOM-BASED STRATEGY FOR SELECTING EQUIVALENT TEST CASES

In this paper, we propose a simple mathematically-based strategy for selecting equivalent test cases.

An algebraic specification of ADTs consists of a syntax declaration and a semantic specification [18,19]. The syntax declaration lists the functions involved, plus their domains and co-domains, corresponding to the input and output variables of methods. The semantic specification consists of axioms which describe the behavioral properties of the functions. The following is an example of an algebraic specification. Bubble sort is chosen because it is familiar to most readers.

Example 1

object *BUBBLESORT* **is**
sorts *Bool Nat List*
inheriting *NAT*
operations
  nil : → *List*
  [_] : Nat → *List*
  sorted : List → *Bool*
  sorting : List → *List*
  _ |_ : List List → *List [associative identity: nil]*
variables
  N N' : Nat
  L L' : List
axioms
  nil . sorted → *true*
  [N] . sorted → *true*

([N] | [N'] | L) . sorted → *([N'] | L) . sorted* **and** *N <= N'*
nil . sorting → *nil*
[N] . sorting → *[N]*
L . sorting → *L* **if** *L . sorted*
(L | [N] | [N'] | L') . sorting → *(L | [N'] | [N] | L') . sorting* **if** *N' < N*
end

A list of functions on an ADT is called a *term* if and only if it conforms to the standard syntax requirements of term algebra [17, 18]. A term can be transformed into another using the axioms of the specification as progressive left-to-right rewriting rules. A term is said to be in *normal form* if and only if no further axiom is applicable. A system of axioms is said to be *canonical* if and only if every sequence of rewriting on the same ground term (that is, a term without variables) eventually reaches a unique normal form, independent of the choice and sequence of rewriting rules used. Thus, any consistent specification should be canonical.

The following is an improved version of the concept of equivalence:

Definition 4.1: Two terms u_1 and u_2 are said to be *equivalent* (denoted by $u_1 \sim u_2$) if and only if both of them can be transformed by canonical axioms into the same normal form.

For instance, the terms *"([5] | [1] | [4] | [2]) . sorting"* and *"([4] | [5] | [2] | [1]) . sorting"* of Example 1 are equivalent because they can both be transformed into the same normal form *[1] | [2] | [4] | [5]*.

Furthermore, we would like to introduce a new concept in our paper:

Definition 4.2: Given a canonical system of axioms, a pair of equivalent terms, formed by replacing all the variables on both sides of an axiom by normal forms, is called a *fundamental pair* induced from the axiom.

The following two definitions are adapted from Frankl for completeness:

Definition 4.3: Given a canonical system of axioms, the series of methods corresponding to the functions in a term is called a sequence of operations corresponding to the term. Two such sequences s_1 and s_2 are *equivalent* (denoted by $s_1 \approx s_2$) if and only if their operations on the same object give observationally equivalent results.

Definition 4.4: An implementation Ψ, which maps ADTs and functions of a canonical specification to classes and methods in a programming language, is said to be *consistent with respect to* the equivalent terms $u_1 \sim u_2$ if and only if the corresponding sequences of operations satisfy $\Psi(u_1) \approx \Psi(u_2)$.

Having defined the fundamental concepts, we recommend a strategy for test case selection: in order to test whether an implementation is consistent with respect to equivalent terms, we need only test fundamental pairs. The testing coverage of fundamental pairs is the same as that of equivalent terms. In other words, any error revealable by equivalent terms can be revealed by some fundamental pair.

For instance, in Example 1, we need only test fundamental pairs such as

([5] | [6] | [3] | [1] | [7] | [9]) . sorting ~ *([5] | [6] | [1] | [3] | [7] | [9]) . sorting*
and *([1] | [3] | [5] | [6] | [7] | [9]) . sorting* ~ *[1] | [3] | [5] | [6] | [7] | [9]*.

We need not test other equivalent pairs such as

([6] | [5] | [3] | [1] | [9] | [7]) . sorting ~ *[1] | [3] | [5] | [6] | [7] | [9]*
or *(([6] | [5]) . sorting | ([3] | [1]) . sorting | ([9] | [7]) . sorting) . sorting* ~
([5] | [6] | [3] | [1] | [7] | [9]) . sorting.

Our strategy has a sound mathematical foundation, simple, and efficient. The testing coverage claim is based on Theorem 4.6 below. The following lemma is required in proving the theorem.

Lemma 4.5: Given a canonical specification, any term u_1 which is not in normal form can be transformed into a unique normal form u_0 via a series of axioms $a_1, a_2, \ldots, a_k$:

$$u_1 \xrightarrow{a_1} u_2 \xrightarrow{a_2} u_3 \xrightarrow{a_3} \dots \xrightarrow{a_{k-1}} u_k \xrightarrow{a_k} u_0$$

such that all the binding variables involved with each step of the transformation are in normal forms.

For example, the term *"([5] / [1] / [4] / [2]) . sorting"* of BUBBLESORT in Example 1 can be transformed into its normal form *[1] / [2] / [4] / [5]* as follows:

([5] / [1] / [4] / [2]) . sorting
→ *([5] / [1] / [2] / [4]) . sorting* {using the last axiom with L = [5] | [1], N = [4], N' = [2], L' = nil}
→ *([1] / [5] / [2] / [4]) . sorting*
→ *([1] / [2] / [5] / [4]) . sorting*
→ *([1] / [2] / [4] / [5]) . sorting*
→ *[1] / [2] / [4] / [5]* {using the second last axiom}

The proof of the general case is straightforward.

Theorem 4.6: For a given canonical specification, an implementation is consistent with respect to all equivalent terms if and only if it is consistent with respect to all fundamental pairs.

Proof of Theorem 4.6: Obviously if an implementation is consistent with respect to all equivalent terms, then it is consistent with respect to all fundamental pairs.

On the contrary, assume that an implementation is consistent with respect to all fundamental pairs. Let $u_1 \sim u_2$ be any two equivalent terms. Suppose the mapping Ψ denotes the implementation, and suppose $\Psi(u_1)=s_1$ and $\Psi(u_2)=s_2$. We would like to prove that $s_1 \approx s_2$.

By Definition 4.1, u_1 and u_2 can be transformed into the same normal form u_0. Then, there exists a series of axioms $a_1, a_2, \dots, a_k$:

$$u_1 \xrightarrow{a_1} u_{12} \xrightarrow{a_2} u_{13} \xrightarrow{a_3} \dots \xrightarrow{a_{k-1}} u_{1k} \xrightarrow{a_k} u_0$$

satisfying Lemma 4.5.

Let $\Psi(u_{1j})=s_{1j}$ $(j=2,\dots,k)$ and $\Psi(u_0)=s_0$.

Suppose (without loss of generality) that *

(1) $u_1 = f_0(A_0).f_1(A_1) \dots f_i(A_i).f_{i+1}(A_{i+1}) \dots f_t(A_t)$
where A_j is either null or a tuple of parameters, containing only ground terms,

(2) a_1 is $O_x.f_1(X_1)\dots f_i(X_i) \rightarrow O_x.g_1(Y_1) \dots g_j(Y_j)$
where O_x is null or an object variable, $X_2, \dots, X_i, Y_1, \dots, Y_j$ are either null or tuples of parameters containing variables and/or ground terms.

Then

$$u_{12} = f_0(A_0).g_1(B_1) \dots g_j(B_j).f_{i+1}(A_{i+1}) \dots f_t(A_t)$$
$$s_1 = \Psi(f_0(A_0)).\Psi(f_1(A_1)) \dots \Psi(f_i(A_i)).\Psi(f_{i+1}(A_{i+1})) \dots \Psi(f_t(A_t))$$
$$s_{12} = \Psi(f_0(A_0)).\Psi(g_1(B_1)) \dots \Psi(g_j(B_j)).\Psi(f_{i+1}(A_{i+1})) \dots \Psi(f_t(A_t))$$

Since the series of axioms $a_1, \dots, a_k$ satisfies Lemma 4.5,

---

* Consider, for example, the class of stacks. Suppose u_1 in (1) is *new . push(4) . pop . push(2)*. Then $f_0(A_0)$ = *new*, $f_1(A_1)$ = *push(4)*, $f_2(A_2)$ = *pop*, $f_3(A_3)$ = *push(2)*. Suppose a_1 in (2) is O_X . *push(I) . pop* → O_X. Then O_X matches *new*, *push(I)* matches *push(4)*, and *pop* matches *pop*. Hence, u_{12} = *new . push(2)*.

$f_0(A_0).f_1(A_1)...f_i(A_i) \sim f_0(A_0).g_1(B_1) \ldots g_j(B_j)$

is a fundamental pair induced from a_1. According to the assumption that the implementation is correct with respect to all fundamental pairs, we have

$$\Psi(f_0(A_0)).\Psi(f_1(A_1)) \ldots \Psi(f_i(A_i)) \approx \Psi(f_0(A_0)).\Psi(g_1(B_1)) \ldots \Psi(g_j(B_j)).$$

Thus,

$$\Psi(f_0(A_0)).\Psi(f_1(A_1)) \ldots \Psi(f_i(A_i)).\Psi(f_{i+1}(A_{i+1})) \ldots \Psi(f_t(A_t))$$
$$\approx \Psi(f_0(A_0)).\Psi(g_1(B_1)) \ldots \Psi(g_j(B_j)).\Psi(f_{i+1}(A_{i+1})) \ldots \Psi(f_t(A_t))$$

i.e., $s_1 \approx s_{12}$. By the same argument, $s_{12} \approx s_{13} \approx \ldots \approx s_{1k} \approx s_0$. Therefore, $s_1 \approx s_0$.

Similarly we can prove that $s_2 \approx s_0$. Hence $s_1 \approx s_2$.

5. CONTRIBUTIONS OF OUR STRATEGY

Compared with Frankl's guidelines for selecting equivalent test cases, our strategy has the following advantages:

(a) Our strategy is based on a sound theoretical foundation and mathematical proof.

(b) The domain of test case selection in Frankl's guidelines is the whole set of all pairs of equivalent terms, but the domain of selection in our strategy is only the set of fundamental pairs induced from the axioms. The original domain is a polynomial function of the set of axioms, whereas the proposed domain is only a linear function of the set. Although our domain of selection is much less than that of Frankl's, our testing coverage is the same. Hence our strategy is more efficient. Furthermore, our strategy is more precise than Frankl's guidelines, and hence easier to be performed.

(c) Our recommendation is very natural since experienced implementors would start their tests with fundamental pairs even in the absence of formal theory. Our strategy simply says that when implementors are satisfied with the test results with respect to fundamental pairs, they do not need to test other equivalent terms.

(d) Given an original term u_1, Frankl's approach searches and reduces an ADT tree to generate a term u_2 such that $u_1 \sim u_2$. "The size of the tree may be exponential in the size of the initial sequence. To deal with this complexity, the simplifier can operate either in batch mode, which builds the entire tree, or in interactive mode, which allows the user to selectively guide the construction of a subtree." [7] The interactive method can only give partial solution, whereas the batch method simply hides the complexity problem from the user. Our strategy avoids the complexity problem entirely by generating equivalent test cases directly from the two sides of each axiom, rather than searching and reducing the ADT trees.

(e) Using our strategy, two of Frankl's tools, the compiler and simplifier, can be replaced by a simple generator which induces equivalent test cases directly from the two sides of each axiom. This will greatly simplify the system.

6. CONCLUSION

In this paper, we take a fresh look at Frankl's functional approach for the testing of object-oriented programs. We find that, although the approach has many general merits, it is based on a fallacious foundation, and the heuristics for the selection of equivalent test cases are supported only by two empirical studies. Hence the correctness and effectiveness of the guidelines are not guaranteed. We define the concept of a fundamental pair as a pair of equivalent terms which are formed by replacing all the variables on both sides of an axiom by normal forms. We prove that an implementation is consistent with respect to all equivalent terms if and only if it is consistent with respect to all fundamental pairs. In other words, the testing coverage of fundamental pairs is identical to that of all equivalent terms, and hence we need only concentrate on the testing of fundamental pairs. We have reduced the domain of test cases from a polynomial function of the set of axioms to a linear function. Our strategy is mathematically based, simple, and much more efficient. Furthermore, it underscores the usefulness of axiom-based specifications.

We note that there may be infinitely many fundamental pairs induced from the same axiom by assigning different normal forms to the variables. Exhaustive testing is of course impossible. How should we select the fundamental pairs, and how does the selection affect the testing coverage? How do we verify whether two resulting objects are observationally equivalent? We are investigating into the application of regularity and uniformity hypotheses as proposed in [15,16] to further enhance our strategy.

REFERENCES

1. SMITH, M.D. and ROBSON, D.J.: 'A framework for testing object-oriented programs', *Journal of Object-Oriented Programming,* 1992, 5 (3): pp.45-53.
2. KUNG, C.H., GAO, J., HSIA, P., LIN, J. and TOYOSHIMA, Y.: 'Design recovery for software testing of object-oriented programs', *Proc. IEEE Workshop on Reverse Engineering,* IEEE Computer Society, Los Alamitos, California, 1993.
3. CHEATHAM, T.J. and MELLINGER, L.: 'Testing object-oriented software systems', *Proc. 18th ACM Computer Science Conference (CSC '90),* ACM Press, New York, 1990, pp. 161-165.
4. DOONG, R.-K. and FRANKL, P.G.: 'Case studies on testing object-oriented programs', *Proc. 4th ACM Annual Symposium on Software Testing, Analysis, and Verification (TAV 4),* ACM Software Engineering Notes, 1991, pp. 165-177.
5. FIEDLER, S.P.: 'Object-oriented unit testing', *Hewlett-Packard Journal,* 1989, 40 (4): pp.69-74.
6. FIRESMITH, D.G.: 'Testing object-oriented software', in *Technology of Object-Oriented Languages and Systems: Proceedings of 11th International Conference (TOOLS 11),* Prentice-Hall, Englewood Cliffs, New Jersey, 1993, pp. 407-426.
7. FRANKL, P.G. and DOONG, R.-K.: 'Tools for testing object-oriented programs', *Proc. 8th Pacific Northwest Conference on Software Quality,* 1990, pp. 309-324.
8. FRANKL, P.G.: 'A framework for testing object-oriented programs', *Computer Science Technical Report PUCS-105-91,* Department of Electrical Engineering and Computer Science, Polytechnic University, Brooklin, New York, 1991.
9. HARROLD, M.J., MCGREGOR, J.D. and FITZPATRICK, K.J.: 'Incremental testing of object-oriented class structures', *Proc. 14th IEEE International Conference on Software Engineering,* IEEE Computer Society, Los Alamitos, California, 1992, pp. 68-80.
10. HOFFMAN, D.M. and STROOPER, P.A.: 'Graph-based class testing', *Proc. 7th Australian Software Engineering Conference (ASWEC '93),* Australian Computer Society, 1993.
11. PERRY, D.E. and KAISER, G.E.: 'Adequate testing and object-oriented programming', *Journal of Object-Oriented Programming,* 1990, 3 (5): pp.13-19.
12. SMITH, M.D. and ROBSON, D.J.: 'Object-oriented programming: the problems of validation', *Proc. 6th International Conference on Software Maintenance,* IEEE Computer Society, Los Alamitos, California, 1990, pp. 272-282.
13. TURNER, C.D. and ROBSON, D.J.: 'State-based testing and inheritance', Technical Report TR-1/93, Computer Science Division, School of Engineering and Computer Science, University of Durham, Durham, UK, 1993.

14. TURNER, C.D. and ROBSON, D.J.: 'Guidance for the testing of object-oriented programs', Technical Report TR-2/93, Computer Science Division, School of Engineering and Computer Science, University of Durham, Durham, UK, 1993.
15. BOUGE, L., CHOGUET, N., FRIBOURG, L. and GAUDEL, M.-C.: 'Test sets generation from algebraic specifications using logic programming', *Journal of Systems and Software*, 1986, 6: pp.343-360.
16. BERNOT, G., GAUDEL, M.-C. and MARRE, B.: 'Software testing based on formal specifications: a theory and a tool', *Software Engineering Journal*, 1991, 6 (6): pp.387-405.
17. EHRIG, H. and MAHR, B.: 'Fundamentals of Algebraic Specifications 1: Equations and Initial Semantics', *EATCS Monographs on Theoretical Computer Science*, 1985, Vol. 6, Springer-Verlag, Berlin.
18. GOGUEN, J.A., THATCHER, J.W. and WAGNER, E.G.: 'An initial algebra approach to specification, correctness and implementation of abstract data types', in *Current Trends in Programming Methodology*, Vol. IV: *Data Structuring*, R.T. Yeh (ed.), Prentice-Hall, Englewood Cliffs, New Jersey, 1978, pp. 80-149.
19. GOGUEN, J.A., WINKLER, T., MESEGUER, J., FUTATSUGI, K. and JOUANNAUD, J.-P.: 'Introducing OBJ3', in *Applications of Algebraic Specification using OBJ*, J.A. Goguen, D. Coleman, and R.M. Gallimore (eds.), Cambridge University Press, Cambridge, 1993.

Notice that a conditional axiom will generate several different fundamental pairs corresponding to different conditions. For instance, in the last axiom of Example 1,

$$L \,/\, [N] \,/\, [N'] \,/\, L'\,.\,sorting \;\rightarrow\; \textbf{if } L \,/\, [N] \,/\, [N'] \,/\, L'\,.\,sorted \textbf{ then } L \,/\, [N] \,/\, [N'] \,/\, L' \;\textbf{ else if } N' < N \textbf{ then } L \,/\, [N'] \,/\, [N] \,/\, L'\,.\,sorting$$

if we take L = [1], N = 3, N' = 5, L' = [7], then we obtain the fundamental pair:

$$[1] \,/\, [3] \,/\, [5] \,/\, [7]\,.\,sorting \;\sim\; [1] \,/\, [3] \,/\, [5] \,/\, [7]$$

On the other hand, if we take L = [5], N = 3, N' = 1, L' = [7], we obtain another pair:

$$[5] \,/\, [3] \,/\, [1] \,/\, [7]\,.\,sorting \;\sim\; [5] \,/\, [1] \,/\, [3] \,/\, [7]\,.\,sorting$$

17

AMI: A Case Tool based on Artificial Intelligence Techniques for an Interactive Modelling for Analysis.

L. LASOUDRIS[a] and M. MAURICE-DEMOURIOUX[a,b] and R. VOYER[c]

[a]Institut National des Télécommunications 9, rue charles Fourier - 91011 EVRY - FRANCE
E-mail: lasoudri@galaxie.int-evry.fr
[b]LAMSADE - Université Paris IX Place du Maréchal de Lathre de Tassigny - 75775 Paris Cedex 16 - FRANCE
[c]LAFORIA - IBP - U. Paris VI Tour 46-00 - 2ème étage - 4, place Jussieu - 75252 Paris Cedex 05 - FRANCE

Abstract

Today, CASE (Computer Aided Software Engineering) tools functionalities give some help in data and process description (mainly in managing the results of analysis). They do not help with efficiency in analysis and design process. Our model brings some aid in O.M.T. (Object Modelling Techniques from Rumbaugh) modelling processing.

AMI uses: Model examples (schema) base, Pattern examples (generic modelling structures of business area) and Generic business area knowledge. AMI allows software analyst or designer both to refine description concepts which is a schema part beeing in progress, and to extend concepts by interpretation of a business area words lattice. AMI implementation uses an A.I. technique: Case-Based-Reasoning (CBR). CBR is very interesting by increasing ability in reasoning activity. In CBR system searches of cases are mainly based on terminology indexing. Indexation system does not allow sufficiently semantical expression. In our area we need more. So we choose for AMI a conceptual graph. In fact, subsumption links and matching possibilities between conceptual graphs allow us to compare different abstraction levels and to realize selective searches for graph verifying some properties.

Today, the implementation of this tool with Smalltalk-80 and its environment VisualWorks is in progress.

Keyword Codes: D.2.1; D.2.2; I.2.4
Keywords: Software, Software Engineering, Requirements Specifications; Tools and Techniques; Computing Methodologies, Artificial Intelligence, Knowledge Representation

1. INTRODUCTION

Modelling activity is the main analysis task in software engineering. Efficiency and quality in modelling activity are two principal criterias for software engineering analysis activity. Using knowledge bringing by previous stored models, works efficiently in modelling tasks. It consists of being able to reuse models or model extracts and to adapt them if it is necessary to satisfy a new analyst need. But, in most cases, it is very difficult to realize a matching between needs expression and previous models. Nowadays in this area, CASE tools "never solve" this problem. So this problem must be solved by the analyst. In this paper, we propose an interactive resolution method using Artificial Intelligence techniques and methods which helps analyst.

In a first part, we present the notion of model as it is used in analysis phase. In a second part, we present modelling process problem in this phase and its limits. We present the main tasks which make problem for the analyst. Then we will show reuse defined in a tool is a good solution to solve this problem. But reuse alone is not sufficient, it must be completed by a concepts emergence techniques. So, we note the state of art in first tools and in second in researches. The last part, before conclusion, presents a tool named AMI, which is in progress in our laboratory.

2.MODEL NOTION

Software life cycle could be decomposed in three phases: requirements/analysis, design and implementation.

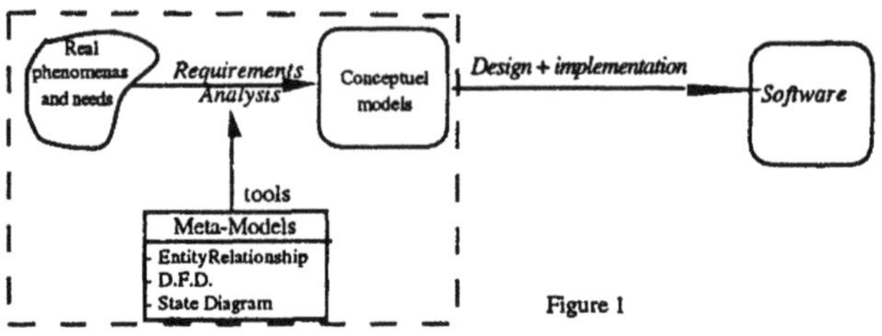

Figure 1

Our paper is relative to requirements/analysis phase (this part corresponds to concepts included in dotted line rectangle, cf. figure 1.).

Software engineering uses model during all phases of its life cycle especially in analysis requirement phase. A model is a particular aspect conceptualization of a system (data, function, behavior). In litterature, the term of model (or diagram, schemata) is used indifferently to designate modelling language or object of this modelization. In this paper, we will use "meta-model" to designate the language and "model" to designate the result of the analysis phase.

Using meta-model leads to a better comprehension of requirements/analysis problem. More, modelling task increases communication between project actors.

Software engineering methods like O.M.T. [1], O.O.A [2], MERISE [3] or OOSA [4, 5] propose specific models, which could be classify according to three types: Entity/Relationship, Data Flow Diagram (D.F.D.) and State Diagram.

In this paper, we will use Object Modelling Techniques (OMT) to illustrate our ideas. For example, OMT suggests to use:

- An "information model", which looks like an extended entity/relationship model with encapsulation of object behavior.
- A classical data flow diagram which illustrates system works.
- A state diagram which describes for a class, possible states and transition states for objects.

3. MODELLING PROCESS PROBLEM IN ANALYSIS PHASE

Existing methods do not well helping during the analyst process. In fact, the reasoning by which we abstract requirements expression to give rise to relevant elements is not well known and not often formalized.

Modelling process is divided, in a company, in several complementary subsets of projects. This leads to analysis models which could be semantically redundant in an unwishing manner (homonymy, synonymy, ...). Company must assure and preserve coherence, non redundancy, and utility of modelized knowledge, especially during new models creation. For these reasons, we propose to use a reuse function.

3.1. It Is a Must To Help Model Components Emergence Process

Modelling process is creative. It is an expert work. Methods using specific meta-model give concepts which must be modelized, and the associated formalism. Nevertheless, they indicate just a little how to realize concepts emergence.

We think that it is necessary:

- to better understand concepts emergence process in requirements/analysis phase
- to know what are indispensable knowledges to realize this emergence.
- to know how this knowledge should be formalized.

We think that this type of formalization is necessary for developping active and intelligent software tools. These tools must be able to help analyst in concepts emergence process.

Today, CASE (Computer Aided Software Engineering) Tools are only able to manage models. They help in model entry using graphic interfaces, storing them into databases, validating and documenting them. They do not help (or a little) in the modelling process because they do not well reuse previous models.

3.2. It Is a Must To Reuse Existing Models or Components of Existing Models

Company view: Set of knowledge bringing by different types of models (data, function, behavior) is the memory structure of a company.

Semantic wealth and precision expressed by models allow a good understanding and communication between actors in a company and consequently reuse of model components is facilitated. In fact, there is an overlapping betwwen concepts using in different models.

Company wishes that coherence, non redundancy, relevance of modelling knowledge are ensured, in particular when new models are elaborated. Consequently, we have to propose an efficiency reuse function which allows analyst to use an adapted structure for new redefined knowledge.

Analyst view: Analyst wishes to work with an existing model then adapts it. He works using existing patterns or model examples and transforms them to reached his specific needs. Then, he gains time in modelling tasks.

4. REUSE

Our goal is to help analyst in his tasks which make problems for him [6].

The first task for which it seems to be helpful to bring an aid is the models storing and researching. This function requires a tool which allows reuse.

Modelization art is complex, analyst needs are very difficult to define. It is also an area in which creativity is very important. So,it seems to be judicious that our tool allows reuse, brings also an help in emergence and definition of analyst needs.

4.1. A Tool Allowing Reuse

Making reuse facility requires to have got a models base, a searching module for picking models or models components which are exactly or closely a response to specific needs for the new model to be built. This latter case requires an adaptation module.

We have to integrate new models (and knowledge they are bringing with) in existing models bases. We must do this integration without forgotten this simple idea "they will be reused later".

These indispensable functionnalities in a tool which allowed reusing models require a high semantic content (specific knowledge). In fact, this tool must have two types of knowledge.

1. Knowledge on existing models components, on reference area, on used meta-model.
2. Knowledge which makes easier models search and capture and which facilitates their adaptation according to expressed needs.

We are seemed to determine necessary knowledge to realize these functionnalities, and in which manner this knowledge should be formalized and manipulated.

4.2. A Tool Which Facilitate Concepts Emergence

Tool must allowed needs expression and understanding. Existing methods do not work totally for the modelling process. Through a specific meta-model, they indicate concepts to be emerged. In fact the reasoning by which people is able to abstract from needs expression the necessary model elements is unwellknown and few or not formalized. Modelling process requires creativity and expertise.

It seems us that it is necessary to have a better understanding of concepts emergence process in analysis phase, to know what is the necessary knowledge which allowed this emergence and in which manner this knowledge should be formalized.

We think that this formalization is necessary for intelligent active software tools development. These tools will be able to help the analyst in concepts emergence process

Help could be bring on two levels:

First level. Analyst must be allowed to formulate information needs (model or component model) by the mean of a query. As far as possible, analyst must express his need with its own terms (its own words) and its own structure (semantic links between concepts of his query). Tool must detect ambiguities into the query, then it must help analyst, according to his wishes, to remove these ambiguities.

Moreover if there is any model in the base which do not satisfy sufficiently the query, the tool could used knowledge about business area to reformulate initial query in terms closed to initial terms (synonym, specialized, generalized, analogous terms, evocated ideas, connected terms, ...).

Second level. Results produced are model extracts which satisfy the expressed needs. Moreover, the obtention of the environment (in model terms) of the results allows an analyst increased thinking and new ideas emergence.

As far as we know, concepts emergence as it is presented in this paper is not integrated into present solutions or tools. There is only some reuse which was made in use.

5. PRESENT TOOLS FOR MODELLING HELP

Present CASE Tools are models manager: they help in getting models using useful graphics interfaces, in storing them in a database, in validating and documenting them They do not well work in producing models because they do not sufficiently integrated necessary knowledge about modelsl extracts emergence.

Present CASE query languages [ERQL (Entity/Relationship Query Langugaes: Gamma International) or GQL (GraphTalk Query Language: Parralax)] allow access to data in repository. The repository is structured on a meta-model composed with segments which concepts of a specific method (Merise [3]) or concepts built before by analyst. Repository is instantiated with model datas described by analyst.

Query languages allow to structure the query around variables defined in meta-model and profit of the advantage of standard functions like count, min, max and so on. Query variables could be parametrized. GraphTalk (Parallax) furnishes some predefined functions which could be utilized in C programs interfacing the GraphTalk tool (links between objects list, model objects list, ...).

The advantages of these tools

These tools allow us to obtain existing models extracts. So it is possible for the analyst to reuse them, and to document applications.

The drawbacks of these tools

It is necessary to well know the model structure to obtain a model extract. In some cases, people must know value of variables to find instantiated concept meta-model.

There is no possibility to look for a component with neither synonym nor evocation links. In others words, search may be efficiency only if the analyst well-knows existing stored models. Queries give model extracts in textual form and not in the form which is associated with the specific meta-model.

6. PRESENT RESEARCH IN MODELLING HELP

Research works show that models reuse process requires to abstract and to structure knowledge stored into them.

The principle is: first take account of model construction process is only possible if modelling tasks and scheduling of process are formalized. This requires that modelling tasks could lie on generic modelling structure. These structures must be independant of specific applications, so they could be reused in many modelling tasks. In others words, their assumptions are that there are many phenomenas which could be modelized by identical structures. Specific model could be built by instanciation of generic structures [7, 8].

The drawback of this approach is the necessity to a-priori build a set of knowledges (generic structures) allowing a large covering of analysis modelling tasks. This approach seems to be difficult taking account of the great number of possible generic structures and the difficulty to find them (choice among abstraction levels and classication criterias).

7. MAIN CARACTERISTICS OF "AMI"

AMI system is a tool which brings help in business application analysis. It is based on the reuse notion of models examples, models patterns, and domain predefined generic knowledge.

An example is a previous existing and validating model (OMT model) or model extract.

A pattern is a stable instanciable generic modelling structure. This concept is based on concepts like Frames [9].

Domain generic knowledges are formalized in a terms conceptual graph (which is named domain graph in the continuation of the paper), which use allows concepts emergence as it is presented in 4-2 paragraph. Links typology induces a specific semantic interpretation. Conceptual graphs are initially developped to represent semantic expressed by natural language. Based on semantic nets, they are used for concepts representation like object, action, activity, event, links (between these OMT concepts). In a formal point of view, a conceptual graph is a bipart graph composed with two types of nodes: concepts nodes and relationships nodes.

AMI helps analyst in refining or extending model part using domain graph interpretation.

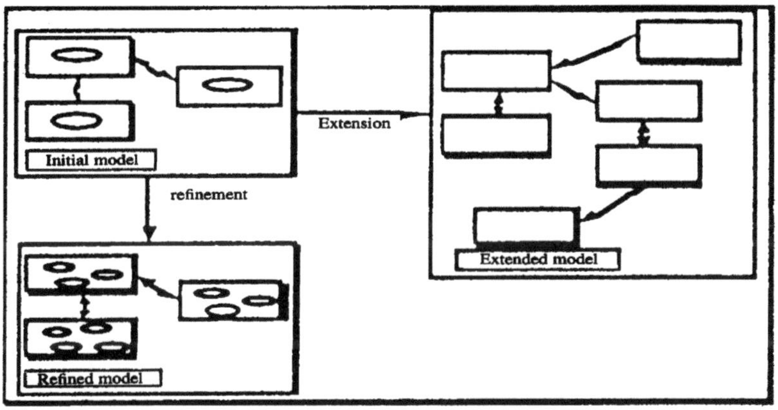

Today, the implementation of this tool with Smalltalk-80 and its environment VisualWorks [10] is in progress.

7.1. Logical Architecture

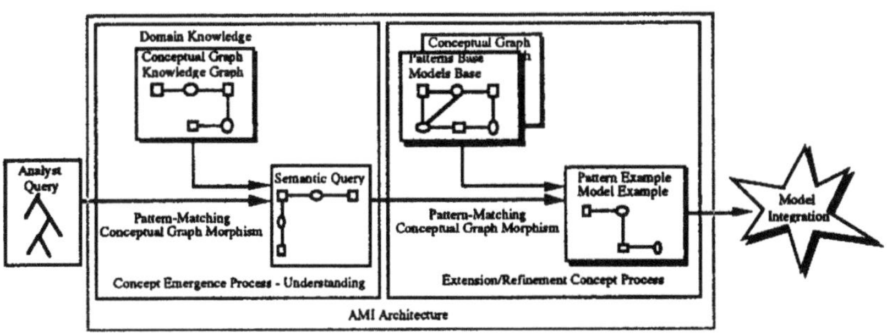

Make use of modelling help is based on case based reasoning (CBR) technics ([11], [6], [12]) and information search [13] and it is done with two phases:

Understanding: It is realized by a flexible, interactive, gradual search in such manner that analyst need formulation progresses step by step. Specified need may be reformulated in interactive manner using knowledge graph. The goal is to obtain a non ambiguous semantic query according to analyst real need.

We could distinguish in conceptual graph several links types: generalization/specialization links, synonymous links, ideas evocation links or closed terms (group terms). Knowledge graph structure is based on the idea of thesaurus in documentation databases area (*Roget's International Thesauraus* and *Webster's 9th New Collegiate Dictionary*).

Matching: Model construction induces an interpretation of its meaning. Matching allowed to select models (or model extracts) not only exclusively those which respond exactly to need expression but also those closed with needs expression.

Matching modules try to satisfy analyst needs just as it is expressed in query, then to compare it with previous stored models examples or patterns.

Matching module quality is associated to model internal representation techniques, to query expression quality, and to matching methods between these two knowledge types.

These latters use indexing and matching functions. They also use strategies: for examples: what we have to do for reducing solutions number if it is necessary, or if we do not find any solutions. Must we have to explicitly and/or implicitly reformulate the query or to build a more generic query ?

By reconstruction of Conceptual Graphs (CG) [14] in terms of more basic "knowledge graphs" [15], we use standard pattern matching techniques [16] for implementing several aspects of the CG theory. In fact, the fundamental CG projection, which determines the specialization/generalization relations between CG, is expressed in terms of pattern matching. So, we can easily modified and/or extended our model since its implementation is fully described by patterns [17]. As a result, this approach improves both the quality of the concept emergence process and the efficiency of the retrieving of model examples and pattern examples.

7.2. Scenarios For Using AMI

It is possible to use AMI at different conception levels. It helps analyst in two tasks. We describe for each of them the using mode of AMI

7.2.1. Help For Definition Concept Phase (refinement)

This phase is composed with four steps which are strictly sequential:

a. **Process Initialization.** This step aims to collect and structure initial term from which analyst wishes an help. Recognition is lexical recognition with a terms dictionnary.

b. **Related Ideas Evocation.** From a recognized term, AMI, using domain terms stored in conceptual graph, proposes main entities closed directly to initial term. We name this entities: ideas. Analyst select one main idea among the proposed ideas.

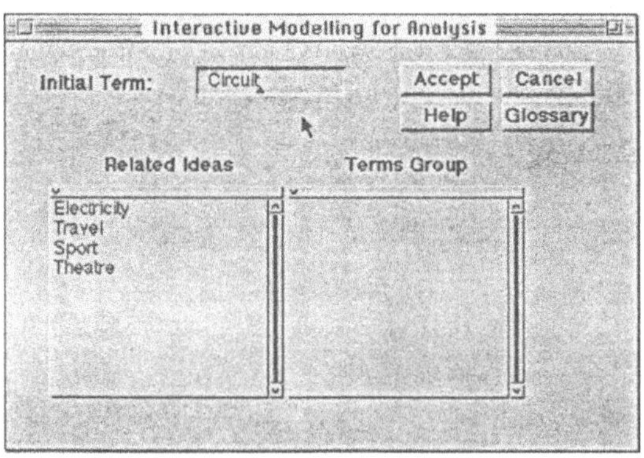

c. **Main Ideas Selection.** Once a main idea is selected, AMI proposes a set of terms synonymous of the initial term.

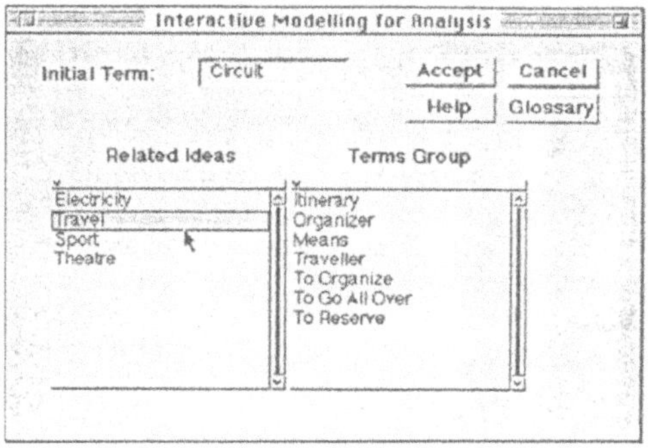

d. **Concept description.** Once a key concept is selected, AMI proposes a pattern (structural description) and/or examples (models extracts of different nature : data, behaviour, functional).

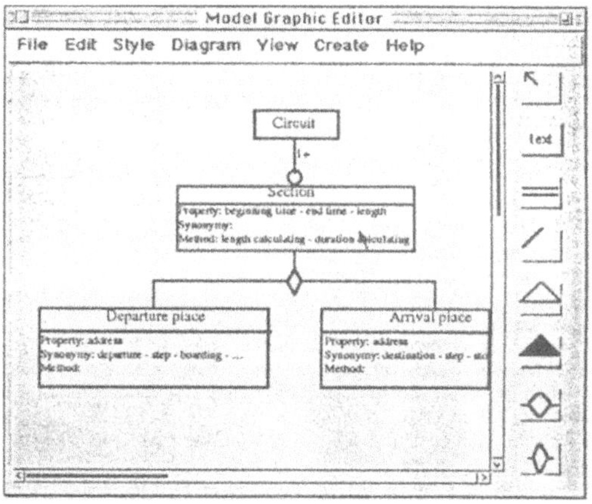

In accordance with selected principles, ideas and concepts evocation phases may be more or less complicated. In fact, it is simple terms equality or at the contrary conceptual graph morphisms.

7.2.2. Help For Concept Extension Phase

From same structure and same conceptual graph, the concept extension phase is equivalent to concept refinement phase described before.

This phase is composed with four steps which are strictly sequential:

a. **Process initialization. (ie 7.2.1)**

b. **Related ideas evocation.(ie 7.2.1)**

c. **Annex concepts evocation.** Once a main idea is selected, AMI proposes a set of group terms obtained from the main idea selected. A group term is obtained using a link from term idea. Then analyst selects the link he wishes to explore.

d. **Concept extension.** Once a key concept is selected, AMI goes through process and sets analyst in concept definition phase.

Now, we have to explicite a scenario using a leisure area example.

7.3. Scenario Example: Help For Concept Extension Phase

Process initialization: Analyst modelizes the concept of "circuit" and looks for defining its modelling environment.
Related ideas evocation: Ideas evocation is done by searching through domain graph.
Annex concepts evocation: From ideas evocation links AMI delivers groups-terms.
Concept extension: From "organize and program" group term AMI proposes to analyst one of the terms of the groups. So it delivers as a result a set of examples and/or a pattern representing the selected term if it is possible. If not, AMI proposes one or several examples and/or pattern relative to others terms of the same group terms.

8. CONCLUSION

In software "requirements/analysis" process, recent tools do not make easy and efficiency previous models reuse. Our tool AMI based on Case Based Reasoning, Production System, Conceptual Graph and Semantic pattern make easy and efficiency Reuse in analysis phase. AMI allows analyst to reuse previous models, or to reuse stable pattern delivered from an analyst query. These queries are matching, by using a production system, to conceptual graph which represents associated knowledge domain. This knowledge is very efficiency because it uses not only synonymous terms but also "generalized/specialized" and analogous terms, evocated ideas, evocated terms. So AMI is able to deliver model or model extract after refinement or extension from an initial term that analyst tries to modelize.

Our future works is both to increase pattern semantic and to adjust thesaurus represented by conceptual graph. Others works should be desirable like different points of view on models, knowledges, coherence, integration of views and so on.

REFERENCES

1. RUMBAUGH Object modeling techniques Prentice Hall 1991
2. COAD and YOURDON, Object-Oriented Analysis ; Prentice Hall International - 1991
3. TARDIEU, ROCHEFELD, COLLETI, (in French) MERISE, Démarche et pratiques ; Edition d'Organisation - 1985
4. SCHLAER and MELLOR, Modelling the world with data ; Yourdon Press - 1991
5. SCHLAER and MELLOR, Modelling the world with states ; Yourdon Press - 1992
6. KOLODNER, Improving human decision making through case-based decision aiding AI Magazine, Vol 12, n°2
7. GROSZ, (in French) Formalisation des connaissances réutilisables pour la conception de systèmes d'information, Thèse de doctorat de l'université de Paris VI - 1991
8. NGUYEN, Un catalogue de type de relation: Une approche sémantique pour la conception dans un formalisme entité-relation étendu, Congrès INFORSID 91 - Paris.
9. MINSKY, A Framework for Representing Knowledge, The Psychology of Computer Vision, pp211-277 ; P. H. Winston Ed., Mc GrawHill - 1975
10. PARCPLACE. "VisualWorks: Reviewer's Guide - release 1". ParcPlace Systems, Inc. 1992.
11. BAREISS, Exemplar-Based Knowledge Acquisition : a Unified Approach to Concept Representation, Classification and Learning ; Boston : Academic
12. SLADE, Case-Based Reasonning : a Research Paradigm ; AI Magazine 12(1) : 42-55
13. Van RIJSBERGEN, A new theorical framework for Information Retrieval, proc. of the ACM Conference on Research and Development in Information Retrieval ; Pisa, sept. 86
14. John F. SOWA, Conceptual Structures: Information Processing in Mind and Machine. Addison-Wesley, London, 1984
15. M. Willems, Generalization of conceptual graphs. In Proceedings of the 6th Annual Workshop on Conceptual Graphs, pp. 27-37, July 11-13, 1991.
16. D.A. Waterman and F. Hayes-Roth, editors. Pattern-Directed Inference Systems.. Academic-Press, New York, 1978
17. J. Bouaud and P. Zweigenbaum, A Reconstruction of Conceptual Graphs on Top of a Production System. In Proceedings of the 7th Annual Workshop on Conceptual Graphs, July 8-10, 1992.

18

Object-oriented Framework for Requirement Specification

[a]Stephen Liao, [a]Jian Ma and [b]Louis Lasoudris

[a]Department of Information Systems, City Polytechnic of HongKong, HongKong
[b]DSI, Institut National des Telecoms, Every, France

Abstract

Object-oriented (OO) approach has been used in the whole life-cycle of software development. Several methods have been proposed for the requirement specification of an application system. However the emphasis of these methods is not put on the specification of dynamic behaviour of classes. This paper presents an OO framework for the specification of an application system at the stage of system analysis. The framework emphasises the description of roles, events and dynamic constraints of classes. It provides a powerful tool to study the roles played by an object at the different stages of its life.

Keyword Codes: D.2.1; D.1.5.
Keywords: Requirement/Specification; Object-Oriented Approach

1. INTRODUCTION

The concepts of object-orientation were originated from a programming language SIMULA [5]. Recently they are being widely used in the whole life cycle of a software sys m development [1], [2], [3]. Requirement specification at the stage of system analysis is also influenced by the OO concepts [1] [2]. Current OO methods for system analysis, e.g. OOA[2] and O*[4], make use of the concepts in OO programming languages, where a same concept can be used from the requirement specification to the system implementation. OO methods also provide rich semantics in modeling an application system. However the emphasis of these methods is not put on the specification of dynamic behaviour of classes. Thus they lack the mechanisms in describing the event sequences and role evolution of a class of objects.

This paper proposes an OO framework for the requirement specification at the stage of system analysis. The framework is object-oriented in the sense that it emphasises the concept of object, class of objects and that it uses the perspective concept in the class of objects to find the subclasses or roles of the class. The framework also emphasises the role description and dynamic behaviour of an application system. It provides a clean and an overall picture of the system.

2. OBJECTS AND CLASSES OF OBJECTS

In the paper, objects are treated as a kind of information resource to an organisation. The state of an object changes constantly and the object operations can be triggered by events. Formally an object is defined as:

Object = <Name, {characteristics}, {context}>

where **Name** is an identifier of an object which is unique in an class. It plays a role of identifying objects at the analysis level.

Characteristics are values which determine the states of objects.

Context is composed of real links about an object.

There are many variations for the class concept. Classification seems to be a trivial process in identifying a class. However a set of rules need to be searched in order to find out classes of objects at the stage of the system analysis.

3. PERSPECTIVES IN CLASSES OF OBJECTS

In OO system analysis, an object may play several roles. These roles may be different during an object life, e.g. a person may have several roles such as student, employee, retired employee at the different stage of his or her life, he or she may also play roles as a student and a soccer player at the same time. Perspective is a means to classify the subclasses of classes of objects . The results of classification help to find the roles of the class and study the role evolution. Perspectives are composed of a set of criteria. These criteria refer to structural and behavioural properties of a class. Results of the perspective application are a set of new classes. Every element of the characteristics or the context of a class is a possible criterion, e.g. the class "Person" may be observed by sex perspective:

Perspective $_{sex}$ Person= ({men}, {women}).

There can be non-evaluative link or evaluative link between two classes of objects . The non-evaluative link implies that an object belongs to a class in a perspective p, but does not belong to another class in the same perspective during all its life, e.g.

Perspective $_{sex}$ Person = ({men},{women}) , men(t1)-/->women(t2)

where a person is a man and can never become a woman.

The evaluative link implies that an object, which belongs to a class at time t1, can belong to another class at time t2 in the same perspective, e.g.

Perspective $_{profession}$ Person = ({student},{employee}) student(t1)-->employee(t2)

where a student can become an employee in the future.

If two classes of objects originating from the same perspective are linked by an evaluative link, they represent roles of the original class on which the perspective is applied. In this case, there is at least one criterion whose value is changeable.

If two classes originating from the same perspective are linked by a non-evaluative link, they represent categories of the original class on which perspective is applied. In this case, the values of all criteria are fixed.

4. SPECIFICATION OF CLASSES OF OBJECTS

Perspective application in classes of objects provides a good mechanism to examine the set of objects and to constitute the new coherent set of objects at both structural and behavioural levels. This leads us to examine the description of a class in a refined way at object model level.

In this research, a specification of classes describes a structure shared by all instances of one class with its associated roles. Formally,

Specification of classes = **<name, static part, dynamic part, [{role description}]>**

Where **name** is the identifier of classes at the user level. **Static part** and **dynamic** part are defined as follows:

Static part = **<{attribute}, {attribute constraints}, {static links}, {static link constraints}>**

Where **attribute** is to describe attributes of all objects associated with the class. **Attribute constraints** are constraints on attribute values, i.e. domain constraints, values ranges. **Static links** describe the authorized links between classes.

An event class means that a fact will arrive in a class because something happens in the exterior of the class or there is a significant internal state change in the class. Significant state change may also trigger other events.

The consequence of the arrival of events in a class can be triggered by one or a set of other events which are either in the same class or in other classes. The consequence or arrival condition of events are fixed by the event rules. Thus the dynamic part is defined as:

Dynamic part = <{event name}, {event rules}>.

Where event name is associated to one specification of classes. Event rules give the precondition which is necessary for the arrival of an event E_i; They also give new attribute values after the arrival of an event. In general:

Precondition-->Event

Where an event on a $class_i$ can not happen if the precondition is not met.

If an event will inevitably occur when a precondition is met, this precondition is a *strong* precondition. Otherwise if an event will not absolutely occur when a precondition is met, this precondition is a *weak* precondition.

A precondition is formed by an expression consisting of events or attribute values.

{Attributes($class_i$)= value, Event($class_j$)} --> Event($class_i$)

The consequence of events in an class consists of modification of attributes in the class and the triggering of events in the same class or in other classes, i.e.,

Event-->Consequence

An event in a class may modify one or several attributes in the same class. Some modifications are not significant for triggering an event, i.e.,

Event($class_i$)-->Change{attributes($class_i$)}

An event in $class_i$ may or may not inevitably trigger one or several events in the same or other classes. Similar to the preconditions, an event can have a strong or a weak consequence on another event. Formally,

Event($class_i$)-->{Event($class_j$)}

5. LINKS BETWEEN TWO EVENTS

It has been indicated that an event can be conditionally triggered by another event. Now the links between two events with the temporal logic are studied in detail.

If there are occurrences of event e1 at the time t1 and of event e2 at the time t2, e1 and e2 can occur at the same time or one after another. The links between two events is expressed by one of the abbreviations: NP, SP, AP, NPS, SPS, APS, NF, SF, AF.

The following formula is used to explain the above elements:

Event1(class,[time])&{[condition]}
--Time formula--> [Time operator].Event2(class,[time])
Time operator= {Always A, Sometimes S, Never N}
Time Formula = (Past P, Future F, Present S) which defined the time of occurrence of the right part of the expression.

6. ROLE DESCRIPTION

The concept of role represents an evolution of characteristics and context of classes. The evolution has to be described as the values and the structures of an class.

Role=<role name, static part, dynamic part>

Where static part is defined as:

static part=<{role attributes}, {role attribute constraints},{static links to the role}>

These components are written in the same manner as those of specification of classes. In fact, they belong to the set of characteristics of the specification of classes, but they define the specific characteristics of each different view on the specification of classes. The specific attributes of the roles will enrich the static part of the specification of classes.

dynamic part=<{role event}, {role event rules}>

The concepts of role event and role event rules are exactly the same as those in a specification of classes that we have already introduced. The dynamic part of role is the evolution between roles.

Role is an interesting concept because it allows us to analyze evolution of an object. With the concept of role, an object can create different events and have different reactions facing same events at different stages of evolution.

SUMMARY

This paper presents an OO framework for the requirement specification at the stage of system analysis. Within the framework, a class is the realization of the concepts of data abstraction and encapsulation. A class can be classified into subclasses and roles using the concept "perspective". Subclasses and roles can inherit properties from the original class.

The proposed framework emphasizes the specification of dynamic behaviors of the application system. Some important concepts in the framework, such as perspective, role, event, and dynamic constraint enable the designers to produce a good presentation about the evolution of roles of objects of the application systems

REFERENCES

1. Booch G., "Object-Oriented Analysis and Design", 2nd ed Benjamin /Cummings 1994.
2. Coad P.and Yourdon E., "Object-Oriented Analysis", 2nd ed., Prentice-Hall, 1991.
3. Pernici B., "Requirements specifications for object-oriented systems", INFORSID 90, Eyrolles, June, 1990 pp41-64.
4. Brunet J., "Modeling the world with semantic objects", Proc. of IFPS object-oriented approach in information systems, North Holland, 1991.
5. Dahl O."Simula"Norwegian Computer Center, Oslo Technical Report, 1965

19

A Structured Object-Oriented View on Systems Modeling

G. Wu and G. Dedene

Section of Information Systems, Department of Applied Economic Sciences, Katholieke Universiteit Leuven, Naamsestraat 69, 3000 Leuven, Belgium

Abstract

Interest in object-oriented methods has been rapidly increasing, as software developers and management demand on producing high quality and productivity softwares. Special features of object-oriented developments can really help to achieve high quality softwares. While this does not mean that object-oriented approaches will automatically obtain high quality software, the special features of object-oriented methods can only guarantee a certain degree of quality. To fully explore the benefit of object-oriented paradigm in software development, extra concepts should be introduced in order to achieve higher quality and productivity. The *structured object-oriented view*(SOOV) on systems modeling to be discussed in this paper is such a concept that can be used to further exploit the power of object-oriented methods to ensure higher quality, especially for large and complex systems. The structured view defines an overall inherent structure on objects and systems. Real world objects and systems are structurally decomposed into several logically and inherently related parts. After decomposition common parts could be discovered and factored out early in the modeling stage. The whole software development process is guided by this view in a quite neat and consistent manner.

Keyword Codes: D.2.1;D.2.2;H.1.0
Keywords: Model-driven, abstract model, real world object, model object, object main, object aspect, structured object-oriented view, object deposition and factoring.

1. INTRODUCTION

The structured object-oriented view on system modeling is part of M.E.R.O.DE. (Model-driven Entity Relationship Object-oriented DEvelopment), a methodology being developed at the faculty of applied economics science of K.U.Leuven. The methodology in fact covers the whole software development cycle from modeling to implementation[1-7]. The objective of this paper is to show an important part of the M.E.R.O.DE. method, that is, the structured object-oriented view on systems modeling. Discussions are based on this method, but applicable to general OOAD. Rather than starting from information requirements (Requirements-driven approach) for systems development, which is indeed a very volatile starting point, development starts with modeling business reality (Model-driven approach) of that part of the real world for the system under development. It turns out to be a much more stable starting point than the system information requirements[4].

The M.E.R.O.DE. development emphasizes on creating an *abstract or business model* of reality. Later on an information model is built, in the design stage, around this abstract model of reality. The abstract model is the basis and source to supply information to end users. Business modeling in M.E.R.O.DE. models the business reality by *business objects* or *model objects*, *business events* and *business rules* concerning the sequence of these events[4],[5]. Business oriented terms or names are used so that end-users can understand and participate in the modeling process. To construct abstract model, modelers first find out relevant *real world objects* in systems under development (problem domain). Real world objects are denoted by R objects. Relationships between R objects are described by ER model. A set of attributes can be identified for each R object and represents the object's static state.

Concerned business events in real world system need also to be identified. For example, "manager gets promoted" and "employee starts training period" are two events in personnel management system. The happening of an event usually causes changes to R objects in a system, for instance, the happening of event "employee joins a project" will cause change to employee's state, i.e., the number of projects that the employee is currently participating in. Similarly, the event affects also project's state, i.e., the number of employees who are participating in the project. When the happening of an event causes changes to the state of a R object, it is said that the event *involves* this R object and an event method is defined in it.

In general, an event may involve several R objects, for instance, the "employee joins a project" event involves both employee and project objects. Events actually represent the *behavior* of R objects and an event sometimes represents the behavior of several R objects, for example, "employee joins a project" event is the behavior of both employee and project objects. A system's behavior is then represented by the behavior of R objects in the system. Behavior of R objects in reality usually can not happen freely. Business rules concerning the sequence or order of these objects' behavior exist, such as that "employee becomes a regular employee" event must follow the event "employee passes trail use period". These business rules are also called *behavior constraints*.

2. BEHAVIOR COMPLEXITY OF REAL WORLD OBJECTS

A simple personnel management example in this paper is used to illustrate the main ideas. Three R objects in this system are of interest to modelers, they are Manager, Employee and Project. Relationships between these R objects are shown in figure 1.

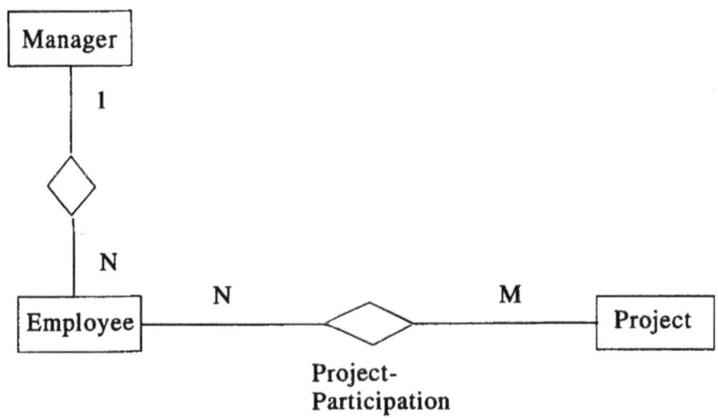

Figure 1. ER model of personnel management example

Concerned events and R objects are given in table 1, the R object/event table. A "*" in the table indicates that the event in the row involves the R object in the corresponding column. An object in reality tends to have a lot of behavior. The employee object in the example has the following behavior: "e-crt", e-start-trial", "e-end-trial", "e-regular", "e-trial-fail", "e-promote", "e-leave", "pp-join", "pp-start-train", "pp-end-train", "pp-disjoin", "e-join-m" and "e-leave-m". Of course employee may have a lot of other behavior which is not concerned or not currently considered in this system. Now considering all behavior of a R object, not only that in a particular system, could we get an inherent structure on it? Simply putting events to R objects can not help modelers to better understand objects' internal structure.

Table 1. R object/event table for personnel management example

	R Object types		
Event types	Manager	Employee	Project
m-crt (new manager)	*		
m-promote (manager gets promoted)	*		
m-end (manager ends)	*		
e-crt (new employee)		*	
e-start-trial (employee starts trial use)		*	
e-end-trial (employee ends trial use)		*	
e-regular (employee becomes regular employee)		*	
e-trial-fail (employee trial use failed)		*	
e-promote (employee gets promoted)		*	
e-leave (employee leaves company)		*	
p-crt (new project)			*
p-end (project ends)			*
pp-join (employee joins project)		*	*
pp-start-train (employee starts training)		*	*
pp-end-train (employee ends training)		*	*
pp-disjoin (employee leaves project)		*	*
e-join-m (employee becomes subordinate)	*	*	
e-leave-m (employee leaves manager)	*	*	

3. STRUCTURED OBJECT-ORIENTED VIEW ON R OBJECTS

This section describes the R object's internal structure and the inter-R objects' structure impact on the state and behavior of objects. First the *R objects' internal structure* is examined. In fact the behavior and states of a R object can be classified or grouped into several logical related groups based on its relationships with other R objects in the ER model, each group is characterized by a relationship. An employee, for instance, has behavior group related to manager (i.e., "e-join-m" and "e-leave-m"), behavior group related to project (i.e., "pp-join", "pp-start-train. "pp-end-train" and "pp-disjoin") and behavior group related to no relationship (i.e., "e-crt", "e-start-trail", "e-end-trail", "e-regular", "e-trail-fail", "e-promote" and "e-leave"). The behavior of a R object now can be partitioned into several disjoined event sets. If the system under development is interested in all potential behavior of a R object in reality, a complete partition of the object's behavior can be obtained. The R object in this case is exactly the same as the one in reality. Similarly a R object's state (attributes) can also be partitioned into several disjoined attribute sets based on relationships.

The *inter-R objects' structure*, a structured view on system, is defined as follows: a R object's behavior and state related to a relationship are actually common to all R objects participating in this relationship, they are the *common part* of these R objects. For example, an employee object's behavior and state related to "project-participation" relationship are common to both employee and project objects, they represent the common part of employee and project objects. To describe these structures, the following concepts are introduced.

Definition 1. A R object's aspect: those parts of a real world object's behavior (events) and state (attributes) which are related to the same relationship, are grouped together and called one aspect of the real world object.

Definition 2. A R object's main: those parts of a real world object's behavior and state which do not concern any relationship in which the object participates are grouped together and called the main of the object.

Note that a R object may have many aspects and a specific system is interested in only some of them. Each aspect contains a set of inherently and logically related events and attributes of a R object and represents a logical unit within the R object. It can be seen that this analysis and study of real world objects' behavior and states can assist modelers to obtain the structure within a R object and the structure among the different related R objects.

4. MODELING REAL WORLD OBJECTS AND SYSTEMS

Real world objects and systems have to be specified by M objects in object model of M.E.R.O.DE., the specification domain objects. M objects stand for model objects. Two approaches can be used to model a R object in object model. One is to model a R object by one M object, the other is to model it by several M objects. The main problem of the first approach is the redundancy caused by specifying the common part (aspect) of two related R objects separately in both of them. This could cause problems of inflexibility and possible inconsistency. The basic problem of the second approach is the loss of R objects in object model, that is, modelers can no longer find R objects in object model. The structured view on R objects can help us to solve these problems, namely to build a bridge between R objects and M objects, and at the same time provide a way to factor out the common parts of R objects in a system to reduce the redundancy in specification. The second approach is better in this sense. The bridge will be discussed in section 7.

Based on the structured view on R objects discussed above, *common parts of R objects are represented by their aspects.* Now factoring out common parts means to factor out aspects of R objects. To do so, each aspect is separated from its related R objects, and is considered or treated as one M object in object model. The mains of R objects are treated also as M objects. The second approach is used here. Two definitions are introduced to describe these more formally.

Definition 3. Aspect object (common part): the model (M) object used to describe an aspect of a R object is called an aspect object.

Definition 4. Main object (non-common part): the model (M) object used to describe the main of a R object is called a main object.

It is clear that there is only one main object for each R object and vice versa. The main object represents the corresponding R object's "identity" in object model, but not completely because some aspects have been taken out and specified in aspect objects. It is also obvious that a R object may have several aspects, therefore the main object is associated with several aspect objects in object model. Aspect objects, in this case, correspond to relationship objects. The choice to use the name "aspect object" is simply because the name itself carries the desired meaning, that is, it represents the aspects of R objects, while the name "relationship object" does not.

All of the events involving R objects need to be transformed into events involving M objects, which can be described by a M object/event table similar to the above discussed R object/event table. M objects, in this case, are listed in columns instead of R objects. There are five M objects in the personnel management example, three main objects, i.e., employee, manager and project main objects, and two aspect objects, i.e., "manager-employee" and "project-participation" aspect objects.

It is important to notice that an event involving a M or R object can actually be classified into two types based on its functions in M or R objects. They are action and response events.

Informal definitions are given below. More formal definitions can be found in [7]. Action and response events of R objects will be discussed in section 7.

Definition 5. An event belongs to a M object: an event E_i is said to belong to an M object o_j if it is existence dependent on M object o_j and there does not exist another M object o_k such that E_i is also existence dependent on o_k and o_k is existence dependent on o_j.

Definition 6. Action event (behavior) of a M object: an event E_i is considered as an action event or the behavior of a M object when it belongs to the object. Example: "pp-join" is an action event of "project-participation" aspect object.

Definition 7. Response event of a M object: an event E_i is said to be a response event of a M object when it involves the object but does not belong to it. Example: "pp-join" is a response event in "employee" main object.

The objective to distinguish between these two types of events is that only the action events of a M object are considered to be its behavior, response events reflect only the impact of other M objects' action events (behavior) on this M object. The behavior constraints to be specified in object model are only specified on the action events of M objects. Definition of "an attribute belongs to a M object" is also given in [7].

5. GRAPHICAL REPRESENTATION OF THE STRUCTURES IN OBJECT MODEL

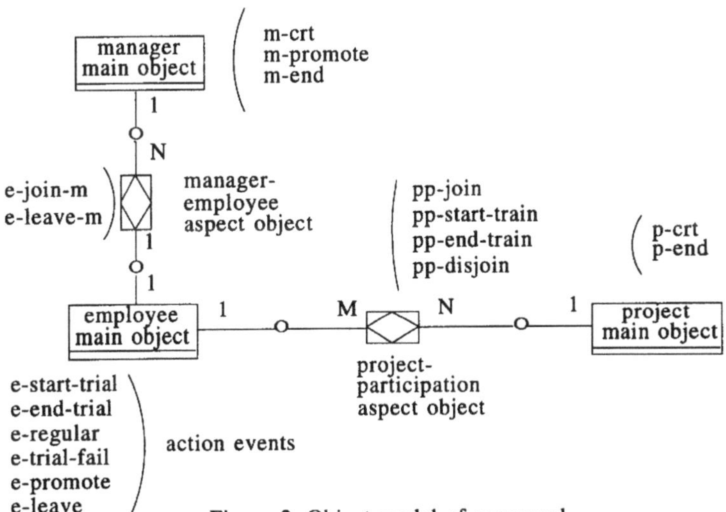

Figure 2. Object model of personnel management system

Object model can be obtained directly from ER model by a concrete procedure. Figure 2 is the object model derived from the ER model of personnel management system. The small circle in the diagram represents the relationship between model objects. There are five M objects in this example. A main object is represented by a box with double lines at its bottom side to show that it is different from the corresponding R object. For example, the employee main model object is different from the R employee object because part of R employee object is taken out and specified in project-participation aspect model object. An aspect object is represented by a box with a diamond within it. In object model, an aspect object is always existence dependent on the related main objects, for example, the "project-participation" aspect object is always existence dependent on main objects "project" and "employee".

Cardinalities of relationships between model objects are represented by the numbers on both sides of the small circles. Action events of the five M objects are assigned to and listed next to them based on definition 6. They are considered as the behavior of these M objects. Response events can also be added to these M objects based on definition 7 [7], they are not shown here in figure 2. Similarly attributes can be assigned to these M objects[7].

In figure 2 "project-participation" aspect object contains the common part of both employee and project objects in ER model, it is one aspect of employee and one aspect of project object as well. "manager-employee" aspect object is then common to both R manager and employee objects. Now it can be seen how the structures can help us to get more information from object model, which could otherwise be ignored.

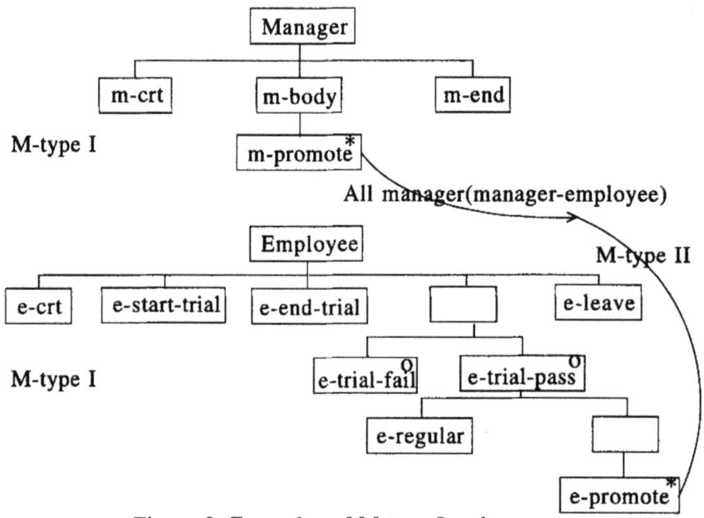

Figure 3. Examples of M-type I and M-type II constraints specification

6. BUSINESS RULES (BEHAVIOR CONSTRAINTS) SPECIFICATION

Besides of attributes and events specified for a model object, business rules in system should also be specified in object model. Recall that business rules are the sequence or order constraints on events, but specified only on action events of M objects in object model. There are two types of constraints, one is the *M object internal behavior constraints* (*M-type I*) which is specified on action events within a model object. This type of behavior constraints can be specified by techniques such as F.S.M., Petri-net, Action diagrams, J.S.D. entity life cycle diagrams and so on. In M.E.R.O.DE, the J.S.D. entity life cycle diagram approach[8] is used. The other is the *inter-M objects behavior constraints* (*M-type II*) which are placed on action events of different model objects. Specification language and graphical means are currently used in M.E.R.O.DE. to specify this type of constraints. Examples of employee and manager main objects' M-type I constraints and M-type II constraints between them are shown in figure 3.

For M object internal behavior constraints, sequence order of events is graphically represented by the left-to-right order of their appearances on the diagrams. "*" means that the event can happen zero or more times and "O" means that only one of the events with "O" can happen[6]. The employee's life cycle can be explained as the follows: an employee is created when he or she enters the company, then starts trial use. If the employee passes the trial use, he or she becomes a regular employee and can get zero or more times of promotions till he or she finally leaves the company. If the employee fails the trial use, he or she has to leave the company. The language specification of the inter-M object behavior constraint "an employee's promotion must follow all of his or her managers' promotion" shown in figure 3 is: ALL Manager (manager-employee).m-promote $\rightarrow_{II}$ Employee.e-promote. It means that the promotion events of all managers related to an employee through relationship "manager-employee" must happen before the employee's promotion events. M object classes now include the following elements: State (attributes), action events (behavior) methods, response events (impact of other M objects) methods, behavior constraints on action events (M-type I and M-type II).

7. RECOVERY OF R OBJECTS IN OBJECT MODEL

To recover a R object is to connect all of its components, i.e., M objects, specified in object model to the R object. Therefore a link or a bridge between R objects and M objects should be established. This link is clearly given by the structures on R objects, that is, a R object is represented by several model objects, its main object and aspect objects, in object model. The big circles in figure 4 actually give the R objects "manager", "employee" and "project". Definitions of R objects' states, behavior and behavior constraints in terms of their related M objects' states, behavior and behavior constraints are given below.

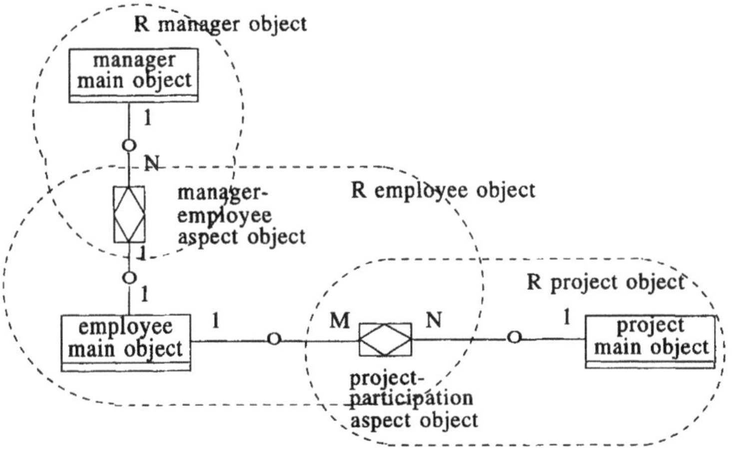

Figure 4. R objects in object model

Definition 8. A R object's state, behavior(or action events) and behavior constraints: a R object's state consists of its main and aspect objects' states(attributes), its behavior consists of its main and aspect objects' behavior(action events), and its behavior constraints consist of its main and aspect objects' internal behavior constraints (M-type I), and inter-M objects' behavior constraints (M-type II) between its related model objects (its main and aspect objects).

Definition 9. A R object's response events: an event is a response event of a R object when it involves the object but is not the behavior of the object.

A R object is now decomposed into several logically related model objects. Object model in this case can support two levels of objects, the real world objects and model objects, thus more information about reality can be provided by the object model. Usually end-users are interested in real world objects and software developers are interested in model objects. In fact end-users can understand object model without difficulties and hence can participate in business modeling.

Properties of a R object can be obtained from the related M objects. The gap between real world objects and model objects is now closed. Arbitrary decompositions could also work, but produce less fruitful and structured specifications. This is the case where modelers arbitrarily or non-systematically introduce M objects to object model without clear ideas about the relationships between the introduced M objects and R objects. Concepts about object, such as, inheritance, reuse, objects' states, behavior and behavior constraints etc., are now applicable to both levels of objects[7].

Finally it should be mentioned that the flexibility, extendibility, maintainability and reusability of the object models obtained based on the structured object-oriented view can be improved[7]. For example, adding (or deleting) a relationship in ER model needs only to add (or delete) one aspect object and the inter-M objects behavior constraints with other model objects. In addition, this structured view in fact provides a way to incrementally specify a real world object and system[7].

8. CONCLUSIONS

This paper introduces a structured object-oriented view (SOOV) on R objects and system, and a way to systematically decompose R objects of a system into M objects of object model. The view can not only solve the redundancy and inconsistency problems and recover the R objects in the specification at the same time, but also increase the software quality and productivity by improved flexibility, extendibility, maintainability and reusability.

REFERENCES

1. Dedene G. and Snoeck M., "M.E.R.O.DE.: A Model-driven Entity-Relationship Object-oriented DEvelopment method", research paper, K.U.Leuven, 1994.
2. Dedene G., " On the mathematical foundations of an object-oriented Business modelling approach ", L.I.R.I.S. K.U.Leuven research note 1990.
3. Dedene G., Snoeck M. and Depuydt A., "On generalisation/Specialisation Hierarchies in M.E.R.O.DE. object-oriented business modelling", research report, K.U.Leuven, 1992.
4. Dedene G., " M.E.R.O.DE. by examples. A tutorial on object-oriented Business modeling.", object technology 93, Cambridge U.K., March 1993.
5. Verhelst M., " Software Development ", Course-notes K.U.Leuven 1991.
6. Wu G., " Structure of objects based on their behavior and the optimized behavior constraint checking in M.E.R.O.D.E. ". Research note Oct., 1992, K.U.Leuven.
7. Wu G., "A systematic approach to M.E.R.O.DE. systems specification", doctoral seminar, April, 1994.
8. Jackson M., " System Development ", Prentice-Hall 1983.

20

Construction of a WYSIWYG LaTeX Typesetting System using Object-oriented Design*

J.H.M. Lee, J.C.K. Leung and C.C.K. Wong
Department of Computer Science
The Chinese University of Hong Kong
Shatin, Hong Kong

Abstract

This paper reports the design of a sophisticated WYSIWYG LaTeX-like typesetting system ViEwTeX. Our approach is based on the Model-View-Controller (MVC) user-interface paradigm, as originated from the Smalltalk community. According to the paradigm, the ViEwTeX system is decomposed into the sub-editor (model) module, the redisplay (view) module, and the user-commands (controller) module. Each module is responsible for a different aspect of ViEwTeX. Represented as separate objects, these modules co-operate by communicating via a controlled and structured pattern. Such decomposition facilitates encapsulation and code reuse. To demonstrate the feasibility of our approach, a prototype implementation of ViEwTeX is constructed according to the design using C and Motif.

Keyword Codes: D.1.5; D.2.10; I.7.2
Keywords: Object-oriented Programming; Design; Document Preparation

1 INTRODUCTION

LaTeX [6], a macros layer built on top of TeX [3], is a sophisticated typesetting system producing high quality mathematical manuscripts and monographs. LaTeX is command-based. Typesetting using LaTeX is no simpler than writing a computer program. This *user-unfriendliness* sets LaTeX back from gaining the acceptance of many potential users. On the other end of the spectrum, there are popular WYSIWYG wordprocessors, such as WordPerfect and Microsoft Word, widely available on personal computers. Output from these wordprocessors is not as aesthetic as that of LaTeX, both in terms of word and line spacing, but they are interactive in nature. Users can view and modify the layout of a document in real-time as it evolves. Wordprocessing is also no longer "programming."

To capture the best of both worlds, we propose ViEwTeX, an interactive WYSIWYG LaTeX wordprocessor. Its design is based on the Model-View-Controller (MVC) user-interface paradigm [5], which originates from the Smalltalk [2] community. According to the MVC paradigm, a user-interface application should be decomposed into a model, a view, and a controller. The *model* is the sub-part containing all of the non-visual non-interactive computer semantic information. The *view* contains all of the visual computer

*This project is supported by a UK/HK Joint Research Scheme grant (A/C 242700500) and a RGC Earmarked grant (A/C 221500260).

semantic information. The *controller* is responsible for capturing the user's attempts to manipulate the object. In this paper, we identify the model, the view, and the controller aspects of VIEWTEX. A reliable and efficient communication protocol among the modules is also proposed. To demonstrate the feasibility of our design, a prototype of VIEWTEX is constructed.

2 VIEWTEX DESIGN USING MVC

We adopt the terminology of [1] and call the model, view, and controller respectively *sub-editor*, *redisplay*, and *user-commands*. The sub-editor hides the details of how an edited text is stored from the rest of VIEWTEX. That includes a basic buffer for storing text, the current position of the cursor, and various markers to remember symbols, special format, and cross-references. The redisplay is responsible for ensuring that all changes to the buffer are promptly reflected on the display. The user-commands captures keystrokes and mouse clicks, and interprets these inputs before informing the sub-editor.

2.1 Overall architecture

The three modules work cooperatively in maintaining a user-interface application. Efficient and reliable communication is essential. A standard communication pattern of the MVC paradigm consists of four separate communications. First, the user performs an action, which is intercepted by the user-commands. Second, the user-commands interprets this action as a request to change the state of the sub-editor, and informs the sub-editor. Third, the sub-editor changes its state and then informs its dependent redisplay that it has changed. Fourth, the redisplay then asks the sub-editor for its current state and updates itself accordingly.

2.2 Sub-editor

In VIEWTEX, the text is stored into a one dimensional array of characters. Besides, the text buffer must also contain two gap pointers (gap-start and gap-end) in order to implement the paged buffer gap technique [1], allowing ease of text insertion. When a user prepares a document, we cannot know, in advance, the amount of work the user will do. Thus, the text buffer should be allocated dynamically. A doubly linked list for text buffers is a suitable choice. Apart from text buffer, mark, symbol and cross-reference information is also necessary in the implementation of the sub-editor.

From time to time, it is useful to be able to remember positions within a text buffer. A mark is an object that can remember position. There can be any number of marks within a text buffer, and more than one mark can remember the same position. In each mark, it contains a mark type (such as `begin` and `end` positions of the centering command) and a position in the text buffer. Each text buffer is associated with a linked list of mark which is maintained into a sorted order of the mark position.

Symbol mark and cross-reference mark are special kinds of mark, which are used to remember positions of mathematical symbols and cross-references. Each text buffer maintains also a sorted linked list of symbol marks and a sorted linked list of cross-reference marks.

2.3 Redisplay

The job of redisplay is to ensure that (1) the state of the sub-editor is displayed on the screen faithfully and (2) the amount of clock time required to make the updates visible is minimized. When the sub-editor has performed a function (e.g. insert character), the redisplay module is required to reflect the changes on the screen in a timely fashion. The redisplay module is also responsible for determining the layout of the text and diagrams on the screen.

The last responsibility is directly related to the *line-breaking* problem: how to divide long paragraphs into individual lines. Traditional algorithms, as adopted by popular wordprocessors such as Microsoft Word, WordPerfect and WordStar, use "*justification*," which considers only the current line and decides how best to finish off that line. The lack of line lookahead often results in awkward word spacing and hyphenation. LaTeX and TeX, using the *optimum* line-breaking algorithm by Knuth and Plass [4], consider a paragraph as a whole, so that the final appearance of a given line might be influenced by the text on succeeding lines.

The core of the redisplay module is Knuth and Plass's algorithm, the function of which is to find the sequence of breakpoints for the current paragraph. The result is stored in a linked-list. The redisplay will then display the content of buffer on screen according to the information stored in the linked-list. The problem of page-breaking is handled by the same algorithm.

2.4 User-commands

The job of the user-commands module is to capture user input, which can be text and commands. While text input must come from key presses, command input can be issued via *hot keys*, *hot buttons*, *pull-down menus*, and *mouse maneuver*. Thus the core of user-commands is a command loop that intercepts user input (via the keyboard and mouse), interprets the input, and informs the sub-editor of users' intention.

3 PROTOTYPE IMPLEMENTATION

The ViEwTeX prototype is realized on a DECstation using the C language, OSF/Motif, Xt Intrinsics, and the Xlib library. The system consists of around 20,000 lines of C code. Features of ViEwTeX can be classified into LaTeX functions and wordprocessor functions.

The main purpose of the current implementation is to verify the feasibility of the MVC design approach. Most but not all LaTeX functions are implemented. In particular, we have left out citation (*a la* BibTeX), floating bodies (*a la* tables and figures), mathematical formulas, and drawing commands, but they can be integrated into ViEwTeX easily. Implemented command categories include sectioning, various symbols, cross-referencing, itemization and enumeration, document style, displayed material, etc. Worth mentioning is that sectioning numbers and reference numbers in cross-referencing are generated automatically by the system.

Wordprocessor functions of ViEwTeX include file commands, copy/cut/paste, and help tools. The most common way to invoke wordprocessor functions is by means of pull-down menus controlled by mouse (or equivalent point-and-click devices). Hot buttons are provided for quick access to some most frequently used functions (both LaTeX and wordprocessor functions). Advanced users or fast typists, who despise the use of mouse, can make use of hot keys. Every function in ViEwTeX has an associated hot key.

Edited documents can be saved in ViEwTEX format for future retrieval or exported to the LaTeX source file format. The latter option provides flexibilities for users to fine tune the edited documents where necessary, such as inserting TEX commands into the documents. ViEwTEX also supports auto-saving function to secure the integrity of an edited document. In case of a system crash, the edited document can be recovered from the incremental log saved periodically during the editing process.

4 CONCLUDING REMARKS

When designing a complex software system, it is essential to *decompose* it into small parts, each of which we may comprehend and refine independently. Design of a word-processor is no exception. In the current project, we have adopted the object-oriented decomposition approach, in which the world is viewed as a set of autonomous agents that collaborate to perform some high level behaviour. In a user-interface application, the collaborating agents are respectively the model, the view, and the controller. The contribution of this paper is three-fold. First, to the best of our knowledge, our work is the first to apply the MVC paradigm outside the Smalltalk-80 environment (which has many MVC required classes pre-defined) and find it practical to do so. The conscious choice of the C language, the most common language in the industry, is a further evidence of the feasibility of our approach. The MVC paradigm, and object-oriented design in general, facilitates encapsulation and code reuse. These properties are proved to be valuable during our implementation process. Second, our design is general enough to be guidelines for the design of other wordprocessors. Third, we have constructed a reliable and practical implementation of a WYSIWYG LaTeX wordprocessor, not yet available in the commercial market. While preparing a document using ViEwTEX, users can concentrate on designing the layout of the document instead of worrying about "programming" LaTeX commands correctly. Most parts of this manuscript were prepared using ViEwTEX.

REFERENCES

1. Finseth C.A., *The Craft of Text Editing: Emacs for the Modern World.* Springer-Verlag, 1991.

2. Goldberg A., *Smalltalk-80: The Interactive Programming Environment.* Addison-Wesley, 1984.

3. Knuth D.E., *The TEXbook.* Addison-Wesley, 1984.

4. Knuth D.E., Plass M.F., Breaking paragraphs into lines. *Software-Practice and Experience*, 11:1119–1184, 1981.

5. Krasner G.E., Pope S.T., A cookbook for using the Model-View-Controller user interface paradigm in Smalltalk-80. *Journal of Object-Oriented Programming*, 1(3):26–49, 1988.

6. Lamport L., LaTeX*: A Document Preparation System.* Addison-Wesley, 1986.

21

An re-engineering Approach for Object-Oriented Database Design

J. Fong[a] and I. Kwan[b]

[a]Department of Computer Science, City Polytechnic of Hong Kong, Kowloon, Hong Kong
[b]Department of Computing, Hong Kong Polytechnic, Kowloon, Hong Kong

Abstract

Applications with databases built by EER model could seek to convert their databases into its OO model for capturing more semantics of application domain. To capture its dynamic semantic, we need users as domain expert for the newly developed database, as they are familiar with the application and can provide domain and relation integrity from the designed database. The objective of this paper is to present an OODB design methodology, which can be used as re-engineering procedure to upgrade database system to OODB through an Object Modelling Techniques(OMT).

Keyword Codes: D.2.10, H.2.1
Keywords: Extended Entity Relationship, Object-Oriented Database, Object Modelling Technique

1. INTRODUCTION

The development of recent object-oriented database(OODB) technology has emphasized on both static and dynamic structure and semantics. The object model to be used in this paper is based on the OMT methodology. The OMT supports the entire software development cycle by the use of its three models: Object model, Dynamic model and Functional model. This three-part model of the system is then refined and optimized to constitute a design. We believe re-engineering a database by taking advantage of new technology, in particular, OODB technology, while maintaining all the features that were proven to be useful in the original database. The translation from an EER-based database to an OODB model can contribute to the development of OODB design methodology.

2. THE HEURISTIC CONVERSION RULES FROM EER MODEL TO OODB MODEL

We will adopt the syntaxes of OODB model by John Hughes[1] using Class, Properties and Operations, instead of Class, Attributes and Methods, and OMT model by James Rumbaugh[2] in this paper.

2.1 Part I- Map EER to OODB in static semantic transformation

<u>Step 1 Entity → class</u>[3]

An EER Model works with entity types and their corresponding attributes. Attributes of a particular entity may be considered as instance variable of the class instance. For example, an entity type Book can be mapped into a class Book as shown in Figure 1. The followings are the mapped OODB with class BOOK where properties are attributes and operations are methods:

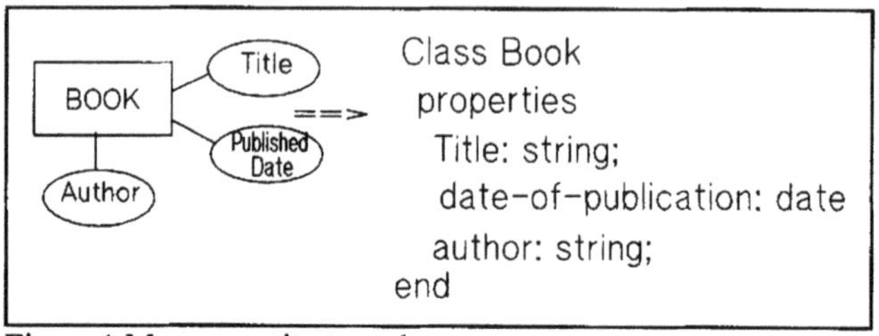

Figure 1 Map an entity to a class

Step 2 Relationship → Association[4]

In EER Model, relationships are represented as named associations among entities. In object-oriented schema, they are links and pointers between superclasses and subclasses. The relationship in the EER model can be mapped into an association in object-oriented schema on a 1:1 basis with its corresponding multiplicity of links/pointers. When constrained by cardinality, relationship need to be mapped according to the constraint. For example, the 1:n relationship in Figure 2 can be mapped into the following OODB where "has" is an association attribute of class Department associating with a set of another class Employee to comply with the 1:n relationship between entity Department and entity Employee in the EER model, and its "hired-by" is an inverse association.

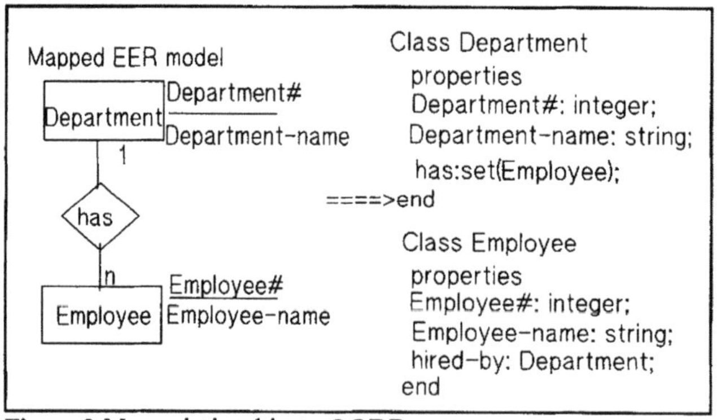

Figure 2 Map relationship to OODB

Step 3 Generalisation → Method[5]

For generalization, the variances among entities are suppressed and their commonalities are identified by generalizing them into one single class. The original entities with each of its unique differences are special subclasses. The mutually exclusive subclasses are called disjoint generalisation. The mutually inclusive subclasses are called overlap generalisation. For example, disjoint generalization in Figure 3 can be mapped into the following OODB where subclasses Contract-Staff and Permanent-Staff inherit the properties and operations of superclass Staff.

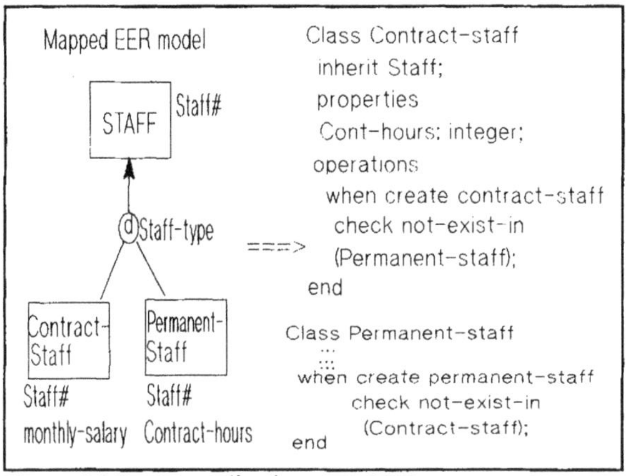

Figure 3 Map generalization to OODB

The mapping of overlap generalization into the object-oriented schema is similar to the mapping of disjoint generalization into the object-oriented schema except that check statement is omitted.

Step 4 Categorisation → Method
A categorisation is derived by mapping isa relationships and their record types to superclass/subclass such that a set of superclass can be united together to form a superclass to a subclass. All these superclasses may have different key attribute as they are originally independent classes. For example, the categorization in Figure 4 can be mapped into the following OODB where subclass Car-owner inherits by associating with only one of the three superclasses: Bank, Person or Company.

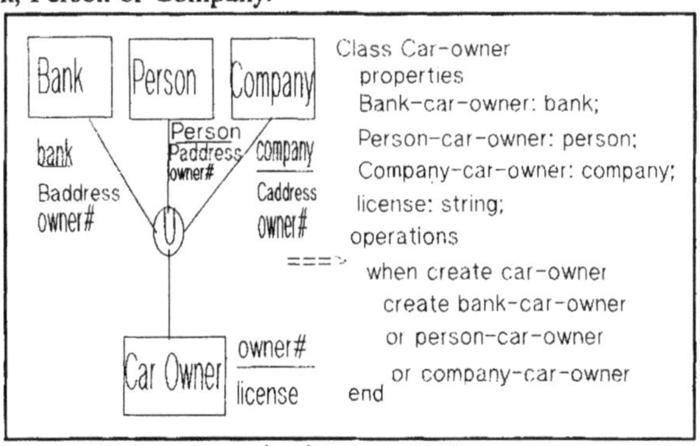

Figure 4 Map categorization to OODB

Step 5 Isa → Inheritance[6]
The concept of inheritance associated with generalization/specification (isa) relationship in object-oriented schema permits classes to be organized in which specialized classes inherit the properties and operations of more generalized class. Class carries common properties while deriving specialized subclass. For example, the isa relationship in Figure 5 can be mapped into the following OODB where subclass Car inherits the properties of its superclass Vehicle.

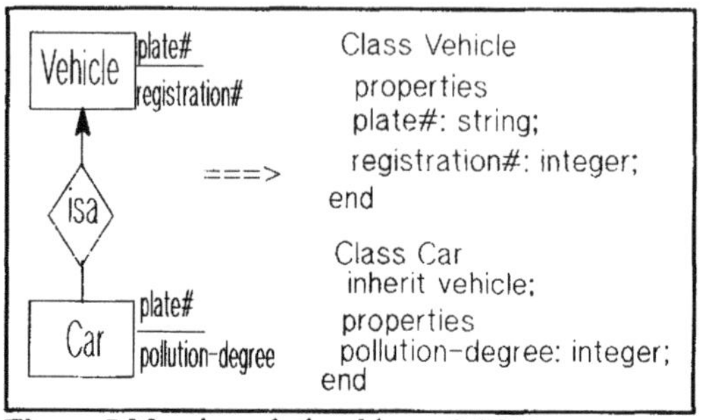

Figure 5 Map isa relationship to OODB

Step 6 Weak entity → Component class

The existence of weak entity in EER model depends on its owner entity. For example, the weak entity Dependent in Figure 6 can be mapped into the following OODB where class Employee is a composite object class which owns a component class Dependent. The own statement implies an existence dependence of component class Dependent such that if an instance of class Employee is deleted, its corresponding component class Dependent instances are also deleted.

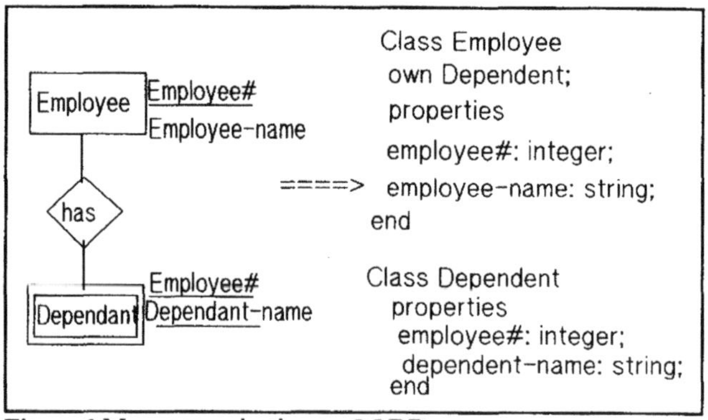

Figure 6 Map categorization to OODB

Step 7 Aggregation → Composite object

The entities and their relationship in EER model can be aggregated to form an entity. In object-oriented model, it permits the combination of classes that are related into a higher level of a composite class. For example, the aggregation in Figure 7 can be mapped into the object-oriented schema in the followings where class Section is an aggregation with two component classes: class Instructor and class Course.

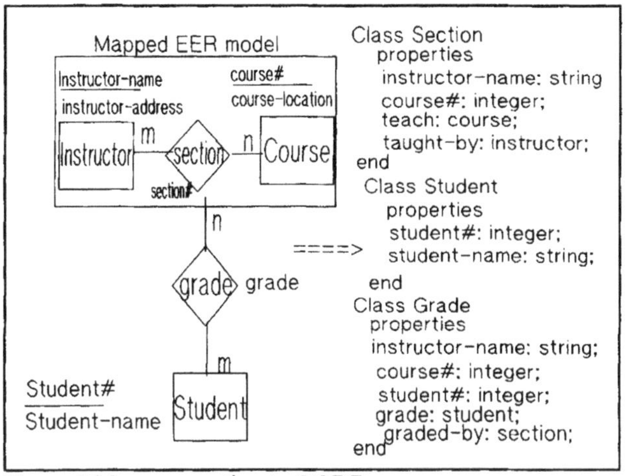

Figure 7 Map aggregation to OODB

2.2 Part II- Knowledge acquisition to obtain the dynamic behaviour semantic of data

Logical schema express data structure with little semantics. To translate an EER schema to OO schema, a direct translation can only map the data structure and relationships but not the extra semantic not represented in original EER and the dynamic semantic recovery. To recapture these dynamic semantics and extra semantic, a knowledge-based approach is therefore useful as users views relies mainly on judgement instead of mechanistic algorithms. The Expert system could then fill in the semantics needed in schema translation by leading users to make knowledgable decision whenever semantics judgment is required[7].

Object-oriented database development is primarily a data abstraction technique. The extra semantic of the object-oriented data model as compared with EER data model are :Schema Evolution and Object Behaviour

The dynamic data modelling which is not catered in EER model would need to be recovered via a knowledge-based approach to elicit the control information of EER model and represent them in OODB model.

The OMT dynamic model which consists of state diagrams and global event flow diagram, specifies allowable sequences of changes to objects from the static object model. Thus, it forms a good representation of changes towards objects and their relationships over time. A set of steps with questions could be asked by the knowledge-based system upon the completion of schema translation process after each schema's properties and relationships in the system have been formed and the resultant object model is created.

These may also be considered and derived in the mapping procedure. This could be best accomplished with the translation rules PLUS users assistance with a knowledge-based approach.

Step 8 : Draw an intermediate OMT Object model(optional)

Operations and state properties are not defined at this stage. They are integrated into the refined Object model after step 8, step 9 and step 10 are processed.

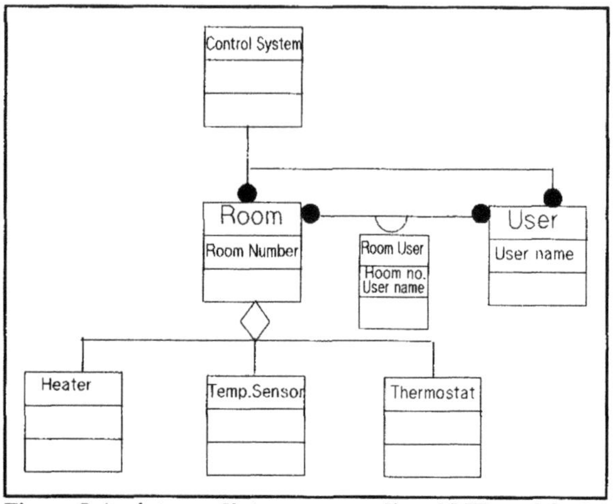

Figure 8 An intermediate corresponding OMT model of a heating system

Step 9 : Derive Dynamic Data Semantic

Q. 1 In light of providing overall picture of the system, what are the expected 'Normal' behaviour in the system?

Answer: A Heater System Scenario

Set a Heater desired temperature by Thermostat, sense temperature by Temp.sensor
If temperature > desired temperature, switch heater off (event 1)
If temperature < desired temperature, switch heater on (event 2)
If temperature = desired temperature, no action (event 3)

Q. 2 What are the causing and resulting event of change of state in each object class ? (for example : heater)

```
Answer:On -> Temp>Desired Temp -> Off -> Temp<Desired Temp -> On
                 event-1                          event-2
Otherwise,
no change of state value when Temp=Desired Temperature (event-3)
```

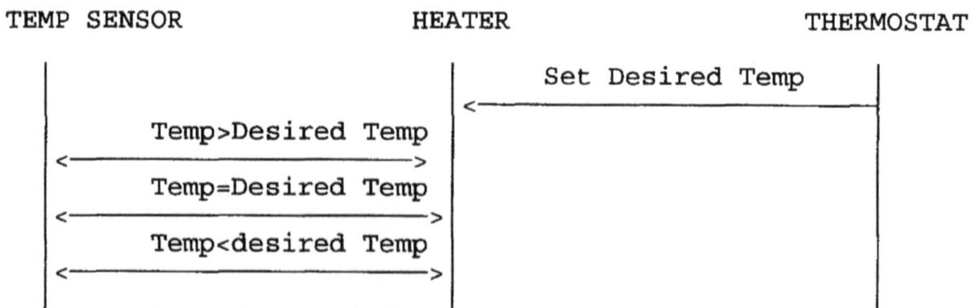

Figure 9 Event-trace diagram for HEATER active object between its related active objects TEMP SENSOR and THERMOSTAT

Q. 3 What is the typical changing sequence for Heater object ?
(ask one object class at a time, for example: heater)
Answer: On->Off->On subject to event that stimuli the object state.

Q. 4 What are the valid state of each object class ?
(ask one object class after the other, for example: heater)
Answer: On or Off, 2 state values only.

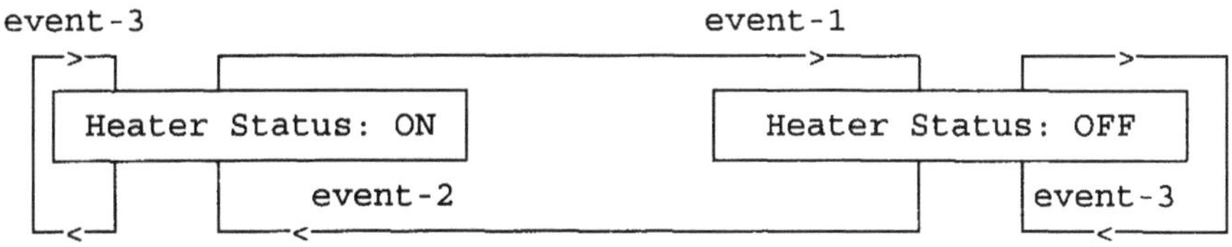

Figure 10 A state diagram of heater

Step 10: Check for consistency and completeness of events between objects and shared among the state diagrams

Q. 5 Are there any state defined in an object class not invoked by a defined event of any object in the event flow diagram ?
Answer: No, (for example, heater object) On -> Temp>Desired Temperature -> Off -> Temp<Desired Temperature -> On

Q. 6 Are there any event causing or resulting a state of a class not being defined in its corresponding state diagram ?
Answer: No, (for example, heater object) On -> Temp>Desired Temperature -> Off -> Temp<Desired Temperature -> On

Action: Put correspond state variable and operation event in each of the related active object class in the object model as in figure 14.

Step 11 : Check consistency between object model and dynamic model

Q. 7 For each state diagram in the dynamic model, is there a corresponding state attribute definition in each active object class in the object model ?
Answer:Yes, Heater status in Heater, Temperature-reading in Temp Sensor and Required Temperature in Thermostat.

Q. 8 For each event causing or resulting the change of state value of an object class, is there a corresponding operation definition in the object class in the object model ?
Answer: Yes, Switch On/Off in Heater, Read Temperature in Temp Sensor and Set Required Temperature in Thermostat.

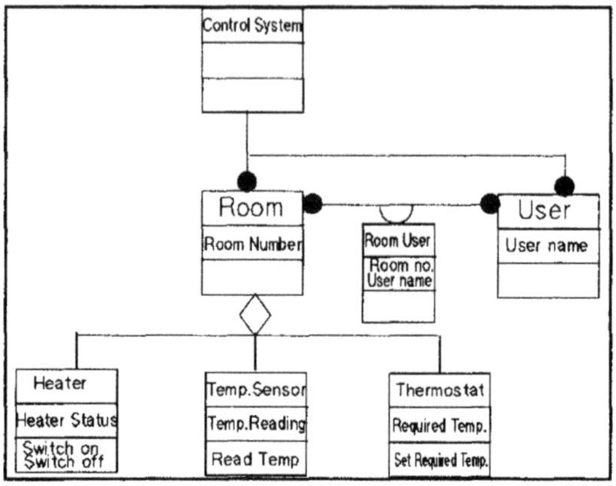

Figure 11 Final OMT model

3. CONCLUSION

This paper proposes a methodology to transform different semantic represented in EER model to OODB schema.

The proposed schema translation procedure from EER to OODB with capturing capabilities of both static data modelling and dynamic data modelling could be semi-automated, tested and verified with a sophisticated case study. The refined methodology, procedures, system/user dialogue and graphical user interface could be automated by implementing it with an appropriate Expert system shell and software, which would certainly open enhancement. The future enhancement of this research is to investigate the knowledge-based approach of capturing dynamic behaviour data semantics and to build CASE tools functionality for OODB design[8].

REFERENCES

1. Hughes J. 'Object-Oriented Databases', *Prentice Hall*, 1991, pp102-106.
2. Rumbaugh J. et al. 'Object-Oriented Modelling and Design', *Prentice Hall*, 1991, pp183-185.
3. Getta J. 'Translation of Extended Entity-Relationship Database Model into Object-oriented Database', *Interoperable Database Systems (DS-5)'*, 1993, pp87-100.
4. Il-Yeol Song 'A Survey of Object-Oriented Database Design Methodologies', *Proceedings of International Conference on Information and Knowledge Management'92*, 1992,pp52-59
5. Chan, J. 'Comparison between OODBMS and RDBMS: A Case Study Approach', *M.Sc Project report of Computer Science, Department at City Polytechnic of Hong Kong* 1994
6. Narasimhan B., Navathe S., Jayaraman S. 'On Mapping ER and Relational into OO Schemas' *Proceedings of the 12th International Conference on Entity-Relationship Approach*, 1993, pp397-692.
7. Fong J., Ho M. 'Knowledge-Based Approach For Abstracting Hierarchical and Network Schema Semantics', *Proceedings of the 12th International Conference on Entity-Relationship Approach*, 1993, pp498-509.
8. Fong J., Kwan I. 'Application of CASE Tool in Database Design By Use Of Semantic Association Model' *Proceedings of the SCS Silver Jubilee Conference on Software Engineering : New Technologies & Business Payoffs*, 1992,pp277-290.

PART FOUR

Software Process and Capability

22

Software Process Model Specification*

M. Baldi and M. L. Jaccheri
Dipartimento di Automatica e Informatica
Corso Duca degli Abruzzi 24, 10129 Torino, Italy

Abstract

The E^3 process model specification method is presented. It consists of a process modeling language based on classes, associations, and inheritance with a graphic representation and a presentation technique based on views and paths. The specification of a real process model is given as example.

Keyword Codes: D.2.0, D.2.2, D.2.6
Keywords: Software Engineering, Tools and Techniques, Programming Environments

1. INTRODUCTION

A software process is the set of real world entities that contribute to the production and maintenance of software systems. A software process model[1] is the description of a software process. A part of a process model is referred to as a process model fragment. A *software process model template* provides a common description for a class of process models [1-2].

E^3 is an academic project that has the goal to provide a methodology to specify, design, execute, and evolve software process models[2]. The E^3 methodology is a meta-process for the production of process models that consists of three meta-phases: specification, design, and implementation. Support for both evolution and reuse is provided in each phase. Each phase exploits a well defined set of object oriented techniques extended with association management. Among these techniques and conventions, some are directly adopted from previous object oriented work, e.g., [3-5], while others have been self developed for specific process modeling support.

This work is about software process model template specification. The E^3 specification method has been used to specify the software process model of FIAT Iveco, an Italian organization. An excerpt of this work is presented as example.

The structure of this work is as follows: section 2 introduces the E^3 specification method by explaining the specification language and a presentation technique. An example is presented in section 3. Conclusions are given in section 4.

2. THE E^3 SPECIFICATION METHOD

The E^3 method for template specification offers:

* This work has been partially supported by MURST 40% project "Metodologie e Strumenti di V&V di Funzionalità, Prestazioni e Affidabilità di Processi e Prodotti nell'Ingegneria del Software" and by EERP project IT-023.

[1] The prefix "software" may be omitted in the following.

[2] E^3: Environment for Experimenting and Evolving software processes.

The E^3 method for template specification offers:

- an object oriented language with graphic representation. The PML offers a set of predefined classes and associations;
- a presentation technique based on views and paths.

The graphic representation gives support for understanding, communicating, browsing, and editing process model fragments as it is difficult to conceptually grasp the nature of the process models in textual forms. The presentation technique allows process specifications to be kept readable independently of their scale.

An E^3 specification consists of a set of classes and associations denoting a process model template. A specification classifies process model elements into sub-classes of predefined classes and poses constraints by means of associations. For example, there are predefined associations to express synchronization constraints among tasks and others to express data flow between tasks. User defined classes and associations are constructed by specialization from the predefined ones.

2.1. Modeling levels

The following three modeling levels are needed:

model level represents a given process model. A process model is represented as an object net, i.e., a set of objects and links.

template level expresses process model templates. A class is a template for a set of objects, while an association is a template for a set of links. Moreover, a cluster (or aggregate) of classes and associations is a template for a set of nets, i.e., process model fragments. Classes and associations are organized in inheritance hierarchies. The template level enables reuse and polymorphism.

meta-model level represents classes of templates. Each class is also an object of class meta-class, as in Smalltalk [5] and each association is also a link of association meta-association. Meta-classes and meta-associations are implicitly declared at the time the respective classes and associations are defined.

2.2. The specification language

The E^3 language for process model template specification is based on the framework depicted in Figure 1. Predefined classes and associations are organized in inheritance hierarchies. The E^3 specification language permits both formal descriptions (by means of classes, associations, and inheritance), and not formal descriptions (by means of comments).

Predefined classes are abstract (i.e., they are never instantiated) and are used to define new classes by means of inheritance; each class must be derived from a predefined class. Classes and associations within a given model must respect the following constraints.

Class inheritance Classes are organized in an inheritance hierarchy whose root is `Object`. Usual semantics of class inheritance is that a class inherits all the attributes and methods of its super-class and in case overrides them. Here, we extend this inheritance definition by saying that a class inherits also the associations to which its super-class participates.

Association inheritance Associations are organized in an inheritance hierarchy rooted by association. The following rule holds for association inheritance.

$$\text{if } R(A_1,\ldots, A_n) \wedge S(B_1,\ldots, B_n) \wedge Inh(S, R) \Rightarrow (m \leq n) \wedge (\forall i,\ 1 \leq i \leq m,\ B_i = A_i \vee Inh(B_i, A_i)).$$

Where R(A,B) denotes an association R defined between classes A and B; Inh(X,Y) denotes that X, being it either a class or an association, inherits from Y. Each class participating to the sub-association S, still participates to the super-association R.

Association overriding An association can be overridden, provided that each class participating to the overridden sub-association, does not participate to the original association. The following rule must be respected:

$$\text{if } R(A_1,\ldots, A_n) \wedge S(B_1,\ldots, B_n) \Rightarrow \exists j, \text{Inh}(B_j, A_j) \wedge (\forall i, 1 \le i \le n, i \ne j, B_i = A_i \vee \text{Inh}(B_i, A_i)).$$

These constraints impact specification of process models, reuse of process model fragments and limit change.

The graphic representation provides a different icon for each predefined class; user defined classes are depicted by means of their own predefined superclass icon. According to the graphical convention introduced in Figure 1(a), each predefined association is uniquely identified by its graphical representation (i.e., it is not necessary to write its name). Even though the same symbol is employed to depict more than one association, the connected classes give context for symbol interpretation.

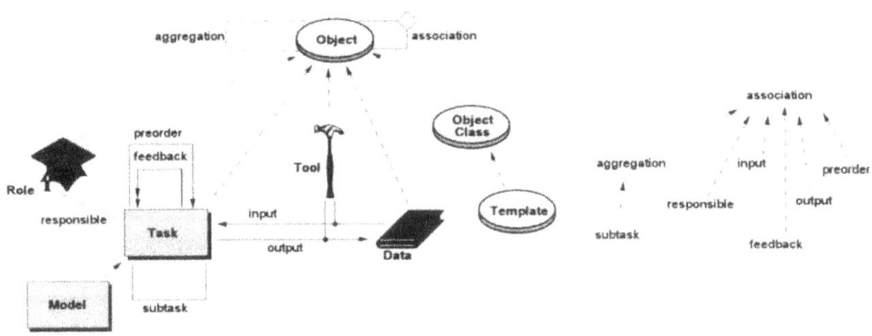

Figure 1. (a) Predefined classes and associations (b) Inheritance hierarchy of predefined associations.

In the following we give the meaning of each predefined class and association.

Object denotes whichever process model element. It is the inheritance root for each class and as each other class it is also an instance of class `ObjectClass`.

association both declares a class of links and constitutes itself a link (arity N). The inheritance hierarchy (rooted by `association`) for associations is displayed in Figure 1(b).

aggregation relates the whole (aggregate) and its parts. When an aggregate is destroyed, its parts are also destroyed, should they not participate in another `aggregation`. It inherits from `association` and its roles[3] are `aggregate` and `parts`.

Task denotes a software development activity. It starts execution, terminates either with success or with failure. In case, it re-starts execution. A software development activity, e.g., design, is represented as a `Task` sub-class.

subtask inherits from `aggregation`. Role names are `father` and `children`[4]. When a `Task` sub-class is connected by `subtask` to a set of children `Task` sub-classes, then father execution is the composition of children executions. Further, when the father is re-started all its children are re-

[3] Here, "role" denotes the role played by a class in the context of an association.

[4] Father and children must not be confused with inheritance role names, as sometimes used in object orientation literature.

started as well. Association `subtask` gives a tree structure, here called *subtask tree*, to a template. Each node of this tree is a `Task` sub-class and each edge is a `subtask` association. In the context of a given `Task` sub-class, association `subtask` declares a synchronization scope, enabling the definition of dependency constraints among sibling activities.

preorder role names are `predecessors` and `successors`. A task must start its execution when all its `predecessors` have terminated.

feedback role names are `giving_feedback` and `waiting_feedback`. A task `T` restarts when a task connected by feedback in the role `giving_feedback` terminates with failure and all `T`'s predecessors are terminated. While `preorder` can exist without `feedback`, `feedback` semantics depends on `preorder` semantics.

Role[5] defines a responsibility. Each sub-class represents a set of skills for a performer.

responsible connects a `Task` sub-class to the `Role` sub-class modeling the role of the activity responsible.

Data has a content that can be read and written. `Data` sub-classes are templates for software process products.

Tool sub-classes model automatic tools or techniques.

input and **output** express data flow among activities and define the manipulating tool.

Model is a particular `Task` sub-class modeling an entire process model, e.g., `Iveco_model` is the model that will be used as an example throughout this paper. Each subtask tree is rooted by a `Model` sub-class.

ObjectClass is a meta-class. It is the super-class of each meta-class. When a class is declared, its meta-class is implicitly declared.

Template is `Model` class. A process model template, i.e., a `Template` instance, is a `Model` sub-class, say `M`. It consists of a set of classes that can be calculated as the sum of: (1) all the `Task` classes in the subtask tree with root `M`; (2) for each of the `Task` sub-classes in the tree, all `Data`, `Tool`, and `Role` classes connected by predefined associations; (3) for each of these classes, all the user defined classes and associations connected to it.

2.3. The presentation technique

Four kinds of views are used in E3 to organize template specifications: Inheritance, Task, Task Synchronization, and User View. Further, each Task and Task Synchronization view for a given model is labeled by a path, that gives the position of the model fragment in the model subtask tree.

Inheritance View Both class and association *Inheritance Views* (IV's) can be build. The class IV shows the standard object orientation inheritance relation among classes. For a given class, there are two IV's: the *super* IV, that is the inheritance hierarchy from `Object` to the given class, and the *sub* IV, that is the inheritance tree rooted by the given class. Figure 3(a) shows an example of class sub IV. Figure 1(b) gives the association IV for the predefined associations.

Task View The *Task View* (TV) gives information about a single `Task` sub-class, by giving the `Data` taken as input and produced as output, and the responsible role. For each `Data` it gives the manipulating tools, i.e., the tools used to process the data. Figure 4(a) is an example of TV.

Task Synchronization View A process model subtask tree models many levels of activity decompositions that are not shown in a single view. Each *Task Synchronization View* (TSV) depicts the synchronization scenario for a single level decomposition of the activity modeled by the

---

[5] Not to be confused with "role" of associations.

Task sub-class given by the path. The TSV specifies the dependency constraints among Task sub-classes by means of the predefined associations preorder and feedback. Figure 2 shows a sample TSV (Association subtask is never shown pictorially, but it is deduced from the path).

User View The *User View* (UV) enables to connect classes by user defined associations. While the three views above impose strict constraints on what can be shown, the UV imposes the only constraint that associations and classes belong to some IV. Figure 4(b) shows a simple product configuration scheme defined in a UV.

Path The position of a given task in the activity breakdown is traced by means of the *path*, starting from the task (Model sub-class) modeling the whole process. As the same task can be subtask of different composite activities, it can have more than one path. Abstract classes do not participate to any subtask tree and root their own path.

3. AN EXAMPLE

In the following, we will refer to the informal process model template that has served as input to our specification as the Iveco process manual. The E^3 specification of the Iveco process manual is referred as the Iveco_model, a Model sub-class.

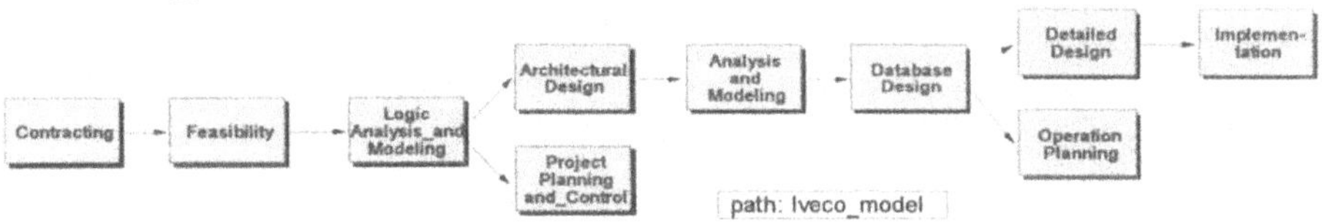

Figure 2. Iveco_model TSV.

Iveco_model is connected by subtask to 10 Phase sub-classes, each denoting one of the 10 main phases stated in the Iveco process manual. Figure 2 gives the TSV of the entire model. The sequencing among the different phases is strict and feedbacks are not allowed. Each of these phases is further decomposed in a production and a V&V sub-phases as inherited from abstract class Phase. Figure 3 shows both the IV and the TSV for class Phase.

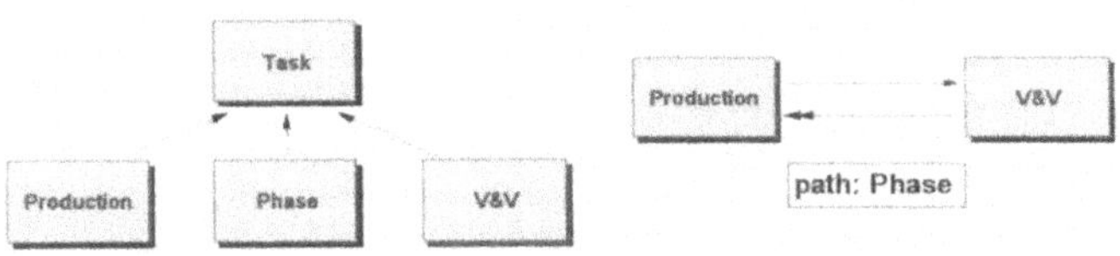

Figure 3. (a) Phase IV. (b) Phase TSV.

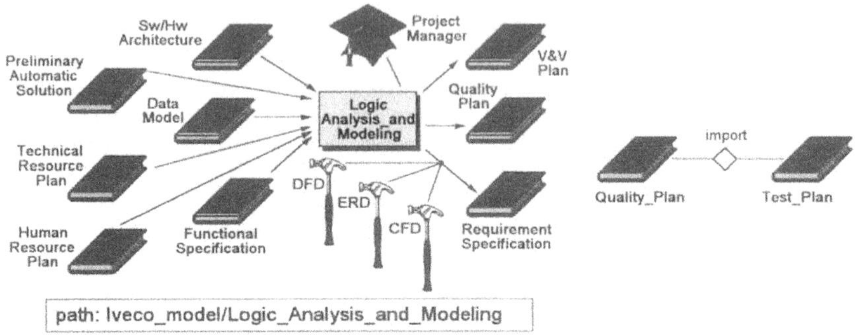

Figure 4. (a) `Logic_Analysis_and_Modeling` **TV. (b)** `Quality_Plan` **UV.**

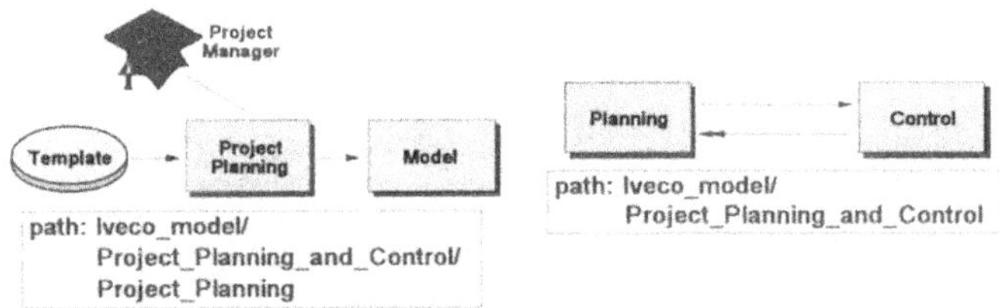

Figure 5. (a) Project_Planning_and_Control TSV. (b) Project_Planning TV.

Figure 4(a) gives the TV of class `Logic_Analysis_and_Modeling`. Class `Quality_Plan` is further specified in the UV depicted in Figure 4(b). Figure 5 shows both the TSV for `Project_Planning_and_Control` and the TV for `Project_Planning`. Project planning and control consists of two main phases, i.e., planning and control. The latter phase is supposed to transform a general process model description, i.e., a template, into a concrete process model, or plan.

4. CONCLUSIONS

In the process modeling arena [6-9], the efforts have been devoted toward definition of an universal process model language that combines different paradigms and that is powerful enough to specify, design, and implement process models. In E^3 , the main efforts are concentrated toward specification, i.e., toward understanding and communicating process models before trying to automate poor process models. A graphical editor that automates the E^3 specification method is under implementation. The E^3 specification language enables classification of process model elements into classes and associations. This helps the discovery of static inconsistencies in a process model definition, i.e., classes and associations play the same role that types play in programming languages. Meta-classes and meta-associations have been introduced to express constraints on process model templates. The meta-model level also enables to model explicitly the meta-process. `Project_Planning_and_Control` is an example of meta-phase specification. These aspects were confirmed by our experiment of specifying the template of Fiat Iveco. A monolithic textual document of 175 pages was transformed into about 200 classes and associations.

References

1. Conradi, R., Fernstrom, C., Fuggetta, A., and Snowdon, R.: "Towards a Reference Framework for Process Concepts", in J.-C. Derniame ed.: *Proc. from EWSPT'92*, Trondheim, Norway, Springer Verlag LNCS, September 1992, pages 3-18.
2. Feiler, P. H. and Humphrey, Watts: "Process Development and Enactment: Concepts and Definitions", in Leon Osterweil ed.: *Proc. from 2nd Int'l Conference on Software Process (ICSP'2)*, Berlin. IEEE-CS Press, March 1993, pages 28-40.
3. Booch, G.: "Object Oriented Design with Application", Benjamin Cummings Publishing Company, Inc., Redwood City, California, 1991.
4. Rumbaugh et al., J.: "Object-Oriented Modeling and Design", Prentice Hall, 500 pages, 1991.
5. Goldberg, A. and Robson, D.: "SmallTalk-80: The Language and its Implementation", Addison Wesley, 1983.
6. Estublier, J., and Melo, W.: "Software Process Model and Work Space Control in the Adele System", in L.Osterweil ed.: *Proc. of the 2nd IEEE International Conference on Software Process (ICSP'2)*, Berlin, Germany, February 1993.
7. Jaccheri, M. L. and Conradi, R.: "Techniques for Process Model Evolution in EPOS", IEEE Trans. on Software Engineering, December 1993, 19(12):1145-1156.
8. Fernström, C.: "Process WEAVER: Adding Process Support to UNIX", In L. Osterweil ed.: *Proc. of the 2nd IEEE International Conference on Software Process (ICSP'2)*, Berlin, Germany, February 1993.
9. Barghouti, N. S. and Kaiser, G. E.: "Scaling up rule-based development environments", *International Journal on Software Engineering and Knowledge*, Engineering, World Scientific, March 1992, 2(1): 59-78.

23

Soft Systems Methodology - A Process View

Graham Tate

Information Systems Department, City Polytechnic of Hong Kong
83 Tat Chee Avenue, Kowloon, HONG KONG

Abstract

Methods from the relatively recent research area of software process modelling are applicable to more than just software processes and methodologies. In this study, software process modelling is applied to the Checkland/Wilson soft systems methodology (SSM). The primary objective is a better understanding of SSM. Advantages and disadvantages of doing so are identified, including the possible disadvantage of over constraining SSM and impairing its spontaneity. A small set of requirements is given for the process modelling and enaction of an instance of SSM. These include low intrusiveness and high practitioner freedom within a basic set of specified activities and products. Goals of modelling and enaction include the observation and better understanding of SSM in action, the better definition of it in situations where this is appropriate, the identification of areas of difficulty for the practitioner(s) involved, the measurement of effort on activities, including iteration and rework, and the possible provision of guidance to inexperienced practitioners. A prototype model is described based on these requirements. Some preliminary findings based on the enaction of a prototype process model in an SSM case study are described.

Keyword Codes: D.2, D.2.1, D.2.9, D.2.m
Keywords: Software Engineering; Requirements/Specifications; Management; Miscellaneous

1. INTRODUCTION

Our primary objective is the application of software process modelling to soft systems methodology (when used for determining information systems requirements) for the purpose of observing SSM in action and understanding it better.

The first and most difficult problem in many information systems (IS) situations is determining requirements. It is also the first essential step in the production of quality systems. No matter how high the quality of information systems is in other respects, if the requirements are wrong, the system will be wrong.

Soft Systems Methodology (SSM) is a purposeful, but relatively unconstrained approach to the determination of requirements for an information system (IS), or indeed for any system. In an IS context it aims to identify the essential information needs of a business operation without too much noise or interference arising from consideration of the way things are done at present. This is in sharp contrast to more traditional methods that examine the current operation in detail in an attempt to determine where changes should be made. One of the more systematic formulations of the latter, the 'change analysis' approach, is given in Lundeberg et al[1]. SSM attempts to take an 'ideal world' view, concentrating on essence rather than accidents, before tempering it with the constraints of the real world.

SSM is intentionally 'soft' in that it addresses unstructured problem situations and tries not to be too dogmatic about how its practitioners go about finding solutions to them. Indeed, there are probably as many variants of SSM as there are active practitioners. We shall therefore concentrate on the fundamentals of SSM as expressed in 7 step Checkland methodology that is the basis of later approaches that claim to be SSM[2,3]. The first six steps are:

1 Investigate the problem situation.

2 Express the problem situation in some suitable form(s).
3 Formulate root definitions of relevant systems.
4 Build conceptual models.
5 Validate the conceptual models against the problem situation expression.
6 Define feasible desirable changes to the existing situation.

The seventh step involves action to solve the problem or improve the situation. If we regard SSM as primarily a requirements methodology, then step seven is concerned with implementation, which we will not consider further here.

This paper is concerned with the application of process modelling to SSM. Process modelling in this context means using an appropriate modelling notation to define the SSM process at a suitable level of detail, including the activities and products of interest. Furthermore it means executing, or in process modelling terms, enacting the defined process, keeping a record of the enaction, modifying the process model if and when necessary to correspond with what is actually done, and measuring aspects of the process, if practicable.

Some care is taken in establishing requirements for SSM modelling, since process models can differ greatly according to their purposes. A modelling architecture is described together with a low-intrusion, large-grain, exploratory process model for SSM. Experience with the use of the model in a case study by a relatively inexperienced SSM practitioner is described. As a result of this exploratory study some preliminary conclusions are drawn about the feasibility and usefulness of process modelling for SSM.

2. WHAT IS A PROCESS VIEW?

Taking a process view of SSM means focusing on the SSM process itself, its activities, products, events, milestones, etc., and their relationships to each other. It involves building one or more models of the process in order to understand, define and enact it. Enaction of a process model is like execution, but with much of the work (in this case almost all the work) being done by the practitioner(s) concerned. If a higher level of computer assistance of the process is used, via a workbench for example, then enaction becomes a sort of symbiosis of practitioner, workbench and model.

A particular process view depends on the viewer, the viewpoint, the goals, purposes and desired outputs of the modelling exercise and the level of definition, e.g. microscopic or macroscopic.

Though process modelling has been done informally for as long as men have used complex processes, the emergence as a major research field of process modelling for software, and software related processes such as SSM, is relatively recent. A major milestone in process modelling was the 1987 paper of Leon Osterweil "Software processes are software too"[4]. As the title indicates, the modelling can be rather formal and detailed, analogous to the manner in which a computer program models a computational or logical process.

2.1 Process modelling

A survey of process modelling is given in Figure 1, taken from Madhavji[5]. In relation to SSM, process engineering is the modelling of the particular SSM process that we have chosen to use. This could be a convenient instantiation of a generic SSM process. Process performance is the enaction of the chosen process by practitioner(s), i.e. the performance of an actual SSM study, including the production of conceptual models and recommendations for feasible desirable changes. Sector B of the diagram relates to the management of the process. This may be minimal for many single practitioner SSM studies, but is obviously important for larger studies and for other more protracted processes, such as software development.

There are a number of process modelling methods and notations. These include:

- process programming in which a process is specified using programming language notation, such as Ada PDL (program design language)
- entity-process modelling in which the states of process objects of interest are modelled together with the events which cause transitions between them[6]
- special process modelling languages and notations, or extensions to existing languages, for example those used in the ambitious Arcadia project[7]

- more conventional IS modelling - after all processes are systems - using for example one of the many structured analysis and design or object-oriented analysis and design notations.

Most of these process modelling methods can be used in most modelling situations, though in any particular situation some will be better than others. Most applications have been to more detailed software processes but the methods are generally applicable, with greater or less convenience, to the modelling of any definable process at any appropriate level of detail, using either fine grain models, or coarse grain models.

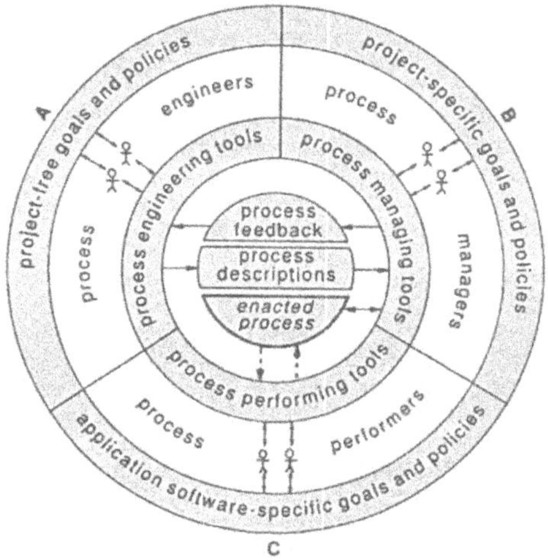

Figure 1: Madhavji's process modelling model

2.2 Process modelling & enaction in practice

The process modelling literature has a great deal to say about how modelling can or should be done, but very little about actual experience of doing it. The requirements for process modelling in practice are seldom made explicit. They can include:

understanding the process
process definition, e.g. for standardisation
measurement and data collection during process enaction
collecting design & decision history during process enaction
guidance of practitioners
control of the process and those performing it
management, including risk management.

Clearly, the nature, granularity, and intrusiveness of a process model will depend on the requirements it has to meet. The modelling notation and tools used in any particular case will depend on requirements and tool availability.

3. WHY TURN A PROCESS SPOTLIGHT ON SSM?

The initial reasons for doing so include a better understanding of the process and explicit observation of the process in practice leading to basic recording, measurement & data collection. Other reasons, which are a little further down the track, include: the identification of common variations of SSM (perhaps different instantiations of the of the same essential generic process); the guidance of practitioners, particularly inexperienced practitioners through, for example the provision of checklists; risk management, covering possible risks in the SSM process itself and also in its products; the identification of needs for tools, e.g. an SSM dictionary of repository. Other possible SSM process modelling advantages include: ensuring that no essential processes are omitted or skimped; the identification of areas of uncertainty, difficulty, high effort, frequent iteration and rework; the possible provision of some problem situation-solution traceability.

There are also a number of possible disadvantages of SSM process modelling which must be borne in mind. The enaction of an SSM process model may unduly interfere with the SSM process itself. This is a potential problem with the enaction of any process model. A balance is necessary between guidance and interference. The process model may over-define the process, over-constrain its enaction and not allow for essential variations, iterations, etc. Enaction may inhibit creativity, spontaneity and enthusiasm, which many practitioners would say are essential elements of SSM. Enaction may also distract from the main aims of SSM, though a good process model should emphasise these.

A further reason for modelling SSM is the future potential for monitoring aspects of the quality the SSM process, particularly in situations where there are a number of practitioners with different backgrounds and experience.

4. REQUIREMENTS FOR AN INITIAL SSM PROCESS MODEL

Where model building is concerned, the importance of determining requirements can scarcely be overemphasised. In spite of the substantial effort required to build and use process models, requirements determination seems either to have been largely overlooked or to have not been explicitly reported in the literature. In the case of SSM, however, where the methodology being modelled is not as well-defined as most others that have been modelled, the question of requirements cannot be brushed aside quite so easily. In brief, our key requirements for an initial SSM process model are those summarised below.

Only key activities and products will be modelled. These are the production of the key products, namely problem situation expression, root definitions, conceptual models, consensus conceptual model, conceptual model validation notes, feasible desirable change report. Subsidiary activities will be subsumed under these major activities. If there are difficulties in doing this, then these will be noted in the enaction records. Flexible sequencing of activities will be permitted to allow for iteration, rework, out of sequence activities, etc. The granularity of the model should be large, on the human time and effort scale rather than the computer scale. The aim is minimal intrusiveness consistent with observing the SSM process and collecting data (such as time, effort and product data) about it. Other requirements include the ability to include useful checklists for practitioner help and guidance, if needed, and interfaces to permit existing or planned tools to be accommodated conveniently within model enaction. Essentially we are seeking to build a management-level SSM shell to support observation, data collection, measurement, tool use, help and possible guidance.

5. APPROACHES TO MODELLING SSM

Figure 2 shows the SSM process modelling architecture used. It will be noted that the SSMer (or SSM practitioner) interacts with the SSM enaction engine, which aims to be an assistant and recorder of all on- & off-workbench SSM activity (or as much as can be easily captured, automatically or in user-friendly exchanges). The SSM process model is essentially a plug-in specification which is interpreted by the enaction engine. Any tools are accessed through enaction so that time spent on tool use can be measured as well as product change (e.g. in size or complexity) as a result of tool use. The design of the SSM enaction engine itself is similar to that described by Tate[8].

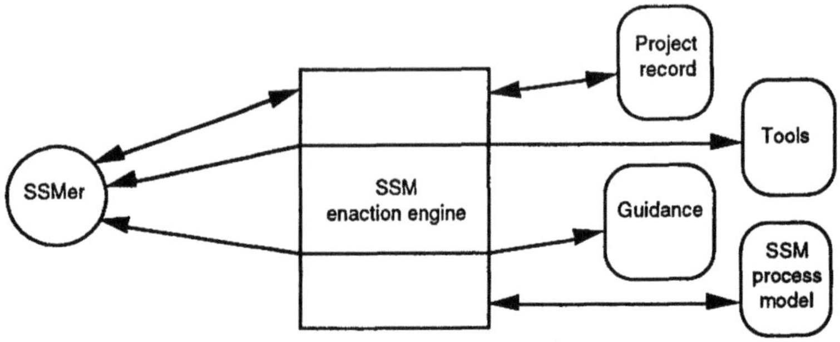

Figure 2: SSM process modelling architecture

Such a workbench-based architecture obviously only covers on-workbench activities directly. Information about off-workbench activities can be collected in several ways. It may be entered during the next on-workbench session. This is the solution we have currently adopted. In future personal digital advisors (PDAs) may be used to help with the incorporation of off-workbench activity into the enaction records.

5.1 A low-intrusion generic model

The initial model used is an instantiation of a simple generic product-based model. The building block of the model is shown in Figure 3. One such block is included for each of the six key SSM products listed in the requirements. Though there are no data flows connecting the blocks, they are dependent on each other through the product base to which they all contribute. No sequence constraints on steps are imposed other than data availability. The SSMer determines the sequence of activities, thus allowing for any pattern of work or rework. Initially we just record simple data and measurements such as the product worked on, what was done and why, when it was done, the effort expended, the product size (if available) at end of the session (e.g. text page or word count, diagram page or object count), and any unresolved problems and consequent actions arising from session.

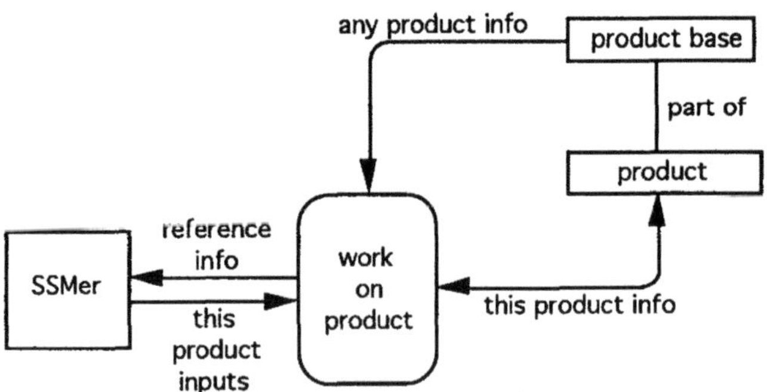

Figure 3: Generic product-based process model building block

6. THE CASE STUDY

The case study itself is not important to this investigation save as a vehicle for the enaction of a prototype of the simple SSM process model outlined above. The case study had to do with the requirements for an information system to support the work of IS journal editors. This may seem a simple and well-defined problem, perhaps even a 'hard' problem in SSM terminology. However, if one considers questions such as special issues, departments, markets, interest and readability, the vagaries of the traditional refereeing process, very limited editorial time and other resources, and so on, the problem becomes somewhat soggy and the views of the main actors rather divergent.

We walked through an enaction of the case study using the process model described. Workbench support was rudimentary, mainly consisting of menu selection of one of the six activities modelled, time recording and the collection of notes and observations about each activity. Products in text form were kept on the workbench, but not at this stage integrated with the enaction engine as the architecture of Figure 2 indicates. Nevertheless, the architecture and model were followed strictly. Other products, such as conceptual models, were paper based, as is traditionally the case in SSM. The findings from our enaction of the case study problem are described below in the conclusions.

7. CONCLUSIONS

Process modelling of SSM is feasible. But is it useful? Our conclusions at this stage are, on balance, yes. It helped an inexperienced practitioner to understand what he was trying to do and where each of his SSM activities fitted into the overall process. At each point, it also helped to focus attention firmly on the activity in hand and its product so that the practitioner was fully aware of his position, the current state of the process, and his immediate target. A good handbook or even a informal model can not quite do this, at least not without the user mentally transforming his references to it into implicit process model fragments which may not be complete and will likely require repeated instantiation, not always in the same form.

Did process modelling stifle creativity? Not in this case. The creative work still had to be done. Model enaction was more intrusive than one would have liked, but not too inconvenient. Observation and measurement intrudes into any process, particularly into complex processes like requirements determination or system development.

What did process model enaction reveal? For this (admittedly inexperienced) practitioner, it showed that SSM involves a great deal of iteration. There was a starting point and a finishing point but the activities in between, while exhibiting a general progression from beginning to end, often occurred rather more in parallel with the practitioner moving from product to product refining and improving them more or less together. In this process, the use of the process model, crude as it was, helped materially to avoid what Raymond Oakes, a well-known SSM practitioner in Northern Ireland, has referred to as "reality seepage", namely the undue intrusion of the 'real' world into the 'ideal' world of conceptual models This was particularly important because of the number of times the practitioner's activities crossed the real/ideal boundary, often within a short period of time.

This practitioner also felt a strong need for tools, particularly in the enaction environment. Without tools the human partner in enaction carries the lion's share of the effort and there is much less integration than the same developer has experienced in a CASE environment[8].

Other conclusions are that SSM process modelling can be done with relatively simple techniques and tools and that it could potentially be a starting point for measuring, better understanding, refining and guiding SSM, particularly for beginners in SSM.

Further experiments are necessary to evaluate the usefulness of SSM modelling and enaction in a wider context.

REFERENCES

1. Lundeberg M., Goldkuhl G. and Nilsson A. *Information Systems Development: A Systematic Approach* Prentice-Hall, Englewood Cliffs, NJ, USA (1981)
2. Checkland P.B. *Systems Thinking, Systems Practice* John Wiley, Chichester, UK (1981)
3. Wilson B. *Systems: Concepts, Methodologies and Applications* 2ed., John Wiley and Sons Ltd., Chichester, UK (1990)
4. Osterweil L., "Software Processes are Software Too" *Proc. 9th ICSE*, (Monterey, CA, March 30-April 2 1987), ACM 2-13
5. Madhavji, N. H. "The process cycle" *Software Engineering Journal* (Sept 1991) 234-242
6. Humphrey, W.S. and Kellner, M.I. "Software Process Modelling: Principles of Entity Process Models" *Proc. 11th ICSE* (Pittsburgh, Pa, May 1989) 331-342
7. Taylor, R. N., Belz, F. C., Clarke, L. A., Osterweil, L., Selby, L., Wileden, J. C., Woll, A. L. and Young, M. "Foundations for the Arcadia environment architecture" in Henderson, P. B. (ed) Proc. 3rd ACM SIGSOFT/SIGPLAN Software Engineering Symposium on Practical Software Development Environments, Boston (Nov 1988) pp 1-13
8. Tate, G. "Software process modelling and metrics: a CASE study" *Information and Software Technology* Vol 35 No 6/7 (June/July 1993) pp 323-330

24

BOOTSTRAP - Improving the Capability of Software Industry with Databas Support

Janne Järvinen

Department of Information Processing Science, University of Oulu, Linnanmaa, FIN-90570 Oulu, Finland. Email: jannej@rieska.oulu.fi

Abstract

Software process assessment approaches, methods and methodologies have gained much attention in both MIS and SE areas recently. Perhaps the most well-known approach is CMM (Capability Maturity Model) which was developed by SEI (Software Engineering Institute at Carnegie Mellon University, Pittsburgh). The most well-known European assessment approach is called BOOTSTRAP methodology. The BOOTSTRAP methodology includes both the CMM and the ISO 9000 standards as its starting points. The methodology includes guided assessment process, questionnaires and algorithm for maturity and capability determination, guidelines for process improvement, assessor training program and licensing policy, and computer-based tools and a database that support the consultancy activities.

The database has a unique role in the BOOTSTRAP methodology for providing a basis for the process improvement of software industry. This role is clarified by explaining the development principles, services and architecture of the software tools used in the BOOTSTRAP methodology. Some sample results are presented using the empirical data collected from over 100 software process assessments made in Europe during 1991-1993 under auspices of the ESPRIT/ Bootstrap project.

Keyword Codes: D.2.0; I.6.0; K.6.3
Keywords: Software Engineering, General; Simulation and Modeling, General; Management of Computing and Information Systems, Software Management

1. INTRODUCTION

Process assessment and improvement methodologies came into the highlight of discussion throughout the software industry since the Software Engineering Institute published its maturity model for software process capability determination in 1987 [4]. This model has further been developed into the CMM framework [9]. During the last three years an ESPRIT project BOOTSTRAP developed a European process assessment and improvement methodology, where the original SEI model was applied as one of the main background approaches. BOOTSTRAP Project assessed also the capability of the European software industry using the methodology developed within the project. [8]

Shortcomings of the SEI model (see for example [2]) and the lack of European and ISO 9000 (see for example [3]) perspective motivated the development of the BOOTSTRAP software process assessment and improvement methodology. BOOTSTRAP extended the SEI approach and adjusted it to suit European software production. This was done mainly by expanding the target group, adapting the ISO 9000 quality standards and adding state-of-the-art software engineering ideas to the methodology.

Firstly, the Bootstrap software process assessment methodology is introduced. Secondly, the role of the database and software tools used by Bootstrap are reviewed. Then a sample of empirical Bootstrap assessment data is presented with a specific interest in presenting the role and meaning of the BOOTSTRAP database for European software industry. Finally, the pros and cons of the database support are considered.

2. BOOTSTRAP METHODOLOGY

The BOOTSTRAP methodology was developed during an ESPRIT technology transfer project whose purpose was to fertilize the soil for the introduction of modern and adequate software technology into European software and software intensive industry. The European assessment methodology was needed because it was felt that the SEI approach was aimed mainly for very large embedded defence systems that did not face the European software production problems.

When developing the methodology BOOTSTRAP Project adopted and extended the original SEI approach with features that were found necessary in the European context, and to attain more detailed diagnosis of the capability of the organizations and their projects ([1]). The aim was to define an improvement path for software producing units with distinct milestones. The software process maturity framework by Humphrey [5] provided a basis for the milestones and ISO 9001 [6] and ISO 9000-3 [7] were used as a framework for the quality system of the BOOTSTRAP methodology in general.

A specific goal of the BOOTSTRAP methodology is to reduce risks related to software production. Management is the key factor to achieve this goal implying that the development should start with development of the organization. In the well-functioning organization the development of the methodology can then commence. When the methodologies are adopted in the organization it is then ready to adopt also the technologies that will support the methodologies in use. It is also important to understand that the technologies are marginal in respect to the growth of productivity and quality - the elements needed to reduce risk.

The BOOTSTRAP methodology includes description of guided assessment process, maturity and capability determination instruments (questionnaires and algorithm), guidelines for process improvement (standards for action plan generation), and assessor training program. The methodology is supported with computer-based tools and a continuously updated European database that provides an excellent opportunity to compare the maturity and capability levels of the company assessed for example with the rolling means of similar companies in Europe.

2.1. The Role of Database in Bootstrap Assessments

The development of the BOOTSTRAP database had two main goals; to assist the Bootstrap assessments and to help in improving the capability of the European software industry.

An important starting point for achieving these goals was the ability to map the state-of-practice of software engineering in Europe. Therefore, as assessments have been conducted, the results have been collected to a database. At present this database is situated in Oulu, Finland and it is maintained by the Finnish Bootstrap partners, the CCC companies and the University of Oulu.

During a BOOTSTRAP assessment when the data is collected it is then transferred into the database and compared with rolling means of similar companies or projects. Therefore, using the Bootstrap database it is possible to view the different average maturity profiles of different segments or countries and compare a new organization to these profiles. This gives a good indication on the status of the organization in relation with others among the chosen segment.

The primary goal of an individual Bootstrap assessment is to measure and develop an SPU quality profile analytically, discovering strengths and weaknesses of the assessed SPU. Secondly the assessment will derive the steps for improvement from the strengths-and-weaknesses profile (see figure 1) in terms of a plan of recommended actions to be taken immediately. The average profiles from the Bootstrap database may be used in creating this profile. The third object of the assessment is to transform the action plan into a series of 'mini-projects' (see table 1) for implementing the recommended improvement steps.

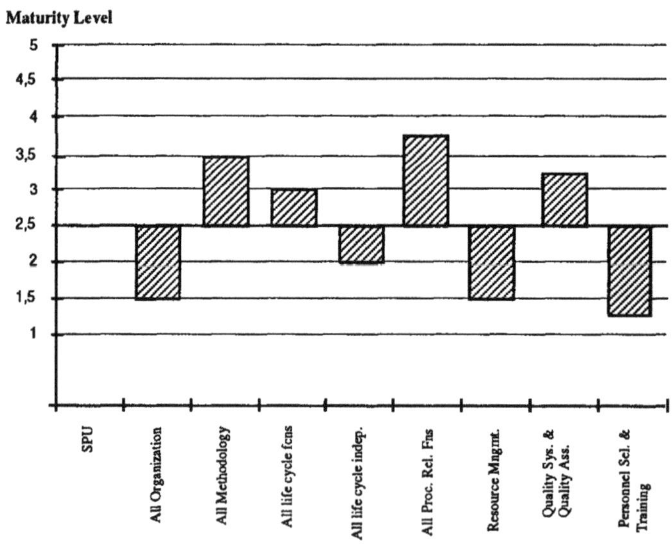

Figure 1. Example of an SPU strengths and weaknesses profile.

3. THE BOOTSTRAP DATABASE SOLUTION AND SOFTWARE TOOL SUPPORT

BOOTSTRAP tools are computer-based facilities that automate parts of the data collection, counting, data analysis, result presentation and data retrieving from the BOOTSTRAP database. The BOOTSTRAP database is a central database that includes all the data captured during the assessments performed by the licensed BOOTSTRAP assessors.

The architecture of Bootstrap Tools and Database is based on a client-server solution (cf. figure 2.). Bootstrap tools are used in client PCs and the complete, central database is located in a unix-based server computer at the Bootstrap Center. Additionally, licencees may have local databases that contain their own assessment data.

Table 1. Example of an SPU action plan table.

Action	Effort	Precon-ditions	Qualifi-cation needed	Priority 1 (impor-tance)	Priority 2 (success)	Final priority
Testing education	3 person months, 10 tmk	Seminar	SW Technology	3	4	3
Develop-ment handbook	6 pm 100 tmk	Documents available	Senior SW Engineer	2	1	1
Purchase evaluation method	2 pm, 40 tmk	Tool study	Junior SW Engineer	5	5	5
...	...	...	...	...	...	...

3.1. BootBase - The Bootstrap Database

The Bootstrap database is called BootBase. It is a database that includes all data collected in the BOOTSTRAP assessments since autumn 1990.

BootBase provides a valuable resource for the European software industry for at least the following reasons:

- The database can be used to generate mean profiles of European and national status of software engineering and especially report the state-of-practice within a specific domain of interest, ie. banking, telecommunications etc.
  A client organization can use the mean profiles to compare themselves to other companies in the field and obtain information on how to focus their improvement efforts.
- BootBase can serve as an aid for generating improvement action plans for an organization as similar organizations may be traced from the database without breaching confidentiality.
- The database will serve as a source of information for comparing the status of software production in Europe to software production in USA and Japan.

3.2. Bootstrap Tools

The Bootstrap tools offer assistance for assessors during the assessment process and enable the data gathering and analyzing functions. These tools are introduced here briefly.

The BootCollector is used for collecting assessment information and supporting the assessors work during an assessment session. The assessment information is then transferred further into the data base and for results processing.

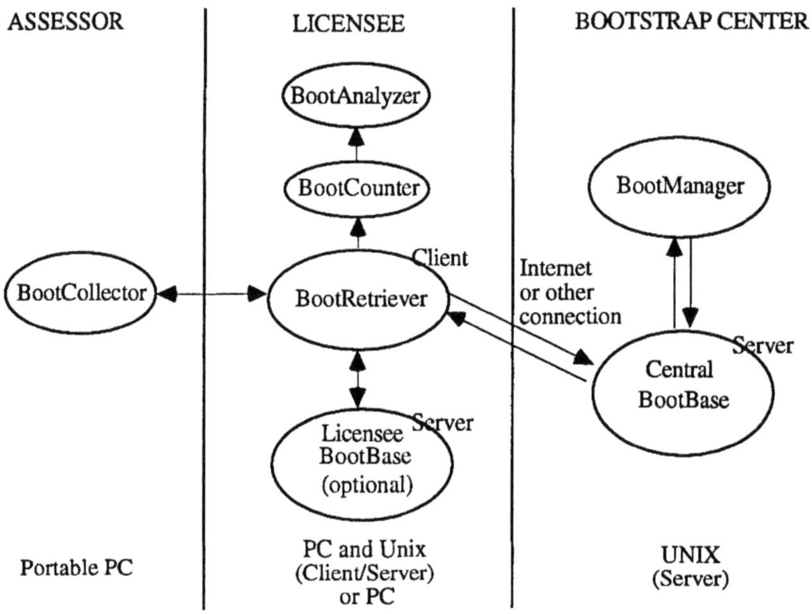

Figure 2. The overall architecture of the Bootstrap Tools and Database.

The BootRetriever, BootCounter and BootAnalyzer form a software package for calculating and displaying the assessment results both in graphical and textual form. The BootManager is a software package for BootBase management and operation in the Bootstrap Center.

The BootRetriever can also be used for performing queries into the Bootstrap database and also as an interface tool between assessors and the Bootstrap Center.

BootAnalyzer also supports assessors in the generation of action plans. The assessment results give detailed description of the strengths and weaknesses of the assessed unit (cf. figure 1). These attributes can be used when designing or verifying the improvement actions. With BootAnalyzer it is also easy to compare possible scenarios of future situations.

Using the Bootstrap database and software tools it is possible to view the different average maturity profiles of different segments or countries and compare a new organization to these profiles. This will give a good indication on the status of the organization in relation with others among the chosen segment.

4. SAMPLE RESULTS FROM BOOTSTRAP ASSESSMENTS

The sample results of the assessments performed during the BOOTSTRAP project contain overall maturity levels of the SPUs and projects and mean values of the key attributes forming capability profiles of the SPUs and projects. Here only the maturity level results will be presented, because the mean values of capability profiles have been kept confidential and counted in different ways for different purposes.

The maturity levels that are presented in the following two figures (Figure 3 and 4) have been counted based on the assessed 37 SPUs and 90 projects during the first and second phases of the BOOTSTRAP project. The figure 3 presents percentage distribution of SPUs on different maturity level quartiles and the figure 4 the same for the projects.

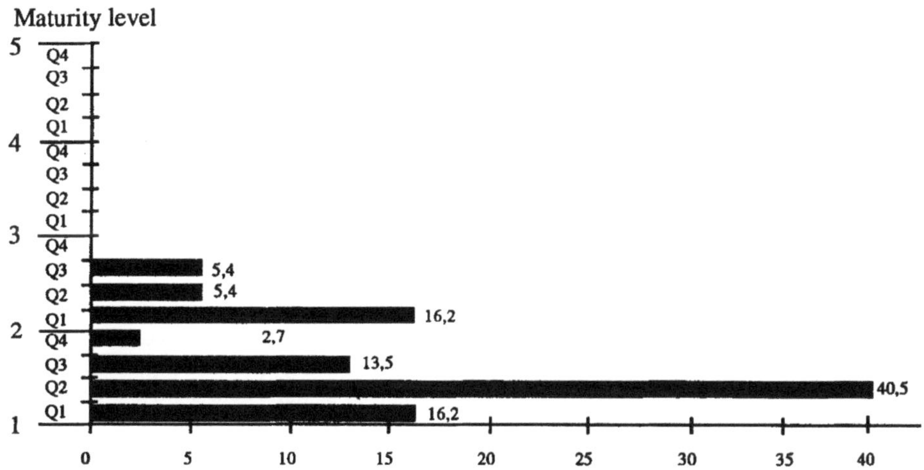

Figure 3.Sample of maturity levels of SPUs in Europe (37 SPUs)

The size of the sample results of the Bootstrap assessments is too small to draw firm conclusions based on it concerning European state of the practice in software production. The only remark that can be made is that the maturity level of the projects seem to be marginally better than with the SPUs. This is the fact when compared the maturity of the SPU with its projects, although the average level computation over the samples above show a slightly opposite result. The tentative explanation for the remark could be that new practice and technology have been adopted first in the projects after that it is perhaps transferred into standard use in the SPU. The result motivates also to use separate questionnaires on the organization and project levels in the way that is included in the BOOTSTRAP methodology.

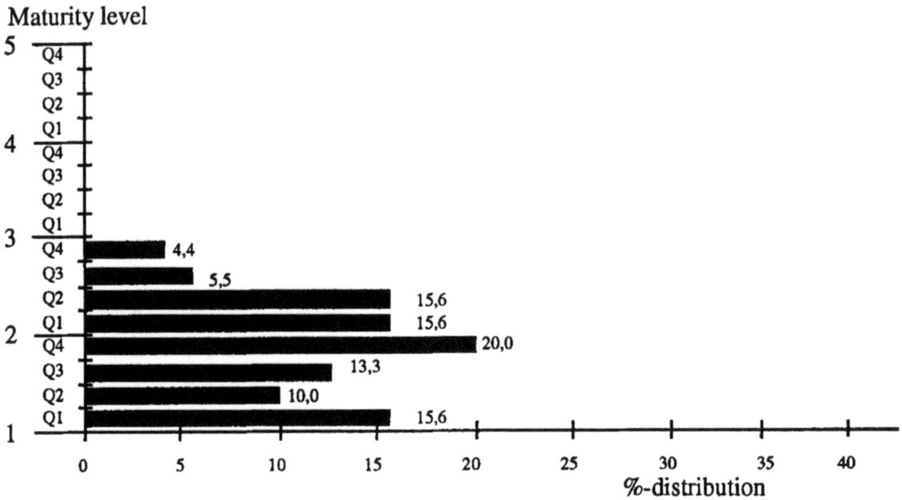

Figure 4. Sample of maturity levels of software projects in Europe (90 projects)

5. DISCUSSION

A well designed and maintained database can be a valuable asset in an attempt to take a broad perspective on the improvement of the software industry. The Bootstrap database contains very current data as the database is continuously being updated with new assessment data from the Bootstrap Licencees. The data should also be quite consistent and comparable because Bootstrap assessments are controlled and can only be performed by assessors who have received proper training.

The Bootstrap database support facilitates the recording and analyzing of the assessment results and helps in designing plans for improvement. For the software industry and its various segments the database provides detailed state-of-practice data that can be used in evaluating the capability and potential of the industry. An individual organization can benefit greatly from the experiences of other similar organizations and also track its progress with the help of the database.

The Bootstrap database can also serve a more general use for the software industry. The database can provide valuable information for the planning of improvement directions for the industry about the areas where improvement is most needed. Also in the process of organizational knowledge creation [10] and in particular inter-organizational knowledge creation and utilization the Bootstrap database can be of help in focusing the resources allocated to the development of the software industry.

As with any other software process assessment methodology, Bootstrap is not a finished product but an evolving one. Many questions remain to be answered. For example, how can we be sure that our method with the database support yields assessment results that represent the reality in an organization? Or what is the true meaning of increased maturity and capability?

6. CONCLUSION

It is difficult to assess software processes and compare the assessment results of software producing units and their processes. Although a general framework is beneficial for the software industry there remains much work in uncovering the specific properties of the different types of software producers. An organization which does telecommunications software is very different from an accounting software company; a real-time process control software company has other requirements for its organization and processes than an in-house MIS unit. With the help of Bootstrap data and feedback from the industry we hope that we are able to identify some of the properties of these different domains and thus participate in the inter-organizational learning process and work of improving the capability and of software industry in general.

REFERENCES

1. Bicego, A., Cachia, R., Haase, V., Koch, G., Krzanik, L., Kuvaja, P., Lancelotti, R., Maiocchi, M., Messnarz, R., Saukkonen, S. Schynoll, W. and Similä, J. 'Bootstrap: Europe's Assessment Method.' *IEEE Software*, pp. 93-95, May, 1993.
2. Bollinger, T. B. and McGowan, C. 'A Critical Look at Software Capability Evaluations', *IEEE Software*, pp. 25 - 41, July, 1991.
3. Bamford, R. C. and Deibler W. J, Comparing, contrasting ISO9001 and the SEI capability maturity model, COMPUTER, October, 1993.
4. Humphrey, W. S. *Characterizing the Software Process: A Maturity Framework.* Software Engineering Institute, CMU/SEI-87-TR-11, DTIC Number ADA182895, June, 1987.
5. Humphrey, W. S. *Managing the Software Process*, Addison-Wesley, Reading, Mass., 1989.
6. ISO 9001, *Quality Systems; Model for Quality Assurance in Design/Development, Production, Installation and Servicing*, 1987.
7. ISO 9000-3, *Quality Management and Quality Assurance Standards, Part 3: Guidelines of ISO 9001 to the Development, Supply and Maintenance of SW*, 1991.
8. Kuvaja, P., Bicego, A. 'Bootstrap: a European Assessment Methodology', *to be published in Software Quality Journal, June 1994.*
9. Paulk, M. C. et al, *Capability Maturity Model for Software, Version 1.1*, Software Engineering Institute, Technical Report CMU/SEI-93-TR24, 1993.
10. Nonaka, Ikujiro, *A Dynamic Theory of Organizational Knowledge Creation*, Organization Science, Vol. 5, No. 1, February 1994.

PART FIVE

Project Management

25

On the Optimal Timing of Software Development Cycle

Hakman A. Wan

Department of Computer Studies, Lingnan College, Hong Kong

Abstract

This paper puts forth a mathematical model and studies the optimal time to start the development cycle of a system before the existing system retires. By assuming a log-linear cost function of maintenance expenses, the solution to the optimization problem can be found.

Keyword Codes: K.6.1; K.6.4
Keywords: Replacement problem, optimization, Lagrangean multiplier

1 INTRODUCTION

Dissatisfactions against an old system pile up until management decides to initiate another round of the system development cycle. But until the new system becomes operational, the existing one remains the only system available to the users. The inappropriateness [1] of the old system still require maintenance which incurs substantial manpower and cost. An early start of the new cycle obviously reduces spending on old system maintenance. But it shortens the operational lifespan of the old system and hence discourages the management to spend time in system development stages. To determine the optimal time for a start to re-write a new system is known as the *Software Replacement Problem.*

The Software Replacement Problem is studied by a handful of researchers among them are Gode *et al.* [2] and Chung [3]. The latter devises a cost function which totals the maintenance and re-writing cost over the planning horizon. A hypothetically perfect productivity of the development team is shown to incur instantaneous replacement. However, we redesign the cost function and produce a solution which differs from instantaneous replacement.

2 THE MODEL

We consider two consecutive system development cycles. Let T_R be the time when the new system cycle begins (ie. re-writing the system starts) and T_N be the time when the new system begins operational. The expenditure during this period includes: 1) maintenance cost between time 0 to T_N, 2) development cost between time T_R to T_N, and 3) maintenance cost between time T_N to T. Our problem is to find the timing of T_R such that the sum of the first two costs is minimized.

Let $m(0)$ represent the number of maintenance requests at time 0, when the old system begins to function. Hence the number of maintenance requests at time t can be expressed as

$$m(t) = m(0)e^{\delta t} \tag{1}$$

where $\delta > 0$ is the logarithmic rate of growth which can be determined by regression analysis. Assuming that every request is entertained by the maintenance team, $m(t)$ becomes the number of requests serviced. It is believed that δ reflects the willingness of the maintenance team to respond to these requests. If the attitude of the team does not change, $m(t)$ is a monotonically increasing function. However, some change of δ is expected and it brings about different considerations which will be mentioned later.

Let $h : R \to R$ be the cost function which maps number of maintenance requests to monetary units of expenses. Thus the total maintenance expenses during the period (0,t) is

$$\int_0^t h(m(t))dt \tag{2}$$

We employ a log-linear cost function h. Then the (present value of the) cost function can be expressed as

$$h(m(t)) = \alpha[m(t)]^\beta e^{-rt} \tag{3}$$

where α and β are defined respectively by the structuredness of the programming technique on the system development and the productivity of the system developers; and $r > 0$ is the rate of interest. The total maintenance cost in the period $(0, T_R)$ is

$$\int_0^{T_R} \alpha[m(t)]^\beta e^{-rt}dt = \frac{\alpha m^\beta(0)}{\delta\beta - r}(e^{(\delta\beta - r)T_R} - 1) \tag{4}$$

The maintenance cost in the period (T_R, T_N) is not included in the integral because we suspect that the system developers may have a different attitude towards maintenance when they learn that the system will soon be replaced. The number of maintenance requests may grow at the same rate δ, but the system team will then be reluctant to entertain as many of these requests as they did before T_R. Here we assume a different rate of growth (ie, we let δ_1 replace δ and let δ_2 represent the rate of growth of maintenance requests that will be serviced. N.B. $\delta_1 > \delta_2$.) Thus expressions (1) and (4) should be

$$m(t) = m(0)e^{\delta_1 t} \quad \text{and} \quad \tfrac{\alpha m^\beta(0)}{\delta_1\beta - r}(e^{(\delta_1\beta - r)T_R} - 1)$$

The last one corresponds to the total cost of maintenance in the period $(0, T_R)$. Following the same argument, the total maintenance cost in the period (T_R, T_N) is found to be

$$\frac{\alpha m^\beta(0)e^{\beta T_R}}{\delta_2\beta - r}(e^{(\delta_2\beta - r)T_N} - e^{(\delta_2\beta - r)T_R}) \tag{5}$$

On the other hand, the rewriting effort is determined by $\int_{T_N}^{T_R} Ldt$ where L represents the daily wages paid to the project team. Hence the total effort, if expressed in terms of its present value, is

$$\frac{\alpha m^\beta(0)}{\delta_1\beta - r}(e^{(\delta_1\beta - r)T_R} - 1) + \frac{\alpha m^\beta(0)e^{\delta_1\beta T_R}}{\delta_2\beta - r}(e^{(\delta_2\beta - r)T_N} - e^{(\delta_2\beta - r)T_R}) - \frac{L}{r}[e^{-rT_R} - e^{-rT_N}] \tag{6}$$

In reality, the effort of developing a system is related to the complexity of the system where complexity can be approximated by the number of function points [3, 4]. Thus $L = \frac{F}{\mu}$ where F is the measure of function points and μ is a proportional constant.

3 THE PROBLEM AND THE SOLUTION

Thus we have an optimization problem:

To minimize $\quad E(T_R, T_N) \equiv$

$$\frac{\alpha m^\beta(0)}{\delta_1\beta - r}(e^{(\delta_1\beta - r)T_R} - 1) + \frac{\alpha m^\beta(0)e^{\delta_1\beta T_R}}{\delta_2\beta - r}(e^{(\delta_2\beta - r)T_N} - e^{(\delta_2\beta - r)T_R}) - \frac{F}{\mu r}[e^{-rT_R} - e^{-rT_N}] \tag{7}$$

such that $T_N \leq T_R$.

Let γ be the Lagrangean multiplier and

$$f(E(T_R, T_N), \gamma) = E(T_R, T_N) + \gamma(T_R - T_N + s^2) \quad (8)$$

be the Lagrangean function. Since $E(T_R, T_N)$ is convex, the Kuhn-Tucker conditions for minimization are

$$\alpha m^{\beta}(0)[e^{(\delta_1\beta-4)T_R} - e^{(\delta_1\beta+\delta_2\beta-r)T_R}] + \frac{\alpha m^{\beta}(0)\delta_1\beta e^{\delta_1\beta T_R}}{\delta_2\beta - r}[e^{(\delta_2\beta-r)T_N} - e^{(\delta_2\beta-r)T_R}] + \frac{F}{\mu}e^{-rT_R} + \gamma = 0 \quad (9)$$

$$\alpha m^{\beta}(0)e^{\delta_1\beta T_R}e(\delta_2\beta - r)T_N - \frac{F}{\mu}e^{-rT_N} + \gamma = 0 \quad (10)$$

$$T_R - T_N + s^2 = 0 \quad (11)$$

$$\gamma s = 0 \quad (12)$$

$$\gamma \geq 0 \quad (13)$$

Solving equations (9)-(13) we look into two different cases:

Case 1 If $s = 0$, then from (11) $T_N = T_R$. It is the so-called instantaneous replacement solution which suggests an non-existent development period for the new system. Assume that $T = T_N = T_R$. Equations (9)-(13) give rise to

$$\frac{2Le^{-\delta_1\beta T}}{\alpha m^{\beta}(0)} = 2e^{\delta_2\beta T} - 1 \quad (14)$$

We can then derive the value of T if all the other variables are known. If we assume further that $\delta = \delta_1 = \delta_2$, (14) can be simplified to

$$T = \frac{1}{\delta\beta}ln(\frac{1 + \sqrt{1 + 8A}}{4}) \quad (15)$$

where $A = \frac{2L}{\delta m^{\beta}(0)}$. Theoretically speaking, $T_N = T_R = T$ is possible if the values are very large numbers (ie. the new system will never begin its development.) It can be accomplished if β is extremely small (ie, the productivity of the development team is extremely high), α is extremely small (ie, the existing system has always been developed in a highly structured way). However, since $T > 0$, A or L must be sufficiently large; ie

$$L > \frac{1}{2}\alpha m^{\beta}(0) \quad (16)$$

Case 2 If $\gamma = 0$ then $s^2 > 0$ or $T_N > TR$. The relation between T_N and T_R is given by (10)

$$\frac{T_R}{T_N} = \frac{1}{\delta_1\beta T_N}ln(\frac{A}{2}) - d \quad (17)$$

where $d = \delta_2/\delta_1$. The optimal timing to start developing the new system can be found by solving (17). However, since $0 < T_R < T_N$

$$1 > \frac{T_R}{T_N} = \frac{1}{\delta_1\beta T_N}ln(\frac{A}{2}) - d > 0 \quad (18)$$

The inequalities can be simplified to

$$h(m(T_N))e^{\delta_2\beta T_N} > L > \alpha m^{\beta}(0)e^{\delta_2\beta T_N} \tag{19}$$

In general, $1 > d > 0$. The right side of (18) ranges from $h(m(T_N))$ and $\alpha m^{\beta}(0)$. When $d = 1$, the inequality gives

$$L > h(m(T_N)) \tag{20}$$

It implies that if all maintenance requests are serviced as if no new system is being developed, the cost of developing a new system is still higher than the maintenance cost at the time when the new system is operational. But if $d = 0$, ie, all maintenance requests are ignored after the new development cycle commences, the left side of (18) gives $h(m(T_N)) > L$. ie, the expenses of developing the new system must be smaller than the maintenance cost at T_N, should there be any.

Again, from (17), the structuredness α of the existing system has a positive effect on the ratio T_R/T_N since a small α (ie, a highly structured old system) prolongs the lifespan of the system by increasing the ratio T_R/T_N .

4 CONCLUSION

Several ideas can be derived from the solutions of the problem:

1. It is discovered that r, the rate of interest, does not appear in any of the solutions. It can be certain that it casts no influence on the value of T_R.

2. If we put the instantaneous replacement strategy to practice, we must expand the lifespan of the existing system as long as possible. It demands a maintenance team of high productivity and an extremely structured development technology, as analyzed in case 1.

3. In both cases, the value of L is bounded by a value proportional to $\alpha m^{\beta}(0)$. From (17), we learn that a highly structured system should last longer than a less structured one, but the influence of α is not very conspicuous since it is hidden in a logarithmic function.

4. The policy of providing selective responses to all the maintenance requests after a new development cycle begins has a positive effect on prolonging the lifespan of the existing system. From (18), the ratio T_R/T_N is increased if a small d is chosen.

References

1 Davis, A.M., Bersoff, E.H., and Comer, E.R., A Strategy for Comparing Alternative Software Development Life Cycle Models, *IEEE Trans. Software Engineering*, vol 14. No. 10, Oct 1988.

2 Gode, D.K, Barua, A., and Mukhopadhyay, T., On the Economics of the Software Replacement Problem, *Proceedings of the 11th International Conference on Information Systems*, 1990.

3 Chung, S.L., Timing of Software Replacement, *preprint.*

4 Albrecht, A.J. and Gaffney, J.E., Software Function, Source Lines of Code, and Development Effort Prediction: A Software Science Validation, *IEEE Trans. Soft. Eng.*, vol SE-9, No. 6, Nov 1983.

26

Information Systems Project Manager's Critical Success Factors: In-house Versus Outsourced Development

Hugo Rehesaar and Andrew Rose

School of Information Systems, University of New South Wales, 2052, Australia.
Information Systems Branch, Pacific Power, Sydney, 2000, Australia.

Abstract

Software quality is measured in many ways; in this paper we look at Client Acceptance.

In order to aid the process of managing and achieving client acceptance, a pilot study has been undertaken to identify the project manager's critical success factors (CSF) for achieving client acceptance. With the increase in outsourcing it is also of interest to determine whether the critical success factors might be different for software developed in-house when compared with that developed by a third party. A previous study (Rehesaar and Rose [1]) found differences in client acceptance criteria between in-house and outsourced projects and these criteria are used here.

This study found that for similar client acceptance criteria there are no differences between in-house and outsourced project manager's critical success factors. However, significant differences were found in the specified critical success factors for different client acceptance criteria. Most notably, eleven of the eighteen critical success factors were applicable to only one client acceptance criterion each.

Therefore, project managers who are changing from in-house to outsourced development or vice versa must be aware that they should apply a different set of critical success factors based on the different set of client acceptance criteria they must satisfy.

Keyword Codes: K.6.1; D.2.9; K.6.m
Keywords: project management, critical success factors; project success; outsourcing

1. INTRODUCTION

To facilitate the acceptance of a project by the client, project managers must at least ensure that their clients' acceptance criteria (CAC) are satisfied. The method proposed to ensure that these client acceptance criteria are satisfied is the critical success factor (CSF) method. The critical success factor method, when applied to client acceptance criteria, identifies the limited number of areas in which results, if they are satisfactory, will allow satisfaction of the criteria that a client will use to evaluate a completed software product for acceptance.

The client acceptance criteria to be used in this study come from previous research by the authors (Rehesaar and Rose [1]). In that study, a list of probable client acceptance criteria was formulated from an analysis of information systems project success literature. This list was provided to a sample of software development clients to determine the criteria they use to evaluate a software product. The result was two lists of top five client acceptance criteria, one each for in-house and outsourced development.

Using this list of client acceptance criteria, a sample of software development project managers was asked to identify the critical success factors for the satisfaction of each of the client's acceptance criteria. The results are critical success factors for each of the client acceptance criteria. Because a difference was found in client acceptance criteria for in-house and outsourced development, this distinction in project management is also investigated.

2. CRITICAL SUCCESS FACTORS

Critical success factors (CSFs) are, for any business, the limited number of areas in which results, if they are satisfactory, will ensure successfully competitive performance in an organisation. If results in these areas are not adequate, the organisation's outcomes will be less than desirable.

The critical success factor concept was first discussed in management literature by Ronald Daniel [2]. He stated that "in reporting internal data, a company's information system must be discriminating and selective. It should focus on 'success factors'. In most industries these are usually three to six factors that determine success; these key jobs that must be done exceedingly well for a company to be successful".

Boynton and Zmud [3] found that the CSF method has attracted considerable attention as a method of supporting both MIS planning and requirements analysis. The research into project critical success factors has been directed towards project implementation success rather than client acceptance criteria, for example, Lasden [4], Wall [5], Wolff [6], Norko [7] (anecdotal), Holt [8], Keller [9], Curtis [10] (single case studies), Rockart [11] (multiple case study), Cleland and King [12], Baker, Fisher and Murphy [13] (normative).

Ashley, Lurie and Jaselskis [14] in research into determinants of construction project success found that a strong relationship existed between the following critical success factors and success measures: planning effort - functionality; project manager's technical capability and technical uncertainty - end user satisfaction; projects manager's administrative capabilities - cost; legal political environment - follow-up work, leading the way to further work on linking success criteria to specific critical success factors.

3. RESEARCH AIMS

a) To investigate the effect of in-house versus outsourced development on project manager's critical success factors.

b) To investigate the effect of client's acceptance criteria on project manager's critical success factors.

4. RESEARCH SETTING AND SAMPLE.

The questionnaires were mailed to fifty project managers, representing ten organisations in Sydney, Australia. Both private and public sectors were represented. Five organisations used in-house developers and five were third party suppliers of outsourcing. Only in-house developers with a charge back in place were chosen so as to not introduce payment/non-payment for services as a variable. Follow up phone interviews were conducted where the completed questionnaires were difficult to interpret accurately.

5. RESEARCH PROCEDURES

The aim of the data collection was to obtain a list of critical success factors for each client acceptance criterion, relevant to in-house and outsourced development organisation types.

The subject project managers were provided with the list of client acceptance criteria for their organisation types sourced from previous research by the authors (Rehesaar and Rose, 1994). They were asked to list CSFs for satisfying each of the CACs. A minimum of three and a maximum of six critical success factors were suggested for each CAC. Additional space was provided for explanation of each CSF to minimise misinterpretation.

The client acceptance criteria for in-house development are shown in Table 1.

The client acceptance criteria for outsourced development are shown in Table 2.

Table 1.

Client Acceptance Criteria and Critical Success Factors for In-house Project Managers

Client Acceptance Criteria	Critical Success Factors
1. Delivery of the completed product with all the functional requirements specified initially or with mutually agreed upon changes.	1. Project Plan/Schedule 2. Requirements/Specifications 3. Involvement of Key Personnel 4. Monitoring and Feedback 5. Project and Change Control 6. System Testing 7. Delivery of Product
2. Completion of the product with the agreed performance level.	1. Performance Criteria 2. Resources Available for Performance Measurement (including personnel, methodologies and tools) 3. Performance Testing
3. The completed product satisfies all the screen, report and data entry requirements specified initially or with mutually agreed upon changes.	1. Project Plan/Schedule 2. Requirements/Specifications 3. System Design 4. Involvement of Key Personnel 5. Monitoring and Feedback 6. Project and Change Control
4. The completed product is likely to directly benefit the intended users: either through increasing efficiency or effectiveness.	1. Project Support 2. Cost/Benefit Analysis 3. Involvement of Key Personnel 4. Training
5. The completed product works as it was intended to work.	1. Requirements/Specifications 2. Involvement of Key Personnel 3. Monitoring and Feedback 4. Project and Change Control 5. System Testing

6. THE SAMPLE

The experience of the respondent in software development and project management was used to evaluate the validity of individual questionnaire results. The project managers from both the internal development and the outsourcing organisations had at least six years experience in software development and at least one year in project management. No questionnaires were rejected based on the respondent's lack of experience. The response rate for questionnaires from the in-house developers was 47% and from the outsourcing developers was 40%.

Table 2. Client Acceptance Criteria and Critical Success Factors for Outsourced Project Managers

Client Acceptance Criteria	Critical Success Factors
1. Acceptance of the completed product by staff for whom it is intended.	1. Requirements/Specifications 2. Involvement of Key Personnel 3. Ergonomic Considerations 4. Monitoring and Feedback 5. Project and Change Control
2. Delivery of the completed product with all the functional requirements specified initially or with mutually agreed upon changes.	1. Project Plan/Schedule 2. Requirements/Specifications 3. Involvement of Key Personnel 4. Monitoring and Feedback 5. Project and Change Control 6. System Testing 7. Delivery of Product
3. The completed product works as it was intended to work.	1. Requirements/Specifications 2. Involvement of Key Personnel 3. Monitoring and Feedback 4. System Testing
4. The completed product is likely to represent a definite improvement in performance over the way the activity used to be performed.	1. Project Mission 2. Cost/Benefit Analysis 3. Involvement of Key Personnel 4. Monitoring and Feedback
5. The completed product is reliable.	1. Requirements/Specifications 2. Resources 3. Reliability Measurement 4. Monitoring and Feedback 5. System Testing

7. RESULTS

7.1 Effect of In-house versus Outsourced Development

Comparison of the two lists of clients acceptance criteria yielded two criteria which were the same for both in-house and outsourced development. The critical success factors for them were compared.

(a) Criterion: 'Delivery of the completed product with all the functional requirements specified initially or with mutually agreed upon changes.'

All seven of the CSFs suggested by the in-house project managers were identical with those of the outsourced developer. The critical success factors are: (1) Project plan/schedule (2) Requirements

/specifications (3) Involvement of key personnel (4) Monitoring and feedback (5) Project and change control (6) System testing (7) Delivery of product.

(b) Criterion: 'The completed product works as it was intended to work.'

For this criterion, the four factors specified by outsourced project managers were shared by in-house project managers, of whom 30% also added 'Project and change control' as a fifth factor. The four shared factors are: (1) Requirements/specifications (2) Involvement of key personnel (3) Monitoring and feedback (4) System testing.

7.2 Effect of Client Acceptance Criteria on Critical Success Factors

In total, 18 critical success factors were identified for the 8 discrete client acceptance criteria.

Of these only two factors (4 and 5) applied to six criteria, of which five were the same; one (13) applied to five criteria; one (8) applied to four; two (10 and 17) applied to three; and one (1) applied to two criteria. The remaining eleven factors were applicable to only one criterion each.

8. DISCUSSION AND FURTHER RESEARCH

Two client acceptance criteria, from the lists of top five criteria, were common to both in-house and outsourced development. For each of these criteria, the critical success factors were the same for both in-house and outsourced project managers, except for one CSF which was specified by less than one third of the in-house project managers.

This suggests that for the same criteria there is no perceived difference in the prioritisation of the work of in-house versus outsourced project managers. That is, the critical success factors are transferable from one environment to the other for similar client acceptance criteria. This is surprising, since the clients in the two environments exhibited marked differences in how they determined whether or not to accept the software product.

Further research is warranted to identify reasons for this disparity and also to determine if the tasks undertaken by the two sets of projects managers to achieve the same critical success factors are different.

The eight discrete client acceptance criteria demonstrated a wide scattering of critical success factors, sharing a total of eighteen CSFs. Only two critical success factors were applicable to six criteria, with eleven factors applicable to only one criterion each. Whilst two criteria (in-house 1 and 3) shared five factors, no pattern emerged linking criteria with sets of factors or vice versa. It is noted that these two criteria were very similar; both referred to satisfaction of requirements.

The results show a strong link between specific client acceptance criteria and their respective critical success factors, with no two criteria sharing critical success factors. Thus project managers will need to be aware of the acceptance criteria employed by their clients and must customise their own critical success factors accordingly if they are to maximise their chances of success.

Despite this strong one-to-one link, three critical success factors were prominent, namely 'monitoring and feedback', 'involvement of key personnel' (both with six criteria) and 'requirements/specification' (with five criteria).

Analysing the data as a whole, showed that one critical success factor 'monitoring and feedback' was applicable to all five of the outsourcing criteria and only three of the in-house criteria. Removing the two common criteria, results in a three to one split. While this suggests a possible influence on critical success factors by in-house versus outsourced in the area of importance ranking of critical success factors, the amount of data in this study does not allow for any more than speculation. Further research with a larger data set may prove interesting.

Whereas no direct link has been established between critical success factors and the in-house versus outsourced environment, the very fact that the critical success factors were strongly linked to the client acceptance criteria does provide an indirect influence on CSF choice, in that the CACs are different between in-house and outsourced development. Hence the project manager in the in-house environment will be working to a markedly different set of critical success factors than the outsourced project manager.

9. CONCLUSION

Previous research on differences between in-house and outsourced development concentrated on the criteria clients use for accepting a software product. It found significant differences in the criteria used. In this study on critical success factors for the same set of client acceptance criteria, no such difference between in-house and outsourcing was found. Significant differences were found in the specified critical success factors for different client acceptance criteria. Most notably, eleven of the eighteen critical success factors were applicable to only one client acceptance criterion each.

Nevertheless, project managers who are changing from in-house to outsourced development or vice versa must be aware that they should apply a different set of critical success factors based on the different set of client acceptance criteria they must satisfy.

REFERENCES

1. Rehesaar, H. and Rose, A. "The Effect of the Client/Developer Environment on Software Acceptance Criteria", ITRC Working Paper 94/14, University of New South Wales, Australia, March, 1994.
2. Daniel, R.D., "Management Information Crisis", *Harvard Business Review*, September-October 1961, pp. 111-121
3. Boynton, A.C. and Zmud, R.W., "An Assessment of Critical Success Factors", *Sloan Management Review*, Summer 1984, pp. 7-27
4. Lasden, M., "Effective Project Management", *Computer and Communication Decisions*, March 1980, pp. 49-59
5. Wall, W.C., "Ten Proverbs for Project Control", *Research Management*, March 1982, pp. 26-29
6. Wolff, M.F., "Rules of Thumb for Project Management", *Research Management*, Vol. 27, July-August 1984, pp. 11-13
7. Norko, W.A., "Steps in Successful Project Management", *Journal of Systems Project Management*, September 1986, pp. 36-38
8. Holt, L., "Project Management Principles Succeed at ICI", *Industrial Management & Data Systems*, March-April 1983, pp. 4-9
9. Keller, R.T. "Predictors of the Performance of Project Groups in R&D Organisations", *Academy of Management Journal*, Vol. 29, 1986, pp. 715-726
10. Curtis, W., Krasner, H. and Iscoe, N., "A field study of the software design for large systems", *Communications of the ACM*, Vol. 31, No. 11, November 1988, pp. 1268-1287
11. Rockart, J.F., "The Changing Role of the Information Systems Executive: A Critical Success Factor Perspective", *Sloan Management Review*, Fall 1982, pp. 3-13
12. Cleland, D.I. and King, W.R., *Systems Analysis and Project Management*, McGraw- Hill, New York, 1983
13. Baker, B.N., Murphy, D.C. and Fisher, D., "Factors Affecting Project Success", in *Project Management Handbook*, Cleland D.I. and King W.R., Van Nostrand Reinhold, New York, 1983, pp. 669-685
14. Ashley, A.B., Lurie, C.S. and Jaselskis, E.J., "Determinants of Construction Project Success", *Project Management Journal*, Vol. 18, No. 2, June 1987, pp. 69-79

27

Measuring the Value and Performance of Your IT Department

Terry Lynch

Western Sydney Area Health Service, Sydney, Australia 2151

Abstract

QUALITY is a cost usually overlooked in software estimation and software valuation. This paper outlines the software quality metrics initiatives developed and being deployed at Western Sydney Area Health Service (WSAHS), Sydney, Australia to address these issues.

WSAHS is a unit of the NSW Health Department employing 8,500 staff in 7 hospitals, 6 community health centres and a dental school. WSAHS has a patient catchment of 1.4 million and is one of the largest VAX and Novelle sites in Australia. WSAHS IS Department has a staff of 56 or whom 20 are software developers working on VAX and PC Workstation applications.

WSAHS needed indicators to demonstrate compliance to quality requirements when delivering systems and to enable corporate planners to monitor trends in software costs. We need also, indicators to use during the software development cycle to determine the cost of quality when negotiating software development and maintenance project funding.

1. OBJECTIVES

To begin with the objectives for software quality indicators were defined as follows:

*To be able to conduct objective evaluations of the quality of software products.

*To provide a measurement to enable the negotiation of the level of quality in a system prior to development beginning.

*To be able to quantify quality so that it can be built into development estimates

*To be able to quantify the quality of production systems to support strategic decisions for resource utilisation and the system replacement planning.

*To be able to predict the production quality of a product whilst still in development and dynamically take steps to ensure that the quality of a product satisfies and predetermined standard.

*To gauge the effectiveness of quality initiatives.

Only the first three of these criteria have been addressed at the time.

2. METRIC CHARACTERISTICS

Having established quality objectives, we established the guidelines for the metrics as being:

a. Objective. The metric must be derivable by a repeatable, quantifiable and auditable process. It must not be intuitive or subjective.

b. Linked to a business need. That is the data has to be gathered for a purpose. That is there must be a clearly defined reason for gathering the data and management must be prepared to act on the indications from the data.

c. Useful. That is to say the data from the metric must be timely and sensitive to of any change in the behaviour or practices the metric is meant to monitor.

d. Economical and easy to gather. If the gathering of the metric data is costly and difficult it will eventually become too much trouble to gather. Especially if there is no perceived benefit to those gathering the data (ie the project teams) and the sponsor or the metrics program. To this end, we designed and constructed three metrics tools in conjunction with the University of Western Sydney. Those tools being an Function Point Tool, a two method estimation tool and a Quality Tracking System. All these tools link to a Project History Data Base and MS-Project tracking tool.

e. Have a Counter Metric. For every metric there has to be a counter metric so that the metrics do not divert the focus of an organisation away from their primary purpose to a secondary purpose - satisfying the metrics.

g. Normalisation. Since the size and complexity of software is so variant, it was recognised that a method of normalising of results be determined. Without it any comparison between projects will be difficult because an allowance cannot be made for size and of products developed and applications developed on different platforms. The normalisation factors choosen were:
- size (function points)
- complexity
- frequency of use and
- the number of users of a system.

3. What to measure?

We identified two distinct groups of metrics we needed to consider to satisfy our objectives:
- Metrics which help us manage the development process and
- Metrics which indicate fit for purpose of software products.

Within those categories we have two sub-categories - Effectiveness and Efficiency.
The efficiency of a software products being how well a product utilises resources (both hardware, consumables and human effort). The effectiveness of a product being how well the product meets the current business need.

For the development process - the software assembly line the objective was to to determine if our tools and techniques are effective and whether we are using them as efficiently as we might.

At this time we have focused on the effectiveness of our products and processes.

3.1 Product Metrics

The measurement criteria of product efficiency and effectiveness chosen was the USAF Rome Laboratories Quality Criteria or RADC Criteria. In this process eleven criteria are identified.
- Conformity to requirements and the business need
- Ease of use
- Reliability
- Flexibility or ease of change
- Maintainability
- Reusability of modules of logic in the system
- Efficiency in execution and utilisation of hardware
- Integrity and security of a system and its data
- Interoperability or the ability of the software to interact with other software in use in the organisation
- Portability of the software to other platforms.
- The ease of testing the software.

Non Functional requirements are defined at the requirements gathering phase of all projects and Business Realisation Reviews (BRR) are conducted 12 months after implementation examine the same criteria. The BRR criteria are each rated from 1 being poor to 5 being excellent the mean score being a Quality Index. All systems are required to meet a QI rating of 3.75 or better. Since introducing this scoring system, four BRRs have been conducted and their results are shown below.

However, the scoring did highlight consistently low ratings for user documentation which is now being addressed.

3.1.1 Other metrics

In addition the following measures have been identified and raw data is now being collected. However, these metrics can not be collated until October when the Function Point Tool comes online.

Ease of Use. How user friendly is the software? The measure used was the number of requests for help received at the help desk. High volumes of request would suggest that the software is difficult to use.

Help desk calls

Function points x number of users x hours of operation

Interoperability. How easy is it for end users to switch between applications? This is be a major concern of clinicians and health workers dealing with the public.

Average steps to exit an application.

The following product efficiency attributes were taken from the IFPUG Function Point Asset Management manual and will :

Reliability. What is the average time to failure of a product? How expensive is it to support a software product compared to other software.

Reliability = cost of repair/ size(x complexity)

Completeness. How often are requests for change received from the clients.

Completeness = Requests for change/ size

Maintainability. What is the application support rate and what is the trend of the costs for a software product.

Maintainability = Maintenance costs / size

3.2 Process Metrics

As mentioned earlier, the metrics gathered need to fit a purpose. The objectives of the quality metrics in the development environment were to:

- Identify good and bad development practices and to introduce practices to promote the good initiatives and impeded counter productive practices.
- Be able to negotiate quality levels to reflect the business need of the organisation.

The development process metrics chosen are :

Testing Proficiency = Defects discovered

Size x Complexity

Efficiency of the process = Defects introduced from previous phases

Total review issues for a phase x size

A defect being an error requiring re-work. For example, a design error not detected until programming.

Again until the FPA tool is ready, these formulations can not be applied however, comparisons of Defects subjectively have highlighted some key issues to address in Requirements gathering. These problems related to our use of JAD sessions and ER- Modelling that had to be addressed immediately.

4. IMPLEMENTATION TACTIC

The first activity was to review metrics programs in a major financial institution and a major Australian airline to establish what were the critical success factors for their metrics programs. This identified 9 critical considerations:

- Sustained management sponsorship. If there is not a strong commitment to the measurement program from the very top then commitment from the metric gatherers will wane.
- The metrics had to be linked to the business needs of the organisation. If there is no purpose for gathering the metrics and no action is taken on trends that the indicators are showing then commitment and enthusiasm and eventually funding will dissipate.
- The metrics had to be relevant to all involved and understood by the players.
- Metrics must not be perceived to be unfair and therefore resisted.
- Care had to be taken not to motivate the wrong behaviour
- Metrics collection must be inexpensive and not cumbersome to collect
- Must act on the indications the metrics are showing.
- Do not try to introduce too many metrics at once. Try to keep the metrics simple and uncomplicated so that they are easily understood.
- Where possible use graphics to represent data and automate the data collection.

5. EARLY INDICATIONS

The development of the tool set in conjunction with the University of Western Sydney has proven to be a critical success factor. For example early attempts to introduce manual Function Point counting proved unsuccessful due to the time consumed and lack of consistency. Likewise the completion of review statistics always required close supervision. When projects began to slip the review details were often not completed. By providing a high level view of review progress and having the review events being designated by a system, reviews could not be missed and had to be completed.

Heavy post implementation support indicated inadequacies in requirements gathering and testing procedures. The defect tracking confirmed this issue enabling corrective action to be initiated to improve staff Entity Relationship Modelling and conducting JAD sessions.

PART SIX

Quality, Reliability, Standards

28

ISO Standards in Software Engineering

J. Billington

University of South Australia, Signal Processing Research Institute, The Levels, Adelaide, S.A., 5095, Australia

Abstract

This paper introduces the work of ISO/IEC JTC1/SC7 Software Engineering. SC7 is going through a period of rapid change, with reorganisations occurring at the last 4 Plenary meetings to meet the needs of the software engineering community.

Keyword Codes: D.2; K.6.2
Keywords: Software Engineering; Software Management

1. INTRODUCTION

International standards in software engineering will play an important role in improving the quality of software during the next decade. The initial thrust is to produce standards for the software development process in the hope that understanding the process, documenting it and then submitting it to continuous improvement will make the development of software repeatable and lead to substantial improvements in quality. A second thrust is to develop standards that directly apply to software products.

The main body entrusted with the development of international standards for information technology is Joint Technical Committee 1 (JTC1) of the International Organisation for Standardisation (ISO) and the International Electrotechnical Commission (IEC). Subcommittee seven (SC7) of JTC1 is the main committee with responsibility for software engineering (SE) standards. This committee liaises with a large number of other committees within JTC1, and other ISO and IEC Technical Committees. An important liaison is with ISO/TC176 which is responsible for the ISO 9000 series of Quality standards.

It is very important that purchasers, suppliers and educators are aware of international standards. This is because purchasers will be able to mandate the use of various standards with the result that suppliers who do not conform will be at a significant disadvantage, particularly in international markets. The purpose of this paper is to provide a brief summary of the activities of ISO/IEC JTC1/SC7, Software Engineering, and to promote the need to become active in the formulation and promulgation of international standards.

2. ISO/IEC JTC1/SC7

The Software Engineering subcommittee, SC7, is chaired by Mr. J. Coté, from Canada which also carries the administrative load. This is handled by the Standards Council of Canada, which runs the secretariat. The current secretary is Mr François Coallier from Bell Canada. Quoting from the Secretariat's Report [2], SC7's area of work comprises: 'Standardization of management techniques, processes, methods and tools necessary for the engineering, development, maintenance and support of software products.'

Every ISO subcommittee comprises a set of member countries, normally represented by their national standards bodies, for example, the British Standards Institute in UK. Members can be active in developing international standards by contributing material and comment and by participating in meetings, in which case they are designated as 'P' members. Members can also be observers, where they can obtain official subcommittee (SC N numbered) documents, but they don't participate. These members are known as 'O' members. As of June 1994, SC7 comprised 25 'P' members (including Australia, USA, Japan, UK and many other European countries), and 15 'O' members.

In ISO, standards are developed using a process of consensus, involving 5 stages: Proposal stage - a new work item is prepared and voted on by 'P' members; Preparatory stage - a working draft (WD) is prepared and voted on for registration as a Committee Draft (CD); Committee stage - CD is revised to take into account member body comments and voted on for registration as a Draft International Standard (DIS); Approval stage - DIS is revised and voted on for approval as an International Standard (IS); Publication stage - IS is published. If there is insufficient support or agreement at any stage, further development and resolution of different positions need to take place, often including further balloting.

An early report on the work of SC7 appeared in IEEE Computer [1]. Since that paper was published in March 1991, major changes in the structure and work of SC7 have occurred. SC7 comprises a set of working groups (WGs) and holds a full meeting (a plenary) once a year in June. The following brief history illustrates the extent of revitalisation. SC7 was re-organised from 5 WGs into 8 WGs in June 1991, and at the June 1992 plenary, decided to disband WG5 and form two new WGs (10 and 11). In June 1993, its WG1 was merged with the new WG11 which obtained full working group status, having operated as an interim WG in its first year. At its Ottawa meeting in June 94, SC7 spawned a new WG 12 'Function Size Measurement', created two ad hoc groups (Quality Aspects of Software Systems and Software-System Relationships), totally changed the emphasis of WG9 to concentrate on software integrity, and significantly changed its WG convenors. SC7 now has 9 WGs, labelled 2 through 12, but excluding 3 and 5. It also has a special work group for SC7 business planning, and an Advisory Group.

The working groups normally meet twice a year, but occasionally there can be more meetings, including special ad hoc or editing meetings when results are wanted quickly. A summary of each meeting is provided as minutes which are circulated as official SC7 numbered documents. Most of the inputs and outputs of the WG meetings are only published as working group documents, and can only be obtained by 'P' members who register a particular individual as the member body's representative.

The SC7 secretariat now runs an electronic mail service to members (SC7_NEWS@qc.bell.ca) which greatly speeds up delivery of some SC7 documents, and provides other useful information (such as conference announcements). SC7 members are strongly encouraged to use email to progress SC7's work programme.

3. SUMMARY OF SC7 PROJECTS

This section provides a very brief summary of the projects undertaken in SC7's working groups. Further information can be found in [2] and the resolutions of the Ottawa Plenary, circulated by email on SC7_NEWS@qc.bell.ca (SC7_NEWS-94-54) on 23 July 1994.

3.1 WG2: System Software Documentation

The convenor of WG2 is Mr. K. Johnson (UK). WG2's scope covers the development of standards for the documentation of software systems. The main project has been the revision of IS 6592 'Guidelines for the Documentation of Computer-Based Application Systems', which is to be circulated as a CD. ISO TR 9294 'Guidelines for the management of Software Documentation' will be revised to ensure consistency with DIS 12207 (see WG7 below). It is proposed to fast track a British Standard 'Guidelines for the design and preparation of documentation for users of application software' through SC7.

3.2 WG4: Tools and Environment

WG4 is convened by Mr. T. Vollman (USA) and has developed Committee Draft 14102 Evaluation and Selection of CASE Tools, which will be revised and distributed for 6 month DIS ballot. A new work item regarding the adoption of CASE Tools into organisations has been accepted.

3.3 WG6: Evaluation and Metrics

This WG, convened by Mr. M. Azuma (Japan), is developing a series of standards for software product evaluation. The first standard, ISO/IEC 9126, Software Product Evaluation - Quality Characteristics, was published in 1992 and will be revised into a 3 part standard. The series comprises a set of 7 follow-on standards (General Guide, Metrics Planning and Implementation, Developer's Guide, Buyer's Guide, Evaluator's Guide, Guide to producing Evaluation Modules and Indicators and Metrics) which are at working draft or committee draft stage. A new standard, IS 12119: Software Quality Requirements and Testing, has recently been approved and will be published shortly. A new project on measurement and rating of data processing performance is currently at the preparatory stage.

3.4 WG7: Life Cycle Management

WG7 is convened by Mr. J. Roberts (USA) and has developed a major standard (DIS 12207-1) on life cycle management that at the time of writing was still under DIS balloting to become an international standard. The standard provides a set of descriptions of processes that can be tailored for a two party supplier-purchaser contract. A follow-on 'Guide Book for Life Cycle Processes' technical report is currently under development. New work will cover the areas of Software Maintenance and Mock-Ups and Prototypes.

3.5 WG8: Support of Life Cycle Processes

Mr. D. Schultz (USA) has recently taken over as convenor of WG8, which is producing a set of standards on various life cycle processes. These include Software Configuration Management (CD 12207-2, to be revised and circulated for DIS ballot, planned 11/94) and working drafts on Project Management, Software Quality Assurance, Verification and Validation, and Formal Review and Audits. A Life Cycle Process Overview standard is also planned once the other standards have been completed.

3.6 WG9: Software Integrity

WG9 was originally established to consider the mapping of standards onto a framework for software engineering standards, which was accepted for publication as a technical report. This work was convened by Richard Ivy (USA), and it has produced a draft technical report 14399, Mapping of Standards Pertinent to Software Engineering, which once published will be maintained by the secretariat. This technical report is a compendium of software engineering standards (and work in progress) produced by various standards bodies. With this work nearly completed, the WG has been refocussed to develop standards on software integrity at the systems level in collaboration with IEC TC56/WG10. It is currently temporarily convened by Mr. L. Tripp (USA).

3.7 WG10: Software Process Assessment

Convened by Mr. Alec Dorling (UK) since its establishment in June 1992, Working Group 10 is developing a set of draft technical reports in the area of process assessment under very tight time scales. The project is known as SPICE (Software Process Improvement and Capability dEtermination). Seven draft TR's are planned to be progressed from Working drafts to DIS by April 1995. These are: Introductory Guide, Process Assessment Guide, Process Improvement Guide, Process Capability Determination Guide, Assessor Training and Qualification Guide, Baseline Practices Guide and Assessment Instrument.

3.8 WG11: Software Engineering Data Definition and Representation

At its June 1992 plenary, SC7 established interim WG11, with Mr. Peter Eirich (USA) as convenor. Its mission was to develop a set of standards for the unambiguous description of software engineering data, such as specifications and designs, and to allow these to be interchanged between different repositories and CASE tools, while preserving their meaning. In June 1993, interim WG11 was merged with WG1, which dealt with human communication of designs and descriptions (such as state event diagrams and data flow diagrams), to form a new WG11. WG1 had nearly finalised ISO/IEC 11411 on state transition diagrams and was in the process of developing a working draft, Diagram eXchange Language (DXL) for tree structured charts, when the merger occurred. It was agreed at the last Plenary that DXL would be circulated as a CD.

The major work of WG11 over the next few years will be developing a set of standards based on the Electronics Industries Association (EIA) interim CASE Data Interchange Format (CDIF) standards. Agreement was reached that a set of 16 CDIF documents would be circulated as WG11 Working Drafts during the next 12 months.

3.9 WG12: Functional Size Measurement

The Ottawa Plenary in June 1994 created WG12 with Mr. H. Rehesaar (Australia) as its convenor, as a group spawned from WG6 to establish a set of practical standards for functional size measurement. They are currently working on a Function Point Analysis standard that will be circulated for CD ballot.

3.10 Ad Hoc Groups

SC7 established two adhoc groups: "Quality Aspects of Software Systems", convened by Mr. Yossi Winograd (USA) and "Software-System Relationship" convened by Dr. Raghu Singh (USA). The main purpose of the first adhoc group is to ensure consistency of the SC7 standards work with that of ISO/TC176 on software specific quality standards, such as ISO 9000.3. The second group was formed to investigate the relationship between systems engineering and software engineering. Both groups are to report to JTC1/SC7 by February 1995.

4. CONCLUSIONS

ISO/IEC JTC1/SC7 has refocussed its efforts to produce standards of considerable importance to industry. The next two years will see the publication of major process and product standards. In particular, the life-cycle management standard ISO/IEC 12207 will be available for two party contracts and this will be supported by specific process standards, such as software configuration management, and a set of draft standards on process assessment. It is vital that the software industry is aware of the status of the standards and it is hoped that this paper will contribute to this objective.

REFERENCES

1 Edelstein D.V., Fujii R., Guerdat C., and Sullo P., 'Internationalizing software engineering standards', *Computer,* March 1991, Vol.24, (3), pp 74-78

2 ISO/IEC JTC1/SC7, 'Secretariat's Report', June 1994, SC7 Standing Document 1, pp 1-38

29

An Investigation of Desired Quality Attributes for Different Types of Software

Tim Musson[a] and Ed Dodman[b]

[a]Department of Computer Studies, Napier University, 219 Colinton Road, Edinburgh, EH14 1DJ, UK
[b]Faculty of Inf & Eng Systems, Leeds Metropolitan University, The Grange, Beckett Park, Leeds, UK

Abstract

The first part of this paper gives an overview of some theoretical issues in software quality: quality models and different approaches to evaluating quality. The second part presents a questionnaire based investigation, concerning both the hypothesis that different software types will have specific profiles of quality attributes and current practice relating to quality attributes, their assurance and their measurement. While failing to confirm the hypothesis the questionnaire allows some interesting observations to be made in relation to the theoretical issues discussed earlier.

Keyword Codes: D.2.1; D.2.8
Keywords: Software Engineering, Requirements/Specifications; Software Engineering, Metrics

1. INTRODUCTION: THEORETICAL ISSUES IN SOFTWARE QUALITY

Current approaches to assuring and measuring software quality are predominantly process based rather than product based. There are two major assumptions here:

1) if we look after the process the product will look after itself

2) quality must be built into the product (can only be assessed when complete and difficult to alter).

These approaches allow the delivery of poor quality software in spite of a seemingly wonderful quality management system: the process functions smoothly, delivering a product on time, within budget and with all appropriate documents approved and signed. However the product may function far from smoothly, rating badly on a variety of quality attributes. Probably the main reason for this emphasis on procedure is that the software product is notoriously difficult to assess for quality whereas the process appears much more amenable. In spite of this, official standards for quality management systems, such as BS 5750, require procedures aimed at continually improving both process and product quality. In order to do this in any meaningful way it is necessary to be able to assess product quality.

1.1 Quality Models

Software quality models are principally of two types: general and specific. Two influential general models are those of McCall et al [1] and Boehm et al [2]. These treat quality as an attribute made up of high level "quality factors" (mainly external attributes such as maintainability, efficiency, reliability, usability) which are decomposed to give "quality criteria". These are associated with low level directly measurable "quality metrics". Factors and decompositions are assumed fixed for all software products.

The problems associated with these fixed general quality models include:

1) a standard set of quality factors and their decomposition is not suitable for all types of software

2) factors, criteria and metrics are of very diverse types (e.g. quality metrics are a mixture of genuine metrics, checklists of design procedures and production standards) [3]

3) managers in different environments may wish to interpret a particular factor in different ways

1.1.1 Gilb's Evolutionary Development and Kitchenham's COQUAMO

More recently general software quality models have been extended by Gilb [4] and Kitchenham [3]. Gilb's model is based on the notion of evolutionary development and delivery together with "measurable objectives": the system is delivered incrementally, always adding the functionality which is likely to give the best value for effort expended and ensuring that the measurable objectives are met. The importance of different aspects of functionality, together with the specification of non-functional attributes (the measurable objectives) are decided by the software engineer and the user in consultation. These non-functional attributes are quality attributes. Gilb [4] argues that they should be decomposed into low-level attributes, with fairly simple measurement procedures. For each of these low-level attributes it is necessary to define: (1) the unit of measurement; (2) the desired value of the measure; (3) the method of objectively determining a value on the scale; (4) the worst acceptable value of the measure; (5) the best known value of the measure anywhere; (6) the current level of the measure, for comparison purposes. This clearly assumes that any desirable attribute must be objectively measurable.

Kitchenham's [3] work attempts to combine Gilb's approach with the earlier work of McCall and Boehm. Her work concentrates on the development of a constructive quality model, "COQUAMO", and also attempts to relate process attributes to objective software measures. This work extracted the following quality factors from the above models:

efficiency, reliability, usability, extendibility, generality, testability, understandability, re-usability, maintainability, correctness, integrity, survivability.

Each of these factors is then classified as one of:

application-specific, requiring application-specific definition,
general with application-independent definition, software production related.

Thus some factors are considered to be totally general and form part of every model. The rest of the model is constructed from factors in other categories: the selection and, possibly, definition of these is carried out in consultation between the software engineer and the user.

1.1.2 Other General Software Quality Models

Delen and Rijsenbrij [5] have proposed a general model specifically for information systems: this restriction made quality assessment more tractable. Their model is based on decomposition, with the top-level product-oriented factors categorised as either static or dynamic. The bottom-level "quality attributes" (quality metrics) are characterised by:

definition means of specifying requirements in verifiable fashion
relevant engineering actions units (e.g. person hours)
measurability (explicit direct, implicit direct, indirect)

The quality attributes are specified by the model, but the requirements for each are specified by the user. While Delen and Rijsenbrij make no claims concerning the success of their approach it seems very reasonable for a restricted domain such as information systems.

A recent development in this area, while not in itself a quality model, is the use of quality function deployment (QFD) [6]. This tool has been well-described in the general quality literature (e.g. [7]) but very little in the software quality literature. In the context of software development QFD facilitates the mapping of customer requirements via software characteristics onto production features. Erikkson and McFadden claim that QFD gives a good structure within which the users' needs are taken into account and progressively refined to give appropriate product metrics. One interesting aspect of this approach is that it implies that development methods should be adapted to the quality attribute requirements.

1.2 Specific Quality Models

A variety of specific quality models have also been proposed. These define quality in terms of one factor, which is decomposed into one or more measurable attributes and usually based on the number of defects found in a software product. The main aim here seems to be to ensure that contractual obligations are met: this coincides with one of Garvin's [8] major approaches to quality - manufacturing-based ("conformance to specification"), whereas the models discussed above relate more to his other major approach - user-based ("fitness for purpose"). This type of approach can assess one aspect, possibly very important for some systems, of software quality. However, it is unlikely that for a complex and multi-dimensional software system, it is best to base quality evaluation on one factor.

AT&T Bell Labs have used such an approach [9]. A variety of measures were used, but all were based on the number of faults found. Such a set of metrics is more a process than a product measure. If many faults are found and fixed this may mean that we now have a very reliable product, or a badly designed, badly constructed product, or both (and fixing the faults may have caused the design to deteriorate further). Even with respect to the process it is not totally clear what these metrics tell us.

Another example of this type of approach is given by Daskalantonakis [10]. He describes the set of metrics used for software evaluation in Motorola. Again, most of these measure defects and failures, with a few specifically relating to the process (e.g. productivity, project duration). The metrics were developed using the Goal/Question/Metric (GQM) approach. A set of goals were established and, for each of these, a set of questions determined, which would allow achievement of the goal to be assessed. Each question was answered using one or more metrics. For example:

Goal 3: Increase Software Reliability

Question 3.1: What is the rate of software failures, and how does it change over time?

Metric 3.1: Failure rate (FR) = number of failures / execution time

Even though this approach seems very restrictive Daskalantonakis claims very substantial benefits from the implementation of the metrics: "There are also many indirect benefits ... improve ship-acceptance criteria, and schedule estimation accuracy... Another long range benefit (which has been actually achieved so far within Motorola) is significant cost reduction due to improved quality". The benefits may well have been even greater if a wider-ranging set of metrics had been used.

An often ignored aspect with this type of approach is the user. For interactive systems it is essential this does not happen: the quality of interaction between the system and the user all important. No amount of internal 'structural' quality or process quality will make up for a lack of external 'functional' quality. The questionnaire results, presented below, give some interesting conclusions with respect to this.

2. THE QUESTIONNAIRE

The above discussion shows that the assessment of product quality is usually based on a generic set of factors applicable to all software. Musson [11] proposed that this could be inappropriate for software and that it might be possible to factor out differing quality requirements for differing software types.

A questionnaire (see Appendix A) was developed to test this hypothesis and to collect information on the actual development processes currently used inside the software industry, the quality attributes considered important and the means used to assess and achieve desired levels of these.

The first group of four questions was designed to locate the responding companies within the software production sector and to define the type of software they produce. The next three questions, relating to the design methods and techniques, computer languages and software tools used, represent an indirect approach to finding out what design paradigms are being utilised.

The next three questions related directly to the quality attributes important to the software producers, how they are assessed and how the achievement of these attributes is measured. Finally respondents were invited to introduce other relevant quality matters ; in general there was very little response to this.

One hundred and forty six questionnaires were sent to firms selected from three sources which were considered to include appropriate companies.

The questionnaire was, wherever possible, mailed to named software managers. Where names were unknown the questionnaires were mailed to the Software Manager or the nearest equivalent title that could be found for the company.

A covering letter explained that the purpose of the questionnaire was to gather information about current industrial thought and practice relating to quality and that all companies responding would receive a full report of the findings of the survey. To ensure anonymity it was made clear that the return slips with names and addresses would be immediately separated from the returned questionnaires.

The questionnaire was designed so that it could be completed in ten to fifteen minutes. As an incentive to completion entry to a free draw was organised with the prize of a free weekend holiday for two offered by the Friendly Hotel Group. In spite of this, and the inclusion of a stamped addressed envelope for the reply, the response rate (23 replies) was disappointingly low.

3. QUESTIONNAIRE RESULTS AND DISCUSSION

In spite of the disappointingly low response rate (23 out of 146), the questionnaires returned showed a wide range of software development activities, in terms of market, industrial sector, mode, design methods and programming languages and some interesting observations may be made. Unsurprisingly, most of the respondents were involved in the development of vertical applications - for specific clients or for inhouse use (effectively, specific clients). The data do not support the hypothesis that different "types" of software have specific profiles of desired quality attributes: e.g. 10 replies (over the full range of software types and modes).showed reliability, maintainability and usability (in any order) as the most important attributes. The response rate was probably too low to determine this type of pattern and the categories used for software were possibly not appropriate.

3.1 Quality Attributes

The main focus of the questionnaire was on quality attributes: their importance, achievement and measurement. The results (Table 3) show clearly that the attributes considered most important were reliability (much more important), usability and maintainability. All others were seen as much less important. The lack of importance for efficiency was encouraging. For some time lecturers have told students that greater processor power at lower cost and higher personnel costs are reducing its efficiency: this is born out by the results. We give below a summary of the reported means of achieving and measuring quality attributes. The number of respondents who seemed unable to distinguish between these activities was surprisingly high.

Rank / **Attribute**	*1*	*2*	*3*	*4*	*5*	*6*
Maintainability	2	6	5	8		
Usability	5	5	7	1		
Reusability		1	3	2	5	3
Portability	2		1		5	3
Reliability	14	5	2	1		
Efficiency		1	4	4	2	1
Others/unknown	2	2				

Table 3. Frequency of rankings of quality attributes

3.2 Achievement of Desired Quality

In general reliability seems to be achieved by the application of standard software engineering and project management methods and the responses seemed to reflect its perceived importance as a quality attribute. While two respondents stated that they used some form of formal method (e.g. Z) as a design method, neither of them mentioned this as a means of achieving reliability. By far the most commonly reported means of achieving reliability were walkthroughs/reviews (both design and code) and testing. Other methods mentioned once or twice included: Fagin reviews, static code analysis, use of a QMS (ISO9001), independent modules and modular design, use of testing tools.

While usability was also considered a very important attribute the means of achieving it were generally much less clear. The usual approach appears to be something like "see whether the customer/user likes it", often while showing the user screen designs. Prototyping was mentioned several times, but, while not totally clear, this usually seemed to either refer to screen designs or just showing the customer a reduced version of the final system. One response suggested a serious approach: "specially trained engineers using videoing and measurement". However, there was a serious lack of use of modern relatively formal approaches to interface design, such as task analysis and cognitive walkthroughs [12], which allow a considerable amount of interface design and evaluation without involving the user.

The means reported for achieving maintainability centred, fairly predictably, around the concept of "good practice". Specifically mentioned were: structured coding methods, modular design, standards (design and coding), reviews (design and code), common code.

The main means reported for achieving other attributes were:

portability: use of appropriate coding standards
efficiency: detailed analysis of task, design reviews
reusability: programming standards, OOD/inheritance, reviews for common procedure identification.

One respondent stated that OOD had been a dismal failure with respect to reusability.

3.3 Measurement/Evaluation of Quality Attributes

The most commonly used approaches to measuring reliability were testing and fault logs. The latter were presumably based on faults reported by users. Other methods mentioned included: third party testing, defect seeding, MTBF, simulation, customer satisfaction. Quite a high level of sophistication was apparent in the methods used to evaluate reliability.

Methods reported for measuring usability ranged from "no formal assessment" to "time taken on user training" to "video, industry standard measures". Most responses were in terms of either user acceptance or customer satisfaction. As with the achievement of this attribute, there was very little attempt to produce any formal or rigorous measurement (for an overview see [13]).

Approaches to measuring maintainability were of two basic types. Indirect measures were based on the means of achievement: clear structured code, specifications and documentation, walkthroughs of module design. Direct measures were based on the effort expended on maintenance - either time or the amount of code needing to be changed: time taken to resolve problems and apply changes, speed of fault resolution, ease of bug fixing, proportion of modules changed. The indirect measures act as predictors of the direct measures. The measurement approaches were fairly sophisticated.

One of the two respondents who reported maintainability as the most important attribute gave as the method of assessment "don't normally assess"!

Respondents did not seem to have too much trouble measuring the other attributes:

portability:	3 supplier platform testing	time taken to port to other platforms
	amount/proportion of code rewritten	
efficiency:	processing/response time	benchmark tests
	speed of volume processing	user's productivity
reusability:	amount/percentage of code reusable	number of common routines
	use of Object Management System.	

One other attribute reported as being measured was defect density (defects per function point).

3.4 Design Methods

Encouragingly, all but three respondents reported using some sort of design method. Most common were prototyping (mentioned 11 times) and SSADM (mentioned 7 times). Those involved in real-time systems were the only users of Yourdon, OOD and formal methods, suggesting that such companies take design issues very seriously. The companies which seemed to take design least seriously also did little to assess quality attributes. The first choice design method (prototyping) was unexpected.

3.5 Other Observations

Several respondents reported using C++ as a programming language but did not use OOD as a design method. This suggests the possibility that the increasing use of C++ is as a "cleaner" version of C, rather than as a vehicle for implementing OOD.

One particularly detailed response reported the use of "incremental, organic development targeted at achieving greatest benefits early in project life": this seems close to the approach advocated by Gilb [4], described above. The same response mentioned a need for better software tools, particularly for the maintenance of old code. Others also desired configuration management and CASE tools.

4. CONCLUSIONS

The results of the questionnaire, while failing to confirm the original hypothesis, allowed some interesting observations. It is planned to continue this work, developing an improved questionnaire in the light of what has been learned. It is clear that other ways of characterising the type of software developed need to be found. An interesting comparison would have been between software developed for specific clients and for a general market. It is also felt that where examples (of languages, attributes etc) are given on the questionnaire, these should either be very few or comprehensive: in the case of the quality attributes listed on the questionnaire these were not comprehensive but the list was probably large enough to discourage respondents from adding their own.

REFERENCES

1. McCall, JA, Richards, PK, Walters, GF: 'Factors in Software Quality' *Vols I, II, III. US Rome Air Development Center Reports NTIS AD/A-049 014, 015, 055,* 1977
2. Boehm, BW, Brown, JR, Kaspar, JR, Lipow, M, MacCleod, GJ, Merrit, MJ: *'Characteristics of Software Quality'.* (North Holland, 1978)
3. Kitchenham, B: 'Towards a Constructive Quality Model. Part I: Software Quality Modelling', Measurement and Prediction' *Software Engineering J,* 1987, Vol.2, (4), pp105-113
4. Gilb, T: *'Principles of Software Engineering Management'.* (Addison Wesley, 1988)
5. Delen, GPAJ and Rijsenbrij, DBB: 'The Specification, Engineering, and Measurement of Information Systems Quality' *J of systems and Software,* 1992, Vol 17, (3), pp 205-217
6. Erikkson, I and McFadden, F: 'Quality Function Deployment: a Tool to Improve Software Quality' *Information and Software Technology,* 1993, Vol 35, (9), pp 491-498
7. Akao, Y: *'Quality Function Deployment: Integrating Customer Requirements into Product Design',* (Productivity Press, Cambridge, MA, 1990)
8. Garvin, DA: 'What Does "Product Quality" really Mean?' *Sloan Mgt Review,* 1984, Vol 25, Fall
9. Inglis, J: 'Standard Software Quality Metrics' *AT&T Technical J,* 1986, Vol 65, (2), pp 113-118
10. Daskalantonakis, MK: 'A Practical View of Software Measurement and Implementation Experiences Within Motorola' *IEEE Trans on Software Eng,* 1992, Vol 18, (11), pp 998-1010
11. Musson, T: 'Towards a Discipline of Software Quality' *Proceedings of the Third Software Quality Workshop, Edinburgh,* 1993
12. Polson, PG, Lewis, C, Rieman, J and Wharton, C: 'Cognitive Walkthroughs: a Method for Theory-based Evaluation of User Interfaces', *Int J Man-Machine Studies,* 1992, Vol 36, pp 741-773
13. Sweeney, M, Maguire, M and Shackel, B: 'Evaluating user-computer interaction: a framework', *Int J Man-Machine Studies,* 1993, Vol 38, pp 689-711.

Appendix A: The text of the questionnaire (omitting additional space left for replies):

Software Quality Profile

1. Is your company more concerned with producing: (please tick)
   a. General Purpose Software (horizontal) b. Specific Software Applications (vertical)
2. Is your software produced mainly for:
   a. In house use b. Specific customers
   c. A specific market sector d. General market
3. If possible give the "industrial sector" in which your software is principally used:
   (e.g. financial, engineering, education, leisure) ....
4. In which of the following modes is your software used:
   a. Real time b. Interactive c. Batch d. Networked e. Other (please specify)
5. What are the most important design methods and techniques (e.g. SSADM, object-oriented, prototyping) which you use in developing your software. (Please list in order of importance)
6. What types of computer language do you use to develop your software (e.g. 3GL, 4GL, database, assembly)? (Please give specific names and if possible indicate your % use of each language)
7. List the software tools you use in developing software (e.g. testbeds, software engineering environments). (Please give name and type of each tool)
8. Below is a list of quality attributes (attached sheet gives interpretation for each). Please indicate which are important to you, ranked in order of importance and if possible give weightings for their relative importance (100 = weight for most important)
   example: if the only attributes important to you are reliability (most important) and maintainability, then rank these 1 & 2 and do not rank any other attributes. If maintainability is only half as important to you as reliability then weight them as 100 & 50.
   (Please add and define any other attributes which are important to you)
   Maintainability Usability Reusability Portability Reliability Efficiency
9. Indicate briefly how you assess those quality attributes which you consider to be important (e.g. efficiency: time taken to process standard test data).
10. Explain briefly how you attain the appropriate quality level for each attribute that is important to you (e.g. reliability: design walkthroughs, static code testing, testbeds). (Please indicate how important you consider each means of achieving the desired level of quality)
11. Please indicate below any other issues which you feel are important to you in ensuring the quality of your software.

30

A Unifying Model for Software Quality Engineering

Ilkka Tervonen

Department of Information Processing Science, University of Oulu,
FIN-90570, Oulu, Finland
e-mail: tervo@rieska.oulu.fi

Abstract

The demand for quality in software production raises new challenges for software engineering process. The solutions proposed for the quality problem are based on standards which provide an abstract frame and drive further tailoring and installation of quality assurance methods and quality control principles. This installing in an enterprise requires a lot of time and effort. The methodologists and persons who are responsible for the choice of the method demand a framework, which helps them to assess the cover and appropriateness of alternative methods from quality engineering viewpoint in particular. The present paper introduces a unifying model which can be used for this assessing of the necessary characteristics of a method. In addition, we briefly illustrate how to apply this model to the definition of a specific review method.

Keyword Codes: D.2.0; K.6.3; K6.5
Keywords: Software Engineering, General; Software Management; Security and Protection

1. MOTIVATION

Following Yourdon [1], "software quality is like loyalty, bravery and thrift: everyone is in favor of it, but it's not always clear that enyone practices it". Although standards (e.g. ISO 9000-3, [2]) form a good starting point for installing of quality assurance in an enterprise and slogans such as "Quality is job number one" motivate emphasis on quality, its installing in an enterprise requires a lot of time and effort. We need also a comprehensive conceptual model (a Unifying Model, [3]) of software quality engineering which defines the quality assessment and quality assurance throughout the software development. This model would not necessarily be of immediate use to a system builder, but it would be a tool for academic analysis that could in turn yield structures and tools useful to a practitioner [3]. It can also be used as a framework which helps a software engineer or a methodologist to assess the necessary characteristics of a method from a quality engineering viewpoint. The Unifying Model can also be applied to the definition of a specific review method.

2. THE UNIFYING MODEL

The Unifying Model is a conceptual model and is defined in a space of three dimensions, levels of abstraction (LoA), software configuration management (SCM) and quality (cf. Figure 1). The dimensions are justified by their necessity in quality engineering with respect to a software object or software product, and there are two-way relationships in each dimension which explain the change from generality/wholeness to specifity/parts and reverse.

The LoA dimension represents a scale of definition specificity and implementation dependence, i.e. the levels of description (different viewpoints), refinements inside a level and mapping between levels. The SCM dimension adds the aspect of a software product intended to focus on software configuration complexity, i.e. software objects (a software description or a software module), their versions or revisions, and their configuration into a software product and further into a software product family.

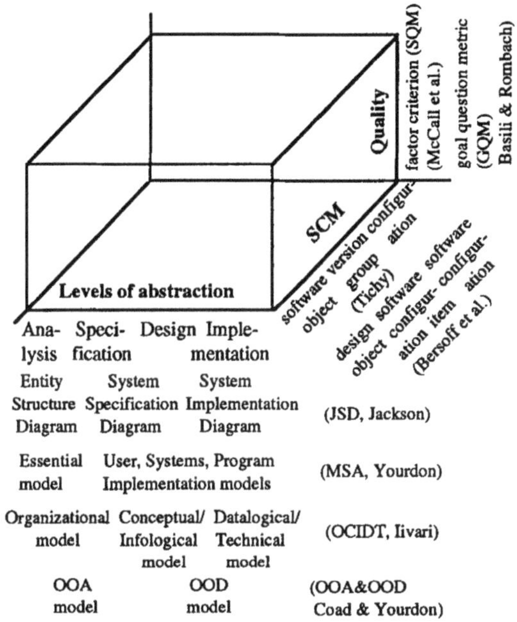

Figure 1. The space of three dimensions

The quality dimension explains the quality of a software object or a software product at a specific level of abstraction and defines quality specificity in terms of a quality factor and criterion, for example.

3. ALTERNATIVE MODELS IN THE UNIFYING MODEL

In the previous section we presented general definitions for the dimensions. We now instantiate and refine these definitions, choosing a specific model for each dimension.

3.1. Levels of abstraction

The levels of abstraction (LoA) dimension encompasses different aspects on the progress of software development such as levels of description (a specific viewpoint at each level), refinements inside a level and mappings between levels. Typically, a specification level depicts a logical viewpoint (implementation independent) and a design level a more implementation dependent viewpoint. The mappings between levels ensure that the characteristics specified at upper levels remain and will be implemented at lower levels. In object-oriented approach the characteristics such as seamless transition cause a blend of refinement and mapping (i.e. an incremental development of a class hierarchy is equal to refinement although the characteristics added are from levels of abstraction).

Among the alternatives (i.e. JSD [4], MSA (Modern Structured Analysis [5], OCIDT [6], [7] and OOA/OOD [8], [9]) we have chosen the OCIDT model, and the OCT (Organizational=O, Conceptual=C, Technical=T) model as its successor. According to Iivari [6] the three levels of abstraction (or modelling) are (1) the organizational level, which defines the organizational role and context of the IS/SW (information system/software) product, (2) the conceptual/infological level, which defines an "implementation independent" specification for the IS/SW product, and (3) the datalogical/technical level, which defines the technical implementation of the IS/SW product. Due to our focus on software engineering, in which the terms infological and datalogical are not very familiar, we use the term OCT model. Although the choice of the OCT model can be seen partly as "taken for granted", we also can justify the choice by its theoretical soundness, i.e. the OCT model is defined by three models, a software model, a process model and a quality model. The software model ties it to information systems research tradition, and the process model defines a hierarchical spiral model which has a number of similarities with the Boehm's spiral model [10]. Both models are tailored to object-oriented approach in our application (cf. [11]). The quality model presents a framework for choices between alternatives and supports the quality dimension, too. The most serious disadvantage of the OCT model is caused by its "unknown" status in the field of software engineering.

The relationships on this dimension are specialization/generalization and decomposition/aggregation. A specialization describes a refinement using transition inside a level and from a higher level of abstraction to a lower one, whereas generalization is the reverse. Decomposition is largely similar to specialization, and describes how a software object is decomposed into more precisely specified software objects, whereas aggregation forms a composite software object from constituent software objects.

3.2. Software configuration management

Software configuration management is an umbrella activity that is applied throughout the software engineering process. It identifies, controls, audits and reports modifications that invariably occur while software is being developed and after it has been released to the customer. A software object [12] or a design object [13] is a core unit in our SCM concept. We borrow the definition of Tichy [12], who defines it as any kind of identifiable, machine-readable document generated during the course of a project (e.g. requirements documents, design documents, specifications, interface descriptions, program code, test programs, test data, binary code, user manuals, etc.). Tichy also places emphasis on two "orthogonal refinements" of software objects, one according to how they were created, the other according to the structure of their body. Creation of a software object depends on its type, since a source object requires human action but a derived object is generated automatically by a program, usually from other software objects. Corrective, adaptive, perfective and preventative maintenance activities produce a steady stream of updates. Since most changes are incremental, they are best viewed as producing related versions of objects rather than separate, unrelated objects. According to Tichy [12], source objects are connected via the relations revision-of and variant-of. The subtypes of a revision-of relation are derived from maintenance activities, being correction-of, adaptation-of, enhancement-of and preventative-of. The revision-of relation forms a directed, acyclic graph reflecting the development history. Each revision may be composed of different variants and thus a variant-of relation identifies the starting points of parallel lines of development.

Although we identify these revisions and versions even in small-scale software development, they will be more inportant in the case of a software product or software product family. The relationships on the SCM dimension also follow this classification. The relationships used here are versioning/configuring, in which versioning describes the change history of the software object or software configuration using an evolution graph, for example, and configuring works in the reverse order, compiling a software composition, a software product and finally a software product family. The major idea is that this grouping allows more flexibility in the evolution of software products and makes the management of software evolution easier.

3.3. Quality

The software engineering area offers some alternative quality "approaches", such as the Software Quality Metrics (SQM) (cf. [14], [15]) and Goal Question Metric (GQM) (cf. [16]) models. Quality is managed in the SQM model by means of quality factors, a set of criteria and metrics for estimating the value of these criteria and of the factors. In the GQM model the terms are goals, a set of questions and metrics for measuring achievement of the goals. Although the terms are slightly different, the models are rather similar because the quality factors selected can be understood as goals, the quality criteria are explained by means of checklists corresponding to the questions, and the metrics are similar in both approaches. In view of its more comprehensive taxonomy of quality factors and criteria, we have chosen the SQM model.

Our synthesis of the SQM model is based mainly on the reports of McCall et al. [14] and Boehm et al. [15], and on the IEEE standard [17]. The factors in the SQM model depict more user-perceived characteristics than do the criteria, which characterize lower-level software-oriented aspects. The IEEE standard [17] defines the factors as management-oriented views of quality. Associated with each factor is a direct metric which serves as a quantitative representation of the quality factor. The second level in the hierarchy consists of quality criteria (sub-factors), which represent technically-oriented concepts. The criteria may correspond to more than one factor, and they are concrete attributes that are more meaningful than factors to the technical staff, i.e. analysts, designers, programmers, testers and maintainers. At the third level in the hierarchy, the criteria are decomposed into metrics used to measure system products and processes during the development life-cycle. The existence of an interrelationship between the factors denotes that they may have cooperative or conflicting relationships, i.e. emphasizing expandability can cause conflicts with efficiency, for example.

The relationships on the quality dimension follow this classification. When the first relationship in quality dimension is a quality break-down, the other one is a quality accumulation. It is based on the fact that direct metric values (factor values) are typically unavailable or expensive to collect early in the software life cycle. For this reason, metrics on the criteria level are used, either collectively or independently, to estimate factor values. There are also some problems, in that the metrics are programming language-dependent (e.g Fortran), their use requires a substantial amount of subjective judgement, and some metrics do not require specific checking if good compilers are used [15].

4. APPLYING THE UNIFYING MODEL TO THE DEFINITION OF A REVIEW METHOD

The characteristics of a Unifying Model are now applied to the definition of a pre-review method - a quality-driven assessment method. The definition of the method is based on object-oriented tailoring of the model. The structure in LoA and SCM dimensions is presented in the form of a class hierarchy. In the LoA dimension it represents a development history and in SCM dimension a evolution history. When defining the quality-driven assessment activities, we focus on a general pre-review aspect and on the specific quality assessment activities defined as relationships earlier in the Unifying Model. From the viewpoint of a pre-review method, quality-driven assessment serves the goal of a review, i.e. it removes defects in software definitions and code. The prefix "pre" implies that quality-driven assessment also supports the essential review process by preparing material which helps reviewing. This material encompasses design rationales which justify trade-off situations in terms of quality issues.

The specific quality assessment activities are derived from relationships in the Unifying Model. Quality break-down activity implements the break-down of a quality factor to a set of quality criteria, whereas in the quality accumulation the value of a quality factor is estimated from a set of criteria. The quality-driven specialization describes the transition of quality requirements from a superclass to subclasses. Quality-driven decomposition is largely similar to quality-driven specialization. The major difference is that decomposition always produces a set of subclasses. Quality-driven association is a constructing activity and works together with quality-driven specialization and quality-driven decomposition. It means link to library components or their further applications, i.e. how the quality of a class can be composed from quality estimates of "used" classes. Quality-driven aggregation is a strong form of association and means constructing inside an application class hierarchy, i.e. how the quality of a superclass can be composed from quality estimates of subclasses. Quality-driven generalization leads to the production of a new and more reusable superclass. Quality-driven versioning describes the change history of a software object, a software configuration, a software product or a product family. The choices are based on a quality estimate of an alternative version or revision and the history can be illustrated by means of an evolution graph, for example. Quality-driven configuring is a reverse activity combining a software composition, a software product and finally a software product family. Collection is also here based on quality estimates and allows different versions of software products which vary in relation to specific quality characteristics, for example.

5. CONCLUSIONS

The present paper formulates a comprehensive conceptual model of software quality engineering which defines quality assessment and quality assurance throughout software development. We define a Unifying Model in a space of three dimensions, levels of abstraction (LoA), software configuration management (SCM) and quality, and choose a specific model for each dimension. The models chosen are the OCT (O=Organizational, C=Conceptual, T=Technical) model on the LoA dimension, a software configuration model of Tichy on the SCM dimension and a SQM (software quality metrics) model on the quality dimension.

When applying the Unifying Model to the definition of the quality-driven assessment, we focus on a general pre-review aspect and on the specific quality assessment activities defined as relationships earlier in the Unifying Model. The specific quality assessment activities are derived from relationships in the Unifying Model, being quality-driven specialization, quality-driven decomposition, quality-driven association, quality-driven aggregation and quality-driven generalization on the LoA dimension, quality-driven versioning and quality-driven configuring on the SCM dimension, and quality break-down and quality accumulation on the quality dimension.

REFERENCES

1. Yourdon E.: 'Editor's notes', *American Programmer*, 1993, vol 6, (6), pp. 1-2
2. ISO: Quality management and quality assurance standards, Part 3: guidelines for the application of ISO 9001 to the development, supply and maintenance of software, ISO 9000-3, International Organization for Standardization, Geneve, 1991
3. CSTB: 'Scaling up: a research agenda for software engineering', *Communications of the ACM*, 1990, vol 33, (3), pp. 281-293
4. Jackson M.: 'System development', Prentice Hall, Englewood Cliffs, NJ, 1983
5. Yourdon E.: 'Modern structured analysis', Prentice Hall, Englewood Cliffs, NJ, 1989
6. Iivari J.: 'Hierarchical spiral model for information system and software development. Part 1: theoretical background', *Information and Software Technology*, 1990, vol 32, (6), pp. 386-399
7. Iivari J.: 'Hierarchical spiral model for information system and software development. Part 2: design process', *Information and Software Technology*, 1990, vol 32, (7), pp. 450-458
8. Coad P. and Yourdon E.: 'Object-oriented analysis', Second Edition, Prentice Hall, Englewood Cliffs, NJ, 1991
9. Coad P. & Yourdon E.: 'Object-oriented design', Prentice Hall, Englewood Cliffs, NJ, 1991
10. Boehm B.W.: 'A spiral model of software development and enhancement', *ACM SIGSOFT Software Engineering Notes*, 1986, vol 11, (4), pp. 14-24
11. Tervonen I.: 'Quality-driven assessment: a pre-review method for object-oriented software development', Dissertation thesis, University of Oulu, Department of Information Processing Science, Reserch papers, Series A19, 1994
12. Tichy W.: 'Tools for software configuration management', In: Winkler J.F.H. (ed.), *Proceedings of the International Workshop on Software Version and Configuration Control*, Stuttgart, 1988, pp. 1-32
13. Bersoff E.H., Henderson V.D. and Siegel S.G: 'Software configuration management: an investment in product integrity', Prentice Hall, Englewood Cliffs, NJ, 1980
14. McCall J.A, Richards P.K and Walters G.F.: 'Factors in software quality', Volumes I, II, and III, RADC reports, 1977
15. Boehm B.W., Brown T.R., Kasper H., Lipow M., Macleod G.J. and Merritt M.J: 'Characteristics of software quality', North-Holland, Amsterdam, 1978
16. Basili V.R. and Rombach H.D.: 'The TAME project: towards improvement-oriented software environments', *IEEE Transactions on Software Engineering*, 1988, vol 14, (6), pp. 758-773
17. IEEE: 'IEEE Standard for a software quality metrics methodology (Draft)', P-1061/D20, IEEE Computer Society Press, New York, NY, 1989

31

Quality Achievement: Current Practices and The Way Ahead

J. Barrie Thompson

School of Computing and Information Systems, University of Sunderland, Priestman Building, Sunderland, SR1 3SD, United Kingdom

Abstract

The efficient production of quality software is a major goal for many organisations and the use of systematic methods, automated tools and quality assurance procedures can all assist in reaching this goal. Results from various surveys and research investigations relating to the acceptance or otherwise of these practices are reported. The major reasons for slow adoption of the practices are given and the problems which are currently restraining progress are identified, in particular those relating to personnel. Proposals are presented concerning the actions which should be taken regarding professionalism, education and technology transfer for there to be a significant improvement in the achievement of quality.

Keyword Codes: D.0, D.2.0, K.7.0
Keywords: Software, Software Engineering, Professionalism

1. INTRODUCTION

A recurring theme within software development has been the problem of poor quality software. This problem has underpinned a 'software crisis' which has lasted since the nineteen sixties and which led to the term Software Engineering (SE) being introduced in 1968 [1]. The concept of SE was originally intended to provide a provocative theme at the conference, but it has evolved over the last 25 years into a technological discipline of considerable importance especially within academic institutions. However, in the call for papers for this conference it was recognised that:

"As the world becomes increasingly dependent on the use of computers, the need for quality software which can be produced at reasonable cost increases. Yet the goal of improving software quality and productivity remains an elusive one. This is so in almost all application areas including business oriented applications. Software development is not yet an engineering practice."

There are many and various reasons why, outside academic institutions, software development has failed to be recognised as an engineering practice and why there has been across industry in general and the commercial sector in particular a failure to adopt SE practices. In the following sections of this paper I will outline what many of the major reasons are and I will suggest how we should approach the future if we are to substantially improve the current situation. Firstly, the results from surveys and research investigations, which my research group have undertaken, and which relate to the acceptance of these SE developments in the UK commercial sector are presented. These investigations have highlighted the reasons for non-adoption of SE practices and the problems which are currently restraining progress. Then, the actions are outlined which I believe must be undertaken for there to be a significant long term improvement.

2. PROBLEMS IN THE ADOPTION OF SOFTWARE ENGINEERING PRACTICES BY THE COMMERCIAL SECTOR WITHIN THE UK

The SE practices which are likely to have the major impact on the quality of software for the commercial/administrative sector are those related to the use of:

- systematic development methods,
- computer based development support environments,
- quality assurance (QA).

Developments in each of these areas are primarily concerned with improvements in the software production process and should reduce the overall software wastage costs which have been estimated [2] for the UK as being in excess of 2,000 million pounds per year.

Evidence that SE practices were probably not being used sufficiently in the mid 1980s can be obtained from the detailed findings of a report produced in 1988 for the UK Department of Trade and Industry by consultants at Price Waterhouse [3] referred to above. However, a more recent picture of the state of the sector with regard to the use of systematic methods, CASE tools, QA approaches and standards can be obtained from work carried out by members of the Commercial SE group at the University of Sunderland. During the last six years members of the group have undertaken in depth investigations of practices within UK data processing departments via four major surveys and follow up case study interviews [4-9]. Within all these surveys the researchers had included questions assess the current state of the industry and assess the actual use of SE practices being investigated. There were also been questions to determine organisations' future plans, the constraints which are placed upon them and the problems that they encounter with regard to the area being surveyed. It is on these latter areas that I will concentrate in the remainder of this section.

2.1 Current and Future Use

Our surveys and related work have indicated that there is a continuing, if slow, increase in the use of methods, CASE and QA procedures. Certainly the situation would appear to have improved from that reported by the consultants from Price Waterhouse [3] but it is often difficult to estimate by how much. The continuing development of SSADM (Structured Systems Analysis and Design Method [10]) and its support from Government is leading to a greater acceptance of the value of the use of systematic methods. We are also sure that the situation regarding the use of CASE tools has improved since our 1990 survey. With regard to QA procedures the situation appears much more positive. Of the respondents to our 1991 survey 22% were already 3rd party assessed and almost half of these had only been certified within the last year, which was double the amount for the previous year. Positive figures for accreditation (24 businesses every three months) has also been reported in the UK Department of Trade and Industry's JFIT NEWS [11]. Nevertheless, given the size of the industry it is obvious that adoption of QA procedures across the whole of the UK software sector has still some way to go. We are sure that pressures from customers will cause a continuing adoption of QA procedures by the software industry but for QA to be really successful its adoption should be due to an internal desire for improvement rather than external forces. Nevertheless, overall what is very clear from our investigations is that there remains a significant proportion of the industry who have not adopted formal SE approaches and there is still a large percentage of software systems being developed without any QA procedures.

2.2 Constraints and Problems

One fundamental constraint on the adoption of SE practices is the lack of clear unbiased information. Another is simply human resistance to change. The major problems we have identified for each area and the common problems relating to human factors and are detailed in the following subsections:-

Methods. The major problems associated with the adoption of cost effective systematic development methods are:-

1. The current wide range of methods and techniques that are available and the lack of experienced staff and information/support. Plus techniques are often seen as too complicated and methods in many cases provide poor coverage of the lifecycle.

2. Unwillingness of organisations to accept change and adopt any new "standardised method". In many cases this is simply due to the costs, primarily in staff time, that are incurred with any major change. In other cases this is due to the fact that organisations have already invested heavily, and in some cases very heavily, in methods of their own.

CASE. The prospective market for CASE tools has been confused by the large variety of different products that are available. In an attempt to clarify matters tools have been categorised to more accurately describe their functions. Unfortunately, tool vendors and manufacturers have not fully agreed on what these terms mean, so such categorisation has simply added to the confusion, and not removed it. The other major problems are:

1. The current high cost of CASE tools. These costs were given as a major reason for not adopting CASE by the respondents to our The actual cost of CASE (per staff member) appeared to be approximately double what non-CASE users were willing to spend.

2. The high costs in terms of extra hardware and initial staff time in the adoption of CASE.

3. Lack of management support to invest in and use tools (and related methods).

Quality Assurance Procedures. Many organisations see no reason to seek accreditation to an external standard as they believe their own internal procedures are more effective. Other major reasons for not seeking an external standard have been identified as:

1. Cost of gaining accreditation and the time to implement new procedures.

2. General confusion over the meaning of quality when applied to software and a lack of knowledge of QA approaches and standards,

Human Problems. In the adoption of methods and tools there can be major problems with staff at all levels. People do not like change, especially if it is a possible threat to their livelihood or the way in which they have to work. Computing professionals are like everyone else in this respect. Managers lack confidence in their ability to understand and control the new technology whilst designers and production staff may believe that the methods and tools will destroy the artistic and creative aspects of their work. It is true that adoption of the new technologies has a large impact on working practices and that many members of staff have been unable (or are unwilling) to alter their working practices. We believe this "Luddite approach" has greatly contributed to the problems of implementing SE practices in the commercial/administrative sector.

Another human problem which we have identified during our work is that there is a deep seated antipathy to the use of standards throughout the industry. Most organisations and individuals formally recognise the value of standards and agree that they are needed. However, when it comes to the actual use of and adherence to standards the situation is in many cases very different [12]. This factor more than any other acts against any rapid increase in the acceptance of QA procedures since these more than any other SE practice depend on standards being adhered to.

3. THE WAY AHEAD

From our surveys and related investigations it has emerged that many of the reasons for the slow adoption of the approaches that should lead to the development of better quality software are related not to technology but to people. In fact I believe that to a great extent over the last 25 years we have concentrated too much on technological aspects and have failed to develop the human aspects that should be associated with any engineering discipline. The areas which I believe we now need to concentrate on, if we are to achieve quality in the future, are: professionalism, SE education within academic institutions, and technology transfer.

3.1 Professionalism

It is absolutely essential that people at ALL levels, both within and outside the software industry, recognise that the production of quality software is as much an engineering discipline as any of the other traditional disciplines such as: mechanical engineering, electronic engineering, and civil engineering. It is vital that a high proportion of staff involved in software related projects are professionally qualified and that they place high regard on their professionalism with regard to ethics, responsibility and the attainment of quality. Traditionally when we attempt to measure quality during a software project we concentrate on metrics associated with the product (ie the code) and on the mechanics of how the product was developed. Little attention appears to be given to the quality of the staff involved in the process. This is despite the obvious fact that high quality staff are likely to produce a high quality product while poor quality staff are not. It would therefore seem that a simple project metric, such as the ratio of the number of professionally qualified staff involved on a project to the total number of staff, [13] is as likely to give a measure of the quality of the final product as established metrics such as that of Halstead [14].

3.2 SE Education within Academic Institutions

Academic institutions have been producing graduates and diplomates in computing-based disciplines in greater and greater number since the late 1970s. However, it would appear that despite all this new blood the "mind set" of the software industry appears not to be as positive towards SE practices and the production of quality products as it should be. Therefore, I must raise the question as to whether or not the students completing these courses are really equipped with the knowledge, skills and abilities which will enable them to immediately operate efficiently and effectively in the industry. Do their courses provide them with the necessary professionalism that should be expected? How do they compare in these areas with graduates in the more traditional engineering disciplines?

To achieve real improvement in the future, educational institutions need to take a much more pro-active role in promoting SE practices and professionalism. Also, this should not only be in named SE courses but in all computing courses from those closely related to business to those related to the more technological aspects of computing. It is also not sufficient to take a traditional computing topic such as algorithms and simply retitle it Software Engineering. There needs to be a change to an underlying approach which places a very high emphasis on aspects such as quality, professionalism, ethics and responsibility. It is important that these aspects need to be introduced at the start of any computing course and used throughout it. It is also important that emphasis is placed within these courses on interpersonal communications as SE practices have as much, if not more, to do with people than with machines. This aspect has been identified by the British Computer Society in its 1990 report on the Future of Information Technology [15] as the single most important skill required for effective participation in the IT society of the 1990s. As they stated "there is no computer substitute for clear thinking and accurate expression".

3.3 Technology Transfer

The achievement of quality in software can only be realised if the appropriate SE practices are implemented and used correctly. However, if the staff who are already in the industry are ill informed or fail to recognise the benefits of SE then any adoption is unlikely to be totally successful. It also must be recognised that, no matter how advanced the technology becomes, without good organisational attitudes it can do little to help surmount the many difficulties that currently face systems development staff. Also, for the correct practices to be adopted there is a clear need for accurate and meaningful information regarding their use. For new developments to be accepted within commercial/administrative organisations, there needs to be much better means of efficient and effective technology transfer.

For particular SE practices to be accepted and used there must be a much better understanding of them, their use and the actual benefits which they can bring. I must emphasise again that the underlying cause for several of the problems identified in the previous section is simply fear of the unknown coupled with a lack of unbiased, easily accessed information. To overcome such problems we need to create enabling mechanisms which will facilitate technology transfer and mutual understanding. In the UK the Institute of Electrical Engineers has already identified a number of such mechanisms [16] which it now intends to progress. However, it is not sufficient to simply produce the technology transfer material. It is imperative that there also is a will within the industry to receive such material with an open mind, appraise it in an impartial manner and where new practices are found to be appropriate, to adopt them willingly and with enthusiasm.

REFERENCES

1. Naur, P. and Randell, B. (Eds.), 1969, "Software Engineering: Report on a Conference Sponsored by the NATO Science Committee" (Garmisch, Germany October 7-11, 1968) published by Scientific Affairs Division, NATO, Brussels.
2. Dennis, M. 1991, TickIT: The DTI Involvement. Management and Design Division Colloquium on TickIT Certification Initiative: Objectives and Practice, IEE, London.
3. Price Waterhouse, 1988, "Software Quality Standards: The Costs and Benefits", Price Waterhouse Management Consultants, London, England.
4. Edwards, H.M., Thompson, J.B., and Smith P., 1989, "Results of a Survey of the Use of SSADM in Commercial and Government Sectors in UK", Information and Software Technology, Vol 31, No 1, 21-28.
5. Edwards, H.M., Thompson, J.B., and Smith P., 1989, " Experiences in the Use of SSADM: A Series of Case-Studies. Part 1: First Time Users.", Information and Software Technology, Vol 31, No 8, 411-419.
6. Edwards, H.M., Thompson, J.B., and Smith P., 1989, " Experiences in the Use of SSADM: A Series of Case-Studies. Part 2: Experienced Users.", Information and Software Technology, Vol 31, No 8, 420-428.
7. Stobart, S.C., Thompson, J.B., and Smith, P., 1991, "Use, problems, benefits and future direction of computer-aided software engineering in United Kingdom", Info. and Software Tech., Vol 33, No 9, 629-636.
8. Davis, C.J., Thompson, J.B., Smith, P., and Gillies, A.J., 1992, "A Survey of Approaches to Software Quality within the UK", Occasional Paper, No 92-5, School of Computing and Information Systems, University of Sunderland, UK.
9. Hardy, C., Thompson, J.B., and Edwards H.M., 1994, "A Preliminary Study of Method Use in the UK", Occasional Paper No 94-12, School of Computing and Information Systems, University of Sunderland.
10. CCTA, 1990 "SSADM Version 4 Reference Manual", NCC Blackwell, Manchester, England.
11. DTI, 1992, "TickIT programme: Launch of 1993 Awards", JFIT NEWS , No 39, DTI, Stevenage, UK.
12. Thompson, J.B., 1990, "A Software Tool and User's Reactions To It", Conference: Computer, Man and Organisation II, May, Nivelles, Belgium.
13. Thompson, J.B., 1993, Discussion following presentation of paper by Davis et al ("Current approaches to software quality assurance within the United Kingdom") at conference Software Quality Management, March, Southampton, England.
14. Halstead, M.H., 1977, "Elements of Software Science", North-Holland, Amsterdam, Holland.
15. BCS, 1990, "Future Impact Of Information Technology", British Computer Society, London, UK.
16. Kemp, A., 1993, "Software- where's the quality?" Computing and Control Engineering Journal, February, 45-47.

32

Software Reliability Models for Practical Applications

M. Xie

Dept of Industrial & Systems Engineering, National University of Singapore, Kent Ridge, Singapore 0511

Abstract

Reliability is one of the most important aspects of product quality. Software reliability research has been going on worldwide and many software reliability models are proposed and studied. In this paper, we first review some of the important software reliability models and then discuss them with respect to their validity and usefulness. The final part of this paper is aimed to present some simple models for the analysis of software failure data. Unlike the conventional approach, we present our model based on the graphical interpretation and this approach allows us to easily test a few models before detailed study based on a selected model is carried out.

Keyword Codes: D.2.0; D.2.5; D.2.8
Keywords: Software Engineering, General; Software, Metrics; Reliability

1. INTRODUCTION

Software reliability, which deals with the study of software related failures and their consequences, is an important aspect of software quality. All products have to be working properly without failure before talking about other quality measures. Software reliability has recently attracted many researchers and practitioners because of the increasing demand of high quality software.

Reliability for both software and hardware is formally defined as the probability that a product will be working without failure during a specified time period and under a specified working environment. However, as software systems are different from the hardware counterparts, conventional technology cannot be applied in software engineering directly and specific models have to be used in the study of the reliability of software [1-4].

The aim of this paper is two-fold. First, we intend to give an overview of some existing software reliability models and their applicability in practice. We mainly discuss model validity and usefulness. Second, we present some recently developed models for software reliability study. Unlike the conventional approach, we present our model based on the graphical interpretation and this approach allows us to easily test a few models before detailed study based on a selected model is carried out.

2. SOFTWARE RELIABILITY MODELS AND THEIR USEFULNESS

2.1. Failure time based models

Reliability of software cannot be predicted without some real information about the software system we are interested in. An important and useful type of information is the failure time data collected during the testing stage. Many software reliability models are developed for the estimation of software reliability based on failure time data. Some well-known models are the exponential model, the logarithmic model and the s-shaped model.

These models are commonly known as nonhomogeneous Poisson process (NHPP) models and the basic assumption is that the failure process can be described by an NHPP. Using different mean value function describing the behaviour of the failure process, the reliability can be predicted.

Denote by $N(t)$ the cumulative number of failures at time t, the NHPP model assumes that the counting process $\{N(t), t \geq 0\}$ has independent increment and $N(t)$ is Poisson distributed with mean value function $m(t)$.

It follows from the standard theory of NHPP that, whenever the mean value function is determined, the reliability function at time t_0 is given as

$$R(t|t_0) = exp\{-[m(t+t_0)-m(t_0)]\}.$$

The Goel-Okumoto model [3], which is also called the exponential model, has the following mean-value function

$$m_{GO}(t) = a(1 - e^{-bt}).$$

The delayed s-shaped model is first proposed by Yamada et al. [4] and the mean value function is given as

$$m_{DS}(t) = a(1 - (1 + bt)e^{-bt}).$$

The Musa-Okumoto model [1], which is of logarithmic type, is another useful NHPP model and the mean value function is

$$m_{MO}(t) = a\ln(1+bt).$$

These models have been widely discussed by many authors and can be seen as the representation of the NHPP software reliability models. The parameter a in the Goel-Okumoto model and the s-shaped model can be interpreted as the total number of faults in the software and the parameter b is a type of fault-detection rate. However, for the Musa-Okumoto model, $m(t)$ is not finite. This is useful when we can interpret the failure process in such a way that not all faults can be removed or new faults can be introduced leading to infinite number of faults in infinite time.

It can be shown that the Goel-Okumoto model has a constant fault detection rate while the delayed s-shaped model has an increasing-then-decreasing failure rate and then the mean value function is s-shaped. For the Musa-Okumoto model, earlier failures reduce the failure rate larger than later failures. In conclusion, these models are able to describe different software failure processes. The practical difficulty is to select a suitable model although a lot of research has focused on the problem of parameter estimation.

2.2. Software-metric based reliability model

It can be argued that software reliability depends on the intrinsic property of the software. Software metrics can be used for the estimation of software reliability. There are many software metrics and a lot of study is going on in finding the most suitable metrics for reliability prediction. In a recent book edited by Fenton and Littlewood [5], some related articles can be found.

Historically, it has been observed at the beginning of the seventies, see e.g. Akiyama [6], that there is a strong dependence between the number of faults and the nature of the program, such as the number of codes, the number of paths and other algorithmic complexity measures. Since then, many software metrics are developed and also applied in software reliability study. Software metrics have been widely applied in different contexts, mainly during the design stage for which software metrics are helpful tools in allocating development resources and making management decisions.

Generally, software metrics can be used in reliability prediction. The main advantage of using software metrics is its applicability at earlier stages of the software development. This is of vital importance since it is helpful for software managers to allocate software testing effort, to decide a preliminary release time and to determine the price of the software product. Empirical software metrics models are simple and they can easily be calculated.

It should be noted that software metrics can only be used to make an overall estimation of software fault content before the testing starts. After the testing, a number of faults are removed and it is important to be able to estimate the number of remaining faults. There are few metrics for making such estimation and this is a problem when using software metrics in estimating software reliability when the prediction is important.

Most existing software metrics, due to their static nature, do not consider the growth of software reliability. A disadvantage of the existing software metrics models is thus that they give only an estimate of the software fault content which is not equal to the probability of software failure, because different faults may have different occurrence rate. An important area of further research is just the relation between the failure intensity of the software and other software metrics or environmental factors which can be used to connect existing static models to other dynamic models.

Existing studies have been concentrated on finding a single metric to give an acceptable estimate of the number of faults. However, this may not be successful and it can be the case that more than one metric will have some impact on the reliability. A better way to utilize several metrics is to combine them using techniques such as multiple-regression analysis, see e.g. [8]. In this respect, more research is needed.

2.3. Combination of information

As discussed previously, both static models and dynamic models are useful. In practice, it is important to combine all available information about the software product and the development process in order to make a better reliability prediction. For example, software complexity measures are useful in estimating the number of software fault content, especially at an earlier stage of software development which is important from a management point of view. The estimate is, however, inaccurate and hence it should be revised as more data have been collected.

In a paper by Yamada, the behaviour of the testing resource expenditures over the testing period can be observed as a consumption curve of testing-effort and the increase in reliability is strongly dependent on the allocated testing-effort. Software reliability models are developed by incorporating some testing-effort models.

A model incorporating various factors related to software testing, such as the number of test workers, is proposed in a paper by Tohma. The applicability of this model and various estimation techniques have also been studied in other papers by Tohma and his co-authors.

The paper by Khoshgoftaar and Munson suggests that software metrics are used in reliability prediction and a neural network approach is used. The approach nicely combines the available software metrics and dynamic software reliability growth models. The model can be trained by including more information and the accuracy of prediction is increased.

Musa [7] presented a theory of software reliability analysis based on the execution time. This well-known software reliability model can be considered a model combining static information with dynamic prediction.

Bayesian estimation is a statistical technique for parameter estimation by combining prior information and the data set. Attempts have been made in using Bayesian techniques in software reliability study. Many Bayesian models have been proposed for the analysis of software failure data in combination with previous knowledge in form of a so-called prior distribution of the unknown parameter.

3. MODELS WITH GRAPHICAL INTERPRETATIONS

Usually, we do not know beforehand which model to use in a particular situation. Even if we have selected a model, we have to determine the parameters of the model. All studies on failure time based models focus on these issues. However, most of the results are difficult to apply in practice. In this section we present a graphical approach which makes the model validation and parameter estimation an easy task.

Usually, the graphical method employs some transformations and finds a linear relationship between the variables of interest. If the required transformation exists, the transformed test data tend to be on a straight line. As a straight line is only characterized by its slope and a point which is through, the number of the unknown parameters in the model with graphical interpretation is limited to one or two. The slope and a point on the straight line, usually the intercept on the vertical axis, provide us the estimates of the parameters [8].

One such model is the Duane model which is a well-known model for reliability growth and it has the following mean value function

$$m_{DU}(t) = at^{b},\ t\geq 0.$$

The Duane model has widely been discussed and applied by practitioners in analysing failure data of repairable systems. In software reliability, the Duane model has also been discussed from various points of view. However, there is little discussion about its graphical interpretation.

The log-power model is a recently developed model with graphical interpretation [8] and it has the mean value function

$$m_{LP}(t) = a\ln^{b}(1+t),\ t\geq 0.$$

Our empirical study on the log-power model shows that the log-power model is able to fit different data sets and has a high prediction ability. It is a very promising model in software reliability modelling.

From the relationship

$$\ln m_{LP}(t) = \ln a + b\ln\ln(1+t),\ t\geq 0$$

we see that if we plot $\ln m(t)$ versus $\ln\ln(1+t)$, the plot should be a straight line. The parameter b is the slope of the straight line and the constant term is just the parameter $\ln a$.

In fact, we can validate a specific model by looking at the fitted line before further analysis is made. If the data cannot be fitted by a straight line, there is then no need to analyze the data and other models should be considered. This *FIRST-MODEL-VALIDATION-THEN-PARAMETER-ESTIMATION* technique is then very simple and convenient for practical applications.

REFERENCES

1. Musa, J.D.; Iannino, A. and Okumoto, K.: '*Software Reliability: Measurement, Prediction, Application*', McGraw-Hill, 1987.
2. Xie, M.: '*Software Reliability Modelling*', World Scientific Publisher, 1991.
3. Goel, A.L. and Okumoto, K.: 'Time-dependent error-detection rate model for software reliability and other performance measures', *IEEE Trans. on Reliability*, 1979, R-28, pp.206-211.
4. Yamada, S. and Osaki, S.: 'Reliability growth models for hardware and software systems based on nonhomogeneous Poisson process: A survey', *Microelectronics and Reliability*, 1983, 23, pp.91-112.
5. Fenton, N.E. and Littlewood, B.: '*Software Reliability and Metrics*'. Elsevier, London.
6. Akiyama, F.: 'An example of software system debugging', *Proc. IFIP Congress, Vol.1*, North-Holland, Amsterdam, 1971, pp.353-359.
7. Musa, J.D.: 'A theory of software reliability and its application', *IEEE Trans. on Software Engineering*, 1975, SE-1, pp.312-327.
8. Xie, M. and Zhao, M.: 'On some reliability growth models with simple graphical interpretations', *Microelectronics and Reliability*, 1993, 33, pp.149-167.

33

Assessing the Quality of Requirements Engineering Products

R E M Champion

Department of Information Systems, City Polytechnic of Hong Kong, Kowloon, Hong Kong

Abstract

The specification of user requirements for software systems provides the foundation for the subsequent development work. This paper examines the criteria for assessing the quality of the products of requirements engineering, and the implications of these criteria on the structure and content of requirements models. In particular, it is argued that the criteria of traceability and and its impact on the maintainability of the final product imply the need for more comprehensive models of requirements statements.

Keyword Codes: D.2.1, D.2.4, D.2.9
Keywords: Requirements Engineering; Conceptual Modelling; Quality Assurance

1. INTRODUCTION

This paper examines the products of the requirements engineering (RE) phase of software systems development, specifically in terms of the quality criteria which are being proposed for these products [1-2]. The intention is to demonstrate that the traditional product of the process is not capable of supporting current demands; and that to satisfy existing quality criteria, new products need to be explicitly described.

The paper first outlines the process of RE in terms of its inputs, transformations and outputs. The nature of the output from the RE process will vary according to the method and models used, and is currently the subject of much debate [3]. Consequently, this paper describes the products in terms of a set of quality criteria, compiled from the literature, which effectively differentiates between good and bad RE products. The quality criteria are then classified according to the purpose of the RE product being measured, and this classification is compared with needs of the various types of personnel who interact with the product. The comparison is used to propose a richer modelling environment for the RE process, which facilitates the representation of requirements knowledge in different models, depending on the aspects of quality which should be addressed by each component.

2. THE PROCESS OF REQUIREMENTS ENGINEERING

Requirements engineering is traditionally viewed as that process which transforms the needs and wishes of potential users of the target computerised system, usually incomplete, and expressed in informal terms, into a complete, precise, and consistent software requirements specification (SRS). The primary process is accepted as being an iteration of the three tasks: elicitation, modelling and validation [4-5]. The cycle of iteration continues until the model is considered to contain sufficient information for the design process to begin and, in practice may continue beyond this point, either as requirements change or designers seek further information [6].

The customers are involved both with the validation of the evolving model and with the review of the SRS as the basis of a contract. The elicitation task may utilise a variety of approaches to gather information for the modelling task, but the sources of the information are limited to people and documents [7]. One special form of documentation is the 'requirements document', which can be used to express an initial version of customers' requirements using natural language, as a starting point for the modelling task [8].

In order to specify the content of the information which is acquired by the analysis phase, it becomes necessary to examine the context in which the people and documents exist. The issues addressed by a full analysis of an enterprise's information system requirements are described in [9-10], but include the organisation, the business processes, the mission and environment. None of these categories of information can be considered as fixed for an enterprise. While much work is being done to facilitate the consensus formation [11], the emphasis is still on the construction of a single view, albeit a view which is acceptable to all parties concerned. While a single view of the required system is essential for the developers, it is less so for system designers, and is a positive disadvantage to other potential users of the RE products who need to understand the complexities of potential futures for the enterprise.

3. EVALUATING THE PRODUCTS OF REQUIREMENTS ENGINEERING

While the products of requirements engineering are generally viewed as consisting of a single artefact, the SRS, there is no standard for the content of this product. Attempts to differentiate between good and bad products have resulted in the formation of quality criteria [2], but these criteria are specified, applied and evaluated with the assumption that a single product is being measured. Consequently, products with different functions are being compared using the same criteria; or, where a single product is precisely defined, that product is subject to the application of all quality criteria, which are often contradictory.

3.1 Fact Elicitation

At the initial stage of analysis, statements concerning any of the aspects of the enterprise may be elicited from the customers, either as the results of observation and interviews, or by the analysis of the initial requirements document. Since the facts may legitimately represent different viewpoints of these different aspects, the only quality criteria which can be realistically applied to the product of this stage are:

(a) Traced; the source of the fact is recorded; (b) Traceable; the inclusion of the fact in any subsequent analysis model can be recorded; and (c) Verifiable; it is possible to determine the truth of the fact from its statement.

The last attribute allows for the removal of any incorrect facts elicited from the customers; no judgements can yet be made about ambiguities or inconsistencies.

3.2 Modelling for System Developers

The traditional end product of the RE process should provide the development team with sufficient information for the design and implementation of an automated information system. Hence, quality criteria for this product can be restricted to:

(a) Complete; everything that the IS is intended to do is included in the product; (b) Consistent; no part of the product conflicts with any other part; (c) Correct; all components of the product describe a required element of the system's behaviour; (d) Minimal; the product should not over-constrain system design; (e) Traced; elements of the product can be traced back to intermediate analysis products; (f) Traceable; elements of the product can be traced forward to design products; and (g) Unambiguous; every element of the product has only one interpretation.

The first two products described above represent the start and end points for the RE process. While the aim of this paper is not to define a process model for RE, it is also necessary to consider intermediate products and their role.

3.3 Intermediate Modelling

The facts obtained from the customers during elicitation may contain knowledge concerning any aspect of the enterprise being analysed, and in any of the modes described above. In order

to organise this information and be able to reason about the implications for the required system, it is necessary for the analysts to construct models of these various issues.
(a) Appropriate; elements of the product describe only features of the issue addressed; (b) Expressive; it is possible to describe any aspect of the issue addressed; (c) Inconsistency tolerant; it is possible that the product may contain legitimate inconsistencies, within different viewpoints; (d) Incompleteness tolerant; the product need only be as complete as the analysts decide; (e) Traced; elements of the product can be traced back to other intermediate analysis products, or directly to facts from the elicitation phase; and (f) Traceable; elements of the product can be traced forward to the final development product, or to other intermediate products.

Traced and traceable now describe a network of links between the initial and final products, through the intermediate models used by the analysts. The quality attribute 'modifiable' can be used to measure the quality of these links rather than of a particular product.

3.4 Modelling for Validation of Requirements Products

Validation of any of the products of RE, by definition, will involve the customers of the system interacting with the analysts. The aim of the interaction is to satisfy the customers that the evolving system description matches their requirements. Two methods of validation exist; either the product being validated is presented to the users for direct evaluation, or the product may be animated or executed to demonstrate aspects of the external behaviour of the target system. The first case adds 'understandable' to the list of quality attributes for the product being validated. For the product to be understandable by non-computer specialists, it may well be necessary to compromise some of the other quality attributes. In the second case, it is assumed that a separate product is involved, allowing the following product-specific quality criteria to be specified.
(a) Complete; everything that the product is expected to demonstrate is included; (b) Consistent; no elements of the product contradict any others; (c) Unambiguous; every element of the product has only one interpretation; and (d) Formal; the notation of the product permits a mechanistic analysis of the content.

The final product may be considered to result from the combination of the products described above, and the way in which the combined products facilitate changes to the requirements for the target IS, either during development or subsequently.

3.5 Modelling for Maintenance and Reuse

The product from this stage may be used by customers, analysts and developers, as well as maintainers. Quality of the product must be measured in terms of the ability of the users to determine the nature and consequences of altering any aspect of an enterprise modelled during the RE process, including the information systems. Since change requests may originate at any level of the enterprise, from its mission and objectives, to the tasks performed by individuals, the need for traceability becomes paramount. The following criteria should be used to measure the quality of the combined product of RE.
(a) Annotated; it should be possible to relate the necessity and stability of requirements to aspects of the intermediate models; (b) Expressive; everything that needs to be considered in evaluating changes is included in the product; (c) Modifiable; the structure of the product allows for alterations of individual components; and (d) Traceable; each component of the product is linked to related components, including 'derived from' relations.

4. CONCLUSIONS

The product description, contained in the SRS, forms only a part of the products of RE, and it is this part which requires consistency, completeness and preciseness. Other products, because of their failure to meet these 'quality' criteria have generally been treated as intermediate, 'throw-away' artefacts, useful only in their contribution to the construction of the SRS. However, such an SRS is only of direct use to the system developers, while other criteria for quality, from other user groups are difficult to match against this single product. The preceding sections have clearly shown the differentiation between the products required for each phase of the process, and the user groups involved at each phase. The advantage of this approach is that products can be evaluated according to criteria which specifically measure the quality required by the phase being addressed.

Finally, the languages and models used for each of the products should reflect the quality attributes addressed. This implies that a single notation may not be sufficient for all products. Consequently, the maintenance product, which involves the combination of other products, may require more sophisticated facilities than currently exist. The linking of concepts represented in different notations, so as to allow tracing of the development, requires further investigation.

REFERENCES

1. Davis, A. *Software Requirements: Objects, Functions, and States*; Prentice Hall, Englewood Cliff, NJ, 1993.
2. Lindland, O. Sindre, G. & Solvberg, A. *Understanding Quality in Conceptual Modeling*; IEEE Software, March 1994.
3. Lubars, M. Potts, C & Richter, C. *A Review of the State of the Practice in Requirements Modeling*; Proc. Int. Symposium on Requirements Engineering, IEEE C. S. Press 1993.
4. Armenise, P. Bandinelli, S. Ghezzi, C Morzenti, A. *Software Processes Representation Languages: Survey and Assessment*; Proc. Int. Conf; SEKE'92, Capri, Italy, June 1992.
5. Loucopoulos, P. and Champion, R. *Concept Acquisition and Analysis in Requirements Specifications*, Software Engineering Journal, Vol 5, No. 2, March 1990.
6. Harker, S. & Eason, K. *The Change and Evolution of Requirements as a Challenge to the Practice of Software Engineering*; Proc. Int. Symp. on Reqs Eng; IEEE C. S. Press 1993.
7. Goguen, J. & Linde, C. *Techniques for Requirements Elicitation*; Proc. International Symposium on Requirements Engineering, IEEE C. S. Press 1993.
8. Kliem, R. *Back to Basics: Developing A Good Requirements Document*; Journal of Systems Management, October 1992.
9. French, J. *The Business Knowledge Investment*; Yourdon Press, Englewood Cliffs, New Jersey, 1990.
10. Mills A, Murgatroyd S, *Organisational Rules: A Framework for Understanding Organisational Action*, OU Press, 1991.
11. Easterbrook, S. *Domain Modelling with Hierarchies of Alternative Viewpoints*; Proc. International Symposium on Requirements Engineering, IEEE C. S. Press 1993.

34

Re-Certification of Software Reliability without Re-Testing

C. Wohlin

Dept. of Communication Systems, Lund Institute of Technology, Box 118, S-221 00 Lund, Sweden, e-mail: claesw@tts.lth.se

Abstract

Usage testing or operational profile testing is depicted as an important test technique to remove the most critical faults from an operational perspective. The technique also allows for determination of the software reliability through application of software reliability models. This is, of course, beneficial, but a problem arises as the usage changes and this can be expected as new services are added to the existing system or the behaviour of the users change due to some reason. Therefore, a method to re-certify software reliability without re-testing the software for all potential changes that may occur is needed. This paper outlines such a procedure based on fault content estimations and by recording a number of measures during usage testing. The procedure gives a basis for determining whether more testing or other means to remove faults is needed prior to the usage changes or if the reliability requirements are fulfilled even after a change in usage. It is concluded that the proposed procedure can be a valuable tool to cope with changes in usage, but more research as well as practical experience from the proposed procedure is needed.

Keyword codes: D.2.0, D.2.5, D.2.8
Keywords: Software Engineering, General; Software reliability, usage testing, operational profile testing, reliability certification, software metrics, fault content estimations, statistical quality control.

1. INTRODUCTION

A reliability estimate based on intended usage gives a good figure of the perceived reliability during operation. The usage profile is used to get an estimate of the reliability experienced during operation. Several profiles may be used during usage testing if different usages are expected based on, for example, the location of the installation or different customers, [1]. The estimate of the reliability based on usage is still the only way to get a realistic estimate, but the change in usage compared to the usage profile applied when estimating the reliability must be handled in some way.

This paper tries to describe one possibility to obtain an estimate of the reliability when the usage is changing. Some different reasons to experience a change in usage compared to the usage profile applied during certification can be identified:

- An erroneous profile was applied during the certification. The change will be experienced as the software is being released.
- A change will occur with the time, either slowly or perhaps quickly due to for example marketing of some specific services

This paper mainly discusses the second item.

Unfortunately, the estimate from usage testing will probably give an optimistic estimation, since if the operational usage is different from the one applied during testing, the reliability will probably be overestimated. The reason is that the certification will be more thorough in the areas where the main usage is supposed to be, but if this is wrong the software will be used more in the less tested regions. Thus it is reasonable to believe that the reliability will drop.

The objective with certification must be remembered, i.e. to certify a specific reliability level, in particular the level that will be perceived during operation. This is done by performing usage testing. The certification objective is not to find faults in general, but to indicate their absence in the frequently executed parts or to locate the faults influencing the reliability the most. Testing, as discussed here, is not primarily supposed to be seen as a fault removal procedure.

2. RELIABILITY ESTIMATE FROM USAGE

Some different opportunities of specifying usage exist, see for example [1, 2, 3]. These methods resemble each other, but have some different properties. The approach discussed in [3] leads to a state explosion for large systems, and the solution proposed in [2] is a further development of the ideas discussed in [3], while the solution proposed in [1] is very similar to the one proposed in [2]. One major difference is the way of modelling the external states. These are modelled explicitly in [2] and more implicitly in [1]. We will here primarily discuss the method presented in [2], which is based on a hierarchical Markov chain.

A usage specification consists of a usage model and a usage profile. The usage model is a structural model of the anticipated usage, while the profile quantifies the actual usage.

In the hierarchical Markov chain model, it is proposed that the probabilities for choosing a particular path in the hierarchy are dynamic, i.e. the probabilities in the hierarchy are changed based on the state of the Markov chain on the lowest level. This level describes the actual state of an external user. The dynamic change of probabilities is a way to capture the difference in load, primarily in terms of capturing the functional interaction that will occur depending on how many users that are in different states. The dynamic behaviour will, however, change around some equilibrium probabilities. A simpler solution in the hierarchical model will therefore be to assign static probabilities in the hierarchy, i.e. the probabilities are independent of the actual states of the external users.

This means that the usage model can either be used with static or dynamic probabilities. If a possible future change in usage shall be modelled it seems unnecessary to model the probabilities dynamically, because of the uncertainty in the future usage. Dynamic probabilities are, however, recommended during usage testing with the expected usage profile, as it, for example, allows that it is more probable that a user who has started a specific sequence continues than that a new specific user enters the system. One way of estimating the reliability based on change in the usage profile is to test the software with a new profile. Thus try to estimate the reliability based on a future possible change in the usage. This approach is feasible but very costly, since it would mean re-testing the whole system as new services are introduced or the usage is expected to change. In particular for large systems which have a long life time and a continuously change of available services, an example of this type of system is a telephony exchange. Another solution would be to make a re-calculation based on the expected future change in usage. The re-calculation is based on the failure data when applying the original usage profile, estimation of fault content and the new profile. This approach is much more tractable and it is the method studied in this paper.

But, before presenting the method, it is essential to realize that even if the usage profile may be slightly incorrect or slowly changing over time, it is better to apply usage testing than to continue performing coverage testing. This is for example emphasized with the results presented in [1, 4].

3. RE-CERTIFICATION OF SOFTWARE RELIABILITY

3.1 Introduction

It is advantageous to make an estimation based on a re-calculation instead of applying new usage profiles in testing. The re-calculation shall be based on the failure data obtained from the usage profile applied during testing, fault content estimations and the new usage profile. A re-calculation procedure would make it possible to calculate the reliability for different profiles without performing new tests. The re-calculation gives an estimate of the reliability after the change in usage has occurred. Hence, providing a valuable input to decide whether the software fulfils the reliability requirements after the change in usage. If it is found that the requirement is not fulfilled then a decision to perform more testing before the change actually occurs can be taken. This means that decisions can be taken based on actual information and not by guessing.

The main problem in reliability estimation is that some faults may be hidden in the software, which were not found in the original usage test but are critical if the usage changes. This is particular problematic if the usage changes dramatically, i.e. a use case which has been very little tested due to little usage in the original case becomes a use case that is used extensively. This will probably make the reliability drop considerably. Therefore, the re-calculation procedure must be based on fault content estimations from either complexity metrics, as discussed in for example [5], or by application of capture-recapture methods as discussed in [6, 7].

3.2 Re-calculation procedure

Several models and measures are needed for the re-calculation procedure. Some of these are normally recorded when performing usage testing, they are:

- Usage model
- Usage profile
- MTBF (Mean Time Between Failures) values

These have to be complemented to allow for a re-calculation, which requires the following models and measures:

Unchanged model:

- The usage model is the same as in the original application. It is assumed that the usage model has not changed as the usage profile changes.

New measures to record:

- Fault content estimations from either complexity metrics or capture-recapture methods must be performed, which primarily must be applied prior to the testing phase to "know" the fault content in different system parts when entering the test phase.
- The locations of the faults found during usage testing must be recorded.
- The probability for failure if the part containing a fault is used has to be determined. It may be the case that a failure does not occur even if the faulty part of the usage model is exercised. This can be determined based on the observed failures and the test cases run in usage testing.
- The mean execution time for a arbitrary transition within a specific service or component as seen from the usage model has to be recorded. This parameter can also be recorded from the test cases executed. The mean execution time shall be used to re-calculate the MTBF values. It is assumed that, if a failure occurs in a service it will take half the execution time to reach the fault.

New input:

- The new usage profile is the reason for performing the re-calculation and it is, of course, an essential input.

During usage testing, it is essential that the usage model is correct and that the profile is as good as possible. The original profile applied results probably in a number of failures. These failure times are recorded, i.e. the MTBF values are noted. This is the normal procedure when applying statistical usage testing.

The re-calculation procedure requires that the fault content prior to usage testing can be estimated and that the actual location of the faults resulting in failures shall be noted. The time to a failure is based on a particular execution. Thus meaning that new MTBF values can be calculated based on the new usage profile and the actual times to reach the parts in the usage model containing the unobserved faults. This also includes the probability for fault detection if the part containing a fault is executed. The probability shall be used in determining whether a fault is found or not, when a part containing a fault is executed. The probability is a measure of fault exposure.

Due to this, it is necessary to record the execution times for different usage parts, e.g. a transition within a service provided to the users. All times to execute a specific abstraction level in the usage model must be recorded, e.g. the services provided to the users or some suitable component level. This figure must be noted, since it has to be used when re-calculating MTBF values based on a new usage profile.

The re-calculation shall be applied, as stated above, when the usage changes or is expected to change. Hence, it is assumed that certification has been performed for one usage profile and a reliability measure has been calculated. The application of re-calculation means that it is possible to prepare for different outcomes in the future. Re-calculation is needed as the change in usage will mean that the perceived reliability changes. The objective is to estimate the new reliability from the experience stored during prior usage tests and the new usage profile.

The re-calculation procedure can be summarized in the following steps:

1. The software reliability requirement to certify is known from the requirements specification.
2. The fault content for different system parts when entering the test phase is estimated applying complexity metrics or capture-recapture methods on, for example, the code.
3. Fault location in the usage model is recorded during testing, hence being able to derive the number of remaining faults in the different system parts.
4. Mean execution time for a suitable level in the usage model is recorded at the testing time.
5. Probability for fault exposure is determined based on experience from usage testing.
6. MTBF values are generated by randomly running through the usage model and adding successful execution time to the current MTBF value, until a fault is reached and executed.

An example is presented in the next section to illustrate the steps in the re-calculation procedure.

3.3 An example

The six step procedure in the previous section will be gone through for a minor example to show how the procedure is intended to work.

Step 1: The software reliability requirement in terms of MTBF is known to be 50 t.u. (time units).

Step 2: The fault content is supposed to have been estimated from phases prior to the test phase. The parts in which the failures reside are assumed to be services in for example a telecommunication system. The following estimates are assumed, based on applying capture-recapture on the code inspections, Service 1: 4 faults, Service 2: 2 faults, Service 3: 5 faults and Service 4: 4 faults.

Step 3: During the ordinary certification, it is assumed that a total of 7 failures were found and assumed corrected, hence leaving an estimate of 8 remaining faults in the software. The usage testing revealing these 7 faults is assumed to result in certification of the required reliability level, i.e 50 t.u., based on the expected usage profile. The usage model and the location of the remaining faults are depicted in figure 1, as well as the new usage profile to be used in the re-certification. The new profile describes an expected change.

The usage modelling technique depicted in figure 1 is further discussed in [2] and the correspondence between system parts, for example services, and model parts is further discussed in [8].

The new usage profile for which the reliability shall be calculated has to be known in terms of the probability for selecting user type 1 from the usage state etc. These probabilities are shown in figure 1. Thus it is possible to run through the usage model by starting in the usage state and then running down in the structure until a specific service is executed.

Step 4: The execution times for each service are supposed to be known from measurements on the system during testing. The times are: Service 1: 2 time units (t.u.); Service 2: 1 t.u.; Service 3: 2.5 t.u. and finally Service 4: 4 t.u. It is assumed that it is not certain that a failure occurs just because the service is executed. Probabilities for fault exposures are given in step 4. It is also assumed that if a failure is executed it will in average happen after half the execution time of the service.

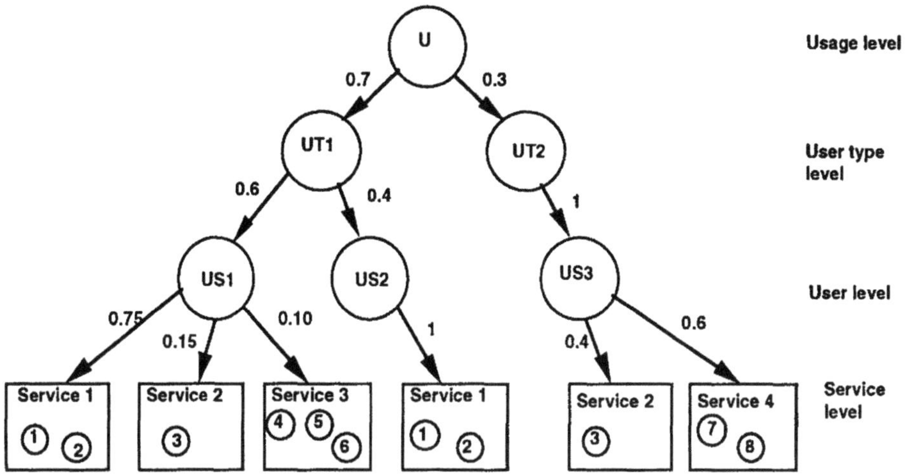

Figure 1. Usage model and new profile with estimated faults remaining.

Step 5: The following fault exposure probabilities are assumed based on the outcome of the usage test performed: Fault 1, 0.05; Fault 2, 0.20; Fault 3, 0.50; Fault 4, 1; Fault 5, 0.30; Fault 6, 0.01; Fault 7, 0.75 and Fault 8, 0.25. The fault exposure probabilities are determined based on the number of test cases run and the faults found in comparison with the estimated number of faults present in the different services.

Step 6: Random numbers are generated to run through the usage model and also to determine whether an actual execution of a service result in a failure or not. The MTBF values are recorded. The outcome became:
Fault no. 4: MTBF(1) = 10.25 t.u.,
Fault no. 2: MTBF(2) = 1 t.u.,
Fault no. 3: MTBF(3) = 6.5 t.u.,
Fault no. 7: MTBF(4) = 20 t.u.,
Fault no. 8: MTBF(5) = 30 t.u.,
Fault no. 1: MTBF(6) = 27 t.u.,
Fault no. 5: MTBF(7) = 75.75 t.u.

Finally, the certification time without failure is found to be 161.5 t.u., i.e. fault no. 6 was not found. The latter indicating that a longer random number sequence has to be generated to find the last known fault. An example of how the outcome was generated is presented in appendix A.

It must be noted that based on the probabilities, the expected order to find the faults are: 7, 2, 3, 8, 4, 1, 5 and 6. The rank correlation between the expected order and the actual outcome in this particular case is 0.69.

These six steps have given new MTBF values. It is seen from these values that if the requirement of MTBF is 50 t.u., then the requirement is not fulfilled and further testing has to be conducted to locate the faults remaining in the software before the usage changes as expected.

3.4 Discussion

A major question remains to be answered: Does this procedure generate the true reliability perceived by the users after the change in usage? The answer to this question is that by applying the procedure it is possible to gain experience from the re-calculation procedure. It is not until it has been tested that the question can be fully answered. Further research is, however, needed to improve both fault content estimations as well as the proposed re-calculation procedure.

The main advantage with this method is that no re-testing has to be performed. The procedure forms a basis for deriving new MTBF values and hence gives an input to taking an informed decision. It can hence be determined whether more testing is needed to remove more faults or if the performed usage test if sufficient to fulfil the software reliability requirement after the usage changes.

It can be concluded that the re-calculation procedure is advantageous compared to applying a new profile directly, since it may not be necessary to re-test. The result from the re-calculation procedure is either that the reliability requirement is still fulfilled or new efforts to locate the faults have to initiated

The re-calculation procedure is a tractable method, hence indicating that it ought to be used because of its simplicity and to gain experience. More research has however to be conducted in the area to make it really useful.

4. CONCLUSION

The change in usage may cause a large fall in the reliability and change in usage is expected over time. It is therefore essential to be able to predict how the change in usage will affect the perceived reliability before it occurs in the operational phase.

The first step is of course to understand that the reliability will change as the usage changes. Then the method presented in this paper can be used to gain experience and then it can be improved. Thus giving a better method of predicting the reliability as the usage changes.

The method presented in this paper is not the optimum method, but possibly the best method available. Further research is needed in the area based on the ideas presented. The method shows, however, that it ought to be possible to predict the reliability based on change in usage, instead of waiting until a fall in reliability is experienced in the field.

5. FUTURE RESEARCH

5.1 Introduction

One disadvantage with usage testing is that correct test cases do not improve the reliability. They only contribute to show that the software has a certain reliability. This is a clear waste of resources, since if it is correct there is no use testing it. To completely eliminate correct test cases seems impossible, but they at least ought to be minimized without losing the opportunity to certify a specific reliability level of the software. It is also well-known that it is impossible to certify the reliability levels required within the available test period, in particular this is the case for safety-critical systems.

5.2 Requirements certification method

What are the characteristics of a good test method?

- From the developer´s point of view, as many as possible of the faults must be found.
- From the procurer´s viewpoint, the software product must be reliable (no faults at all in the software would be preferable)
- The number of erroneous test cases under a given time interval ought to be maximized.
- The length of the test interval must be minimized.
- It would be favourable if the total number of faults and their location could be estimated.
- The software ought to be released with a given reliability (within confidence bounds).
- Future failure occurrences ought to be predicted.

- A certain degree of coverage of the code ought to be obtained.
- Automatic control if the test cases go right or wrong would be beneficial.

Does this test methodology exist? The answer is clearly no.

The objective of the future research is to improve the existing test methods so they better fulfil the characteristics outlined above.

ACKNOWLEDGEMENT

I am grateful to Jan-Eric Johansson, Telia (Swedish Telecommunication Administration), Sweden for granting permission to base this research on a prestudy conducted by Telia.

REFERENCES

1. Musa, J. D.: 'Operational Profiles in Software Reliability Engineering', IEEE Software, 1993, Vol. 11, No. 2, pp. 14-32.
2. Runeson, P., and Wohlin, C.: 'Usage Modelling: The Basis for Statistical Quality Control', Proceedings 10th Annual Software Reliability Symposium, Denver, Colorado, USA, June 1992, pp. 77-84,.
3. Whittaker, J. A. and Poore, J. H.: 'Markov Analysis of Software Specifications', ACM Transactions on Software Engineering and Methodology, 1993, Vol. 2, No. 1, pp. 93-106.
4. Adams, E. N.: 'Optimizing Preventive Service of Software Products', IBM Journal of Research and Development, January 1984.
5. Munson, J. C., and Ravenel, R. H.: 'Designing Reliable Software', Proceedings Fourth International Symposium on Software Reliability Engineering, Denver, Colorado, USA, November 1993, pp. 45-54,.
6. Eick, S. G., Loader, C.R., Long, M.D:, Votta, L.G and Vander Wiel, S. A.: 'Estimating Software Fault Content Before Coding', Proceedings 14th International Conference on Software Engineering, Melbourne, Australia, 1992. pp. 59-65.
7. Vander Wiel, S.A., and Votta, L.G.: 'Assessing Software Designs Using Capture-Recapture Methods', IEEE Transactions on Software Engineering, 1993, Vol. 19, No. 11, pp. 1045-1054.
8. Wohlin, C., and Runeson, P.: 'Certification of Software Components', IEEE Transactions on Software Engineering, 1994, Vol. 20, No. 6, pp. 494-499.

APPENDIX A: EXAMPLE OF RE-CALCULATION

The objective of this appendix is to illustrate the derivation of MTBF values for a new usage profile, see section 3.3, step 6.

1. Random numbers are generated. For example: 0.4077, 0.0433, 0.3966, 0.6597 and 0.7538. A total of 450 random numbers were generated to get the MTBF values presented in section 3.3.
2. The five random numbers give a specific sequence in the usage model, see figure 1. The following is obtained:
   0.4077 < 0.7 => transition U -> UT1
   0.0433 < 0.6 => transition UT1 -> US1
   0.3966 < 0.75 => transition US1 -> Service 1 (i.e. service 1 is executed)
   Two faults are located in service 1. It is now necessary to find out if these are found or not. The probabilities for fault exposure are given in section 3.3, step 5.
   0.6597 > 0.05 => Fault 1 is not found.
   0.7538 > 0.20 => Fault 2 is not found.

3. Thus the total execution time so far is equal to the execution time of Service 1, let the execution time be denoted S1.
4. New random numbers are generated and the usage model is run through from state U over and over again until a fault is found.
5. The first MTBF value is determined based on the sum of the execution times of the services until the first failure occurs. The MTBF becomes:
   MTBF = S1 + S2 + S1 + S1+ S1 + S3/2.
   It was assumed that half the execution time occurred before the fault was encountered, hence explaining S3/2. It was fault number 4 that was found, which is located in service 3.
6. The actual value of the MTBF is determined from the execution times of the services, see section 3.3, step 4.
   MTBF = 2 + 1 + 2 + 2 + 2 + 2.5 / 2 = 10.25 t.u.
7. The usage model is run through until 7 failures have been found and a long execution time has passed without encountering the last known fault. The MTBF values are given in section 3.3, step 6.

35

SAFE [1]: A Programming Language for Software Quality

B.K.Oliver and R.G.Dromey

Software Quality Institute, Griffith University, QLD, 4111, Australia

email: sqi@cit.gu.edu.au

ABSTRACT

A heavy responsibility for ensuring the quality of programs currently rests with programmers. Existing languages do little to reduce this burden.

Here a new imperative programming language called SAFE is introduced, which is designed to facilitate the construction of quality software. It shifts much of the unnecessary responsibility for ensuring quality away from the programmer and into the language.

Keyword Codes: D.3.0; D.3.3; D.2.6

Keywords: Programming Languages, General; Language Constructs & Features; Programming Environments.

1. INTRODUCTION

"You cannot inspect quality into products"

(Deming, [1])

Imperative programming languages do little to facilitate the production of quality software. Some even would argue that they hinder the development of good software. The Von-Neumann bottleneck and the relatively low expressive power of imperative languages means programs are frequently complex, error-prone and difficult to comprehend. Their continued extension, proliferation, and prospect for continued popularity poses a major problem for the development of quality software in the future.

Until we have quality tools for development to improve software quality, other efforts such as quality management will always be of limited benefit to end product quality.

Appropriately designed programming languages can make a significant contribution to improving the quality of software. Computer science must focus on constructing tools which facilitate building quality into software rather than burdening developers with the responsibility for ensuring quality. Unless we adopt this philosophy, software engineering will not make substantial progress in the development of quality software [2].

2. IMPERATIVE LANGUAGES AND SOFTWARE QUALITY.

"...there is no point in making mistakes unless thereafter we are able to learn from them."

(E.W.Dijkstra, [3])

Despite the great deal of research effort which has been spent on imperative programming languages, many serious flaws still remain [4]. From compiler theory to language design, a plethora of material has been written concerning the defective features of programming languages. For example, Landin[5], Minsky[6], Dijkstra[3], Backus[7], Floyd[8], Hoare[9] and Wirth[10] have all made strong comments concerning the use of imperative programming languages. With the exception of ADA [2], imperative languages are still in a poor state because they have never been designed with quality *explicitly* in mind. Three factors contribute to the current state of imperative programming languages.

---

[1] An acronym derived from the principle constructive features of the language: Sequence, Assignment, Functions, Encapsulation

[2] ADA has failed as a programming language for developing quality software due to its inherent complexity and the difficulty in developing a secure compiler. Hoare[9] strongly recommended that ADA be disbanded as the standard programming language for military systems as ADA program run-time security could not be guaranteed. In fact, ADA still suffers from many quality problems [4].

i). Languages are being continuously extended, but not becoming stronger. Design focus has been on optimization and featurization rather than rectifying their defects at the most basic levels [7].

ii). The problems of imperative programming languages have not been collected in a single publication. This suggests a lack of interest in language design from the quality perspective.

iii). The problems identified have not been structured into a comprehensive framework and directly classified according to their impacts on software quality. This has hindered the formation of comprehensive views of imperative programming languages, particularly in relation to the production of quality software.

3. SAFE: DESIGN GOALS AND SEMANTICS

"Everything has been thought of before the problem is to think of it again"

Goethe.

SAFE is an imperative programming language that has been designed specifically to facilitate building quality into software. The decision to design this language arose directly from a related study pertaining to the development of quality software [11]. The study found,

i). Programming languages were deficient in supporting the production of quality software. Programmers were unnecessarily burdened with a large responsibility for ensuring quality assurance during development. These burdens should be shifted to language designers and compiler writers.

ii). Imperative programming languages are by far the most popular programming languages in use and will continue to be so for many years. Given this situation, the most constructive way to develop quality software is to design imperative languages that actively facilitate building quality into software.

Here we present a language which designs out flaws in past imperative languages and thereby supports the development of quality software.

Ideally, we have sought to design an imperative programming language that <u>prevents</u> programmers from introducing quality defects in the first place. Because language design can not guarantee to make programs quality-defect-proof, we have used a second line of defense: *detection of correctness violations occurs during compilation and where needed execution.*

With so much water under the bridge, the major problem facing any contemporary programming language designer is not just to make an interesting contribution, but making an original and <u>useful</u> contribution. Uniquely, our approach has been to focus on language design solely from the quality perspective, explicitly concentrating on learning from the past but not being restricted by it, shaving existing concepts where needed, removing distinctions which are artificial, creating distinctions worthy of separate existence and filling conceptual gaps that are apparent [12]. At the highest level we seek a language that not only facilitates building quality into software, but also:

i). provides an alternative to other imperative programming languages, such as C++, C, PASCAL, FORTRAN, COBOL, and MODULA-2, which in the past have not been effective in efficiently producing quality software. [4]

ii). augments the imperative programming with the security, expressive power and virtues of the functional paradigm, without producing a PL/I (that is, a programming language which tried to be everything for everyone).

iii). demonstrates that it is possible to design imperative programming languages which facilitate building quality into software, simply, efficiently, consistently and coherently.

iv). demonstrates that an imperative programming language may efficiently exhibit the expressive power, computational security and simplicity of functional programs written in functional programming languages.

We do not imply that a language which satisfies these above goals will be the ultimate imperative programming language. We do however suggest that our objectives will be an interesting and effective starting point for future language research in relation to software quality.

3.1. Features of SAFE

The following features have been included in SAFE because of their contribution to the development of quality software.

• Parameterized profunctions [3] are used to localize the effect of computations associated with each statement in language. **ALL** statements and expressions must be parameterized with respect to their inputs and outputs. *No statement in the language has the capacity to produce side-effects* as all state changes must be specified at the level they occur.

For example: The following quotient remainder solution has completely parameterised input and output variables. In this example, an assignment to either input variables X or D would result in a compilation error.

```
r, q := QuotientRemainder ! do(X, D][.r, q := X, 0)
        [] r≥D → r, q := r-D, q+1
        .QuotientRemainder
```

• The computational model employed by SAFE is more secure than most conventional imperative languages as it traps the execution of statements with undefined (unassigned) variables at compile time.

• The notion of type restriction provides a powerful yet simple mechanism for the declaration and manipulation of data-types. Inheritance, Relational abstraction and Concurrency are consistent and natural extensions of the basic declaration mechanism.

• First class profunction abstractions admit the technique of parameter-hiding, a powerful form of information hiding. Parameter hiding tightens data-coupling, increases efficiency, highlights information-flow and reduces the number of variables and explicit assignments required by the programmer.

• An efficient style of relational computing is introduced based on access rather than on searching.

• A powerful high-level programming methodology called Meta-programming is introduced for the composition of entire programs into systems rather than just the composition of profunctions into programs. Meta-programming is further extended to permit the composition of sub-systems from systems to create larger, higher-level systems.

Enforcement of Modulisation

The majority of current programming languages provide facilities for the modulisation of abstract data-types. Although this may encourage structured programming, programmers still have the responsibility for doing so. SAFE however actively encourages software reuse by requiring that only user-defined types are permitted within programs and systems. As all data-types must be declared and encapsulated within modules, structured programming is enforced.

Enforcement of Encapsulation.

The enforced modulisation of SAFE programs would be ineffective without also placing restrictions on the content of our modules. The content restrictions on modules are as follows:

i). Each abstract-data-type must be contained within its own module.

ii). A constant may only be declared within the module which defines its type. This means constants are completely encapsulated.

iii). Function abstractions (profunctions) may only be declared within modules and not within programs.

iv). Profunctions within modules must take or return one or more variables of the data type defined by the module.

[3] A *Profunction* in SAFE represents a parameterised and encapsulated computation that returns the values of one or more variables.

Furthermore, enforced modulisation and encapsulation:

i). Encourages software reuse; as programming becomes a strict application of data-types from modules.

ii). Makes higher level composition of programs and sub-systems largely declarative as its focus is upon defining data-flows.

iii). Decreases coupling between executable's and data-types, thereby positively influencing analysability, maintainability and testability.

iv). Programming no longer remains a completely creative process where functions, constants and data-types may be declared where needed. Instead programming becomes an applicative process of using previously declared encapsulated data-types.

4. CONCLUSION

The majority of current imperative programming languages still allow programmers to construct programs not far removed in quality from those which were written more than a decade ago. SAFE offers an alternative to these traditional programming languages. It shifts a significant amount of the quality burden away from programmers and into the language. SAFE's unique design philosophy focuses upon building quality into software and making it harder for programmers to introduce quality defects into programs.

Its strict scoping and declaration rules *enforce* structured programming, encapsulation and reuse philosophies, rather than just supporting them as do traditional programming languages. SAFE also manages to augment the imperative programming paradigm with the security, expressive power and virtues of languages from the functional paradigm, without producing a PL/I. It makes an important contribution to imperative programming by facilitating the development of quality software. In superseding traditional imperative programming languages, it provides a model for what imperative programming could be.

REFERENCES

1 Deming W.E., *Out of the Crisis*, MIT Press, 1986, Cambridge, Mass

2 Dromey, R.G:'A Model for Software Product Quality', *IEEE Transactions on Software Engineering* (in press)

3 Dijkstra, E.W, (1972): "The Humble Programmer", *ACM Turning Award Lectures-The First Twenty Years 1966-1985*, ACM Press, 1987, pp.17-32.

4 Oliver, B.K: 'SAFE: A Programming Language For Software Quality', Honours Thesis, 1993, Griffith Univeristy, Australia.

5 Landin, P.J: 'The next 700 Programming Languages', *Communications of the ACM* 9 (1966), pp.157-166.

6 Minsky, M. (1969): 'Form and Content in Computer Science', *ACM Turning Award Lectures-The First Twenty Years 1966-1985*, ACM Press, 1987, pp.219-242.

7 Backus, J: 'Can programming be liberated from the von Neumann Style? A functional style and its algebra of programs', *Communications of the ACM*, 1987, 21, pp.613-640.

8 Floyd, R.W, (1978):'The Paradigms of Programming', *ACM Turning Award Lectures-The First Twenty Years 1966-1985*, ACM Press, 1987, pp.131-142.

9 Hoare, C.A.R, (1980):'The Emperor's Old Clothes', *ACM Turning Award Lectures-The First Twenty Years 1966-1985*, ACM Press, 1987, pp.143-162.

10 Wirth, N: 'From Programming Language Design to Computer Construction', *ACM Turning Award Lectures-The First Twenty Years 1966-1985*, ACM Press, 1987, pp.179-190

11 Dromey, R.G, and McGettrick, A.D: 'On specifying Software Quality', *Software Quality Journal* 1. No. 1, 1992, pp. 1-31.

12 Dromey, R.G: 'SAFE: A Programming language for Software Quality', DRAFT Report. Unpublished (1991), Griffith University, Australia.

Impact of Organisational Maturity on Software Quality

Margaret Tan[a] and Chee Yuen Yap[b]

[a] Department of Decision Sciences, National University of Singapore, Kent Ridge Crescent, Singapore 0511
b Acer Computer International Pte Ltd, Singapore

Abstract
Introducing quality process improvements in software development is a challenge. The organisation requires a certain level of maturity to undertake a quality management programme. Often such programme involves a process re-engineering paradigm. It also embodies a new culture that encourages relentless and continuous improvement of the way all the activities are executed. An exploratory study investigating the impact of organizational maturity on software quality practices is conducted on 280 companies in Singapore. The objective of the study is to understand the issues underlying the implementation of software quality management concepts.

Keyword Codes: D.2.9; K.6.3; K6.4
Keywords: Software Engineering, Management; Software Management; System Management

1. INTRODUCTION

Software quality is very important with increasing application of information technology to critical areas like medicine, safety, and security. Poor quality software is no longer tolerable. Customers are now shifting their attention from prices at the time of purchase to life cycle costs that include expenditures on services and maintenance - the total costs.

Because software engineering has evolved into a highly complex process with its high impact on the organization, the only way to incorporate quality is to manage it on a corporate-wide basis that reaches every level in the organization. However, the organisation that introduces quality management must have a sophisticated level of maturity. A maturity level where there is strategic planning and a mission definition with multi-year implementation techniques.

The traditional software development environment where quality of the software rests in the hands of individual developers is inadequate. Software developers have realized that quality cannot be effectively and efficiently attained by only the developers. All parties involved in the software development processes must be motivated and committed to quality. Quality has to be 'built in" to be co-ordinated in the management processes. In other words, it must be "managed in" as part of strategic planning and not merely as a "control in" function [1].

The purpose of this study is to see how rigorous IT companies in Singapore are in adopting a disciplined process to software development. The objective is also to understand the issues underlying the implementation of software quality process management concepts. This study uses the Software Engineering Institute (SEI) software capability maturity model (CMM) [2] as a yardstick to measure the organisational maturity in adopting good software development practices.

2. SOFTWARE QUALITY MANAGEMENT

Quality is defined as "both a philosophy and a set of guiding principles that represent the foundation for a continuously improving organization. ...... (and which) integrates fundamental management techniques, existing improvement efforts, and technical tools under a disciplined approach focused on continuous improvement" [3]. This definition encompasses an organization-wide relationship of people, technologies, processes, and management to work towards customer satisfaction. It embodies a culture of motivating staff through involvement, empowerment, and communication; education, training and learning; improving work processes and systems; instilling management commitment, leadership, and support; and establishing quality assurance policies, objectives and mission. It encourages relentless, continuous improvement of the way all the activities of an organization are executed, the end result of which will lead to products and services of consistent and dependable quality at low cost [4].

Quality process improvement model institutionalizes the systems of making permanent fundamental changes in all processes and activities of the organization to reduce or eliminate waste, to enhance good management practices, and to enrich the working environment to increase management yields. To be successful, it must be part of corporate planning so that there is a sharing of the vision and objectives by all members of the organization. As the organisation needs to be re-structured, and the old processes challenged, the implementation is a multi-year incremental re-engineering design and process. Like any other management initiative, a successful transformation or re-engineering of software development processes need clearly defined objectives, roles, policies, and accountabilities.

The objective of the process-oriented approach is to "build in" quality at every phase of the development cycle and involving every member of the team. Quality should be designed at the beginning of each process and not at the end by inspection (testing) after the product (system) is developed. Final testing does not ensure quality [5]. Failures or errors are much more expensive to fix after the system has been built. Besides, the "quick fix" provides few lasting gains.

3. SOFTWARE PROCESS MATURITY MODEL

Before an organisation embarks on software quality planning, it is necessary for it to assess and understand the current state of its software development process. There are many ways in which an organization can assess its state of practice. The SEI software process maturity assessment is one such method. It uses a 120-question assessment model that identifies the organization's capability to plan, define, manage, execute, and improve the software development processes and it then categorizes the organization across five process levels of maturity. By establishing the organisation's position in this framework, management can identify areas where improvement actions will be most effective.

The first level, which is the lowest level is also called the "initial" or "ad hoc" level. This level characterizes an organization as having a laissez-faire approach where development procedures are ill defined. There is no formal or consistent procedure, nor is there a mechanism to ensure systematic procedures are followed. Change control is laxed and there is little understanding on key issues of configuration management nor quality assurance.

The second level, the "repeatable" process or "intuitive" level, characterizes an organization as having a management framework with some practiced sets of methods and tools. In other words, a project management approach maybe used. However, it lacks some process focus and technical standards. The organisation at this level learns from past experience to repeat its future performance.

The third level, the "defined" or "qualitative" level, characterizes the organization as having defined functional processes institutionalized in the use of modern software engineering tools, techniques, and standards. The organization has a systematic and methodological process analysis. However, it has not yet begin to take process data for benchmark improvements.

The fourth level, a fairly advanced level, is called the "managed" or "quantitative" level. At this level processes are well defined and they are quantified, measured, and controlled. An organisation in this level uses a process and statistical database to control and drive software quality. When a process is under a statistical benchmark, repeating the work in roughly the same way will produce a sustained and consistent result.

Finally, the fifth level, the highest level, is called the "optimizing" level. It characterizes an organization as having reached an advanced, sophisticated environment that focuses on rigorous defect-cause analysis and prevention for continuous improvement. There is a mechanism to identify the weakest process elements, correct the process to achieve optimum performance.

4. RESEARCH METHOD

A field study using survey questionnaire, adapted from the SEI CMM framework, is used to collect data on the organisational maturity of software development practice in Singapore. A pilot study was conducted to test for comprehensiveness and validity.

The questionnaire is sent out to the chief information officer and it measures the company profile in terms of revenue, size, ownership, age, software development purpose, and number of developers. It also measures the technical and management characteristics of the software development practices.

280 companies in Singapore which have software development either for in-house use or sale to external customers participated. The sample is stratified to include software vendors, private enterprises, and government organisations.

5. RESULTS

The response rate of 45.7 percent consists of 128 responses, out of 280 organisations. However, only 88 responses have software development, thus, giving a valid response rate of 31.4 percent that is used for data analysis. The biggest group of respondents comes from software vendors, representing 42 percent, followed by private enterprises, 34 percent, and finally the government representing 24 percent.

Table 1 shows the distribution of the process maturity levels of the organisation. It is not surprising that most organizations - 72 percent - are in Level 1, the "ad hoc" level. As level 1 characterizes the organization as not having any well-defined procedure and process for development, such organization lacks a mechanism for management reviews in terms of performance tracking and change control. Often the cost and schedule estimates made are unpredictable.

It is interesting to observe that the organisation profile of the responses show that most organizations are fairly young (31 percent are less than 8 years old), have small revenue (35 percent having less than S$10 million), have a small number of developers (64 percent of organisations have less than 26 developers). Therefore, it is no surprise that most organizations may not have the necessary sophistication in quality assurance programme. Another plausible explanation may be that most organizations do not have the necessary expertise in terms of resources, or priorities in terms of strategy to understand the structured software development approach. On the other hand, they may not consider it necessary to have a disciplined approach as most of their projects may have fairly narrow scope like projects for modifications and enhancements on existing systems.

Table 1: Distribution of Software Capability Maturity Level

Maturity Level	Software Vendor	Private Enterprise	Government Organisation	Total
1	28	25	19	72
2	2	5	3	10
3	6	2	2	10
4	0	1	0	1
5	6	1	0	7

The results show that only 10 percent of the organisations are at Level 2 - "repeatable" process that describes an organization as having some structured procedure to software development. However, these organisations lack process standards and definitions to assign process resources. It appears that the majority of this level is represented by private organizations - 5 percent, followed by the government - 3 percent. Unfortunately, the vendors are the least represented with only 2 percent. A plausible explanation is that private organizations having higher revenue (26 percent having more than S$100 million), maybe be said to have better management resources and skills to expend greater effort on project management. As the government is the initiator of IT usage since the mid 1980s, it is no surprise that most of their projects would have adopted a fairly well-structured procedure (National Computer Board being the developer of most government computerization programmes).

On the other hand, Level 3 having 10 percent overall representation, is mostly found in vendors - 6 percent. This is followed by equal representation of 2 percent each by the private and government organisations. It is encouraging to see that vendors are having greater awareness and concern for establishing a quality process measurement system that requires identification of quantitative quality goals, plans, tracking, and measurements. It appears that this defined level may not be the priority of private and government organisations if their applications are not of a critical nature. However, in the vendor organization, because software development is the core activity, reaching Level 3 indicates their involvement and commitment in pursuing quality product and services. It is interesting to observe that 5 percent of organizations reaching this level also have a fairly large number of developers (more than 100 persons). A simple explanation is that with a large number of developers, "building in" quality is necessary to co-ordinate the tasks to enforce the consistency and dependency that is required of the products. Of course, with higher human resources, "organizational decomposition is effective in just the same way as software decomposition" [7]. The organization is able to explore greater avenues of process management, like design and code reviews, change controls, and the use of sophisticated tools and techniques. Organisations with small numbers of developers, on the other hand, constrained by their resources, may be preoccupied with "fire-fighting" techniques of error detection. It must be noted that reaching this level of maturity requires committed resource investment in the quality system.

The higher levels of 4 and 5, however, are poorly represented. Only 1 percent of the organisation, and surprisingly this comes from the private enterprises, reach level 4 maturity. Level 4 characterizes the organisations as having some reasonable statistical and benchmarking control over product quality. Level 5 characterizes the organization as one that emphasizes continuous process improvements through error-cause analysis. Interestingly, 7 percent of the organisations have attained this level. It is encouraging to see 6 percent of software vendor out of the overall 7 percent embracing Level 5 maturity. Developing software for external customers may require different levels of rigour than developing software for internal customers. Internal customers may be less stringent on the quality than external customers who are more likely to be more demanding to ensure the systems developed are to their specifications and satisfaction.

It is not surprising to note that 5 percent of these 7 percent are companies with foreign-equity. It appears that foreign-equity companies are more conscious of the increasing importance of quality management for competitive advantage. It could also represent that there is a well managed software development process in its home country. This trend indicates that software process quality is still at its preliminary stage amongst local equity.

6. CONCLUSION

The understanding of quality management goes far beyond a simple concern for the reliability of inspection methods used. Instead, it encourages relentless, never-ending improvement of the way all the activities of an organization are executed. It seeks to provide products and services that satisfy the customers with their consistent and dependable quality, at low cost [8, 9]. Increased productivity will only come from increased quality at every input to the computer development chain. Good process management techniques may provide the impetus to resolving the software crisis of missed schedules, overrun budgeted, software defects, and increasing backlog vis-a-vis applications demand. Further, it would increase the company's reputation that in turn would increase market share.

The government of Singapore has generated tremendous interests and enthusiasm in encouraging globalization as strategies for Singapore to compete in the 1990s. As such, having quality in its software products and services is a strategic way to compete and sustain its competitiveness. However, quality is a relatively new concept in the software development environment in Singapore, the results are not surprising. To obtain continuous improvement, a formal system of quality planning, auditing, and goal setting is necessary. As most organizations are very weak in understanding and having an organizational structure in terms of its maturity level for a quality process-oriented environment, it is equally no surprise that the elements of quality system concept are poorly understood, what more embraced. It is quite clear that a lot of work is needed to introduce the quality concept in software development.

REFERENCES

1. Garvin, D.A. Quality on the Line. *Harvard Business Review*, Sept-Oct 1983, pp 65-75.
2. Humphrey, W.S. *Managing the Software Process*. Reading, Ma: Addison-Wesley, 1989.
3. Schulmeyer, G.G. *Zero Defect Software*. New York: McGraw-Hill, 1990.
4. Hames, R.D. Total Quality Management: The strategic advantage. *Total Quality Management*, 1991, 2, 1.
5. Aeh, R.K. Focus on the process. *Journal of Systems Management*, November 1990, p 20.
6. Humphrey, W.S. and W.L.Street A Method for Assessing the Software Engineering Capability of Contractors, *Technical Report*, Software Engineering Institute, Carnegie Mellon University, Sept 1987, pp 219-244.
7. Daly, E.B. Organizing for successful software development. *Datamation*, 1979, pp 107-116.
8. Deming, W.E.*Quality, Productivity, and competitive Position*. Cambridge: MIT Press, 1982.
9. Feigenbaum, A.V. *Total Quality Control*. New York: McGraw-Hill, 1986.

37

Using Strongest Postconditions To Improve Software Quality

Si Pan, R. Geoff Dromey

Australian Software Quality Research Institute,
Griffith University, Nathan, Queensland, AUSTRALIA 4111

Abstract

The cost of developing and maintaining high quality software remains at a premium. In this paper we introduce a practical approach for enhancement of software quality, based on calculation of strongest postconditions of program components. The method provides a powerful means for detecting and removing by transformation various forms of redundancy and inconsistency in programs. The feasibility of this approach depends upon calculations of strongest postconditions for iterative constructs and assignments.

Keyword Codes: D.2.1; D.2.4, D.2.8; F.3.1, F.3.2
Keywords: Software Engineering, Reasoning about Programs, Formal Methods, Reengineering

1. INTRODUCTION

Many previous studies [1,3,5] have focused on calculation of Weakest Preconditions to assist with program derivation and program proof. Recently a number of authors [1,3,15] have studied the calculation of the strongest postcondition of a program statement S satisfying a precondition P. Calculation of postconditions has applications in program verification [15], quality improvement [1,15], deriving specifications from programs [15] and quality measurement [16]. For existing programs, without any accompanying formal specifications, improving program quality cannot be done effectively until the postcondition is calculated using the initial precondition and the program statements. In this paper, a major focus is upon finding the computable Strongest Postcondition Q of S under the precondition P.

Methods [7] to enhance program quality involve either Rule-Based approaches [6] or Computational approaches. The former are useful for detecting some classes of static quality defects, but they tend to lack generality and the necessary transformation machinery. Typical computational-based approaches, such as Symbolic Evaluation and Information/Data-Flow Analysis [2,8,9,11,12], focus on data dependence/independence and enable detection of some computational redundancy and inconsistency, but they are weak in enhancing the logical and structural quality of programs. The relations they use are localized and unable to detect many forms of defects and redundancy. Localized preconditions also prevent the method from achieving the ideal that has been recently suggested by Hoare, He & Sampaio [10].

The model we propose uses the strongest precondition at a given point to calculate the strongest postcondition for the current statement which is also the strongest precondition for the next statement. The process of strongest postcondition calculation is integrated with the transformations necessary to improve the quality of programs in line with the strongest postcondition results. This model, which includes a practical means for calculating strongest postconditions for loops has a number of potential applications.

2. BACKGROUND

In order to model practical programs, we have to introduce I/O statements, denoted by ***read***(x) and ***write***(E), and procedures/functions into *Dijkstra's Guarded Command Language* [4] to support our theoretical development.

2.1. Problems With Strongest Postcondition Calculations

Previous studies [1,3] characterize the semantics of a small imperative language in terms of strongest postconditions for given a precondition, P, as follows:

DS0: $sp(P \vee R, S) \equiv sp(P, S) \vee sp(R, S)$ DS1: $sp(P, \emptyset) \equiv P$

DS2a: $sp(P, n:=E) \equiv (n=E) \wedge \exists n:P$ DS2b: $sp(P, n:=E(n)) \equiv P[E^{-1}(n)/n]$

DS3: $sp(P,$ *if* $C \rightarrow S_1 [] \neg C \rightarrow S_2$ *fi*$) \equiv sp(P \wedge C, S_1) \vee sp(P \wedge \neg C, S_2)$

DS4: $sp(P,$ *do* $G \rightarrow S$ *od*$) \equiv \neg G \wedge (\exists i: 0 \leq i: sp(P, ($*if* $G \rightarrow S$ *fi*$)^i)$ DS5: $sp(P, S_1; S_2) \equiv sp(sp(P, S_1), S_2)$

Although these results give, in principal, a calculation method for strongest postconditions, they are limited for a number reasons. Firstly, the term $\exists n:P$ in DS2a is not explicitly indicated since it only stipulates that the variable n is bounded by the precondition P. This makes direct calculation difficult. Secondly, the inverse function $E^{-1}(n)$ in DS2b may be undefined or difficult to calculate. Thirdly, the depth i of the calculation in DS4 is not fixed. This again makes direct calculation of strongest postconditions for loops difficult. A result of DS4, improved by Back [1] on loops involving a *non-deterministic assignment statement*, indicates that the calculation depth i may be bounded. However it is not fixed.

2.2. Functions

We define the following function (*Reassignment Rules*) to preserve the integrity of strongest postcondition calculations when a variable is initialized (either by input or assignment) or reassigned:

Given any **P**, the function takes **P** and a variable x as arguments and returns $\mathbf{P}^{V-\{x\}}$ which is independent of x has the following properties:

when $\mathbf{P} \Rightarrow (x=e)$: $\mathbf{P}^{V-\{x\}} \equiv \mathbf{P}[e/x]$; R1

otherwise: $\mathbf{P}^{V-\{x\}} \equiv \mathbf{P}[y/x]$, where y is a fresh variable R2

where **P**[e/x] represents the expression in which all occurrences of x in **P** are replaced by e. More importantly, these reassignment rules provide a renaming method to detect and correct quality defects where the variable (x) is used for two purposes (R2) or the program contains redundancy (R1). When reassignment of a variable takes place, it must be replaced by its value throughout the precondition. This effectively removes redundancy or renames a two-purpose variable in the program.

Another useful function is the *Split Function*:

For any (conjunctive) guard expression **C** and a (conjunctive) precondition **P**, the ***Split Function***, which is denoted by $\mathbf{C} \psi \mathbf{P}$, takes **C** and **P** as its arguments and returns a (conjunctive) redundancy-free guard expression **R** such that

$$\exists ! \mathbf{R}((\mathbf{P} \wedge \mathbf{C} \equiv \mathbf{P} \wedge \mathbf{R}) \wedge \forall r((\mathbf{P} \wedge \mathbf{C} \equiv \mathbf{P} \wedge r) \Rightarrow (r \Rightarrow \mathbf{R})))$$

To illustrate this, let us consider a guard $i \neq j \wedge a[i] < X$ under the precondition $X < a[j]$. If we use only the precondition $X < a[j]$ to evaluate $i \neq j$ and $a[i] < X$ respectively, each of them is not redundant. However if we employ the definition $X < a[j] \wedge (i \neq j \wedge a[i] < X)$ then to simply, we have $X < a[j] \wedge (i \neq j \wedge a[i] < X) \equiv X < a[j] \wedge a[i] < X$ because $a[i] < X < a[j] \Rightarrow i \neq j$ which identifies that $i \neq j$ is a redundant component of the guard. This example provides the justification for the definition we have introduced. This definition provides not only mathematical rigour and consistency but also the basis for calculating the level of redundancy in any guard expression [15].

3. STRONGEST POSTCONDITIONS FOR NON-ITERATIVE STATEMENTS

Non-Iterative Statements include assignments, I/Os, branch statements and procedures. We will review the calculation of strongest postconditions for assignments, I/Os and procedures.

3.1 Strongest Postconditions for I/O Statements

When ***read***(x) is successfully executed (independent of any previous value of x), x will always be assigned a value in the type domain $D_T(x)$ which is independent of its precondition. The statement ***write***(E) is successfully executed if and only if the variables of the expression E are assigned and their types-match. What we are interested in is its strongest postcondition under P that ***write***(E) does not change the variable state. So that we simply define:

$sp(P,$ ***read***$(x)) \equiv P^{V-\{x\}} \wedge x \in D_T(x)$ $sp(P,$ ***write***$(E)) \equiv P$

3.2 Strongest Postconditions for Assignments

To overcome the difficulty with strongest postcondition for assignments, we prove [15]

$sp(P, x:=E) \equiv P^{V-\{x\}} \wedge x=E$,

$sp(P, x:=E(x)) \equiv P[E_1^{-1}(x)/x] \vee P[E_2^{-1}(x)/x] \vee \ldots \vee P[E_n^{-1}(x)/x]$,

where $E_1^{-1}(x)$, $E_2^{-1}(x)$, ... and $E_n^{-1}(x)$ are all inverse functions of x=E(x)

In practice, these theoretical formulas may make the calculations difficult. Firstly, $P(x)^{V-\{x\}}$ may not be easily obtained from P(x). Secondly, the inverse functions of x=E(x) may be undefined (*e.g. x=x/0*) or difficult to capture (*e.g.* $x=Ax^{25}+Bx$) or an infinite number of inverse functions (*e.g. x=x mod 2*). However from a theoretical viewpoint, for any assignment x:=e, sp(P, x:=e) $\equiv$ $sp(P, t:=x; x:=e[t/x])^{V-\{t\}}$, where t is a fresh variable and sp(P, t:=x; x:=e[t/x]) can always be calculated. Since the following calculation/evaluation never uses such an auxiliary variable t again, we need not remove the auxiliary variable t from sp(P, t:=x; x:=e[t/x]), because it does not affect any subsequent calculation/ evaluation. This auxiliary variable gives us a really practical but also simple approach to solve the problem of calculating strongest postconditions involving assignments. More importantly, these calculation difficulties reflect the presence of quality defects in a program: that is, variables are being used for two purposes. The treatment indicates a consistent structure of the program. For example, the variable x in ***read***(x); $y:=Ax^{25}+Bx$; x:=3; ... is used for two purposes (one to record the value of the input and another the value 3). The ideal code should be ***read***(t); $y:=At^{25}+Bt$; x:=3; ....

Examples:

1. $sp(a[i]>a[j], x:=a[i]; a[i]:=a[j]; a[j]:=x) \equiv sp(sp(a[i]>a[j]^{V-\{x\}} \wedge x=a[i], a[i]:=a[j]), a[j]:=x)$ (DS5)

$\equiv sp(sp(a[i]>a[j] \wedge x=a[i], a[i]:=a[j]), a[j]:=x)$ (R2)

$\equiv sp((a[i]>a[j] \wedge x=a[i])^{V-\{a[i]\}} \wedge a[i]=a[j], a[j]:=x)$

$\equiv sp((a[i]>a[j])[x/a[i]] \wedge a[i]=a[j], a[j]:=x)$ (R1)

$\equiv (x>a[j] \wedge a[i]=a[j])^{V-\{a[j]\}} \wedge a[j]=x$

$\equiv x>a[i] \wedge a[j]=x$ (R1)

2. $sp(\neg p(y) \wedge \neg p(a) \wedge p(f(a)) \wedge x=a, x:=f(x)) \equiv \neg p(y) \wedge \neg p(a) \wedge p(f(a)) \wedge f^{-1}(x)=a$ (for the abstracted function *f*)

$\equiv \neg p(y) \wedge \neg p(a) \wedge p(f(a)) \wedge x=f(a)$

3. $sp(x>-1 \wedge y>0, x:=x^2) \equiv (\sqrt{x}>-1 \vee -\sqrt{x}>-1) \wedge y>0 \equiv (\sqrt{x}\geq 0 \vee \sqrt{x}<1) \wedge y>0 \equiv \sqrt{x}\geq 0 \wedge y>0 \equiv x\geq 0 \wedge y>0$

3.3 Strongest Postcondition for Procedures/Functions

Since a procedure/function without side-effects can be treated as a normal statement/expression (where the local variables should be removed from their strongest postconditions), we will therefore focus upon defining strongest postconditions for procedures/function with side-effects.

Given a precondition P for a procedure Q with side-effects, the strongest postcondition should be sp(P, Q). During calculation, the state-changing statements (i.e., assignments and ***read***-statements) in Q change the initial states of variables in P. As a result, the final variable states in sp(P, Q) may be different from the states in P.

When a function has a side-effect, it may change some variable states in the expression. For example, consider an expression x+*f*(x)+x*x, where the side-effect function *f*(x) increases x by 1 then returns the current value of x. When the initial value of x is 1, the expression may correspond to either 1+2+2*2 if x*x is evaluated after *f*(x), or 1+2+1*1 if x*x is evaluated before *f*(x). The value of the expression depends on the evaluation-order that the selected compiler chooses. In order to model the evaluation-order problem, we denote an expression E containing a side-effect function *f*(...) as E(**x**,*f*(...),**y**), where the variable sets **x** and **y** are evaluated before and after execution of *f*(...) respectively. Given any precondition P for such an E(**x**,*f*(...),**y**), the strongest postcondition is defined as

$$sp(P, E(\mathbf{x},f(\ldots),\mathbf{y})) \equiv sp(P, \mathbf{x}':=\mathbf{x}; f':=f(\ldots); E(\mathbf{x}',f',\mathbf{y}))^{V-\{\mathbf{x}',f'\}}$$

Where **x'** and *f'* are fresh variables (set). This formula corresponds to the following steps:

1. storing **x** using a fresh variable set **x'**, i.e., sp(P, **x'**:=**x**);

2. evaluating function $f(\ldots)$, i.e., $sp(sp(P, x':=x), f':=f(\ldots))$;
3. evaluating 'normal' expression $E(x',f',y)$, i.e., $sp(P, \ldots; E(x',f',y))$
4. removing the auxiliary variables, i.e., $sp(P, x':=x; f':=f(\ldots); E(x',f',y))^{V-\{x',f'\}}$

Example:

$sp(x=1 \wedge y>x,\ t:=x+f(x)+x*x)$

$\equiv sp(x=1 \wedge y>x,\ x':=x;\ f':=f(x);\ t:=x'+f'+x*x)^{V-\{x',f'\}}$ where $f(x)$: x:=x+1; ***return***(x)

$\equiv sp(x-1=1 \wedge y>x-1 \wedge x'=x-1 \wedge f'=x,\ t:=x'+f'+x*x)^{V-\{x',f'\}}$

$\equiv sp(x=2 \wedge y>x-1 \wedge x'=1 \wedge f'=x \wedge t=x'+f'+x*x)^{V-\{x',f'\}}$

$\equiv x=2 \wedge y>x-1 \wedge t=1+2+x*x$

3.4 Non-iterative Statement Optimization

Using strongest postcondition calculations, we can define and detect directly various quality defects, such as uninitialized variables, mystery numbers, two-purpose variables and so on. In addition, a statement S is called *(logically) redundant* under a given precondition P if and only if $sp(P, S) \equiv P$. A guard C is called *(logically) redundant* under a given precondition P if and only if C is *pre-determined* under P (i.e., $P \Rightarrow C$ or $P \Rightarrow \neg C$). Any redundant statement S, although it executes successfully, can be removed because although it executes successfully, does not change the domain of the initial state. Any redundant C has its value (**true** or **false**) determined before execution. Instead, we can use its value directly in a program which will not change any state domains over the execution path. All (logical) redundancy can be removed while still preserving correctness [15].

During the process of calculation of the strongest postcondition, the result for each statement (including procedures) can be used to remove redundant components using a set of transformation rules, such as:

$\{P\}\ x:=E \quad \models \{P\}\ \emptyset \quad$ when $P \Rightarrow (x=E)$, $P \neq$ **false**

$\{P\}$ *if* $C \rightarrow S_1\ []\ \neg C \rightarrow S_2$ *fi* $\models \{P\}$ *if* $C \psi P \rightarrow S_1\ []\ \neg(C \psi P) \rightarrow S_2$ *fi* where $P \neq$ **false**

The first rule removes self-assignment x:=x and any ineffective assignment x:=E that establishes an already established condition in P. The second rule guarantee that each branch guard is not pre-determined under the precondition. The definition for any redundant procedure Q under a precondition P still follows $sp(P, Q) \equiv P$. In addition, another type of redundant procedure occurs where only output variables other than global variables (i.e., it is a side-effect free procedure) are employed, if all output variables are never used before they are reassigned.

The strongest postcondition calculation can allow an arbitrary pair of two non-iterative statements to change their order and preserve logical equivalence. This results in a small number (10) of equivalence transformation rules being required for removing redundancy from non-iterative statement sequences [15].

4. STRONGEST POSTCONDITION FOR LOOPS

Before proceeding with the strongest postcondition for loops, we briefly review some issues relating to use of strongest postcondition calculations to improve loop structures.

4.1. Loop Normalization

Major quality improvement tasks are detecting and removing redundancy and detecting defects (including non-termination). To assist in handling these problems, a procedure, called *Loop Normalization* [15], has been developed, based on strongest postcondition calculations, graph theory and recursion. It transforms any loop into an equivalent segment containing only *Well-Structured* loops, from which redundancy has been removed and each guard (including branch-guards and nested subloop guards) is not pre-determined under its precondition during iteration.

Here we use an example -- List Merge [14], which contains considerable inefficiencies:

out:=Nil;

do $\neg C_1 \vee \neg C_2 \rightarrow$ ***if*** $C_2 \vee (\neg C_1 \wedge \neg C_2 \wedge \neg C_3) \rightarrow S_1\ []\ \neg C_2 \wedge (C_1 \vee C_2 \vee C_3) \rightarrow S_2$ ***fi od***

where C_i=(in_i=Nil), S_i=(out:=out++in_i.head; in_i=in_i.tail) for $i \in [1,2]$, and C_3=(in_1.head$\leq$ in_2.head).

to illustrate briefly how loop normalization reconstructs loops. Firstly, this loop body indicates four branches, that is

if $C_1 \wedge \neg C_2 \rightarrow S_2$ [] $C_2 \wedge \neg C_1 \rightarrow S_1$ [] $\neg C_1 \wedge \neg C_2 \wedge C_3 \rightarrow S_1$ [] $\neg C_1 \wedge \neg C_2 \wedge \neg C_3 \rightarrow S_2$ *fi*

Using strongest postcondition calculations, we know that after execution of the first or second branch, the control-flow may terminate or enter the same branch again (as $sp(C_1 \wedge \neg C_2, S_2) \Rightarrow C_1$ and $sp(C_2 \wedge \neg C_1, S_1) \Rightarrow C_2$). And, after execution of the last branch the control-flow may terminate or enter one of the last three branches. The third branch has a similar property to the last branch. From these results we can construct the *Branch Successor Graph* (BSG) for this loop:

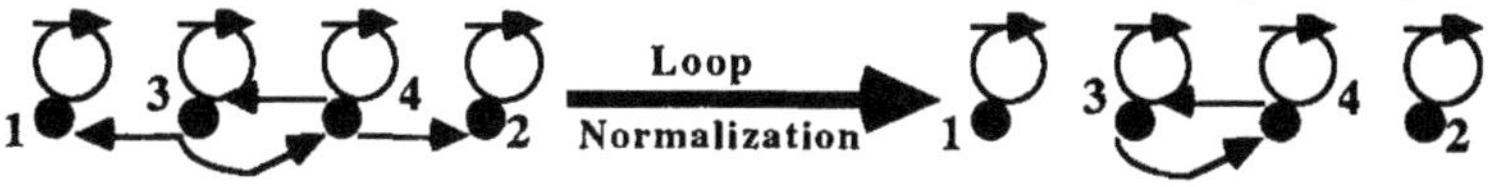

The BSG is constructed as follows: we first calculate the strongest postcondition that applies when each branch has been executed. By comparing this condition (using implication) with the condition for executing each possible branch we can identify which branches are directly reachable (i.e., successors) after executing a given branch. Obviously, a quality loop structure should exhibit a *strongly connected* BSG. This means, any node should be connected to all nodes (i.e., after execution of any branch, the control-flow should be able to access all branches if the loop guard holds). In carrying out the *structural refinement* of loops the ultimate goal is to transform every BSG into a single or a set of strongly connected components. For example, with List Merge, there are three strongly connected components in its BSG (corresponding to three loops). So the normalized loop is:

out:=Nil;

do $C_1 \wedge C_2 \rightarrow$ *if* $C_3 \rightarrow S_1$ [] $\neg C_3 \rightarrow S_2$ *fi od*; *do* $\neg C_1 \rightarrow S_1$ *od*; *do* $\neg C_2 \rightarrow S_2$ *od*

4.2. Strongest Accessible Conjunctive Postcondition

We use a computational model to calculate the *Strongest Accessible Conjunctive Postconditions* [15] for well-structured loops. The formal definition is:

Given a conjunctive precondition P of a loop *do* G $\rightarrow$ S *od*, the *Strongest Accessible Conjunctive Postcondition*, denoted by sp_{ac}(P, *do* G $\rightarrow$ S *od*), is the conjunctive condition such that: $V(sp_{ac}(P, do\ G \rightarrow S\ od)) \subseteq V(P) \cup V(S)$ (Accessibility)

$sp(P, do\ G \rightarrow S\ od) \Rightarrow sp_{ac}(P, do\ G \rightarrow S\ od)$ (Strongest Conjunctive)

and $\forall q((sp(P, do\ G \rightarrow S\ od) \Rightarrow q) \Rightarrow (sp_{ac}(P, do\ G \rightarrow S\ od) \Rightarrow q))$

where V(S) represents the variable set which is assigned by S, and q is a conjunctive formula and $q \neq$ **true**.

The desired relationship $sp_{ac}(P, do\ G \rightarrow S\ od) \equiv sp(P, do\ G \rightarrow S\ od)$ may hold. When it does not hold, the former is the strongest (accessible) conjunctive condition that the latter implies. Even in those cases, the former is still strong enough to be useful for improving program quality and deriving specifications from programs [15] because of their conjunctive form and accessibility. In contrast to DS4 and Back's result [1], the calculation depth of our process [15] to obtain $sp_{ac}(P, do\ G \rightarrow S\ od)$ is fixed.

Example:

The Finding-First-Maximum-Position program [5]:

{$1 \leq N$} i:=1; p:=i;

do $i \neq N \rightarrow$ *if* $A[i+1] \leq A[p] \rightarrow$ i:=i+1 [] $A[p] < A[i+1] \rightarrow$ i:=i+1; p:=i *fi od*;

Our calculation method yields the strongest accessible conjunctive postcondition $\exists j \in [1,i] p=j \wedge \forall j \in [1,p-1]\ A[j] < A[p] \wedge \forall j \in [p+1,i] A[j] \leq A[p] \wedge i=N$, which is also its strongest postcondition. More importantly, after removal of the local variable (i.e., using R1 to remove i), we end up with its (post-)specification $\exists j \in [1,N] p=j \wedge \forall j \in [1,p-1] A[j] < A[p] \wedge \forall j \in [p+1,N] A[j] \leq A[p]$.

4.3 Using Strongest Postcondition To Improve Software Quality

We now use the example of the Abstract Program *AP* suggested by Manna [13]:

if $p(y) \rightarrow$ x:=y; *do* $\neg p(x) \rightarrow$ x:=f(x) *od*

[] $\neg p(y) \rightarrow$ x:=a;

if p(x) → ***do*** ¬p(x) → x:=f(x) ***od*** [] ¬p(x) → x:=f(x); ***if*** p(x) → x:=a; ***do*** ¬p(x) → x:=f(x) ***od fi***
fi
fi

to show the strongest postcondition calculation for ***AP*** under the initial precondition **true**. A summary of the calculations is as follows:

sp(**true**, ***AP***)
≡ sp(**true**∧p(y), x:=y; ***do*** ... ***od***) ∨ sp(**true**∧¬p(y), x:=a; ***if*** ... ***fi***)
(DS3)
≡ sp(p(y)∧x=y, ***do*** ¬p(x) → ... ***od***) ∨ sp(¬p(y)∧x=a∧p(x), ***do*** ... ***od***)∨ sp(¬p(y)∧x=a∧¬p(x), x:=f(x); ***if*** ... ***fi***)
≡ sp(p(y)∧x=y, ∅) ∨ sp(¬p(y)∧x=a∧p(x), ∅)∨ sp(¬p(y)∧¬p(a)∧x=f(a); ***if*** ... ***fi***) (since p(y)∧x=y⇒p(x) and)
≡ (p(y)∧x=y) ∨ (¬p(y)∧x=a∧p(x)) ∨ (¬p(y)∧¬p(a)∧x=f(a)∧¬p(x)) ∨ sp(¬p(y)∧¬p(a)∧x=f(a)∧p(x), x:=a; ***do*** ...)
≡ (p(y)∧x=y) ∨ (¬p(y)∧...) ∨ (¬p(y)∧...) ∨ sp(¬p(y)∧¬p(a)∧p(f(a))∧x=a, x:=f(x); ***do*** ¬p(x) → x:=f(x) ***od***)
(since(...∧¬p(a)∧x=a)⇒¬p(x), separating the 1st iteration from the loop)
≡ (p(y)...) ∨ (¬p(y)...) ∨ (¬p(y)...) ∨ sp(¬p(y)∧¬p(a)∧p(f(a))∧x=f(a), ∅) (since(...∧p(f(a))∧x=f(a)⇒¬p(x))
≡ (p(y)∧x=y) ∨ (¬p(y)∧p(a)∧x=a) ∨ (¬p(y)∧¬p(a)∧x=f(a))

We not only discover ***AP***'s function through the calculation of its strongest postcondition but we also prove ***AP***'s termination because it has been reduced to a branch statement. The resulting program with all logical redundancy removed, is transformed into the equivalent much simpler program as follows:

if p(y) → x:=y [] ¬p(y) → ***if*** p(a) → x:=a [] ¬p(a) → x:=f(a) ***fi fi***

5. CONCLUSION

In this paper we have shown how the concept of strongest postconditions provides the basis for a formal and powerful computational model that may be used to enhance the quality of imperative programs. When these calculations are combined with optimizing transformations a very effective method is obtained for removing various forms of redundancy and inconsistency from programs. The closed form for calculation of the strongest postcondition (including loops) makes the whole approach of significant practical interest for monitoring, controlling and improving the quality of new and existing software.

References:

1. Back, R.J.R.: *A Calculus of Refinements for program Derivations*, Acta Informatica 25, 593-625, 1988.
2. Beageretti, J., et al.: *Information-Flow and Data-Flow Analysis of While-Programs*, ACM/TPLS 7(1), 1985.
3. Dijkstra, E.W., Scholten, C.S.: *Predicate Calculus and Program Semantics*, Springer-Verlag Press, 1989.
4. Dijkstra, E.W.: *A Discipline of Programming*. Englewood Cliffs. Prentice Hall 1976.
5. Dromey, R.G.: *Program Derivation*, Addison-Wesley Press, 1989.
6. Dromey, R.G., et al.: *A Program Quality Control System*, Tech. Report, Griffith Uni., Australia, 1990.
7. Dromey, R.G., McGettrick, A.D.: *On Specifying Software Quality*, Software Quality J. 1, 43-74, 1992.
8. Fosdick, L.D., Osterwell, L.J.: *Data Flow Analysis in Software Reliability*, ACM Comput. Surv. 8, 1976.
9. Hecht, M.S.: *Flow Analysis of Computer Programs*, E. North-Holand, N.Y., 1977.
10. Hoare, C.A.R., He, J., Sampaio: *Normal Form Approach to Complier Design*, Acta Informatica 30, 1993.
11. Kennedy, K.: *A Survey of Data Flow Analysis Techniques in Program Flow Analysis: Theory and Applications*, Prentice-Hall Englewood Cliffs, N.J., 1981.
12. King, J.C.: *Symbolic Execution and Program Testing*, CACM 19(7), 384-394, 1976.
13. Manna, Z: *Properties of Programs and the First-Order Predicate Calculation*, CACM 16(2), 1969.
14. McDermid, J.A.: *Software Engineer's Reference Book*, Butterworth-Heinemann, 1991.
15. Pan, S.: *Software Quality Improvement, Specification Derivatiion and Quality measurement Using Formal Methods*, Ph.D Thesis, Griffith Uni., Australia, 1994.
16. Pan, S., Dromey, R.G.: *A Formal Basis for Software Quality Measurement*, Proc. of 17th Annual Comput. Sci. Conf., Chrischurch, New Zealand, 1994.

PART SEVEN

Specifications, Metrics, Assessment

38

Experience in Software Inspection Techniques

David A Brunskill and Alan Samuel

School of Computing, Staffordshire University, P.O. Box 334, Beaconside, Stafford, Staffs ST18 0DG, UK.

Abstract

It is generally accepted that every programmer checks his or her code before submitting it to testing. This process has been formalised by means of 'reviews', 'walkthroughs' and 'inspections'. Inspections were used in industry by the author, following Fagan, but were not well-metricated: others have shown that the quantifiable benefits of inspections may be considerable. A final-year project at Staffordshire University has produced results for software inspection compared both to computer-based testing alone and to computer-based testing following inspection in which metrics were collected throughout the process, allowing comparisons of effectiveness and efficiency.

Keyword codes: D.2.4, D.2.5, D.2.8
Keywords: Program verification, Testing and Debugging, Metrics.

1. INTRODUCTION

Every programmer checks his or her code before submitting it to testing, and always has done. However, it is a well-established psychological fact [1], [2] that the reading of the program by a second, independent person is a useful technique for discovering errors that would otherwise go unnoticed. It appears that the independent checker does not need to be more experienced in the language, or better-informed in terms of likely sources of error; simply coming to the program fresh appears to lend a perspective denied the originator.

Basili [3] showed, in a controlled study, that code reading was more effective than either functional testing, or structural testing, although the participants believed the contrary. In practice, informal "cross-checking" of each other's work has been common in many development environments, as programmers recognised that a second view of a program could quickly highlight errors that would otherwise be missed, or not be discovered until formal testing, when a considerable amount of rework would result.

In his seminal work on software testing, Myers [2], following Fagan [4], recognised the significance of code inspection in the process of developing correct programs, and gave some of the earliest and most practical guidelines for conducting the process. More recently, Gilb and Graham have gathered together the threads of universal best practice in this area [5], and proposed a comprehensive methodology for the process of software inspection, including the use of metrics.

2. METHODS FOR PROGRAM VERIFICATION

This paper does not discount software testing as a necessary technique in the process of producing correct software; however, the role of testing *per se* is considered separately in Section 5. For now, however, we wish to concentrate on methods other than computer-based testing techniques.

2.1 Desk-checking

The process of program evaluation by means of peer assessment is well-established in general. The way in which this cross-checking of work is conducted, however, varies from establishment to establishment.

In some situations, it may be that such verification is never formally stated as a requirement of the software development process, but has merely evolved over time. In the author's experience, this has tended to arise quite naturally among teams which have worked together successfully on a number of projects, with relatively few personnel changes. In such an environment, staff tend to be relaxed, confident of their own abilities, and unthreatened by criticism.

Alternatively, program verification by desk-checking may be an institutionalised, formal process, in which programs produced by junior programmers are evaluated by more senior personnel - often the designers - and/or by the project leader. Such a process tends to evolve quite naturally into one of the methods considered below.

2.2 Reviews and Walkthroughs

As noted by Yourdon [6] and others, the distinction between a Formal Technical Review and a structured walkthrough is not always clear: the phrases are frequently used interchangeably in practice.

However, current best practice suggests that the word 'Review' should be reserved for a consideration of project development at milestone points: statistical data may also be produced at such a time for QA purposes (see, for example, [7]). The personnel involved will typically be a chairman, the author of the work under review, a QA representative, plus one other independent reviewer, who has some expertise in the area under consideration. Reviews may apply to any stage of the lifecycle, and their primary purpose is to provide information to management, to answer the question, "Does this product do what it is supposed to do?" [8].

A structured walkthrough applies normally to the analysis and/or design stages of software development, and records data on issues such as completeness, correctness and integrity of the entity-relationship diagrams, data dictionary, and process specifications; and on structure charts, module specifications, etc. A *code walkthrough* is usually equivalent to a code inspection, as originally defined by Michael Fagan at IBM [4].

2.3 Software Inspections

Inspections are now primarily seen as a part of the software quality improvement process, in which defect detection occurs routinely, and as a result of which the development process is improved. There is, additionally, much evidence in the literature (e.g., [9], [10], [11]) as well as anecdotally, of considerable cost-benefit.

As originally proposed by Fagan, design and code inspections were seen as a formal, efficient and economical way of finding errors; an inspection team was assumed to comprise members with specific roles to play, viz:

- moderator: a competent technical member of staff specially trained in inspection techniques who should have a galvanising and synergistic effect on the team members;

- designer: the person who produced the piece of work under inspection;

- coder/implementer: the person responsible for translating the design into code;

- tester: the programmer responsible for writing and executing test cases.

It has been recognised during the intervening years that all personnel involved in inspections must be committed to the use of this method. This implies that managers require at least one day's training to familiarise them with the technique, moderators require three days' training, and participants need at least a half-day introduction.

The most impressive results, in terms of defect reduction and cost-benefit, have been realised where senior management are committed to this method of working, as an integral part of the process of quality improvement.

3. AN INDUSTRIAL PERSPECTIVE

3.1 Background

During 1990 and 1991, the author led a software development team whose brief was to design an electricity prepayment metering system, making use of contactless smart cards. This involved considerations of data security, communications, and the human-computer interface, as well as database management, and inspections were introduced at the design stage in order to improve the quality of the resulting system.

3.2 Introduction of Inspections

None of the team members involved in inspections were specially trained in the techniques, but all were impressed with the results claimed. A member of the Quality department was present at the inspections in addition to the suggested team members, and a senior designer from another project was co-opted as moderator. No meeting lasted more than 2 hours.

As each module was designed, its author made a formal request for inspection, and the relevant documents were circulated in advance to all participating staff. Subsequently, the inspection meeting was convened, and the design checked, under the direction of the originator. Errors were categorised as 'Missing', 'Wrong' or 'Extra', and were also categorised by problem type. The log was then circulated to all participants, and a follow-up meeting rechecked the design, after the errors originally identified had been dealt with; if necessary, a third iteration of the process occurred.

3.3 Results

It is clear, with hindsight, that the major weakness in the process as described above was the lack of senior management commitment. It was the software developers who initiated the process, believing it would improve quality and reduce overall development time, and in the event the use of inspections was vindicated. The final product was delivered on schedule and worked correctly. Errors did occur subsequently in operation, but the delivery of correctly-working software on the originally-scheduled date was in contrast to experience both with projects which had preceded this, and others which were under development at about the same time.

Fagan identifies six operations as essential in the inspection process: Planning, Overview, Preparation, Inspection, Rework and Follow-up [9]. In the work as described above, these stages were not strictly adhered to: in particular, there were unclear entry and exit criteria; the process did not follow best practice; and the preparation was haphazard. Further, no metrics were formally collected for the inspections, along the lines of, for example, defects found/page, defects found/hour, time for correction, or even time spent in inspections, and time for software testing. Nevertheless, the experience was enough to persuade the personnel involved that the process had produced real quality-improvement results, and that it should be retained and cultivated for future projects.

4. AN ACADEMIC PERSPECTIVE

4.1 Background

A final-year student at Staffordshire University, Alan Samuel, compared human-based testing techniques with computer-based testing techniques, on three small program units, written in C, COBOL, and FORTRAN. The inspection and testing processes were monitored by collecting metrics from start to finish, allowing calculation of effectiveness, efficiency, and cost saving.

The experiment was prompted in part because, as noted by Bisant and Lyle [12], inspections were developed in the industrial sector, rather than in an academic environment, and most of the data available to date has been produced in industry. A further motivation was the desire to attempt to evalute the extent to which the use of inspections could be incorporated in the undergraduate curriculum.

4.2 Methods Used

The software inspection technique was the process as originally defined, and as developed and amplified by Jones and others [13], [5]. The computer-based testing required some consideration: since all the programs were small (about 300 lines of code) and of only moderate complexity, it was decided to use structural testing based on loop-modified path coverage. Thus, a set of test inputs was generated whose number was quite manageable, but which were sufficient to provide test effectiveness at the TER3 = 1 level.

The participants in the inspection process were also students, many of whom were reading for higher degrees following a period of industrial experience. In all, 12 different personnel were involved in the code inspections, their backgrounds ranging from system administration to mechanical engineering. None of these volunteers had any prior experience of software inspection, and so had to be introduced to the method, its aims, techniques, and outcomes. The testing was performed by Samuel, who proceeded in each case by drawing the program flowgraph, determining the McCabe complexity of the program, and then deriving the basis test cases. The overall strategy involved each program being first inspected, as desribed above, and metrics noted for time taken, number of majors/hour etc. The program was also compiled, debugged, and tested independently, and metrics noted for this process. Finally, each program was tested *after* corrections due to inspection, and similar data collected for this combined process.

The C and Fortran programs were specifically written for this experiment, making use of standard programming methods and techniques as taught at Staffordshire University. They were not evaluated in any other way prior to the experiment taking place, and so represented typical 'first-cut' programs. The COBOL program was a module taken from a much larger order-processing system which was running live at that time in business, but which suffered extremely high maintenance costs, and typical downtime of 3 - 5 hours per week. This module was of particular interest for these reasons: however, because the 'copy' and data files were unavailable, it was not possible to compile the module, and so for testing, only static analysis was possible, and results for effectiveness and time saved may be estimated only by inference.

4.3 Results

The results may be summarised as shown in Tables 1, 2 and 3 below.

Table 1: Time taken for code verification.

	C Program (hrs)	Fortran Program (hrs)	COBOL Program (hrs)
inspection alone	13.6	10.9	10.4
test alone	16.5	9.5	n/a
inspection + test	5.5	14.9	n/a

Table 2: C program Statistics.

	Efficiency (Majors/hr)	Effectiveness* (Majors)	Time saved (hrs)
inspection alone	0.73	60%	2.9
test alone	0.34	35%	-
inspection + test	0.54	60%	11.0

Table 3: Fortran program statistics.

	Efficiency (Majors/hr)	Effectiveness* (Majors)	Time saved (hrs)
inspection alone	0.55	60%	4.0
test alone	0.63	30%	5.4
inspection + test	0.40	60%	-

*Effectiveness calculated as follows: assume inspection discovers 60% of all errors (historically acceptable). Then testing effectiveness is determined as the proportion of known *and assumed* errors discovered by this method.

For the COBOL program, a total of 24 issues were raised during inspection, at a rate of 0.5 issues/minute. A total of 5 majors was discovered. The total time taken to correct the major defectives was 10.4 hours, i.e., an average rate of 2.1 per major. If the assumption is made that the time to fix a typical error on the live system is 5 hours (representing a single corrective maintenance effort), then the total maintenance time required to correct the faults will be 25 hours, representing a notional time saving due to code inspection of 14.6 hours.

5 SUMMARY AND CONCLUSIONS

Clearly, this experiment is limited in its scope and no very general conclusions may be drawn from such an exercise. A number of points are relevant, however, in the context of the activity.

5.1 Some Metrics for this Experiment

Inspection proceeded at a rate of approximately 1 page per hour; this compares favourably with Fagan's recommended rates of 90 noncommentary source code statements per hour as a rule-of-thumb, and 125 noncommentary source code statements per hour at a maximum. The errors uncovered implied an error rate immediately after coding of 1 per 8 lines for Fortran, 1 per 30 lines for C, and 1 per 40 lines for COBOL. These figures are higher than one would expect for the Fortran program, but not untypical for the others (e.g., 1 error per 18 lines of C code is not uncommon [14]).

It should also be noted that

- the participants were untrained in software inspection
- the programs considered were small
- it was not possible to compile and dynamically test the COBOL module.

Additionally, the time taken for structural testing assumed that the whole process was being done by hand. This perhaps gives a fairer comparison of the efficacy and efficiency of the two methods, but clearly, static and dynamic analysis tools have much to offer in this area: the best of the currently-available tools are capable of discovering quite subtle errors. Additionally, of course, inspection cannot do many of the things that testing alone can do: for example, give a measure of performance or reliability.

5.2 Pedagogical Issues

A subsidiary reason for conducting the project was to establish the extent to which software inspection would be useful as a technique by means of which undergraduate students could improve both their productivity and the quality of their programs. It is clear that inspections would be of real value in this sense, as well as having a bonus effect in preparing students for current best practice in software development when they graduate. There are some administrative and pedagogical issues to be considered, however, in that for the most part, university students are expected to produce individual pieces of work, and collaboration is discouraged. Nevertheless, group projects are undertaken at various stages in the course of a degree, at Staffordshire and other universities, and it would seem appropriate to introduce this method in that area. This would allow the students to apply the techniques of software inspection in accordance with the latest thinking, and in an environment which would allow them to develop the skill without the constraints of commercial practice. As well as the introduction of software inspections in this way, it is intended to develop the work described in this paper with a future final-year or Master's student: ideally, a metric relating correctness of code prior to testing as a function of (among other things) effort devoted to software inspection would be the result of such work.

As software systems develop in size and complexity, and the number of systems which are in some sense mission-critical increases, the question of software quality assumes an increasing importance, and defect prevention becomes more of an issue than defect detection. The relevance and effectiveness of software inspection in achieving higher-quality software is probably no longer debatable, but difficulties still exist in persuading industry at large of this. The terms 'walkthrough', 'inspection' and 'review' are also widely misused, or misinterpreted, in the commercial environment. However, the data in this paper suggests strongly that a properly-managed combination of inspection and computer-testing offers the most effective and efficient way to produce reliable software. Additionally, the adoption of inspections, as currently formulated, as an integral part of software engineering undergratuate education, would play a useful role in disseminating this expertise more widely in practice, and in altering the perception of the activity of producing high-quality software, as a quantifiable, cost-effective process resulting in continuous improvement.

REFERENCES:

1. WEINBERG, G M, 'The Psychology of Computer Programming', (Van Nostrand Reinhold, 1971).
2. MYERS, G J, 'The Art of Software Testing', (Wiley-Interscience, 1979).
3. BASILI, V, 'Software Metrics', *Programme for the Open University, U.K.*, 1987.
4. FAGAN, M E, 'Design and code inspections to reduce errors in program development', *IBM Systems Journal,* 1976, Vol 3.
5. GILB, T and GRAHAM, G, 'Software Inspection', (Addison-Wesley, 1993).
6. YOURDON, E, 'Structured Walkthroughs', (Prentice-Hall, 1977).
7. ARTHUR, L J, 'Improving Software Quality: An Insider's Guide to TQM', (Wiley, 1993).
8. WEINBERG, G M, and FREEDMAN, D P, 'Reviews, Walkthroughs, and Inspections', *IEEE Transactions on Software Engineering,* Jan 1984, 10-1.
9. FAGAN, M E, 'Advances in Software Inspections', *IEEE Transactions on Software Engineering,* July 1986, 12-7.
10. ACKERMAN, A F, BUCHWALD, L S, and LEWSKI, F H, 'Software Inspections: An Effective Verification Process', *IEEE Software,* May 1989.
11. CHRISTENSON, D A, HUANG, S T, and LAMPEREZ, A J, 'Statistical Quality Control Applied to Code Inspections', *IEEE Jnl Selected Areas in Communications,* Feb 1990, 8-2.
12. BISANT, D B, and LYLE, J R, 'A Two-Person Method to Improve Programming Productivity', *IEEE Transactions on Software Engineering,* Oct 1989, 15-10.
13. JONES, C L, 'A Process-Integrated Approach to Defect Prevention', *IBM Systems Journal,* 1985, 24-2.
14. HATTON, L, 'Automated Incremental Improvement of Software Product Quality: A Case History', *Proc. Software Testing, Analysis and Review Conference (STAR '93), London, Oct 1993.*

39

Measuring Process Improvement:
Integrating Software Process Assessment With Quality Cost Evaluation

M.P. Neilson and T.P. Rout

Australian Software Quality Research Institute, School of Computing and Information Technology, Griffith University, Queensland 4111 AUSTRALIA

Abstract

This paper reports an extension of a commonly used method for Software Process Assessment by incorporating a detailed breakdown and analysis of quality costs.

The quality cost assessment is based on evaluating a set of baseline activities and corresponding indicators. The results of a case study indicate that the combination of software process assessment and quality cost measurement provides a good indication of the success of process improvement programs.

Keyword Codes: D.2; D.2.2; D.2.8
Keywords: Software Engineering; Tools and Techniques; Metrics

1. INTRODUCTION

In 1990, Schulmeyer [1] declared that "we are in the midst of a software crisis", following a Price Waterhouse [2] study that revealed non-conformance costs accounted for over 50% of total effort. Schulmeyer [1] called for a "complete restructuring of the software development process" suggesting that the fundamental philosophies of Total Quality Management could be applied to software.

TQM focuses on the process, describing an overall philosophy of continuous process improvement, working to the goal of continually improving the development process. The key notion of TQM is that increasing quality will decrease development costs and consequently increase productivity. Productivity increases as quality costs decrease because of less rework, fewer mistakes and fewer delays. Customers receive higher quality products at a lower cost causing the organisation to dominate the market.

Quality costs are an effective means of controlling the process, ie. quantifying the disadvantages of poor quality and the benefits of quality improvement.

The International Standard for Quality Vocabulary [3], provides the following definition:

"Quality Cost: the difference between the actual cost to a company of making and selling products and the cost which would exist if there were no failure, and no possibility of failure, of the product to conform to specification during manufacture and use. Quality cost is the sum of prevention, appraisal and failure costs".

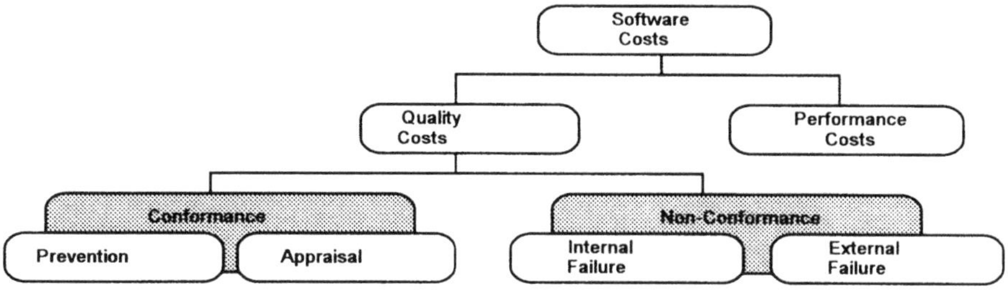

•Quality Planning	•Design Appraisal	•Scrap	•Complaints
•Quality Auditing	•Receiving Inspection	•Replacement, rework or repair	•Warranty Claim
•Assuring vendor/ subcontractor quality	•Inspection and Testing	•Reinspection and Retesting	•Products rejected and Returned
•Reviewing and verifying designs	•Inspection and Test Equipment	•Defect diagnosis	•Concessions
•Process Control Engineering	•Materials consumed during inspection and testing	•Disposition Determination	•Loss of Sales
•Design and development of quality measurement and equipment	•Analysis and reporting of test and inspection results	•Downtime	•Recall Costs
•Quality Training	•Field Performance testing	•Downgrading	•Product Liability
•Acquisition, analysis and reporting of quality data	•Approvals and Endorsements		
•Quality Improvement Programs	•Stock Evaluation		
•Product recall and liability insurance	•Record Storage		
•Planning of Product recall			

Figure 1: Quality Cost Framework

Based upon this definition, a model of quality costs can be constructed that provides a clear delineation of the components of these costs, based on the *Guide to the Determination and Use of Quality Costs* [4]. Initially, a distinction is drawn between the costs of conformance and non-conformance; each of these can then be further broken down, giving a series of individual quality cost components.

Figure 1 shows a conceptual view of Quality Costs. Costs of Conformance can be divided into prevention and appraisal elements. Prevention costs are costs involved in taking measures to ensure that things are done "right first time"; appraisal costs are costs incurred by checking that things have been done right first time. Non-conformance costs comprise internal failure costs - the cost of fixing failures before the product is released to the customer - and external failure costs - the cost of fixing failures after delivery to the customer. Performance costs are the costs that would be incurred during development if the product was 100% defect free or there was no chance of it being otherwise.

2. QUALITY COSTS AS A MEASURE OF PROCESS IMPROVEMENT

Process improvement is a long-term incremental activity [5]. The key challenge is to continuously capture and apply knowledge about the limitations of the current processes with the eventual goal of Zero Defects. The limitations can be captured by carrying out a capability evaluation as a result of a process assessment. Several methods for process assessment exist; the best known and most widely used is the Capability Maturity Model (CMM) developed by the Software Engineering Institute [6].

The CMM is a five stage maturity model, based on Crosby's generic structure of quality maturity and the principles of Total Quality Management. An organisation's process is assessed as characterising one of the five "Maturity Levels", Initial, Repeatable, Defined, Managed or Optimising. Each *maturity level* is composed of several *key process areas*. Each key process area comprises a number of *key practices*, organised into five sections called *common features*. The common features specify the key practices that, when collectively addressed, accomplish the goals of the key process area. The common features are attributes that indicate whether the implementation and institutionalisation of a key process area is effective, repeatable, and lasting; the five common features are: Commitment to Perform; Ability to Perform; Activities Performed; Measurement and Analysis; and Verifying Implementation.

Process improvement can be facilitated by Software process assessment. Process assessment is the measurement and evaluation of processes to identify strengths and weaknesses, enabling continuous improvement. The conduct of an assessment involves a disciplined examination of the processes against a set of criteria to perform within quality cost and schedule. The aim of an assessment is to identify the strengths and weaknesses of current practice and the ability of the process to control or avoid significant causes of poor quality, cost and schedule performance [7]. However, there is currently no way of repeatably or comparably quantifying improvement of the process.

Process assessment models can indicate the route to significant progress, by highlighting strengths and weaknesses, but as Lai [8] noted there are two key elements missing. First, there is a lack of valid process-related metrics, especially those that can be used with the CMM; and secondly, there needs to be an economic and business case model of process improvement again based on the CMM. Improvements can be achieved in two ways; by increasing gains and/or reducing costs although "the biggest cost reductions can be gotten by determining what we are spending now for the costs associated with defects, and constantly measuring and monitoring to determine new cost of quality opportunities to reduce [9]". A quality cost assessment framework that would enable valid comparisons across organisations to be made would satisfy both these needs.

The first step toward quantitative analysis is identifying the good and bad practices - process improvement "requires both planting good practices and weeding out bad practices" [10]. This can be achieved by a process assessment. The second step is to put into place the necessary mechanisms to gain statistical control of the process [10], [11]. This can be achieved by measuring Quality Costs.

Software development organisations are already using process assessment methods and quality cost data to measure process improvement and highlight areas for improvement [12]. In 1993 Raytheon reported that they had evolved from a level 1 (on the CMM 5-point scale of capability) in 1988 to a level 3 in 1993. They reported a continuing decrease in the cost of rework. Boehm [13] estimated that eliminating rework might reduce software costs by 30 to 50 percent. During the last four years Raytheon have reduced their rework costs by 30 percent from 41 to 11 percent. However, these measures of improvement are not comparable across organisations and therefore there is no way of valid benchmarking to be carried out.

We have developed a framework that provides a view of quality costs that is directly linked to an overall assessment of organisational and process capability, therefore providing a repeatable and comparable assessment of quality costs. The development process can be examined and improved, targeting failure costs and investing in prevention. It is a tool that can be used to gain senior management commitment to quality improvement, - "the purpose of comparisons is to get those moving who aren't moving" [14].

3. DEFINITION OF THE FRAMEWORK

The framework supports the PAF approach outlined earlier. This approach highlights the strengths and weaknesses and consequently areas for improvement. The purpose of a quality cost assessment is to focus on areas of high expenditure and to identify potential cost-reducing opportunities and more importantly measurement is the first step to control and improvement.

Baseline activities were identified for the quality cost elements of the conformance category. Initially, the goals of the key process areas of the CMM and the activities that included the intent of ISO 9000 from the Trillium model [15] were mapped onto the quality cost elements. The goals of the CMM are a summary of the key practices and are used to determine if an organisation or project have effectively implemented a key process area. The goals were chosen as opposed to the key activities to maintain the simplicity of the framework. Like the Trillium and the Bootstrap models, the intent of ISO 9000 was included because it contains guidelines for an organisation wide quality management system, providing a solid foundation for improvement.

A pilot study revealed that the level of granularity in the framework was inadequate and did not cover specific issues. It was necessary, therefore, to consider a lower level of detail within the CMM in order to achieve the desired level of granularity. Not all of the Common Features contain practices that can be mapped clearly and unambiguously to cost indicators; after investigation, it was decided to restrict the framework to the common feature, "Activities Performed". The ISO 9000 activities from Trillium were found to be satisfactory and were retained.

A set of indicators were defined for each activity, based on the [16] measurable process attributes: time, effort and number of incidents. These indicators are used to determine the quality cost of each activity. Each indicator is classed as:

- a full quality cost,
- a partial quality cost,
- subsumed under other costs, or
- a performance cost.

The costs that are partial quality costs are labelled along with the indicator. The cost of some activities are unavoidably subsumed under other indicators. This does not allow the cost of such an activity to be assessed separately. In some instances it was possible to indicate the activity under which the cost is subsumed. Others are not specifically subsumed under one particular activity and consequently can not be specified. The four examples below serve to demonstrate the nature of the framework:

	Maturity Level	Key Process Area	Activity Performed	Indicator	Cost Category	Cost Status
1	Two	Requirements Management	"The software engineering group reviews the allocated requirements before they are incorporated into the software project."	Effort expended by SE group on reviewing allocated requirements	Prevention - Quality Planning	FULL QUALITY COST
2	Three	Intergroup Co-ordination	"The software engineering group and the other engineering groups participate with the customer and end users, as appropriate, to establish the system requirements."	Effort expended by those other than the SE group with customer and end users establishing requirements.	Prevention - Quality Planning	PARTIAL QUALITY COST
3	Two	Software Quality Assurance	"The SQA group's activities are performed in accordance with the SQA plan."	Costs subsumed under indicators for related activity, "A SQA plan is prepared for the software project according to a documented procedure.	Prevention - Quality Planning	FULL QUALITY COST
4	Three	Software Product Engineering	"The software design is developed, maintained, documented, and verified, according to the project's defined software process, to accommodate the software requirements and to form the framework for coding."	None	Performance Cost	NON-QUALITY COST

Effort is of primary importance in measuring process improvement because it is usually the largest element of cost. In the early 1980's the notion of measuring effort to measure project cost was conceived [17], [18]. Recently, the Software Engineering Institute [19] defined the first repeatable framework for measuring effort and cost specifically for the purpose of tracking project costs. The SEI model allows the project manager to track the actual and planned expenditure of personnel resources. The manager then uses other indicators; such as, progress, cost and quality, to interpret the data. This approach was adopted by Hughes Aircraft to assess process improvement [20]. This method is used to control projects and therefore can not be used to control organisation-wide quality improvement. The SEI framework for measuring effort is not applicable for the purpose of measuring quality costs because it does not support the organisation-wide assessment of a baseline set of activities, and because of this would not facilitate repeatability or comparability.

4. AN EMPIRICAL EXAMPLE

The power and usefulness of the combination of an assessment model with measurement of quality costs was investigated through a case study; the results indicate that the added precision of cost measurement gives added weight to the outcomes of assessment.

4.1 Study Description

The case study was conducted in the IT development unit of a large organisation, employing 120 full time staff. This case study was opportunistic, as the researcher was invited by the organisation's quality manager to assess the quality costs of the unit. The three day, cross-sectional snap shot placed some limitations on the validity of the findings and also had some distinct advantages. It was not possible to view a series of projects to gain an indication of what extent the process is institutionalised. However, the importance of this is not paramount because the organisation can not be assessed by averaging a number of projects, the quality costs may be no better than the worst project. Although a detailed analysis of organisational characteristics such as culture, power structure, etc was impossible in such a short time frame, most of the responses to the researcher were automatic, highlighting the consensus issues [21] and while the social barriers were erect, the individuals within the organisation were reacting naturally.

During the three day period, fifteen hours of semi-structured interviewing was carried out. In addition, six hours of informal discussions were held with five other staff besides those involved with the interviewing. The quality manager who initiated the study became the primary contact, giving as much background and assistance as possible. The senior manager provided job descriptions to assist with the selection of individuals for interviewing.

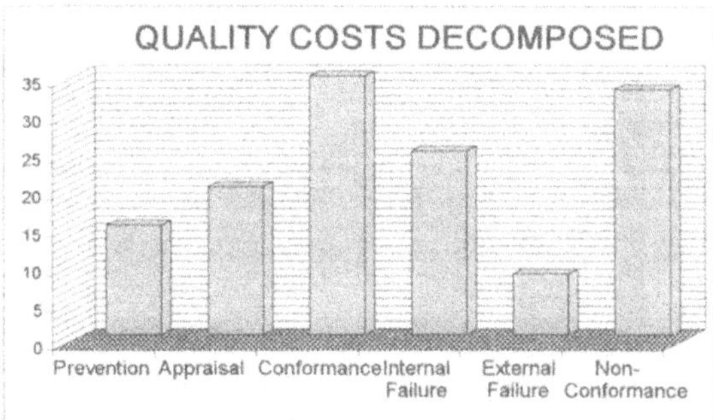

Figure 2: Quality Costs Decomposed

4.2 Research Findings

Non-project specific quality costs were calculated for an 7.5 month period. Project specific quality costs were calculated based on a notional 50 000 person-hour project over 12 months. The assist with the calculations, the organisation provided other relevant figures. Each activity studied was graded as Fully Satisfied (FS), Not Satisfied (NS) or Partially satisfied (PS).

The measurement of the cost of non-conformance was outside the realm of the framework. Figures were given by the organisation based on design and customer trouble reports for the same period that the cost of conformance referenced. These figures did not include machine-time for failure, or any retesting costs. Considering these costs the total cost of non-conformance would be approximately 43% of total development costs. This is still a very conservative figure, it would certainly be much higher taking into consideration the amount of time programmers spend "debugging", if they were to give an honest estimate!

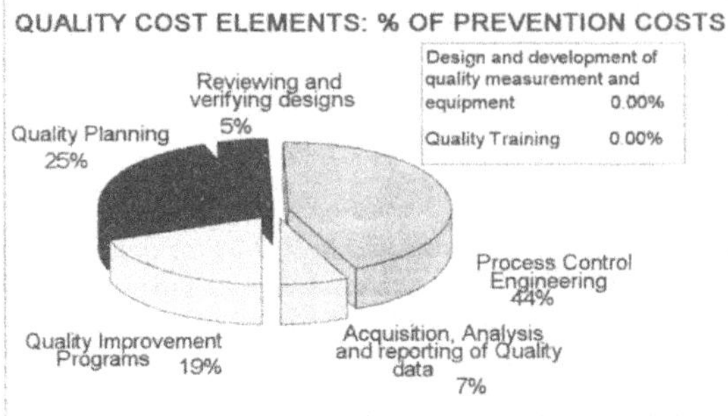

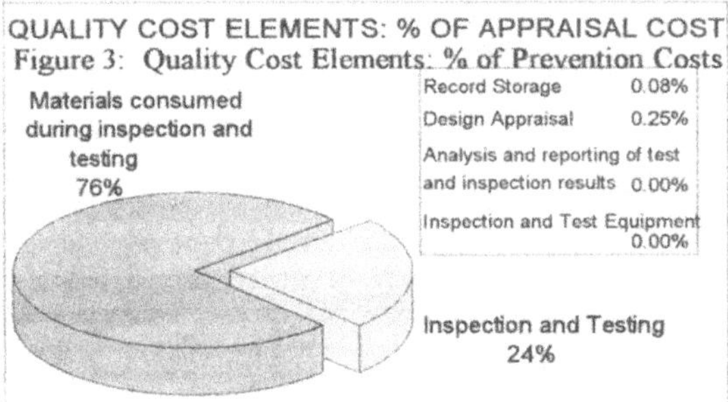

Figure 3: Quality Cost Elements: % of Prevention Costs

Figure 4: Quality Cost Elements: % of Appraisal Costs

Figure 2 demonstrates the relationship between each category, Prevention, Appraisal, Internal Failure and External Failure, and as a sum of Prevention and Appraisal - conformance and a sum of Internal Failure and External Failure - non-conformance. The results demonstrate that there are problems with the organisation's processes. The organisation invests large amounts in Appraisal (26.33%) and Internal Failure costs (8.16%) are still high.

Figure 3 shows a detailed breakdown of Prevention costs. Comparisons can be made with the Raytheon study [12] during the level one period where only few prevention activities are carried out. The Raytheon study reported [12] that at level one prevention costs were approximately 5%. This organisation was assessed at a level one and prevention costs are 4.85%.

Figure 4 shows a detailed breakdown of Appraisal costs. The problem with the Inspection and Testing process may be that no effort is expended on Analysis and Reporting of Test and Inspection Results (0%). The same errors could be happening repeatedly and there is no procedure to correct the problems, consequently a continuously high Internal Failure rate.

5. DISCUSSION AND CONCLUSIONS

Mandeville [9] defines quality improvement as "the deliberate, planned approach to preventing defects from occurring". The are two approaches to process improvement; analysis and benchmarking [3], [5]. Analysis requires quantitative evidence to determine where improvement needs to be made and where improvements have been made, demonstrating the value of the investment. Benchmarking involves the identification of an "excellent" organisation and striving to match or surpass it.

The main benefit of a framework of this nature is that it provides a view of quality in the context of an overall process assessment which is useful to organisations who are beginning or who have begun a continuous process improvement program. It is important to measure quality costs using the PAF approach, especially for organisations who are currently not competitive. The categorisation will demonstrate dramatically how much is expended on Internal and External failure costs and contrast how little is expended on prevention. Appraisal costs analyse the relationship between prevention and failure costs [9]. The development process can be examined and improved, targeting failure costs and investing in prevention.

The case study shows that the framework is a useful tool for assessing quality costs in software development in an organisational and process capability context. The standardised set of baseline activities ensures that the results are repeatable and comparable.

The other distinct advantage of the framework is that because it is based on a standard set of baseline activities it can be easily migrated from the CMM to any other suitable set of baseline practices to enable the appropriate comparisons to be made. It is envisaged that the framework could be used over time in parallel with software process assessment as an indicator of process improvement, similar to Raytheon Equipment Division [12]. The advantage of this framework is not only that it can be used for internal quantitative analysis but it can also be a very useful benchmarking tool. It provides a standardised approach to assessing process quality from an economical perspective, that allows comparisons to be made across organisations of the same capability.

REFERENCES

1 Schulmeyer, G., "Zero Defect Software", NY: McGraw-Hill, 1990.

2 Price-Waterhouse, "Software Quality Standards: The Costs and Benefits", A Report for the UK Department of Trade and Industry, April 1988.

3 ISO 8402 - 1993, "Quality - Vocabulary", Geneva: International Organisation for Standardisation, 1993.

4 AS 2561, "Guide to the determination and use of quality costs", Australian Standards Association, 1982.

5 Humphrey, W.S., "Introduction to Software Process Improvement", Technical Report, CMU/SEI-92-TR-7, 1992.

6 Paulk, M.C., Curtis B. and Chrissis M.P., "Capability Maturity Model for Software, Version 1.1", CMU/SEI-93-TR-24, February, 1993.

7 ISO/IEC JTC1/SC7, "The Need and Requirements for a Software Process Assessment Standard", Study Report N944R, Issue 2.0, 11 June, 1992.

8 Lai, R., "The Move to Mature Processes", *IEEE Software*, July 1993, pp 14-17.

9 Mandeville, W.A., "Software Costs of Quality", *IEEE Journal* on Selected Areas in Communications, February 1990.

10 Card, D.N. (ed.),"Understanding Process Improvement", *IEEE Software*, July 1991.

11 Jones and Tabberer (1993), "Process Quality Costing adapted to Software Development", Software Quality J., Vol 2, pp 199-208.

12 Dion, R., "Process Improvement and the Corporate Balance Sheet", *IEEE Software*, July 1993.

13 Boehm, B. W., "Industrial Software Metrics Top 10 List." *IEEE Software*, September 1987: 84-85.

14 Crosby, P.B., "Quality is Free", NY: McGraw-Hill, 1979.

15 Bell Canada, "Trillium: Telecom Software Product Development Capability Assessment Model", Draft 2.2. Montreal: Bell Canada, July 1992.

16 Fenton, N.E., "Software Metrics: A rigorous Approach" London, UK: Chapman and Hall, 1991.

17 Boehm, B.W., "Software Engineering Economics", Englewood Cliffs, NJ: Prentice-Hall, 1981.

18 DeMarco, T., "Controlling Software Projects: management, measurement, estimation.", Englewood Cliffs, NJ: Prentice-Hall, 1982.

19 Goethert, W.B., E.K. Bailey and M.B. Busby, "Software Effort and Schedule Measurement: A Framework for counting Staff Hours and reporting Schedule Information", Technical Report CMU/SEI-92-TR-21, Software Engineering Institute, Pittsburgh, 1992.

20 Humphrey, W.S., Snyder B.R. and Willis R.R., "Software process improvement at Hughes Aircraft", *IEEE Software*, July 1991.

21 Pressman, R., "Software Engineering: A Practitioner's Approach", 3rd Ed., NY: McGraw-Hill, 1988.

Mutation versus All-uses: An Empirical Evaluation of Cost, Strength and Effectiveness

W. Eric Wong[a], Aditya P. Mathur[b] and José C. Maldonado[c]

[a]Department of Software Technology, Hughes Network Systems, Germantown, MD 20876.

[b]Department of Computer Sciences, Purdue University, W. Lafayette, IN 47907.

[c]Department of Computer Science and Statistics, University of São Paulo, 13560-970, São Carlos, Brazil.

Abstract

Although mutation has been empirically found to be effective in detecting faults, it often imposes unacceptable demands on computing and human resources because of the large number of mutants that need to be compiled and executed on one or more test cases. We designed a case study to explore two alternatives of mutation to reduce its cost without significantly deteriorating its strength and effectiveness. The alternatives are (1) constrained *abs/ror* mutation which examines only the *abs* and *ror* mutants and ignores the others, and (2) randomly selected 10% mutation which examines only 10% of the randomly selected mutants of each mutation operator in Mothra. Data collected during experimentation have shown that both alternatives provide a significant *cost* reduction in terms of the number of test cases required to satisfy an adequacy criterion and the number of mutants to be examined. Such gain is accompanied by a small *strength* loss in the ability to distinguish non-equivalent mutants and cover feasible all-uses. In terms of decreasing order of fault detection effectiveness the ranking is mutation, constrained *abs/ror* mutation, all-uses, and randomly selected 10% mutation. These data suggest that examining only a small percentage of the mutants may be a useful heuristic for evaluating and constructing test sets in practice.

Keyword Codes: D.2.5; D.2.8
Keywords: Software Testing, Cost, Strength, Effectiveness, Mutation, All-uses

1 Introduction

Although mutation testing has been empirically found to be effective in detecting faults[3, 7], it suffers from a problem of performance. The complexity of mutation is $O(n^2)$, where n is the number of variable references in the program. The number of mutants generated can be prohibitively large even for programs that are less than 100K lines of code. These mutants have to be compiled, executed, and often examined by the tester to determine equivalence, which makes mutation testing too expensive to be used in practice. Different algorithms were proposed to reduce the time to execute all mutants on a parallel [9] and a sequential [11] machine. These algorithms suffer either a conversion between different operating environments or extra memory requirement to store the program state, which limits their usability. As a significant portion of the computational cost of mutation testing is incurred in executing mutants against test cases, this cost can be reduced significantly by reducing the number of mutants to be examined. We, therefore, propose the randomly selected 10% mutation and the constrained *abs/ror* mutation criteria described below. The major difference between our approach and the algorithms discussed above is that those algorithms do not reduce the number of mutants to be examined; it is the time to execute the mutants that is targeted for reduction whereas both of them are reduced in our approach.

Cost, difficulty of satisfaction, and fault detection effectiveness [12] are three meaningful bases against which test adequacy criteria should be compared. Cost refers to the *work* necessary to satisfy it. Difficulty of satisfaction is also known as the subsumption relationship [5] and strength [10]. Fault detection effectiveness refers to the fault detection capability of a criterion. We conducted experiments to explore the two alternatives of mutation described above with respect to the all-uses and mutation criteria in terms of these three factors. Data collected during experimentation will help us to answer the questions: Will reducing the number of mutants to be examined be a cost-effective alternative to the mutation testing? Will examining only a small percentage of the mutants be a useful heuristic for evaluating and constructing test sets in practice?

The remainder of this paper is organized as follows. Section 2 provides a brief overview of mutation and data flow based adequacy criteria used in the remainder of this paper. In Section 3, we explain how we compared the cost, strength, and effectiveness of various test adequacy criteria. Our experimental methodology is described in detail in Section 4. Data collected from experiments and its analysis appear in Section 5. Our conclusions appear in Section 6.

2 All-uses and mutation based test adequacy criteria

In this section we provide an overview of all-uses and mutation based test adequacy criteria by presenting only the information required for an understanding of the rest of the paper. More details can be found in [5, 7]. Let P denote the program under test with $\mathcal{D}$ as its input domain. Test cases are selected from the input domain. A test set $T \subseteq \mathcal{D}$ consists of one or more test cases.

2.1 All-uses criterion

Let s_i and $s_j, 1 \leq i, j \leq n$ be two statements in P at which variable x is defined, $d_i(x)$, and used, $u_j(x)$, respectively. The pair $(d_i(x), u_j(x))$ is a def-use pair. A def-use pair is a *p-use* or a *c-use* pair depending on whether s_j is a predicate or not, respectively. We say that any such pair is *feasible* if there exists a test case $t \in D$ such that the execution of P on t causes control to transfer from s_i to s_j, traversing one or more statements, without defining x at any statement other than at s_i. Such a path is also considered a *definition clear path* with respect to x. A test case $t \in T$ covers a c-use pair $(d_i(x), u_j(x))$ if the execution of P on t causes the execution of a definition clear path with respect to x from s_i to s_j. A p-use pair $(d_i(x), u_j(x))$ is considered covered if a definition clear path with respect to x from s_i to s_j to s_k is executed for each successor s_k of s_j. We refer to the set of all c-uses and p-uses as *all-uses* [5]. A test set T may be evaluated against the all-uses criterion by computing the ratio of the total number of all-uses covered to the total number of feasible all-uses. A ratio of unity implies that T is adequate with respect to the all-uses criterion.

2.2 Mutation criterion

Let m be a syntactically correct program obtained by making a syntactic change in P; m is known as a *mutant* of P. Let r be a rule according to which P is changed; r is known as a *mutant operator*. There could potentially be an infinite number of mutant operators. To keep mutation testing practical, the set of mutant operators is kept small and consists of simple mutant operators [4]. The application of a set of mutant operators MO to P results in a set of mutants $m_1, m_2, \ldots, m_n, n \geq 0$. Mutant m_i is considered *equivalent* to P if for all $t \in \mathcal{D}$, $P(t) = m_i(t)$. When executed against a test case t, mutant m_i is considered *distinguished* from P if $P(t) \neq m_i(t)$. Unless distinguished, a non-equivalent mutant is considered *live*. One can obtain a variety of mutation based criteria by varying MO. Hereafter, we refer to the mutation based criterion with respect to the set of all 22 mutant operators in Mothra [4] as the *mutation* criterion. A test set T may be evaluated against the mutation criterion by executing each mutant against elements of T. The ratio of the number of mutants distinguished to the number of non-equivalent mutants is the *mutation score* of T for P. T is considered adequate with respect to the mutation criterion if the mutation score is unity.

One mechanism for reducing the cost of mutation testing is to examine a small percentage, say 10%, of randomly selected mutants of each mutant type and ignore the others. Earlier empirical investigations by Acree [1], Sayward, and Budd [3] have shown that even with test cases generated using only 10% of the mutants, no more than 1% of the non-equivalent mutants were overlooked. In this paper we present results not only to verify this aspect but also to investigate the cost and effectiveness of the randomly selected 10% mutation. Hereafter, we refer to such alternate mutation as 10% mutation.

Another mechanism for reducing the cost of mutation testing is constrained mutation. Using constrained mutation, one examines only a few specified types of mutants and ignores the others. For example, the constrained *abs/ror* mutation studied in this paper examines only the *abs* and *ror* mutants. The *abs* mutant operator generates mutants by replacing each use of x by $abs(x)$, $-abs(x)$, and $zpush(x)$ wherever possible. The terms, $abs(x)$ and $-abs(x)$ represent the absolute value and the negative absolute value of x, respectively. A mutant containing $zpush(x)$ is considered distinguished if a test case causes the value of x to be zero when execution reaches the mutated expression. When applied to a program containing an assignment statement $z := x + 1$, the *abs* operator generates six mutants obtained by replacing this assignment by $z := abs(x) + 1$, $z := -abs(x) + 1$, $z := zpush(x) + 1$, $z := abs(x + 1)$, $z := -abs(x + 1)$, and $z := zpush(x + 1)$. The *ror* mutant operator generates mutants by replacing each relational operator by other relational operators. In addition, it also replaces each condition consisting of at least one relational operator by the boolean constants `true` and `false`. For example, when applied to a program containing a predicate "if $(x = 0)$ then", this mutant operator generates the following seven conditions: "if $(x < 0)$ then", "if $(x \leq 0)$ then", "if $(x \neq 0)$ then", "if $(x > 0)$ then", "if $(x \geq 0)$ then", "if (`true`) then", and "if (`false`) then". A detailed rationale of such selection can be found in [14]. Hereafter, we refer to the constrained mutation using *abs* and *ror* mutation operators as *abs/ror* mutation.

3 Comparison methodology

The cost of the alternative mutation testing is measured by two metrics. One is the number of test cases required to satisfy it [10]. The other is the number of mutants to be examined [14]. We use Equations (1) and (2) to compute the cost reduction in terms of the number of test cases required with respect to the mutation or all-uses adequacy criteria, respectively, and the cost reduction in terms of the number of mutants examined with respect to the mutation adequacy criterion.

$$\left(1 - \frac{\text{average size of test sets adequate with respect to alternate mutation}}{\text{average size of mutation (or all-uses) adequate test sets}}\right) * 100\% \quad (1)$$

$$\left(1 - \frac{\text{total number of mutants examined when using alternate mutation}}{\text{total number of mutants examined in mutation}}\right) * 100\% \quad (2)$$

Two measures were selected for the strength of the alternative mutation testing. In one, the strength is measured in terms of the mutation scores by Equation (3). In the other, the strength is measured in terms of the all-uses scores by Equation (4).

$$\frac{\text{number of mutants distinguished by a test set}}{\text{total number of non-equivalent mutants}} * 100\% \quad (3)$$

$$\frac{\text{number of all-uses covered by a test set}}{\text{total number of feasible all-uses}} * 100\% \tag{4}$$

Given a program P, a specification S, and a test set T adequate with respect to a criterion C, T is said to be able to expose faults in P if there exists a test case $t \in T$ which makes P behave differently from S. As long as T detects at least one fault in P, T is counted as a fault-revealing test set. Equation (5), defined below, is used to compute the percentage of C fault-revealing adequate test sets.

$$\frac{\text{number of } C \text{ adequate test sets which expose at least one fault}}{\text{number of } C \text{ adequate test sets generated}} * 100\% \tag{5}$$

4 Experimental methodology

4.1 Subject programs

For cost and strength comparison, we used a suite of the four programs described below. Faults discovered while preparing the programs were removed. This was done as the goal of our experiments was to investigate which one of the adequacy criteria is more expensive and difficult to satisfy and not to investigate their fault detection capability. A source listing of each of these programs and removed faults can be found in [13].

- `FIND`: This program takes two inputs, an array a and an index f, and permutes the elements of a so that elements to the right of position f are greater than or equal to $a[f]$ and elements to the left of position f are less than or equal to $a[f]$.
- `STRMAT1` and `STRMAT2`: Each program takes a text and a pattern of zero or more characters. If the pattern appears in the text then the position of the first occurrence of the pattern in the text is returned, otherwise a zero is returned.
- `TEXTFMT`: This program takes a text as input and formats it.

For effectiveness comparison, we used another suite of four programs with naturally occurring faults described below. A source listing of each of these programs and their faults can also be found in [13].

- `SORT`: This program takes an array and sorts it in descending order.
- `STRMAT3`: This program is similar to `STRMAT1` and `STRMAT2` with faults not removed.
- `POSITION`: This program takes two inputs, an array a and a value max, and sums the elements of a until the sum meets or exceeds max. If such an element exists, its position is returned, otherwise, a zero is returned.
- `STAT`: This program takes an array a and computes its sum, minimum, and maximum.

4.2 Experiments & testing tools

We generated mutants in our experiments using all 22 mutant operators in `Mothra` except the *goto*. Two testing tools, `Mothra` and `ATAC` [8] were used. `Mothra` is a mutation testing tool for testing Fortran 77 programs. Given a program and a test set, `Mothra` generates a set of mutants, executes them against test cases in the test set, and computes the mutation score. `ATAC` is a data flow coverage measurement tool for C programs. Given a program and a test set, `ATAC` computes the block, decision, c-use, p-use, and all-uses coverage. While using these tools, it is the tester's responsibility to determine equivalent mutants and infeasible data flow attributes.

Thirty adequate test sets with respect to mutation, *abs/ror* mutation, 10% mutation, and all-uses adequacy criteria were randomly generated with the exception that there are only five 10% mutation adequate test sets for `FIND`, `STRMAT1`, `STRMAT2`, and `TEXTFMT`. Details of test case generation can be found in [13].

Table 1: Program size metrics

		Number of mutants†			Number of decisions‡	Number of all-uses
		mutation	*abs/ror* mutation	10% mutation		
Cost & strength comparison	FIND	916	166 (18.12 %)§	94 (10.26 %)	17	119
	STRMAT1	627	125 (19.94 %)	65 (10.37 %)	16	63
	STRMAT2	510	99 (19.41 %)	50 (9.80 %)	12	66
	TEXTFMT	938	135 (14.39 %)	103 (10.98 %)	18	53
Effectiveness comparison	SORT	490	90 (18.37 %)	50 (10.20 %)	5	37
	STRMAT3	415	85 (20.48 %)	43 (10.36 %)	8	53
	POSITION	251	37 (14.80 %)	26 (10.36 %)	6	22
	STAT	446	72 (16.14 %)	44 (9.87 %)	8	54

†Mutants include both non-equivalent and equivalent.

‡Decisions and all-uses include both feasible and infeasible.

$\S\% = \frac{\text{number of mutants examined using alternate mutation}}{\text{number of mutants examined in mutation}} * 100$

Table 2: Average size of mutation, 10% mutation, *abs/ror* mutation, and all-uses adequate test sets

	FIND	STRMAT1	STRMAT2	TEXTFMT
mutation	24.57	20.23	17.57	16.67
10% mutation	9.20	10.00	8.60	9.60
abs/ror mutation	14.73	12.00	8.27	6.97
all-uses	6.67	6.07	6.40	5.23

5 Experimental results and analysis

Table 1 lists the number of mutants, decisions and all-uses for the programs used. These metrics serve as indicators of the relative complexity of programs considered in our experiments. Table 2 lists the average size of mutation, 10% mutation, *abs/ror* mutation, and all-uses adequate tests, respectively. Tables 3 and 4 contain the average all-uses and mutation scores using mutation, 10% mutation, *abs/ror* mutation, and all-uses adequate test sets, respectively. Scores in the above tables are computed as percentages. Table 5 contains statistics on fault-revealing adequate test sets with respect to mutation, 10% mutation, *abs/ror* mutation, and all-uses criteria.

Cost comparison

From our experimental data and the summary in Table 2 we make the following observations:

- 42% to 63% and 40% to 58% fewer test cases are required to satisfy 10% mutation and *abs/ror* mutation adequacy, respectively, than to satisfy mutation adequacy.
- 35% to 84% and 33% to 121% more test cases are required to satisfy 10% mutation and *abs/ror* mutation adequacy, respectively, than to satisfy all-uses adequacy.
- 175% to 268% more test cases are required to satisfy mutation adequacy than to satisfy all-uses adequacy.
- 89% to 90% and 80% to 85% cost reduction in terms of number of mutants to be examined for 10% mutation and *abs/ror* mutation adequacy, respectively.

Table 3: Average all-uses scores using mutation, 10% mutation, *abs/ror* mutation, and all-uses adequate test sets

	FIND	STRMAT1	STRMAT2	TEXTFMT
mutation	100.00	100.00	100.00	99.39
10% mutation	99.59	97.93	98.62	96.97
abs/ror mutation	99.56	97.13	96.27	95.45
all-uses	100.00	100.00	100.00	100.00

Table 4: Average mutation scores using mutation, 10% mutation, *abs/ror* mutation, and all-uses adequate test sets

	FIND	STRMAT1	STRMAT2	TEXTFMT
mutation	100.00	100.00	100.00	100.00
10% mutation	97.59	97.25	96.37	99.01
abs/ror mutation	98.29	98.84	95.70	95.90
all-uses	92.31	86.01	91.60	92.86

Strength comparison

From our experimental data and the summary in Tables 3 and 4 we make the following observations:

(1) All-uses scores:

- For FIND: Each mutation, three of the five 10% mutation, and seventeen of the thirty *abs/ror* mutation adequate test sets are all-uses adequate.
- For STRMAT1: Each mutation, two of the five 10% mutation, and eighteen of the thirty *abs/ror* mutation adequate test sets are all-uses adequate.
- For STRMAT2: Each mutation, three of the five 10% mutation, and six of the thirty *abs/ror* mutation adequate test sets are all-uses adequate.
- For TEXTFMT: Twenty-four of the thirty mutation, one of the five 10% mutation, and two of the thirty *abs/ror* mutation adequate test sets are all-uses adequate.

(2) Mutation scores:

- None of the 10% mutation, *abs/ror* mutation, and all-uses adequate test set is mutation adequate.

In summary, 10% and *abs/ror* mutation adequate test sets suffer less than 5% loss on average mutation and all-uses scores when compared with the mutation and all-uses adequate test sets, respectively. Notice that when compared with the all-uses adequacy, both 10% and *abs/ror* mutation provide higher mutation scores.

Effectiveness comparison

From our experimental data and the summary in Table 5, we make the following observations:

- For all four experiments, the mutation criterion is the most effective in exposing program faults.
- The average effectiveness for the mutation, *abs/ror* mutation, 10% mutation and all-uses criteria is 92.50%, 88.33%, 81.66%, and 83.33%, respectively.

The above observations indicate that in our study mutation criterion is the most effective followed, in order, by *abs/ror* mutation, all-uses and 10% mutation.

Table 5: Number of fault-revealing adequate test sets

Program	mutation	*abs/ror* mutation	10% mutation	All-uses
SORT	30 (100.00 %)‡	30 (100.00 %)	29 (96.67 %)	29 (96.67 %)
STRMAT3	21 (70.00 %)	16 (53.33 %)	18 (60.00 %)	12 (40.00 %)
POSITION	30 (100.00 %)	30 (100.00 %)	28 (93.33 %)	30 (100.00 %)
STAT	30 (100.00 %)	30 (100.00 %)	23 (76.67 %)	29 (96.67 %)

‡The percentage was computed using Equation (5) in Section 3.

6 Conclusions and future work

In this study we find that compared to the mutation criterion, both the randomly selected 10% mutation and the constrained *abs/ror* mutation provide significant cost reductions in terms of the number of test cases required and the number of mutants examined. This gain is, however, accompanied by a small strength loss in the ability to distinguish non-equivalent mutants and cover feasible all-uses. On the other hand, when compared to the all-uses criterion both alternate mutation criteria require more test cases and suffer a small strength loss in the ability to cover feasible all-uses. However, both of them also show a better effectiveness and a stronger strength in the ability to distinguish non-equivalent mutants than the all-uses criterion. Our overall conclusions are:

- In terms of decreasing order of cost (the number of test cases required) the ranking is mutation, *abs/ror* mutation, 10% mutation, and all-uses.
- In terms of decreasing order of fault detection effectiveness the ranking is mutation, *abs/ror* mutation, all-uses, and 10% mutation.

These data suggest that examining only a small percentage of the mutants may be a useful heuristic for evaluating and constructing test sets in practice. While testing software under time pressure and budget constraints, testers may use mutation testing for the safety-critical parts and leave the other parts to be tested by a cost-effective alternative such as the *abs/ror* mutation or the all-uses criteria.

As discussed in Section 4.2, the tools we used support different programming languages, Mothra for Fortran 77 and ATAC for C. Although it has been shown that the effect of using different languages is negligible on the conclusions reported here [10], it is certainly desirable to avoid any language translation in the experiments. We are currently using PROTEUM [6], a C mutation tool implemented based on [2], to conduct experiments with constrained mutation using different combinations of mutant operators directly on larger size C programs. Such studies have the advantage of eliminating any possible language bias and will shed more light on how to reduce the cost of mutation testing.

References

1 Acree, T. A.: *'On mutation'*, PhD thesis, School of Information and Computer Science, Georgia Institute of Technology, Atlanta, GA, August 1980.

2 Agrawal, H., DeMillo, R. A., Hathaway, R., Hsu, Wm., Hsu, W., Krauser, E. W., Martin, R. J., Mathur, A. P. and Spafford, E. H.: 'Design of mutant operators for the C programming language', Technical Report SERC-TR-41-P, Software Engineering Research Center, Purdue University, W. Lafayette, IN, March 1989.

3 Budd, T. A.: *'Mutation Analysis of Program Test Data'*, PhD thesis, Yale University, New Haven, CT, May 1980.

4 Choi, B. J., DeMillo, R. A., Krauser, E. W., Mathur, A. P., Martin, R. J., Offutt, A. J., Pan, H. and Spafford, E. H.: 'The Mothra toolset', *Proc. of the Twenty-Second Annual Hawaii International Conference on System Sciences*, HI, January 1989.

5 Clarke, L. A., Podgurski, A., Richardson, D. J. and Zeil S. J.: 'A formal evaluation of data flow path selection criteria', *IEEE Trans. on Software Engineering*, 15(11):1318-1332, November 1989.

6 Delamaro, M. E., Maldonado, J. C., Jino, M. and Chaim, M.: 'PROTEUM: A testing tool based on mutation analysis', *Proc. of the Seventh Brazilian Symposium on Software Engineering*, Rio de Janeiro, Brazil, October 1993.

7 DeMillo, R. A., Lipton, R. J. and Sayward, F. G.: 'Hints on test data selection: Help for the practicing programmer', *IEEE Computer*, 11(4):34-41, April 1978.

8 Horgan, J. R. and London, S. A.: 'ATAC: A data flow coverage testing tool for C', *Proc. of Symposium on Assessment of Quality Software Development Tools*, New Orleans, LA, May 1992, pp 2-10

9 Krauser, E. W., Mathur, A. P. and Rego, V. J.: 'High performance software testing on SIMD machines', *IEEE Trans. on Software Engineering*, 17(5):403-423, May 1991.

10 Mathur, A. P. and Wong, W. E.: 'An empirical comparison of data flow and mutation based test adequacy criteria', *The Journal of Software Testing, Verification, and Reliability*, 4(1):9-31, March 1994.

11 Weiss, S. N. and Fleyshgakker, V. N.: 'Improved serial algorithms for mutation analysis', *Proc. of International Symposium on Software Testing and Analysis*, Cambridge, MA, June 1993, pp 149-158

12 Weyuker, E. J., Weiss, S. N. and Hamlet, R. G.: 'Comparison of program testing strategies', *Proc. of the Fourth Symposium on Software Testing, Analysis and Verification*, Victoria, British Columbia, Canada, October 1991, pp 154-164

13 Wong, W. E.: *'On Mutation and Data Flow'*, PhD thesis, Department of Computer Science, Purdue University, W. Lafayette, IN, December 1993.

14 Wong, W. E. and Mathur, A. P.: 'Reducing the cost of mutation testing: An empirical study', *The Journal of Systems and Software*, 1995. (To appear)

41

Software Quality: The user's point of view

M. Xenos and D. Christodoulakis

Computer Technology Institue, 3 Kolokotroni Str., Patras 26221, Greece

Abstract

In this paper is presented a methodological approach for the measurement and the evaluation of users' opinion for a software product. The methodology is general and applicable for every product and, as a concept, in every situation. The basic principle for the methodology is that each user's opinion should be evaluated in analogy to this user's qualifications in respect to computers in general, to this particular product and to the application automated by this. Therefore, the measurement and the analysis of the users' qualifications is performed before users are asked for their opinion about the product. Afterwards, the users will be asked their opinion about the product. This opinion counts equally to their pre-measured qualifications.

In addition, in this paper are presented some techniques about how to set-up customized questionnaires, about how to collect and analyze the measurements and about how to overcome human aspects related to human disapproval, or even refusal to measurements.

Keyword Codes: D.2.4; D.2.8
Keywords: Software Engineering; Program Verification; Metrics

1. INTRODUCTION

Currently programming techniques differ greatly from those of a few years ago. The broad use of object oriented programming languages, visual programming tools and computer aided software engineering (CASE) tools, have facilitated and accelerated programmers' work. Traditional quantities/metrics for measuring software quality -such as LOC, software science metrics[1], software complexity Metrics[2]- are not fully able to measure the particular characteristics, the programming effort, nor the quality of programs which have been created using new techniques. New metrics and models[3] designed especially for such programming techniques will eventually also become inadequate, as the programming languages, techniques and tools continue to evolve. What has remained unchanged in software engineering throughout the years, regardless of programming styles, languages and techniques, is that there will always be one or more users who will work using the product. From a software product written in machine code to a product developed under a sophisticated CASE tool, there will always be a way to evaluate its quality by weighting user critique.

This paper presents a methodology for the evaluation of software quality, based on the critique provided from possible, or actual users of this product. The methodology is not "stand-alone" on measuring and improving the quality of the software product. It must be used within an overall and systematic approach[4] to ensure software quality with the aid of measurements. The main principle, that is presented in section 2, is to be able to estimate each user's ability to evaluate the product, based on user expertise as far as syntactic and semantic knowledge within the field and the overall user qualifications. Consequently, the more qualified the user is, the more value will be given to his critique. Some guidelines are provided in section 3, in order to set up such a user evaluation method. Some instructions are also provided in section 4, about the questionnaires related to the product itself. Additionally, techniques and guidelines are proposed in order to select a statistical sample, to set up questionnaires for measuring users' ability to serve as "software evaluators", to measure the results of their evaluation, to identify the "experts" (those users whose opinion must weight the most), and finally (in section 5), to analyze and interpret the answers to these questionnaires.

2. THE BASIC PRINCIPLES OF THE PROPOSED METHODOLOGY

The fundamental principle for this methodology is to value each user's critique according to the user's overall qualifications in the field. To the opinion of each user will be given as much value as qualified in the field the user is. Therefore, the result of the measurements of the user's critique is not the average (Avg.) that is shown by the equation 1:

$$Avg = \frac{\sum_{i=1}^{i=n} O_i}{n}$$

where $O_i \in [0,100]$, is the opinion of the user i for the program that is measured , but the average (Avg.) that is shown by the following equation 2:

$$Avg = \frac{\sum_{i=1}^{i=n} O_i \cdot E_i}{\sum_{i=1}^{i=n} E_i}$$

where $E_i \in \Re 1$ is the measurement of the user's i qualifications. Using the above equation, the opinions of users with different qualifications within the field of application are contributed in the overall software evaluation, in analogy to their qualifications.

In fact the equation 2 is also not complete. It does not include terms like how tired the user was, when measurements took place, how seriously the measurements were contacted, how well the user was feeling that day, etc. Such unpredictable factors are included in the following equation 3:

$$Avg = F(O_i, E_i, X1_i, K, Xk_i, n)$$

where $X1_i, K, Xk_i$ represents these factors. The authors opinion is that this equation is solvable, but since all of its elements are very difficult to be measured, in this paper the analysis will focus on the equation 2. Solving equation 2 is an important step toward the solution of the complete equation 3. In the next two sections the method both O_i and E_i are measured is presented.

3. EVALUATING THE USER

As shown in figure 1 the user is considered to have three different parts of knowledge related to the subject that is measured. These three parts are the personal background, the syntactic knowledge about the product and the semantic knowledge about the application[5]. These three parts are not consider to contribute equally to form the user's profile. The personal background contributes the half of the other equally contributing parts. Therefore the 20% is assigned for the user's personal background and the 40% for both the user's syntactic and semantic knowledge. These three parts are further analyzed below.

figure 1

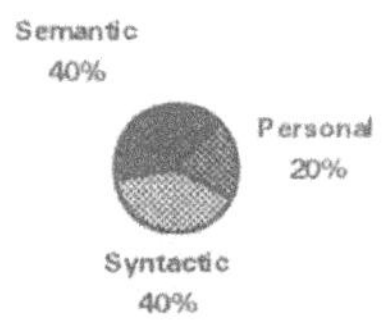

The personal background: All the user's attributes which are not related to the product or the application are collected in this name. Such attributes are, the user's age, his general education, his culture, etc. The user's age has to do with his ability to adopt new technologies and working styles and be open minded in changes. His education helps him to be able to express serious critique, and the nearer to the subject of his studies is the subject of the product, the more objective he will be.

figure 2

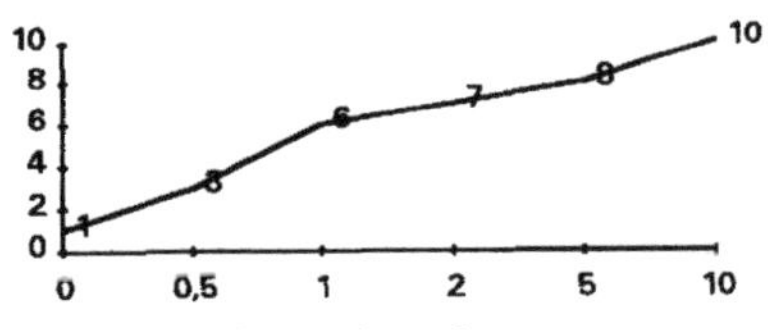

The syntactic knowledge: Syntactic knowledge is the knowledge of the existing computer applications, and the familiarization with the use of computers in general. The more similar to the measured application those applications are, the better for the user.

The years of experience are also a subject for measurement. As illustrated in figure 2, a user is considered to gain experience faster in the very first years when working with a program and slowly after these years. The key point here, is to understand that the subject for measurements is not the user's ability to operate a program, but his ability to provide critique for a similar program. This ability is considered to be equal to 3 out of 10 after half a year of experience and 6 out of 10 in the first whole year. The user gradually reaches 10, after ten years of experience. No user is consider to gain any further experience after working more than 10 years on the same program. The aim of the questions on the users syntactic knowledge is to evaluate the user's interaction with the program, the use of similar systems, the general use of computer systems and of course the years of experience for each one of the above.

The semantic knowledge: The extreme majority of computer programs are not constructed to offer something new, but to automate an pre-existing activity. In most of the cases, new programs are build to offer an new automation, replacing an existing product. This activity (automated or not) is known by many users with different expertise levels. The semantic knowledge defines how well a user knows this activity -meaning how well a user understands the semantics of the under automation problem. Measuring semantic experience, the years of experience are also important and the diagram in figure 2 applies the same.

4. MEASURING USER'S CRITIQUE

The need to measure user's critique was firstly described as a concept by Boehm et al.[6] and McCall et al.[7]. The McCall's quality model has been the basis for the ISO Metrics standard[8]. This standard reduces the complexity of the McCall's model by using the following six quality attributes: Functionality, Reliability, Usability, Efficiency, Maintainability, and Portability.

In order to be in compliance with the ISO Standards this methodology embodies all the six quality characteristics of the ISO9126, and two more from the first 11 quality attributes from McCall's model (Simplicity and Expandability). Therefore the proposed set of attributes is the following eight quality characteristics:

- Functionality,
- Simplicity,
- Reliability,
- Usability,
- Efficiency,
- Maintainability,
- Expandability and
- Portability.

These attributes were found sufficient in order to describe all the aspects of the user's critique about the measured product. Additionally, these attributes could be decomposed to lower-level attributes (according to McCall's model), and finally into direct questions to the user.

The five proposed rated levels for the products are the following:

- poor,
- average,
- good,
- excellent, and
- optimum.

The scoring system is also simple. A 20% of the overall score of the question is assigned for the selection of "poor", 40% for the "average", 60% for the "good", 80% for the "excellent", and 100% for the "optimum". Using this approach, the lower level of user satisfaction which could be measured, is 20% of the expected product and the best level is, naturally, 100%. An example of how the functionality could be measured, is the following question:

"How does the product perform user's functions?" with the available choices:

Poor The product does not provide the required functions.
Average The product provides the required functions, except some limitations. These limitations may be overcame by using manual procedures.
Good The product provides the required functions, except minor limitations, that may be ignored.
Excellent The product provides all required functions, except a few minor limitations. These limitations may also be overcame by using other automated functions.
Optimum The product performs all user's requirements without any limitation at all.

This methodology suggests that the user must be given only multiple choice sheets with the question and the choices (Poor, Average, Good, Excellent, Optimum) and to be guided by an expert analyst, in order to mark the suitable answer. Further explanation about why this is suggested, is provided in the following section.

The scoring system of the questionnaires, measuring the users' opinion for a product, is very simple. An equal amount of contribution is given to each of the eight quality attributes: 12.5% for each attribute. The participation of each question in the overall 12.5% of the attribute is related with the measured application and is to be defined by the expert analyst. For example, in a telematics application the **availability** characteristic is highly the most important characteristic of the **reliability** attribute. For an non telematics application this characteristic might not be considered important.

5. COLLECTING AND ANALYZING THE MEASUREMENTS

The collection of the answers to the measurements is a vivid aspect of the methodology. Human aspects related with the tendency not to take seriously these measurements, or to exaggerate about their abilities, may affect the reality of measurements. The kind of answers which are required is equally important. Multiple choice sheets have been used in our experiments and our suggestion is to follow this example. It's easy to analyze the multiple choice answers, the collection of answers may be automated and the users are guided to choose a preset answer. The problem of multiple choice sheets is that the user may not find a suitable answer, or may not understand which answer is the one that suits better. In order to solve this, in our first examples the users were provided plenty of comments, explaining each question and guide them to the right selection. The experiments shown that in the most cases the users tend to ignore long comment lines and as a result they tend to chose carelessly. It has been found that the best solution is to provide plain questionnaires without any comments, but not just give them to the users to mark them. An expert is the one who must ask the questions to the users, must advise them about the best category that fits to them, and must mark the answers for them. Using this approach, the user's tendency to exaggerate about their abilities is limited, due to the expert's present.

The size of the questionnaires is important too. In the early experiments, when the questionnaires were just given to the users, has been measured a big tendency to mark carelessly the last answers of the questionnaires. This tendency grows when the size of the questionnaires becomes bigger. Humans do not like filling questionnaires, especially when the questions have to do with their abilities. Therefore they never take this task seriously. Furthermore the bigger the questionnaire is, the more careless they tend to be, when they choose their answers. Our suggestions are that the questionnaires must be small. It would be better to divide a questionnaire into three parts and to repeat the measurements three times.

The methodology that analyze the measurements is graphically illustrated in figure 3. The selection of the statistical sample, (how many users will be asked to fill in the questionnaires **Q1,...,Qm** and how these users will be selected), is not the subject of this paper. There is a well defined theory of how to perform a statistical analysis. From the set of **m** questionnaires the analysts extract the **Ei** and the **Oi** (the user evaluation and the user opinion). Analyzing this result, the **Avg** of the equation 2 is extracted. In addition the analysis of a users' subset, **EUS**, consisted only from the "expert users", results in the expert users' opinion. This opinion, **EUA**, is of a great importance and significantly more important from the result of equation 1. In the next paragraphs two techniques are proposed in order to identify the "experts" .

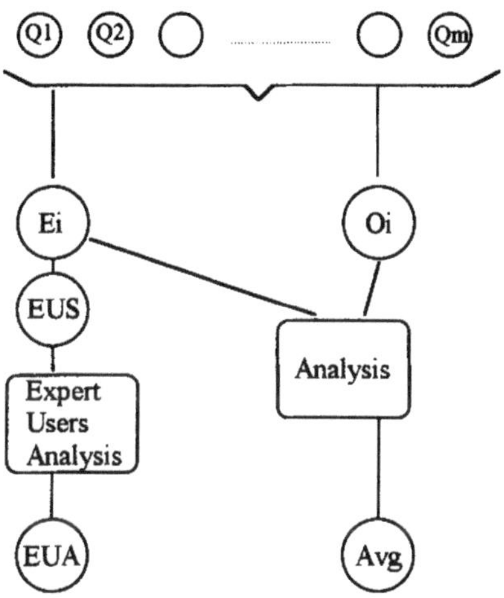

Figure 3

The first technique is the one that is chosen in our experiments. According to this technique, the analysts set a minimum standard for the expert user, select a statistical sample, collect the answers to questionnaires and finally, identify the users who exceed this minimum standard as experts. Using this technique, the analysts have the opportunity to work besides the limits of the statistical sample, by heuristically selecting "candidate expert users". Those users are persons who the analysts believe that there is a great possibility to exceed the minimum expert level.

The second technique is more simple than the first one, but it might fail to identify the real expert users. According to this technique, the analysts after the collection of the answers to the questionnaires, consider the upper 5% of the users as experts. This technique requires a homogenous statistical sample, so as there will be within an actual 5% of expert users. The choice of 5% as the limit for the expert user selection, is based on our experimentally measurements, but in other environments might be different. In other situations a different users' percentage might be chosen as experts, according to the user profile analysis performed before the measurements. In order to estimate this percentage, pre-analysis like the first technique must be carried out before the measurements.

6. OPEN PROBLEMS AND FURTHER RESEARCH

The methodology that is presented in this paper, is not complete so as to measure the quality of a software product. It must be used in parallel with other software metrics and under an overall rigorous quality assurance approach for optimum software engineering. Though this methodology will be valuable throughout time because it is not depended on programming languages, techniques and tools, but it evaluates the product itself.

The aim of this paper, was not to provide same sample questionnaires, that an analysts will take them as they are and apply them, but to provide a way of analyzing user's opinions. This approach is formed under a methodology that is applicable as a concept in all cases. Though, the analysts must operate within the scope of this methodology and define their own suitable questionnaires. The answer to the question "How to measure users' critique?" is a methodological and rigorous collection and analysis of measurements by using customized, dynamically changed, and always suitable questionnaires.

Solving equation 3 is an open problem. Our estimation based on our current research reveals that the result of the measurements of the "expert users opinion" might be the best approximation to this equation's solution. This measurement might be better than both the results of equations 1 and 2. Proving this estimation is also a future goal.

REFERENCES

1. HALSTEAD, M.: 'Elements of Software Science', McGraw-Hill, 1968.
2. McCABE, T.: 'A Complexity Measure', *IEEE Transactions on Software Engineering*, 1976, SE-2, (4), pp 156-167.
3. XENOS, M. and TSALIDIS C. and CHRISTODOULAKIS D.: 'Measuring software complexity using software metrics', *3rd European Conference on Software Quality Proc.*, Madrit Spain, 1992, pp 167-178.
4. FENTON, N.: 'Software Metrics - A rigorous approach', Chapman & Hall, 1991.
5. PRESSMAN, R.: 'Software Engineering - A practitioners approach', McGraw-Hill, 1992, pp 457-480.
6. BOEHM, B.: 'Software Engineering Economics', *IEEE Transactions on Software Engineering*, 1978, SE-10, (1), pp 37-46.
7. McCALL, J. and RICHARDS P. and WALTERS G.: 'Factors in software quality', US Rome Air Development Centre Reports, 1977.
8. ISO9126: ISO/DP 9126.: 'Software Quality Characteristics', ISO9126, 1987.

42

Complexity Measures for System Development Models

E.H. Ferneley[1], D.A. Howcroft[2] and C.G. Davies

[1]Department of Computing, Manchester Metropolitan University, Manchester, M1 5GD, UK
[2] Department of Computation, UMIST, P.O. Box 88, Manchester, M60 1QD, UK

Abstract

This paper discusses mechanisms to measure the inherent complexity of the formative stages of the software development process. The techniques presented concentrate on two major specification and design modelling techniques, namely hierarchy and network diagrams, which may be found in many current structured development methods. The measurement of hierarchy models considers the level of nesting or *inherited* complexity of processing activity. The measurement of network models considers the implicit complexity of the information flows terminating at and emanating from processes.

Keyword Codes: D2.7, D2.8, D2.10
Keywords: Maintenance, metrics, design methods

1. INTRODUCTION

The advent of system development methods was hailed as the way forward to the production of quality, reliable software systems. However, throughout the past two decades it has become increasingly obvious that this has not always been the case. In fact there is now a major crisis facing the software development community. Increasing amounts of development resources are being devoted to the maintenance of existing systems. It has been estimated that by the mid 1990s nearly 90% of the system development resources will be consumed by the maintenance of existing systems [1]. A major area of concern, therefore, is the ability to control and monitor the development process, the assumption being that this will reduce the costs of quality software production. This raises a major issue, how does one monitor and control the development of quality software?

To this end there are many active research areas. One such avenue of research, suggests that the utilisation of complexity assessment techniques will aid in the reduction of the problem, by guiding the developers towards the reduction of the inherent complexity of systems under development. This, then is the subject of this paper.

The crisis in the software community can be summarised as the product of poor quality software [2, 3]. As a result, software quality quantitative estimation has become a major issue. Most studies have concentrated on the measurement of the later stages of the development lifecycle, such as the count of lines of code. However, it is also important to direct attention to the earlier stages of the software lifecycle since many of the software quality problems have been considered as originating in these early phases [4]. Incorrect decisions at this stage can result in the most costly of problems and have a major impact on software quality. Attempts to correct errors at the implementation stage is considerably more expensive than rectification of errors during the earlier stages of the lifecycle [5] and so measurement at the initial design stage enables an assessment of quality before committing to code. ·A key factor in the enhancement of quality, in these early stages of the development cycle, is the ability to keep the complexity of the models as simple as possible. Thus the concept of complexity is vital to this study. *Complexity* can be defined as the degree of difficulty in analysis, design, testing and implementation of software [6]. Quantitative software metrics, when defined and used correctly, have been shown to be useful indicators of software complexity [7], and maintainability [8].

In many design methods the modelling of individual processing units precedes the modelling of the communication of these units with each other and the outside world. The modelling of processes is frequently concerned with the representation of the sequential time-ordering of individual process actions. Later, consideration is given to how these processes communicate with each other in terms of information flow. Consideration, will therefore be given first to the measurement of sequential time-ordered models and then how this measurement can be applied to network models.

2. THE MEASUREMENT OF HIERARCHY DIAGRAMS

A hierarchy diagram is a sequential time-ordered model of a processing unit (for an example refer to figure 1). This consists of four structural component types - iteration, selection, sequence and the atomic elementary. The diagram is always read from left to right, it may be considered as an inverted tree with the top most node being the root component of the tree, and the elementary components being the leaf nodes.

In order to evaluate the design complexity of hierarchical models it is necessary to consider each individual path through the diagram. To derive an overall complexity rating for hierarchy diagrams a measurement is obtained based upon the number of linearly independent paths through a process. This value has to take into account the complexity that occurs as we traverse *up* the hierarchical tree from the leaf component. This is known as the nesting level or *embedded complexity*.

The hierarchy metrics assign gradings to branches in a structure, these grades are drawn from the theories of *control flow metrics* [9, 10]. These metrics are concerned with the flow of control through the structure of a program. The control structure, thus defined, is modelled by the utilisation of directed graphs where the nodes correspond to program statements and an arc from one node to another represents a flow of control between statements. This measure is useful because, assuming that the graph is strongly connected, it indicates the number of *basic paths* (or linearly independent circuits) which, when combined, generate all possible paths throughout the program.

2.1 Hierarchy Complexity Metrics

The hierarchy metrics presented below have their foundation in the 'classical' complexity metric as defined by McCabe [11]. Empirical studies have suggested that there is a relationship between McCabe's cyclomatic complexity measure, which measures the *basic paths* through a given process, and the future reliability and maintainability of that process [7; 12]. The mechanism for the measurement of hierarchy diagrams is as follows:

- Because elementary components are the simplest component type they are assigned an initial design complexity grade of **1**. Elementary components have an implicit complexity as they represent sequential processing, this complexity must be considered.

- Sequential components within the body of the diagram are not graded, since they do not increase the processing complexity in terms of path structure. Sequential components are essential to the decomposition of a structure. Any such sequential decomposition requires the sub-division of the model into logical processing tasks.
- Selectable components are graded by applying principles derived from McCabe's cyclomatic complexity measure by considering the number of *basic paths*. The complexity grade for selections is determined by the number of selectable branches. Hence, when a selection is encountered the corresponding grade is the number of selectable possibilities. To illustrate, consider component *H* in figure 1, this has been awarded a rating of **3** as there are three distinct paths. Similarly, should there be four selectable children then the node would be given a complexity grade of **4**.

Iterative components are assigned a grade of **2**. This decision is based on the premise that when an iteration is encountered the number of *basic paths* is **2**, because the iteration may or may not be invoked. Given that an iteration has a potentially infinite number of paths due to the nature of the construct, a more meaningful measure is to count the number of distinct paths. Although distinct iteration loops are not counted, the weight of the component will be reflected in the *Hierarchy Complexity Totals* (see below).

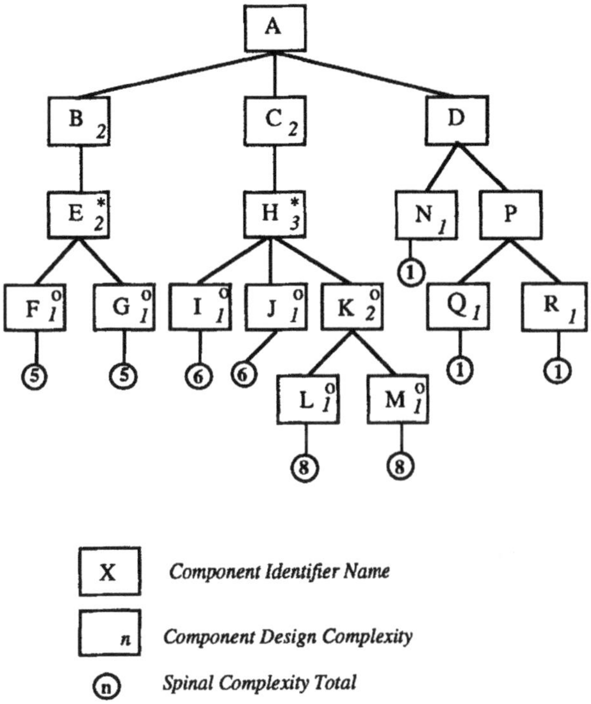

Figure 1: Example of Calculation of Spinal Complexity Total and Hierarchy Complexity Total

A grade for each *spine* in the hierarchy diagram is then calculated following examination of the spine from the root component to the specified elementary component, this is known as the *Spinal Complexity Total*. Such a traversal through the hierarchical diagram takes into account embedded design complexity. An overall grade for the diagram, the Hierarchy Complexity Total, may be attained by adding the constituent Spinal Complexity Totals as follows:

$$\text{Hierarchy Complexity Total} = \sum_{1}^{s} \text{Spinal Complexity Total} \quad (1)$$

where Spinal Complexity Total is the individual spinal design complexity values and s is the number of individual spines. In the case of the diagram in figure 1 this would be 41.

The theoretical and practical basis of McCabe's metric has been heavily criticised [13, 14]. However, the application presented in this paper avoids the more contentious aspects of his work.

It considers embedded complexity that results from the nesting of structures, and also allows for distinct measurement of subsets of a program, rather than offering a single definitive value. Most metrics quantify the complexity of a process or program by means of a single global value. The use of a single-value number tends to conceal important internal aspects of the module, and thus degrades its usefulness. The metrics presented in this paper define a measurement technique that will integrate the embedded structural complexity of a process or program. This enables appreciation of every aspect of the hierarchy model and its contribution to complexity, rather than evaluating complexity as a whole.

3. THE MEASUREMENT OF NETWORK DIAGRAMS

A network diagram is a set of connected nodes, where the nodes represent processes (modules, functions or procedures, i.e. processing elements) and the connections represent the passage of data. To evaluate the complexity of network diagrams the connectivity of processes is examined. In order to achieve this the number of inter-process connections, along with their implicit structural complexity, is assessed. No distinction is made between local and global information flows, since complexity values are only based on an individual process' connectivity. The metric for individual processes therefore, reflects both the connectivity of the process and the implicit complexity of the structure of the data flowing into and out of that process.

3.1 Network Complexity Metrics

The network metrics presented here are loosely based on *information flow metrics* [15, 16] which measure the number of distinct information processing paths through a given process. To assess the complexity of process coupling, the total number of linearly independent paths through a process may be calculated. This is achieved by multiplying the number of information flows terminating at a process (known as *fan-in*) by the number of information flows emanating from a process (known as *fan-out*). Empirical studies have concluded that the level of information flow is closely correlated with development time [17]. These metrics are relevant to <u>any</u> system developed using a structured design technique which can be represented in terms of a network diagram (for example [18, 19, 20]).

The mechanism by which a total network complexity value for a given process node is achieved is as follows::

- Each information flow terminating at and emanating from the specified process is given a *Hierarchy Complexity Total* figure. This is based on the specified information flow's implicit data structure. For example, if a single parameter was being passed this would be **1**.

- To calculate a weighting for the overall complexity of information terminating at (or emanating from) the process the individual input (or output) *Hierarchy Complexity Total* figures are accumulated. The metric for the *total complexity* of information fanning-in to the process is therefore:

$$\textit{Fan-In Complexity Total} = \sum_{0}^{n} \textit{Hierarchy Complexity Total} \text{ terminating at the process} \quad (2)$$

Similarly, the metric for the *total complexity* of information fanning-out of the process is therefore:

$$\textit{Fan-Out Complexity Total} = \sum_{0}^{n} \textit{Hierarchy Complexity Total} \text{ emanating from the process} \quad (3)$$

Addition is used instead of multiplication to arrive at a value for the fan-ins (or fan-outs) of a node. The reasoning is best illustrated by example. Consider a single fan-in where the Hierarchy Complexity Total = 30; this could be perceived to have an equivalent complexity of three fan-in's with a Hierarchy Complexity Total of 10 each. If Multiplication was applied this would give a composite total of 1000, however, with addition this would give only a value of 30. It may be considered that multiplication tends to inordinately distort the usefulness of the metric by severely skewing the total.

- The calculation for the composite figure for the module as a whole is weighted to reflect the difference between a single input (or output) source and multiple input (or output) sources. Therefore, in order to account for this, the *Fan-In Complexity Total* is multiplied by the total number of individual fan-in's giving a *Fan-In Multiplicity Complexity Total.* The *Fan-Out Multiplicity Complexity Total* metrics are derived in the same manner. This may be summarised as follows:

  Fan-In Multiplicity Complexity Total = (*Fan-In Complexity Total* * Σfan-in) (4)

  Fan-Out Multiplicity Complexity Total = (*Fan-Out Complexity Total* * Σfan-out) (5)

- Finally, to gain an assessment of the overall complexity for a given process the *Fan-In Multiplicity Complexity Total* is multiplied by the *Fan-Out Multiplicity Complexity Total.* Multiplication is used in deriving this value to reflect the total number of possible information processing paths through a given process. A problem would arise if either the number of fan-in's or fan-out's for a process is zero, since this would result in an instance of zero complexity. The solution proposed in such specialised cases is to assign a value of 1 whenever a zero fan-in or fan-out is encountered. The metric for arriving at a value for individual processes may be summarised as follows:

  Process Complexity Total =
  (*Fan-In Multiplicity Complexity Total* * *Fan-Out Multiplicity Complexity Total*) (6)

The metrics presented assess the complexity of the information entering and leaving the process and an overall information flow complexity measure is attained for each process. An example of the application of these metrics can be seen by considering figure 2.

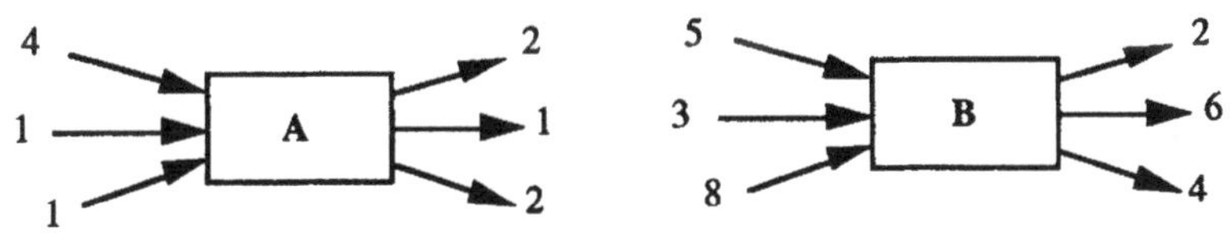

A
Fan-in Multiplicity Complexity Total = (4 + 1 + 1) * 3 = 18
Fan-out Multiplicity Complexity Total = (2 + 1 + 2) * 3 = 15
Process Complexity Total = (18 * 15)

B
Fan-in Multiplicity Complexity Total = (5 + 3 + 8) * 3 = 48
Fan-out Multiplicity Complexity Total = (2 + 6 + 4) * 3 = 36
Process Complexity Total = (48 * 36)

Figure 2: Example of Calculation of Network Metrics

Traditional information flow metrics suffer from the inability to distinguish differing levels of complexity inherent within information flows. This deficiency would mean that the two processes illustrated in figure 2 would result in the same measure of complexity. Such traditional metrics would only distinguish three fan-in's and three fan-out's for each process. But this clearly is not so. It has already been shown in the discussion regarding hierarchy metrics that individual data models necessarily have differing values of complexity. It follows therefore that the complexity of the individual information flows must also be variable. Any measurement of process and network complexity must take this into account. To this end, the network metrics presented here, permit a more meaningful measurement to be given to process and network complexity.

4. CONCLUSION

This paper has illustrated how two key complexity measurement techniques can be applied to two major forms of design specification. Enhanced quality may be brought about by attempting to maintain low levels of complexity. In order to achieve this the development process must be controlled. An essential part of this process is the ability to obtain meaningful measurements for complexity. This paper has attempted to show how the adaptation and modification of accepted metrics may be refined and thus applied.

The work presented in this paper has developed from a long-standing research project at UMIST into the construction of IPSE's and CASE tools. The latest CASE tool being developed is centred on the concept of method-configurable tools. This tool is being built incorporating the quantitative complexity measurement aids presented above. The research has shown, by the application of reverse engineering, a significant correlation between high values of complexity and error prone software. Consequently, the inclusion of such measurements is seen as an essential aid to the successful development of quality software products.

References

1. MOAD, J., Maintaining the Competetive Edge *Datamation*,, Feb. 1990, pp 60 -61.
2. FENTON, N. E., *Software Metrics: A Rigorous Approach,* Chapman and Hall, London, 1991.
3. SOMMERVILLE, I., *Software Engineering,* Addison-Wesley 4th Edition 1992.
4. HIRAYAMA, M., SATO, H., YAMADA, A. AND TSUDA, J. Practice of quality modelling and measurement on software life-cycle, *IEEE*, 1990.
5. BOEHM, B.W. *Software Engineering Economics* Prentice Hall, 1981.
6. FERNELEY, E. H., HOWCROFT, D. A. & DAVIES, C. G., Design Metrics as an Aid to Cost Estimation, Proc. ESCOM 1994, Ivrea, Italy, 11th - 13th May 1994.
7. CONTE, S. D., DUNSMORE, H. E. AND SHENN, Y. Y., *Software Engineering Metrics and Models*, Benjamin/Cummings, 1986.
8. KAFURA, D. & REDDY, R. R., The Use of Software Complexity Metrics in Software Maintenance in *IEEE Transactions on Software Engineering*, Vol. SE-13, No. 3, Mar. 1987, pp. 335-343.
9. WILSON, R. I., *Introduction to Graph Theory,* Academic Press, 1972
10. LEGARD, H. & MARCOTTY, M., A Generalogy of Control Structure, *Communications of the ACM,* Vol. 18, Nov. 1975, pp. 629-639.
11. MCCABE, T. J., A Complexity Measure in *IEEE Transactions of Software Engineering,* Vol. SE-2, No. 4, 1976.
12. WARD, W. T., Software Defect Prevention using McCabe's Complexity Metric in *Hewlettt-Packard Journal,* Vol. 39, No. 3, 1989, pp. 30-35.
13. SHEPPERD, M., A Critique of Cyclomatic Complexity as a Software Metric in *Software Engineering Journal*, 3(2), 1988, pp. 30-36.
14. FENTON, N.E., Software Measurement and Analysis: A Case Study in Collaborative Research in *22nd International Conference on Systems Science*, IEEE, January 1989.
15. HENRY, S. & KAFURA, D., Software Structure Metrics Based on Information Flow in *IEEE Transactions on Software Engineering,* Vol. SE-7, No. 5, 1981, pp. 510-518.
16. SHEPPERD, M., Early Life-cycle Metrics and Software Quality Models in *Information and Software Technology*, Vol. 32, No. 4, May 1990, pp. 311-316.
17. SHEPPERD, M., Design Metrics: An Empirical Analysis in *Software Engineering Journal,* 5(1), 1990, pp. 3-10.
18. MYERS, G., *Composite Structured Design*, Van Nostrand, 1978.
19. JACKSON, M., *System Development,* Prentice Hall, 1983.
20. YOURDON, E. AND CONSTANTINE, L.L., *Structured Design*, Prentice-Hall Inc., 1979.

43

Composite Complexity Measures (CCM)

P.S. GROVER[a] AND N.S. GILL[b]

[a] Department of Computer Science, University of Delhi, India
[b] Department of Computer Science & Applications, M. D. University Rohtak, Haryana, India

Abstract

Studies based on Halstead and McCabe's metrics use different attributes of a program to measure the software complexity. There are certain characteristics which are used by software science measures but the same are not used by cyclomatic number measure to ascertain the complexity and vice-a-versa. Here, we report the results of our study which uses the combined characteristics of the program to measure the software complexity. This has been done by employing the concept of weights for the various tokens occurring in control/iterative structures in a program.

Keyword Codes: D.2.8; D.4.8
Keywords: Complexity Measures, Software science, Cyclomatic number; Development effort; Composite measure.

1. INTRODUCTION

The complexity of software systems affects its design, testability, reliability and maintainability. In order to produce reliable software, its complexity must be controlled by suitably decomposing the software systems into smaller subsystems [1]. The ever increasing cost of program development has made the measurement of software complexity much more important than it has ever been before [2]. There are several ways of perceiving the software systems for the purpose of complexity measurement. Out of these software science complexity measures and the cyclomatic complexity measure are prominent ones [3,4]. Though both these methods measure software complexity, but basis for measuring software complexity is completely different.

In software science measure, the basis of detecting and measuring the software complexity is the size of software systems only and it doesn't keep track of other characteristics of software systems such as program flow control, iteration and so on [3,5]. Similarly, cyclomatic number measures the software complexity due to program flow control only, but doesn't keep track of other characteristics of software systems such as operators, operands, etc. In this paper we have attempted to take into account the complexities both due to size of software systems as well as due to presence of various control/iterative structures in modules of the software systems.

Recently, Bina Ramamurthy and Austin Melton [6] have tried to measure the weighted complexity of software modules by assigning additional weights to total operator and operand counts. But they did not take into account the multiple-test predicates, GOTO statements, etc. In present study, we have examined these issues as well. We have used our three-term model [7] and taken into account these various multiple-test predicates. We call this a Composite Model. The measures will be referred to as *Composite Complexity Measure.*

Before defining our composite measure, we briefly introduce software science measures (Halstead as well as our three-term model) and McCabe's cyclomatic complexity measure [3,7,4].

2. HALSTEAD's SOFTWARE SCIENCE MEASURE

In software science [3] approach,
vocabulary size is given as : $n = n_1 + n_2$
where n_1 , n_2 are number of unique operators and operands respectively.

The length of program is $N = N_1 + N_2$, where N_1 and N_2 are total occurrences of operators and operands respectively. Other metrics such as program volume (V), language level (l), programming effort and time etc. are defined using these basic metrics.

As the modern languages are very rich in functions/reserve-words/keywords so it is better to count keywords/reserve-words/functions separately besides operators and operands [7]. Using this model, the results for estimating program lengths have also been found encouraging. We apply this model to our present study.

Here n_1 , n_2 are the unique number of operators, operands respectively whereas n_3 is the number of unique keywords/ reserve-words/ functions which was earlier considered a part of operators. Similarly, N_1 , N_2 , N_3 are the total count of n_1 , n_2 , n_3 respectively.

Following Halstead measures, vocabulary size is defined as : $n = n_1 + n_2 + n_3$ and the length of program is $N = N_1 + N_2 + N_3$.

These are now used to estimate other measures such as program volume, language level, effort and so on.

3. McCabe's CYCLOMATIC COMPLEXITY MEASURE

McCabe measure [4] is based upon the study of program control graphs. If G is the program control graph for a given program, then the cyclomatic number is : $V(G) = m - n + p$, where m is number of arcs, n is number of nodes, p is number of connected components (p=1 for strongly connected control graphs). McCabe's measure has been reasonable for control cyclomatic complexity but doesn't take into account the software complexity due to size as mentioned earlier.

4. COMPOSITE COMPLEXITY MEASURES

Composite measure takes into account both the complexities due to software size as well as control flow. It has been done by associating extra weights to the total occurrences of software tokens in our model. We assign weights to the nonsequential structures so that length, volume, effort, language level, programming time etc. can detect complexities due to nonsequential structures [6,8,9].

Rules for assigning extra weights and levels are as follows :

i) If there is no non-sequential structure present in the software module, then extra weights will be zero for all occurrences of operators,operand,keywords/reserve-words/functions.

ii) List of the nonsequential structures/predicates irrespective of the level of control structure with their corresponding weights are :

	STRUCTURE /Predicates	*Weights*
a)	if-then/if-then-else/ repeat-until/do-while/ for-do	1
b)	GOTO/Computed GOTO (or CASE)	1
c)	AND/OR/EQV/XOR	2

iii) Level of the control structures will be increased by one for a single occurrence of any control structure within its body (nesting) and so on.

iv) Only the control structures will be examined for assigning weights and levels to all the operators, operands and keywords/reserve-words/functions respectively so that additional values due to weight and level could be added to the present values of N_1, N_2, N_3 respectively.

v) Nesting of heterogeneous (different types) control structures will also be considered in the same fashion as nesting of homogeneous control structures.

vi) The control structures such as if-then-else-if will be considered as a multilevel nesting and will be converted into simple structures using the control structure if-then-else for the purpose of assigning weights.

Following the above mentioned rules for assigning weights and levels, the weighted metrics are given as :

$$Nw = Nw_1 + Nw_2 + Nw_3$$

where Nw_1, Nw_2, Nw_3 are weighted total count of n_1, n_2, n_3 respectively and are defined as :

$$Nw_1 = N_1 + \sum_{n_1} DX(n_1) * L(n_1)$$

$$Nw_2 = N_2 + \sum_{n_2} DX(n_2) * L(n_2)$$

$$Nw_3 = N_3 + \sum_{n_3} DX(n_3) * L(n_3)$$

where DX(t) is the weight attached to token t and L(t) is the level at which the token t is positioned.

Weighted volume, $Vw = Nw * \log_2 n$, Weighted effort, $Ew = V_w / \hat{L}$

Weighted Language level, $lw = \hat{L}w * Vw^*$, Weighted time, $Tw = Ew / 18$.

We have applied these rules to various languages like FORTRAN, Pascal, C and BASIC. But, here we report our results for FORTRAN 77 only.

5. EXPERIMENTAL MENTAL RESULTS

We take two test programs P1 and P2 listed below :

```
C      Test program P1
       REAL U, V, W, X
       READ(*,*)U,V,W
       X=U
       U=V
       W=X
       X=U+V+W
       WRITE(*,*)X
       END
```

```
C      Test program P2
       REAL U, V, W, X
       X=U
       IF (X .LT. V) X=V
       IF (X .LT. W) X=W
       WRITE(*,*)X
       END
```

Applying theory of software science with revised basic metrics [7], we get the following results :

For P1	*For P2*
$n_1=3$, $n_2=4$, $n_3=3$; $N_1=9$, $N_2=16$, $N_3=3$	$n_1=3$, $n_2=4$, $n_3=4$; $N_1=7$, $N_2=14$, $N_3=5$
$n = 3+4+3 = 10$; $N = 9+16+3 = 28$	$n = 3+4+4 = 11$; $N = 7+14+5 = 26$
$V = 93$, $l = .67$, $E = 1116$, $T = 62$	$V = 90$, $l = .57$, $E = 1103$, $T = 61$

By looking at the values of different metrics, it seems that both the programs P1 and P2 need the same programming effort and time but by looking at the programs, program P1 is found less complex than program P2. In other words, this study doesn't reflect the effect of control structures.

Applying McCabe's theory of complexity for the same programs Pl and P2 the results are :

$V(G1) = m - n + 1 = 1$; $V(G2) = m - n + 1 = 3$.

Thus by looking at the cyclomatic numbers, we infer that program P2 is more complex than program P1. But, this study does not take care of the complexity which will arise due to size of software modules.

Now, by applying the composite measures, we get the following weighted results :

For P1:	*For P2:*
$Nw_1=N_1+0=9$; $Nw_2=N_2+0=16$;	$Nw_1= N_1+((1+1))=9$; $Nw_2= N_2+(1+1+(1+1))=18$
$Nw_3=N_3+0=3$; $n = 3 + 4 + 3 = 10$	$Nw_3= N_3+((1+1))=7$; $n = 3 + 4 + 4 = 11$
$Nw = 9+16+3=28$; $Vw = 93$	$Nw = 9+18+7=34$; $Vw = 118$
$Ew = 1116$, $Tw = 62$, $lw = .67$	$Ew = 1858$, $Tw = 103$, $lw = .44$

From these calculations we infer that program Pl is less complex than program P2. Differences arise due to two factors : size and control/iterative structures.

We have studied a set of thirty two FORTRAN 77 language programs for all the three measures. Following the weighted results we have computed program volume, language level, development effort and time which are given in Table I along with the values of lines of code (LOC) and McCabe's cyclomatic number, V(G). We have also estimated the relative differences between composite metric Ew and E as a function of McCabe cyclomatic number, V(G) and has been plotted in Fig. 1. We observe that with the rise in McCabe's complexity the effort increases.

The results of composite measures can be used for modularizing the software systems rather than using both software science metric E and McCabe's cyclomatic number V(G).

6. CONCLUSIONS

In the present study we have applied the three term model taking into account the effect of control/repetitive structures on the software science metrics. Our study shows that the effect of these structures on complexity is quite significant.

ACKNOWLEDGMENTS

We would like to thank Prof. D.R. Taneja of M.D. University, Rohtak for the many useful suggestions and kind help he has given during the preparation of this paper.

REFERENCES

1. Lew, Ken S., Dillon, T.S. and Forward, K.E. : 'Software Complexity and Its impact on Software Reliability', IEEE Trans. on SW Engg., November 1988, Vol. 14, (11).
2. Shen, Conte, and Dunsmore : 'Software Science Revisited : A critical analysis of the theory and its empirical support', IEEE Trans. on SW Engg, March 1983, Vol. SE-9,(2), pp. 156-165.
3. Halstead, M.H. : 'Elements of Software Science', (New York, Elsevier, North-Holland, 1977).
4. McCabe, T.J. : 'A Complexity Measure', IEEE Trans. on SW Engg., December 1976 Vol. SE-2, (4), pp. 308-320.
5. Conte, S.D. and Shen, Dunsmore : 'Software Engineering Metrics and Models', (The Benjamin/Cummigs Pub. Company, Inc.. 1986).
6. Ramamurthy, Bina and Melton, Austin : 'A Synthesis of Software Science Measures and the Cyclomatic Number', IEEE Trans. on SW Engg., August 1988, Vol. 14, (8), pp. 1116-1121.
7. Grover, P.S., Gill, N.S. and Singh, R. : 'Measuring Software Systems', Proc. Annual National Seminar on "Operations Research and Management Decision Making", New Delhi, Nov. 19-20. 1993.
8. Prather, Ronald E. : 'An Axiomatic Theory of Software Complexity Measure', The Computer Journal, 1984, Vol. 27, (4).
9. Harrison, W. and Magel, K. : 'A Complexity Measure Based On Nesting Level', SIGPLAN , March 1981, 16(3).

Table - I
Composite Metrics for FORTRAN 77 Language

P.No.	V	Vw	LOC	λ	λw	V(G)	E	Ew	T	Tw
1	904	1067	15	2.07	1.75	4	18794	26216	1044	1456
2	443	568	10	1.31	1.09	5	8099	13028	450	724
3	606	691	14	3.21	2.83	5	8288	10747	460	597
4	198	250	9	0.7	0.5	3	3379	5482	188	306
5	495	807	17	0.41	0.28	7	16952	43869	942	2437
6	781	1177	20	0.47	0.34	10	31748	69645	1764	3869
7	803	960	17	0.79	0.69	6	25331	36090	1407	2005
8	1489	2598	51	0.35	0.21	11	97320	288667	5407	16037
9	721	1178	28	0.74	0.49	9	22322	57745	1240	3208
10	1900	2519	50	0.57	0.44	11	109195	190833	6066	10602
11	348	719	15	0.42	0.2	6	10029	42544	557	2364
12	768	902	26	0.47	0.44	5	30968	41000	1720	2278
13	835	1184	33	0.64	0.48	7	30036	59497	1669	3305
14	1472	1611	20	0.89	0.81	5	59595	71283	3311	3960
15	644	1199	29	0.19	0.1	9	37225	128926	2068	7163
16	664	1136	17	0.54	0.32	7	23380	67964	1299	3776
17	554	636	19	0.97	0.9	3	13097	16916	728	940
18	1174	1638	23	1.16	0.8	7	37508	73784	2084	4099
19	1191	1850	29	0.86	0.66	9	44440	105714	2469	5873
20	3732	4685	50	2.04	1.65	10	159487	250535	8860	13919
21	954	1183	13	0.47	0.38	5	42780	65722	2377	3651
22	502	701	17	0.34	0.28	4	18943	35584	1052	1977
23	1106	1432	29	0.41	0.32	9	57254	95467	3181	5304
24	1768	2542	41	0.54	0.38	11	102197	206667	5678	11482
25	263	291	11	2.18	1.98	2	2893	3523	161	196
26	260	520	12	0.56	0.28	5	5652	22222	314	1235
27	201	309	7	0.33	0.25	4	4926	11196	274	622
28	53	53	3	1.54	1.54	1	309	309	17	17
29	405	590	16	0.55	0.42	5	11066	22433	615	1246
30	619	856	20	0.53	0.42	5	20983	38514	1166	2140
31	93	93	7	0.67	0.67	1	1116	1116	62	62
32	90	118	5	0.57	0.44	3	1103	1858	61	103

Fig. 1 : Plot Between V(G) and (Ew−E)

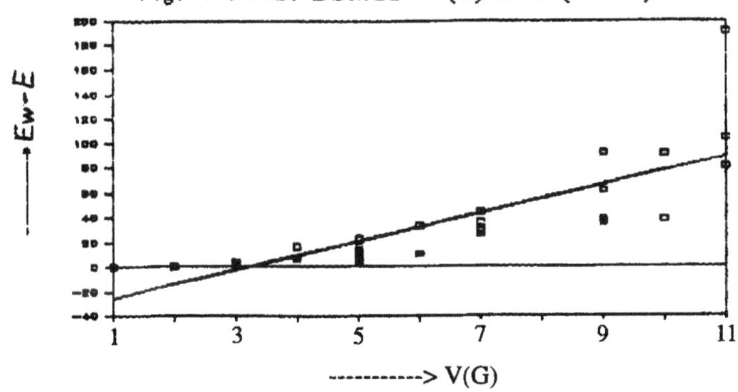

44

Automated Testing Tool for NATURAL®

Sheung-lun Hung, Lam-for Kwok, Ken Chee-keung Law

Department of Computer Science, City Polytechnic of Hong Kong
83 Tat Chee Avenue, Kowloon, Hong Kong

Abstract

Traditional manual testing procedures are time-consuming and unreliable. As program gets larger and more complex, automated testing is an essential step in the software development cycle. This project aims at developing the prototype of an automated coverage testing tool for NATURAL® on a range of platforms including UNIX® and MS-Window. The prototype has proven to be applicable to a large number of programs of various sizes. This work represents a first step towards the complete automation of the coverage testing process and further development is on the way to produce an operational tool.

Keyword Codes: D.2.5; D.2.2
Keywords: Software Engineering, Testing and Debugging; Software Engineering, Tools and Techniques

1. INTRODUCTION

Software testing is a crucial component of the software development process. The traditional manual approach to testing is both time consuming and error prone. It is the aim of the present study to investigate into the feasibility of automating one aspect of testing, namely coverage testing. This paper describes the prototype of an automated coverage testing tool for the 4GL NATURAL® running under both the MS-Window and the UNIX® environment. Minor modifications is needed to extend the testing functions for other environments.

In coverage testing [1], the goal is to execute all the possible test paths for a given program. The selection of a particular test path is determined by conditions of the decision constructs in the program under test. Exhaustive testing of all the paths by manual methods is normally impractical as the number of distinct test paths is usually very large. The automated coverage testing procedures chosen is based on a test path selection technique proposed by Thomas J.

McCabe[2,3]. In McCabe's Baseline method, the total number of test paths is first determined by computing the cyclomatic complexity [4,5]. The other steps are:

- derive the flow graph from analysis of the source program under test;
- select a baseline path that preferably satisfy the following criteria:
  - perform a major function in the program and not an error path, and
  - intersects a maximum number of decisions in the flow graph;
- select second test path by flipping the condition of the first decision statement on the baseline path while keeping the other conditions of the original path unchanged;
- the third, fourth and subsequent test paths can be generated by flipping the conditions of the second, third .. decision statements etc.

There are three stages in the testing. The first stage is to compute the cyclomatic complexity and to obtain the flow graph for a given program module. The second stage is to select a test path. The third stage is to generate the test data so as to execute the selected test path. Only one set of input data for all the test paths is used instead of generating a large number of test data sets for all the test paths. The path selection is affected by automatically substituting 'true' or 'false' in the conditions of the decision statements as required by the baseline method.

This paper is organized into four sections. Section two describes the testing procedure. Section three gives the functional components of the system and provides a sample execution summary report. Section 4 concludes and identifies areas for further developments.

2. TESTING PROCEDURE IMPLEMENTATION

The automated testing procedure consists of six steps is depicted in the diagram below:

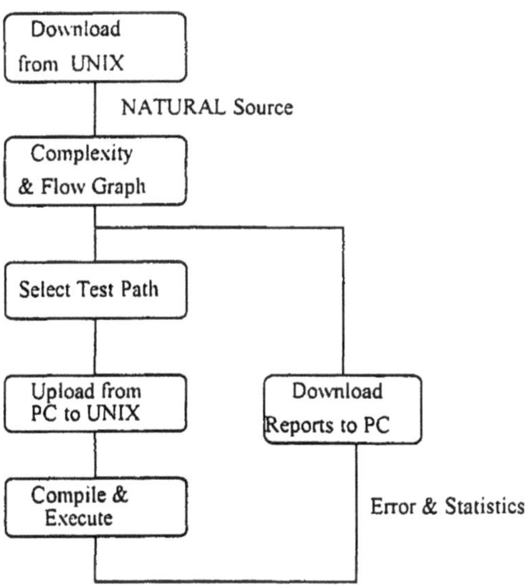

Figure 1. Testing Procedures

NATURAL® source code is assumed to reside on a SUN SPARC workstation. The six steps are:

1. Source code is downloaded to a PC platform under MS-Window from UNIX.
2. The cyclomatic complexity and flow graph are obtained.
3. McCabe's Baseline method is used to select the appropriate test path by modifying conditions of decision statements in the source program.
4. A copy of the source with selected test path is uploaded to UNIX.
5. The source is compiled and executed on the SUN SPARC.
6. Statistics and run-time errors are recorded and downloaded to MS-Window for analysis and storge.

Another test path is then selected and the whole process is repeated until all the test paths have been exhausted. It is important to ensure that only one copy of the source program is kept in the system. The same set of test data will be used for all the test paths. A summary report of all errors is provided at the end of the testing.

3. FUNCTIONAL COMPONENTS OF THE AUTOMATED TESTING TOOL

The automated coverage testing tool besides selecting test paths has to collect statistical and error information. The tool has six major functional components: Lexical Analyzer, Flow Graph Generator, Test Path Generator, Test File Generator, File Transfer, and Error Report Analzer.

♦ **Lexical Analyzer**

The lexical analyzer captures the NATURAL source code information and convert source statements into tokens. The major task of the lexical analyzer is to derive flow graph information from the tokens. The analyzer therefore focuses on capturing conditional constructs such as IF.., REPEAT.., DECIDE .. etc. The information stored for each conditional construct include:

- token_type - the token value for the conditional construct ;
- start_line - the starting line number of the conditional construct in the program;
- end_line - the line number for the next construct.

The information is fed into the flow graph generator.

♦ **Flow Graph Generator**

The flow graph generator is capable of computing the cyclomatic complexity as well as deriving the flow graph for the program under test. The flow graph provides a visual means of showing the flow control structure of the program. A sample flow graph is given in figure 2 with the associated cyclomatic complexity V(G) which is 17 in this case.

Each node in the flow graph can represent one of the four different classes of constructs for NATURAL®. They are:

- decision statements - e.g. IF..THEN, DECIDE ON;
- loop statements - e.g. REPEAT..UNTIL, READ, FIND;
- end statements - e.g. END-IF, END-DECIDE, END-REPEAT;
- sequential statements.

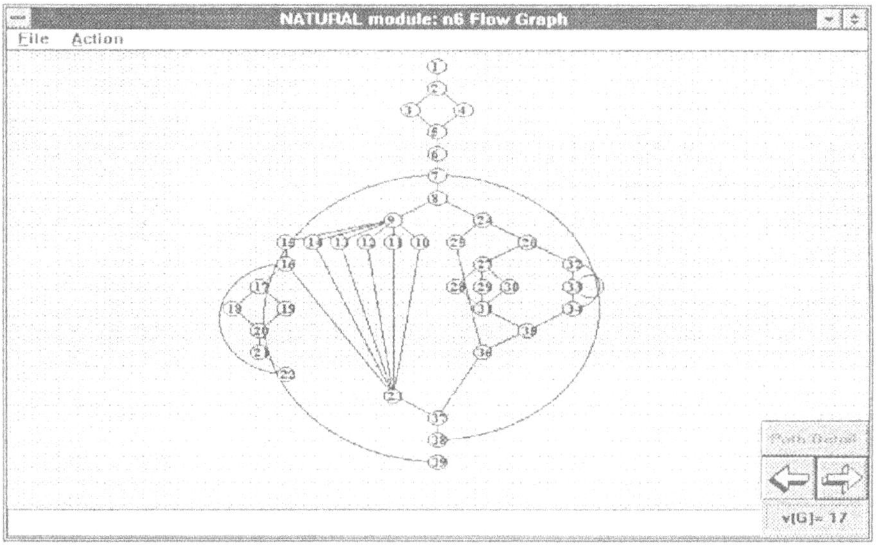

Figure 2. Sample flow graph

In the construction of the flow graph, input characters are arranged in the same order as they appear in the original source program. One complication arises as a result of the nesting nature of conditional constructs. Backtracking is normally required to locate previous nodes. Two separate data structures are used in the construction of flow graphs. They are the node information table and the edge information table.

♦ Test Path Generator

The test path generator generates all the test paths based on the Baseline technique of McCabe. The path selection technique comprises of three phases. The first phase is to create a look-up table for all branching nodes. The second phase is to invoke the algorithm for selecting the baseline path. In the final phase, a path selection algorithm is invoked to select the different test paths in accordance with the baseline technique. Each test path can be displayed. Figure 3 is a sample of the flow graph with the test path highlighted.

The nodes falling within the test path is displayed at the bottom of the screen.

♦ Test File Generator

The test path generator creates test files which are to be used in the coverage testing. Each test file corresponds to the enforcement of execution of a particular test path. The module examines each decision statement of the concerned path and by substitutes the conditions by either an always 'true' or 'false' expression as deemed necessary.

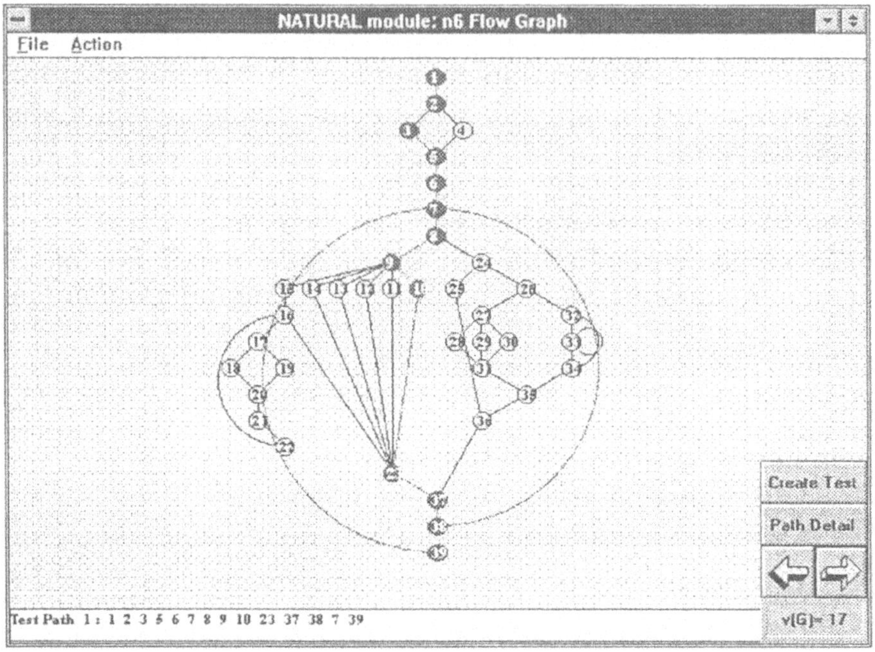

Figure 3. Sample test path applying on the flow graph

♦ File Transfer Software

The uploading and downloading of files between UNIX and PC are carried out with the help of typical FTP programs. Both operations are automated through executing upload and download script files.

♦ Error Report Analyzer

The module resides on the PC platform and provides analysis and summary of execution errors in the different test runs. The main report from the analyzer is an execution summary report. The report contains a line by line error summary of the test program. The format of the report is as given in figure 4.

Execution Summary Report

Total Number of Test Paths =32

Source Statement Number	Last Tested #test	Number of items exercise	Error Message if any
1	8	5	Nil
2	2	2	divide by zero

Figure 4. A Sample Execution Summary Report

4. CONCLUSION AND FUTURE DEVELOPMENT

A prototype for automating the coverage testing process has been implemented and tested with 35 NATURAL programs of various sizes. Overall it has been found to be extremely useful and can in effect be used to reduce some of the workload of program testers. There are still many problems needed to be resolved before the tool can become operational. On the more fundamental issues:

- The arbitrary way of setting the conditions in the decision constructs is debatable. A proper way is to derive input data from output requirements for each test path.
- The lexical analyzer at present has difficulty in recognizing multi-words keywords such as AT END OF DATA.. etc. (keywords are also embedded).

Other issues include:

- Line crossing in flow graph is difficult to handle and should be avoided.
- The lexical analysis is a time-consuming process because of the large vocabulary of NATURAL.

Future work should look at ways of deriving input test data automatically for each test path. The ability to detect features such as the existence of dead code will be most useful.

ACKNOWLEDGEMENT

We would like to thank Mr. Wilson Hau for his asistance on this paper.

REFERENCES

1. Beizer, B.: 'Software System Testing and Quality Assurance', (Van Nostrand Reinhold, 1984)
2. McCabe, T.J. and Schulmeyer, G.G.: 'System Testing Aided by Structured Analysis - A Practical Experience', *IEEE Proceedings of COMPSAC*, pp.522-8, 1982
3. McCabe, T.J.: 'Structured Testing: A Testing Methodology Using the McCabe Complexity Metric', NBS Special Publication, 1982, pp.82-119
4. McCabe T.J.: 'A Complexity Measure', *IEEE Trans. on Software Engineering*, December 1976, pp.308-20,
5. McCabe, T.J., Young, L.F., Calybaugh, K.W., and McManus, J.: 'Design Basis Paths: A Complexity Driven Design Inspection Methodology', *Proceedings of the Total Systems Reliability Symposium*, 1983, pp.67-72

45

Analysis of Data Collected from Software Development Case Studies

Robin Hunter

Department of Computer Science, University of Strathclyde, Richmond Street, Glasgow,UK.

Abstract

The ESPRIT project, SCOPE, on software product evaluation, collected data from 27 case studies in order to experiment with and evaluate software assessment modules. Data from 14 of the case studies was transferred to a central database held at the University of Strathclyde. Data in the database belonging to individual case studies was analysed in a number of ways within the SCOPE project, and a limited amount of analysis across the case studies was also performed. Since the project was completed, further analysis has been performed across the case studies with the aid of the database's SQL interface. The paper describes some of the results obtained and points to how further useful analysis might be performed.

Keyword Codes: D.2.8
Keywords: Metrics

1 INTRODUCTION

The SCOPE (Software CertificatiOn Project for Europe) was an ESPRIT project funded by the European Community from 1989 until 1993. The Project was led by Verilog, a software tool developer based in Toulouse, France. There were eleven other partners and four associate partners involved in the project from a total of eight European countries. One of the partners was the University of Strathclyde in Glasgow. The Computer Science Department in the University was involved in the project from a Software Engineering point of view, while the Law School in the University was involved in legal aspects of the project. The SCOPE database, which will be discussed in this paper, was also developed (in conjunction with other partners) at Strathclyde.

The SCOPE project was concerned with software *product* evaluation for certification. Thus it contrasted with (and complemented) other concurrent projects such as the UK based TickIT project based on the application of ISO 9001[7] to the software process, and the work of the SPICE (Software Process Improvement and Capability dEtermination) Project based on the work of the US Software Engineering Institute and its Capability Maturity Model[5].

The approach taken by the SCOPE project was based on the Software Product Standard ISO 9126[8] which identified six quality characteristics for software products viz Portability, Efficiency, Reliability, Functionality, Usability and Maintainability. Prior to SCOPE, the main initiatives concerning software product quality were compiler validation which was based on language standards, and the German Gutegemeinschaft Software scheme based on the German Standard DIN 66 285(now ISO 12119)[9]. This scheme provided a basic assessment of the functionality of software packages mainly to ensure that the package description (required by the Standard) accurately described the behaviour of the software.

SCOPE was more ambitious than either of these schemes in that it was concerned with quality characteristics other than functionality. It was also modular in its approach, in that it defined stand alone modules that were able to assess a particular quality characteristic, to a particular level, by a particular method.

2 ASSESSMENT MODULES

The SCOPE assessment modules were mostly of one of three forms: modules based on static analysis, modules based on dynamic analysis, modules based on predefined check-lists.

2.1 Modules based on Static Analysis

These modules used results obtained by measuring source code statically (ie without running it). Two static analysers were used, Logiscope[12] and QUALMS[13], Logiscope evaluated a range of metrics from Halstead and McCabes' metrics to call graph metrics and certain types of user-defined metrics. QUALMS was mainly concerned with control graph metrics. Data from the static analysers was used in connection with the derivation of evaluation modules for quality characteristics such as maintainability and functionality.

2.2 Modules based on Dynamic Analysis

Two types of modules were developed based on dynamic analysis. One type was for reliability modelling and the other dealt with test coverage. Our understanding of reliability differed somewhat from that of ISO 9126. We used the generic definition of reliability being *the probability that a software system would not fail in a given period under a given usage.* Using this definition reliability may be predicted with the aid of a reliability growth model of which there are a number available. The project made use of a commercially available product (details in acknowledgement at end of paper) which chooses, on the basis of best fit so far, which of nine models should be used to predict the future reliability of a system.

Test coverage was chosen as a measure of functionality and a number of code coverage measures were defined. It was realised that, this type of data would be most easily collected by means of a dynamic analysis tool with capabilities such as Logiscope provides, integrated with its static analysis capabilities.

2.3 Modules based on check-lists

Many of the evaluation modules were based on check-lists supported by a check-list manager tool used by the project. Initially most of the check-lists were developed by a single partner for a single case study. However towards the end of the project there was a merging of ideas and a number of check-lists were produced which represented the consensus view of the project as a whole, being in many cases, amalgams of existing checklists.

3 THE CASE STUDIES

The SCOPE evaluation modules were experimented with, validated and refined through 27 software development case studies monitored in eight European countries. The data collected from the case studies was analysed locally and/or centrally at the University of Strathclyde.

4 DATA COLLECTION AND STORAGE

4.1 Data collection

SCOPE was fortunate to have two phases, the first one of 18 months (March 89 - September 90) and the second one of 34 months (October 90 - June 93). Six of the case studies were in phase 1 thus the project had the opportunity to experiment with data collection in phase 1 and to try and 'get it right' in phase 2.

A number of lessons were learnt from phase 1[10].

- different tools can give different values for the same measurement
- naming software product parts is not trivial
- data required is often held by tools, making manual collection redundant

4.2 Data transfer

In many cases data had to be transferred from a software development or analysis tool to a central repository. In practice a stream of metrics were transferred at a time and a simple interface language was defined to represent such a stream.

4.3 Data storage

In phase 1 of SCOPE the repository used for the data held centrally was a relational database with an object-oriented interface developed by the REQUEST Project[3]. This was successful, but in phase 2 the use of a simple relational data base was attractive in that it would be more portable, would offer a more usable SQL interface for exploratory investigations, and would be more likely to be compatible with other software data collection initiatives.

Along with the database were developed, with the aid of the Unix compiler tools, simple routines for transferring metric data streams to and from the database.The metrics mainly comprised static analysis metrics, code coverage metrics and reliability data

5 DATA ANALYSIS

5.1 Analysis performed for individual case studies

It is not possible to describe all the analysis performed by SCOPE partners and their case study providers on individual case studies. One case study used the inter-failure times of the most serious failures from failure data describing 1010 failures, to identify the 'best fit' reliability growth model using the reliability module already described. The model identified in this case was the Goel-Okumoto model[2]. Other investigations involved seeking correlations between metrics collected for a particular case study. Test coverage data for one case study, for example, was found to correlate with McCabe's metric[11], depth of nesting and largest prime metrics.

5.2 Analysis performed centrally

Certain basic checks were performed on case study data when it as transferred to the central site. These were mainly to ensure consistency of data and to catch any obvious 'problems'. In addition, static metrics were analysed to detect anomalies, as well as for indicators of structuredness, maintainability etc.

5.3 Analysis performed across case studies during SCOPE

A number of simple comparisons across the case studies were made centrally. Five case studies provided both Logiscope and Qualms metrics, three provided only Logiscope metrics and five case studies only Qualms metrics. Bar graphs and histograms showing characteristics of the various case studies such as mean and maximum values of numbers of statements per module, depth of nesting, values of various complexity metrics were produced for all the case studies for which data was available. These were produced mainly to identify case studies with anomalous values of these metrics compared with the case studies as a whole.

5.4 Analysis performed after the end of SCOPE

Just before the end of SCOPE the database was 'sanitised' in order that none of the data in the data base, or results from it which might later be published, could be traced to the original supplier of the data. In particular, program names, identifier names etc. were all replaced by symbols of no mnemonic significance. Some exploratory analysis of the data has been performed at the University of Strathclyde and in this section we describe the work done so far. It falls into a number of categories.

visual browsing: Visual browsing was used to confirm the reasonableness of the data, for example that the total number of operands was never less than the number of distinct operands. It was also used to look for possible correlations deserving further investigation.

effect of language on metric values: Some simple analysis was performed to look for correlations between particular metric values and the source language in which the software was written. No such correlations were found.

Halstead's metrics : Halstead's length metric is known [1] not to correlate well with the actual length of a source code program or module. Analysis of the Case Studies confirmed this lack of correlation.

browsing with SQL: SQL proved to be a powerful tool in detecting anomalies and possible correlations in the database. For example it was easy to show that our two static analysers did not always produce consistent results as has been shown by Hunter and Roper[6], where it was concluded that the inconsistencies stemmed from inadequate definitions of the metrics, rather than from deficencies in the tools themselves.

6 CONCLUSIONS

We have tried to identify some of the issues involved in implementing a simple metrics database. We feel that some of the issues are not generally appreciated and it is not surprising that few such databases currently exist. SCOPE was successful in setting up a database containing a large number of source code metrics by paying close attention to the issues of data collection, data transfer and data analysis described earlier. In particular the use of SQL as a browsing tool is advocated in situations where it is not known in advance what types of analysis will be performed. A database of the type described might be used industrially to predict size, cost and other attributes of a software product to be developed, based on comparisons of known attributes of previously developed software products and the new product to be produced. It is from exploratory analysis of the type described in this paper that useful predictors, perhaps specific to a particular environment, may be found.

Acknowledgements

The contributions of the following towards the data capture, transfer and storage work of the SCOPE project at the University of Strathclyde is gratefully acknowledged: Paul Carson, Stephen Church, Kenneth Kirkwood, Martin Neil, Andrew Rae and Marc Roper.The support of Reliability and Statistical Consultants Ltd, Surrey, UK in supplying their reliability programs under special terms is also gratefully acknowledged.

REFERENCES

1. Bache, R. and Bazzana, G.: 'Software Metrics for Software Assessment', (McGraw Hill, 1994)
2. Goel, A. L. and Okumoto, K.: 'Time-dependent error-detection rate model for software reliability and other performance measures', *IEEE Trans. Reliability*, 1979
3. Dale, C.: 'The REQUEST Database for Software Reliability and Software Development Data', *4th annual ESPRIT conference*, Brussels, 1987
4. Halstead, M.: 'Elements of Software Science', (Elsevier North Holland, 1977)
5. Humphrey, W. S.: 'Managing the Software Process', (Addison Wesley, 1989)
6. Hunter, R. B. and Roper, R. M. F.: 'Standardisation of Source Code Metrics', *EUROMETRICS91*, Paris, 1991
7. ISO 9001, 'Quality Systems, Model for Quality Assurance in Design/Development, Installation and Servicing', (International Standards Organisation, 1987)
8. ISO 9126, 'Software Product Evaluation - Quality Characteristics and Guide-lines for their Use', (International Standards Organisation, 1987)
9. ISO 12119, 'Information Technology-Software Packages - Quality requirements and testing', (International Standards Organisation, 1994)
10. Kirkwood, K. B., Hunter, R. B. and Rae, A. K.: 'Experiences of Automated Data Collection from Software Development Projects', *Proceedings of the IFIP WG 5.4 Conference on Approving Software Products(ASP 90)*, Garmisch-Partenkirchen, published by North Holland, 1990
11. McCabe, T. J.: 'A Complexity Measure', *IEEE Trans. in Software Engineering*, vol 2, 1976
12. Verilog; Logiscope Technical Presentation, Toulouse, 1989
13. Wilson. L. and Leelasena. L.: The QUALMS program documentation, Alvey project SE/69, South Bank Polytechnic, London, 1988

46

A Framework for Software Development Technical Reviews

Lesley Pek Wee Kim [a], Chris Sauer [b], and Ross Jeffery [c]

[a] School of Computer Science and Engineering
[b] Fujitsu Centre, Australian Graduate School of Management
[c] School of Information Systems

The University of New South Wales, Sydney 2052, Australia.

Abstract

Reviews are seen as an important aid to achieving high quality software. But, there is considerable variance in the literature. Three seminal review types – Fagan's inspection, Freedman and Weinburg's technical review, and Yourdon's structured walkthrough are briefly described. A framework is presented to identify core features and variants. The core components represent an implicit normative theory of reviews; the variants indicate possible variations to the theory. There are indications emerging that this theory may be flawed. This framework provides a foundation from which to empirically test the core components of the theory and its variants.

Keyword Codes: D.2, D.2.0, D.2.9
Keywords: software engineering, quality, inspection, structured walkthrough, technical review.

1. INTRODUCTION

Software engineering is said to be 'a strategy for producing quality software' [5]. It is widely agreed that the traditional approach of defect testing just before product delivery is far too late [1], especially if we consider the popular 6Σ characterisation of quality which translates to approximately 3 to 4 defects per million lines of code [8]. The software review technique is seen as a method of removing errors throughout the software life cycle. The literature offers competing prescriptions. These prescriptions appear to be similar in a number of basic features, but detailed examination reveals many differences. It is possible that these variations complicate the application of reviews within organisations. Moreover, researchers in the field have no common ground on which to base their research because it is not clear what is essential and what is inessential in the differing prescriptions. This paper attempts to build a framework to remedy this by analysing three seminal review types. Section 2 summarises each of the review types. Section 3 describes the SDTR (Software Development Technical Reviews) framework, via the common and different characteristics of the review types. Finally, we conclude the paper by outlining the contributions of this framework, and giving suggestions for future research in the area.

2. THE THREE REVIEW TYPES

Three major review types stand out in the literature: Fagan's inspection (FI), Freedman and Weinburg's technical review (FWTR), and Yourdon's structured walkthrough (YSW). They have been selected for their completeness and high volume of citation. This section summarises them.

2.1 Fagan's Inspection

Fagan's inspection (1972) can be tailored to control any software quality attribute [9]. Major claimed quantitative benefits are error detection, cost effectiveness, productivity, software quality, predictability, and information on development operations. Nonquantitative benefits include better service to users, and a professional development environment.

Among recommendations for the structure of FI, an important part is the presence of a good moderator [1,2]. Each of the other reviewers plays a role: author, reader, or tester. Management's presence in meetings need not adversely affect review outcomes, but reviews should not be used for staff appraisal [2]. Recommended FI team size is 4, but can vary with the review object. Prescriptions for reviewer training are also given [1]. The inspection process can be divided into six operations [1]: *planning* (moderator plans the meeting), *overview* (meeting for product education, document distribution, role assignment), *preparation* (reviewer preparation), *inspection* (meeting for defect finding, reader paraphrases the object), *rework* (error correction), and *follow-up* (moderator ensures proper rework, determines need for reinspection).

The FI process thus consists of pre-inspection activities, the FI meeting, and post-inspection activities. It contains at least one meeting, the aim of which is to find defects only [1]. Error classes and checklists assist reviewing. The FI process must have a well-defined software development process, and a proper description and execution of FI at each stage. FI serves to detect errors, provides error control, and provides feedback to the producer. It was first devised for design and code, but can be tailored for any development product. Specification, design changes, unit test, test case, and documentation [2] can also be inspected. The meeting duration should be a maximum of 2 hours [2]. The physical outputs are reports on defects, and meeting details. They are detailed and of fixed formats, and enable management to perform statistical analysis of the reviews. A database exists to record defect classes [1]. Other matters discussed include starting inspections, defect definitions, prerequisites for using FI, and inspection scheduling.

2.2 Freedman and Weinburg's Technical Review

The claimed quantitative benefits are the detection and correction of errors, reduction of errors reaching testing stage, and reduction in maintenance costs. Nonquantitative benefits claimed include providing management with reliable technical information for project control, education for reviewers, communication between reviewers, and favourable effects and appreciation on staff competence.

The structure of FWTR includes role assignments: review leader, recorder, and reviewers. Two types of roles are not differentiated in the literature: project and meeting roles. A *project role* relates to project responsibilities (eg designer). A *meeting role* relates to meeting responsibilities (eg moderator). Hence FWTR has meeting roles only and has no reader or presenter. Managers usually do not participate in meetings [3]. It is not specified whether FWTR can be used for staff evaluation. Team size should be kept small (minimum 2). The same team should be used throughout a project [3]. No formal reviewer training is mentioned (except for review leader); reviewers are best trained by experience [3]. The FWTR process consists of pre-FWTR activities (planning, preparation), meeting activities, and post-FWTR activities (report production and distribution). Review aids exist for the review leader and recorder [3,5]. Anything tangible used in software development can be reviewed [3]. A review object can be broken down by form (seeking different perspectives on the same material) and by function (breaking it into smaller pieces) [3,5]. The meeting should last 2 hours maximum[3]. A review summary report, issues list (addressed by producer), and the related issues report are produced. The latter two are kept in the history file. Recommendations are given on the use of history file [3,5]. Other matters discussed include error explanations, scheduling [3,5], starting reviews, and physical recorder placement.

2.3 Yourdon's Structured Walkthrough

Yourdon's structured walkthrough is viewed as a natural complement to the software structured development techniques [8]. The purpose is to get a group of people from roughly the same level to scrutinise a piece of work from different perspectives. The review is 'structured' so that it may be conducted in an organised way. The stated YSW quantitative benefits are error detection and establishment of standards [8]. Nonquantitative benefits claimed are providing training to staff and 'insurance'[8] for incomplete work (more chance to salvage work when someone leaves the project).

YSW requires project and meeting roles: presenter, coordinator, secretary/scribe, maintenance oracle, standards bearer, user representative, and outsider [8]. Team size should be 5 or 6 [8]. No reviewer training is mentioned. Yourdon discusses the psychological games played in walkthroughs and how they affect the outcome [5,8]. Yourdon also provides guidelines for forming programming teams [5,8]. Management roles and staff performance evaluation are also discussed [8]. The overall structure of the YSW process consists of pre-YSW activities (planning, preparation), meeting activities, and post-YSW activities (report production, error correction). Analysis, design and code guidelines are tailored for structured methods only. Standards are used to aid reviews. YSW objects are either product-related, or operational prototypes [8]. The meeting should be 30 minutes minimum, and 2 hours maximum [8]. Outputs consist of a public meeting summary, and an action list (addressed by producer) [8]. Other matters discussed include the varying degrees of formality of YSW [5,8], cases when YSW are not worthwhile [5,8], use of structured methodologies, prescriptions for reviewers' responsibilities, and defects.

3. THE SDTR FRAMEWORK

The existing literature on reviews consists of many publications originating mostly from the three review types we have described [1–3,6,8,10–16]. The major purpose of this paper then is to expose the principles underlying these review types. We accomplish this by scrutinising the literature in search of their core similarities and differences. The resulting SDTR framework consists of a dichotomy of review features: *key features* (common to the three review types) and *significant variations* (differing in at least one of the three review types).

The framework does not purport to say what reviews should be, nor does it capture all the existing knowledge on reviews. Rather, it seeks to specify the features that are agreed on by the major writers and which might be deemed essential to successful reviews. It also identifies areas of significant disagreement which could be expected to influence the choice of review type by a developer.

3.1 The Components of the SDTR Framework

One of the major contributions of the SDTR framework is to organise and structure the existing knowledge on reviews. Review characteristics can be categorised as follows: *review aims and benefits* which list the claimed aims and benefits of reviews; *human elements* which describe the human aspects of reviews; *review process* which describes the overall review process; *review output* which describes the physical outputs from a review process; and *other matters* which covers anything else. These components are not necessarily mutually exclusive, and do not impose constraints on assembling new review types.

3.2 Key Features and Variations of SDTR

In this section, we discuss for each SDTR component, the key features (in italics), followed by the possible variations reviews can take. Table 1 lists the key features and the major variations using the SDTR components.

<u>Review Aims and Benefits</u>

A review is used to improve the quality of software. It is agreed that the major aim of reviews is to improve the quality of software. The key quantitative benefit is that all reviews aim for error detection.

Variations to the quantitative benefits are error correction, reduction in cost of testing, reduction in maintenance costs, improved predictability and productivity, and the establishment of standards [1–3,5,6,8]. Next, *a review has nonquantitative benefits.* It is agreed that nonquantitative benefits exist, but there is no agreement on a key nonquantitative benefit. This need not be that the authors totally disagree; rather they place different emphases on what they perceive reviews should be. Variations to the nonquantitative benefits include providing reliable technical information for project control, reviewer education and communication, improving staff competence, providing management staff appreciation, creating better service to users, creating a more professional development environment, providing training to staff, and the ability to salvage incomplete work due to staff changes [1–3,5,6,8].

Aims/Benefits	Human Elements	Review Process	Review Outputs	Other Matters
		keys:		
–software quality by error detection –some intangible benefits	–moderator –roles	–meetings –review process, aids –variety of objects –max. meeting duration	–report production	
		variations:		
–*quantitative benefits:* error correction cost effectiveness predictability productivity establish standards –*nonquantitative benefits:* project control education, training staff competence service to users professionalism job recovery	–moderator tasks –role varieties,types –team size –driver of meeting –training needs –management involvement –staff evaluation –team formation	–number of meetings per review process –process variability –break down of objects –types of review aids –software process control	–types of reports –report contents –use of reports or history file –formats of reports	–defect definitions –review prerequisites –physical placement of reviewers –criteria for success –starting reviews –review scheduling –when not to have reviews

Table 1: The SDTR Framework – Key Features and Variations

Human Elements

A review must have a moderator or equivalent role. Each review type has a person responsible for the organisation and conduct of reviews (FI moderator, FWTR review leader, YSW coordinator). The variations lie in the moderator's tasks and task distribution. The FWTR review leader's tasks are similar to the FI moderator except that the recording is performed separately. The YSW recorder (secretary) produces the reports. Thus, the recording and report production are performed by either the moderator or recorder. *Each reviewer must be assigned a role for the review meeting.* Project and meeting roles are not differentiated. The authors agree that role assignment is essential in reviews. The variations lie in the variety of roles for each review type and the type of role represented (meeting or project role). Yourdon recommends three meeting roles. FWTR and FI have two meeting roles respectively.

One review variation is the review team size (4 for FI, at least 2 for FWTR, and 5 or 6 for YSW). The optimal team size is unknown. The driver of the FI meeting (absent in FWTR) is the author and the sequence of review discussions depends on this role. The equivalent YSW role is the presenter, whose task is to introduce the project. It is not clear to what extent the YSW presenter drives the meeting. Training requirements differ with review types. FI reviewers' training needs vary with roles;

FWTR reviewers train by experience; and the training issue is not mentioned in YSW. There is some agreement that line supervisors should not be present at reviews. However, management can gain useful information depending on the distribution of reports. Yourdon suggests using reviews for staff evaluation. Fagan advises against it. The attitude of FI management and their acceptance of FI are important for success. Fagan also indicates when management is permitted to attend review meetings. Freedman and Weinburg, and Yourdon discuss the importance of using the same team for a project, over a period of time, for building effective teams.

Review Process

A review process must contain at least one meeting. A meeting is a formal physical gathering of people to carry out some common tasks. It requires some planning and organisation to ensure smooth running. The FI process contains up to two meetings: overview and review meetings (sometimes the overview is optional). The FWTR and YSW processes have one meeting only. *A review process consists of a meeting, and pre- and post-review activities.* The basic structure of all reviews consists of a meeting whereby reviewers agree on the set of errors present in the review object. The review meeting and the pre- and post-review activities make up the review process. The activities can change with the review object. *A review process has aids to assist reviewers.* For FI, error type checklists and frequently occurring errors are used. FWTR reviewer aids are more to help reviewers be good reviewers. YSW reviewer aids include standards, and recommendations for each role's responsibilities. *A review process is applicable to various software development objects.* However the objects suggested by the authors are different. The two types of YSW objects are operational prototypes, and product-related objects. FI objects are all product-related, whereas YSW and FWTR include operational prototypes. Variations include ways to break up an object. *A review meeting usually lasts a maximum of two hours.* It is agreed that a meeting should last 2 hours maximum. Only Yourdon recommends a minimum of half an hour.

A significant variation on the review process is in the use of reports to analyse review performance. Fagan recommends the use of statistical analysis on review data to improve future review processes. Freedman and Weinburg have similar ideas on review feedback and present practical advice on how the history file can be used [5]. Yourdon does not present any of these ideas.

Review Output

A review has as its output two or more reports. The report is central to the output of any review. It provides information that can be used to control software development. The variations in the reports lie in their contents, formats, and use. The review summary reports are usually of a fixed format and for management use. There is little consensus on report contents and why they are needed.

Other Matters

There is no obvious key feature in this category. However the variations are many. Defect definitions differ with review types. A defect in FI is an instance where the requirements and the exit criteria are violated. The standards against which errors in FWTR and YSW are considered are unknown. Yourdon implies that some defects are subjective (design) and are influenced by underlying assumptions. The prerequisites for each review type differ. FI requires well-defined development stages and entry/exit criteria to control the start/end of inspections. No prerequisites exist for FWTR, but YSW requires the use of structured development methodologies. Reviewers' placement is only discussed by Freedman and Weinburg (the recorder should be visible to everyone). FI's scheduling estimates are for systems programming only. No estimates are given for FWTR; Yourdon discusses some scheduling factors. Recommendations for starting reviews are varied. FI checklists can be developed from initial inspections. Freedman and Weinburg also give some tips for starting reviews [3]. Yourdon does not discuss it. Lastly, Yourdon discusses cases when it is not worthwhile having reviews.

4. CONCLUSIONS

The SDTR framework identifies key features and differences among the seminal review types. The key features form the core of a normative theory of reviews. However, this theory (including the variations) is not as yet well tested. The theoretical status of the variations is less clear. Since they are not common to all review types, any given variation will be regarded as unnecessary by the proponents of the other review types. The categorisation of review attributes provides a foundation from which research can be conducted.

Systematic research of this kind is warranted for three reasons. First, there is limited knowledge of the actual performance of the three review types, and no substantial basis for comparison. Second, results from the study of group decision-making, highlight elements of reviews which are worthy of attention [19,20]. Third, Votta et al [17,18] have begun to explore alternative approaches to inspections with encouraging results. The SDTR framework provides the basis for a sound understanding of the value of the elements of the core normative theory and its variants.

REFERENCES

1. Fagan M. E., 'Advances in software inspections', *IEEE Transactions on Software Engineering*, Vol SE–12(7), 1986.
2. Fagan M. E., 'Design and code inspections to reduce errors in program development', *IBM Systems Journal*, Vol 15(3), 1979.
3. Freedman D. P., Weinburg G. M., Handbook of walkthroughs, inspections and technical reviews: evaluating programs, projects, and products, 3rd (Ed), Little, Brown and Company, 1982.
4. Pflegeer S. L., Software engineering: the production of quality software, 2nd (Ed), Macmillan, 1991.
5. Kim L. P. W., Sauer C., Jeffery R., 'A critical survey of software development technical reviews a non–method specific approach to sofware quality assurance', ITRC Report #94/34, School of Information Systems, University of New South Wales, Apr 1994.
6. Weinburg G. M., Freedman D. P., 'Reviews, walkthroughs, and inspections', *IEEE Transactions on Software Engineering*, Vol SE–10(1), Jan 1984.
7. Yourdon E., 'Quality: what it means and how to achieve it', *MIS*, Feb 1993.
8. Yourdon E., Structured Walkthroughs, 4th (Ed), Yourdon Press, 1989.
9. Boehm et al B., Characteristics of software quality, New York, American Elsevier, 1978.
10. Myers G. J., 'A controlled experiment in program testing and code walkthroughs/inspections', *Communications of ACM*, Sep 1978.
11. Parnas D. L., Weiss D. M., 'Active design reviews: principles and practices', *Journal of Systems and Software*, Vol 7, pp 259–265, 1987.
12. Reeve J. T., 'Applying the Fagan inspection technique', Quality Forum, Vol 17(1), Mar 1991.
13. Russell G. W., 'Experience with inspection in ultra large–scale developments', *IEEE Software*, pp25–31, Jan 1991.
14. Bush M., 'Improving software quality: the use of formal inspections at the Jet Propulsion Laboratory', *IEEE*, pp196–198, 1990.
15. Doolan E. P., 'Experience with Fagan's inspection method', Software – Practice and Experience, Vol 22(2), pp173–182, Feb 1992.
16. Weller E. F., 'Lessons from three years of inspection data', *IEEE Software*, pp38–45, Sep 1993.
17. Votta L. G. Jr., 'Does every inspection need a meeting ?', *SIGSOFT'93*, Dec 1993.
18. Porter L. G., Votta L. G., 'An experiment to assess different defect detection methods for software requirements inspections', forthcoming.
19. Levine R. E., Moreland R. L., 'Progress in small group research', Annual Review of Psychology, Vol(1), pp585–634, 1990.
20. ME Shaw, Group dynamics: the psychology of small group behaviour, McGraw–Hill, 1981.

47

A Model-based Approach for Software Test Process Improvement

Lin Lian[a], Fusayuki Fujita[b], Shinji Kusumoto[a], Ken-ichi Matsumoto[c], Tohru Kikuno[a] and Koji Torii[c]

[a]Department of Information and Computer Sciences, Faculty of Engineering Science, Osaka University, 1-3 Machikaneyama, Toyonaka, Osaka 560, JAPAN

[b]Software Laboratory, Sharp Corporation, Nara, JAPAN

[c]Nara Institute of Science and Technology, 8916-5 Takayama, Ikoma, Nara 630-01, JAPAN

Abstract

Reducing the effort or cost of testing is a key issue to high productivity in software development. This paper proposes a test process model which aims to grasp the current status of test processes and to provide several metrics to evaluate efficiency of test processes in order to construct the process improvement plan. The model defines test process as an iterated process of four kinds of hypotheses development and verification which deal with: correctness of the program to be tested, location of failure, location of faults, and correction of the faults, respectively. The analysis results of experimental data collected from the test process show the validity of the proposed model and usefulness of the metrics.

Keyword Codes: D.2.5; D.2.8
Keywords: Software Engineering, Testing and Debugging; Software Engineering, Metrics.

1. INTRODUCTION

There are numerous research studies towards the improvement of software development process[1][2]. Basili and Rombach have proposed *Goal/Question/Metric paradigm* (simply called *G/Q/M paradigm*) in the *TAME* project[1]. The *G/Q/M paradigm* has a mechanism to describe explicitly the relation between the goal, to be achieved in the process, and the metric to be applied to the process. Humphrey has proposed SEI Software Process Maturity Self-Assessment[2]. Based on a *process maturity model*, SEI Self-Assessment builds a consensus view of an organization's maturity and the key issues facing it. Then ultimately it presents an improvement plan for software development process endorsed by general management.

The importance of the following key attributes (a)-(c) is commonly stressed in these proposals for the improvement of software development process: (a) software development process is strictly defined, (b) for each activity, quality data are collected and analyzed statistically, and (c) based on the analysis result, improvement of each activity is executed.

This paper proposes a test process model which aims to grasp the current status of test processes and to provide several metrics to evaluate efficiency of test processes in order to construct the test process improvement plan. The key idea of the proposed model is to define test process as an iterated process of four kinds of hypotheses development and verification that deal with (1)correctness of the program to be tested, (2)location of failure, (3)location of faults (that is cause of the failure), and (4)correction of the faults, respectively. Then, we apply the proposed model and metrics to test process in an academic environment.

2. HYPOTHESIS-BASED DEBUGGING

Test process consists of two sub-processes[3]: testing and debugging. Testing is the process of analyzing a software item to detect the differences between existing and required conditions [1] and to evaluate the features of the software items. Debugging is the process to detect, locate, and correct faults [3].

There are two general approaches to debugging: induction and deduction [4]. The inductive approach first formulates a single working hypothesis and then proves or disproves it based on data and the analysis of the data; while the deductive approach begins by enumerating all possible causes or hypotheses and then rules out particular causes one by one until a single one remains for validation.

Araki et al. proposed debugging process model based on deductive debugging approach [5]. They consider debugging process as the process of locating and correcting errors in a program in which errors[2] have been detected. In locating the errors and grasping their causes, programmers develop hypotheses about the errors and their causes, and verify or refute these hypotheses by examining the program. In correcting the errors, programmers again develop hypotheses about how to modify the program and verify or refute them.

3. TEST PROCESS MODEL

3.1. Hypothesis-based approach

We propose a hypothesis-based test process model as shown in Figure 1. In this model, we assume that test data set to be used is given, and test process is completed when we obtain the program finally, which executes what the specification of the program requires for the test data set, in inductive approach.

The model consists of two subprocesses; *testing* and *debugging*, and both of them are further divided into two primitive activities: *Hypothesis Development* and *Hypothesis Verification.*

The Hypothesis Development is an activity to formulate a single working hypothesis by

[1] In this paper, we follow the IEEE standard [3] with respect to the definition of error and fault. In the IEEE standard, an error is defined as a human action that results in software which contains a fault. Examples include omission or misinterpretation of user requirements in software specification and incorrect translation or omission of a requirement in the design specification. A fault is defined as a manifestation of an error in software. A fault, if encountered, may cause a failure (synonymous with bug). Thus "the difference between existing and required conditions" correspond to failure.

[2] "Errors" in [5] corresponds to "faults" in the IEEE Standard.

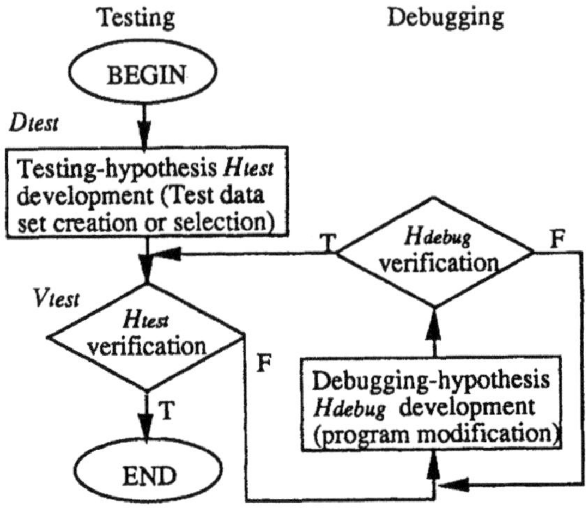

Figure 1: Test Process Model

instantiating *Hypothesis Templates*, i.e., by substituting the parameters of the *Hypothesis Templates* by data. The Hypothesis Verification is an activity to prove or disprove the working hypothesis. In the following part of this section, we shall describe Hypothesis Development and Verification in the test process in detail. Before giving the definition of the test process, we introduce the following notations:

- P: A program to be tested.
- P_0: An ideal program that executes correctly required specification.
- T: A set of given test data.
- $t_j \in T$: It is defined to be a sequence of pairs space (input,output) of P_0: $(i_{j_1}, o_{j_1})(i_{j_2}, o_{j_2})\ldots(i_{j_{n(j)}}, o_{j_{n(j)}})$, where i_{j_r} is the rth input of t_j, o_{j_r} is the rth output corresponding to i_{j_r}, and $n(j)$ is the number of inputs of t_j.
- t_j^P: A sequence of pairs space (input,output) of P. It can be also denoted like t_j: $(i_{j_1}, o_{j_1}^P)(i_{j_2}, o_{j_2}^P)\ldots(i_{j_{n(j)}}, o_{j_{n(j)}}^P)$

3.2. Testing subprocess

Testing is a process that checks if program P executes correctly required specification or not for each element of T.

Definition 1: Testing subprocess is verification of hypothesis:

$$H_{test}: \quad (\forall t_j \in T(1 \leq j \leq |T|))\ t_j^P = t_j$$

where

$$t_j^P = t_j \text{ iff } (\forall l,\ 1 \leq l \leq n(j))\ o_{j_l}^P = o_{j_l} \text{ (See Figure 2).}$$

Testing-hypothesis Template:

$$HT_{test}(\rho): \quad (\forall t_j \in T(1 \leq j \leq |T|))\ t_j^\rho = t_j$$

where ρ is a parameter which is a program to be tested. And a working hypothesis for the testing is defined as $HT_{test}(P)$ where P is a program to be tested. We denote $HT_{test}(P)$ development by D_{test} and $HT_{test}(P)$ verification by V_{test}, respectively (See Figure 1).

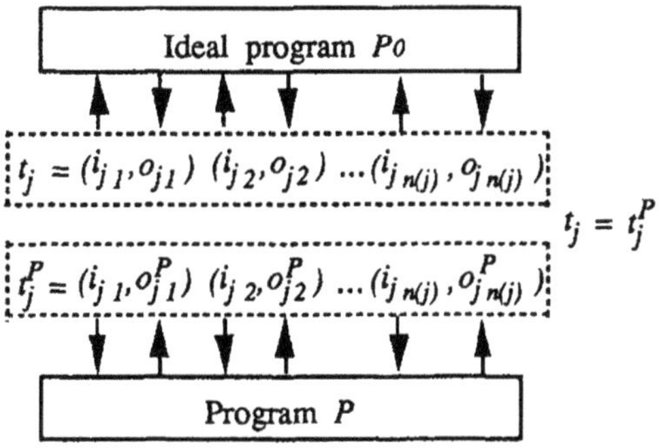

Figure 2: Testing-hypothesis H_{test}

3.3. Debugging subprocess

Debugging process is executed if the working hypothesis $HT_{test}(P)$ is refuted. Debugging is a process that creates a program which could execute correctly required specification for the given test data set T. The program, denoted by P' in this model, is constructed by modifying P.

Definition 2: Debugging subprocess is verification of hypothesis:

$H_{debug} : (\exists P')t_\tau^{P'} = t_\tau$.

In general, in order to construct P', several activities have to be done. In this model, debugging is further divided into the following three subprocesses: (1) Failure location, (2) Fault location, and (3) Fault correction. Each of them is defined as an iterated process of hypothesis development and verification, and has a hypothesis template, respectively (See Figure 3).

(1) Failure location

The failure location is a process that clarifies a statement of the program P which provides incorrect output (or incorrect state of P, e.g., hang up, infinite loop) in the testing.

Definition 3: Failure location is verification of hypothesis:

$H_{fll} : \exists\tau(1 \le \tau \le |T|)\exists o_1(1 \le o_1 \le n(\tau))\exists\sigma_1(1 \le \sigma_1 \le \tau_N)(output(s^P_{\tau_{\sigma_1}}) = o^P_{\tau_{o_1}}, o^P_{\tau_{o_1}} \neq o_{\tau_{o_1}})$.

where $s^P_{\tau_{\sigma_1}}$ is σ_1-th statement of P executed for t_τ. $output(s^P_{\tau_{\sigma_1}})$ is an output of the statement $s^P_{\tau_{\sigma_1}}$ for t_τ (See Figure 4). The value of $output(s^P_{\tau_{\sigma_1}})$ is $NULL$ when $s^P_{\tau_{\sigma_1}}$ is not an output statement.

Failure-location-hypothesis Template:

$HT_{fll}(\tau, o_1, \sigma_1) : output(s^P_{\tau_{\sigma_1}}) = o^P_{\tau_{o_1}}, o^P_{\tau_{o_1}} \neq o_{\tau_{o_1}}$.

where τ, o_1, σ_1 are parameters. τ is a test data number, o_1 is an output number, and σ_1 is a statement execution number of P, respectively. We denote $HT_{fll}(\tau, o_1, \sigma_1)$ development by D_{fll} and $HT_{fll}(\tau, o_1, \sigma_1)$ verification by V_{fll} (See Figure 3).

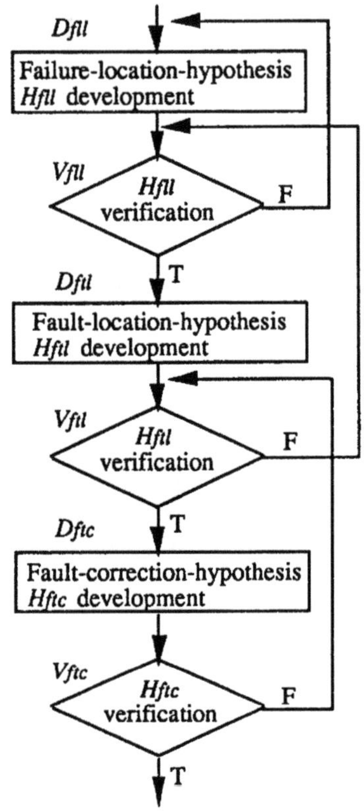

Figure 3: Debugging Process Model

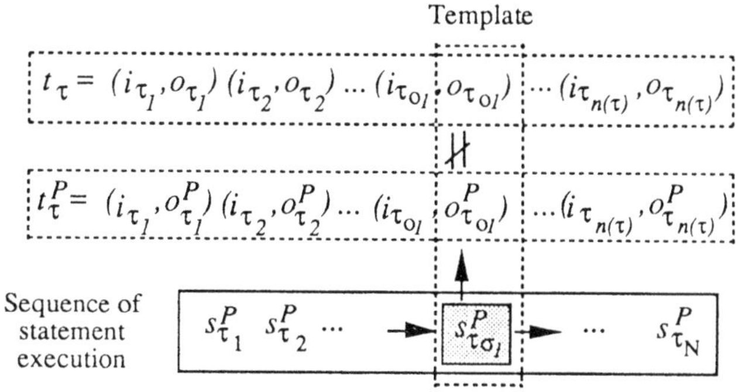

Figure 4: Failure-location-hypothesis H_{fll}

(2) Fault location

A fault is the cause of the failure. And fault location is a process that clarifies statement of the program P which causes incorrect state (an ordered set of internal and/or external variable values) of P during the testing.

Definition 4: Fault location is verification of hypothesis:

$H_{ftl} : (\exists o_2(1 \leq o_2 \leq o_1), \exists \sigma_2(1 \leq \sigma_2 \leq M))\ E^P_{\tau_{\sigma'_1 - 1}} = E_{\tau_{\sigma_2 - 1}}(1 \leq \sigma'_1 \leq \sigma_1), E^P_{\tau_{\sigma'_1}} \neq E_{\tau_{\sigma_2}}$, $output(s^P_{\tau_{\sigma'_1}}) = o^P_{\tau_{o_2}}(1 \leq o_2 \leq o_1), output(s_{\tau_{\sigma_2}}) = o_{\tau_{o_2}}, HT_{fll}(\tau, o_1, \sigma_1)$.

where $s_{\tau_{\sigma_2}}$ is σ_2-th statement of P^0 executed for t_τ. And $E^P_{\tau_{\sigma'_1}}$ and $E_{\tau_{\sigma_2}}$ indicate the state (an ordered set of internal and/or external variable values) of P and P^0 after executing $s^P_{\tau_{\sigma'_1}}$ and $s_{\tau_{\sigma_2}}$ for t_τ, respectively (See Figure 5).

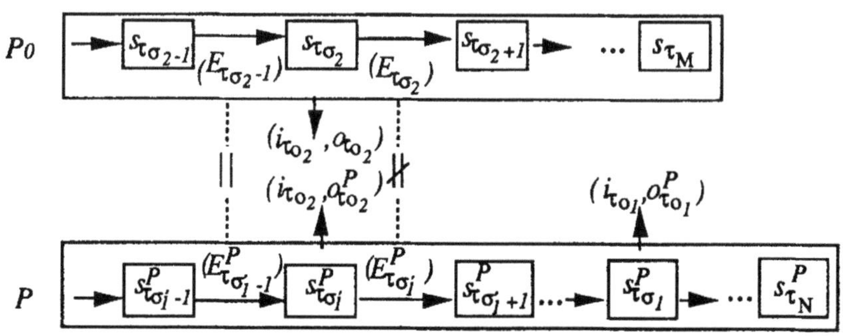

Figure 5: Fault-location-hypothesis H_{ftl}

Fault-location-hypothesis Template:

$HT_{ftl}(\tau, o_1, \sigma_1, o_2, \sigma_2)$: $E^P_{\tau_{\sigma'_1-1}} = E_{\tau_{\sigma_2}-1}(1 < \sigma'_1 \leq \sigma_1), E^P_{\tau_{\sigma'_1}} \neq E_{\tau_{\sigma_2}}, output(s^P_{\tau_{\sigma'_1}}) = o^P_{\tau_{o_2}}(1 < o_2 \leq o_1), output(s_{\tau_{\sigma_2}}) = o_{\tau_{o_2}}, HT_{fll}(\tau, o_1, \sigma_1)$.

where $\tau, o_1, \sigma_1, o_2, \sigma_2$ are parameters. τ, o_1, σ_1 are the same as $HT_{fll}(\tau, o_1, \sigma_1)$, respectively. o_2 is an output number, and σ_2 is a statement execution number of P^0, respectively. We denote $HT_{ftl}(\tau, o_1, \sigma_1, o_2, \sigma_2)$ development by D_{ftl} and $HT_{ftl}(\tau, o_1, \sigma_1, o_2, \sigma_2)$ verification by V_{ftl}, respectively (See Figure 3).

(3) Fault correction

Fault correction is a process that constructs program P' by replacing the faulty part of program P with a complete one.

Definition 5: Fault correction is verification of hypothesis:

H_{ftc} : $(\exists P')\ t^{P'}_\tau = t_\tau, output(s^{P'}_{\tau_{\sigma_3}}) = o_{\tau_{o_1}}(1 \leq \sigma_3 \leq L), E^{P'}_{\tau_{\sigma'_3-1}} = E_{\tau_{\sigma_2}-1}(1 \leq \sigma'_3 \leq \sigma_3), output(s^{P'}_{\tau_{\sigma'_3}}) = o_{\tau_{o_2}}, E^{P'}_{\tau_{\sigma'_3}} = E_{\tau_{\sigma_2}}, HT_{ftl}(\tau, o_1, \sigma_1, o_2, \sigma_2)$.

where $s^{P'}_{\tau_{\sigma_3}}$ is σ_3-th statement of P' executed for t_τ.

Fault-correction-hypothesis Template:

$HT_{ftc}(\tau, o_1, \sigma_1, o_2, \sigma_2, P')$: $t^{P'}_\tau = t_\tau, output(s^{P'}_{\tau_{\sigma_3}}) = o_{\tau_{o_1}}(1 \leq \sigma_3 \leq L), E^{P'}_{\tau_{\sigma'_3-1}} = E_{\tau_{\sigma_2}-1}(1 \leq \sigma'_3 \leq \sigma_3), output(s^{P'}_{\tau_{\sigma'_3}}) = o_{\tau_{o_2}}, E^{P'}_{\tau_{\sigma'_3}} = E_{\tau_{\sigma_2}}, HT_{ftl}(\tau, o_1, \sigma_1, o_2, \sigma_2)$.

where $\tau, o_1, \sigma_1, o_2, \sigma_2, P'$ are parameters. $\tau, o_1, \sigma_1, o_2, \sigma_2$ are the same parameters of $HT_{ftl}(\tau, o_1, \sigma_1, o_2, \sigma_2)$, respectively. P' is a program. We denote $HT_{ftc}(\tau, o_1, \sigma_1, o_2, \sigma_2, P')$ development by D_{ftc} and $HT_{ftc}(\tau, o_1, \sigma_1, o_2, \sigma_2, P')$ verification by V_{ftc} (See Figure 3).

4. METRICS FOR EFFICIENCY OF TEST PROCESS

In this section, we provide several metrics to evaluate efficiency of test processes and then to construct the improvement plan for the processes based on them. The computations of those metrics are based on the following test process parameters.

$\Gamma = D_{test}V_{test}D_{fll}\ldots V_{test}$: Sequence of operations till termination of the test process.

n_α: Number of operation α in Γ, $num(\delta, \Gamma)$: Number of δ in Γ.

The numbers of repetitions of H_{fll}, H_{ftl}, H_{ftc} for correcting a single fault, denoted by HE_{fll}, HE_{ftl} and HE_{ftc} respectively, are computed as follows:

Failure location error rate: $HE_{fll} = \frac{num(V_{fll}D_{fll}, \Gamma)}{n_{V_{test}} - 1}$

Fault location error rate: $HE_{ftl} = \frac{num(V_{ftl}V_{fll}D_{ftl}, \Gamma)}{n_{V_{test}} - 1}$

Fault correction error rate: $HE_{ftc} = \frac{num(V_{ftc}V_{ftl}D_{ftc}, \Gamma)}{n_{V_{test}} - 1}$

We consider that the nearer the values of HE_{fll}, HE_{ftl} and/or HE_{ftc} approximate 0, the higher the testing efficiency is.

Let VE_{fll} be the number of repetitions of V_{fll} and VE_{ftl} the number of repetitions of V_{ftl} respectively for correcting a single fault, they are calculated as follows:

Verification error rate for failure location $VE_{fll} = \frac{num(V_{ftl}V_{fll}D_{fll}, \Gamma)}{n_{V_{test}} - 1}$

Verification error rate for fault location $VE_{ftl} = \frac{num(V_{ftc}V_{ftl}V_{fll}D_{ftl}, \Gamma)}{n_{V_{test}} - 1}$

5. DISCUSSIONS

In order to show the validity of the proposed model and usefulness of the metrics, we apply the model and the metrics to test processes in academic environment[9].

The main characteristics of the test processes in this experiment are: (1) Two graduate students (A and B) designed, implemented and tested a kind of data processing program based on a specification, written by natural language, by using C language. (2) One UNIX workstation was assigned to each of them. While student tested his program, we recorded image on the workstation's display by video camera and VCR, key stroke on the keyboard by *PAM* system [6].

By analyzing image on the display and key stroke on the keyboard, we could obtain a lot of data about the students' activities on testing. From such data, we could know which operation of the model was being performed by the students, and construct the sequence of operations during testing. Almost all parts of the sequence complied with the model. We may, therefore, reasonably conclude that the proposed model can describe the actual test process in student project. We could analyze their test process based on the values of the metrics. Based on results, we advised Student B to use tools for fault location, e.g., program slicing tool *SPYDER* [7], and error-cause-chasing tool *CHASE* [8]. Then, we advised Student A to use tools for fault location mentioned above, and to use some tools supporting fault correction.

REFERENCES

1. BASILI V. R. and ROMBACH H. D.: 'The TAME project: Towards improvement-oriented software environment', *IEEE Trans. Software Eng.*, 1988, Vol.14, (6), pp.758-773.
2. HUMPHREY W.S.: 'Characterizing the software process: A maturity framework', *IEEE Software*, 1988, Vol.5, (2), pp.73-79.
3. 'IEEE Standard Glossary of Software Engineering Terminology', *IEEE, ANSI/IEEE Std 610.12-1990*, 1990.
4. SHOOMAN M. L.: 'Software Engineering', (McGraw-Hill, 1983).
5. ARAKI K., FUKUZAWA Z. and CHENG J.: 'A general framework for debugging', *IEEE Software*, 1991, Vol.8, (3), pp.14-20.
6. TAKADA Y., MATSUMOTO K. and TORII K.: 'A programmer performance measure based on programmer state transitions in testing and debugging process', *Proc. of 16th International Conference on Software Engineering*, May 1994, pp.123-132.
7. AGRAWAL H., DEMILLO R.A. and SPAFFORD E.H.: 'Debugging with dynamic slicing and backtracking', *Software: Practice and Experience*, 1993, Vol.23, (6), pp.589-616.
8. SHIMOMURA T.: 'Bug localization based on error-cause-chasing methods', *Trans. of IPS*, 1993, Vol.34, (3), pp.489-500.
9. FUJITA F.: 'A software testing process model for evaluating capability of testing in software engineers education', *Master Thesis of Osaka University*, March 1994 (in Japanese).

48

Size Estimation for C Programs with Different Applications

Christopher J. Lokan

Department of Computer Science, Australian Defence Force Academy, Canberra, Australia.

Abstract

Cost estimation is an important aspect of the management of software development projects. Most cost estimation models require an estimate of the size of the program to be developed. Accurate size estimation is thus critically important. Earlier work has shown that weighted counts of conceptually unique variables (where each variable is weighted by the number of functions in which it is referenced) are good predictors of the final size of Pascal and C programs. Simple equations using only that information give acceptable accuracy, even across a range of sizes and applications. For Pascal programs, the accuracy is acceptable by the end of high level design; for C programs, it is acceptable by the end of detailed design. In this study, C programs are classified by application, instead of being treated as a single class. Different estimation equations are then used for programs in each class. Overall estimation accuracy improves at each stage of design. A broad classification scheme is sufficient to give estimates of acceptable accuracy by the completion of high level design.

Keyword Codes: D.2.8; K.6.1.
Keywords: Software Engineering, Metrics; Project and People Management.

1 INTRODUCTION

An important aspect of software project management is the assessment and allocation of the resources required during development. Numerous software cost estimation models exist to help managers with this task. An essential input to all such models is an estimate of the size of the software to be developed. Accurate estimation of software size is thus vital. Unfortunately it is very difficult, especially during the early stages of development.

Many approaches to size estimation are used in industry. Several are supported by commercial size estimation tools and services. Most involve subjective estimation, particularly through comparison with completed projects whose size is known. An alternative approach, in which this work falls, is to develop algorithmic models that predict the size of a program from quantitative measurements of some of its attributes (see for example [1, 2, 3, 4, 5, 6, 7]).

The research described here concentrates on the variables in a program as the key factor. Lokan and Conte[8] have shown that very simple equations can estimate the final size of Pascal programs with acceptable accuracy, from as early as the completion of high level design, across a range of program applications and sizes. These equations were based on a weighted count of conceptually unique variables, in which each variable in a program was weighted by the number of procedures in which it was used. A similar study of C programs [9] supports these findings, except that accuracy was not quite acceptable after high level design (by detailed design it was acceptable).

Figure 1: LOC vs. weighted variables

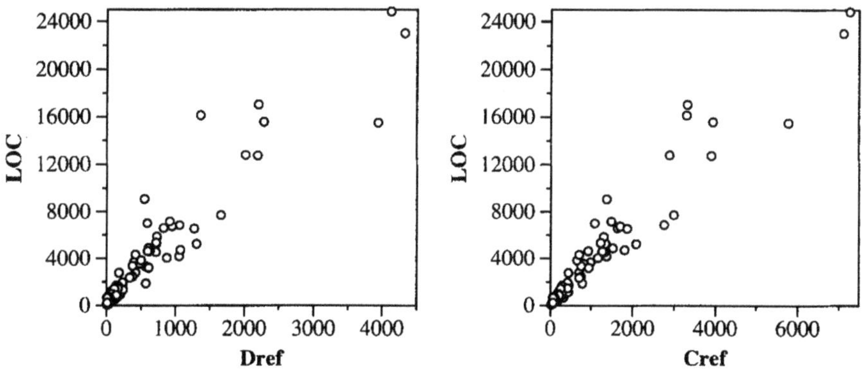

This study looks more closely at the C programs, to try to improve the accuracy of the size estimates by classifying programs into groups for estimation. Rather than considering all programs as one class, with a single estimation equation for them all, separate estimation equations are used for programs in different classes. The programs are classified by application.

2 METHOD OF STUDY

2.1 Data collection

One hundred and fourteen C programs, covering a broad range of applications, were analyzed. In total the programs amounted to almost 340,000 lines of source code. They ranged in size from 71 to 24,836 lines, with a mean of 2,975 and a median of 998 lines.

Three attributes were measured for each program: *LOC* (the number of source lines, excluding blank lines and lines that only contain comments), *Dref* and *Cref* (weighted counts of the conceptually unique variables[1] identifiable after high level design and detailed design respectively). Each identifier was weighted by the number of functions in which it was used. The difference between *Dref* and *Cref* is that *Cref* includes local names within functions, and implementation-dependent constants (*eg* array sizes), while *Dref* does not.

Figure 1 plots the size of each program against *Dref* and *Cref*. Both plots show clear linear relationships; the scatter is slightly wider with *Dref*.

2.2 Classifying programs by application

The sample programs were classified into fifteen types of application. These were grouped further into four broad classes: computation-intensive programs, interactive programs with a rich user interface, batch-oriented file translation programs, and system programs. Table 1 summarizes the programs in each class.

[1] "Variables" includes identifiers defined as variables, struct fields, or values of an enumerated type; identifiers that are passed as parameters in function calls; identifiers defined in `#define` directives. System-defined names, like those defined in files such as `stdio.h`, were not counted. Neither were identifiers declared by the programmer but not used.

Table 1: Summary of the programs in each classification

Class	Application	No. of programs	Program sizes			
			Mean	Median	Smallest	Largest
Computation-intensive	AI	2	5073	5073	3311	6835
	astronomy	4	4353	5063	698	6589
	cryptography	5	1397	1578	305	2764
	data analysis	10	3575	530	151	23022
	simulation	3	1775	687	595	4044
Interactive: sophisticated user interface	email, news	5	13889	16132	2356	24836
	communications	3	5500	4725	4615	7161
	database	6	1356	951	683	3360
	editor	7	7723	6733	783	15511
	games	4	5471	2420	1464	15578
File or program translation	file compression	7	3533	1705	1156	7718
	filter	9	836	295	122	3549
	parser	9	1839	1085	199	6995
	translator	10	1219	859	322	4181
System	system	30	1086	580	71	6536
Total		114	2975	998	71	24836

There are two reasons for grouping programs into broad classes as well as individual applications. First, it is desirable to have estimation models that are as general as possible; broad classifications should be investigated before more detailed ones. Second, each class that is analyzed separately needs to be large enough for the statistics to have some meaning.

2.3 Estimation equations

Simple linear equations are desirable, as they are intuitive and easy to apply. Earlier work [8, 9] has shown that other forms of equation are no more accurate than linear equations. Hence only linear equations were sought here.

The measures used to evaluate the accuracy of each equation were the mean magnitude of relative error (denoted $\overline{MRE}$), and the proportion of programs predicted with $MRE \leq .30$ (denoted *Pred*(.30)). R^2 (the *coefficient of multiple determination*, which indicates the extent to which estimated and actual values are linearly related[10]) is reported here for information, but is not used to assess the predictive ability of any equation.

Campbell *et al.*[4] consider an equation acceptable if $\overline{MRE} \leq .30$ and $Pred(.30) \geq .70$. Although this criterion is arbitrary, it has been widely accepted in software engineering. It is used here.

A form of trial and error was used to derive the estimation equations. Ordinary regression was used to provide initial guesses for the coefficients. A range of values around the initial guess was then defined for each coefficient, based on a visual inspection of a graph of size against the dependent variable (*Dref* or *Cref*). An exhaustive search through all combinations was then made to find the best-performed equation in terms of $\overline{MRE}$ and *Pred*(.30). This approach usually improved $\overline{MRE}$ and *Pred*(.30) substantially, compared to the regression-derived equation.

Table 2: Best equations after high level design

Class	Equation	R^2	$\overline{MRE}$	$Pred(.30)$
All programs	$6.50 \times Dref + 150$	0.90	0.31	0.64
Interactive	$5.20 \times Dref + 510$	0.85	0.22	0.84
Computation	$5.60 \times Dref + 170$	0.97	0.23	0.71
Translation	$6.50 \times Dref + 150$	0.80	0.36	0.57
System	$6.50 \times Dref + 150$	0.91	0.35	0.60
filter	$7.25 \times Dref + 110$	0.98	0.34	0.67
compression	$7.50 \times Dref + 450$	0.90	0.16	0.86
parser	$8.87 \times Dref + 180$	0.93	0.35	0.67
translator	$3.50 \times Dref + 440$	0.95	0.28	0.80

Table 3: Overall accuracy after high level design

Classes	R^2	$\overline{MRE}$	$Pred(.30)$
All together	0.90	0.31	0.64
4 classes	0.90	0.29	0.64
7 classes	0.90	0.27	0.72

3 RESULTS

3.1 High level design

Table 2 shows the performance of the best equation for estimating the size of programs in each class, based on *Dref*. The first line gives the best equation, and its accuracy, when all programs are considered as a single class. The next four lines give this information for each broad class, and the last four lines give it for the subclasses of the file translation programs.

Two of the four broad classes (interactive and computation-intensive programs) appear to represent distinct subclasses. They were already estimated with acceptable accuracy; defining their own estimation equations improves the accuracy further.

The translation programs and system programs cannot be distinguished as useful subclasses from the original full sample. These programs were estimated most poorly in the first place. Classifying them as translation-oriented or system-oriented has gained nothing. A more fine-grained classification by application is the next step to try. System programs cannot be broken down further by application. Translation programs can be broken down by application into four subclasses.

The last four lines of Table 2 show the best equations for each separate application within the translation programs. They appear to represent quite distinct subclasses. Each is estimated more accurately by its own separate equation than by the equation for the class as a whole. It appears that two subclasses are estimated with acceptable accuracy; the other two fall slightly short. With only 7–10 programs for each application, though, firm conclusions cannot be drawn.

Overall estimation accuracy for the sample of 114 programs is shown in Table 3. The first line shows the overall accuracy when each program is estimated with the same equation. The second line shows the overall accuracy when the programs are grouped into four classes. The

Table 4: Best equations after detailed design

Class	Equation	R^2	$\overline{MRE}$	$Pred(.30)$
All programs	$4.00 \times Cref + 30$	0.94	0.24	0.73
Interactive	$3.53 \times Cref + 300$	0.91	0.18	0.88
Computation	$3.09 \times Cref$	0.98	0.22	0.83
Translation	$4.62 \times Cref$	0.85	0.26	0.69
System	$4.30 \times Cref$	0.92	0.23	0.87
filter	$4.34 \times Cref$	0.99	0.23	0.67
compression	$4.20 \times Cref + 330$	0.90	0.14	0.86
parser	$4.55 \times Cref$	0.88	0.20	0.89
translator	$2.40 \times Cref + 300$	0.94	0.24	0.80

Table 5: Overall accuracy after detailed design

Classes	R^2	$\overline{MRE}$	$Pred(.30)$
All together	0.94	0.24	0.73
4 classes	0.93	0.23	0.81
7 classes	0.94	0.21	0.84

last line shows the overall accuracy when seven classes (three broad classes, and a breakdown of the fourth into four separate applications) are used. Classifying the programs into seven classes improves $\overline{MRE}$ by 4% and $Pred(.30)$ by 8%. These represent relative improvements of 13% in the values of each of $\overline{MRE}$ and $Pred(.30)$.

In summary, classifying programs by application has identified some distinct classes which are worth estimating separately, and overall accuracy now appears acceptable.

3.2 Detailed design

Table 4 shows the performance of the best equation for estimating the size of programs in each class, based on *Cref*. It has the same structure as Table 2.

Each class is estimated with greater accuracy by its own estimation equation. There are substantial differences between the four equations, and between each of them and the single equation used for the sample as a whole. Classifying programs broadly by application finds real differences after detailed design.

The size of interactive, computation-intensive, and system programs is estimated well as a function of *Cref*. For these three classes, $\overline{MRE}$ is at most 23% and $Pred(.30)$ is at least 83%. Even the translation programs are almost estimated acceptably as a single class. The previous section showed that they should be broken down further by application. The last four lines of Table 4 show the best equations when this is done. Although the accuracy generally looks good, firm conclusions cannot be drawn because the subclasses contain too few members.

Overall estimation accuracy for the sample of 114 programs is shown in Table 5. Even without classifying the programs at all, estimation accuracy is acceptable. Classifying the programs into four classes helps; classifying them into the more sensible seven classes helps further.

4 CONCLUSIONS

The main findings of this study are:

- Classifying programs by application, and using a separate estimation equation for each class, improves the accuracy of the estimates.
- When programs are classified into only a few classes, $\overline{MRE}$ and $Pred(.30)$ each improve in relative terms by about 10–17%.
- For three of the four broad classes, size estimation is acceptably accurate after high level design. The fourth class needs to be broken down to a finer level, whereupon it too can be estimated with acceptable accuracy after high level design.
- It is enough to classify programs broadly by application, in order for estimates based on weighted counts of distinct variables (using equations like those in Tables 2 and 4) to be acceptable from high level design onwards.

Several avenues are open for further research. A direct follow-on to this study would be to assess the value of a fine-grained classification by application. This general approach to size estimation could also be investigated with other languages, and with large industrial programs.

REFERENCES

1. Albrecht A., 'Measuring application development productivity', *Proc. IBM Applications Development Symposium*, October 1979, pp 83–92

2. DeMarco T., 'Controlling Software Projects', (Yourdon Press, 1982)

3. Dunsmore H., Wang A., 'A step toward early size estimation for use in productivity models', *Proc. 1985 National Joint Computer Conference on Software Quality*, Williamsburg VA, March 1985

4. Campbell R., Conte S.D., Rathi M.K., 'Early prediction of software size and effort', Purdue University Technical Report SERC-TR-10-P, March 1988

5. Rathi M.K., 'An Objective Methodology for Early Software Size Estimation', PhD thesis, Purdue University, August 1988

6. Bourque P., Côté V., 'An experiment in software sizing with structured analysis metrics', *Journal of Systems and Software*, 1991, Vol. 15, (2), pp 159–172

7. Verner J., Tate G., 'A software size model', *IEEE Transactions on Software Engineering*, 1992, Vol. 18, (4), pp 265–278

8. Lokan C.J., Conte S.D., 'Size estimation for Pascal programs', Purdue University Technical Report SERC-TR-129-P, December 1992. To appear in *Journal of Computer and Software Engineering*

9. Lokan C.J., 'Early size prediction for C programs', Purdue University Technical Report SERC-TR-139-P, June 1993

10. Conte S.D., Dunsmore H., Shen V., 'Software Engineering Metrics and Models', (Benjamin-Cummings, 1986)

49

Cyclomatic complexity as a measure of the structure of knowledge-based/expert systems

T. T. Moores

Department of Information Systems, City Polytechnic of Hong Kong, 83 Tat Chee Avenue, Kowloon, HONG KONG.

Abstract

The "structure" of a program is often used as an indicator of the likely error-proneness of a system (and thus its quality). This paper reviews the applicability of cyclomatic complexity as a measure of the structure of knowledge-based systems (KBSs). Threshold values are sought above which 80% of error-prone programs are captured. The results obtained suggest that cyclomatic complexity substantially outperforms lines of code as a measure of the error-proneness of KBSs.

Keyword Codes: D.2.2; D.2.5; D.2.8
Keywords: Tools and Techniques; Testing and Debugging; Metrics

1. INTRODUCTION

Measures of complexity is seen as the best indicator of error-proneness, or the likelihood of a piece of software to have an operational fault (e.g., [1,2]). "Good structure" has often been described as the ability of a system to resist errors even when changes are made to some part of its sub-structure [3,4]. It is on this basis that controlling the structure of a program has a direct bearing on the quality of the overall system. The classic studies for conventional systems are McCabe[5] and Henry & Kafura [6,7]. Clearly, "quality" is not simply an issue of the number of bugs, but it can often be reduced to such a judgement. The question to be addressed in this paper is whether similar metrics can be derived for KBS languages such as Prolog. For the sake of simplicity, the terms "knowledge-based system" and "expert system" will be considered to be interchangeable and the term KBS will be used throughout this paper.

Very few metrics have been developed for knowledge-based systems (KBSs). Those KBS metrics which do exist have not been extensively validated and are mainly suggestions of the types of measurements to make [8-10]. Attempts to define 'structure' have included: counting the different types of node in a Rete-network [11], modelling the way data is partitioned within a Prolog clause [12], or modelling the location of data within a clause and then measuring the structure of the resultant model [13]. Outside these references, however, there is little or no work being done on metrics for KBSs.

This paper will test the assumption that structure metrics can be developed for Prolog-based systems without needing to specifically address the "KBS-ness" of the system. This simplification would lead to the useful conclusion that characteristics of a development environment becomes an inherent part of any metrics model and there is no need for any special (KBS) definition of the term "structure". On the grounds of its relative popularity, the attempt here will be to apply cyclomatic complexity[5] to Prolog, with lines of code (LOC) taken as a baseline metric. It will be expected that LOC is *not* a good structure metric. Section 2 will describe the two main variants of the cyclomatic complexity metric ($v(G)=e-n+2$ and $v(G)=$No.of conditionals+1). Section 3 will present the results of applying the cyclomatic complexity metric to 80 commercially-developed LPA Prolog programs. For a description of the Prolog language, the interested reader is refered to [14-16].

2. CYCLOMATIC COMPLEXITY

Cyclomatic complexity [5] is a graph-theoretic structure metric which attempts to define the procedural complexity of a program in terms of flows through a graph. Blocks of code are represented as nodes while decision-points are represented as arcs joining one node to another. By transforming a program into a graph, a measure of program complexity would then be a measure of the number of paths through this graph. Paths are identified by defining a program as a strongly connected graph, G, which has n vertices, e edges and p connected components. The cyclomatic number, v(G), can then be calculated as:

$$v(G) = e - n + 2p$$

where, p = 1 (for one component). The component count, p, signifies the number of separate routines within a program. In most studies, p is taken to be one. The equation for cyclomatic complexity can also be reduced to a count of the number of predicates (such as IFs, WHILEs, etc.), plus one. In practice, McCabe suggests that it is more convenient to count conditionals and so the refined measure of cyclomatic complexity becomes:

$$v(G) = \text{No. of conditionals} + 1$$

Some care needs to be taken over the fact that compound conditionals are actually disguised IFs (e.g., IF "C1 AND C2" THEN.. becomes IF C1 and IF C2 THEN..); while CASE statements are actually multiple IFs, where a CASE statement with N conditions would have to be re-written as N-1 IF statements. The distinction between well-structured and badly-structured programs is that the program graph of well-structured programs can be reduced sequentially by removing nodes with only one input and one output until there is only one node left.

The idea of transforming a program into a graph of pathways proved to be an appealing and influential concept. The first reactions, however, were to redefine the metric in order to accommodate problems in the way the graph represented certain program structures. New variations of the metric quickly emerged where more emphasis was placed on the bounds of ELSE statements[17], arcs at a node forming "knots"[18], the flow of both control and data[19] and the nesting depth of statements (e.g., [20]). The most important use of these graph-theoretic measures of complexity has been to explain the number and distribution of errors[21,22]. The complexity of a program has also been related to the difficulty of developing the program[23], the use or reachability of particular nodes[24], while later studies generated similar graphs on the basis of the system design or specification (e.g., [25]).

Similar to many structure metrics, however, it is sometimes difficult to detect how the elements of the program are to be mapped onto the appropriate metric elements. By abstracting what a program is to a graph of nodes and arcs it becomes confusing to know whether we are measuring syntactical or psychological program complexity[26]. McCabe clearly wants to measure both syntactical and psychological complexity, but the bridge from its syntactical measurement to its psychological impact is uncertain[27]. For instance, Halstead's model of effort, E, has been found to correlate with construction time, the number of errors, and debugging time significantly better than cyclomatic complexity[28]. The lack of support for relating measures of complexity to what programmers see as "complex" and thus being error-prone is a typical criticism of structure metrics (e.g., [29]). Even in view of these criticisms it still appears that cyclomatic complexity remains an appealing (if unproven) structure metric.

3. APPLYING STRUCTURE METRICS TO PROLOG

The aim of the structural analysis here is to deduce a metric threshold value, T, for LOC and v(G) above which Prolog programs tend to be error-prone. A set of 80 commercially-developed LPA Prolog programs were analysed, of which 46 had a total of 115 post-release errors (i.e., 57.5% of the programs had errors). Such errors record faults found by users and beta-testers after the product had been released. Although structure metrics are more typically related to errors found during testing, no reports detailing coding or testing errors were available. The analysis will focus on detecting an error-prone program regardless of how many errors a particular program might have. The structure metrics being used are:

- lines of code (defined as non-comment, non-blank lines of code);
- cyclomatic complexity, $v(G)_1 = e - n + 2$; and,
- cyclomatic complexity, $v(G)_2$ = No. of conditionals + 1.

The two variants are assessed together because it is not clear at this point which version is likely to work best. The theoretical version, $v(G)_1$, requires a definition of Prolog decision points (edges) and blocks of code (nodes). The practical version, $v(G)_2$, requires a count of Prolog conditionals only. Cyclomatic complexity is defined here for Prolog in terms of the calls from one predicate to another and has the following properties:

- a single node, *n*, replaces all instantiations of the predicate (such that, a call by any predicate with the same name is represented as a call from a single node with that name);
- a predicate in the body of a clause is represented as an arc, *e*, from the clause head node to the clause body node (where one arc represents all calls between predicates of the same name);
- the number of conditionals contained within a program is equated to the number of unique predicate names, *P*;
- The calculation of cyclomatic complexity is defined as either:

  $$v(G)_1 = e - n + 2$$

  or,

  $$v(G)_2 = P + 1$$

Using these definitions a program can be represented as a directed flow-graph from which a measure of cyclomatic complexity can be taken.

Typically, the justification for a good structure metric is one which has a reasonably high (ranked) correlation between the metric value and programs with errors. However, this is of little value to the developers who are more interested in pinpointing exactly those programs within the system which are likely to have errors. Rather than using correlation, therefore, the analysis here will aim to identify a metric threshold value, T, which identifies most (say, 80%) of those programs with errors. This would allow more directed testing to be carried out and, hence, increase the overall quality of the delivered system with the minimum of effort. For arbitrary reasons, the threshold chosen is the point at which those programs above the threshold represent at least 80% of programs with one or more recorded errors. Since there are 46 programs with errors, this means looking for the point at which 37 or more of the error-prone programs are above T.

Along with this condition, however, it also seems necessary to maximise the proportion of programs which exceed T and have recorded errors ($Prop_R$=max) and minimise the proportion of programs which have recorded errors but do not exceed T ($Prop_W$=min). These two conditions show the success of the metric in terms of its 'strike rate' of identifying error-prone programs ($Prop_R$), and its fallibility in terms of its failure to flag programs which do, in fact, have errors ($Prop_W$). These conditions are therefore defined as:

$S_T(T)$ = the proportion of programs with errors that exceed T

$= E / N_E = E / 46$

$Prop_R$ = the proportion of programs which exceed T that have errors

$= E / N_T$

$Prop_W$ = the proportion of programs which do not exceed T but have errors
= $(N_E - E) / (N_{total} - N_T)$ = $46 - E / 80 - N_T$

where,

E = number of programs above T which have errors (max=46)
N_E = number of programs with errors (total=46)
N_T = number of programs above T (max=80)
N_{total} = number of programs (total=80)

The value of $S_T(T)$ will vary between 0.00 and 1.00. In comparing the performance of each of the three structure metrics, therefore, the threshold for each is taken be the highest value of T for which the following are true:

$S_T(T) \geq 0.80$ (and where **$Prop_R$=max** and **$Prop_W$=min**)

Table 1.
Results of metrics at $S_T(T)=0.80$

Metric	Highest value of T for which $S_T(T)=0.80$	N_T	$Prop_R$	$Prop_W$
LOC	74	61	0.607	0.474
$v(G)_1$	33	58	0.638	0.409
$v(G)_2$	34	53	0.698	0.333

The thresholds for each structure metric are calculated as the highest value of T for which $S_T(T)=0.80$ (see Table 1). As can be seen, the best metric appears to be the practical version of cyclomatic complexity, $v(G)_2$, on the grounds that it:

- requires the fewest number of programs to be tested in order to capture 80% of the programs with errors (53, as opposed to 58 or 61);
- has the highest $Prop_R$ and lowest $Prop_W$ at the required 80% cut-off point (0.698 and 0.333, respectively).

In other words, by using the threshold $v(G)_2>34$, the developers can reduce the number of programs tested by 34%, and still capture 80% of error-prone programs. The actual threshold chosen for $v(G)_2$, however, would depend on the limits placed on the number of error-prone programs which are allowed to be released, and the number of programs which can be reasonably tested during the final development phase.

It should be noted that six of the largest programs exceed the threshold for all three structure metrics and yet have no documented post-release errors. This appears to be because all six programs are core to the functionality of the system and so were extensively tested before release. Hence, it could be argued that the metrics defined here have only captured programs which have been inadequately tested rather than which have overly-complex structures that make them error-prone. On the other hand, it could also be argued that since fixing a "bug" during testing is cheaper than post-release "fixes" (e.g., [30]), the errors detected within the sample of 80 programs by $v(G)_2$ are the sort of expensive repairs which the standard testing procedure has clearly not captured.

4. SUMMARY OF RESULTS

The results of the analysis carried out in the previous sections have shown that knowledge-based systems developed using Prolog are amenable to metrics analysis using measurements previously designed for conventional languages. In particular, models of structure have been deduced from the sample of 80 LPA Prolog programs, where a program is likely to contain at least one documented post-release error when,

$v(G)_2 > 34$

where,

$v(G)_2$ = No.of unique predicate names + 1

Although the values of $v(G)_1$ and $v(G)_2$ are quite similar (33 and 34, respectively), $v(G)_2$ is clearly the better structure metric because it has a better $Prop_R$ 'strike rate', and misclassifies the fewest proportion of error-prone program as being defect-free. The use of $v(G)_2$ is also important since it clearly out-performs LOC and is based on a feature of the Prolog language which is important to the developers: The number of different predicate names that need to be defined in order to implement the system. It is interesting to note that the number of unique predicate names used within a program has also been found to be the dominant variable in models which estimate the size of Prolog programs (e.g., see [31]).

Calculating v(G) early - for instance at the design stage - is a problem which has been investigated recently for conventional systems' development and shows some promise (e.g., [32]). Whether similar early quality assessments can be made for KBSs is a matter of further investigation.

The importance of this study is the clear result that metrics *can* be applied to KBS development. In its most naïve form, metrics are simply used to assign a value to attributes of system development which can help to answer "How much?" and "How long?" questions. With answers to these questions, the risks associated with KBS development are reduced because the cost and duration of the project can be better estimated. If the results of this study can be repeated, then the conclusion must be that KBS development no longer becomes a risky venture and can be measured and controlled as well as any other form of systems development.

REFERENCES

1. SCHNEIDEWIND, N.: 'Software metrics for aiding program development and debugging', *Proc. AFIPS National Computer Conference*, New York, June 1979, pp989-994.
2. DUNSMORE, H. and GANNON, J.: 'An analysis of the effects of programming factors on programming effort', *Journal of Systems and Software*, 1980, Vol.1, (2), pp.144-153.
3. SOONG, N.: 'A program stability measure', *Proc. AFIPS National Computer Conference*, 1977, pp163-173.
4. YAU, S, and COLLOFELLO, J.: 'Some stability measures for software maintenance', *IEEE Transactions on Software Engineering*, 1980, Vol.6, (6), pp.545-552.
5. McCABE, T.: 'A complexity measure', *IEEE Transactions on Software Engineering*, 1976, Vol.2, (4), pp.308-320.
6. HENRY, S. and KAFURA, D.: 'Software structure metrics based on information flow', *IEEE Transactions on Software Engineering*, 1981, Vol.7, (5), pp.510-518.
7. HENRY, S. and KAFURA, D.: 'The evaluation of software systems' structure using quantitative software metrics', *Software - Practice and Experience*, 1984, Vol.14, (6), pp.561-571.
8. KAISLER, S.: 'Expert system metrics', *Proc. International Conference on Neural Networks*, Atlanta, October 1986, pp.114-120.
9. READDIE, M., STRENG, K.-H. and WERMSER, D.: 'KADS metrication', ESPRIT Project 1098, Report SD-G10-001. Produced by SD(Europe) Ltd. & NTE NeuTech Entwicklungsgesellschaft + Co. KG, 1989.

10. BEHRENDT, W., LAMBERT, S., RINGLAND, G., HUGHES, P. and POULTER, K.: 'GATEWAY: Metrics for knowledge based systems', *Proc. First World Congress on Expert Systems*, Miami, December 1991, pp.1056-1067.
11. GUPTA, A. and FORGY, C.: 'Static and run-time characteristics of OPS5 production systems', *Journal of Parallel and Distributed Computing*, 1989, Vol.7, pp.64-95.
12. MARKUSZ, Z. and KAPOSI, A.: 'Complexity control in logic-based programming', *The Computer Journal*, 1985, Vol.28, (5), pp.487-495.
13. MYERS, M. and KAPOSI, A.: 'Modelling and measurement of Prolog data', *Software Engineering Journal*, 1991, Vol.6, (4), pp.413-434.
14. CLOCKSHIN, F. and MELLISH, C.: 'Programming in Prolog', (Springer-Verlag, 1981).
15. BRATKO, I.: 'Prolog Programming for Artificial Intelligence', (Addison-Wesley, 1986).
16. O'KEEFE, R.: 'The Craft of Prolog', (The MIT Press, 1990).
17. MYERS, G.: 'An extension to the cyclomatic measure of program complexity', *ACM SIGPLAN Notices*, 1977, Vol.12, (10), pp.61-64.
18. WOODWARD, M., HENNELL, M. and HEDLEY, D.: 'A measure of control flow complexity in program test', *IEEE Transactions on Software Engineering*, 1979, Vol.5, (1), pp.45-50.
19. OVIEDO, E.: 'Control flow, data flow and program complexity', *Proc. IEEE Computer Software and Applications Conference*, November 1980, pp146-152.
20. HARRISON, W. and MAGEL, K.: 'A complexity measure based on nesting level', *ACM SIGPLAN Notices*, 1981, Vol.16, (3), pp.63-74.
21. KITCHENHAM, B.: 'Measures of programming complexity', *ICL Technical Journal*, 1981, May, pp.298-316.
22. BASILI, V. and PERRICONE, B.: 'Software errors and complexity: An empirical investigation', *Communications of the ACM*, 1984, Vol.27, (1), pp.42-52.
23. BASILI, V., SELBY, R. and PHILLIPS, T.: 'Metric analysis and data validation across Fortran projects', *IEEE Transactions on Software Engineering*, 1983, Vol.9, (6), pp.652-663.
24. IYENGAR, S., PARAMESWARAN, N. and FULLER, J.: 'A measure of logical complexity of programs', *Computer Languages*, 1982, Vol.7, pp.147-160.
25. SANSOM, W., NEVILL, D. and DOGARD, P.: 'Predictive software metrics based on a formal specification', *Information and Software Technology*, 1987, Vol.29, (5), pp.242-248.
26. CURTIS, B., SHEPPARD, S., MILLIMAN, P., BORST, M. and LOVE, T.: 'Measuring the psychological complexity of software maintenance tasks with Halstead and McCabe metrics', *IEEE Transactions on Software Engineering*, 1979, Vol.5, (2), pp.96-104.
27. PRATHER, R.: 'An axiomatic theory of software complexity measure', *The Computer Journal*, 1984, Vol.27, (4), pp.340-347.
28. DAVIS, J. and LeBLANC, R.: 'A study of the applicability of complexity measures', *IEEE Transactions on Software Engineering*, 1988, Vol.14, (9), pp.1366-1372.
29. SHEPPERD, M.: 'A critique of cyclomatic complexity as a software metric', *Software Engineering Journal*, 1988, Vol.3, (2), pp.30-36.
30. BOEHM, B.: 'Software Engineering Economics', (Prentice-Hall, 1981).
31. MOORES, T.: 'A model to size the development of Prolog programs', Department of Information Systems, City Polytechnic of Hong Kong, Hong Kong, Working Paper No.13, April 1994.
32. McCABE, T. and BUTLER, C.: 'Design complexity measurement and testing', *Communications of the ACM*, 1989, Vol.32, (12), pp.1415-1425.

50

S/C: a Software Size/Complexity Measure

Y.R. Pant[a], J.M. Verner[b] and B. Henderson-Sellers[c]

[a] MacDonald Dettwiler Pty. Ltd., Sydney

[b] Department of Information Systems, City Polytechnic of Hong Kong

[c] School of Computing Systems, University of Technology, Sydney

Abstract

A new software structural complexity metric is proposed which is a simple, yet powerful, extension of the normal lines of code count. This measure is shown to account for the differences in complexity of program statements in high-order languages and is useful in assessing control complexity of source programs objectively when the source code is available. The proposed measure also satisfies the seventh axiom of Weyuker's software complexity measures (complexity is dependent on permutation of source statements). The measure has the potential (not fully evaluated here) for use in assessing the effort related to understanding software for software maintenance, debugging and generalization. In our pilot project, we found that the time taken to trace artificial bugs introduced in programs is explained better by S/C counts than by lines of code counts.

Keyword Codes: D.2.8, D.2.5
Keywords: Metrics, Testing

1. INTRODUCTION

The lines of code measure does not account for the complexity of an individual line of code. This may reduce the effectiveness of the lines of code measure as a representation of structural complexity on which models of external characteristics[1] such as understandability may be based.

Program understandability and maintainability/generalizability are parallel concepts. The more difficult a program is to understand, the more difficult it is to enhance/modify. A program fragment has to be understood and analyzed fully before it can be generalized and enhanced. Program analysis consists of an examination of source code to find out what the program is supposed to do and how various program segments are connected together. Without a proper understanding of a program segment, it may be difficult to predict or detect the ripple effects of change within the program and affecting other programs (although the reverse is not true — we may understand the segment and still not be able to predict e.g. maintenance costs and ripple effects). Both intra- and inter-module structures may well affect the cost of software maintenance. There are several factors (in addition to the following) affecting program maintenance costs[2]:

- control flow: the consequences of executing each path of the program logic.
- program structure types (e.g. procedural, control, data and input/output);
- data flow, their origin, aliases and uses; and

Table 1
Classification of C++ control keywords.

Class I	break, case, continue, default, return, switch, throw
Class II	do, else, for, goto, if, while

1.1 Control complexity

Control statements specify the order in which a computation is carried out. Traditionally, cyclomatic complexity[3] was used to assess control flow complexity of programs, especially for providing a "basis set" for testing. The cyclomatic number of a single-entry, single-exit program is equal to the total number of individual decisions (of the program) plus one[4]. The problem with this approach is that the complexity of different control statements constructed with the keywords like `if/else`, `while`, `for` and `switch` is deemed to be the same. However, intuitively, some of these statements/keywords (SKs) are inherently more complex than others. Furthermore, in cyclomatic complexity, program text excluding control statements *do not* add any complexity; for extrapolation to program comprehension this is frequently inappropriate.

In a high-order programming language, decision-making and iterative statements are normally more complex than assignment statements[5,6]. Ledgard and Marcotty[5] discuss the relative power of control structures. They introduce the idea of a hierarchy of difficulty of understanding different executable statements. Iyengar *et al.*[6] classify control statements into three categories: *sequencing, conditional* and *repetitive*. They conclude that the repetitive statements are the most logically complex structures, since they demand the values of the variables during the ith iteration to be expressed recursively in terms of the values of the variables at the $(i-1)$th iteration.

There are 13 control keywords in C++: `break`, `case`, `continue`, `default`, `do`, `else`, `for`, `goto`, `if`, `return`, `switch`, `throw` and `while`. Some of these SKs do not take any optional parameters (e.g. `continue`, `break`) while others take a varying number of parameters (e.g. `if`, `for`) in different contexts. Thus (inherently) different control keywords have differing complexity. Furthermore, the SKs e.g. `if` and `for` (taking a varying number of parameters) also group a number of statements to make a block of code.

A block of code is similar to a subprogram but without a name[7]. In some sense, the abstraction mechanisms[8,9] provided by a subprogram and a block of code can be considered to be equivalent. Thus, the SKs e.g. `if` and `for` are at a higher abstraction level than the SKs e.g. `break` and `continue`. Therefore, to assess control complexity, it may be necessary to analyze the specific uses of SKs. Based on these observations, we classify (Table 1) the control keywords of the C++ programming language into the following two categories:

- *Class I:* those that do not take any optional parameters or only fixed parameters (e.g. switch) and
- *Class II:* those that take a varying number of parameters.

We think that Class II SKs carry more 'functionality' or contain more 'logical stuff' (and hence are more difficult to comprehend) than Class I SKs. In order to avoid the problems in straightforward application of SLOC counts and cyclomatic complexity (discussed by many authors), complex statements realized with Class II keywords should be broken into simple or primitive statements for which the effort for understanding is approximately the same.

Indeed, the classification of C++ keywords is difficult as the members of Class I and Class II can overlap. For example, the keyword `goto` does not introduce any repetitions nor conditions, and supports a low-level programming style[7]. Since the `goto` only sequences the flow of control, it should have been a member of Class I. However, it may introduce an arbitrary transfer of control that may span a large amount of program text. As a result, the program may be difficult to understand and maintain since immediacy of resolving variable dependencies is lost[10]. This makes it a suitable member of Class II.

Since a `for` loop allows grouping of statements like declarative, assignment, comparison and arithmetic, we have placed it into Class II. The following `for` loop

```
for (int i = 0; i <= 50; i++) {
    /* Repeats 50 times */
}                                        (E1)
```

has a declaration/assignment statement, comparison and arithmetic statement and takes three parameters. These parameters can have wide ranges of values which makes some `for` statements much more complex than others. For instance, to create an infinite loop (E2), we do not specify any parameters:

```
for ( ; ; ) {
    /* An infinite loop */
}                                                    (E2)
```

The following statement (E3) has two declaration/assignment, two comparison and two arithmetic statements. Because of the differences in the number of parameters, (we believe that) this `for` loop (E3) will take greater effort to understand and modify than the previous `for` loops (E1 & E2).

```
for (int i = 0, j = 500; i <= 50, j >= 70; i++, j- -) {
    /* A more complex loop */
}                                                    (E3)
```

1.2 The repetitive and conditional constructs

There are three repetitive statements in C++/C: `for`, `while` and `do/while`. As they are generally equivalent[11], only the `for` loop will be discussed in detail here. All the loops have three parts: `expr1`, `expr2` and `expr3`.

```
for loop:
    for (expr1; expr2; expr3) {                      (E4)
    }
while loop:
    expr1;
    while (expr2) {                                  (E5)
        expr3;
    }
do/while loop:
    do{
        expr1;
        expr3;                                       (E6)
    }while (expr2);
```

Generally, `expr1` and `expr3` initialize, increment or otherwise change some variables that are used by the loop; `expr2` is normally a conditional statement that is used for controlling the repetition of the loop.

```
for (int i = 0; i < 10; i++) {
    /* do something */                               (E7)
}
```

To illustrate the method of obtaining the S/C measure, we consider the `for` loop (E7). We can think of this loop as consisting of the following four parts:

- initialization: `int i = 0`
- comparison: `i < 10`
- increment: `i++`
- binder: `for (; ;) {...}`

Thus, the S/C counts of the loop (E7) is four. We have named the group of elements `for (; ;) {...}` as a "binder". The binder logically groups the first three parts (`int i = 0, i < 10` and `i++`) together. We consider that a binder contributes one unit of S/C. However, it is possible to assign varying subjective weights (similar to that of ref 12) to the control keywords.

Had there been two comparisons (E8) like:

```
for (int i = 0; i < 10 && j > 2; i++) {
    /* For loop with two comparisons */              (E8)
}
```

then the S/C counts would be seven because the two comparisons can have four outcomes, creating four distinct execution (or mental) paths. This should be reasonable because E8 is intuitively more difficult to construct, comprehend and debug than E7, as all the four distinct paths must be traversed mentally. In other words, because of the four possible (different) execution paths, E8 requires more effort (for understanding, for maintenance and for testing) than E7.

The proposed model differs from the complexity measure [3] which is simply a count of the total number of individual *conditions* (not decisions) plus one whilst having some similarity with the NPATH measure[13].

A more complex `for` loop (E9) is shown below:

```
for (int i = 0; ((i < lim - 1) && ((c = getchar()) != EOF)
    && (c != 8)); i++ ) {
/* More effort is required to understand this loop */
}
```
(E9)

In this loop, the initialization and assignment parts are no different to those discussed above (e.g. E7, E8). However, the decision making part is complex and has the three conditions `i < lim-1`, `(c = getchar()) != EOF` and `c != 8`. The three comparisons are *anded* together such that they have 8 different outcomes. With the keyword `for` and the statements `int i = 0` and `i++`, the S/C count of this line is 11.

```
if (a < b) {
    /* A simple if statement */
}
```
(E10)

The simple `if` statement (E10) can be broken into two parts:

- comparison: `a < b`
- binder: `if (){...}`

Thus it contributes 2 units of S/C.

1.3 Nested statements

Nested statements have been a source of considerable debate in the context of software complexity metrics[14,15]. The following nested `if` (E11)

```
if (expr1) {
    if (expr2) {
        s2;
    }
}
```
(E11)

can be theoretically considered as a subset of (E12)

```
if ((expr1) logical-operator (expr2)) {
    /* logical-operators can be && or || */
    s2;
}
```
(E12)

when the `logical-operator` is `&&`, and commonalities can be traced. For example, in the C language, the predicates are always evaluated from left to right, and evaluation stops as soon as the truth or falsehood of the result is known[16]. In this case, if the first predicate (`expr1`) evaluates to be false, the second will not be evaluated. The same criterion is also true in the nested `if`s (E11); the second `if` statement will not be evaluated if the first predicate evaluates to be false. In other words, for the statements `s2` to be executed, both the predicates must evaluate to true. We can also consider a *logical* and (`&&`) to be *implicit* in the first *nested* construct.

One of the important differences between the *nested* and the *and*ed construct is that the execution history of the statements `s1` may alter the evaluation of the second predicate, thus causing the statements `s2` to be executed. McCabe's[3] metric fails to account for differences such as this. In McCabe's measure, each conditional expression in a complex Boolean expression adds the same level of difficulty as an entire conditional structure. McCabe's measure does not have any provisions for distinguishing between a series of nested `if` statements and a single (equivalent) `if` statement in which all the conditions are grouped together.

The differences can be accounted for by identifying the property that a *nested* construct has one more `if` and has more static properties than its corresponding *and*ed version. Neglecting `s1` and `s2` and assuming that `expr1` and `expr2` each has only one predicate, the S/C counts of the first construct is 6; while that of the second is 5.

As a second example, the statements equivalent to the following construct (E13) is 4.

```
if (exprl) {
}
                                                          (E13)
if (expr2) {
}

while ((c = getchar()) != EOF) {
     s1;
     if (a >= b) {                                        (E14)
          /* do something */
     }
}
```

In E17, the execution of the inner `if` loop is controlled by the outer `while` loop. When programmers attempt to understand the inner `if` block, they should consider the effect of the variable 'c' on the condition '`a >= b`'. For example, the statements `s1` might affect the values of the variables 'a' and 'b' as a result of different values of 'c'. The programmers might think that if the variable 'c' is true *and* the variable 'a' is greater than or equal to the variable 'b' then only the code inside the inner `if` loop will be executed. This is similar to logical anding (`&&`) of 'c' and (`a <= b`) which creates four execution paths (total S/C counts = 6).

Thus, this model is in accordance with our intuitive understanding that a module gets more complex if there are more embedded or nested control statements in it.

2. EXPERIMENTAL SUPPORT

For our experiment, we selected two programs (Figure 1) each of 41 source lines of code in C. The S/C counts of the first program was 50; while that of the second was 81.

The first program computes some simple statistics (mean, standard deviation, maximum and minimum value) from a set of data. The second program prompts for a number to be entered and validates it. If a user enters characters other than the digits (including one decimal point), the number will not be accepted and the user is prompted again to enter a correct real number.

2.1 Experiment

As the 'effort for understanding a program' is a difficult measure to quantify, we sought to measure the time required to trace bugs artificially introduced in the programs. The buggy statements are shown within a framebox for both the programs (Figure 1). Different types of bugs were introduced in the programs to reduce the likelihood of formulating similar debugging strategies (in the subsequent program) when the subjects found the bug(s) in the initial program.

- In the 'statistical' program (Figure 1(a)), the statement `for (i = 0; i < size; i++)` was changed to `for (i = 1; i <= size; i++)` and the statement `sum = 0.0` was deleted.
- In the 'input validation' program (Figure 1(b)), the statement `only_digits = 1` was changed to `only_digits = 0`; the statement `if(!isdigit(buffer[i]))` was changed to `if(isdigit(buffer[i])`

Let μ be the mean difference of the time taken to debug the 'input validation' and the 'statistical' program, then

$$\text{Null hypothesis:} \quad H_0 : \mu = 0,$$
$$\text{Alternative hypothesis:} \quad H_a : \mu > 0.$$

The null hypothesis states that there is no difference between the debugging times, and H_a states that the 'input validation' program takes more time to debug (its S/C counts are greater) than the 'statistical' program.

The debugging order of the two programs was randomized by tossing a coin. The programs were given to 15 subjects, who were asked to record exactly the time taken to trace the bugs. The subjects were either currently working on C projects or had previously developed programs in C. The subjects were closely monitored without any interference while they were fixing the bugs.

```
# include <stdio.h>
# include <math.h>
# define MAXSIZE 500

void compute_stat()
{
  int i, size;
  float sum = 0.0, temp, avg, stddv, max, min, data[MAXSIZE];

  printf("\nEnter data size :  ");
  scanf("%d", &size);

  printf("\nEnter data separated by a space :  ");

  for (i = 0; i < size; i++) {
    scanf("%f",&data[i]);
  }

  max = min = data[0];

  for (i = 0; i < size; i++) {
    if (data[i] > max) {
      max = data[i];
    }
    if (data[i] < min) {
      min = data[i];
    }
    sum = sum + data[i];
  }
  avg = sum/size;

  sum = 0.0;
  for (i=0; i < size; i++) {
    temp = avg - data[i];
    if (temp < 0) {
      temp = -temp;
    }
    sum = sum + (temp * temp);
  }

  stddv = sum/size;
  stddv = sqrt(stddv);
  printf("\nmean = %5.2f std.  dev.  = %5.2f max = %5.2f, min =
%5.2f\n", avg, stddv, max, min);
}


int main()
{
  compute_stat();
  return 0;
}
```

```
#include <stdio.h>
#include <stdlib.h>

char buffer[500];

double read_dbl (const char *prompt)
{
  int i, only_digits, no_decimals;
  double num;
  do {
    printf(prompt);
    scanf("%s", buffer);

    only_digits = 1;

    no_decimals = 0;

    for (i = 0; buffer[i]; i++) {
      if (buffer[i] == '.') {
        no_decimals++;
      }
    }

    if (no_decimals > 1) {
      only_digits = 0;
    }
    else {
      for (i = 0; buffer[i]; i++) {
        if (! isdigit(buffer[i])) {
          if (buffer[i] ≠ '.') {
            only_digits = 0;
            break;
          }
        }
      }
    }
    if (only_digits) {
      num = atof (buffer);
    }
  } while (! only_digits);
  printf ("the digit is = %f\n", num);
  return num;
}
```

Figure 1 (a) 'Statistical' program; and (b) 'Input validation' program.

2.2 Results and interpretation

The results are shown in Table 2. The first column assigns an identification number to the different subjects. The second column indicates the time (in minutes) spent to trace the bugs of the program in Figure 1(a) while the last column indicates the time needed to find the bugs of the program in Figure 1(b). In columns 2 and 3, the letter N within the brackets indicates that the corresponding subject did not identify the correct answer.

A program may be difficult to debug until it is fully understood. In addition, the 'understanding'

Table 2
Experimental results.

Subject identification	1	2	3	4	5	6	7	8	9
Time to debug programs (in minutes)									
'statistical'	10.2	13.5	6.8	9.2	12.6	7.3	8.5	11.2	17.8
'input validation'	8.5	17.3	13.4	11.8	20.5	12.8	15.2	21.7	20.8

Subject identification	10	11	12	13	14	15	ave.	s.d. (σ)
Time to debug programs (in minutes)								
'statistical'	12.3	8.7	10.9	9.8	8.4	13.4	10.7	2.88
'input validation'	10.5	25.6	13.8	18.9	9.3	16.5	15.8	4.99

component may take a major portion (up to 70%) of the total debugging time[17]. Thus we assume that debugging time is highly correlated with time for understanding a piece of code. This means that it would be incorrect to ignore the pairs and analyze the data as if we had two samples, one for the 'statistical' and the other for the 'input validation' programs. The difference in debugging time of programs in Figure 1(a) and 1(b) was significant (Wilcoxon signed ranks text, $T^+ = 115$, no. of subjects = 15). For a sample size of 15, it is not unreasonable to use a normal approximation with a mean of $n(n+1)/4 = 60$ and a variance of $n(n+1)(2n+1)/24 = 310$. This gives a normal test statistic (z-value) of 3.10 which is statistically significant at the 1% level ($z_{crit} = 2.576$ for a two-tailed test).

The 'input validation' program (Figure 1(b)) had $\frac{81}{50} = 1.62$ times more units of S/C than the 'statistical' (Figure 1(a)) program although both had the same size in terms of lines of code (41 LOC). The ratio of average values of debugging time for the two similarly sized (in LOC) programs was $\frac{15.8}{10.7} = 1.48$. These results are encouraging, albeit from a small pilot project. Further large scale empirical experiments are planned as a full validation of the newly proposed S/C metric.

3. CONCLUSIONS

In high-order programming languages, program statements (constructed even with the same keyword) can have a varying degree of "complexity". In this paper, an objective size/complexity measure is proposed which is sensitive to the complexity of individual control statements as well as the length of the code ("number of lines") and nesting levels.

A pilot study undertaken in this paper indicates that the S/C metric is highly correlated with the effort (time) for finding artificially introduced bugs in C programs (than with the source lines of code measure). A large scale experiment is planned as a full validation of the newly proposed S/C metric.

The proposed metric can be useful for assessing the control complexity of program statements for the purpose of software maintenance, generalization, debugging and testing. The proposed metric may also be more suitable than the normal lines of code for quantifying the effort related to understanding a piece of code for a number of post-delivery activities and, incidentally, can be shown to satisfy Weyuker's[18] seventh axiom.

4. ACKNOWLEGEMENTS

We wish to acknowledge the support of a Small Research Grant (grant number C450.301) from the Australian Research Council. We also wish to thank Graham Tate of City Polytechnic of Hong Kong for his useful comments on an earlier draft of this manuscript.

REFERENCES

1. FENTON, N.E., 'Software assessment: a necessary scientific basis', *IEEE Trans. Soft. Eng.*, 1994, Vol. 20, (3), pp. 199–206
2. MARTIN, J. and McCLURE, M., 'Software Maintenance: The Problem and Its Solutions', (Prentice-Hall, Englewood Cliffs, New Jersey, 1983)
3. McCABE, T., 'A complexity measure', *IEEE Trans. Software Eng.*, 1976, Vol. 2, (4), pp. 308–320
4. CONTE, S., DUNSMORE, H. and SHEN, V., 'Software Engineering Metrics and Models', (Benjamin/Cummings, Menlo Park, California, 1986)

5. LEDGARD, H. and MARCOTTY, M., 'A genealogy of control structures', *Comm. ACM*, 1975, Vol. 18, (11), pp. 629–639
6. IYENGAR, S., PARAMESWARAN, N. and FULLER, J., 'A measure of logical complexity of programs', *Comp. Lang.*, 1982, Vol. 7, pp. 147–160
7. GHEZZI, C. and JAZAYERI, M., 'Programming Languages Concepts', (John Wiley and Sons, New York, 1987)
8. SHAW, M., 'Abstraction techniques in modern programming languages', *IEEE Software*, 1984, Vol. 1, (4), pp. 10–26
9. LISKOV, B. and GUTTAG, J., 'Abstraction and Specification in Program Development', (MIT Press, Cambridge, Massachusetts, 1986)
10. CANT, S., JEFFERY, R. and HENDERSON-SELLERS, B., 1992, 'A conceptual model of cognitive complexity of elements of the programming process', Centre for Information Technology Research Report No. 57, University of New South Wales, Sydney, Australia, 1992
11. LIPPMAN, S., 'C++ Primer', (Addison-Wesley, Reading, Massachusetts, 1991)
12. BERNS, G., 'Assessing software maintainability', *Comm. ACM*, 1984, Vol. 27, (1), pp. 14–23
13. NEJMEH, B., 'NPATH: a measure of execution path complexity and its applications', *Commun. ACM*, 1988, Vol. 31, (2), pp. 188–200
14. HARRISON, W. and MAGEL, K., 'A complexity measure based on nesting level', *ACM SIGPLAN Not.*, 1981, Vol. 16, (3), pp. 63–74
15. PIWOWARSKI, P., 'A nesting level complexity measure', *ACM SIGPLAN Not.*, 1982, Vol. 17, (9), pp. 44–50
16. KERNIGHAN, B. and RITCHIE, D., 'The C Programming Language', (Prentice-Hall, Englewood Cliffs, New Jersey, 1990)
17. GUGERTY, L. and OLSON, G., 'Comprehension differences in debugging by skilled and novice programmers', *First Workshop on Empirical Studies of Programmers*, eds E. Soloway and S. Iyengar, Washington D.C., June 5–6, 1986, pp. 13–27
18. WEYUKER, E. 'Evaluating software complexity measures', *IEEE Trans. Software Eng.*, 1988, Vol. 14, (9), pp. 1357–1365

51

A Critical Re-examination of Cyclomatic Complexity Measures

B. Henderson-Sellers[a] and D. Tegarden[b]

[a] School of Computing Sciences, University of Technology, Sydney, Australia

[b] Department of Accounting, Virginia Tech., USA

Abstract

Cyclomatic complexity is a recognized measure of one aspect of structural complexity. Here two measures are re-examined theoretically for four cases: (a) modularization to eliminate duplicate code, (b) multiple entry, single exit modules, (c) single entry, multiple exit modules and (d) multiple entry, multiple exit modules.

Keyword Codes: D.2.8, D.2.5
Keywords: Metrics, Testing

1. INTRODUCTION

In this paper, we clarify the differences between the original, standard McCabe[1] metric, $V(G)$ and a new cyclomatic complexity metric, which we[2] denote by $V_{LI}(G)$. Both metrics will be discussed in terms of (a) decision structures, (b) number of linearly independent (LI) paths for the formation of a basis set (both of these initially for single-module programs and then for larger systems) and then considered with respect to (c) modularization, (d) modularization to remove duplicate code, (e) programs containing multiple entry modules and (f) programs containing multiple exit modules. Initially we outline the complexity framework within which these cyclomatic complexity metrics are placed — they characterize "internal attributes" which contribute to the overall structural complexity of the document (i.e. design document or code). We then introduce a detailed mathematical discussion of two forms of the cyclomatic complexity metric which are theoretically valid and immediately applicable to testing. Since the measures are conceptually well-validated, it is inappropriate, and indeed unnecessary, to seek statistical corroboration.

2. FRAMEWORK FOR COMPLEXITY METRICS

Software has several characteristics which can, for the purpose of this discussion, be divided into two groups: internal characteristics and external characteristics[3]. Internal characteristics include size and control flow complexity. These are items for which it is possible to derive measures/metrics which can be applied objectively — control flow complexity being the focus of this paper. External characteristics (e.g. maintainability, reliability) are much harder to measure since, as Fenton notes, they must involve human and/or environmental considerations. One aim of metrics research is to identify functional relationships between these external characteristics and the measurable internal characteristics. One component of this research agenda is to ensure the theoretical, and hence practical, validity of the measures of the internal characteristics. The validity of the internal measures is thus of paramount importance in ensuring that good prognostic models for external characteristics can be built in this way.

In the interim, however, one use of internal metrics which may be justifiable and pragmatically useful, even in the absence of any link to an external characteristic, is as "alarms"[4,5]. An alarm would occur

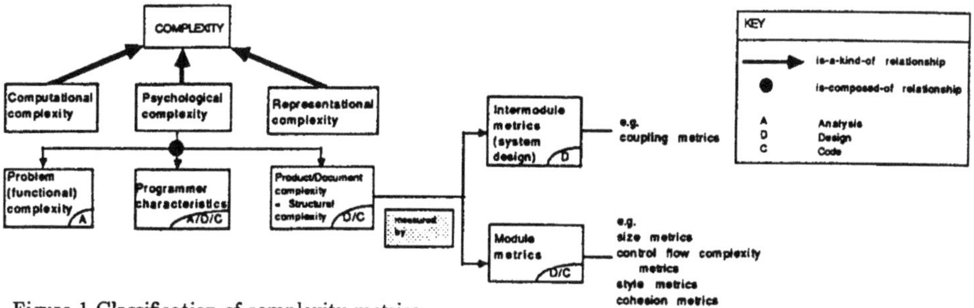

Figure 1 Classification of complexity metrics

whenever the value of a specific internal metric exceeded some pre-determined threshold which would draw attention to that particular part of the code.

Complexity, itself an external characteristic or attribute, has three "flavours": computational, psychological and representational (Figure 1). The most important of these is psychological[6] which encompasses programmer characteristics, structural complexity and problem complexity. Programmer characteristics are hard to measure objectively[7] and little work has been done to date on measures of problem complexity. The prime focus of "complexity research" has thus been on structural complexity which is measured by module metrics and intermodule metrics[5]. Modularity metrics are focussed at the individual module level (subprogram) and may be measures for (i) the internals of the module (procedural complexity) such as size, data structure or logic structure (control flow complexity) or (ii) the external specification of the module (semantic complexity) — typical module cohesion as viewed externally to the module. Intermodule metrics (measuring systems design complexity), on the other hand, describe the connections ***between*** modules and thus characterize the system level complexity.

Here we focus on measures for control flow complexity and specifically on two variants of the cyclomatic complexity measure.

3. CYCLOMATIC COMPLEXITY

McCabe's[1] cyclomatic complexity, $V(G)$, is a measure in widespread use for assessing the control complexity (an internal characteristic) in a program. It aims to provide a basis set for constructing a testing programme (at the unit level) as well as identifying heuristically subprograms which might be regarded as "overly complex".

A basis set comprises a number of linearly independent (LI) paths through the program such that all other paths can be constructed from members of the basis set by using a vector-based approach. It has also been shown[3] that for a program in which there are only ***binary*** decisions (viz. all nodes have outdegree ≤ 2), the magnitude of this basis set is equally given as (no of decisions + 1) or, by Euler's theorem, as the number of discrete regions of the 2-D flowgraph. However, it is important to stress that, despite numerous claims to the contrary[8], the cyclomatic complexity ***does not*** measure external characteristics such as reliability, development effort, understandibility etc. Neither we nor McCabe make any claim that these metrics are theoretically related to psychological complexity which itself must include a strong, cognitive component.

Henderson-Sellers[9] has introduced a revised equation for quantifying "cyclomatic complexity" which has properties upon code modularization not exhibited by the original[1] cyclomatic complexity — a concern raised initially by Shepperd[8]. Feghali and Watson[10] have shown this to be equivalent to "integration complexity"[11] but with the module design complexity, $iv(G)$, replaced by $V(G)$. As such, this new formula, as pointed out[10] represents the "integration complexity without design reduction" and "gives the cardinality of a basis set of paths through an entire program ...".

4. UNDERPINNING BY GRAPH THEORY

The cyclomatic complexity is based on graph theory[12] which says that for a *connected* graph, the graph cyclomatic number[13], v, also called the first Betti number, the nullity or the cycle rank, is given as

$$v = e - n + 1 \tag{1}$$

and for a graph with p components

$$v = e - n + p \tag{2}$$

where e is the number of edges and n the number of nodes. A connected graph (Equation (1)) is a graph where *all* nodes are reachable from every other node. A disconnected graph is one with p components which are disjoint, but which could, with the addition of $(p-1)$ additional edges, be turned into a connected graph (see figure 1 of ref 2). Since in a connected graph, a path from a to b is equivalently a path from b to a, there is no notion of "strongly connected" until the graph becomes directed, as in software representations. This means that, for a single program or program module, the connected, directed acyclic graph (DAG), does not satisfy the definition of connectedness until an edge is added from the stop node to the start node. The resultant graph is thus known as a strongly connected graph and has one more edge than its corresponding undirected graph (or the regular DAG equivalent). Thus the cyclomatic complexity, or cycle rank, is given for a single, strongly connected DAG by

$$V(G) = e - n + 2 \tag{3}$$

— a form frequently quoted in the literature[14–16] as representing the standard McCabe metric. McCabe's[1] Theorem 1 says that in a strongly connected graph i.e. one in which p must have a value of unity, $V(G)$ is equal to the maximum number of linearly independent circuits. This is the basis set from which all other circuits (or for a DAG all other paths) can be created. This is seen as an important guideline and one we shall return to frequently below.

Equation (3) is useful for the cyclomatic complexity of a single component DAG. However, with respect to the extension of $V(G)$ to more than one component, there appear to be two options. Assuming that we are trying to describe a measurement effectively for a connected graph but expressed in terms of, say, three disjoint components, then the argument there is easily extended to give, inductively,

$$V_{LI}(G) = e - n + p + 1 \tag{4}$$

This is the form proposed by Henderson-Sellers[9] and relabelled here with a subscript LI (linearly independent) as we shall later show that this metric (Equation (4)) is strongly related to the cycle rank of the graph.

Feghali and Watson[10] point out that a different approach was taken by McCabe[1]. He argued that *each* of the p components needs to be converted into a strongly connected graph, thus giving p graphs, themselves strongly connected, but not connected to each other. Here $V(G)$ is given by

$$V(G) = e - n + 2p \tag{5}$$

Thus each component is treated independently and the value given by Equation (5) is relevant to each component but not really to the integrated system. Indeed, Shepperd[8] noted that this means that a program with several subroutines is "treated as unconnected components within the control graph" which has "the bizarre result of increasing overall complexity if a program is divided into more, presumably simpler, modules". Each additional subprogram isolated from the rest of the program increases the value of $V(G)$ by 1. Feghali and Watson[10] interpret this additional complexity upon "brute-force modularization" as a test for the interface, rather than an addition to the integration test path basis, which is the focus of $V_{LI}(G)$ and the discussion here.

This concern led to the proposal[9] of Equation (4) which has the properties that

1) modularization (prior to removal of repetitive code) has no effect on $V_{LI}(G)$.
2) the value of $V_{LI}(G)$ for the full program is equal to the total number of decisions, D, plus one.
3) the value of $V_{LI}(G)$ is unchanged when subroutines are merged back into the program either by nesting or sequence. This ties in with the argument that the integration testing procedures (for the present limited to single calls to single entry, single exit components) are unchanged by modularization.
4) the value of $V_{LI}(G)$ provides a basis set for integration testing or for unit testing of a single module.

A simple example will help here to illustrate the differences between $V(G)$ and $V_{LI}(G)$. In Figure 2, there is a main routine and two subroutines, A1 and A2. The values of $V(G)$ and $V_{LI}(G)$ are $V(G) =$

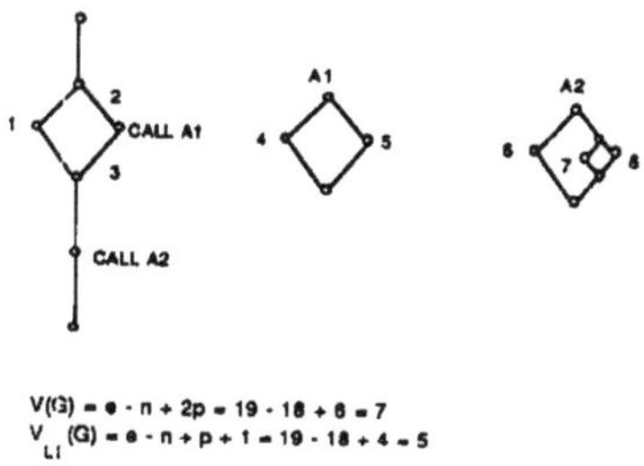

Figure 2 Main routine and two subroutines (A1 and A2) — depicted as three disconnected components.

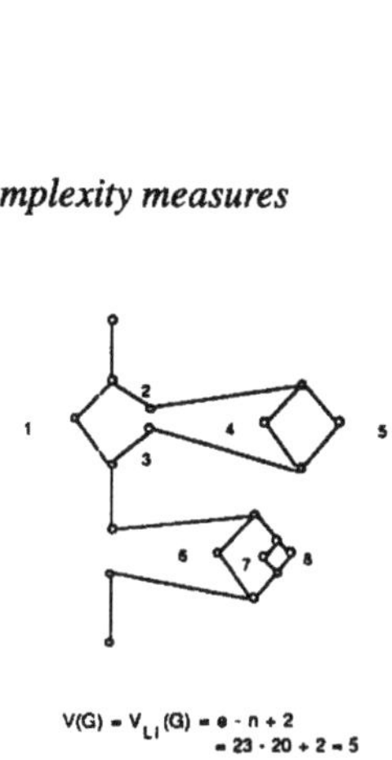

Figure 3 Example of Figure 2 redrawn in terms of a single connected graph.

$19-18+2*3=7$ and $V_{LI}(G)=19-18+3+1=5$. In terms of testing paths, these graphs are equivalent to a single DAG, using the node splitting technique[9], as shown in Figure 3, for which both $V(G)$ and $V_{LI}(G)$ have the same value, given by Equation (3) viz. $23-20+2=5$. In both figures, there are four decisions, whilst the basis set is more easily obtained from Figure 3. The (non-unique) basis set is

1 6; 2 4 3 7; 2 5 3 6; 2 5 3 8; 1 7

All other paths (1 8; 2 4 3 6; 2 4 3 8; 2 5 3 7) are expressible as linear combinations of elements of the basis set. For example, (1 8) = (1 6) + (2 5 3 8) − (2 5 3 6). Finally, both Figures 2 and 3 depict the infinite 2-D plane divided into five regions.

The relationship between the whole and the sum of the parts is also different. McCabe[1] shows that

$$V(G)=\sum V(G_i) \tag{6}$$

whereas it can be shown[9,17] that, for subroutines merged, by nesting or sequence, into a main routine,

$$V_{LI}(G)=\sum V_{LI}(G_i)+1-p \tag{7}$$

Thus $V(G)$ (or more accurately $V_{LI}(G)$) is given by

$$V(G)\equiv V_{LI}(G)=\sum_{i=1}^{p}(e_i-n_i+2)-p+1=e^*-n^*+2p-p+1=e^*-n^*+p+1 \tag{8}$$

where e^* and n^* are the total edges and nodes respectively. The difference here is that Fenton and Kaposi[17] as well as Henderson-Sellers[9] are considering that summing components means merging them (by sequence or iteration); whereas the McCabe approach (Equation (6)) sums *without* merging. Thus the focus is at the *module* level, where the most appropriate formula is Equation (3). $V_{LI}(G)$ retains an interpretation with respect to testing paths both at the unit and at the program level, whereas $V(G)$ treats modules in a program essentially independently.

For the example discussed above, Figure 2 has three components with component $V(G_i)$ values equal to 2, 2 and 3 respectively. Thus from Equation (7) we get $V_{LI}(G)=2+2+3+1-3=5$ as derivable directly in Figure 3. On the other hand, Equation (6) gives $V(G)=7$ which does not relate to criterion of the number of LI paths which is clearly 5.

Henderson-Sellers[9] only considered modularization in the sense of dividing a program into modules and did not address the consequence of the second reason for modularization: the elimination of duplicate code chunks. Based on our Equations (4) and (7), we now extend the $V_{LI}(G)$ metric to cases beyond these single entry/single exit modules[9] i.e. to (i) modularization in order to eliminate duplicate code, (ii) multiple entry single exit modules, (iii) single entry multiple exit modules and (iv) multiple entry multiple exit modules.

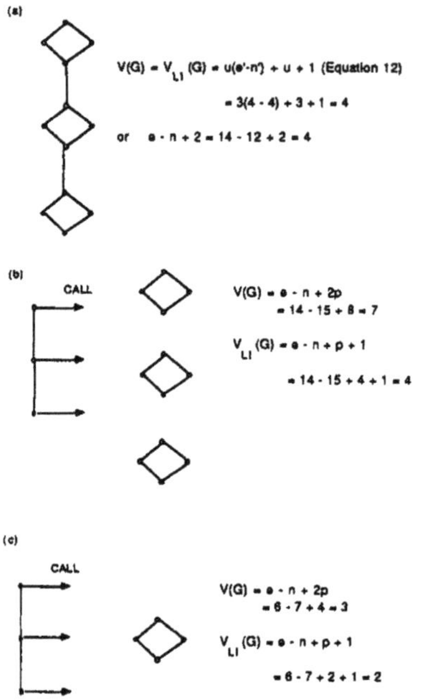

Figure 4 (a) Three modules (single IF THEN ELSE blocks) linked linearly ($p = 1$); (b) modularization into main routine and three subroutines ($p = 4$); (c) elimination of duplicate code ($p = 2$).

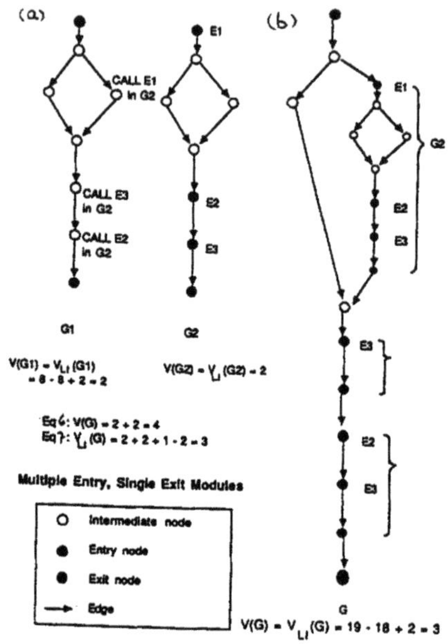

Figure 5 Multiple entry, single exit modules — example DAGs

4.1 Modularization to Eliminate Duplicate Code

Consider a single program which contains u blocks of duplicate code, each with e' edges and n' nodes embedded within it. Let us consider the simplest case: that these u blocks are connected by simple edges (Figure 4(a)). Since there are u "chunks" of duplicate code connected together linearly, there are $u - 1$ edges of connection. The total complexity of this single module ($p = 1$) is thus given as

$$V_{LI}(G) = (ue' + u - 1) - un' + 2 = u(e' - n') + u + 1 \tag{9}$$

We now consider the modularization of this program. Since there are u duplicate chunks, the modularized program has one main routine which has u nodes and $u - 1$ edges and u other components (viz. $p = u+1$) (Figure 4(b)). The value of $V_{LI}(G)$ is unchanged. The concept that these $p-1$ components are duplicates and can be replaced by a single module (Figure 4(c)) is introduced. Now there is the main routine plus only one other module: that of the duplicated chunk. This has e' edges and n' nodes. For the main module, $V_{LI}(G_1) = (u - 1) - u + 2 = 1$ and for the submodule, $V_{LI}(G_2) = e' - n' + 2$. Hence, from Equation (7)

$$V_{LI}(G) = V_{LI}(G_1) + V_{LI}(G_2) + 1 - 2 = 1 + e' - n' + 2 + 1 - 2 = (e' - n') + 2 \tag{10}$$

Since the value of the unmodularized code is given by Equation (9) above, it can be seen that the modularization to deal with each chunk of repeated code gives a reduction in the value of the cyclomatic complexity of $(ue' - un' + u + 1) - (e' - n' + 2) = (u - 1)(e' - n' + 1)$. In other words, as noted in ref 10 yet consistently with ref 9, the cyclomatic complexity of a program containing duplicate chunks explicitly embedded in the main program (Figure 4(a)) is greater than the modularized version where the duplication is removed from the graph depicting the program (Figure 4(c)). Additional CALLs to the same subprogram engender no extra *structural* complexity since no additional test paths are created. Feghali and Watson's[10] comment on the dramatic increase of "complexity" in this situation is relevant to cognitive complexity but not structural complexity or the testing paths approach.

As a corollary, since the complexity of the repeated module can be expressed as $v = e' - n' + 2$, we can substitute this expression for v and calculate a decrease in complexity which gives a result identical to that given in ref 8. Summed over all k repeated modules leads to a decrease of $\sum_{i=1}^{k}(u_i - 1) \times (v_i - 1)$ where v is the complexity of the module being extracted. This reduction also reflects the smaller cyclic basis so that the test strategy avoids duplicate testing of the duplicate code chunks.

In contrast, the identical analysis using $V(G)$, rather than $V_{LI}(G)$, gives

(a) as one module $V(G) = u(e' - n') + u + 1$ (cf. Equation (9) for $V_{LI}(G)$)
(b) as $u + 1$ modules $V(G) = u(e' - n' + 2) + 1$ (cf. Equation (9) for $V_{LI}(G)$)
(c) as two modules $V(G) = e' - n' + 3$ (cf. Equation (10) for $V_{LI}(G)$)
(d) reduction (between (c) and (a)) $\Delta V(G) = (u-1)(e' - n') + u - 2 = (u-1)(v-1) - 1$
(e) reduction (between (c) and (b)) $\Delta V(G) = (u-1)(e' - n' + 2) = (u-1)v$

In terms of calculating $V_{LI}(G)$ for a program with several CALLs to the same subroutine, then additional CALLs in excess of one do not add to the value of $V_{LI}(G)$ since they introduce no further entries in the cyclic basis. Thus Equation (7) holds for subroutines with multiple CALLs. However, it should be noted that this conclusion should not be extrapolated to other classes of complexity measures, such as psychological complexity or understandability — for example, intuitively multiple CALLs may make a program harder to comprehend and debug (a topic which cannot be addressed by the structural cyclomatic complexity measures discussed here).

4.2 Multiple Entry, Single Exit Modules

Whilst multiple entry modules are generally not frequently encountered, and indeed discouraged by some authors, it is important that any validated metric be equally applicable to multiple entry modules as to single entry modules. In the context of cyclomatic complexity metrics, the results of the previous section apply directly. Multiple entries are simply a method of code reuse. Thus the arguments for duplicate code expressed above remain valid and $V_{LI}(G)$ is calculated from Equation (7).

For example, Figure 5(a) depicts two simple program modules each with a cyclomatic number of two (one decision per module). There are clearly three vectors in the cycle basis. We suppose that the subprogram module, G_2, has the normal entry point at the beginning of the module, but that it also has an entry point at node E_2 and E_3 as indicated. The value of $V_{LI}(G)$ from Equation (7) is found to be 3 (=2 + 2 + 1 − 2). This has 2 decisions so again we expect $V_{LI}(G) = 1 + 2 = 3$. There are also three planar regions as anticipated from Euler's formula. This is shown as a single connected graph in Figure 5(b).

4.3 Single Entry, Multiple Exit Modules

Multiple exit points are frequently used in structured programming. Generally these occur in branches of IF structures where an immediate return to the CALLing module occurs (Figure 6(a)). In this case, the addition of a second RETURN at X_1 (in addition to the normal RETURN at the end of the module at X_2) can be represented in one of three ways (Figures 6(b–d)). Either an additional (fictitious) edge can be drawn to the exit node of the subroutine (Figure 6(b)), in which case one is added to the value of $V_{LI}(G)$ for every such RETURN; or, using node splitting to change the disconnected components of Figure 6(b) to the connected graph of Figure 6(c), an additional edge is drawn direct to the main module; and finally (Figure 6(d)), the subroutine can be fully embedded. In all cases, we can easily capture this additional complexity explicitly by adding one to $V_{LI}(G)$ for every additional exit point. Thus Equation (4) becomes

$$V_{LI}(G) = e - n + p + 1 + \sum_{j=1}^{p-1}(r_j - 1) \tag{11}$$

where e is the number of edges, n the number of nodes, p the number of connected components (modules), and r_j the number of exit points in the DAG representation of the j-th module (where there are $p - 1$

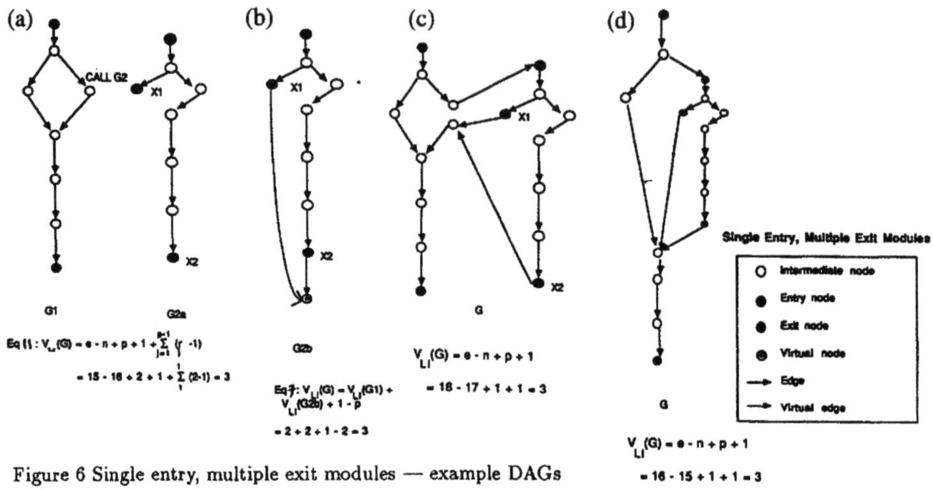

Figure 6 Single entry, multiple exit modules — example DAGs

such modules e.g. subroutines). This can be interpreted as an increase in the complexity of the program (cf. one not using multiple exits) by

$$\Delta V_{LI}(G) = \sum_{j=1}^{p-1}(r_j - 1) \tag{12}$$

— an approach also used in ref 15. In this example, the value of $V_{LI}(G)$ is found to be 3 (=18 − 17 + 2: Figure 6(c) or 16 − 15 + 2: Figure 6(d)). Alternatively, Equation (11) can be applied directly to the disjoint graphs of Figure 6(a) to give $V_{LI}(G) = 15 - 16 + 3 + 1 = 3$. There are clearly 2 decisions and 3 regions.

4.4 Multiple Entry, Multiple Exit Modules

Multiple entry multiple exit (MEME) point modules are seldom encountered in structured programming. However, for completeness sake, we note briefly that since multiple entries do not change $V_{LI}(G)$, MEME modules can be treated identically to multiple exit modules to which Equation (11) applies.

5. DISCUSSION

The focus of both the measures $V(G)$ and $V_{LI}(G)$ is that of structural complexity. They can be related (with varying degrees of success) to the number of decisions and the provision of a basis set of testing paths (unit and system level, as discussed above). One difference relates to whether $V(G) = \sum V(G_i)$ which is true for McCabe's $V(G)$ but not for $V_{LI}(G_i)$; although the latter retains consistency with the notion of a basis set. At the system level, $V_{LI}(G)$ maintains a description of the basis set with regard to a testing methodology and complements the notion of integration complexity[11], $iv(G)$. The connection, as Feghali and Watson[10] correctly note, is that $V_{LI}(G)$ provides a test-paths view equivalent to this integration complexity without design reduction, whereby decision nodes not involved in subprogram CALLs are ignored. Thus the formula for integration complexity[11], S_1, given by

$$S_1 = \sum iv(G) + 1 - p \tag{13}$$

is closely paralleled by Equation (7) for $V_{LI}(G)$.

In closing, we propose that a modification to the $V_{LI}(G)$ approach also may be worth exploring. Rather than Equation (4), it is worth evaluating the measure

$$C(G) = e - n + p \tag{14}$$

This has the advantage that it represents, both at module and program level, the number of decisions rather than the number of decisions plus one; that is measurable on a ratio scale since it has an absolute zero such that transformations of the type $g)x) = a\ x$ are possible[6]; that the sum of the components is equal to complexity of the total program (thus satisfying Weyuker's[18] 5th axiom). Conversely, the basis set is given by $C(G)+1$. At the same time, $C(G)$ does not change upon modularization and is unchanged when subprograms are nested or sequenced back into the main program. When a program is modularized to remove duplicate code, $C(G)$ is reduced by an amount $(u-1)v$ (cf. $(u-1)\times(v-1)$ for $V_{LI}(G)$). Finally, both $C(G)$ and $V_{LI}(G)$ provide the dimension of the cycle rank for developing integration testing methodologies.

Consequently, $C(G)$ may be a possible candidate for inclusion in compound psychological complexity measures; although it should be stressed that neither analytical nor empirical work yet undertaken seems convincing[8].

6. ACKNOWLEDGEMENTS

We wish to thank David Monarchi for constructive discussions during the preparation of this paper. We wish to thank Ross Jeffery, June Verner and Yagna Pant for comments on an earlier draft of this paper.

REFERENCES

1. McCABE, T., 'A complexity measure', *IEEE Trans. Software Eng.*, 1976, Vol. SE-2, (4), pp. 308–320
2. HENDERSON-SELLERS, B. and TEGARDEN, D., Response to 'Clarification concerning modularization and McCabe's cyclomatic complexity', *Comm. ACM*, 1994, Vol. 37, (4), pp. 92–94
3. FENTON, N.E., 'Software Metrics: A Rigorous Approach', (Chapman and Hall, London, 1991)
5. SZENTES, J. and GRAS, J., 'Some practical views of software complexity metrics and a universal measurement tool', First Australian Software Engineering Conference (ASWEC), Canberra, 14–16 May, 1986
6. KITCHENHAM, B.A. and LINKMAN, S.J., 'Design metrics in practice', *Inf. Soft. Technol.*, 1990, Vol. 32, (4), pp. 304–310
7. ZUSE, H., 'Software Complexity: Measures and Methods', (Walter de Gruyter, Berlin, 1990)
9. KEARNEY, J.K., SEDLMEYER, R.L., THOMPSON, W.B., GRAY, M.A. and ADLER, M.A., 'Software complexity measurement', *Comm. ACM*, 1986, Vol. 29, (11), pp. 1044–1050
10. SHEPPERD, M., 'A critique of cyclomatic complexity as a software metric', *Software Engineering Journal*, 1988, Vol. 3, pp. 30–36
11. HENDERSON-SELLERS, B., 'Modularization and McCabe's cyclomatic complexity', *Comm. ACM*, 1992, Vol. 35, (12), pp. 17–19
12. FEGHALI, I. and WATSON, A.H., 'Clarification concerning modularization and McCabe's cyclomatic complexity', *Comm. ACM*, 1994, Vol. 37, (4), pp. 91–92
13. McCABE, T.J. and BUTLER, C.W., 'Design complexity measurement and testing', *Comm. ACM*, 1989, Vol. 32, (12), pp. 1415–1425
14. BOLLOBÁS, B., 'Graph Theory. An Introductory Course', (Springer–Verlag, New York, 1979)
15. BERGE, C., 'Graphs', 2nd ed., (North-Holland, Amsterdam, 1985)
20. BAKER, A.L. and ZWEBEN, S.H., 'A comparison of measures of control flow complexity', *IEEE Trans. Software Eng.*, 1980, Vol. SE-6, (6), pp. 506–512
21. HARRISON, W.A., 'Applying McCabe's complexity measure to multiple-exit programs', *Software — Practice and Experience*, 1984, Vol. 14, (10), pp. 1004–1007
22. CONTE, S.D., DUNSMORE, H.E. and SHEN, V.Y., 'Software Engineering Metrics and Models', (Benjamin/Cummings, Menlo Park, CA, 1986)
24. FENTON, N.E. and KAPOSI, A.A., 'Metrics and software structure', *Inf. Software Technol.*, 1987, Vol. 29, (6), pp. 301–320
25. WEYUKER, E.J., 'Evaluating software complexity measures', *IEEE Trans. Software Eng.*, 1988, Vol. 14, (9), pp. 1357–1365

52

Reliability through Cooperative Work in Software Testing*

Tuomo Tuikka

Department of Information Processing Science, University of Oulu,
Linnanmaa, FIN-90570, Oulu, Finland, email:ttu@rieska.oulu.fi

Abstract

There are many papers pointing out ways to reach reliability in the product. Those papers are mostly dealing with the issue in quantitative manner. However, the reliability we in our everyday software production try to reach depends more or less on an agreement between people producing a product. This agreement is reached through cooperation during the process of software production. This is a paper to take a look at software testing and reliability with a view of cooperative work. Surely, all work is essentially cooperative work in that it depends upon others for its successful performance and software testing is no exception of this. Open question is what is the role of cooperative work in software testing and reliability of the product? The ideas presented here are examples based on the experience of the writer in the field of software testing. As a result cooperative work is seen to play essential role for reliability. Furthermore, a view of articulation work is suggested to be useful for further studies of cooperative work in software testing.

Keyword Codes: D.2.5; J.4; K.6.3;
Keywords: Software Engineering, Testing and Debugging; Social and Behavioral Sciences; Management of Computing and Information Systems, Software Management;

1. SOFTWARE TESTING AND RELIABILITY

Software testing is one part of the software production process and important phase so that reliable products can eventually be sent out to world market. As software producers we also have a responsibility of our products because people using them might lose their time and money due to errors in the program. Thus, we have goals for software testing such as high quality, user satisfaction, cost benefits.[1] Perhaps we could see software testing to be useful in two spheres like [1] does: "When carried out effectively in the commercial sphere, software testing will contribute to the delivery of higher quality software products, more satisfied users and lower maintenance costs. In the scientific sphere, good testing will result in more accurate and reliable results." Considering this division the goals of these two spheres could sometimes be contradictory. Questions like what is the level of results for (scientifical) testing or when is the product good enough for release arise (commercial pressure). Although software testing has a different significance to different people, usually quality of the product is we all aim at. Furthermore, quality of other kind, the quality of software process, certainly affects the ultimate quality, reliability, and safety of the software. While testing is no substitute for improving

*This work has been done in the Finnish part of the ESPRIT project 6225 COMIC, funded by F. C. T D. (Tekes). Author wishes to thank Tauno Tönning foundation for additional funding and Peter Carstensen and Carsten Sørensen of Risø National Laboratory in Roskilde, Denmark for comments and suggestions.

the process, it does occupy crucial role in the overall software development process[2] and it is an integral part of any quality programme.[1] As [3] puts it: "Testing is one of the methods used by the Software Quality Assurance (SQA) group to ensure the quality of systems..." and [4] "The purpose of testing is to make quality visible". More accurately program testing could be defined as simply: "Testing is the process of executing a program with the intent of finding errors"[5]. Hetzel defines testing further by determining meeting requirements: "Testing is any activity aimed at evaluating an attribute or capability of a program or system and determining that it meets its required results" [4] There are several stages of testing including unit, integration, system, product, customer, and regression testing. These terms usually refer to the stage of the testing, not its form. This paper refers more to regression testing which is meant to assure that a new version of a system faithfully reproduces the desirable behaviour of the previous system [2]. Software testing techniques are discussed in [6, 7].

What we intuitively call "software reliability" is the probability of not encountering a sequence of inputs that leads to failure.[8] Reliability estimation, viewed by [2], attempts to predict the mean time to failure of software based on the experience of testing against an operational profile of the software use. Safety evaluation attempts to find and eliminate sources of failure and risk in software based on an understanding of the code, its requirements, and its environment of use.[2] Software reliability analysis, the estimation of the probability of software failure during a specified exposure period, as a subject of research is related to the well-established work on general system reliability theory. Many papers have been written on software reliability models. Overview e.g. [9]

Software is a difficult object to develop [8]: "Problems or fundamental limitations in software are: 1) Complexity, it takes time to develop, 2) Error sensitivity, no useful interpretation of tolerance is known for software, 3) Hard to test, software is notoriously difficult to test adequately. Moreover, it has been pointed out that testing carried out by selected test cases, no matter how carefully and well-planned, can provide nothing but anecdotes. 4) Correlated failures, in contrast to the situation with hardware systems, one cannot obtain higher reliability by duplication of software components. One simply duplicates the errors. 5) Lack of professional standard."[2] Thus, besides difficult to develop, an important problem is whether test is adequate, that is, not only what test cases should be tested but also when testing should start and stop. We do have measures to lean on in trying to determine if our product is ready for release, but it is impossible to tell if our software is error free. Apparently there is a lot true of what is said about belief on a product trustworthiness: "We cannot test software for correctness, it is difficult to make accurate predictions of software reliability and availability, it is not practical to measure the trustworthiness of software. We consider a product to be trustworthy if we believe that the probability of it having a potentially catastrophic flaw is acceptably low."[8] There has been also critics on statistical methods for calculating the reliability of program. There is consensus among several researchers that there are some serious shortcomings of these models which need to be remedied before they can be used.[2] Many of the models rely on assumptions that are often not satisfied in practice. Another drawback of these models as [2] mentions is that they do not deal directly and thoroughly with the crucial question of when to stop testing the software. Well, if we cannot test software for correctness how do we get products out anyway? How do we agree on product reliability?

Objective of this paper is not to show problems of any models, but to present a view to co-operative work in software testing when reliability of the product is sought-after.Suggestion presented here is that agreement of reliability of software emerges through cooperative work in software production. Thus, e.g. required results (cf.[4]) of software are negotiable. To illustrate this argument I give an example of my personal experience in the field of software testing and especially in this case from work in regression testing.

3. COOPERATIVE WORK IN SOFTWARE TESTING

The first place we find cooperation useful in software testing is the situation where we are trying to test our own product. Like [1] says:"We normally perceive our own products as correct. This means that, once we have made an error during the development phase, this becomes part of our product. Having made an erroneous assumption once, in reviewing or testing the product we are likely to make the same assumption again. To operate successfully, anyone testing their own software must be prepared to question every aspect of the product, ignoring any inclinations to assume the correctness of any previous work. For most of us this is difficult: our thought processes will follow the previously trodden path - to repeat the error"[1]. In case we work in a large software production environment, however, say for example 60 or more people, the role of software tester and programmer is usually divided. The nature of test situation determines then the nature of cooperation.[6]

All work is essentially cooperative work in a sense that it depends upon others for its successful performance (cf. [10]), and it is constituted by work processes that are related as to content, that is, processes pertaining to the production of a particular product or service. The definition for cooperative work used here is: "At the core of this conception of cooperative work is the notion of interdependence in work. In the sense that cooperative work occurs when multiple actors are required to do the work and therefore are mutually dependent in their work and must coordinate and integrate their individual activities to get the work done "[11]

Next example is a description how regression testing can happen. The problem studied is when software testing can be stopped and release sent out. Let's assume a software corporation has 65 people working on a product. That means we have many *mutually interdependent actors* in working on a product. In that group we have software developers, testing groups, and marketing people who are waiting for the delivery date to come. Figure 1 is simplified view where a circle means a position in a team.

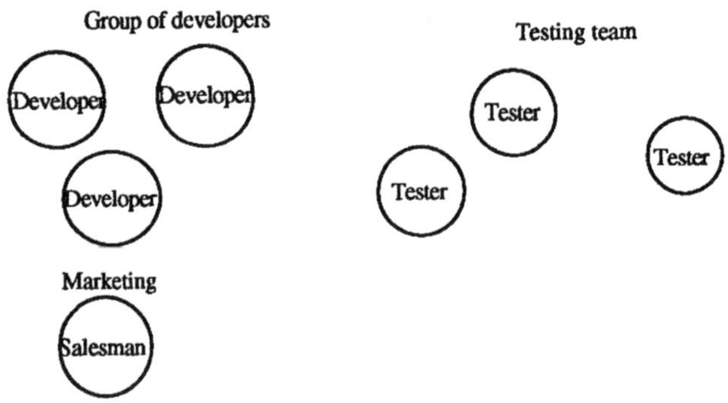

Figure 1. Simple description of software production group.

When we try to see 65 of them we get a little idea of the *complexity* we might be in when studying the organisation and work in it. In this simplified example we think that programmers and testers are those people who develop the product. Programmers are those who write the code, and testers test product, collect errors, and inform of them. However, if someone else finds an error, responsibles are notified. Every tester has his/her own area of responsibility, which is some part of the product. Product may consist of different parts which can be also products themselves. This part can be the user interface and its functions, compiler or a unit which can be thought to be tested as a whole. Usually everyone has several of these responsibility areas. Here we can see that *many highly interconnected parts*, components, concepts, lines of code created etc. are in the field of work. There are many actions for tester who tries to find errors in the program. Let's assume a tester finds a new error. This information must be told further, so that error can be repaired. Of course the founder of an error can be anyone in the company. At this stage the error goes for correction if it is thought to be worth correcting. Worthyness is examined by the group working on the development and programmer, because correction should be done in a reasonable time period and be relative to other work. When the error is corrected, information of it is given further, with data on how it should be tested. This way we ensure it will not happen again. (Figure 2)

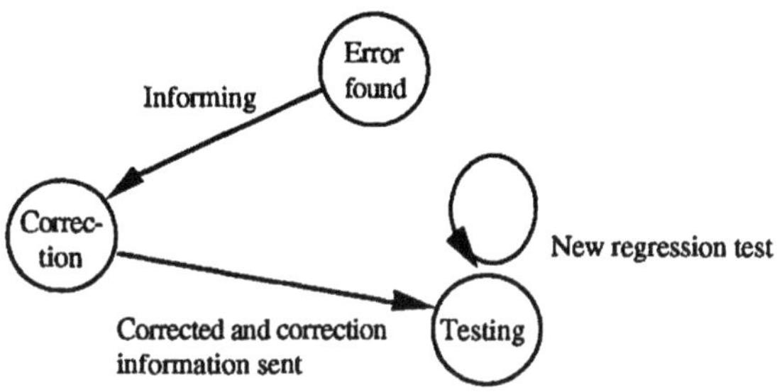

Figure 2. Simplified work process in case of finding an error.

New version of program should not include the error anymore. We need to be certain of that further on and a test operation is decided on it. This way we close the earlier problems of the product and also collect information of the product history. Test operation is decided by the test group leader usually, but with enough experience also tester is able to do it. Automatic test macro will be written for regression tests and finally the test operation is done automatically, unless the case is so difficult it needs special arrangements. When new version of the product is taken for tests, we can now ensure old error is fixed. This happens by automatic tests which are driven to new version. This phase is a mechanical procedure after automatic environment has been built. New tests can be added to the test set which can consist hundreds of tests. The result of testdrive should be that all tests pass, but sometimes you can find that old problem has come back again. Many broken errors might indicate a severe problem in product. For example, wrong file has been compiled during build up. One of the criterias for the maturity of the product could be error count and type of errors. Sometimes error type is needed to decide whether problem is important or not. In serious cases error must be fixed right away because leaving it would jeopardize the whole development process. Small problems could be cosmetic problems like wrong error messages etc. One generally interesting issue is where error has been. It might be possible to track the true cause of problems if we know where the bugs appear. This also could give a clue if the problem is very serious. With this knowledge it is possible to design further procedures and time it takes compare to other actions.

Previous description shows how work should go and usually goes. However, in final stages of product, date of release coming, everyone is doing their best to get all errors found and fixed. However, behind the curtains it is possible to find many problems. We have *uncertainty* of the real nature of an error, is the problem really how it looks like? There is also uncertainty how the test set is covering problem areas and what happens when error is fixed, does a fix create more and even worse problems. There is a constant change in utilisation of machines and equipment need to be renewed while technology develops. Learning and adaptation of new information is essential to get tests to right use environment. This is *dynamism*, and it is often caused from the fact that the work situations are characterised by handling a number of concepts, requirements, etc. that are dynamic by nature, i.e., events can happen at indeterminate times. This might result in change of the problem to be solved. Finally, supposing that we cannot test for correctness, how can we tell our product is ready. Can we trust the product enough for release? This is a question of negotiation. The marketing department may want to get a release despite of few minor bugs. But what is a minor bug? A minor bug may be a symptom for a far deeper problem. And a week or two more testing and fixing might hurt company stocks and investors.

In cooperative work people have to coordinate their work due to their mutual interdependency. Easiest way to see how this is done in our example is to look at how reliability is reached. Final reliability of product is a result of negotiations. There are several points that illustrate this in our example. First we need to inform responsible people of an error. Second, we have to do negotiations of worthiness of correction, the nature of error, probably about the results of tests and error severity in possible deliverable software. Issues for negotiation could be: What parameters of the product to discuss? What kind of errors could be acceptable in the product or worth correction? What new errors you could get from correcting old ones? Are we going to change anything we have earlier accepted as a standards? Through this process we finally reach an agreement (or not) that our product is good for release. Much information can be attained from formal reliability models, but they are only an aid for software testing work. Thus, the decision of release is made in meetings, discussions and negotiations and we can argue that cooperative work plays important role in software testing.

Furthermore, in a large software production company we can see that, besides mutually interdependent actors, many highly interconnected parts, uncertainty and dynamism characterise work environment and work. By Woods (1988) [12] they characterise the dimensions of complexity. Complex work situations are most often handled in a distributed cooperative work arrangement with mutually interdependent actors. In this case all activities are heavily intertwined and a decomposition into small isolated test activities is impossible [13], this means that division of labor in software testing is not only a matter of structuring the program properly[14]. Thus, many actors and perspectives are involved. This, in turn, requires *articulation work* to be performed by the people involved.[15] In the words of Strauss [16], articulation work is "a kind of supra-type work in any division of labor, done by various actors. Articulation work amounts to the following. First, the meshing of the often numerous tasks, clusters of tasks, and segments of the total arc. Second, the meshing of efforts of various workers (individuals, departments, etc.). Third, the meshing of actors with their various types of work and implicated tasks." For articulation purposes, activities such as allocating resources, planning and scheduling tasks, monitoring the state of affairs in the development and test process, classifying and prioritizing, distributing information, and negotiating requirements, priorities, etc. are essential.[15] Consequently the agreement of software maturity is reached through articulation work and reliability is more like common understanding on state of software and belief that software works on certain conditions.

4. DISCUSSION

A cooperative ensemble of people in software production and in testing process must find an agreement that the product is reliable enough for release. Still, disagreement can be possible even though the product has been released and market forces decide the success of the product. More studies of cooperative work and its computer support can be found in reseach field of Computer Supported Cooperative Work [17-19]. However, nature of software testing and articulation work are seldom addressed directly in the literature although cooperative work affects deeply into the quality of our products. Further studies of cooperative work would be useful for developing tools to support cooperative work in software testing which is one goal of my research.

REFERENCES

1. Parrington N. and Roper M., Understanding Software Testing. 1989, Chichester, England: Ellis Horwood Limited.
2. Dalal S. R., Hogan J. R. and Kettering J. R.. Reliable Software and Communication: Software Quality, Reliability, and Safety. in *15th International Conference on Software Engineering*. 1993. Baltimore, Maryland, USA: IEEE Computer Society Press, Los Alamitos, California, USA. p. 425-435.
3. Yourdon E., Software Quality Assurance in the 1990s. in *Sixth Annual Pacific Northwest Software Quality Conference*. 1988. Portland, Oregon, USA: p. 3-33.
4. Hetzel B., The Complete Guide to Software Testing. 1988, Wellesley, MA, USA: QED Information Sciences Inc. 284.
5. Myers G.J., The Art of Software Testing. 1979, New York: John Wiley and Sons.
6. Beizer B., Software Testing Techniques. Second Edition ed. 1990, New York: Van Nostrand Reinhold.
7. Beizer B., Software System Testing and Quality Assurance. 1984, New York: Van Nostrand Reinhold Company Inc. 358.
8. Parnas D. L., Schouwen A. J. v. and Kwan S. P., Evaluation of Safety-Critical Software. *Communications of the ACM*, 1990. **33**(6): p. 636-648.
9. Malaiya Y. K. and Srimani P. K., Software Reliability Models: Theoretical Developments, Evaluation and Applications. 1990, Los Alamitos, California, USA: IEEE Computer Society Press.
10. Bannon L. and Schmidt K., CSCW: Four Characters in Search of a Context, in Studies in Computer Supported Cooperative Work. Theory, Practice and Design, J. M. Bowers and S. D. Benford, Editors. 1991, North-Holland: Amsterdam etc. p. 3-16.
11. Simone C.and Schmidt K., Computational Mechanisms of Interaction for CSCW1993, COMIC, ESPRIT Basic Research Project 6225: Lancaster, United Kingdom.
12. Woods D. D., Coping with complexity: the psychology of human behavior in complex systems, in Tasks, Errors and Mental Models. A Festschrift to celebrate the 60th birthday of Professor Jens Rasmussen, L. P. Goodstein, H. B. Andersen and S. E. Olsen, Editors. 1988, Taylor & Francis: London etc. p. 128-148.
13. Petchenik N. H., Practical Priorities in System Testing. *IEEE Software*, 1985. **2**(5): p. 18-23.
14. Parnas D. L., Software Aspects of Strategic Defense Systems. *Communications of the ACM*, 1985. **28**(12): p. 1326-1335.
15. Carstensen P. H., Tuikka T. and Sørensen C., "Are we done now?" Towards Requirements for Computer Supported Cooperative Software Testing. in *Precedings of the 17th Information systems Research seminar In Scandinavia (IRIS 17)*. 1994. Iso-Syöte Conference Centre, Finland: University of Oulu, Department of Inf. Processing Science, Finland. p. 424-438.
16. Strauss A., Work and the Division of Labor. *The Sociological Quarterly*, 1985. **26**(1): p. 1-19.
17. Schmidt K., Simone C., Carstensen P., Hewitt B. and Sørensen C., Computational Mechanisms of Interaction: Notations and Facilities, in Computational Mechanisms of Interaction for CSCW, C. Simone and K. Schmidt, Editors. 1993, Esprit BRA 6225 COMIC: Lancaster, England. p. 109-164.
18. Greif I., ed. Computer-Supported Cooperative Work:A Book of Readings. 1988, Morgan Kaufmann Publishers Inc.: San Mateo, USA.
19. Michelis G. D., Simone C. and Schmidt K., Proceedings of the Third European Conference on Computer-Supported Cooperative Work. 1993. Milan, Italy: Kluwer Academic Publishers. .[1] N. Parrington and M. Roper, Understanding Software Testing. 1989, Chichester, England: Ellis Horwood Limited.

PART EIGHT

Reusability

53

Code Reusability Mechanisms

Xavier Castellani and Hong Jiang

CEDRIC-IIE (CNAM) research laboratory, 18 allée Jean Rostand, 91025 Evry Cedex, France
Tel 33 1 69 36 73 50 - Fax 33 1 69 36 73 05, castellani@iie.cnam.fr, jiang@iie.cnam.fr

Abstract

This paper describes standardized reusability mechanisms of program code using a metric and a guideline. These mechanisms find five results of code reusability which allow us to merge programs, to store programs in a library and to include them in other programs, and to store common sequences code of programs in a library and to include them in programs. These mechanisms show how programs can be built in a standardized manner on using a metric and a guideline.

These mechanisms are based on the standardized reusability mechanisms of objects of the object-oriented analysis and design methodology MCO. They can be used with any programming language.

Keyword codes: D.2.3; D.2.6; D.2.8; D.2.10
Keywords: Program design. Reusability. Metrics. Guideline.

1. INTRODUCTION

According to Nauer and Randell [14], *software reuse is the process of creating software systems from existing software rather than building software systems from scratch.*

According to Meyer [13], *reusability is the ability of software products to be reused, in whole or in part, for new applications.*

The software reuse in developing new software is a well known field in software engineering for about twenty years [11]. There is an increasing need for a corresponding maturity in reutilisability, assessment and measurement. The assessment of a component's quality and reutilisability are critical to a successful reuse effort. Components must be easily comprehensible, easily incorporated into new systems. Unfortunately, no consensus currently exists on how to go about measuring component's reutilisability [3].

The success of reuse technology depends on the integration of reuse libraries into the design and programming environments. To reuse software, it is necessary to have specifications of the software. Without these specifications the reuse is impossible. Furthermore, it is very inefficient to look through manually the specifications [6]. When the number of reusable components is quite big, this is not practical. Therefore, reutilisability mechanisms and on-line searching mechanisms are required. With the support of an on-line searching tool [2], software can be shared easily.

The idea of using metrics to normalize program code reusability has been proposed by several specialists. We can mention Cox [7] and groups of the Annual Workshop on Software

Reuse [16]. To our knowledge, it does not exist rational utilization of metrics to normalize the reusability of programs.

This paper presents a solution to normalize the reusability of programs with mechanisms which use a metric and a guideline. These mechanisms find five results of code reusability which allow us to merge programs, to store programs in a library and to include them in other programs, and to store common sequences code of programs in a library and to include them in programs.

The mechanisms of code reusability allow us to find common programs and common sequences in different programs to store them in libraries and to include in programs. The common sequences code and the particular sequences code of two programs are presented in Section 2. The five results of program code reusability are presented in Section 3. Metrics to measure program code are presented in Section 4. The mechanisms of code reusability are presented in Section 5.

2. COMMON SEQUENCES CODE AND PARTICULAR SEQUENCES CODE OF TWO PROGRAMS

A sequence code is a set of lines of code. We distinguish *declaration sequences (DS) which are data declarations and the other declarations: declarations of macros, of "include", of "copy", etc. which can be used, from processing sequences (PS) which can be performed.*

The common declaration sequences of two programs are the data declarations of the same types and the other declarations which are identical: declarations of macros, declarations of "include" or of "copy", etc.

Data declarations of the same types may be declarations of data which have not the same names. Common declarations sequences may be not contiguous sequences and may be not ordered with the same order. Numerous programs have common sequences. It is in particular the case for input/output programs.

The particular declaration sequences of two programs are the declarations which are not common declaration sequences.

The common processing sequences of two programs are processing sequences which provide the same processing.

Two processing sequences provide the same processing if their specifications are syntactically identical or if a tool or an analyst must certify that they ensure the same processing. It is especially necessary to study processing sequences that use named data differently but of the same types, and to study processing sequences not specified with the same statements, for example "case" statements specified with "if" statements.

The common processing sequences may be not contiguous sequences. For example in Cobol, a processing sequence may be defined with statements using "Perform" blocks and these blocks.

Common processing sequences may be not ordered with the same order. For example "Allocation" statements, blocks of the different cases of "case" statements and parallel blocks of statements.

The particular processing sequences of two programs are the processing sequences which are not common processing sequences.

3. THE FIVE RESULTS OF PROGRAM CODE REUSABILITY

In this Section we apply the principle of the object reusability mechanisms [5] to program reusability. These object reusability mechanisms allow the creation of object merges, simple inheritances and abstract objects. The five possible results of program code reusability between two programs P-a and P-b presented in Figure 1 are deduced from the results of object reusability .

1 - P-b is identical to P-a.
2 - P-b is merged with P-a.
3 - P-a is stored in a library and is "included" in P-b.
4 - P-b is stored in a library and is "included" in P-a.

---

5 - One or several common sequences existing in both programs P-a and P-b are stored in a library and are "included" in P-a and in P-b.

Figure 1: The five results of reusability between two programs

For the results 2, 3, 4, the particular sequences of P-b and of P-a (result 2), or of P-a or P-b (results 3 or 4) are defined in case sequences and the program is parameterized to perform these particular sequences.

For the result 5, one or several common sequences existing in both programs P-a and P-b are stored in a library and are "included" in P-a and in P-b. This result allows us to create separately declaration sequences from processing sequences.

The result 5 allows us to define common sequences in two programs. We do not present the study of identical sequences of a same program.

To simplify, we say here that a program is stored in a library and is "included" in another program. According to the used language, this mechanism is obtained with the statements "Include" in C or Pascal, "Copy" in Cobol, or by defining sub-program, or with other mechanisms.

The five results of reusability are defined between two programs which have the most important common sequences. The reusability between several programs is studied successively between these programs considered two by two. For example between two programs P-a and P-b, P-b is stored in a library and is "included" in P-a. After, the reusability is studied between two programs P-a and P-c, P-c is stored in a library and is "included" in P-a.

4. METRICS TO MEASURE PROGRAM CODE

Numerous software experts have proposed metrics to measure software components. Some of them are mentioned by Fenton [8]. The simplest unit to measure source program code length is Lines of Code (LOC). Others prefer the Used Instructions (UI): the COCOMO method (COst COnstructive MOdel) [4] of Boehm for example. Others use the Function Points (FPs) [1]. However, most companies use LOC in spite of their deficiencies [9].

Software engineering specialists have defined other metrics than the sizes of the programs to measure the quality of the software. Among the most used the metrics to measure numbers of operators and numbers of operands, mention the metrics of Halstead [10], the metrics to measure program control graphs, mention the metrics of McCabe [12] and the metrics to measure program call graphs, the hierarchical complexity which is the average number of modules by level.

In this article we use the sizes to measure programs code and we measure these sizes with lines.

5. MECHANISMS OF CODE REUSABILITY

5.1. Guideline of Code Reusability

A code reusability guideline fixes for two programs:

. the minimum size of their common sequences (MinCL),

. and the maximum size of the particular sequences of a program with regard to the other (MaxPL),

in order that these two programs may be merged, or one may be stored in a library and "included" in the other.

For two identical sequences of code, MinCL fixes their minimum size in order that one of them may be stored in a library and "included" in their programs.

- Which code reusability guideline should we choose?

It is not difficult to define a code reusability guideline in an information department because analysts and developers have precise ideas of their values.

Generally, the average size of a written in C, Pascal, Cobol, ..., is comprised between 800 and 3000 lines; some programs even pass beyond 5000 lines. With these languages, the sequences which are stored in libraries to be reused in several programs with the statements "Include" in C or Pascal, "Copy" in Cobol, ..., have generally minimal sizes comprise between 30 and 100 lines according to the programming recommendations: "it is forbidden to store too little sequences in a library". These minimal sizes (30 and 100 lines), are possible values of MinCL. MinCL must be superior to one line. With non object-oriented programming languages the masking is not usable, hence MaxPL must be count in tens lines (and the particular sequences are defined in case sequences).

5.2. Presentation of Mechanisms of Code Reusability

The code reusability mechanisms optimize the reusability of program code with the following criteria:

. a similar program code reused in several programs and satisfying the reusability guideline constraints must be defined once in a library,

. a sequence code reused several times in programs and satisfying the reusability guideline constraints must be defined once in a library,

. the reusability must be made in priority with programs otherwise with sequences,

. and the number of programs and of sequences reused must be minimized.

The mechanisms of reusability of a new program P-b with an existing program P-a which has the most lines in common with P-b, are defined by the algorithm presented in Figure 2. The five results of this algorithm are presented in Section 3.

```
If the code of P-a and the code of P-b are identical
    then P-b is identical to P-a
    else If number of lines of common sequences of P-a and P-b: Number(CL-ab)
            is superior to MinCL
            then If number of lines of the particular sequences of P-a: Number(PL-a)
                    is inferior to MaxPL
                    then If number of lines of the particular sequences of P-b:
                            Number(PL-b) is inferior to MaxPL
                            then P-b is merged with P-a
                            else P-a is stored in a library and is "included" in P-b
                         Endif
                    else If number of lines of the particular sequences of P-b:
                            Number(PL-b) is inferior to MaxPL
                            then P-b is stored in a library and is "included" in P-a
                            else For each common sequence of data declarations
                                          or of processing statements of
                                          P-a and P-b: Number(CL-ij)
                                     If Number(CL-ij) is superior to MinCL
                                        then The common sequence will be stored in a
                                             library and are "included" in P-a and in P-b
                                        else No reusability between P-a and P-b
                                     Endif
                                 Endfor
                         Endif
                 Endif
            else No reusability between P-a and P-b
         Endif
Endif
```

Figure 2: Algorithm to study the reusability between two programs P-a and P-b

5.3. Example of Application of Code Standardized Reusability

Two C functions presented in [15] are in Figure 3:

- a function to be created: Write_vert_str which writes a string of characters to the screen vertically, beginning at a specified pixel position (x, y) and having specified foreground and background colors,
- and an existing function: Write_horz_str which writes a string of characters to the screen horizontally, beginning at a specified pixel position (x, y) and having specified foreground and background colors.

Write_horz_str is the existing function which has the most lines in common with Write_vert_str. It is similar to the previous function. It is a particular case but these functions are short and can be wholly presented in this paper. The common declaration sequences of these functions and their common processing sequences are contiguous except DS1, and are ordered with the same orders. We study the reusability of these two functions on considering the lines of code.

Program to be created P-b: **Function to write a string of characters to the screen vertically using the custom characters**	**Existing program P-a:** **Function to write a string of characters to the screen horizontally using the custom characters** (function which has the most lines in common with P-b)

P-b:

```
void write_vert_str (int x, int y, char *string, int color)
{
                                                    DS1 7 lines
    #define seq_out (index, val)        {outp (0x3C4, index) ; \
                                          outp (0x3C5, val) ;}
    #define graph_out (index, val)      {outp (0x3CE, index) ; \
                                          outp (0x3CF, val) ;}
    unsigned int offset;
    char far * mem_address;

    int char_offset, point_color, dummy, i, j, mask, p=0;

    unsigned char char_test, exist_color;
                                                    PS1 2 lines
    couvert (x, y);
    while (string[p]);

    {
                                                    PS2 6 lines
        #ifdef CGA
        char_offset = (string[p] - 32) * 8;
        #endif
        #ifndef CGA
        char_offset = (string[p] - 32) * 14;
        #endif

        plot_char (x, y, char_offset, color, 1);
        y -= 8;
        if (y<8)
        {
          #ifdef VGA
          y=472;
          x += 14;
          #endif
          #ifdef EGA
          y=342;
          x += 14;
          #endif
          #ifdef VGA
          y=192;
          x += 8;
          #endif
        }
        p++;
    }
}
```

P-a:

```
void write_horz_str (int x, int y, char *string, int color)
{
                                                    DS1 7 lines
    #define seq_out (index, val)        {outp (0x3C4, index) ; \
                                          outp (0x3C5, val) ;}
    #define graph_out (index, val)      {outp (0x3CE, index) ; \
                                          outp (0x3CF, val) ;}
    unsigned int offset;
    char far * mem_address;

    int char_offset, dummy, i, j, mask, p=0;

    unsigned char char_test, exist_color;
                                                    PS1 2 lines
    couvert (x, y);
    while (string[p]);

    {
                                                    PS2 6 lines
        #ifdef CGA
        char_offset = (string[p] - 32) * 8;
        #endif
        #ifndef CGA
        char_offset = (string[p] - 32) * 14;
        #endif

        plot_char (x, y, char_offset, color, 0);
        x += 8;
        #ifdef CGA
        if (x>312)
        {
          x=0;
          y -= 8;
        }
        #endif
        #ifdef CGA
        if (x>632)
        {
          x=0;
          y -= 14;
        }
        #endif
        p++;
    }
}
```

Legend ▒ **DSi** : Declaration Sequence. ☐ **PSi** : Processing Sequence.

Number of lines of the common sequences of P-a and P-b: **Number(CL-ab) = 15 lines**

Number of lines of the particular sequences of P-b: **Number(PL-b) = 24 lines**	Number of lines of the particular sequences of P-a: **Number(PL-a) = 23 lines**

Figure 3: Example of C program reusability study

The results of the program reusability mechanisms are presented in Figure 4 according to several values of the code reusability guideline. The links "is included in" are represented with arrows.

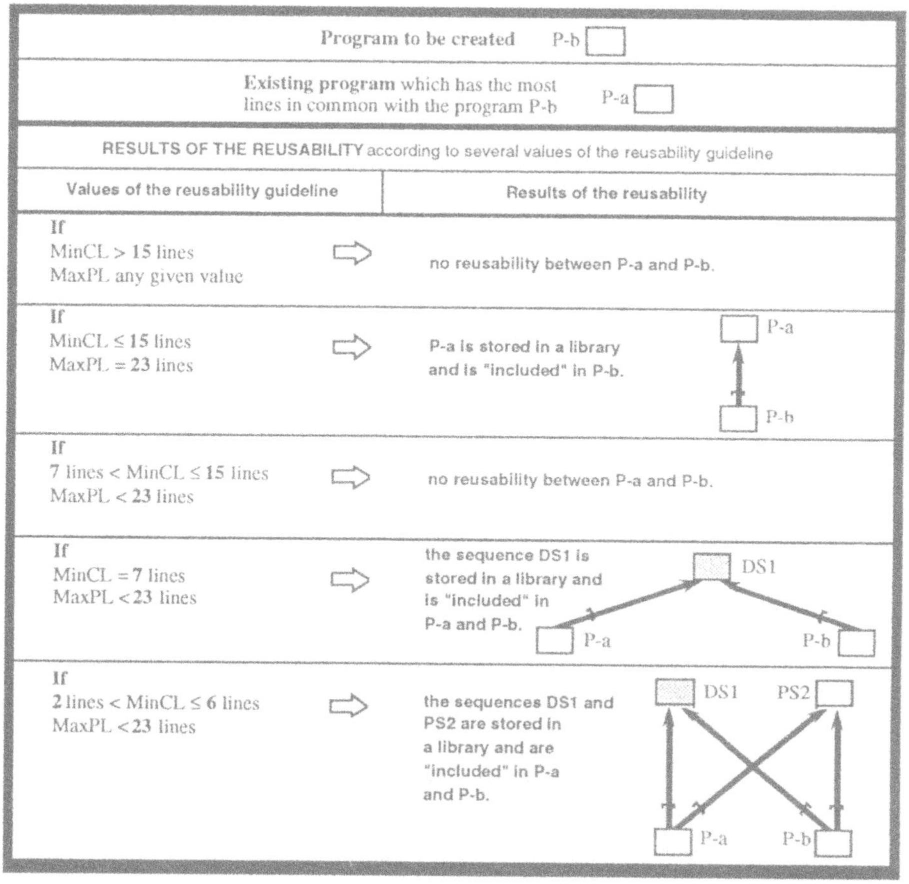

Figure 4: Examples of results of program standardized reusability (obtained with several values of the reusability guideline)

6. CONCLUSION

The reusability guidelines allow comparison of programs to study if they are similar by measuring respectively their common sequences and their particular sequences.

We have adopted the solution which consists in measuring the likeness between programs with guidelines and not with percentages of common and of particular sequences because this last approach does not allow comparison of programs with a reference (a guideline). The use of guidelines supposes that a good metric may be chosen. For program studies we have used the sizes of the declaration and the processing sequences measured with the same metric: the number of lines. It is possible to measure these sizes with numbers of statements or other metrics. Furthermore it is possible to use two different metrics and two guidelines to measure the declaration and the processing sequences.

The reusability mechanisms are mechanisms of pattern recognition because they allow us to compare programs and to study their resemblance. Furthermore they can also create sequences which are stored in libraries of which the reusability must be studied. So the algorithm of the reusability mechanisms is recursive and these mechanisms do not only make pattern recognition.

The reusability mechanisms allow us to find reusable components which can be stored in libraries and reused. So the reusability mechanisms allow us to begin a reverse engineering. They should be implemented in CASE tools, in DBMS and in programming environments of languages.

An outstanding research is on the possibility to take into account programs and sequences code which are syntactically different but which have nearly the same control graph and/or the same call graph.

References

1. Albrecht A. J.: 'Measuring Application Development Effort Productivity', *Proceedings Joint IBM/SHARE/GUIDE App. Symp.*, October 1979.
2. Blaise G.: 'Implantation de l'algorithme de réutilisabilité uniforme d'objets MCO en Smalltalk-80', Graduate thesis engineer cycle C CNAM, 1992.
3. Boetticher G., Srinivas K., Eichmann D.: 'A neural net-based approach to software metrics', *The fifth international conference on software engineering and knowledge engineering*, 1993.
4. Boehm B. W.: 'Software Engineering Economics', Prentice-Hall, New York, 1981.
5. Castellani X.: 'Mechanisms of Standardized Reusability of Objects', *IFIP WG 8.1 Working Conference on Information System Development Process Como*, September 1-3, 1993, proceedings published by North-Holland.
6. Cheng J.: 'Improving the software reusability in object-oriented programming', *ACM Press*, Oct. 1993.
7. Cox B.: 'Planning the software industrial revolution', *IEEE Software*, 7(6), November 1990.
8. Fenton N. E.: 'Software metrics, A Rigorous Approach', Chapman & Hall, 1991.
9. Firesmith D. G.: 'Managing Ada projects; the people issues', *Proceedings TRI Ada'88*, Charleston, WV, 24-27 October 1988.
10. Halstead M. H.: 'Element of Software Science', Elsevier, North Holland, 1975.
11. Krueger C.: 'Software reuse', *ACM Computing Surveys*, 24(2), 1992.
12. McCabe T. J.: 'A complexity measure', *IEEE Transactions on Software Engineering*, SE-2(4), December 1976.
13. Meyer B.: 'Object-oriented Software Construction', Prentice Hall international, Series in computer science, 1988.
14. Nauer P.and Randell B.: 'Software Engineering', Report on a Conference by the NATO Science Committee. NATO Scientific Affairs Division, Brussels, Belgium, 1968.
15. Stevens R. T.: 'Graphics Programming in C', 1990, M&T Publishing, Inc.
16. WISR'92: 5th Annual Workshop on Software Reuse Working Group Reports, M. Griss and Will Tracz editors, Software Engineering Notes, ACM Press, Volume 18, Number 2, April 1993.

54

Rule-based Reasoning Approach for Reusable Design Component Retrieval

Sen-Tarng Lai[a,b] and Chien-Chiao Yang[a]

[a]Dept. of Electronic Engineering, National Taiwan Institute of Technology, 43 Keelung Road, Section 4 Taipei, TAIWAN

[b]Telecommunication Laboratories, Ministry of Transportation and Communications, 9 Lane 74, Hsin-Yi Road, Sec. 4 Taipei, TAIWAN

Abstract

Each phase of software development life cycle has the potential for reuse. However, according to the viewpoint of cost and reusability, the design phase is the most suitable phase for packaging the reusable software components. In this paper, we describe the design component knowledge extraction and representation method for component retrieval. The design knowledge is based on the principle of structured design and object-oriented design. According to the valuable and clearly design component knowledge, we generate a rule-based system which contains the component matching rules and retrieval supporting rules. Using these rules not only can assist the potential reusers retrieve the more suitable design component but also can improve component retrieval performance.

Keyword Codes: D.2.m; H.3.3; I.2.4; I.2.m
Keywords: Software Reuse; Component Retrieval; Knowledge Representation; Rule-based System.

1. INTRODUCTION

The heart of large software project is design. Software design is conducted in two steps. Preliminary design is concerned with the transformation of requirements into data and software architecture. Detail design focuses on refinements to the architectural representation that lead to *detailed data structure* and *algorithmic representations* for software.

Code reuse is better understand and more prevalent by far than other software development phase of reuse[1]. Since code components have a high degree of specificity, the most highly reusable components tend to be small. A code component in a reuse library is likely to be of little value and the detailed design documents should be very valuable in understanding code component. Thus it is extremely important that detailed design documents associated with code modules to be a reusable design component [2-3]. This reusable design component is the most suitable software component for reuse.

In this paper, we detailed describe the important design knowledge for component classification and retrieval, and specify how to extract the knowledge from detailed design documents. We also propose the methods for represent the design component knowledge and transfer the design component knowledge into the rule-based system for assisting component's retrieval. In Section 2, we describe the existing software component's representation approaches for classification and retrieval. In Section 3, we specify the important attributes of design component and package them into *a frame-based representation*. In Section 4, we explain the features of rule-based component retrieval system. At last, we make a summary and discuss our future works in Section 5.

2. LIMITATIONS OF EXISTING COMPONENT REPRESENTATION METHODS

In the Priteto-Diaz's faceted classification method which describe *the unit functional component classification* in coding phase [4-5], each component is characterized by a six-item structure consisting of

<function, object, medium, system type, functional area, setting>

and each tuple can only be specified by one term (keyword).

In [6], the authors applied the idea of conceptual dependency to represent software component descriptions and software component requests.

These methods have been published many years and applied to the many software library systems. There are also several drawbacks and limitations need to modify or enhance: (1) An action verb or a functional keyword just can represent the smaller components which process the primitive function. Larger numbers of smaller components forces the reuser to spend more time comparing components to determine the one best suited for the current application. (2) Internal data structure is a very important item for software component's retrieval, modification, and adaptation. They did not pay much attention to it. (3) Thesaurus is not a good approach for resolving the conceptual similar verbs in different applications. (4) They are not suitable for object-oriented design. For example, to represent the object of stack, it is necessary to separate three primitive functions in the faceted classification scheme of Priteto-Diaz and Freeman: <empty, character, table>, <push, character, table>, and <pop, character, table>. For resolving these limitations and drawbacks, we propose a flexibility knowledge representation method which describes in next Section.

3. COMPONENTS KNOWLEDGE REPRESENTATION

There are many attributes to represent the software design phase components. Only three important attributes are suitable for the criteria of software component retrieval. The three basic component's attributes are: *processing action, internal data structure* and *component's interface*. In this section, we will discuss how to represent, extract and package the component's attributes for component retrieval.

3.1. Action statements

In software detailed design phase, one of the task is describe the program logic. In component retrieval, it is meaningless for the reuser to describe the detailed logic of software components. They just concern whether the functional specifications of software components match their requirement or not. There are many approaches to represent the component function (such as keywords, natural language). It is difficulty to build the common recognition for using natural language to represent component function. Using an action verb or a functional keyword to represent the component function is too rough. An action statement can represent five or more program instruction statements. An action statement contains a single strong action verb and a singular object (such as, open a file, delete a record). A series of action statements not only can represent the processing action of component but also can build the common recognition for component designers and component reusers.

The objective of thesaurus is to resolve the trouble of synonym. But the thesaurus did not consider the relationship of semantic and limitation of application domain. Based on the thesaurus, the component designers and the component users can not get common recognition. In this paper, we propose the uniform action verbs to represent the action statement of component processing action. Table 1 is the action verbs' table for action statements.

Table 1.
Action verbs' table for action statements

accept	delete	handle	put
add	dequeue	identify	queue
allocate	detach	increment	read
analyze	determine	initialize	record
build	display	insert	release
calculate	edit	issue	resolve
check	encode	locate	restore
clear	enqueue	link	scan
close	enter	load	schedule
complete	establish	look_up	search
construct	execute	merge	select
control	extract	modify	set
convert	find	move	store
copy	fix	obtain	transfer
create	format	open	translate
decrement	get	place	updat
			write

3.2. Internal data structure

Program consists of *data structure* and *algorithms* [7]. Thus it is not surprising that data and program structure are important and need to be properly related to achieve the goal of successful programming. Data structures not only affect the operation style of program algorithm but also contain information and are operated on during the execution of a program. Two software components doing exactly the same function may look entirely different, because they use different internal data structures. Clearly define data structure of software component can assist us to classify software component. In like manner, software component retrieval, modification and adaptation also need to use the attribute of internal data structure. It is important to specify the data structure of software components. The C++ Booch Components [8] provide classes for the domain independent data structure: *Bag, Deque, Graph, List, Map, Queue, Ring, Set, Stack, Variable_string* and *Tree*.

For enhancing forenamed data structure, we also consider the file structure (such as Sequential_File, Indexed_File, and Relative_File) and primitive data type (such as integer, character, real, array, record).

3.3. Component's interfaces

Each component can not stand alone. One of the software design process is establishing relationships and interconnections among components. In [9], the authors used I/O parameters to deduce the software component behavior and retrieve the retrieve software. Interfaces of software components are one of important attributes for retrieval.

3.4. Design component knowledge extraction

In [10], we use *module definition*, *module description*, and *module data representation* to specify the detailed design documents. These documents are very useful for module understanding, modification, adaptation. It is not necessary to utilize all of items of these documents as the attributes of component retrieval. We need extract the useful attributes which include internal data structure, action statements and component interface from these detailed design documents. The internal data structure can be gotten from module definition and module data representation. The action statements can be extracted from module logic description. The component interface can be abstracted from module definition and module data representation (see Figure 1).

Based on these valuable attributes, we can package the design component knowledge into *design knowledge frame*. In this frame-based knowledge representation, each slot can contain more than one item. According to the importance, each slot and item can be set different weight values for component retrieval (see Figure 2).

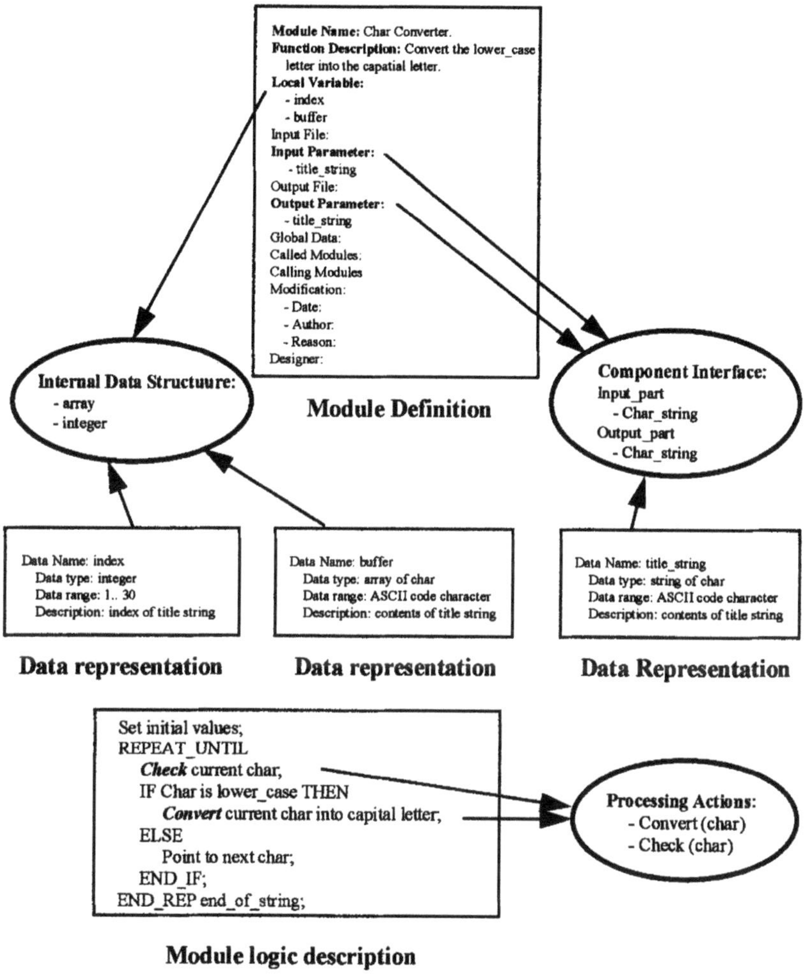

Figure 1. Extract the important attributes from detailed design documents

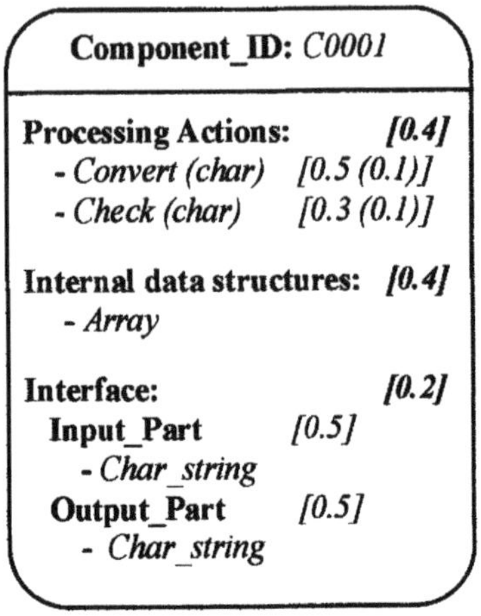

Figure 2. Frame-based representation for design component

4. COMPONENT RETRIEVAL RULES GENERATION

In the Section 3, we extract and package the design knowledge into a frame-based representation. In this Section, we will discuss the rule-based system generation which based on the frame-based representation. We give an example to describe the rule generation. This is a typical component which converts the lower-case letter into the capital letter (see Figure 2).

According to *frame-based knowledge* and *weight values*, system can generate the difference match ratio rules for component retrieval:

(a) The first set is fully match rules. If reusers provide the query information all meet the component attributes then these rules will be filed. For example,

Input (char) ^ Output (char) -> Interface (C0001) ***[0.5+0.5 = 1.0]***

Convert(char) ^ Check(char) -> Process(C0001) ***[(0.5+0.1) + (0.3+0.1) = 1.0]***

Data_Structure(array)^ Interface(C0001) ^ Process(C0001) -> Component (C0001) ***[0.4 + 0.2 * 1.0 + 0.4 * 1.0 = 1.0]***

(b) The second set is partial match rules. According to the query information of reusers, these rules can be filed and computed the match ratio for reference. For example,

Convert( ) ^ Check( ) -> Process(C0001) ***[(0.5 + 0.3) = 0.8]***

Data_Structure(array) ^ Process(C0001) -> Component (C0001) ***[0.4 + 0.4 * 0.8 = 0.72]***

Data_Structure(array) ^ Process(Convert) -> Component (C0001) ***[0.4 + 0.4 * 0.5 = 0.6]***

We also provide the more useful rules for assisting component retrieval before reasoning these basic rules. We call them as *retrieval supporting rules.* These rules are generated by analyzing and computing the appearance frequency of action statements in specific internal data structure of existing software components (see Table 2). Based on the retrieval supporting rules, reuser can be guided to modify the unreasonable query information and get the suitable software components. Reducing the unreasonable query information can great improve the performance of component retrieval.

Table 2.
The table of appearance frequency of action statements in specific internal data structure

Internal Data Structure	Action Statements	Frequence
Array		
	Search	97
	Get	53
	Check	47
	Convert	7
	:	:
	:	:
Bag		
:		
:		

5. CONCLUSIONS

To improve software quality and productivity are major benefits of software reuse. However, for increase efficiency, reuse should be considered at design time, not after the implementation has been completed. Design reuse is more valuable than code reuse. Design documents combine the knowledge and the experience from software design engineers. It is very important how to reuse the existing knowledge and experience. In this paper, we detailed describe the important design component knowledge for component retrieval, and specify how to extract the knowledge from detailed design documents. Finally, we propose the methods for represent the design component knowledge and transfer the design component knowledge into the rule-based system for assisting component's retrieval.

Four major advantages of rule-based component retrieval system are:

(1) *high hit-ratio* -- the uniform keywords can build the common recognition between component designers and reusers. According to the common recognition and extension of component knowledge items for retrieval, reusers have the high hit-ratio for component retrieval.

(2) *high adaptability* -- the design knowledge representation not only suit for structured design methodology but also can apply to the object-oriented design approach.

(3) *high maintainability* -- it is very easy to insert or delete a reusable software design component.

(4) *high performance* -- based on the history data and experience, this system can avoid the unreasonable query information and great improve the retrieval performance.

Some software metrics can help us extract and identify reusable software components. Including these metrics to the attributes of software component, can not only relies the characteristics of software components but also can help reuser select the suitable software components. Our future work will consider the metrics of software design. Based on the result of software design components' measurement, we can extract the more suitable components.

REFERENCES

1. LANERGAN, R.G. and GRASSO, C.A.: '**SOFTWARE ENGINEERING WITH REUSABLE DESIGNS AND CODE**', *IEEE Trans. Software Eng.*, 1984, Vol.10, (5), pp.498-501
2. JOHNSON, R. E. and FOOTE, B.: '**DESIGNING REUSABLE CLASSES**', *Journal of Object-Oriented Programming*, 1988, Vol. 1, (2), pp.22-35
3. TRACZ, W.: '**SOFTWARE REUSE MYTHS**', *ACM SIGSOFT Software Engineering Notes*, 1988, Vol. 13, (1), pp.17-21
4. PRIETO-DIAZ, R. and FREEMAN, P.: '**CLASSIFYING SOFTWARE FOR REUSABILITY**', *IEEE Software*, 1987, Vol.4, (1), pp. 6-16
5. PRIETO-DIAZ, R.: '**IMPLEMENTATION FACETED CLASSIFICATION FOR SOFTWARE REUSE**', *Proc. of the 12th Internalational Conference on Software Engineering*, March, 1990, pp. 300-304
6. WOOD, M. and Sommerville, I.: '**AN INFORMATION RETRIEVAL SYSTEM FOR SOFTWARE COMPONENTS**', *Software engineering Journal*, 1988, Vol.3, (5), pp. 198-207
7. WIRTH, N.: '**ALGORITHM + DATA STRUCTURES = PROGRAM**', (Prentice-Hall, 1976)
8. BOOCH, G.: '**OBJECT-ORIENTED ANALYSIS AND DESIGN**', (Benjamin/Cummings, 1994)
9. PODGURSKI, A. and PIERCE, L.: '**RETRIEVING REUSABLE SOFTWARE BY SAMPLING BEHAVIOR**', *ACM Trans. on Software Engineering and Methodology*, 1993, Vol.2, (3), pp. 286-303
10. LAI, S.T. and CHOU, L.Y.: '**MODULE DESIGN DOCUMENT ASSISTANT SYSTEM**', *TL Technical Journal*, 1987, Vol.17, (2), pp. 93-108 (in Chinese)

55

A Multi-layer Metrics Combination Model for Reusable Software Components

Sen-Tarng Lai[a b] and Chien-Chiao Yang[a]

[a]Dept. of Electronic Engineering, National Taiwan Institute of Technology, 43 Keelung Road, Section 4 Taipei, TAIWAN

[b]Telecommunication Laboratories, Ministry of Transportation and Communications, 9 Lane 74, Hsin-Yi Road, Sec. 4 Taipei, TAIWAN

Abstract

Software reuse is an important approach to increase software quality and productivity. There are many factors may affect the result of software reuse, however, software component extraction is one of the most important and influential factors. Defining a perfect software reuse metric is a necessary condition for identify high reusable software components and retrieve the more suitable candidate components. In this paper, we propose a multi-layer metrics combination model for reusable component extraction. In this model, each layer combination can apply different linear combination models for specific purpose. This feature provides high flexibility to adjust the weighting value of combination model and high capability to improve measurement of reusable software component. Based on the multi-layer metrics combination model, we also can create a qualification threshold for extracting the reusable software component and defining a ranking schema for candidate components in component retrieval.

Keyword Codes: D.2.m; D.2.8
Keywords: Software Reuse; Software Metrics; Combination Model; Primitive Metrics.

1. INTRODUCTION

Software reuse has the potential to *improve software quality, reduce development costs,* and *increase productivity.* Improving software quality and productivity is the primary objective of software reuse. There are many problems must be resolved for attaching this objective. For example, five major steps of software reuse are: extracting reusable software components, packaging software components, classifying and retrieving software components, modifying software components, and adapting software components to the new software system. In first step, software component extraction is one of the most important and influential factors. Each phase's products of software life cycle has the potential for reuse. Code reuse is better understand and more prevalent by far than other software development phase of reuse [1]. Since code components have a high degree of specificity, the most highly reusable components tend to be small. A code component in a reuse library is likely to be of little value and the detailed design documents should be very valuable in understanding code component. Thus it is extremely important that detailed design documents associated with code modules to be a reusable component [2].

Similarly, each module of the detailed design and coding phase has the opportunity to be a reusable software component in existing system. In software reuse, to determine the qualification of reusable software components is one of the most important job [3]. Reusing high quality software components is a necessary condition for improving software quality and productivity. Quality of software component is a key point for judge the qualification of reusable software components. In an important paper by Boehm [4], an attempt is made to define software quality in terms of some high-level software characteristics. These characteristics are: reliability, portability, efficiency, human engineering, testability, understandability, modifiability.

Some software characteristics can help us extract and identify reusable software components. These software characteristics are high-level software characteristics which can be decomposed into several primitive characteristics. On the other side, it is necessary to combine the primitive characteristics for measuring a particular characteristic. In this paper, we propose ***a multi-layer metric combination model*** which is based on the linear combination models. In this model, each layer combination can apply different linear combination models for increasing flexibility. Separate combination for different purposes can improve the efficiency and capability of measurement. In Section two, we describe the existing software metrics for design and coding phase. Then we describe the metrics' data collection and normalization in Section three. In Section four, we discuss the metric combination model and define the multi-layer metric combination model. Finally, we make a summary and discuss our future work in Section 5.

2. SOFTWARE METRICS FOR DESIGN AND CODING PHASES

Although, some metrics are impossible to measure or predict directly, there are still exist many software metrics for measuring the characteristic of software. According to the ***meta-metrics*** defined by the conte [5], we are interested in metrics that are ***simple, robust, useful for design and coding phase***, and that *can be analyzed properly*. These metrics include:

(a) *Size metric (Lines of code):* A line of code is any line of program text that is not a comment or blank line, regardless of the number of statements or fragments of statements on the line. It is one of the most familiar software measure.

(b) *Data structure metric:* An intra-modular measure of the information flow complexity of each module *M* in a system is defined by the Henry-Kafura [6], as follow:

*Complexity of module M = length (M) * (fan-in (M) * fan-out (M)) ** 2*

The Shepperd [4] refines the above formation like the following:

*Complexity of module M = (fan-in (M) * fan-out (M)) ** 2*

(c) *Logic structure metric (McCabe's Cyclomatic complexity):* McCabe has observed that the difficulty of understanding a program is largely determined by the complexity of the control flow graph for that program [7]. For each module of a system, we can draw the control flow graph G for that module. The cyclomatic complexity metric for the module, denoted V(G), is the number of regions into which G divided the page. McCabe has shown that V(G) is equivalent to one more than the number of decisions in the flow diagram.

(d) *Nesting level of program construct:* As a general guideline, nesting of program constructs to deprhs greater than three or four levels should be avoided.

(e) *Ratio of statement and branch coverage:* There are many coverage measures for unit programs testability: statement coverage, branch coverage, decision coverage, and path coverage. Statement and branch coverage are more useful in unit testing.

(f) *Coupling and cohesion:* Coupling is a measure of the degree of interdependence between modules. Cohesion is an attribute of individual modules, describing their functional strength.

3. DATA COLLECTION AND SCALE NORMALIZATION

In this Section, we describe how to collect the metric data and normalize the metric data for combination.

3.1. Data collection

Using *static program analyzer* and each *metric definition* or *formula*, we can compute the values of Halstead's Measure, Information Flow Structure Metric, McCabe's Cyclomatic Complexity and nesting level of programming structure. Based on *the test coverage analyzer*, we can get the values of statement coverage and branch coverage of unit testing. About the coupling and cohesion, there are a number of proposed classes of coupling and cohesion that are believed to provide an ordinal scale of measurement. It is difficult to determine the scale of coupling and cohesion by traditional software tools. According to the clearly definitions of scale of coupling and cohesion, we apply them into a rule-based system which can help us determine the scale of coupling and cohesion, from highest to lowest.

3.2. Scale normalization

In general case, a potential software characteristic is combined by several primitive characteristics. Some software primitive metrics which are concerned with the quality of software component, have different scale values in their representation. For combining these primitive metrics, we recommend all scale values of the primitive metrics shall be normalized among 0 and 1. Near to 1 represent the most desirable value, and near to 0 represent the least desirable value. The following two tables are the examples to represent the normalized value of primitive metrics: Table 1 is the normalized value of lines of code and Table 2 is the normalized value of nesting level of program construct.

Table 1.
Normalized value of Lines of Code

LOC	Normalized Value
1 - 50	1.0
51 - 100	0.8
100 - 150	0.6
150 - 200	0.4
200 - 250	0.2
> 250	0.0

Table 2.
Normalized value of nesting level of program construct

Level of nesting of program construct	Normalized Value
0 - 1	1.0
2 - 3	0.8
4 - 5	0.5
6 - 7	0.3
8 - 9	0.1
> 9	0.0

4. METRICS COMBINATION

In [4], each high-level software characteristic can be decomposed into several primitive characteristics. On the other side, it is necessary to combine the primitive metrics for measuring a particular characteristic. In this Section, we will discuss the metric combination models.

4.1. The linear combination

The goal of metrics combination is to improve the measurement capability and flexibility. In this Section, we consider three linear combination models:

(a) *Equally Weighted Linear Combination:*

This model is the simplest combination to form. Each primitive metric has an equal weight constant.

$$HLM = \frac{1}{n}\sum_{i=1}^{n} PM_i$$

where,

- *PM:* Normalized value of Primitive Metric
- *HLM:* High-level Metric

(b) *Unequally Weighted Linear Combination:*

In this model, according to the optimistic and pessimistic predications, different weights are assigned to different primitive metrics. Such that,

$$HLM = \sum_{i=1}^{n} W_i PM_i$$

, and

$$1 = \sum_{i=1}^{n} W_i$$

where W_i is the weight constant of ith primitive metricPM_i.

(c) *Dynamically Weighted Linear Combination:*

In this model, we can adjust the weights of any primitive metric for adapting different applications.

4.2. Multi-layer metrics combination model

In this paper, we select six primitive metrics to measure the reusable characteristic of software component. These metrics are simple, valid, robust, useful for development, and that can be analyzed properly. According to the different characteristics of primitive metrics, we divide them into three groups:

(a) *Complexity metrics:* include control flow, information flow, line of code, and nesting level of program construct.

(b) *Modularity metrics:* include coupling and cohesion.

(c) *Testability metrics:* include statement coverage and branch coverage.

For combining these primitive metrics, we take three steps. In first step, we consider the characteristics which are potentially contradictory. For example, reduces in logic structure complexity usually result in increased data structure complexity. Then, we combine the primitive metrics which belong to same class in step two. Finally, we combine these three classes' metrics into a software reuse metric. We call this combination model *a multi-layer metrics combination (MLMC) model* (see Figure 1). In this model, each layer combination can apply different linear combination models for increasing flexibility. Separate combination for different purposes can improve the efficiency and capability of measurement.

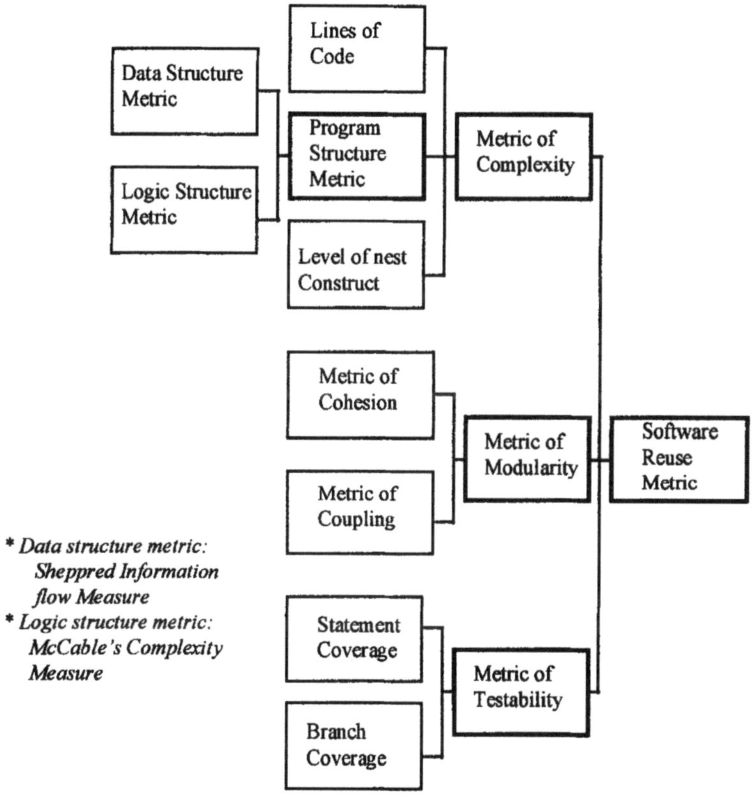

Figure 1. The Mutli-layer metrics combination model

5. CONCLUSIONS

A potential software characteristic is composed of several primitive characteristics. Combination these primitive characteristics is a major approach to measure the potential characteristic. In software reuse, it is necessary to consider more than one primitive characteristic for extracting suitable and reusable software components. In this paper, we propose the multi-layer metric combination model which based on the linear combination models for reusable components. The goal of this combination model is to improve *the measurement capability and flexibility* for reusable software components. In *MLMC* model, each layer combination can apply different linear combination models for specific purpose. This feature provides high flexibility to adjust the weighting value of combination model and high capability to improve measurement of reusable software component.

Based on the *MLMC* model, we also can create an automatic extraction tool for extracting the reusable components from existing software and define a ranking schema for candidate components in component retrieval. We propose a component extraction approach which based on the primitive metric's combination model. Using this approach, we can clear define the extraction qualification for reusable components.

Our future work is to define the qualification threshold for extracting reusable software components from existing software with the *MLMC* model. For improving the practically of this model, we will use mass experiment data help us adjust the weight constants and normalization value of primitive metrics. Further, to develop an automatic reusable software component extraction tool is helpful in software reuse.

REFERENCES

1. LANERGAN, R.G. and GRASSO, C.A.: '**SOFTWARE ENGINEERING WITH REUSABLE DESIGNS AND CODE**', *IEEE Trans. Software Eng.*, 1984, Vol.10, (5), pp.498-501
2. TRACZ, W.: '**SOFTWARE REUSE MYTHS**', *ACM SIGSOFT Software Emgineering Notes*, 1988, Vol.13, (1), pp.17-21
3. CALDIERA, G. and BASILI, V.R.: '**IDENTIFYING AND QUALIFYING REUSABLE SOFTWARE COMPONENTS**', *IEEE Computer*, 1991, Vol.24, (2), pp. 61-70
4. BOEHM, B.W., BROWN, J.R. and LIPOW, M.: '**QUANTITATIVE EVALUATION OF SOFTWARE QUALITY**', *Proceedings of the Secondard International Conference on Software Engineering*, 1976, pp. 592-605
5. CONTE, S.D., DUNSMORE, H.E. and SHEN, V.Y.: '**SOFTWARE ENGINEERING METRICS AND MODELS**', Benjamin/Cummings, (Menlo Park, 1986)
6. FENTON, N.E.: '**SOFTWARE METRICS - A REIGOROUS APPROACH**', (Chapman & Hall, 1991)
7. MCCABE, T.: '**A COMPLEXITY MEASURE**', *IEEE Trans. Software Eng.*, 1976, Vol.2, (4), pp.308-320

PART NINE

Integrated Environments, Case Tools

56

Environment For Three Dimensional Graphics User Interface Development

Y. K. Chan, Sam Kwong, C. H. Lee, and K. L. Chan

Department of Computer Science, City Polytechnic of Hong Kong, 83 Tat Chee Avenue, Kowloon Tong, Hong Kong

Abstract

Graphics User Interface(GUI) serves as a link between the end user of an application and the application itself. Run time GUI is characterized by its look-and-feel and interaction style. Characteristics of a run time GUI system depends on the particular GUI building tool used and its underlying architecture. Current implementation of GUI are in two-dimensions(2D) and the trend is to extend GUI into three-dimensions(3D) in order to provide a natural interface for applications in 3D. It is expected that 3D specific GUI builder will become available when methodology for automating 3D GUI building process for a large class of 3D application is better understood. Until then, it is proposed that a 3D development and debugging environment should be available for building such interfaces for individual application as required. This paper describes the overall framework and some details that enables the building of 3D GUI.

Keycodes: D.1.7; D.2.5; I.3.2
Keywords: Visual Programming Language, Problem Analysis Diagram, Computer Aided Diagram, Visual Programming Environment, Graphics Kernal System, XLIB, Graphics User Interface

1. Introduction

Progress in the area of visual languages[1,2] for different applications have been reported and in turn motivated a visual programming environment(VPE)[3] that is specially architected to support the development and debugging of graphics applications.

The VPE can be considered as a lower CASE tool and is therefore suitable in developing applications[4] in which the software architecture is already specified. The VPE can also be applied to implement the Xlib part of the X Window System which is a network-transparent window based graphics system. As the Xt Intrinsic defines an architectural model for widget, GUI run time system such as Motif[5] can also be implemented by the VPE. It should be noted that although the Motif widget set is 3D in appearance, the contents of icon objects are not truly 3D. The need for rapid prototyping of GUI is reflected both in the area of research[6] and in the area of products[7]. However, existing User Interface methodology and tools can not adequately meet User Interface requirement of a 3D nature[8]. Until rapid prototyping for 3D GUI becomes mature, it is envisaged that complex 3D User Interface architecture will have to be derived through specification obtained by formal methods. The subsequent specification that yields the corresponding architecture can then be implemented in VPE and the appropriate use of functions in GKS-3D[9].

2. The VPE: the visual programming language(VPL)

The VPE is a visual programming environment that separates 'C' source code procedure into three parts. These three parts are the "Data Declaration and Initialization" part, the "Control of Flow using Problem Analysis Diagram(PAD)[10]" part and the "Executable Assignment Statements" part, respectively. A subset of the VPL syntax is presented as an extended BNF notation in Appendix 1.

The three parts in the VPL are illustrated in Figures 1, 2 and 3. Figure 1 and 2 illustrate how flow and execution are presented in VPL. It can also be deduced that, from Figures 1 and 2, icons can be inserted and deleted at will to alter the control flow and that there are certain viewing flexibility in the VPL system. Figure 3 is self explanatory by virtue of its contents for data declaration and initialization.

It is advantages to use VPL instead of representing a program procedure in terms of a piece of flat text when referred to the dimensional analysis proposed by Shu[11]. The visual extent[11] of VPL over a piece of 'C' source code increases the readability and maintainability of the target software. The VPL enforces programmer discipline by imposing structure at the program development stage.

3. The VPE: the debugger for graphics applications

Figures 4, 5, 6 and 7 are four snap shots during the debugging of a simple graphics application. The upper right window is the debugger and the lower left window is the debuggee. It should be noted that the two windows should really have been initiated to larger sizes to cover more of the display surface of the graphics workstation display monitor. The default 'trace' level during debugging is at icon trace level which means that a 'step' command advances execution by one icon. In Figure 5, the lines of code for 'graphics initialization for debuggee', 'clear graphics and text contents in debuggee', 'initialize locator input class with mouse as a physical input device', 'initialize x=y=0' has NOT yet been executed. These four statements will be executed if user types in either 'step<cr>' or simply '<cr>' from keyboard. The visual appearance of Figure 7 indicates that the 'locator position has been defined' and that 'the line positioned between x=y=0 and locator'. It should be noted that the code in Figure 6 would not have been executed if the cross-hair cursor position is not moved to the debuggee window. The sharing of input resources between debugger and debuggee and that the debuggee execution may either be suspended or runable based on input context has also been reported[12].

Other debugging features include variable trace, execution until breakpoint, etc..

4. Similarity between GKS-2D functionality and Interactive Objects[13]

The Interactive Objects(IO) as proposed by Wood and Gray have three common attributes(visibility, selectability and movability). In the context of GKS-2D, the contents of an Object are OUTPUT PRIMITIVES and the Object itself is a NAMED SEGMENT containing all the output primitives. Visibility and selectability as defined in [13] can then be implemented by GKS-2D segment attribute such as invisible/visible, undetectable/detectable. The movability attribute can be implemented by SEGMENT transform in which translate-x and translate-y are the magnitudes to define distance moved. Additional settable segment attributes are highlighting and priority. Other SEGMENT manipulation capability through the use of segment transform include segment scaling and rotation.

5. An example of IO implementation using GKS-2D

Implementation of IO attributes by GKS-2D functionality is illustrated in Appendix 2. The implementation is in Fortran binding.

Appendix 2a defines the transformation number. All GKS segments(IO) are within this transformation number 10. In the context of GUI, it is useful to have a transformation number for IOs categorized under application and another number for IOs categorized under development tools, etc..

Appendix 2b illustrate how the fourth segment can be created.

Appendix 2c illustrates how a segment can be picked and then subsequently translated if required.

6. Conclusion

Infrastructure for developing 2D IO based on VPE and the suitable use of GKS-2D functions have been presented. Extension of VPE capability to cater for 3D graphics development and debugging requires no more than perspective and parallel projection[14] of 3D data. Such additional capability does not require structural change in the VPE and therefore modification to VPE is straight forward to catering for 3D IO development resulting in an enhanced VPE for 3D application development. The advantage of structural compatibility between 2D run time GUI system and 3D run time GUI system developed using the same methodology is obvious not be overlook in terms of compatibility and maintenance and well as programmer portability.

REFERENCES

1. Chang S.K., "Visual Languages", Principles of Pictorial Information Systems Design, Prentic-Hall International Editions, 1989, pp262-300.
2. Williams C.S., Rasure J.R., "A Visual Language for Image Processing", *IEEE Workshop on Visual Languages*, 1990, pp86-91.
3. Tam S.S. and Chan Y.K., "Graphics Application Development under Window Environment", *Proc. of 2nd Int. Conf. in Software Eng. & Knowledge Eng.*, Illinois, U.S.A., June 1990, pp234-238.
4. International Organisation for Standardization: Information Processing Systems - Computer Graphics - Graphics Kernel System(GKS) - Functional Description. ISO 7942(1985).
5. Open Software Foundation, OSF/Motif Style Guide, 1990.
6. Philip G. Gray, Alistair C. Kilgour and Catherine A. Wood, "Dynamic reconfigurability for fast prototyping of user interfaces", *Software Engineering Journal*, November 1988, pp257-262.
7. Asymetrix Corporation, "Using Toolbook, a Guide to Building and Working with Books", Bellevue, WA. 1989.
8. A. D. Bimbo, M. Campanai and P. Nesi, "A Three-Dimensional Iconic Environment for Image Database Querying", *IEEE Trans. on Software Engineering*, vol. 19, no. 10. Oct 1993, pp997-1011.
9. International Organisation for Standardization: Information Processing Systems - Computer Graphics - Graphics Kernel System for Three Dimension(GKS-3D) - Functional Description. ISO/DIS 8805(1986).
10. Futamura Y., Kawai T., Horikoshi H. and Tsutsumi M., "Development of Computer Program by PAD(Problem Analysis Diagram)", *Proceedings of the 5th International Software Engineering Conference*, 1981, pp.325-332.
11. Shu Nan C., "Visual Programming Languages: A Perspective & A Dimensional Analysis", Visual Languages edited by S. K. Chang et al., Plenum Press, New York, 1986.
12. Elliot A. and Sachs G.M., "Shering Input Devices in the Starbase/X11 Merge System", *Hewlett-Packard Journal*, Dec., 1989, pp.38-41
13. Wood C.A. and Gray P.D., "User Interface - Application Communication in the Chimera User Interface Management System", *SOFTWARE Practice & Experience*, Vol. 22, No. 1, Jan. 1992. pp. 63-84.
14. Rogers D.F. and Adams J.A.,"Mathematical Elements for Computer Graphics", McGraw Hill, 1976. ISBN 0-07-053527-2.

Appendix I
A subset of the VPL syntax

The followings are the extended BNF representation for the meta-language of the visual language used on the PAD diagram.

<program>	::=	<declaration file><modules>
<modules>	::=	<module>|<module><modules>
<module>	::=	<DDI file><PAD file>
<declaration file>	::=	<structure specifier list><declaration specifier list>
<structure specifier list>	::=	<structure specifier>|<structure specifier><structure specifier list>
<structure specifier>	::=	struct <structure identifier>{<structure declaration>};
<structure identifier>	::=	<identifier>
<identifier>	::=	<letter>|<identifier><digit>|<identifier><letter>|<identifier><symbol letter>
<letter>	::=	<upper-case letter>|<lower-case letter>
<upper-case letter>	::=	A|B|C|D|E|F|G|H|I|J|K|L|M|N|O|P|Q|R|S|T|U|V|W|X|Y|Z
<lower-case letter>	::=	a|b|c|d|e|f|g|h|i|j|k|l|m|n|o|p|q|r|s|t|u|v|w|x|y|z
<symbol letter>	::=	_|-|$
<digit>	::=	0|1|2|3|4|5|6|7|8|9
<structure declaration list>	::=	<structure declaration>|<structure declaration><structure declaration list>
<PAD file>	::=	

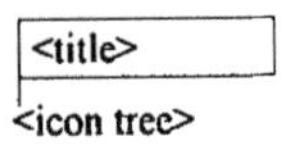

<icon tree> ::= <empty>

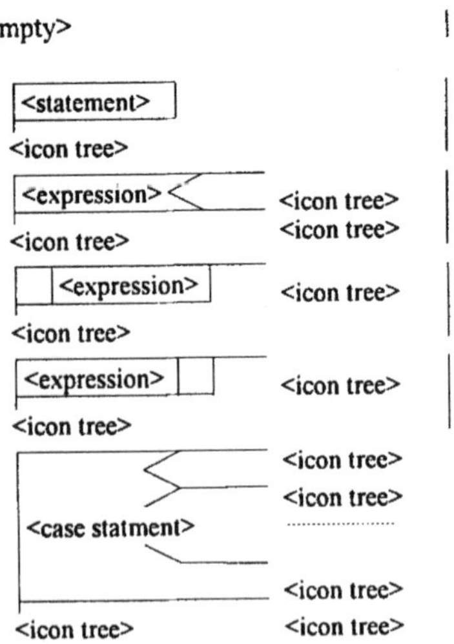

<structure declaration> ::= <type specifier><declaration>;

Appendix II

a)

```
c    all segments defined inside transformation number 10
c    TRANSFORMATION number 10
c    by setting window, setting viewport, select transformation number
         CALL GSWN ( 10, 0.0, 10.0, 0.0, 10.0 )
         CALL GSVP ( 10, 0.0, 1.0, 0.0, 0.72 )
         CALL GSELNT ( 10 )
c    set input priority for transform 10 greater than transform 0
         CALL GSVPIP ( 10, 0, 0 )
c    set workstation windown and workstation viewport
         CALL GSWKWN (IWKID, 0.0, 1.0 , 0.0, 0.72 )
         CALL GSWKVP (IWKID, 0.0, 0.27, 0.0, 0.195 )
```

(b)

```
c    now create segment for DUCK
         CALL GCRSG(IFOUR)
         CALL GFA ( NUMDUCK, DUCKX, DUCKY )
         CALL GCLSG
```

c)

```
c    PICK any one of the six segments
c    default Prompt & Echo Type is Device Coordinate echo plus pick symbol
c                       mouse, {none,ok},   segment,   pickid
7700     CALL GRQPK ( IWKID, IONE, ISTATUS, ISEGMENT, IPKID )
         IF ( ISTATUS .EQ. 0 ) GOTO 7700

c    TRANSLATE the segment that has been picked (selected)
c    Prompt & Echo Type 12 is World Coordinate digital value plus cross-hair
         CALL GINLC( IWKID, 1, 10, XINITLC(ISEGMENT), YINITLC(ISEGMENT),
           12, 0.0,0.1,0.0,0.1,0,NULLSTR80 )
         CALL GSLCM ( IWKID, 1, 1, 1 )
7010     NORTRANS = 10
         CALL GSMLC ( IWKID, 1, NORTRANS, XLC, YLC )
         IF ( NORTRANS .NE. 10 ) GOTO 7010
         DXLC = XLC - XINITLC(ISEGMENT)
         DYLC = YLC - YINITLC(ISEGMENT)
         TM(I,J) = ETM(ISEGMENT,I,J)          [ I=1,2; J=1,3 ]
         CALL GACTM ( TM, XINITLC(ISEGMENT),YINITLC(ISEGMENT),
           DXLC,DYLC, 0.0, 1.0,1.0, 0, TMO )
         XINITLC(ISEGMENT) = XLC
         YINITLC(ISEGMENT) = YLC
         ETM(ISEGMENT,I,J) = TMO(I,J)         [ I=1,2; J=1,3 ]
         IF ( DXLC.NE.0.0 .OR. DYLC.NE.0.0 )CALL GSSGT ( ISEGMENT,TMO )
         CALL GESC ( 100, 1, STR80 )
         IF ( STR80(1:1) .EQ.'2' .OR. STR80(2:2) .EQ. '0' ) GOTO 7010
         CALL GSLCM ( IWKID, 1, 0, 1 )
         CALL GRSGWK ( IWKID )
```

Appendix III

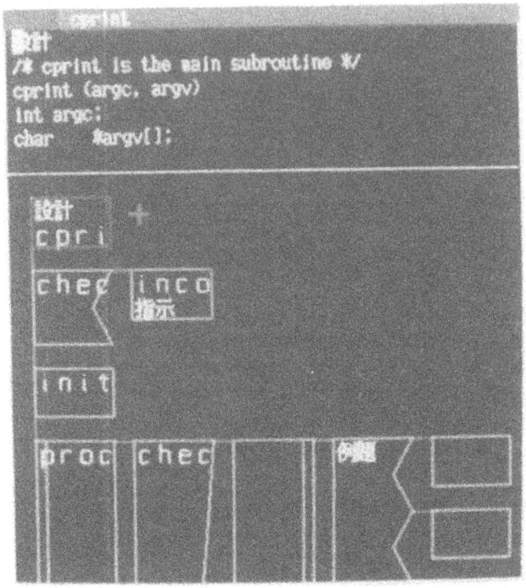

Figure 1. a Problem Analysis Diagram example

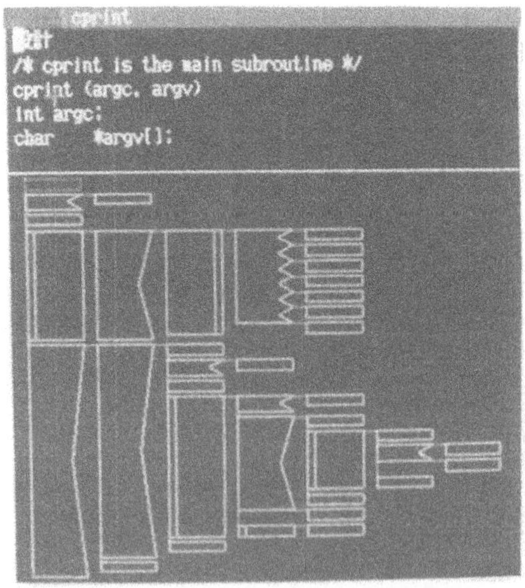

Figure 2. a shrunk Problem Analysis Diagram

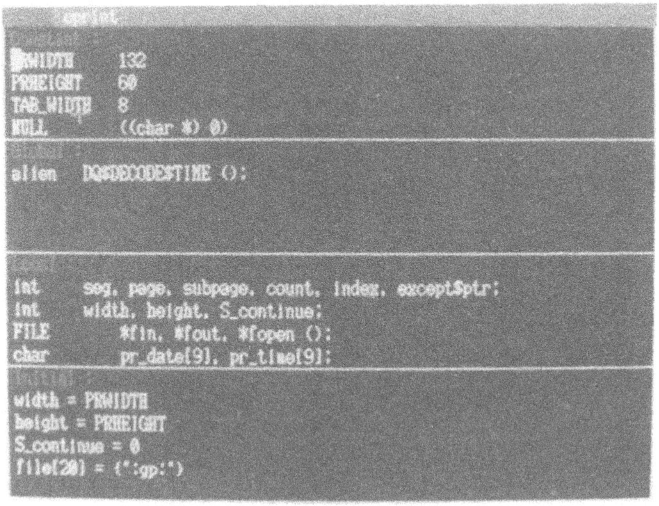

Figure 3. a Data Declaration and Initialization example

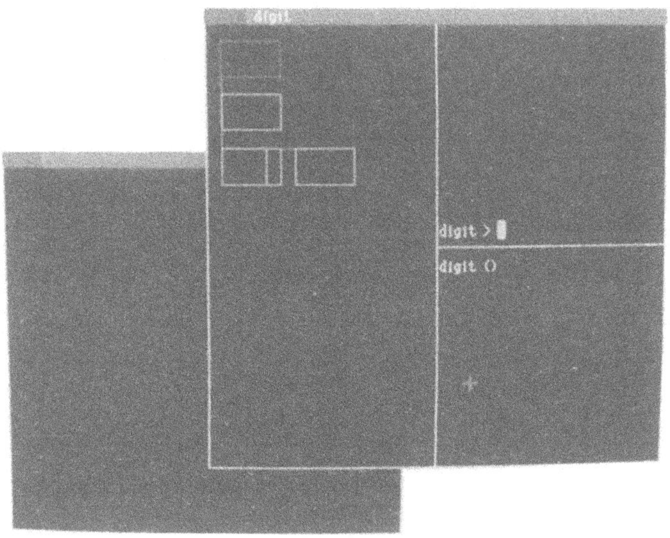

Figure 4. Initializing Debugger and Debuggee

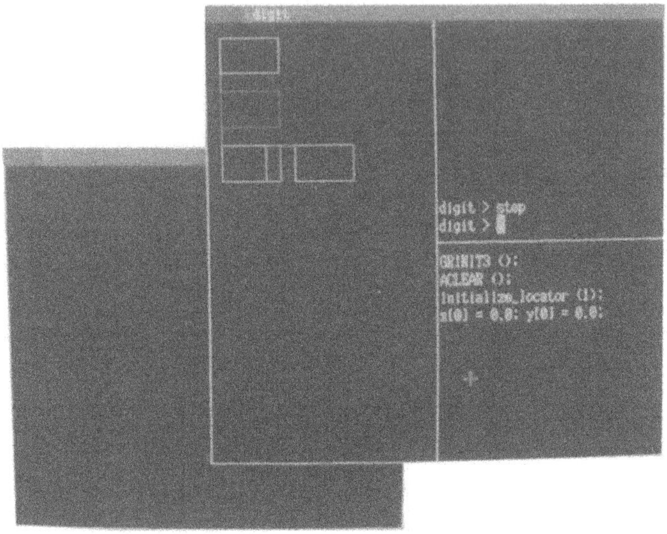

Figure 5. single stepping debugging

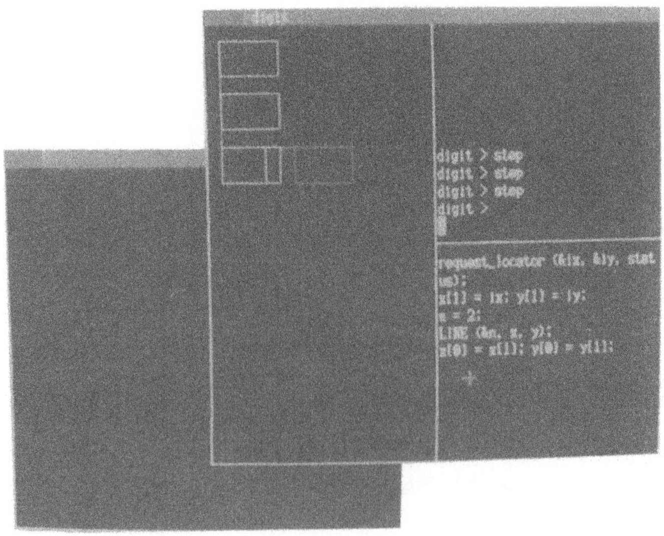

Figure 6. graphics application debugging

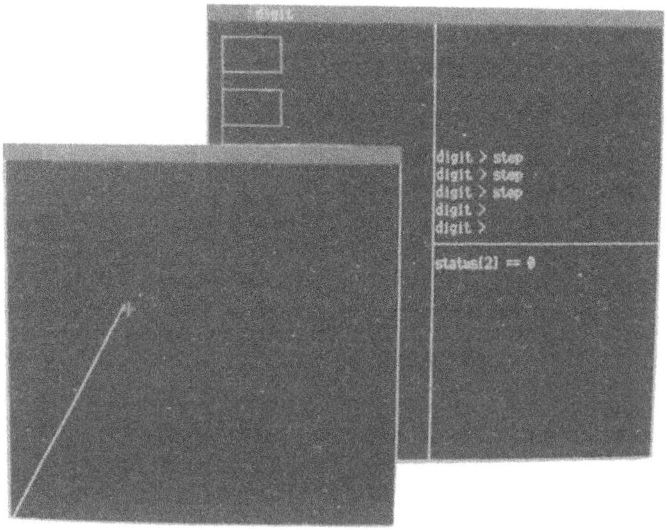

Figure 7. sharing of debugger/debuggee input resource

PEACE: Process Evolution and Adaptation CASE Environment - Its Framework and Requirements

Takeshi Yoshida, Atsunori Murata and Motoei Azuma

Department of Industrial Engineering and Management, Waseda University,
{yoshi | murata | azuma }@azuma.mgmt.waseda.ac.jp

Abstract

The *PEACE* (*P*rocess *E*volution and *A*daptation *C*ASE *E*nvironment) is a process support environment based on the process management paradigm, the *DREAM* (*D*esign, *R*efine, *E*volve and *A*dapt paradig*m*). The Darwin's theory of evolution and object oriented concept which encapsulates process and product are applied. The environment consists of three sub-systems co-operating to each other to support human agents: the *D*esign and *Re*finement *S*ub-*s*ystem (*DRESS*), the *E*volution and *A*daptation *S*ub-*s*ystem (*EASS*), and the *P*rocess *O*bject *M*anagement *S*ub-*s*ystem (*POMSS*). The aim of this research is to support designing and managing evolutional and adaptive software life cycle processes, and reduce gigantic human loads caused by diversity of software products and changing requirements. In this paper its concept, framework, and requirements are presented.

Keyword Codes: D.2.2; D.2.6: D.2.9
Keywords: Tools and Techniques; Programming Environments; Management

1. INTRODUCTION

Various methodologies for software development were proposed. These experiences implies that a good product is produced by a good process. It is widely accepted that the key concept of modern quality assurance is to produce a good product not by testing but by managing the process.

Early studies about software process were based on rigid process model such as [1]. Following the conventional process models, many process models were proposed such as [2]. Recently a focus of software quality management is shifting from products to processes. In spite of great efforts, most of software process stays at premature level, and most software management still depends on human creativity. Process assessment and process improvement require more flexibility because users want to see the interface before designing, and no matter how carefully and deliberately requirements are analyzed, they tend to change. These facts lead to the need of more sophisticated management support environment, which supports manager to improve their processes by evolving and adapting the environment itself to changes in its environment.

2. DREAM PARADIGM

The *DREAM* paradigm (*d*esign, *r*efine, *e*volve, and *a*dapt paradig*m*) is a new process paradigm which *PEACE* environment is based on. Using PEACE a manager can design and manage the evolutional and adaptive software life cycle processes, and reduce gigantic human loads caused by diversity of software processes and products. We apply the Darwinian concept and the object-oriented concept to implement three meta-processes.

Design a Process: Because of the fact that a process management still depends on human works, we recognized necessity of designing processes from requirements. We proposed a process design and assessment method [3] in which processes were to be designed based on quality requirement of the software product, and then each process were assessed. We believe that designing a process from requirements can increase quality and productivity.

Refine a Process: While configuration of products are carefully designed and iteratively refined to deal with their diversity, processes are stiffly prepared before process execution. We believe that it makes processes flexible and adaptive to refine the configuration of both processes and products concurrently and iteratively.

Evolve and Adapt a Process: Productivity and quality of products depends on processes. An environment where processes are executed is unstable and changing over time. To obtain better processes it is needed to evolve processes over and over. Through evolving processes the organization can achieve higher productivity and quality of software products and increase and keep competitiveness of the organization.

3. PEACE ARCHITECTURE

PEACE environment which are our target and under development consists of three sub-systems (fig.1). Harmony of them and human agents such as manager, developer, and so on enables processes easily designed, enacted, assessed, and improved and human efforts reduced.

DRESS (*D*esign and *R*efinement *S*ub-*s*ystem): DRESS is the *C*omputer *A*ided *P*rocess *D*esign (CAPD) system. Using this human agents can design and refine processes easily. The system contains two facilities; *process-object-retrieving facility* (PORF) and *process-object-browsing facility* (POBF). PORF searches the possible process objects which has product attributes similar to those that human agents input from all PO (*p*rocess *o*bject) stored and managed by POMSS. It provides a list of the POs searched for human agents. Human agents can browse POs by POBF. Because POMSS manages POs like class library human agents can track the objects lined to their ancestors and descendent and reach at the objects about which they want to know the information.

EASS (*E*volution and *A*daptation *S*ub-*s*ystem): EASS is the *C*omputer *A*ided *P*rocess *I*mprovement (CAPI) system. Using the system human agents can evolve and adapt processes easily. While process improvement now depends on talented persons, this system introduces computational assists to process evolution so it can reduce management loads that manager responsible for process improvement must face. The system includes two facilities; the *trouble-searching facility* (TSF) and the *success-searching facility* (SSF). TSF searches the POs that was unsuccessfully completed. In contrast the SSF searches the POs finished successfully. Successful process is one that met the process specification and produced the products that met the products requirements. These facilities provides a list of the POs searched.

POMSS (*P*rocess *O*bject *M*anagement *S*ub-*s*ystem): POMSS stores POs designed and refined. During and after enactment experiences that human agents wrote and measured values of process attributes and products attributes are collected and stored by this system. And this provides them to DRESS and EASS when two sub-systems require. In this sub-system POs are handled in class-library manner.

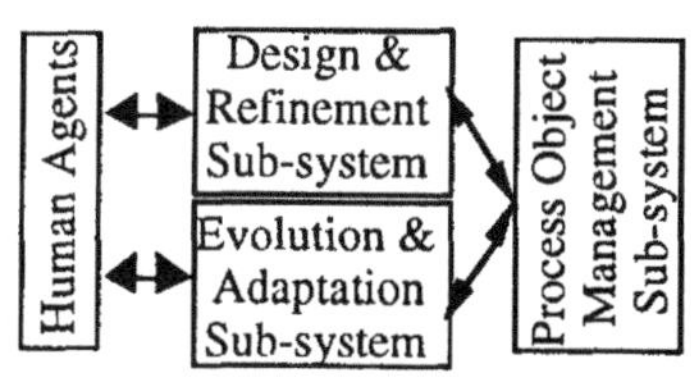

fig.1 PEACE Architecture

4. PROCESS IMPLEMENTATION BY PEACE

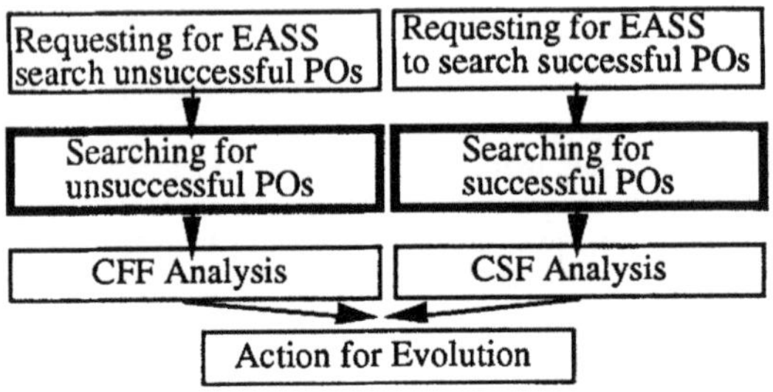

fig.3 Evolving and Adapting a Process

In this chapter we explain the method to design, refine, and evolve process by using sub-systems. The procedures for design and refinement of processes is shown in fig.2. The procedures for evolving processes is illustrated in fig.3. Bold rectangle in fig.2 means activity assisted by DRESS. Bold rectangle in fig.3 means activity assisted by EASS. Normal rectangle means human agents' task in both figures.

Designing a Process by DRESS: Human agents such as managers specify product attributes from requirements received. Following it they can request for DRESS to search standard process for the product with specified attributes. If it is not existing one more search is performed by making the abstraction level of object higher. If existing they can use it and tailor it to the products. Following them human agents conforming the searched process to the situation they face.

Refining a Process by DRESS: After searching for standard one human agents refine the process and make process object sub-class(es). This is performed in the case such as menu display design process where similar displays are required but they are slightly different from each other. This situation needs one super-process-object-class and some sub-process-object-class. The refinement of processes does not have to be performed before enactment of the process. It is possibly performed iteratively with product-refinement or enactment of the portion of the process.

Evolving and Adapting a Process by EASS: Human agents can request for EASS to search both successful and unsuccessful objects from all objects stored by POMSS in anytime. Following them they perform critical success factor (CSF) analysis and critical failing factor (CFF) analysis by carefully considering lists of both kinds of objects. Relying the results of analysis they can plan the effective action strategy and can design new standard processes.

5. CONCLUSION

Gigantic human loads can be reduced by using PEACE environment. While tasks in process management were depend on human creativity and special talents, some portion of works human agents must face can be assisted by our environment. Especially process improvement activity can be made easier although it has been supported by little tools.

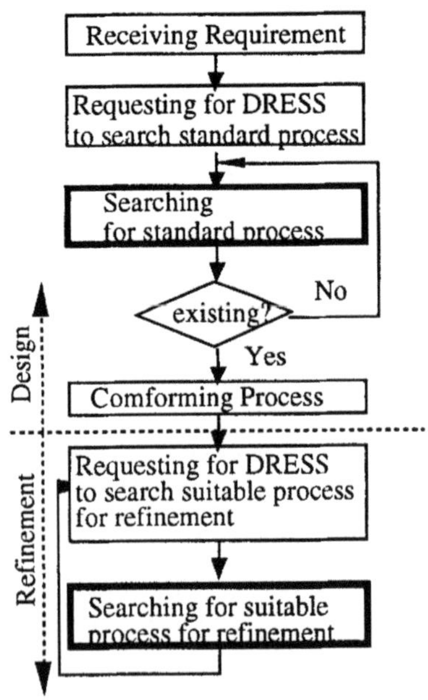

fig.2 Process Design and Refinement

Software processes can become very flexible and adaptive while they were very stiffly prepared and most process paradigms forced processes to be designed totally before their enactment. This benefit can be produced by encapsulation of process and product.

We mentioned the effects of PEACE but some details should be clarified. They will be presented in further papers.

References

1. Royce, W.W.: 'Managing the Development of Large Software Systems', *Proc. WESCOM*, 1970, pp.1-9
2. Boehm, B.W.: 'A Spiral Model of Software Development and Enhancement', *Computer*, Vol.21, (5), May 1988, pp.61-72
3. Yamaguti, T. and Azuma, M.: 'Quality Management of Software Processes', *Proc. 45th Nat'l Conf. of IPSJ*, 1992, pp.141-142 (written in Japanese)

58

Software Development Environments to Support Model Consistency

V.E.Veraart and S.L. Wright

Computer Science Programme, Murdoch University, Perth, Western Australia.

Abstract

A major problem affecting software quality and software development productivity is the use of incorrect and inconsistent models of the problem solution domains during the software development process. Our solution is firstly to make the methods and models more precise by defining their semantics, and secondly to ensure that partially overlapping models are semantically and syntactically consistent over their *alias components*. Our approach is expose the operations a tool performs on its model to other tools via semantic events. We maintain tool independence by using a co-ordinator to translate semantic events in one model into appropriate semantic events on alias components in other models.

Keyword codes: D.2.6; D.2.1; D.2.2.
Keywords:Programming Environments; Requirements/Specifications; Tools and Techniques.

1. INTRODUCTION - METHODS AND TOOLS

The use of methods for modelling various aspects of a proposed system has been an accepted part of systems analysis and design for many years. As software development proceeds through the lifecycle the nature of the models changes as the information contained in individual functional, data and time models is aggregated into models that become more concrete in respect to the final system. Development converges to the "final solution" models. These may be represented as source code fragments, database queries, library functions, etc. As convergence proceeds many of the inconsistencies are usually discovered, often after considerable economic investment in the project. We believe that the creation of consistent, complementary models enhances the capability, correctness, and therefore quality, of the final, implementation. Our particular area of interest is ir the application of analysis and high-level design methods to produce complementary models for the early phases of the software development lifecycle (SDLC).

2. MODEL CONSISTENCY

The *deliverables* of the analysis and design phases of the SDLC are usually a set of models representing particular views of the system. These models are not a deliverable as far as the client is concerned, but the information they contain is a deliverable to some downstream activity in the software manufacturing process. (If this is not the case, then there is no justification for building them.) As such, they form an important part of the infrastructure required for software development and as with any infrastructure component, contribute indirectly to the quality of the final product.

2.1 Alias components

If we consider that each of the models represents a*view* of the problem domain or system under development, then by definition these concurrent models possess a degree of commonality. This commonality arises from the *alias components* that occur in the models. We define an alias component to be an entity (in its broadest sense of an item, place, event, role, policy etc) that appears in a number of method-models but with different semantics and representations in each model. The analyst naturally identifies items as alias components as part of the model-development process.

2.2 Model evolution

Software development proceeds in an iterative manner. Once the initial models have been created, we often need to update domain information. Typically, this is done from within a particular tool. This tool can maintain its internal model consistency. However, in order for inter-model consistency to be preserved any changes we make to the model components must be propagated to all relevant alias components in other models. If consistent change propagation is not incorporated into the development process, we can have a set of models that are no longer consistent in reflecting the state of our knowledge of the problem domain or system [6].

3. SEMANTIC TOOL INTEGRATION

Our work seeks to identify some of the reasons that tool integration is important, in terms of the needs of the users of an environment, and to propose an integration mechanism that meets those needs. We propose that the solution to the problem of model consistency is to integrate method-tools with respect to the commonality between the models they manipulate.

3.1 Syntactic and semantic specification of method-models

All method-models have a syntax, a notation that describes the valid components of the model and its structure. This syntax can be expressed as a concrete syntax using either graphical components or textual lexemes. For graphical models the syntax is most often expressed as a set of "rules" describing the shape and placement of their components, using narrative text.

Within a model some combinations of components, although syntactically valid may be semantically meaningless Model semantics involves the rules, relating to the types of components, that govern the consistency between a model and its"owner" ie method. Thus flow, transform, store, etc, are the 'data types' of the DFD method and there is a set of rules that constrains how they can be operated upon, eg combination. We use a type system that allows us to introduce the notion of semantic checks to eliminate many obvious semantic errors

Once we move beyond the simple creation operations, the definition of the method semantics for many operations is often left to the individual tool implementer; there are no ISO or ANSI standards in this area. Clearly, the semantics of any operation should be clearly specified, unambiguously, in terms of its effect on its models. Failure to achieve this<u>within</u> any single method-tool makes integration with any other tool impossible.

To achieve consistency between models that are the product of different method-tools, we must be able to map operations on the components of one method-model onto alias components represented in other models. Since the differences between models are likely to be both syntactic and semantic (depending on the semantic-gap between tools) the mapping operation must be able to operate at both syntactic and semantic levels. We define models having a high degree of similarity of form and expression as exhibiting a small semantic gap. Semantic-closeness is generally low for method-tools that are used in the earlier phases of the SDLC, ie analysis and high-level design.

A commonly proposed solution to the semantic-gap problem is to create unified operation sets that can operate on all method-models of the environment. However, reducing all the semantic operations to a common, canonical set has obvious problems.

4. A COOPERATIVE APPROACH TO TOOL INTEGRATION

Our alternative approach is to express the required "consistency" operations in terms of each tool's own operation set. This allows independent tools to be inserted into, and removed from, an integrated environment without requiring modifications to any other tool in the environment. This is achieved by specifying each method's operation-set as a formal, concise semantic definition. Once the set of alias components for the methods in the environment has been identified, we determine which operations of their operations have the potential to produce model inconsistencies. Finally we define the operation-mappings that are necessary across tools whose models are affected by these operations.

Most analysis tools are not directly integrable due to the semantic gap between them in terms of their operations and data components. We group these tools into a *cluster*, and all the tools are linked to a *coordinator*. The coordinator is a programmable component that gives us flexiblity in defining an environment's toolset. Our tools are required to publicise their behaviour, this establishing a basis for a communication method between tools. When a tool cooperates with other tools in its cluster it informs them of any relevant actions on its own model by issuing *semantic events*. A semantic event is an operation on a method-model, by its tool, that is syntactically and semantically valid for the model and causes a change in the state of the model. Each tool defines a set of semantic events that are equivalent to operations on its models.

The cluster coordinator handles mapping of outgoing tool-events into semantically consistent ingoing events by table lookup, simple translation or by invocation of specified computation fragments. By introducing both a coordinator-cluster mechanism, and semantic events, we can ensure that tools in the environment are totally independent of one another. The coordination component is a fully programmable part of the system. For example, when a tool is modified, or a new tool added to the environment, other tools are not directly affected by any new semantic events. Rather, the coordinator is modified to translate any new events into events that are meaningful in terms of other existing tools.

For very simple semantic operations automatic consistency control may be possible, however at this stage we envisage that user intervention will be necessary and a tool's response to events may be to inform the user of the need for changes to the model and to identify the affected components. To handle consistency control automatically one solution is to include an expert-system as an additional component in the environment, whose rules encapsulate "consistency policies".

5. TECHNICAL ISSUES

To take advantage of the event-coordination strategy, tools will usually be written specifically for the environment. Method tools are implemented as small, cohesive micro-tools, and assembled around a cluster coordinator This allows for a high degree of reuse, between tools, of the common components that are found in many tools eg as object drawing functions, cut-and-paste editing functions, etc.

To integrate a tool into the environment it requires:

- an executable component that implements each tool's functions and can be directly integrated into a cluster
- a place to store their model data structures - a file store, or similar mechanism
- a set of method-model data structure definitions that can be installed into the store
- an external interface definition, that is a tool's events; a method-tool must have a well - defined set of operations in terms of syntax (notation) and semantics (model manipulation)

a set of fragments to handle the events as defined by each tool's external interface definition.
the ability to execute in an identical manner whether they are run in stand-alone mode or in a cluster.

The interface descriptions are used to decide how tools can be connected, and to validate the connections in terms of correct data type matching, etc. Architectural requirements for the environment include:

- an event handling mechanism
- ability to run tools and coordinators as separately executing processes, or threads

- the means to communicate data between tools
- facilities for setting up communication paths between tools, and/or perform broadcasts.

Many current operating systems, for example UNIX, provide the basic technical mechanisms that enable us to build a prototype. We are currently building a prototype to test our concepts, and highlight inadequacies, using C++, UNIX, and Glish [4] to provide the inter-process communication.

6. RELATED WORK

Very little work on integration is done from an environment user's perspective, ie of what use is integration to them. Brinkkemper adopts a similar approach to our work with alias components. He uses meta-data modelling to derive method-companionship[1] that is used in defining editor transfer charts, in the context of switching between editors, on the execution of certain editing operations concerned with common components. We apply meta-modelling at the level of events on models of *data structures* rather than to diagrammatic representations. A number of recent papers have appeared in the literature concerning integration of structured methods such as entity-modelling and data flow diagramming with formal methods [5] [3] [2]. In general, these deal with uni-directional translation, rather than method integration which we consider to be bi-directional. Our approach allows updates to be made in any of the clustered tools, and to be notified to other tools with models containing common components.

7. CONCLUSION

We have proposed that one method for improving the quality of software is by exerting some control over the models created during the development process. The control takes the form of requiring consistency between the models. Ensuring that inconsistencies are noted and corrected as soon as possible ensures that flaws relating to missing or ambiguous information do not become apparent in the latter stages on the development process.

Implementing integration at the tool level means that the actual methods remain unchanged. To achieve model-consistency via tool-integration we identify the alias components of the method models and ensure that operations on these components, executed within the method-tool, are made available to any other tools, sharing a common responsibility for the component, in a manner that is semantically consistent for each tool. We achieve this by clustering the tools about a coordination tool that acts as a semantic event translator and despatcher. The tools communicate via events that are comprehensible within each tool in terms of its own model semantics.

In our cooperative approach there is no requirement for tools to agree on common data types, structures and/or message formats, thus it prevents loss of independence and flexibility. The definitions for a tool's data structures, as well as its control over instantiated data structures, are encapsulated within the tool itself. This differs from the common approach of data being maintained in a common repository where access is only available via the repository manager. From the perspective of its user the tool behaves as any normal independent tool, and can be used in a totally stand-alone capacity. Cooperative tools can easily be reused and can be attached to other groups of tools, providing a very flexible integration arrangement. These benefits are achieved through each tool working at a high-level of abstraction (manipulating its method-models) and exposing its operations, at that model level, to other tools using semantic events.

An extended version of this paper is available, via FTP on ftp.cs.murdoch.edu.au as Murdoch University Computer Science Technical Report CS/94/05.

REFERENCES

1. Brinkkemper, S., deLange, M., Looman, R., van der Steen, F.H.G.C., 'On the derivation method-companionship by meta-modelling', *Soft. Eng. Notes*, (15) 1, January 1990, pp 49-58.
2. Misic, V., Velasevic, D., Lazarevic, B., 'Formal specification of a data dictionary for an extende ER data model', *Computer Journal*, (35) 6, 1992, pp 611-622.
3. Polack, Fiona, 'Integrating formal notations and systems analysis: using entity relation-ship diagrams", *Software Engineering Journal*, September 1992, pp 363-371.
4. Paxson, Vern., Saltmarsh, Chris., '*Glish*: A user-level software bus for loosely-couplec distribution systems', *Proceedings of 1993 Winter USENIX Technical Conference*, 1993.
5. Semmens, L.T., France, R.B., Docker, T.W.G., 'Integrated structured analysis and form specification techniques', *Computer Journal*, (35) 6, 1992, pp 600-610.
6. Veraart, V.E., Wright, S.L., 'Consistent models enhance software quality*Proceedings of SQM94*,
   Computational Mechanics Institute, Edinburgh, July 94, pp 159-174.

PART TEN

Education and Training

Process Oriented Instruction for Software Engineers (POISE): Perspectives and Experiences

Srinivas Thummalapalli and Rajat Kumar Todi

Centre for Development of Telematics, 11/6B Shanti Chambers, Main Pusa Road, New Delhi - 110 005, India.

Abstract

This paper briefly describes the training model for imparting the process view of software development to the graduate engineer trainees in a Level 2 telecom research and development organization. The design of the approach was predicated on the concepts of ETVX model for software development. Its structure and features were designed to align the training objectives with the organizational goals.

It provides an insight into the operational aspects and their underlying objectives. It provides structured learning experience to the trainees and enable them to assimilate, appreciate and apply the concepts of software engineering to the software development.

It narrates the difficulties after implementing the approach and proposes requisite measures to make the approach responsive and vibrant. The paper also refers to similar such exercises in the academic arena and the relevance of some aspects in the organizational environment.

Key words Codes: D.2.m; K.4.3; K.6.1

Key words: Software Engineering, Miscellaneous; Computers and Society, Organizational Impact; Management of Computing and Information Systems, Project and People Management.

1. INTRODUCTION

Centre for Development of Telematics (C-DOT) is the telecommunications technology research centre of Government Of India. C-DOT's mission, its products, and its future perspective can be found from [9], [11]. C-DOT is a level 2 organization [6], [10]. Its software quality objective is to migrate to level 3 on SEI CMM [10] and to attain ISO 9000 certification for its software development process. It follows the spiral model [1], [6] for the development of its software products.

C-DOT recruits fresh engineering graduates (GETs) and engineers who have at most one or two year's of experience. GETs were from Electrical & Electronics Engineering (ECE) and Computer Science (CS) disciplines. Detail of first three batches of GETs are given in table 1.

It was felt that GETs require an introduction to software engineering, and to software development process model that is being followed in C-DOT. They should be exposed to C-DOT's software environment. Other desirable and essential skills are like communication, project management, team-work and quality consciousness. The aforesaid needs are realized through Software Development Methodology workshop (SDM w/s).

Table 1

Attributes of GETs batches

	GET 1	GET 2	GET 3
Total Number	42	35	64
CS	35	24	38
ECE	7	11	26
No. of Teams	14	16	22
No. of Mentors	7	8	11
Trainees/Teams	3	2-3	2-3

2. SOFTWARE DEVELOPMENT METHODOLOGY WORKSHOP

The accent of the workshop is on making the trainee to appreciate:

- significance of process in the successful realization of the product.
- bearing of individual effectiveness on the quality software development.
- interplay of persons and processes to develop real-time software solutions.
- constraints and compulsions of real time software working environment.

The structure and features of SDM w/s with its underlying intent was also presented. For the detailed exposition refer to [3].

2.1. Structure

1. Task Force: A task force (TF) on SDM w/s was constituted to implement the approach. It consisted of technical group (TG) and process group (PG). Technical group consists of mentors who were engineers from switching software division and process group consists of members from technical training division.

2. Selection: Members of both the groups were nominated by their respective divisional managers. A typical mentor has a working experience of at least 1.5 years. The details of the earlier batches are presented in table 1.

3. Teams: A team (TR) consists of 2 to 3 trainees. It was formed by the process group by considering the following factors viz. educational qualifications (whether from CS or ECE), qualification level (undergraduate or graduate) and gender, disposition of individuals (whether an individual is extrovert or introvert).

It is a conscious attempt to re-transform existing groups into new associations. The experience with three batches of GETs (refer table 1) corroborates that the criteria for composition of successful teams in the arena of the academic world [8] are equally applicable in an industrial environment.

4. Roles: The roles and responsibilities of technical group, process group, and trainees were clearly defined and documented for easy reference [5], [14].

5. Communication: The nature of communication between different groups is depicted in figure 1. Brief about the different channels is given below.

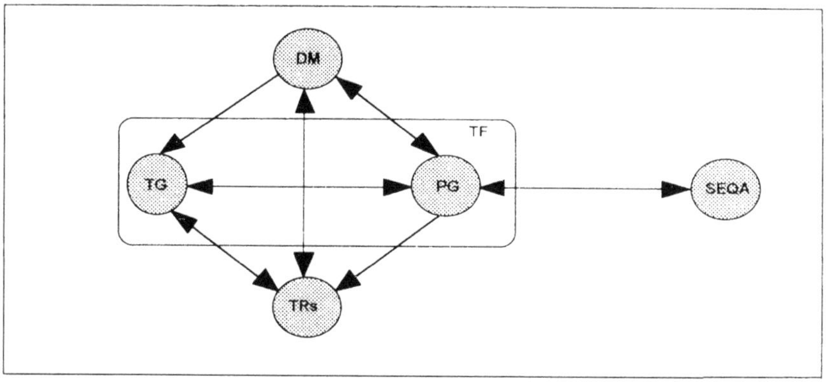

FIGURE 1: COMMUNICATION MODEL

Communication between:

- Technical Group and Process Group: to select assignments, to modulate the approach, and to track the progress of the trainees during the workshop.
- Process Group and Divisional Manager (DM): to update the status of progress, and to seek resource allocation.
- Technical Group and the teams: to help the trainees to solve their conceptual difficulties.
- Process Group and the teams: to give and receive the feedback for continuous process improvements, to make the trainees aware of process.
- Divisional managers and trainees: to convey the organizational vision and seek the first hand feedback from trainees.
- Process group and Software Engineering and Quality Assurance (SEQA): to identify the leverage areas for software process improvement.

6. Medium: Through e-mail, personal dialogue and through internal courier.

7. Assignments: Problems were either designed or selected from the problem bank. Process group provides the criteria of selection. Normally the criteria [1] are: degree of complexity of the problem should be such that it enables the implementation of processual aspects such as reviews, documentation, etc. and it provides practical insight into product development cycle.

8. Allocation: The assignments were allocated to the trainees after the presentation of the problem statements by the mentors. During the presentation, mentors state the problem, their expectations and requisite understanding that is essential to carry out the assignment. Each mentor guides 2 teams.

9. Duration: 2 months

10. Resources: Standard learning resources on Software Engineering were made available. Systems laboratory has one VAX and two VME systems with 18 terminals.

2.2. Features

1. INTERFACE: To create a sense of expectancy about the workshop, and to build the requisite tempo to practice software engineering, a series of thematic outlines entitled INTERFACE on software engineering was released. The details of the themes can be found in [3], [7], [12].

2. PACT: To simulate the concept of contractual obligation between the user and the developer on the process level, Process Adoption and Conformance Treaty was made to be executed between the teams and the respective mentors. It is also to clarify the roles, expectations and responsibilities of the mentors and trainees. The text was adapted from [10].

3. ETVX Model: The concepts of ETVX model [5], [13] have been applied to the development process. A notion of the same was applied to the workshop operations. Precise entry criterion (E), task descriptions (T), validation procedures (V), and exit criteria (X) has been outlined both for the development process and the various phases of the workshop. The details of the model are depicted in figure 2.

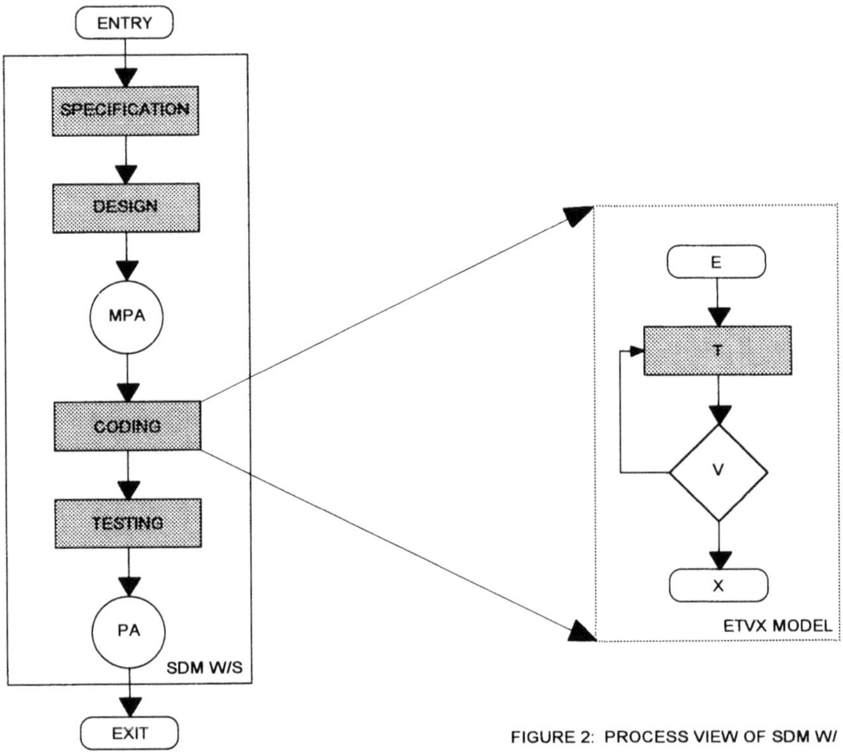

FIGURE 2: PROCESS VIEW OF SDM W/

4. Plans: The salient features of approach are strategic, operational and software quality plans [11]. They explain how the training objectives are aligned with the organizational goals.

5. Focus areas: Error prevention and early error detection were given due significance. Reviews, simultaneous documentation and strict adherence to schedules were identified as focus areas to achieve the needed behavioral change in the trainee.

6. Schedules: The schedule for the SDM w/s was designed based upon [12], with an explicit mention of reviews and milestones. Trainees were introduced to software project planning aspects.

7. Orientation: Process group introduces the trainees to approach and development process model of SDM w/s. During the SDM w/s, a variant of waterfall model was followed.

8. Lectures: GETs were exposed to the language module and digital switching software (DSS) architecture module prior to the SDM w/s. During a given phase of SDM w/s, generic, specific and

practice lectures were delivered. Lectures were also presented on review process and inspection cycle. Inspection cycle consists of problem data resolution, inspection, causal analysis, and fixing of errors.

9. Documentation: Specific deliverables were identified. Guidelines on documentation were provided to the GETs.

10. Self Learning Instruments: At the end of each phase questionnaire from [12] were compiled and released to trainees. It is to reinforce the conceptual understanding specific to a phase.

11. Accomplishment Review: Presentations were conducted for teams after the completion of all the exit criterion for all phases. Trainees are expected to *reflect* on *how* aspects of the development of the solution and discuss with the other teams.

12. Feedback: Trainees and mentors gave feedback on speakers' performance, on the workshop, and on the resource utilization. This was analyzed and necessary measures were incorporated in the design of the next SDM w/s.

13. Metrics: Seven process measurements were collected from the teams to gain the visibility into the process and fine-tune the approach for the future batches of GETs. The type of measurements can be found in [3].

14. Assessments: The performance appraisal form in C-DOT [3], [4] was adapted to meet the needs of SDM w/s. The scheme has one mid-term appraisal (MPA) and final performance appraisal (PA). They are carried out by the mentors.

15. Recognition Awards: Peer to peer recognition program (PEPUP) was instituted basing on the essence of [2]. The details of awards and nominations are in [3].

16. Newsletter: A newsletter named *STRIDES: for excellence* is brought out exclusively for sharing of experiences, information and insights during the workshop amongst the constituent members.

17. Meetings: The meeting process consists of agenda distribution, preparation, meeting and release of minutes. It was found that meetings were 80% effective. Criteria of effectiveness are the extent to which agenda was discussed and action items were finalized. On average 1.75 hours were spent on each of 6 meetings.

3. DIFFICULTIES

The salient difficulties that were encountered during SDM w/s were:

- Teams felt that the checklists and guidelines were generic.
- The deadlines were common to all the teams irrespective of the complexity of the assignment. It does not reflect the inherent complexities and in turn the need for different deadlines for different assignments.
- The propensity to realize the product at the expense of process has its bearing.
- GETs felt that documentation hampers the product development though they agree to the philosophy of documentation.
- Process group could not provide timely analysis of the inspection summary's data owing to high volume.
- Mentors had difficulties in assessing team members' involvement for the interactions were limited to review and consultative meetings.

4. FUTURE DIRECTIONS

The following measures are to be incorporated in the approach for the future SDM w/s. They are based on the feedback from the constituents of the communication model.

- Formalization of the meeting process.

- Introducing the prospective mentors to consulting skills.
- Conducting formal practice sessions on reviews.
- Increasing the variety of assignments.
- Strength of the team to be decided basing on the man-hours' requirement for a given assignment.
- Team specific deadlines to be decided.
- Providing the checklists with examples.
- Project management practices and configuration management procedures to be incorporated.

REFERENCES

1. Bruegge, Bernd: "Teaching an Industry-oriented Software Engineering Course", *Software Engineering Education: SEI conference 1992 proceedings.* Springer-Verlag, LNCS 640, 1992, pages 64-79.
2. Carder, Brooks and Clark, James D.: "The Theory and Practice of Employee Recognition", Quality Progress, December 1992, pages 25-30.
3. C-DOT. Approach to Software Development Methodology Workshop - A primer. Centre For Development of Telematics, N. Delhi, December 1993.
4. C-DOT. C-DOT Performance Appraisal Manual. Centre For Development of Telematics, N. Delhi, March 1993.
5. Fowler P.and Rifkin, P: "Software Engineering Process Group Guide", Technical Report CMU/SEI-90-TR-24 ESD-90-TR-225. Carnegie Mellon University, Software Engineering Institute, February 1993.
6. Ghosh, H.: "Current Software Engineering Practices in C-DOT", Technical Report, C-DOT TR 001-1993, Centre For Development of Telematics, N. Delhi, June 1993.
7. Gibbs et. al., N. E., "The Carnegie Mellon University Master of Software Engineering Training Program", *Software Engineering Education: SEI Conference Proceedings,* Pittsburgh, Pennsylvania, July 1989, pages 152-154.
8. Kantipudi et. al., M.: "Software Engineering Course Projects: Failures and Recommendations", *Software Engineering Education: SEI conference 1992 proceedings,* Springer-Verlag, LNCS 640, 1992, pages 324-337.
9. G. B. Meemamsi. C-DOT story. Kedar Publications, N. Delhi, 1993.
10. M. C. Paulk et al. Capacity Maturity Model for Software, Version 1.1. Technical Report CMU/SEI-93-TR-24 ESC-TR-93-177. Carnegie Mellon University, Software Engineering Institute, February 1993.
11. B. D. Pradhan. Telecommunication: At least a phone in every village. IEEE Spectrum, March 1994, pages 43-47.
12. R. S. Pressman. Making Software Engineering Happen. A Guide for Instituting the Technology. Prentice-Hall, 1988.
13. R. A. Radice et. al. A programming process architecture. IBM Systems Journal vol. 24, no. 2, 1985, pages 79-95.
14. T. Srinivas. Role of Mentors. Process Document of Technical Training Division, Centre For Development of Telematics, N. Delhi, December 1992.

60

OO Methods in Teaching: Current Experience and Future Possibilities

Gillian Lovegrove[a], Phil McLaughlin[a], Jakub Chabik[a], Pippa Standen[b]

[a]School of Computing, Staffordshire University, Stafford UK
[b]School of Information Systems, SIHE, Southampton UK

Keyword Codes: D.1.5; D.2.10
Keywords: OO teaching, OO analysis and design, OO methods

Abstract

The potential of object-oriented technology (OOT) to ease the problems of complexity, maintenance costs and reuse is now being realised for large systems. OOT is now recognised as a technique for "serious" software engineering, such that the number of commercial products built using OOT is on the increase. A significant amount of research and commercial activity in the object-oriented database field is seen as another sign of the importance of the OO paradigm. The Object Management Group (OMG) has produced an object model which is acceptable to over 100 companies world-wide.

OOT is sufficiently important for it to be included in every undergraduate curriculum. Introducing students to the object paradigm within traditional computing and information systems courses is a difficult task. There is a need to choose a suitable language that supports objects (OOPL) and/or the need to teach an OO analysis and design method appropriate for the newer paradigm. The timing for these is crucial and discussed in the paper.

However the paper focuses on the choice of method, which, given the plethora of OO methods on the market, is not easy. Criteria for assessing methods for teaching are given, together with an evaluation for two well known methods. The potential of two recent "hopeful" methods is assessed and guidelines given for using methods within the curriculum.

1. INTRODUCTION

Object orientation is now accepted as a software engineering technique, resulting in an increasing number of commercial products, driven partly by a trend towards componentware [1]. Object-oriented databases are seen as a significant addition to relational databases, though the technology for their integration appears to be taking a long time to mature. Nevertheless the focus on the standardisation of the object model for databases is likely to have an impact on OO technology in general.

2. LIFE CYCLES, METHODS AND LANGUAGES

Typically structured development proceeds down the waterfall cycle from requirements capture to analysis, design implementation and maintenance; systems development models are constructed involving entity relationship models, data flow diagrams, and entity life histories.

In contrast, OO analysis and design (OOAD) is an inherently iterative process with the distinction between the analysis and design processes being less well defined. Analysis might be said to be the identification of objects from the problem space, whereas design is the refinement of objects and class hierarchies in the solution space. This refinement of classes becomes somewhat dependent on the coding language. All in all therefore, the notion of a waterfall cycle is less appropriate to OOAD than traditional methods.

2.1 Analysis and design

OO analysis starts by an attempt to identify objects and their relationship with each other (client, server, responsibility); this is a difficult task. Ideally the analyst would have previous experience in OO modelling which has implications with respect to teaching.

The design phase consists of the generation of the class hierarchies, subsystems and modules. In practice it is rare that any software system is so fully specified that no further changes are required during design and before implementation. Also, the design phase can be affected by characteristics of the implementation language such as the existence of single or multiple inheritance and file structures.

2.2 The different methods

The design and use of OO methods is currently an area of great debate with at least 40 different methods available to choose from [2,3,4]. Methods have been developed from different backgrounds, such as modelling and simulation, or more traditional information systems background. Some concentrate more on analysis and some mainly on design.

Each of the methods hopes to achieve a dominant position in the market. With the experience of traditional methods in mind, it is unlikely that any one method will dominate for all domains and situations, but as the technology matures a smaller number of methods will become popular. These will undoubtedly have a good CASE tool associated with them for a reasonable price, and capable of producing code.

3. OVERVIEW OF CURRENT STATE OF THE ART

There are many books which teach an OOPL first and incorporate little in the way of design[5,6,7,8,9,10]; Meyer encourages formal approaches to software specification, construction and verification [11,12]. Others concentrate on a design method but incorporate examples in languages [17,18]. Weiner and Pinson describe current practice in university courses, short courses and seminars [13]. They assert that in general four steps are followed: providing an understanding of the OOP approach, illustration of the properties and features of OOP by teaching an OOP language, presentation of a features analysis, and integration of the first three steps into a logical approach to problem solving.

Wu describes a three-stage, incremental approach in teaching OOP [13]. The first stage includes making students able to write a simple program, unlearning old methods of programming. The second stage introduces the benefits of code reuse, abstraction and encapsulation. Stage three introduces students to client/server programming, the concept of inheritance and polymorphism, and introduces an OO design method. A later article [15] gives more detail of the design stage. He asserts that OOP is ultimately learned only through constant use and experimentation.

We see that there is support for a broad approach in the USA integrating OO concepts with language and design, allowing the student time to merge the ideas arising from theory and practice. The fundamental differences between the American and the European methods for systems development may be partly due to cultural differences between America and Europe and in part by the different educational systems [16]. American methods are strongly focused on pragmatism and informality, whereas European methods are more formal, resulting in better predictability and system quality. The dilemma for the European teacher is that a pragmatic approach during teaching aids faster understanding, whilst teaching a design method more formally, runs the risk of overloading the students with the details of the method at the expense of understanding the underlying principles of object technology.

4. CRITERIA FOR METHODS FOR TEACHING

In the light of the experience above, the amount of familiarity students have with object-oriented concepts before they start concentrating on analysis and design is a factor in deciding which method would be a good one to adopt. It is assumed here that the previous experience is likely to exist but be limited. The criteria for choosing a method are given below:

(a) students can do it: it is conceptually simple; draws on previous experience
(b) it is well documented (in a book)
(c) it is easy to visualise and the notation is simple
(d) it is useful in industry, well tested and popular
(e) there is a CASE tool for the method which is affordable
(f) it encourages group work

Criteria (a), (b), (c), (d) and (e) are self-explanatory. The last one reflects the increased emphasis on group activities which arises from using object-oriented methods. It also reflects the need in the undergraduate curriculum to include group activities, since this experience will be a support for their careers at a later date.

5. ASSESSMENT OF SELECTED METHODS

CRC cards were designed and used especially for the teaching environment [20] before the book associated with the method [21] was published. The method appeared effective and cheap and was adopted at the University of Southampton. OMT is the method promoted by Rumbaugh, whose book was one of the first to appear [18] and offered a more detailed prescriptive view of objects; this was adopted at Staffordshire University. A number of other methods are known to have been used in other UK universities; these include Booch, Coad/Yourdon and Shlaer/Mellor, chosen largely because of the availability of the books.

5.1 CRC or Wirfs-Brock method

This method might be said to have an exploratory, then analysis and design phase. The exploratory phase deals with gathering of information, in particular the identification of classes and their associated responsibilities. This phase relies heavily on heuristics and uses CRC cards (Class, Responsibility and Collaboration) as the primary vehicle for team communication. CRC cards are index cards or PostIts on which designers write information about proposed classes.

(a) students can do it: it is conceptually simple; draws on previous experience

CRC is simple and students can pick it up easily. It does not draw on past experience.

(b) it is well documented (in a book)

The book [Wirfs-Brock 90] is a good one with well explained examples and heuristics.

(c) it is easy to visualise and the notation is simple

The notation is simpler, good for teaching though it may be lacking for commercial needs.

(d) it is useful in industry, well tested and popular

It is currently less well known in industry and less used.

(e) there is a CASE tool for the method which is affordable

The method, being based on group work and heuristics, does not lend itself to a CASE tool; if there are CASE tools, they are not well known.

(f) it encourages group work

This method is designed for group work though it can be used singly.

5.2 OMT

OMT [18] is a very popular method in the software engineering community. Having been developed from a modelling and simulation background it has been adapted for use in what would normally be considered mainstream information systems applications.

(a) students can do it: it is conceptually simple; draws on previous experience

OMT consists of three basic models. The first is the object model represented using object structure diagrams, close to the conventional entity relationship models. This allowed them to model the object structures fairly quickly. Similarly, the dynamic model shows object behaviour using state diagrams(c.f. entity life histories), and the functional model shows value mapping and functional dependencies with data flow diagrams. The three models are complementary and for simple models OMT is very clear.

(b) it is well documented (in a book)

The book [18] is clear, and Rumbaugh writes regularly in JOOP, presenting case studies.

(c) it is easy to visualise and the notation is simple

The notation is not too complex for students to grasp.

(d) it is useful in industry, well tested and popular

OMT has been applied fairly extensively. It is less of an academic tool than a practical method and has thus found acceptance with C++ and Smalltalk developers

(e) there is a CASE tool which is affordable

A number of CASE tools support OMT, including low cost tools (e.g. Select OMT).

(f) it encourages group work

OMT neither enforces or discourages group working.

6. EXPERIENCE WITH THESE TWO METHODS

Experience with students is mixed. Some students are able to grasp the modelling concepts with ease, whilst some have great difficulty; students rarely perceive the importance of analysis and design, and tend to divorce it from system development. Thus their analytical ability is below what would be expected in industry. Often they lack general business or industrial knowledge. Modelling requires some understanding of the domain, but more importantly an understanding of the concepts of object technology. Initial identification of object structures and relationships is vital; CRC is better than OMT in this respect. Having identified the classes, students find it difficult to classify them into inheritance hierarchies and aggregations due to their relative lack of experience.

A more radical change in concept for students to come to grips with, is the notion of object to object communication via message passing. In CRC this concept is exercised by groups working through scenarios, in contrast to OMT where it is modelled using state diagrams. Experience shows that stronger students gain an understanding of the basic OO concepts relatively easily, but weaker students find they are a significant hurdle to be overcome before they can concentrate on using the chosen method.

7. NEW METHODS THAT MIGHT HELP

ObjectOry and Fusion are relatively recent methods which may prove of greater use with students. Jacobson's method, ObjectOry, would arguably build on students' familiarity with the traditional SDLC. Fusion combines the best of several methods and is a mix of Rumbaugh's OMT, Wirfs-Brock's method, Booch's OOAD and formal methods.

7.1 ObjectOry

Jacobson's ObjectOry method takes a global view and centres on an analysis of the way a system is actually used; his use of three types of objects (Interface, Entity and Control) which separate interface behaviour from entity objects and keep these independent of controls, helps to construct sophisticated designs and provides a robust model. Both the processes and the method are represented as objects; in the opinion of some people, this may lead to software which is not truly object-oriented.

Central to ObjectOry is the concept of Use Cases, which identify a scenario, process, particular pattern or usage, which link the complete SDLC. Organisation analysis and design models around user interaction and actual usage scenarios. Each Use Case is identified through the actors of each scenario and the students can decide the actors' roles for each process, identifying the main tasks of each actor. The thread provided by Use Cases runs through the whole project.

(a) students can do it: it is conceptually simple; draws on previous experience
Use Cases call for a degree of role play which can appeal to students. The method is conceptually simple, with some underpinning by traditional and structured SDLC methods.

(b) it is well documented (in a book)
The book is a good one [3].

(c) it is easy to visualise and the notation is simple
ObjectOry is good here too.

(d) it is useful in industry, well tested and popular
It appears to becoming quite popular.

(e) there is a CASE tool which is affordable
ObjectOrySE, ObjectOry Support Environment
is the CASE tool.

(f) it encourages group work
Use Case role play encourages supportive and participative group work.

7.2 Fusion

(a) students can do it: it is conceptually simple; draws on previous experience
Fusion is very easy to pick up. In contrast to OMT, it supports the earliest stage - object identification - and focuses on analysis.

(b) it is well documented (in a book)
The book [23] is excellent, especially for students, in that it is short, communicative and based on examples rather than high level formality.

(c) it is easy to visualise and the notation is simple
The notation is simple and has similarities with OMT.

(d) it is useful in industry, well tested and popular
of several methods and also supports invariants, preconditions and postconditions.

(e) there is a CASE tool which is affordable
There are three CASE tools mentioned in the book.

(f) it encourages group work
Not explicitly.

8. CONCLUSIONS

Our experience supports that of Weiner and Wu [13,14,15]. In addition, it appears that the more formal approach of European education may lead to greater difficulties in students understanding and using object-oriented technology. Thus whilst many methods may be highly thought of in a commercial setting, it is useful for students inexperienced in OO to learn a method in a curriculum that strengthens these weaknesses. Existing methods, like OMT, may be used more successfully with the addition of working through scenarios and role playing. Alternatively, a new method like Fusion, with a greater emphasis on finding objects, might be an improvement. There is some concern about ObjectOry in that it may not lead to strictly object-oriented systems, but since this whole technology is relatively young, this appealing method should not be ignored.

Undergraduate curricula need to contain many more contact hours for object technology, including experience with concepts and use of a suitable language before methods can be taught successfully. In time we believe this will happen, but meanwhile many students may find themselves baffled. For them, the power and potential of OO may be obscure.

References

1. Byte Magazine, May 1994.
2. Graham, I. *Object-Oriented Methods* (2nd edition). Addison Wesley.
3. Jacobson, I. et al. *Object-Oriented Software Engineering: A Use Case Driven Approach.* Addison Wesley 1992.
4. Hutt, A. *Object Analysis and Design: Description of Methods.* John Wiley 1994.
5. Graham, N. *Learning C++.* McGraw Hill 1991.
6. Kaehler, T. & Patterson, D. *A Taste of Smalltalk.* Norton and Co. 1986.
7. Lippman, S. *C++ Primer.* Addison Wesley 1990.
8. Shafer, D. & Ritz, A.D. *Practical Smalltalk.* Springer Verlag 1991.
9. Shafer, D. *Smalltalk Programming for Windows.* Prima Publishing 1993.
10. Stroustrup, B. *The C++ Programming Language.* Addison Wesley 1987.
11. Meyer, B. *Eiffel: the language.* Prentice Hall 1992.
12. Meyer, B. *Toward an object-oriented curriculum.* JOOP May 1993 v6 n2.
13. Weiner, R. & Pinson, L. *OOP: an academic perspective.* JOOP June 1993 v6 n3.
14. Wu, C.T. *Three-stage, incremental approach in teaching OOP.* JOOP July-August 1993 v6 n4.
15. Wu, C.T. *Teaching OOP in three stages, stage 3.* JOOP September 1993 v6 n5
16. Kristen, G. *From European Methods to Object Orientation. Objects in Europe.* Vol 1 No 2 Spring 1994
17. Booch, G. *Object-oriented Design* (2nd Edition). Addison Wesley 1994.
18. Rumbaugh, J et al. *Object-oriented modelling.* Prentice Hall 1991.
19. D'Souza, D. *Working with OMT.* JOOP October 1993 v6.
20. Wirfs-Brock, R & Wilkerson, B. *Object-oriented design: a responsibility approach.* OOPSLA Proceedings, Sigplan Notices, 24. ACM Press 1989.
21. Wirfs-Brock, R et al. *Designing Object-oriented Software.* Prentice Hall 1990.
22. Coleman, D et al. *Object-oriented Development:the Fusion Method.* Prentice Hall 1994

INDEX OF CONTRIBUTORS

Azuma, M. 3, 378

Baldi, M. 149
Billington, J. 189
Brookes, A. 62
Brunskill, D.A. 243
Bustard, D.W. 29

Castellani, X. 345
Chabik, J. 395
Champion, R.E.M. 215
Chan, F.T. 107
Chan, K.L. 369
Chan, Y.K. 369
Chen, H.Y. 107
Chen, J. 99
Christodoulakis, D. 266
Coakes, E. 45
Coakes, J. 45

Darroch, G. 62
Davies, C.G. 273
Dedene, G. 127
Dodman, E. 193
Dromey, R.G. 10, 227, 235
Dunne, P. 37
Durnota, B. 99

Evans, J.B. 92

Ferneley, E.H. 273
Ferguson, R.I. 37
Fong, J. 139
Fujita, F. 300

Gill, N.S. 279
Gorton, I. 50
Grover, P.S. 279
Guinan, P.J. 78

Hall, P.A.V. 88
Henderson-Sellers, B. 320, 328
Howcroft, D.A. 273
Hung, S.-L. 284
Hunter, R. 290

Jaccheri, M.L. 149
Järvinen, J. 162
Jeffery, R. 294
Jiang, H. 345

Katayama, T. 72
Kikuno, T. 300
Kim, L.P.W. 294
Kokol, P. 56
Kusumoto, S. 300
Kwan, I. 139
Kwok, L.-F. 284
Kwong, S. 369

Lai, S.-T. 353, 361
Lasoudris, L. 115, 123
Law, K.C.-K. 284
Lee, C.H. 369
Lee, J.H.M. 135
Leung, J.C.K. 135
Liao, S. 123
Lian, L. 300
Lokan, C.J. 308
Lovegrove, G. 395
Lynch, T. 183

Ma, J. 123
Maldonado, J.C. 258
Mathur, A.P. 25
Matsumoto, K.-I. 300
Maurice-Demourioux, M. 115
McLaughlin, P. 395
Miller, J. 62
Millington, D. 66
Mochizuki, S. 72
Moores, T.T. 314
Motwani, S. 50
Murata, A. 378
Musson, T. 193

Neilson, M.P. 250

Oliver, B.K. 227

Pan, S. 235
Pant, Y.R. 320
Parrington, N.F. 37

Rehesaar, H. 177
Roper, M. 62
Rose, A. 177
Rout, T.P. 250

Samuel, A. 243
Sateesh, T.K. 88
Sauer, C. 294
Sawyer, S. 78
Standen, P. 395
Stiglic, B. 56

Tan, M. 231
Tate, G. 156
Tegarden, D. 328
Tervonen, I. 200
Theaker, C.J. 84
Thompson, J.B. 206
Thummalapalli, S. 389
Todi, R.K. 389
Torii, K. 300
Tse, T.H. 107
Tuikka, T. 336
Tulloch, I.M. 66

Veraart, V.E. 382
Verner, J.M. 320
Voyer, R. 115

Wan, H.A. 173
Whitworth, J. 84
Wohlin, C. 219
Wood, M. 62
Wong, C.C.K. 135
Wong, W.E. 258
Wright, S.L. 382
Wu, G. 127

Xenos, M. 266
Xie, M. 211

Yang, C.-C. 353, 361
Yap, C.Y. 231
Yoshida, T. 378

SUBJECT INDEX

Abstract model 127
Algebraic specifications 107
All uses 258
Artificial intelligence 115

CASE and workbench tools 84
Combination model 361
Component retrieval 353
Computer aided diagram 369
Computer and information science
education 72
Computers and society 389
Complexity measures 279
Composite measure 279
Computing methodologies 115
Conceptual modelling 215
Cost 258
Critical success factors 177
Cyclomatic number 279

Design 135
methods 273
Development effort 279
Distribution and maintenance 37
Document preparation 135

Effectiveness 258
Extended entity relationship 139

Formal methods 235
Functional testing 107

Graphics kernal system 369
Graphics user interface 369
Group and organization interfaces 78
Guideline 345

Information systems
applications 45
general 56, 72
Inspection 294

Knowledge representation 115, 353

Langrangean multiplier 173

Language constructs and features 92, 227

Maintenance 273
Management 156, 378
of computing and information systems 162, 336, 389
Metrics 62, 243, 250, 266, 273, 290, 314, 320, 328, 345
Miscellaneous 156
Model
driven 127
object 127
Mutation 258

Non-functional requirements 84

Object
aspect 127
deposition and factoring 127
main 127
modelling technique 139
orientation 84, 123
Object-oriented
analysis and design 395
database 139
methods 395
programming 37, 62, 92, 99, 107, 135
teaching 395
Office automation 45
Optimization 173
Organizational impact 389
Outsourcing 177

Primitive metrics 361
Process modelling 84
Professionalism 206
Program
design 345
verification 243, 266
Programming
environments 149, 227, 378, 382
languages
general 227
Problem analysis diagram 369

Project
  and management 177
  and people management 50, 308, 389
  success 177
Quality 294
  assurance 215

Real-time systems 84
Real world object 127
Reasoning about programs 235
Reengineering 10, 235
Reliability 211
Replacement problem 173
Requirements 45, 88
  engineering 215
  and specifications 29, 56, 66, 99, 115, 123, 156, 193, 382
Reuse 10, 345
Rule-based system 353

Security and protection 200
Simulation and modelling, general 162
Social and behavioural sciences 326
Software 115, 206
  engineering 10, 45, 50, 56, 66, 115, 149, 156, 189, 193, 206, 235, 250, 266, 284, 294
    design 72
    general 88, 162, 200, 211, 219
    management 231
    miscellaneous 389
  fault content estimations 219
  management 50, 72, 162, 189, 200, 231, 336
  metrics 10, 193, 211, 219, 300, 308, 361
  operational profile testing 219
  reliability 219
    certification 219
  reuse 353, 361
  science 279
  statistical quality control 219
  testing 258, 300, 336
  tools and techniques 284
  usage testing 219
Strength 258
Structured object-oriented view 127
Structured walkthrough 294
System
  attributes 84
  management 231

Technical review 294
Testing and debugging 243, 284, 314, 320, 328
Tools and techniques 29, 37, 66, 78, 88, 99, 115, 149, 250, 314, 378, 382

Visual programming
  environment 369

www.ingramcontent.com/pod-product-compliance
Ingram Content Group UK Ltd.
Pitfield, Milton Keynes, MK11 3LW, UK
UKHW020131290926
15471UKWH00003B/420
9781475765434